THE TRANSLATIONS OF SEAMUS HEANEY

THE TRANSLATIONS OF
SEAMUS HEANEY

Edited by Marco Sonzogni

FARRAR, STRAUS AND GIROUX

NEW YORK

Farrar, Straus and Giroux
120 Broadway, New York 10271

The Library of Congress has cataloged the hardcover edition as follows:
Names: Heaney, Seamus, 1939–2013 author. | Sonzogni, Marco, editor.
Title: The translations of Seamus Heaney / edited by Marco Sonzogni.
Other titles: Works. English
Description: First American edition. | New York : Farrar, Straus and Giroux,
    2023. | Includes bibliographical references and index. |
Identifiers: LCCN 2022055010 | ISBN 9780374277734 (hardcover)
Subjects: LCSH: Poetry—Translations into English. | LCGFT: Poetry.
Classification: LCC PR6058.E2 A6 2023 | DDC 821.914—dc23/eng/20221127
LC record available at https://lccn.loc.gov/2022055010

Paperback ISBN: 978-0-374-61284-9

Our books may be purchased in bulk for promotional,
educational, or business use. Please contact your local bookseller or
the Macmillan Corporate and Premium Sales Department at 1-800-221-7945,
extension 5442, or by email at MacmillanSpecialMarkets@macmillan.com.

www.fsgbooks.com
Follow us on social media at @fsgbooks

1 3 5 7 9 10 8 6 4 2

Contents

Abbreviations

100P	*100 Poems* (2018)
ABVIa	*Aeneid Book VI* (2016)
ABVIb	*Aeneid Book VI* (FSG, 2016)
Beowulf	*Beowulf* (1999)
Beowulf BE	*Beowulf: Bilingual Edition* (FSG, 2000; Norton, 2001; Faber & Faber, 2007)
BTa	*The Burial at Thebes* (2004)
BTb	*The Burial at Thebes* (FSG, 2004)
CP	*Crediting Poetry* (Gallery Press, 1995)
CTa	*The Cure at Troy* (Field Day/Faber & Faber, 1990)
CTb	*The Cure at Troy* (FSG, 1991)
DC	*District and Circle* (2006)
DD	*Door into the Dark* (1969, 2002)
DN	*Death of a Naturalist* (1966, 2006)
DOWV	*Diary of One Who Vanished* (1999)
EL	*Electric Light* (2001)
EP	*Eleven Poems* (Queen's University Belfast, 1965)
FK	*Finders Keepers: Selected Prose 1971–2001* (2002)
FW	*Field Work* (1979, 2001)
GT	*The Government of the Tongue* (1988)
HC	*Human Chain* (2010)
HL	*The Haw Lantern* (1987)
Laments	*Jan Kochanowski: Laments* (1995)
LW	*The Last Walk* (Gallery Press, 2013)
MV	*The Midnight Verdict* (Gallery Press, 1993, 2000)
North	*North* (1975, 2001)
NSP1990	*New Selected Poems 1966–1987* (1990)
NSP2014	*New Selected Poems 1988–2013* (2014)
OG	*Opened Ground: Poems 1966–1996* (1998)
P1980	*Poems 1965–1975* (1980)
PM	*Poems and a Memoir* (Limited Editions Club, 1982)
Preoccupations	*Preoccupations: Selected Prose 1968–1978* (1980)
RP	*The Redress of Poetry* (1995)
SA	*Sweeney Astray* (Field Day, 1983; Faber & Faber, 2001)
SD	*Stone from Delphi: Poems with Classical References* (Arion Press, 2012)

SF	*Sweeney's Flight* (Faber & Faber and FSG, 1992)
SI	*Station Island* (1984, 2001)
SL	*The Spirit Level* (1996, 2001)
SP	*Selected Poems 1965–1975* (1980)
SS	*Stepping Stones* (with Dennis O'Driscoll, 2008)
ST	*Seeing Things* (1991)
Stations	*Stations* (Ulsterman Publications, 1975)
TCSF	*The Testament of Cresseid & Seven Fables* (2009)
TSH	*The Translations of Seamus Heaney* (2023, the present edition)
WO	*Wintering Out* (1972)

(The publisher is Faber & Faber unless stated otherwise.)

Introduction

THE POET-TRANSLATOR

This volume collects all the translations of Seamus Heaney: 101 texts from fourteen languages that demonstrate how prominent, powerful and personal a role translation played in the poet's imagination and work. It testifies also to the form's enduring importance to the author across time: he began the first of them before the publication of his 1966 debut, *Death of a Naturalist*; he was working on the last of them in the months before his death in 2013.

Most of the texts in this edition were published during SH's lifetime, some posthumously; several appeared multiple times, a few once; one is published here for the first time. It is a body of writing carefully and confidently accomplished – even if, 'in the case of translation,' as he observed, 'it is even truer than usual that a poem is never completed, merely abandoned' (*SF*, viii).

From school to Stockholm, from scriptorium to stage, a striking and humbling cohesion underscores this volume. Translation after translation, and decade after decade, the poet-translator weaves his own word-hoard and story-board. This was Heaney's characteristic way of building confidence in his personal and poetic stance through the continuity of thoughts and words, commitment and testimony, visibility and accessibility, inspiration and education. It is the hope of the editor of this volume that its readers will confirm for themselves that each of his translations have what Heaney, quoting Anna Swir, referred to as a poem's 'biological right to life' (*SS*, 159).

Titled 'Prayer', the unpublished translation in this edition has come to us as a clean, unmarked typescript discovered in the archives of the National Library of Ireland. Whether it was intended to be revised by the author, or perhaps be submitted for publication, we cannot be sure, but we do have a guide as a precedent. 'To a Wine Jar', the text that opens this book, found its way from typescript to publication thirty years after it was finished and did so without revision.

SH was exacting about disseminating his work. When a text was published, it was invariably in a state of advanced completion. Still, the 'double-take of feeling' influencing the poet-translator – being simultaneously accountable to 'the inner literalist' and to 'the writer of verse' – is a force that is always operating upon the author to an extent that can be considered 'self-revealing' (*CTb*, 77; *TSH*, 251, *l.* 1606). The line between completion and abandonment is not always a clear one. After all, as SH himself asks in a poem stemming from translation, and titled 'The Fragment', '"Since when . . ./Are first line and last line of any poem/Where the poem begins and ends?"' (*EL*, 57).

For translation in particular, finding an answer to that question poses a special challenge, but for SH the response lay in the composition process itself. He gave equal care to translation as to his original work and held the forms in a level of literary equivalence. But he also understood an instinctive difference between the two: that a translation was already a variant of an original, and therefore bore a differing relationship to composition than did a poem that he might have originated himself.

Capturing every stage of that distinction – registering every alteration in draft, each forward or sideways step – did not hold the same intrinsic value for SH as might accompany the creation of an original work, because variance was an essential component in the transformation of a poem from one language to another. It was a flux built into the process, and was the element that he was seeking to excise in achieving a version of sufficient fixity that might mark it as ready for publication – like 'The unpredictable fantail of sparks/Or hiss when a new shoe toughens in water' (*DD*, 9). The toughest challenge for any translator, and especially for the literary translator, is to arrive at a stage of completion where the 'tense diaphragm' (*DN*, 44) between translator and poet, and between translation and original, can finally be relaxed so that the text can breathe naturally.

In the opening remarks of his Robert Lowell Memorial Lecture (Heaney 2008b) SH quotes a line from one of his own poems as the translator's motto: 'I had your measure and you had mine' (*DC*, 61). Achieving that measure – that completion – required in SH a process of constant sounding and refining in order to stabilise the movement of the text in place and time. Even so, some published variants do stand out as illuminating of his creative process, as signals of his pathway to completion through 'the ongoing vigour of the "translated" knowledge' and 'the aspiration of all translation to live a free and independent life' (Heaney 1999b, 331).

Sweeney Astray (1983–4), Heaney's first major translation, is in progress for over a decade, for example, with more than a dozen excerpts published (1976–82) before the appearance of the complete translation; a further decade elapses before the publication of the revised translation in *Sweeney's Flight* (1992). 'For one thing,' as SH explains in his Preface to that revised edition, 'there is a slightly different rhythmic imperative in operation when a piece stands on its own than when it is a constituent element in some longer structure' (*SF*, viii). In the 1992 text, 'grievously' becomes 'sacrilegiously', a revision that charges Ronan's private grief with religious defilement, making him curse Sweeney (*SF*, 91; *TSH*, 136, §6, *l*. 2).

Beowulf (1999; *Beowulf BE*, 2007), SH's most domineering translation, is the result of an even longer gestation that spanned nearly two decades and spawned many published excerpts (1980s–1990s). After that book was published, SH made further revisions: 'clearly' to 'brightly' for example, in the text of a 1999 Gallery Press Christmas card (*Beowulf*, 51; *BE*, 109; *TSH*, 326, *l*. 1572), and, invited to contribute to an anthology titled *Irish Writers Against War* (2003), adapting some lines into an independent poem titled 'News of the Raven' (*Beowulf*, 91–5; *BE*, 195–203; *TSH*, 359–62, *ll*. 2897–3027).

SH's version of Sophocles' *Philoctetes* comes out in the USA on 4 December 1991, more than a year after the play premiered at the Guildhall in Derry on 1 October 1990 and was published in Ireland and Britain. SH takes this opportunity to weave his title of the play, *The Cure at Troy*, into the text, where it appears (*TSH*, 252, *ll*. 1654–5) spoken by Philoctetes in his last speech: 'I can see/The cure at Troy' (*CTb*, 80). This supplementary line strengthens the connection already established by translator and translation between Ancient Greece and Ireland, 'north and south', he told Dennis O'Driscoll in conversation, where 'the idea of a miraculous cure is deeply lodged in the religious subculture, whether it involves faith healing or the Lourdes pilgrimage' (*SS*, 422). The title would also serve as a model for SH's second Sophocles translation, *The Burial at Thebes* (2004), where an original poem SH had published in the *New Yorker* under the title 'Sophoclean' provides the basis for a key chorus (*BTa*, 16–17; *TSH*, 389–90, *ll*. 356–89). The 2008 Peacock production of the play enables SH to refine his version: the text in this edition is what SH regarded as 'the final correct version'.

The words, lines and punctuation of 'The Yellow Bittern' and 'The Glamoured' – SH's translations of two canonical and rhythmical texts in the Irish tradition, '*An Bonnán Buí*' and '*Gile na gile*' – jigged their way into print multiple times across two decades (1997–2016). The inclusion of Canto II from Dante's *Inferno* in a new anthology in 1998 provides SH with the opportunity to re-read the translation he had published in 1993. So Virgil's desire to honour Beatrice's plea and aid Dante – 'I yearned the more to come' – becomes more explicit – 'I yearned the more to help' (Havely 1998, 264; *TSH*, 36, *l*. 117). When Billy Connolly was recording Henryson's fable 'The Fox, the Wolf and the Carter', SH readily adjusted his 2009 translation of

'Lent-feed' to 'Lent-food' (*TCSF*, 141; *TSH*, 470, *l*. 172) to improve clarity and flow. In 2009 SH also committed to print his first Pascoli translation, 'The Kite', which he had encountered in Italian in 2001 and which would form the basis for 'A Kite for Aibhín', the last poem in his last book, *Human Chain*, published in 2010.

SH was exacting about titles too. As bibliographer Rand Brandes notes, for SH effective titles would be 'successfully embodying the spirit of the poem or book in a way that resonates with the reader' and 'serve as emblems capable of calling forth the essence of the book or poem from memory' (Brandes 2008b, 19). That said, an excerpt from the translation in progress of *Aeneid Book VI* (*ll*. 638–78 of the standard Latin edition by R. A. B. Mynors; *ABVIa*, 35–7; *TSH*, 512–13, *ll*. 867–914) appears in print with two different titles: 'The Fields of Light' (2008) and 'The Elysian Fields' (2012).

Each of these occasions demonstrates that SH never downplayed his debt to the source text as he strove to achieve with his translations the same independence as in his original works. Even when the process involved languages he did not know or required working with scholars and co-translators, the translations become unmistakably his. In a panel on translating poetry and poetic prose (1999), SH described the translator as 'a creative stealer', arguing that the writer and the translator share the same 'artistic task': 'to make something of the given, to move it through a certain imaginative and linguistic distance' (Heaney 1999b, 331). 'All language,' he maintained, 'is an entry to further language' (Delanty 2012, xii).

SH did not have an overarching theory of translation, and he could be cautious about pronouncing upon it; what insights he did share, however, are illuminating. Reflecting on *The Burial at Thebes* (2004), his version of Sophocles' *Antigone*, he affirms that 'verse translation is not all that different from original composition' and that 'in order to get a project under way, there has to be a note to which the lines, and especially the first lines, can be tuned' (Heaney 2005, 169).

It is an analogy that illustrates exactly how he went about his translation and poetry alike. 'Until this register is established,' he explains, 'your words [. . .] cannot induce that blessed sensation of being on the right track, musically and rhythmically' (Heaney 2005, 169). A description of translation, this account nonetheless seems also to evoke a line in 'Song' in which SH describes 'that moment when the bird sings very close / To the music of what happens' (*FW*, 53). In another poem, 'The Given Note', he describes the moment of inspiration as a process of translation: 'spirit music' that is surprisingly and mysteriously received and that 'Rephrases itself into the air' (*DD*, 36). This image returns in conversation with George O'Brien at Georgetown University (1988) when SH mentions Osip Mandelstam's definition of great poets as 'air stealers' (Heaney 1998b, 20:42–20:52), akin to the musician of 'The Given Note'.

Another metaphor of translation as creative transfer can be found in 'The Settle Bed', in which SH writes 'whatever is given // Can always be reimagined' (*ST*, 29). It is not surprising that, when translating, SH embraced the 'liberating idea' that 'an original work exists not in order to be perfect but in order to engender itself repeatedly in new translations' (Heaney 1999b, 331). An event 'out of the marvellous' reported in *Lebor Laignech* ('Book of Leinster'), in *Lebor Bretnach* (Irish Nennius) and also in *Konungs skuggsjá* ('The King's Mirror') reaches SH's imagination through Kenneth Hurlstone Jackson's English translation, 'The Air Ship' (Jackson 1971, 165). This transmission – 'hung out on the limb of a translated phrase' (*SI*, 57), 'Needy and ever needier for translation' (*HC*, 58) – exemplifies the evolutionary impact of translation as SH practised it. 'I Lightenings viii' (*ST*, 62), which is known also as 'The annals say . . .' – one of the poems singled out by the Swedish Academy to illustrate how the 'lyrical beauty and ethical depth' of SH's poetry 'exalt everyday miracles and the living past' (Nobel 1995) – could arguably have found space in this edition. This original text, like all the translated texts here, exemplifies the poet-translator's 'light-headed credo' in 'Discovering what survives translation true', as he says in 'Remembered Columns' (*SL*, 45).

SH's translations – to be listened to as given notes that give back 'the clear song of a skilled poet' (*Beowulf*, 5; *BE*, 9; *TSH*, 287, *l.* 90) – are arranged here in two sections: texts that can be classified as short or long poems, and those of book length that have been previously published under their own title; in each, obvious printers' errors have been silently corrected.

An editor's Commentary, arranged by decade, provides information on the original source text, a publication history of the translation, and an account of its background and significance drawn from SH's discussions of his own translations: his prefaces, introductions, essays and interviews in which he discusses materials and motivations. Secondary sources helped to further document that SH turned to translation as an ideal space to connect his experiences in Ireland, north and south of the border, with experiences outside Ireland, and to comment on societal issues near and far with personal and artistic integrity.

The universal dimension of SH's local preoccupations and the redressing power of literature across confines and cultures are made evident in an interview with Jon Snow for Britain's *Channel 4 News* (1999) in which SH draws a parallel between the situation in Northern Ireland and events in *Beowulf*, which he had recently completed. Because of their 'extreme ordeal, a little exhaustion, and tremor', the people of Ulster, like those in the Old English epic poem, he said, 'know a lot' about danger, dread, hurt and suffering. This is 'the general condition of species at the end of the century', observes SH, 'and the particular condition of people in Northern Ireland' (Heaney 1999e, 4:34–5:49).

In Northern Ireland, SH's life, education and work developed 'to the tick of two clocks' (*North*, x): Catholic and Protestant mindsets; Nationalist and Unionist agendas; Irish and British cultures. This inherited homeplace, an inescapable middle ground – 'Two buckets were easier carried than one./I grew up in between', he writes in 'Terminus' (*HL*, 5) – is the natural habitat of the translator. Seamus Heaney was a born translator.

Marco Sonzogni
Autumn 2022

THE TRANSLATIONS

To a Wine Jar

HORACE

When Manlius was consul you were filled,
Venerable pitcher, and I was born.
Now we meet. For what? Regrets or laughter?
Rows or old maudlin loves or boozy sleep?

No matter. The rare Massic that you store   5
Is only to be savoured on a day
Like this: Corvinus is insisting on
A wine that is a wine. So down you come.

Corvinus will appreciate you, though he looks
The real ascetic and sounds so terribly   10
Socratic. Anyhow, even Old Cato's
Frosty precepts thawed in the heat of wine.

You are a sugared poison to the souls
Of puritans, a sweet forbidden fruit.
The canny man relaxes when you smile,   15
Unloads his worst fears, leaks his secret plans.

You'll flush a worried wretch with sudden hope
And boost the small man up into heroics:
Who will go brazen into royal courts
Or face the firing line after a glass.   20

Join us, then, to-night. Here's company! Bacchus
And the jealous Graces. Venus too.
The lamps flicker. Down you come. We'll drink
Till Phoebus, returning, routs the morning star.

Prayer

GABRIELLE DE COIGNARD

The fear of death disturbs me constantly;
For those in hell there can be no redemption;
Though I have sinned I cannot feel contrition;
The further I go, the worse my agony.

5   You will consume me like a brittle leaf
On that appalling day of tribulation:
Let me at last repent of my transgression,
For fastened to my soul is bitter grief.

You made me out of flesh, tendons, and veins,
10   Of blood and bones, of liver, lungs, and brains –
I'm dust and ashes, Lord; remember this.

Like straw that winds rend from little to less,
Your wrath can sweep me into nothingness.
Ah, do not let me fall in the abyss!

The Digging Skeleton

CHARLES BAUDELAIRE

After Baudelaire

I

You find anatomical plates
Buried along these dusty quays
Among books yellowed like mummies
Slumbering in forgotten crates,

Drawings touched with an odd beauty,   5
As if the illustrator had
Responded gravely to the sad
Mementoes of anatomy –

Mysterious candid studies
Of red slobland around the bones.   10
Like this one: flayed men and skeletons
Digging the earth like navvies.

II

Sad gang of apparitions,
Your skinned muscles like plaited sedge
And your spines hooped towards the sunk edge
Of the spade, my patient ones,

Tell me, as you labour hard   5
To break this unrelenting soil,
What barns are there for you to fill?
What farmer dragged you from the boneyard?

Or are you emblems of the truth,
Death's lifers, hauled from the narrow cell   10
And stripped of night-shirt shrouds, to tell:
'This is the reward of faith

In rest eternal. Even death
Lies. The void deceives.
We do not fall like autumn leaves   15
To sleep in peace. Some traitor breath

Revives our clay, sends us abroad
And by the sweat of our stripped brows
We earn our deaths; our one repose
When the bleeding instep finds its spade.'   20

We had already left him. I walked the ice
And saw two soldered in a frozen hole
On top of other, one's skull capping the other's,
Gnawing at him where the neck and head
5   Are grafted to the sweet fruit of the brain,
Like a famine victim at a loaf of bread.
So the berserk Tydeus gnashed and fed
Upon the severed head of Menalippus
As if it were some spattered carnal melon.
10   'You,' I shouted, 'you on top, what hate
Makes you so ravenous and insatiable?
What keeps you so monstrously at rut?
Is there any story I can tell
For you, in the world above, against him?
15   If my tongue by then's not withered in my throat
I will report the truth and clear your name.'

That sinner eased his mouth up off his meal
To answer me, and wiped it with the hair
Left growing on his victim's ravaged skull,
20   Then said, 'Even before I speak
The thought of having to relive all that
Desperate time makes my heart sick;
Yet while I weep to say them, I would sow
My words like curses – that they might increase
25   And multiply upon this head I gnaw.
I know you come from Florence by your accent
But I have no idea who you are
Nor how you ever managed your descent.
Still, you should know my name, for I was Count
30   Ugolino, this was Archbishop Roger,
And why I act the jockey to his mount
Is surely common knowledge; how my good faith
Was easy prey to his malignancy,
How I was taken, held, and put to death.
35   But you must hear something you cannot know
If you're to judge him – the cruelty
Of my death at his hands. So listen now.

Others will pine as I pined in that jail
Which is called Hunger after me, and watch
As I watched through a narrow hole   40
Moon after moon, bright and somnambulant,
Pass overhead, until that night I dreamt
The bad dream and my future's veil was rent.
I saw a wolf-hunt: this man rode the hill
Between Pisa and Lucca, hounding down   45
The wolf and wolf-cubs. He was lordly and masterful,
His pack in keen condition, his company
Deployed ahead of him, Gualandi
And Sismundi as well, and Lanfranchi,
Who soon wore down wolf-father and wolf-sons   50
And my hallucination
Was all sharp teeth and bleeding flanks ripped open.
When I awoke before the dawn, my head
Swam with cries of my sons who slept in tears
Beside me there, crying out for bread.   55
(If your sympathy has not already started
At all that my heart was foresuffering
And if you are not crying, you are hardhearted.)

They were awake now, it was near the time
For food to be brought in as usual,   60
Each one of them disturbed after his dream,
When I heard the door being nailed and hammered
Shut, far down in the nightmare tower.
I stared in my sons' faces and spoke no word.
My eyes were dry and my heart was stony.   65
They cried and my little Anselm said,
"What's wrong? Why are you staring, Daddy?"
But I shed no tears, I made no reply
All through that day, all through the night that followed
Until another sun blushed in the sky   70
And sent a small beam probing the distress
Inside those prison walls. Then when I saw
The image of my face in their four faces
I bit on my two hands in desperation
And they, since they thought hunger drove me to it,   75
Rose up suddenly in agitation
Saying, "Father, it will greatly ease our pain
If you eat us instead, and you who dressed us

In this sad flesh undress us here again."
80 So then I calmed myself to keep them calm.
We hushed. That day and the next stole past us
And earth seemed hardened against me and them.
For four days we let the silence gather.
Then, throwing himself flat in front of me,
85 Gaddo said, "Why don't you help me, Father?"
He died like that, and surely as you see
Me here, one by one I saw my three
Drop dead during the fifth day and the sixth day
Until I saw no more. Searching, blinded,
90 For two days I groped over them and called them.
Then hunger killed where grief had only wounded.'
When he had said all this, his eyes rolled
And his teeth, like a dog's teeth clamping round a bone,
Bit into the skull and again took hold.

95 Pisa! Pisa, your sounds are like a hiss
Sizzling in our country's grassy language.
And since the neighbour states have been remiss
In your extermination, let a huge
Dyke of islands bar the Arno's mouth, let
100 Capraia and Gorgona dam and deluge
You and your population. For the sins
Of Ugolino, who betrayed your forts,
Should never have been visited on his sons.
Your atrocity was Theban. They were young
105 And innocent: Hugh and Brigata
And the other two whose names are in my song.

'The small bird'

ANONYMOUS

The small bird
let a chirp
from its beak:
  I heard
woodnotes, whin-
gold, sudden.
the Lagan
  blackbird!

5

'Look far. Cast'

ANONYMOUS

Look far. Cast
eyes northeast
over tossed
    seascapes.
5   There's the seal!
And tides fill
and run, all
    whitecaps.

The Names of the Hare

ANONYMOUS

The man the hare has met
will never be the better for it
except he lay down on the land
what he carries in his hand –
be it staff or be it bow –   5
and bless him with his elbow
and come out with this litany
with devotion and sincerity
to speak the praises of the hare.
Then the man will better fare.   10

'The hare, call him scotart,
big-fellow, bouchart,
the O'Hare, the jumper,
the rascal, the racer.

Beat-the-pad, white-face,   15
funk-the-ditch, shit-ass.

The wimount, the messer,
the skidaddler, the nibbler,
the ill-met, the slabber.

The quick-scut, the dew-flirt,   20
the grass-biter, the goibert,
the home-late, the do-the-dirt.

The starer, the wood-cat,
the purblind, the furze cat,
the skulker, the bleary-eyed,   25
the wall-eyed, the glance-aside
and also the hedge-springer.

The stubble-stag, the long lugs,
the stook-deer, the frisky legs,
the wild one, the skipper,   30
the hug-the-ground, the lurker,
the race-the-wind, the skiver,
the shag-the-hare, the hedge-squatter,
the dew-hammer, the dew-hoppper,

COMMENTARY 546–8 | 11

35 the sit-tight, the grass-bounder,
the jig-foot, the earth-sitter,
the light-foot, the fern-sitter,
the kail-stag, the herb-cropper.

The creep-along, the sitter-still,
40 the pintail, the ring-the-hill,
the sudden start,
the shake-the-heart,
the belly-white,
the lambs-in-flight.

45 The gobshite, the gum-sucker,
the scare-the-man, the faith-breaker,
the snuff-the-ground, the baldy skull
(his chief name is scoundrel).

The stag sprouting a suede horn,
50 the creature living in the corn,
the creature bearing all men's scorn,
the creature no one dares to name.'

When you have got all this said
then the hare's strength has been laid.
55 Then you might go faring forth –
east and west and south and north,
wherever you incline to go –
but only if you're skilful too.
And now, Sir Hare, good-day to you.
60 God guide you to a how-d'ye-do
with me: come to me dead
in either onion broth or bread.

Song of the soul that delights in knowing God by faith

JOHN OF THE CROSS

How well I know that fountain, filling, running,
    although it is the night.

That eternal fountain, hidden away,
I know its haven and its secrecy
    although it is the night.   5

But not its source because it does not have one,
which is all sources' source and origin
    although it is the night.

No other thing can be so beautiful.
Here the earth and heaven drink their fill   10
    although it is the night.

So pellucid it never can be muddied,
and I know that all light radiates from it
    although it is the night.

I know no sounding-line can find its bottom,   15
nobody ford or plumb its deepest fathom
    although it is the night.

And its current so in flood it overspills
to water hell and heaven and all peoples
    although it is the night.   20

And the current that is generated there,
as far as it wills to, it can flow that far
    although it is the night.

And from these two a third current proceeds
which neither of these two, I know, precedes   25
    although it is the night.

This eternal fountain hides and splashes
within this living bread that is life to us
    although it is the night.

30   Hear it calling out to every creature.
      And they drink these waters, although it is dark here
            because it is the night.

      I am repining for this living fountain.
      Within this bread of life I see it plain
35   although it is the night.

Fountains in the sea

MARIN SORESCU

Water: no matter how much, there is still not enough.
Cunning life keeps asking for more and then a drop more.
Our ankles are weighted with lead, we delve under the wave.
We bend to our spades, we survive the force of the gusher.

Our bodies fountain with sweat in the deeps of the sea,   5
Our forehead aches and holds like a sunken prow.
We are out of breath, divining the heart of the geyser,
Constellations are bobbing like corks above on the swell.

Earth is a waterwheel, the buckets go up and go down,
But to keep the whole aqueous architecture standing its ground   10
We must make a ring with our bodies and dance out a round
On the dreamt eye of water, the dreamt eye of water, the dreamt
     eye of water.

Water: no matter how much, there is still not enough.
Come rain, come thunder, come deluged dams washed away,
Our thirst is unquenchable. A cloud in the water's a siren.   15
We become two shades, deliquescent, drowning in song.

My love, under the tall sky of hope
Our love and our love alone
Keeps dowsing for water.
Sinking the well of each other, digging together.   20
Each one the other's phantom limb in the sea.

Angle

MARIN SORESCU

Overhead, the traditional lines
Of cranes:
Sonnets for countrymen.

The tear

MARIN SORESCU

I weep and weep a tear
Which will not fall
No matter how much I weep.

Its pang in me
Is like the birth of an icicle.

5

Colder and colder, the earth
Curves on my eyelid,
The northern ice-cap keeps rising.

O, my arctic eyelid.

Old people in the shade

You get tired quickly, you forget easily,
You start talking to yourself,
You move your lips
And come on yourself in the mirror moving your lips.

5   I have a fair notion of how old age will be for me.
For a day or two every summer, for a week
I am old.
Wrinkled, shrunk like a peach stone
In the kernel of the luscious day.

10   A Ulysses who keeps drifting off,
Forgetting where he's going back to,
Why he's astray on the sea,
Whether the war in Troy is over or coming.
A Ulysses unlikely to kiss smoke from the chimneys
15   Of home.

Are you straightening your tie there
Or strangling yourself?

40 degrees in the sun. I go into the house
And, with an ultimate effort of memory, remember
20   My name.
Torrid weather is much the same as old age.
The same sensations.

You trip on the rugs
You stumble over the slippers –
25   One of your nails has turned septic,
One of your teeth seems to be looser.

In the summer, we all come together.
We are all old,
Even the foetus in its mother's womb.

18 | COMMENTARY 550–1

The first words

MARIN SORESCU

The first words were polluted
Like river water in the morning
Flowing with the dirt
Of the blurbs and the front pages.
My only drink is meaning from the deep brain,   5
What the birds and grasses and stones drink.
Let everything flow
Up to the four elements,
Up to water and earth and fire and air.

Proper names

When the ancient world foundered
Bottles had not been invented
So whatever was valuable there
Was rolled up
5   Into a few proper names
And set afloat on the water.

They have reached us safely, those names.

And when we uncork one,
Homer, say, or Pythagoras or Tacitus,
10   Great sheaves of light break open in the sky,
Millennial chaff falls on our shoulders.

Let us do all we can to increase
The store of proper names in the world
So that if the earth goes down
15   They will keep on floating,
Trojan horses with the whole of mankind in their bellies,
Headed for the gates of other planets.

Miraculous Grass

NUALA NÍ DHOMHNAILL

There you were in your purple vestments
half-way through the Mass, an ordained priest
under your linen alb and chasuble and stole:
and when you saw my face in the crowd
for Holy Communion   5
the consecrated host fell from your fingers.

I felt shame, I never
mentioned it once,
my lips were sealed.
But still it lurked in my heart   10
like a thorn under mud, and it
worked itself in so deep and sheer
it nearly killed me.

Next thing then, I was laid up in bed.
Consultants came in their hundreds,   15
doctors and brothers and priests,
but I baffled them all: I was
incurable, they left me for dead.

So out you go, men,
out with the spades and the scythes,   20
the hooks and shovels and hoes.
Tackle the rubble,
cut back the bushes, clear off the rubbish,
the sappy growth, the whole straggle and mess
that infests my green unfortunate field.   25

And there where the sacred wafer fell
you will discover
in the middle of the shooting weeds
a clump of miraculous grass.

The priest will have to come then   30
with his delicate fingers, and lift the host
and bring it to me and put it on my tongue.
Where it will melt, and I will rise in the bed
as fit and well as the youngster I used to be.

Mo Mhíle Stór

NUALA NÍ DHOMHNAILL

I was under your spell from the start:
I was young, I was soft,
and you well knew you could turn my head
with your talk about whitewashed courts
5   and big long sleeps on a duck-down bed
and gloves made out of the skins of fish.

When you sailed away
my goodbyes were the gulls in your wake.
I put up with rows and with blame
10   from every side; there was a time
when I could number my friends
on the fingers of one hand.

You sailed through life, you came back home,
your boat beached on my bed.
15   As I covered you all in honey,
I saw your hair had gone grey
and straight;
but in my memory the curls grew on,
twelve coils in the ripening
20   crop on your head.

Will Travel

CATHAL Ó SEARCAIGH

for Rachel Brown

To-morrow I travel on to a haven
Beyond the pitch and brawl of the sea:
The flats round here are a run-down graveyard
Where my young self walks like a nameless zombie.

In an open house over there, the hearth   5
Is the heart and soul of every welcome;
When I hear that candid, soothing accent
I'll be flush with health and my step will quicken.

O I'm travelling on to a sheltering haven
And hope is bellying out in my sail.   10
In a warmer place, I'll mend and be safe
From streets as cold as the wind round headstones.

Exile's Return

CATHAL Ó SEARCAIGH

for Peigí Rose

He's back tonight to a deserted house.
On the doorstep, under a brilliant moon, a stark
shadow: the tree he planted years ago is an old tree.

The Clay Pipes

CATHAL Ó SEARCAIGH

You won't be the one to turn away when death
rolls in towards you like the ocean.

You will hold to your steadfast gaze,
as it comes tiding in, all plash and glitter
from the rim of eternity.   5
You will keep your head.
You will come to your senses again as it
foams over the ridged beaches of your brain
and you will take it all in
and know it completely: 10
you will be a child again, out on the strand
at Magheraroarty, your body
abandoned altogether
to the lift of the Atlantic.
But before you went the whole way then away   15
into nothingness, you would touch the bottom.
And this will be what happens to you here:
you'll go through a black hole of initiation,
then reach the land of the living;
but the seal of the brine will be on you forever   20
and you'll have depth as a person.
You'll walk from danger of death into the truth.

Here is the best image I can find:
you are like the forest people of Colombia
I read about in the library,   25
a tribe who smoke clay pipes, coloured pipes
that used to have to be made from this one thing:
basketfuls of clay
scooped out in fatal danger
in enemy country, in a scaresome place   30
full of traps and guards and poisoned arrows.
According to this article, they believe
that the only fully perfect pipes
are ones made out of the clay
collected under such extreme conditions.   35

Lament

CATHAL Ó SEARCAIGH

in memory of my mother

I cried on my mother's breast, cried sore
The day Mollie died, our old pet ewe
Trapped on a rockface up at Beithí
It was a sultry heat, we'd been looking for her,
5   Sweating and panting, driving sheep back
From the cliff-edge when we saw her attacked
On a ledge far down. Crows and more crows
Were eating at her. We heard the cries
But couldn't get near. She was ripped to death
10 As we suffered her terrible, wild, last breath
And my child's heart broke. I couldn't be calmed
No matter how much she'd tighten her arms
And gather me close. I just cried on
Till she hushed me at last with a piggyback
15 And the promise of treats of potato-cake.

To-day it's my language that's in its throes,
The poets' passion, my mothers' fathers'
Mothers' language, abandoned and trapped
On a fatal ledge that we won't attempt.
20 She's in agony, I can hear her heave
And gasp and struggle as they arrive,
The beaked and ravenous scavengers
Who are never far. Oh if only anger
Came howling wild out of her grief,
25 If only she'd bare the teeth of her love
And rout the pack. But she's giving in,
She's quivering badly, my mother's gone
And promises now won't ease the pain.

After Liberation

J. C. BLOEM

I

Sheer, bright-shining spring, spring as it used to be,
Cold in the morning, but as broad daylight
Swings open, the everlasting sky
Is a marvel to survivors.

In a pearly clarity that bathes the fields   5
Things as they were come back; slow horses
Plough the fallow, war rumbles away
In the near distance.

To have lived it through and now be free to give
Utterance, body and soul – to wake and know   10
Every time that it's gone and gone for good, the thing
That nearly broke you –

Is worth it all, the five years on the rack,
The fighting back, the being resigned, and not
One of the unborn will appreciate   15
Freedom like this ever.

II

Turning tides, their regularities!
What is the heart, that it ever was afraid,
Knowing as it must know spring's release,
Shining heart, heart constant as a tide?

Omnipresent, imperturbable   5
Is the life that death springs from.
And complaint is wrong, the slightest complaint at all,
Now that the rye crop waves beside the ruins.

Inferno: Canto I

DANTE

In the middle of the journey of our life
I found myself astray in a dark wood
where the straight road had been lost sight of.

How hard it is to say what it was like
5 in the thick of thickets, in a wood so dense and gnarled
the very thought of it renews my panic.

It is bitter almost as death itself is bitter.
But to rehearse the good it also brought me
I will speak about the other things I saw there.

10 How I got into it I cannot clearly say
for I was moving like a sleepwalker
the moment I stepped out of the right way,

But when I came to the bottom of a hill
standing off at the far end of that valley
15 where a great terror had disheartened me

I looked up, and saw how its shoulders glowed
already in the rays of the planet
which leads and keeps men straight on every road.

Then I sensed a quiet influence settling
20 into those depths in me that had been rocked
and pitifully troubled all night long

And as a survivor gasping on the sand
turns his head back to study in a daze
the dangerous combers, so my mind

25 Turned back, although it was reeling forward,
back to inspect a pass that had proved fatal
heretofore to everyone who entered.

I rested a little then, for I was weary,
then began to climb up the waste slopes once more
30 with my firm foot always the lower one beneath me

When suddenly the spotted fluent shape
of a leopard crossed my path
not far up from the bottom of the slope,

Harrying me, confronting my advance,
loping round me, leaping in my face   35
so that I turned back downhill more than once.

The morning was beginning all above,
the sun was rising up among the stars
that rose with him when the Divine Love

First set those lovely things in motion,   40
so I was encouraged to face with better hope
the beast skipping in its merry skin

By the time of day, the sweetness of the season:
but not enough not to be frightened by
the sudden apparition of a lion   45

That came for me with his head in the air
and so maddened by hunger that it seemed
the air itself was bristling with fear.

And a she-wolf, so thin she looked as if
all her appetites were gnawing at her.   50
She had already brought many to grief

And I was so overcome at the sight of her
my courage broke and I immediately lost heart
in climbing the mountain any farther.

And as somebody who thinks he is going to win   55
every time will be the most distressed one
whenever his turn comes to be the loser –

I was like that as I retreated from
the animal's turbulent head-on attack
gradually, to where the sun is dumb.   60

While I was slipping back, about to sink
back to the depths, I caught sight of one
who seemed through a long silence indistinct.

When I saw him in that great waste land
65 I cried out to him, 'Pity me,
whatever you are, shade or a living man.'

He answered me, 'No, not a living man
though I was once alive, and had Lombards
for parents, both of them Mantuan.

70 Although I was born *sub Julio*, my prime
was spent in the heyday of the false gods
when I lived in Rome, in good Augustus' time.

I was a poet, and I sang of that just son
of Anchises who came out of Troy
75 after the burning of proud Ilion.

But why do you face back into misery?
Why do you not keep on up the sweet hill,
the source and cause of all felicity?'

'Oh, are you then Virgil, are you the fountainhead
80 of that wide river of speech constantly brimming?'
I answered and for shame kept my head bowed.

'You are the light and glory of other poets.
O let it avail me now, the long devotion
that made me love your book and cleave to it.

85 You are my master, my authority.
I learned from you and from you alone
the illustrious style for which they honour me.

Look at the beast that has forced me to turn back.
Help me, O famous sage, to confront her
90 for she makes my veins race and my pulses shake.'

'You will have to go another way around,'
he answered, when he saw me weeping,
'to escape the toils and thickets of this ground;

Because this animal you are troubled by
95 lets no man pass but harasses him
until she kills him by her savagery,

And she is so consumed by viciousness
that nothing fills her, and so insatiable
that feeding only makes her ravenous.

There are many animals she couples with   100
and there will be more of them, until the Hound
shall come and grind her in the jaws of death.

He will not glut himself on ground or riches,
but wisdom, love, and virtue will sustain him
and the two Feltros will vie to be his birthplace.   105

To humble Italy, for which the virgin
Camilla died bleeding, and Turnus died, and Nisus
and Euryalus, he will bring salvation.

He will pursue the wolf through every town
until he has hunted and hounded her to hell   110
where envy unleashed her first and set her on.

Therefore, for your own good, I think the best course
is to follow me and I will be your guide
and lead you from here through an eternal place

Where you will hear desperate screaming and will see   115
those long-lost spirits in torment suffering
the second death in perpetuity.

And then you will see those who are not distressed
in the fire because they hope to come,
whenever their time comes, among the blessed.   120

If you want to ascend among these, then you
will be guided by a soul worthier than I
and I will leave you with her when I go;

For that Emperor above does not allow
me or my like to come into His city   125
because I was a rebel to His law.

His empire is everywhere but His high seat
and city are there, in His proper kingdom.
O happy is the man He calls to it.'

130 And I said to him, 'I ask you, poet,
     in the name of that God you were ignorant of
     and to help me to escape my own worst fate,

     Lead me to that place described by you
     so that I may see St. Peter's Gate
135 and those other ones you spoke of in their sorrow.'

     Then he set off and I began to follow.

Daylight was going and the umber air
soothing every creature on the earth,
freeing them from their labours everywhere:

I alone was girding myself to face
the ordeal of the journey and my duty   5
which literal memory will now retrace.

Now, O muses, and now, high genius, help me.
And memory, that recorded what I saw,
be manifest in me, sheer faculty.

'Poet,' I began, 'who are my guide,   10
consider what my strength is able for
before you set me on the arduous road.

You tell how the father of Silvius
went into eternity and was there
in the living flesh, with all his bodily senses,   15

And yet the thoughtful man will understand
why the Adversary of all things evil,
considering the greatness he would found

And who and what spring from him, showed him favour –
for he was chosen in the empyrean   20
to father glorious Rome and her empire

And we cannot speak of Rome or of the empire
truly, except as the holy seat
founded to keep great Peter's successor.

On that journey, celebrated by your skill,   25
he was enlightened and set upon the way
toward victory and the papal mantle.

Then the Chosen Vessel went there and returned
with confirmation of that faith which is
the beginning of the way into salvation.   30

But I, why should I go? Who grants me passage?
I am not Aeneas and I am not Paul.
My unworthiness is plain for all to judge.

Therefore, were I to undertake this journey
35   I fear it would be madness. But you are wise.
What I can hardly grasp, you know completely.'

And like a man reneging his decision,
having second thoughts and shifting ground,
withdrawing from the course he has embarked on,

40   On that dark hillside there and then I weakened,
for once I admitted doubts about a purpose
so hastily conceived, the purpose went.

'If I have understood you rightly in this,'
the shade of that magnanimous one replied,
45   'your spirit is being plagued by cowardice

Which often weighs on a man, makes him distrust
an honourable course and turns him from it
as seeing wrong will turn a shying beast.

So to rid you of this fear, I will tell you
50   why I have come and everything I've heard
from the moment I began to care for you.

I was among those who are in suspense
when a lady called me, so blessed and beautiful
I pleaded with her to let me do her service.

55   Her eyes were shining brighter than the stars
and she began to speak with an angel's voice
in that gentle and quiet speech of hers:

'O courteous spirit of Mantua, whose fame
is lasting in the world, and for as long
60   as the world lasts will always last the same,

My friend – no friend of fortune's – on his trek
up the desolate slope is so overcome
and panic-stricken that he has turned back

And from the news I heard of him in heaven
he may already be so far astray   65
that I have roused myself too late to help him.

Hurry to him, speak in your eloquent way
and do whatever else is necessary
to help him through, and that will comfort me.

I am Beatrice who am sending you.   70
I come from the place I am yearning to return to.
It was love that moved me and love makes me speak.

When I am in the presence of my Lord
I will talk about you often and every word
will praise you.' She was silent then and I began,   75

'O lady of virtue, through you and you alone
mankind surpasses all that is contained
within the close sphere of the circling moon.

To do your bidding gratifies me so
that were it done already, it would be late.   80
Your will is my will, you need only say.

Yet tell me also why it holds no terror
for you to descend here into this deep centre
out of that spacious zone you are homesick for.'

'Since you are so penetrating and eager   85
for knowledge,' she answered, 'I will tell you briefly
why I am not afraid to enter here.

Only things with the power to do harm
deserve our fear, and those things alone –
nothing else, for nothing else is fearsome.   90

What you are suffering does not affect me
because God, by His grace, made me immune
and none of the flames burning here afflicts me.

In heaven above there is a gentle lady
so concerned for the vexed soul I direct you to   95
that the stern judgment has been eased on high.

And this lady was moved to intercede
with Lucy, saying, "I commend your faithful one
to you, who is sorely beset now and in need."

100   And Lucy, who abhors all cruelty,
arose and made her way to where I was
seated in ancient Rachel's company.

"You, Beatrice," she said, "true praise of God,
why won't you help the man who loved you so
105   that for your sake he broke from the common crowd?

Do you not hear the sorrow in his cry?
Do you not see the death assailing him
on that water which outsways the very sea?"

Nobody with more alacrity
110   ever sought the advantage or fled harm's way
than I, when I had heard these speeches uttered,

Sought to come down here from my heavenly seat
and put my whole trust in your noble language
which honours you and everyone who hears it.'

115   When she had finished persuading me
she turned her eyes away, shining with tears,
so I yearned the more to help, and accordingly

Have come to you because of her reasons
and taken you out of the path of that wild beast
120   which barred the short way to the lovely mountain.

What is it, then? Why are you hesitating?
Why do you let cowardice skulk inside your heart?
Why are you not daring and liberated

When three such blessed ladies have sued
125   on your behalf in the court of heaven
and my own words to you promise so much good?'

As little flowers, that were all bowed and shut
by the night chills, rise on their stems and open
as soon as they have felt a touch of sunlight,

So I revived in my own wilting powers   130
and my heart was flushed up with such bravery
that I began like somebody set free:

'Oh, what compassion she had who relieved me!
And what courtesy you have who obeyed
so quickly the true words of her plea.   135

What you have said has turned my heart around
so that I am now as ready to proceed
as I was before I started losing ground.

Go on, then, for one will informs us both.
You are my guide, my master and my teacher.'   140
This is what I said, and when he moved

I entered on the deep and savage path.

THROUGH ME IT LEADS TO THE CITY SORROWFUL.
THROUGH ME IT LEADS TO THE ETERNAL PAIN.
THROUGH ME IT LEADS AMONG THE LOST PEOPLE.

JUSTICE INSPIRED MY MAKER ABOVE.
5   IT WAS DIVINE POWER THAT FORMED ME,
SUPREME WISDOM AND ORIGINAL LOVE.

BEFORE ME NO THING WAS CREATED EXCEPT THINGS
EVERLASTING. AND I AM EVERLASTING.
LEAVE EVERY HOPE BEHIND YOU, YOU WHO ENTER.

10 I saw these words inscribed above a gate
in obscure characters; and so I said,
'Master, I find their sense hard to interpret.'

And he said to me like one experienced,
'All your distrust must be abandoned here,
15 here and now all cowardice must be ended.

We have come to the place I told you to expect,
where you would see that people in their sorrow
who have forfeited the good of intellect.'

And he put his hand on my hand then
20 with a glad look on his face which soothed me
as he led me in to the realm of things hidden.

Here sighing and laments and wailing cries
went harrowing the air where no stars shone
so that at first the tears came to my eyes.

25 A garble of languages, high baying sounds,
beseeching cadences, surges of rage,
screeches and moans and the plash of beating hands

Made pandemonium which does not relent
but keeps that darkened and timeless element
30 in turbulence, like sand in a whirlwind.

Horror reeled round my head and ringed me in
so that I said, 'Master, what am I hearing?
Who are these people who seem so lost to pain?'

And he said to me, 'Such are the sorrows
undergone by the stricken souls of those   35
whose lives were lived without disgrace or praise.

They belong here with that choir of angels,
the cowardly ones, self-seekers, self-preservers,
who did not stand with God yet were not rebels.

Heaven banished them, to keep its beauty pristine,   40
and deep hell does not admit them, in case the wicked
might show the fairer by comparison.'

And I asked him, 'Master, what kind of affliction
do they suffer, they lament so bitterly?'
And he, 'I will explain it to you briefly.   45

These ones do not have any hope of death,
and their life is so blind and abased that they envy
every other fate that souls can meet with.

The world lets no report of them survive.
Both Mercy and Justice hold them in disdain.   50
Let us not talk of them. Move on. Observe.'

And as I looked again I saw a banner
swirling and swept about at such great speed
it seemed compelled to shift like that forever,

And behind it such a long procession   55
of people, I should never have believed
death had brought so many to their ruin.

Among them were ones I could recognise
and when I saw and knew the shade of him
who made the great refusal through cowardice   60

Immediately there and then it came to me
that this was the useless crew who are repugnant
not just to God, but to God's enemies even.

These unfortunates, whose lives were without life,
65   went naked and were stung unmercifully
        by hornets and wasps that the place was swarming with;

        Their faces bled; the blood ran down in streams
        that mixed with tears and fell about their feet
        where it was ingested by repulsive worms.

70   Then, when I looked a bit ahead, I saw
        people on the shore of a great river
        and so I said to him, 'Now, Master, will you

        Instruct me about them and what it is dictates
        their readiness to cross over, or what seems
75   like readiness to me in this dim light?'

        'To you, these things are going to be plain,'
        he answered, 'the moment you set foot
        on the sad riverbank of Acheron.'

        Then, because I feared my words displeased him,
80   I walked on with a downcast, shamefaced look
        and until we reached the river I did not speak.

        And there in a boat that came heading toward us
        was an old man, his hair snow-white with age,
        bawling out, 'Woe to you, wicked spirits!

85   Never hope to see the heavenly skies.
        I come to bring you to the other shore,
        to eternal darkness, to the fire and ice.

        And you there, you, the living soul, separate
        yourself from these others who are dead.'
90   But when he saw that I did not stand aside

        He said, 'By another way, by other harbours
        you shall reach a different shore and pass over.
        A lighter boat must be your carrier.'

        And my guide said, 'Quiet your anger, Charon.
95   There where all can be done that has been willed
        this has been willed; and there can be no question.'

Then straightaway he shut his grizzled jaws,
the ferryman of that livid marsh,
who had wheels of fire flaming round his eyes.

But as soon as they had heard the cruel words,   100
those lost souls, all naked and exhausted,
changed their colour and their teeth chattered;

They blasphemed God and their parents on the earth,
the human race, the pace and date and seedbed
of their own begetting and of their birth,   105

Then all together, bitterly weeping, made
their way toward the accursed shore that waits
for every man who does not fear his God.

The demon Charon's eyes are like hot coals fanned.
He beckons them and herds all of them in   110
and beats with his oar whoever drops behind.

As one by one the leaves fall off in autumn
until at length the branch is bared and sees
all that was looted from it on the ground,

So the bad seed of Adam, at a signal   115
pitch themselves from that shore one by one,
each like a falcon answering its call.

They go away like this over the brown waters
and before they have landed on the other side
upon this side once more a new crowd gathers.   120

'My son,' the courteous master said to me,
'all those who die under the wrath of God
come together here from every country

And they are eager to go across the river
because Divine Justice goads them with its spur   125
so that their fear is turned into desire.

No good spirits ever pass this way
and therefore, if Charon objects to you,
understand well what his words imply.'

130　　When he had ended, such a violent tremor
　　　　shook the dark plain I still run with sweat
　　　　at the very memory of my terror.

　　　　The tear-soaked ground blew up a wind
　　　　that went foundering and flaring and flashed crimson
135　　so that all my faculties were stunned

　　　　And I fell like a man whom sleep has overcome.

Do you remember the beach

ANA BLANDIANA

Do you remember the beach
Covered with splintered glass,
That beach
Where we couldn't walk barefoot?
And the way you would gaze   5
At the sea, and gaze, all absorbed, and say
You were listening to me?
Do you remember
The gulls going wild, wheeling
Round and round as the bells   10
Chimed out behind us somewhere
In churches that had
Fish for their patron saints?
And how you headed away
At a run   15
Towards the surf, yelling back
That you needed distance
To be able to see me.
Then the gulls,
The swirl of the snow,   20
The spray, all of them mingled,
And I would look on
With a kind of desperate elation
As your feet marked the sea,
The sea that would close like an eyelid then   25
Where I waited and looked.

The country we come from

Let's talk about
The country we come from.
I am from summer,
A homeland so frail
5   The fall of a leaf
Could crush it to nothing.
Still, the sky there is gravid with stars
And sags so near to the earth, sometimes
Before you know where you are it is all
10   Brushed air, grass-tickle, star-giggles
And flowers: so many flowers
Ablaze like so many suns
Hurting your eyes,
Drying them up in their sockets.
15   And meanwhile round suns are hanging
From every tree.
Where I come from
The only thing missing is death.
There happiness is so abounding,
20   You keep drifting off, you are sleepy,
So sleepy, so sleepy.

Sometimes I dream

ANA BLANDIANA

Sometimes I dream of my body
Caught in a trawl-net of wrinkles
And pulled like a dead weight through snow;
This happens on a hard-frozen, dazzling beach
Beside a clear bay.   5
I never see the fisherman
But I know he's your father:
What I do see each time
Is the wrinkle-net and my body
Like a catch in its meshes, hauled up   10
Into the pure, unknowable dream
Of the morning I die,
        So peaceful
You do not enter it,
So silent I do not call out: 15

Everything is sleeping open-eyed
And the one thing that moves –
A light within that light, an echo –
Is a whisper-weak curse
That frays and unravels the net   20
So that I slip out again
To the timeless, immaculate waters.

Maybe there's somebody dreaming me ANA BLANDIANA

Maybe there's somebody dreaming me
And that's why my gestures have turned
So slack and soft-edged,
Their purpose forgotten half-way,
5   My every move idiotic,
Backsliding and groggy.
It explains these states of collapse
When my profile keeps fading
And all that I do melts away . . .
10   And whoever is dreaming me, maybe
Every now and again
He comes to his senses, dragged
Forcibly up from his sleep
And into his life,
15   The one that is real.
Which is why the shadows unnerve me
And I'm sometimes left hanging
On a melting thread of wet snow,
Not knowing if ever
20   He'll be able to get back to dreaming
So that something in my own life
Can happen to me.

It's snowing hostility

ANA BLANDIANA

It's snowing hostility.
There's hate in this snow coming down
On waters deep-frozen with hate,
On orchards that bloom for sheer badness,
On the embittered, suffering birds.   5
It's snowing as if the snow meant
To smother the life of this people
Aswim in their gifts.
It's snowing with a ferocity
That's only too human,   10
It's snowing with venom.
And is no one surprised?
Is there nobody else who remembers
That in the beginning this snow
Was a snowfall of love?   15
Now it is late
And the terrible blizzard's still blowing
And there's nothing for it, I think,
But to wait
And be there   20
For the famishing wolves,
At their disposal.

The morning after I die

ANA BLANDIANA

The morning after I die
Will be cool, like those misty September dawns
When the dog-days are over
And I blink awake in white air, making strange
5　At a woolly light in the trees.
And because it's September, I'll have come to
Very early and – again like September –
Be lonely enough to keep hearing
The air drip-dripping towards noon
10　Down the wet cheeks of quinces;
I'll be in a drowse,
Praying to get back to sleep
For a little while longer,
Lying there, never moving,
15　Eyes closed, my face in the pillow,
As the deafening silence beats louder
And louder and wakens me up more and more.

The start
Of that eternal day
20　Will be like a morning in autumn.

Inhabited by a song

ANA BLANDIANA

The song isn't mine,
It just passes through me sometimes,
Uncomprehended, untamed,
Lightly dressed in my name;
The way the gods in the old days   5
Would pass among people
Dressed in a cloud.

I don't know when it will come,
I don't know when it will go
Or where it is all the while   10
It isn't inside me:
My whole destiny is to attend
On the whim of a marvellous thing.

Inhabited by a song,
Forsaken by a song,   15
Maybe even the widow of a song
(My unknown beloved)
I am not the one for your laurels –
Except insofar as I've been
Its servant, humble and faithful   20
Right to the end.

Loneliness

ANA BLANDIANA

Loneliness is a town
Where everyone else is dead.
The streets are clean,
The street-markets empty,
5   Suddenly everything's in a true light
Through being deserted – exactly
The way it was meant to be.
Loneliness is a city
Where it's always snowing
10   Prodigiously, and no footsteps ever
Profane the layered
Drift of the light.
And you alone, the unsleeping eye
Keeping an eye on the sleepers, you
15   See, comprehend, and can't have enough
Of a silence so pristine
Nobody fights there,
Nobody's lied to,
And even the tear in the eye
20   Of the abandoned animal
Is too pure to hurt.
On the border
Between suffering and death,
Loneliness is a happy town.

Hunt

ANA BLANDIANA

I never have been in pursuit of words.
All I ever looked for
Was traces of their passage
Like the long silver haul
Of sunlight sweeping the grass   5
Or moonblinds drawn on the sea.
The shadows of words
Are what I hunted –
And hunting these is a skill
Best learned from the elders.   10
The elders know
That nothing is more precious
In a word
Than the shadow it casts
And words with no shadow to cast   15
Have lost their word-souls.

As if

ANA BLANDIANA

As if the light itself
Were merely a plant, as if the stars
Sent down their thin rays
Like capillary roots
5 Sucking at me, to extract
Their mysterious nutrient.
Astral blooms flock to the scalpel
Like crows to the plough.

The size of this field of light scares me.
10 With so many flowers to feed, I'm worn
To the bone, fulfilled and woozy with love.
And whom can I call for assistance?
Will nobody rid me, root, stem and branch,
Of this star-sprouting garden,
15 Burst the galactic, numinous dykes
And make way for the ocean of darkness?

Lament for Timoleague

SEÁN Ó COILEÁIN

for Benedict Kiely

One night, moody, troubled,
   I walked out near the sea.
Shaken, overwhelmed,
   Thinking compulsively.

Moon, stars up in heaven.   5
   A hush along the strand.
Perfect stillness. Treelines.
Tide resting. And the wind.

I walked like a sleepwalker –
   In a daze, lost to the world –   10
When next thing a church doorway
   Looms up in the road.

I stood in its ancient arch
   Where lepers had stood in their day
For their dole of alms; and I thought   15
   Of that lost community.

Broken forms lay nearby,
   Old benches all collapsed.
Scholars and clerics had sat there
   And road-worn travellers.   20

I sat myself. I pondered.
   I covered my head in my hands.
My tears were dew on the grass,
   My sorrows grain on the ground.

And I raved to myself about it,   25
   Lamenting on, heartsore.
'There was a time,' I said, 'when life
   Was whole in this enclosure;

A time of bells and brothers
   When sacred texts were read,   30
When choirs sang plainsong, and music
   Maintained the praise of God.

And God knows too what storms
    Bore down and beat these walls,
35 The tower, the mound, the entire
    Cloister-walks and gables.

Abbey, consecrated
    To the King of Hope Divine,
Abbey, you have endured
40   Hard frost and wind and rain.

O mossy mullioned rampart!
    O absence sanctified!
Your saints have been scattered far,
    Your sanctuary destroyed.

45 Desolate now, abandoned,
    No choir, no choir-stall,
The voice in your wilderness
    Is the screech of the night-owl.

Ivy sprouts on your arches,
50   Nettles root in the floor
And a fox keeps barking above
    The constant rush of water.

No meals in refectory,
    No beds in the sleeping quarters,
55 No order in possession,
    No mass being said at altars.

No abbot, rule or office,
    No round of disciplines.
All that remains is a pile
60   Of sticky, clay-streaked bones.'

And then I saw myself
    Like the monastery I mourned for,
Buffeted, exposed,
    And fated to endure.

The Yellow Bittern   CATHAL BUÍ MAC GIOLLA GHUNNA

Yellow bittern, there you are now,
Skin and bone on the frozen shore,
It wasn't hunger but thirst for a mouthful,
That left you foundered and me heartsore.
What odds is it now about Troy's destruction   5
With you on the flagstones upside down,
Who never injured or hurt a creature
And preferred bog-water to any wine?

Bittern, bittern, your end was awful,
Your perished skull there on the road,   10
You that would call me every morning
With your gargler's song as you guzzled mud!
And that's what's ahead of your brother Cathal
(You know what they say about me and the stuff)
But they've got it wrong and the truth is simple: 15
A drop would have saved the croaker's life.

I am saddened, bittern, and broken-hearted
To find you in scrags in the rushy tufts,
And the big rats scampering down the ratpaths
To wake your carcass and have their fun.   20
If you could have got word to me in time, bird,
That you were in trouble and craved a sup,
I'd have struck the fetters off those lough waters
And wet your thrapple with the blow I struck.

Your common birds do not concern me,   25
The blackbird, say, or the thrush or crane,
But the yellow bittern, my heartsome namesake
With my looks and locks, he's the one I mourn.
Constantly he was drinking, drinking,
And by all accounts I've a name for it too,   30
But every drop I get I'll sink it
For fear I might get my end from drouth.

The woman I love says to give it up now
Or else I'll go to an early grave,
But I say no and keep resisting   35
For taking drink's what prolongs your days.

You saw for yourselves a while ago
What happened the bird when its throat went dry;
So, my friends and neighbours, let it flow:
40   You'll be stood no rounds in eternity.

Raftery's Killeadan

in memory of Michael Durkan

Now spring is arriving and evenings are stretching
And after the feast of St Brigid I'll go
For I've taken a notion and grown impatient
To be back in the heart of the County Mayo.
The town of Claremorris will be my first station,   5
In Balla beyond it the strong drink will flow,
In Kiltimagh next I'll put up and be feted
And in Ballina too, a few miles down the road.

I swear and declare that my heart begins soaring
Like a freshening breeze or a mist the winds blow   10
When I think about Carra and crossing on over
To Gallen and all of the plains of Mayo.
Killeadan's the place that is fruitful and fertile,
There's blackberries, raspberries, plenty of growth,
And the minute I land there among my own people   15
The years will drop off and I'll get back my youth.

There's wheat and there's barley, flax-crops and oats there,
Rye with fine awns, red meat and white bread,
Poteen distilling, illegal shebeening,
People eating and drinking and out of their head.   20
There's ploughing and sowing and moulding and hoeing
And other activities yet to relate,
The mills and the lime-kilns at work unabating,
A heaven on earth and no paying of rent.

The lough laps with water, the river keeps running,   25
The weirs are in order, the nets in good shape,
The pike and the trout and the eel swim down under,
There are crabs on the bottom and seals on the top.
The mackerel shoals there, at night comes the salmon,
And elvers in millions awash in the surf,   30
And lobster and tortoise and turbot and gurnet
And the sea full of fish like a bog full of turf.

There's all of the timber that you could imagine,
Sycamore, beech, fir, hazel and ash,
Boxwood and holly, the yew, birch and rowan,   35

COMMENTARY 572 | 57

And green oak that's chosen for hull and for mast;
Mahogany, logwood, fine-grained and expensive,
That instrument makers esteem and expect,
The apple and whitethorn being cut down and seasoned,
40   And sally and willow for creel and for skep.

There the thrush and the cuckoo answer each other,
The hen-blackbird nests there, watched by the cock.
There goldfinch and linnet are birds of a feather,
The snipe whirring up and the lark on the bog;
45   The eagle of Achill, the Kesh Corran raven,
The hawk from Lough Erne and the white swan from Rome,
And if you were up with the sun in the morning
You'd hear every one of them sing in the grove.

The orphan and widow get aid and redress there,
50   Their means are restored, their holdings are free,
Poor scholars find schools there, get teaching their lessons,
And the street is a haven for buskers like me.
It's the first in the world for decent behaviour.
Raftery says so and gives it the palm.
55   So now it's long life to Frank Taafe who lives there
And his people before him in Raftery's home.

I am Raftery

ANTOINE Ó RAIFTEIRÍ

I am Raftery the poet,
Full of hope and love,
My eyes without eyesight,
My spirit untroubled.

Tramping west   5
By the light of my heart,
Worn down, worn out
To the end of the road.

Take a look at me now,
Facing for Balla,   10
Playing the fiddle
To empty pockets.

A School of Poetry Closes

TADHG ÓG Ó HUIGÍNN

Tonight the schools break up,
The beds will be deserted
And we who occupied them
Will weep and separate.

5   Too bad so many of us
Who bedded down last night
Here in our usual places
Won't close an eye tonight.

My God, how will I bear it?
10   My home from home abandoned,
And all its past fame cancelled.
What is the sense of it?

Towards Samhain the poetry class
Would reassemble always:
15   If one man were still with us
This break-up would not happen.

Whoever came here to him
For lodging and art-training
Would come to hate it, once
20   The cuckoo started calling.

For then the school broke up
And students headed homeward –
But now they won't be back here
For art or training ever.

25   I would think long when that break came,
I missed my class and master,
But thinking long won't soothe me
For the death of Fearghal Rua.

Since no one can replace him
30   It is better to disperse now:
Another teacher's lessons
Would be like going to prison.

For thirty years and over –
Let me be the first to say it –
His esteem kept me alive.   35
Now grief has dug my grave.

My God, how will I bear it?
I have drunk a bitter glassful,
And, God, it is all the sorer
In the aftermath of pleasure.   40

Without fail, every night,
I was close to him and working:
I shared the hut with Ó hUigínn
Until I was fully fledged.

And if anyone badmouthed me   45
Behind backs to my tutor
He never deigned to notice.
I basked in his good favour.

From childhood I was party
To his every plan and notion   50
(Ó hUigínn, God reward you!)
Then next thing we were parted.

Whatever poetry teaching
I give my students now
Was got from Fearghal Rua,   55
But it cannot match his teaching.

Through his death I realise
How I value poetry:
O hut of our mystery, empty
And isolated always.   60

Áine's son is dead.
Poetry is daunted.
A stave of the barrel is smashed
And the wall of learning broken.

Poet to Blacksmith

EOGHAN RUA Ó SÚILLEABHÁIN

Séamus, make me a side-arm to take on the earth,
A suitable tool for digging and grubbing the ground,
Lightsome and pleasant to lean on or cut with or lift,
Tastily finished and trim and right for the hand.

5   No trace of the hammer to show on the sheen of the blade,
The thing to have purchase and spring and be fit for the strain,
The shaft to be socketed in dead true and dead straight,
And I'll work with the gang till I drop and never complain.

The plate and the edge of it not to be wrinkly or crooked –
10 I see it well shaped from the anvil and sharp from the file;
The grain of the wood and the line of the shaft nicely fitted,
And best thing of all, the ring of it, sweet as a bell.

Colmcille the Scribe

ST COLMCILLE

My hand is cramped from penwork.
My quill has a tapered point.
Its bird-mouth issues a blue-dark
Beetle-sparkle of ink.

Wisdom keeps welling in streams   5
From my fine-drawn sallow hand:
Riverrun on the vellum
Of ink from green-skinned holly.

My small runny pen keeps going
Through books, through thick and thin,   10
To enrich the scholars' holdings –
Penwork that cramps my hand.

The Glamoured   AODHAGÁN Ó RATHAILLE

Brightening brightness, alone on the road, she appears,
Crystalline crystal and sparkle of blue in green eyes,
Sweetness of sweetness in her unembittered young voice
And a high colour dawning behind the pearl of her face.

5   Ringlets and ringlets, a curl in every tress
Of her fair hair trailing and brushing the dew on the grass;
And a gem from her birthplace far in the high universe
Outglittering glass and gracing the groove of her breasts.

News that was secret she whispered to soothe her aloneness,
10   News of one due to return and reclaim his true place,
News of the ruin of those who had cast him in darkness,
News that was awesome, too awesome to utter in verse.

My head got lighter and lighter but still I approached her,
Enthralled by her thraldom, helplessly held and bewildered,
15   Choking and calling Christ's name: then she fled in a shimmer
To Luachra Fort where only the glamoured can enter.

I hurtled and hurled myself madly following after
Over keshes and marshes and mosses and treacherous moors
And arrived at that stronghold unsure about how I had got there,
20   That earthwork of earth the orders of magic once reared.

A gang of thick louts were shouting loud insults and jeering
And a curly-haired coven in fits of sniggers and sneers:
Next thing I was taken and cruelly shackled in fetters
As the breasts of the maiden were groped by a thick-witted boor.

25   I tried then as hard as I could to make her hear truth,
How wrong she was to be linked to that lazarous swine
When the pride of the pure Scottish stock, a prince of the blood,
Was ardent and eager to wed her and make her his bride.

When she heard me, she started to weep, but pride was the cause
30   Of those tears that came wetting her cheeks and shone in her eyes;
Then she sent me a guard to guide me out of the fortress,
Who'd appeared to me, lone on the road, a brightening brightness.

*

Calamity, shock, collapse, heartbreak and grief
To think of her sweetness, her beauty, her mildness, her life
Defiled at the hands of a hornmaster sprung from riff-raff,   35
And no hope of redress till the lions ride back on the wave.

Jesus and the Sparrows

ANONYMOUS

When Jesus, Son of the living God,
    Was still a child, five years of age,
He played in twelve small water puddles
    That he blessed and fenced around with clay.

5   And Jesus made twelve little bird-shapes –
    The ones that are called *passeres*:
Out of the smooth clay he had modelled
    Twelve sparrows on a Sabbath day.

Then comes a Jew who cautions Jesus,
10   Son of the almighty God,
And takes him by the hand to Joseph
    To have him chide his foster son.

'Give your son a scolding, Joseph,
    Caution him for his misdeed.
15   On the Sabbath he has fashioned
    Clay images of birds.'

Then Jesus claps his hands together.
    They hear his child-voice give a shout.
Before their eyes the prince of graces
20   Scares a flock of sparrows up.

They hear him speak the clear small words.
    The pure lips of Jesus move:
'So that you may know who made you
    Fly home now. Away! Be off!'

25   A witness spread the news: a story
    Everybody marvelled at.
They listened and could hear distinctly
    The little cries of the birds in flight.

Saint Brigid's Wish

ATTRIBUTED TO ST BRIGID

I'd like the King of Kings to have
   The full of a deep bog hole of beer
And all of Heaven's kith and kin
   To be drinking out of it forever.

I'd like belief to be fermenting   5
   And stills to be running holiness;
I'd like the flails of penitence
   To beat a rhythm through the house.

I'd like the menfolk of high heaven
   To be the men of the house I own.   10
I would broach the barrels of my patience
   And draw the draught of satisfaction.

I'd like the cup of good to pass,
   Alms and dole to go the rounds,
Bumpers of mercy on the house   15
   And whatever they're having for all hands.

Elegy: The God in the Sea Greets Bran
in the Land of the Waves
ANONYMOUS

When Bran and his companions had been at sea for two days and two
nights, they saw a man in a chariot coming toward them over the sea.
The man sang to them and made himself known, saying he was
Manannan. These are some of the verses he sang:

Bran is astonished at the beauty of the waters;
his coracle lifts on the clear wave.
I ride where he rows; my chariot plunges, I
surge through a blossoming plain.

5   Bran rolls with his boat, the sea lifts and
lays him, he leans to the prow.
My chariot axle threshes a surf of wildflowers,
my wheels are spattered with flower juice.

Bran sees the backs of the waves like the quick
10   backs of dolphins; the sea surface glitters.
I see greensward, wild roses and clover,
the pelt of the grazing.

You look and next thing salmon leap out
of the foam; mother-wet silver.
15   They are my calves, my calves' licks, my
lambs, my bleating cavorters.

One chariot, one charioteer – me at full tilt –
that's all you can see.
You are blind to what's here. The land is a drumming
20   of hoofbeats, a mane-flow, a host at full gallop.

The land is immense, we swarm in its
bounty, it flourishes for us.
You are welcome; from the prow, gather up
the fruit of the branches.

25   Men and women, lovely, at ease among
windfalls. No sin and no forcing.
They rise off the forest floor, they pour
out the wine.

We are from the beginning, won't grow
old or go under the earth.   30
We cannot imagine debility; we
are unmarked by guilt.

Arion

ALEXANDER PUSHKIN

We were all there in the boat;
Some of us tightening sail,
Some at the heave and haul
Of the oars, vessel and load
5   Deep surging, our passage silent,
The helmsman buoyed at the helm.
And I, taking all for granted,
Sang to the sailors.
                    A wind
10 Struck then, a boiling maelstrom.
Helmsman and sailors perished.
Only I, still singing, washed
Ashore by the swell, sing on,
A mystery to myself,
15 Safe and sound on a rock-shelf
Where my clothes dry in the sun.

The Civil Power

When the great event was happening on the cross
And the racked godhead perished *in extremis*,
Then, at that solemn moment, on either side
Of the life-abounding tree, two women stood
        Steadfast and in pain: 5
The Virgin Mary and Mary Magdalene.
But nowadays beneath that blessed crossbar
What you see's not holy women but two guards
Like sentries at the city governor's door,
Armed men in shakoes, stern and sinister.   10
Can someone say why the area is secured?
Is the crucifixion now state-owned and sponsored?
A facility sealed off from thieves and vermin?
Or can it be the authorities imagine
This adds distinction to the king of kings?   15
Or that this show of force, this sentry-posting,
Can save the master whose obedience
Commits his flesh to the scourge and nail and lance?
Or are they scared that the common people's presence
Will offend the one who died with criminals   20
For the whole tribe of Adam? And refuse them entry
So as not to overcrowd the strolling gentry?

'Imagine striking a match that night in the cave'

JOSEPH BRODSKY

Imagine striking a match that night in the cave:
use the cracks in the floor to feel the cold.
Use crockery in order to feel the hunger.
And to feel the desert – but the desert is everywhere.

5   Imagine striking a match in that midnight cave,
the fire, the farm beasts in outline, the farm tools and stuff;
and imagine, as you towel your face in the towel's folds,
the bundled up Infant. And Mary and Joseph.

Imagine the kings, the caravans' stilted procession
10   as they make for the cave, or rather three beams closing in
and in on the star; the creaking of loads, the clink of a cowbell;
(but in the cerulean thickening over the Infant

no bell and no echo of bell: He hasn't yet earned it.)
Imagine the Lord, for the first time, from darkness, and stranded
15   immensely in distance, recognising Himself in the Son
of Man: homeless, going out to Himself in a homeless one.

Flight into Egypt

JOSEPH BRODSKY

In the cave – it sheltered them, at least,
safer than four square-set right angles –
in the cave the threesome felt secure
in the reek of straw and old clobber.

Straw for bedding. Outside the door,   5
blizzard, sandstorm, howling air.
Mule rubbed ox; they stirred and groaned
like sand and snowflake scourged in wind.

Mary prays; the fire soughs;
Joseph frowns into the blaze.   10
Too small to be fit to do a thing
but sleep, the infant is just sleeping.

Another day behind them now,
its worries past. And the 'ho, ho, ho!'
of Herod who had sent the troops.   15
And the centuries a day closer too.

That night, as three, they were at peace.
Smoke like a retiring guest
slipped out the door. There was one far-off
heavy sigh from the mule. Or the ox.   20

The star looked in across the threshold.
The only one of them who could
know the meaning of that look
was the infant. But He did not speak.

LYCIDAS
Where are you headed, Moeris? Into town?

MOERIS
The things we have lived to see . . . The last thing
You could've imagined happening has happened.
An outsider lands and says that he has the rights
5   To our bit of ground. 'Out, old hands,' he says,
'This place is mine.'And these kid-goats in the creel –
Bad cess to him – these kids are his. All's changed.

LYCIDAS
The story I heard was about Menalcas,
How your song-man's singing saved the place,
10   Starting from where the hills go doubling back
And the ridge keeps sloping gently to the water,
Right down to those old scraggy-headed beech trees.

MOERIS
That's what you would have heard. But songs and tunes
Can no more hold out against brute force than doves
15   When eagles swoop. The truth is, Lycidas,
If I hadn't heard the crow caw on my left
In our hollow oak, I'd have kept on arguing
And that would've been the end of the road, for me
That's talking to you, and for Menalcas even.

LYCIDAS
20   Shocking times. Our very music, our one consolation,
Confiscated, all but. And Menalcas himself
Nearly one of the missing. Who would there be to sing
Praise songs to the nymphs? Who hymn the earth
To grow wild flowers and grass, and shade the wells
25   With overhanging green? Who sing the song
I listened to in silence the other day
And learned by heart as you went warbling it,
Off to the Amaryllis we all love?
The one that goes, 'O herd my goats for me,
30   Tityrus, till I come back. I won't be long.

Graze them and then water them, and watch
The boyo with the horns doesn't go for you.'

MOERIS

And then there was that one he never finished,
Addressed to Varus, about a choir of swans
Chanting his name to the stars, 'should Mantua   35
Survive, Mantua too close to sad Cremona.'

LYCIDAS

If you've any song to sing, then sing it now
So that your bees may swerve off past the yew trees,
Your cows in clover thrive with canted teats
And tightening udders. The Pierian muses   40
Made me a poet too, I too have songs,
And people in the country call me a bard,
But I'm not sure: I have done nothing yet
That Varius or Cinna would take note of.
I'm a squawking goose among sweet-throated swans.   45

MOERIS

I'm quiet because I'm trying to piece together
As best I can a song I think you'd know:
'Galatea,' it goes, 'come here to me.
What's in the sea and the waves that keeps you spellbound?
Here earth breaks out in wildflowers, she rills and rolls   50
The streams in waterweed, here poplars bend
Where the bank is undermined and vines in thickets
Are meshing shade with light. Come here to me.
Let the mad white horses paw and pound the shore.'

LYCIDAS

There was something I heard you singing by yourself   55
One night when the sky was clear. I have the air
So maybe I'll get the words. 'Daphnis, Daphnis, why
Do you concentrate your gaze on the old stars?
Look for the star of Caesar, rising now,
Star of corn in the fields and hay in haggards,   60
Of clustered grapes gone purple in the heat
On hillsides facing south. Daphnis, now is the time
To plant the pear slips for your children's children.'

MOERIS

Age robs us of everything, of our very mind.
65   Many a time I remember as a boy
Serenading the slow sun down to rest,
But nowadays I'm forgetting song after song
And my voice is going: maybe the wolves have blinked it.
But Menalcas will keep singing and keep the songs.

LYCIDAS

70   Come on, don't make excuses, I want to hear you
And now's your chance, now this hush has fallen
Everywhere – look – on the plain, and every breeze
Has calmed and quietened. We've come half-way.
Already you can see Bianor's tomb
75   Just up ahead. Here where they've trimmed and faced
The old green hedge, here's where we're going to sing.
Set that creel and those kid-goats on the ground.
We'll make it into town in all good time.
Or if it looks like rain when it's getting dark,
80   Singing shortens the road, so we'll walk and sing.
Walk then, Moeris, and sing. I'll take the kids.

MOERIS

That's enough of that, young fellow. We've a job to do.
When the real singer comes, we'll sing in earnest.

Anything Can Happen

HORACE

Anything can happen. You know how Jupiter
Will mostly wait for clouds to gather head
Before he hurls the lightning? Well, just now
He galloped his thunder cart and his horses

Across a clear blue sky. It shook the earth   5
And the clogged underearth, the River Styx,
The winding streams, the Atlantic shore itself.
Anything can happen, the tallest towers

Be overturned, those in high places daunted,
Those overlooked regarded. Stropped-beak Fortune   10
Swoops, making the air gasp, tearing the crest off one,
Setting it down bleeding on the next.

Ground gives. The heaven's weight
Lifts up off Atlas like a kettle-lid.
Capstones shift, nothing resettles right.   15
Telluric ash and fire-spores boil away.

Summer

ANONYMOUS

Early summer, loveliest season,
World is being coloured in.
While daylight lasts on the horizon,
Sudden, throaty blackbirds sing.

5   The dusty-coloured cuckoo cuckoos.
'Welcome, summer,' 's what he says.
Winter's unimaginable.
The wood's a wicker-work of boughs.

Summer, and the river's shallow,
10   Thirsty horses nose at pools.
Heather spreads on bogland pillows,
White bog-cotton droops in bloom.

The deer's heart skips a beat; he startles.
The sea's tide fills, it rests, it runs.
15   Season of the drowsy ocean.
Tufts of yellow-blossoming whins.

Weak-kneed bees have gathered strength
To carry in loads reaped from flowers.
Mud wattles the hill-cattle's flanks.
20   Ant-swarms shine and feed for hours.

The forest is a wind-thrummed harp.
The tide fills now: now holds its breath.
Hillsides are ablaze with colour.
Heat haze veils the brimming lough.

25   The corncrake crakes away, a bard
True to his form; the cold mare's tail
Of a waterfall falls to the pool;
Rushes rustle, lake is still.

Swallows swerve and flicker up.
30   Music starts behind the mountain.
There's moss, a lush growth underfoot.
Spongy marshland glugs and stutters.

Bogbanks shine like ravens' wings.
The cuckoo keeps on calling welcome.
The speckled fish jumps; and the strong   35
Warrior is up and running.

Man's in his prime; the maiden proud
-ly budding into womanhood.
The wood stands tall; there's perfect calm
In treetops, on the level plain.   40

You've this mad urge to gallop horses;
Excitement stirs in gathered crowds.
Sun sends an arrow-shower of light
Into the ground, turns gold to iris.

A little, jumpy, chirpy fellow   45
Hits the highest note there is;
The lark sings out his clear tidings.
Summer, shimmer, perfect days.

Moling's Gloss

Among my elders, I know better
   And frown on any carry-on;
Among the brat-pack on the batter
   I'm taken for a younger man.

Colmcille's Derry

Why I love Derry:
  it is calm, it is clear,
transparent angels in every
  breath of air.

The Monk's Tryst

ANONYMOUS

Sweet-striking bell
   a-brangle in the small hours gale:
   better up with you for chapel
   than up late with some Jezebel.

Gráinne's Words about Diarmait

ANONYMOUS

There's one I want to look and look at,
   to whom I'd give the light-drenched world,
   all of it, all of it, and not care.
   I'd give it all and think it worth it.

Pangur Bán

ANONYMOUS

Pangur Bán and I at work,
Adepts, equals, cat and clerk:
   His whole instinct is to hunt,
   Mine to free the meaning pent.

5   More than loud acclaim, I love
Books, silence, thought, my alcove.
   Happy for me, Pangur Bán
   Child-plays round some mouse's den.

Truth to tell, just being here,
10 Housed alone, housed together,
   Adds up to its own reward:
   Concentration, stealthy art.

Next thing an unwary mouse
Bares his flank: Pangur pounces.
15   Next thing lines that held and held
   Meaning back begin to yield.

All the while, his round bright eye
Fixes on the wall, while I
   Focus my less piercing gaze
20 On the challenge of the page.

With his unsheathed, perfect nails
Pangur springs, exults and kills.
   When the longed-for, difficult
   Answers come, I too exult.

25 So it goes. To each his own.
No vying. No vexation.
   Taking pleasure, taking pains,
   Kindred spirits, veterans.

Day and night, soft purr, soft pad,
30 Pangur Bán has learned his trade.
   Day and night, my own hard work
   Solves the cruxes, makes a mark.

Hallaig

SORLEY MACLEAN

'Time, the deer, is in Hallaig Wood'

There's a board nailed across the window
I looked through to see the west
And my love is a birch forever
By Hallaig stream, at her tryst 5

Between Inver and Milk Hollow,
Somewhere around Baile-Chuirn,
A flickering birch, a hazel,
A trim, straight sapling rowan.

In Screapadal, where my people 10
Hail from, the seed and breed
Of Hector Mor and Norman
By the banks of the stream are a wood.

To-night the pine-cocks crowing
On Cnoc an Ra, there above, 15
And the trees standing tall in moonlight –
They are not the wood I love.

I will wait for the birches to move,
The wood to come up past the cairn
Until it has veiled the mountain 20
Down from Beinn na Lice in shade.

If it doesn't, I'll go to Hallaig,
To the sabbath of the dead,
Down to where each departed
Generation has gathered. 25

Hallaig is where they survive,
All the MacLeans and MacLeods
Who were there in the time of Mac Gille Chaluim:
The dead have been seen alive,

The men at their length on the grass 30
At the gable of every house,
The girls a wood of birch trees
Standing tall, with their heads bowed.

Between the Leac and Fearns
35   The road is plush with moss
And the girls in a noiseless procession
Going to Clachan as always

And coming back from Clachan
And Suisnish, their land of the living,
40   Still lightsome and unheartbroken,
Their stories only beginning.

From Fearns burn to the raised beach
Showing clear in the shrouded hills
There are only girls congregating,
45   Endlessly walking along

Back through the gloaming to Hallaig
Through the vivid speechless air,
Pouring down the steep slopes,
Their laughter misting my ear

50   And their beauty a glaze on my heart.
Then as the kyles go dim
And the sun sets behind Dun Cana
Love's loaded gun will take aim.

It will bring down the lightheaded deer
55   As he sniffs the grass round the wallsteads
And his eye will freeze: while I live,
His blood won't be traced in the woods.

'I sing of a maiden'

ANONYMOUS

I sing of a maiden   beyond compare:
King of all kings   she chose to bear.

He came all so still   where his mother was
As dew in April   that falleth on the grass.

He came all so still   to his mother's bower   5
As dew in April   that falleth on the flower.

He came all so still   where his mother lay
As dew in April   that falleth on the spray.

Mother and maiden   was never none but she:
Well may such a lady   God's mother be.   10

Cædmon's Hymn

CÆDMON

Praise we the Fashioner now of Heaven's fabric,
The majesty of his might and his mind's wisdom,
Work of the world warden, worker of all wonders,
How he the Lord of Glory everlasting
5   Wrought Heaven's rooftree for the race of men,
Then made Middle Earth to be their mansion.

The Light of Heaven

DANTE

With a smile Saint Bernard indicated
That I should raise my eyes; but already
Of my own accord I had anticipated

His wish, for my gaze was holding steady
And growing pure as it focused on that beam   5
Of the high Light which is *sui generis*

True. And thenceforth my vision was aswim
With sights beyond speech, which fails such witnessing
As memory fails when its contents overbrim.

Like somebody who sees things when he's dreaming   10
And after the dream has nothing to report
Except a recollection of the feeling,

So I live now, for the things I saw depart
And are almost gone, although a distilled sweetness
Still drops from them into my inner heart.   15

It is the same with snow the sun releases,
The same as when in wind, on swirled-up leaves,
The Sibyl's message eddies and disperses.

O Supreme Light, elevated so above
What mortal minds can rise to, restore to mine   20
Something of what You were when shown forth,

And empower my tongue so that I may illumine
The generations who are still to come
With a spark at least of Your pure serene,

Because, by returning to my memory some-   25
What, and being celebrated in these tercets,
Your overallness will be more brought home.

I believe – such was the sheerness of the light
I endured from the living ray – I would have been
Utterly lost if my eyes had been averted.   30

And it was on that account that I kept on
Looking directly into it, until
With the Infinite Worth my gaze made one.

O abounding grace, whereby I could still
35 Presume to look through the eternal light
So searchingly my absorption there was total!

In the depths of it I beheld infolded,
Bound by love into one single volume,
What is loose-leafed through the cosmos, far and wide:

40 Substances, accidents, and what connects them,
Diamond-bonded, fused so brilliantly
That compared with it my verse is a dim flame.

Everness of form I believe I saw,
Its knit and knot, because as I repeat this
45 I experience more and more onsets of joy.

Yet this very memory of it entails loss,
Oblivion greater than millennia have wrought
On the Argonauts and the Argo and their shadows

That astonished Neptune. And so my mind, all rapt,
50 Stood motionless and marvelled, concentrated,
Growing more eager the more it was absorbed.

In that light a person is translated
So far beyond it is impossible to consent
To turn away to any other sight –

55 Because the good, which is the will's intent,
Is all encompassed in it, and outside it
That which is perfect inside is much lessened

In perfection. But my language cannot
Equal what I remember: an infant's tongue
60 Bubbly with breast-milk would be more articulate.

Not because there was change within the one
Semblance apparent in the light I gazed on –
Which is ever simple, showing forth as shown –

But because in me my own altering vision
Was strengthened as it gazed, that same appearance   65
Seemed of itself to suffer alteration.

Within the incandescent deep subsistence
Of the Light on high, there appeared to me three circles
In three colours but of the one dimension

And one by the other as a rainbow by a rainbow   70
Seemed to be reflected, and the third seemed fire
Exhaled equally by those other two.

O how inadequate language is, how far
Short of my conception! Compared to what I witnessed,
My verse is weak, words barely register.   75

O Eternal Light who abide in your onliness
Who know only Yourself and, self-known and knowing,
Love and smile on Your own radiance.

That circling – those rings born from this glowing,
Made manifest in You as reflected light –   80
When my eyes had watched it for a while, kept showing

Forth from within itself, where it shone bright
In its own colour, the Image of us; and for that reason
My look was entirely concentrated on it.

As the geometer, lost in contemplation   85
While he tries to square the circle, won't give up
Although bewildered and balked of his solution,

So I was lost in study of that sight:
I yearned to see how the Image had inscaped
The circle and is co-extensive with it.   90

But my own wings were not equal to the flight
Except that my mind was struck by a bright bolt
And in a flash was granted all it sought.

Here power upholding high imagining failed,
But as a balanced wheel revolves and whirrs   95
My will and my desire were now revolved

By the love which moves the sun and the other stars.

Testimony: What Passed at Colonus

in memory of Czesław Miłosz

His instruction calmed us, his company and voice
Were like high tidings in the summer trees,
Except this time he turned away and left us.
He walked to where the stream goes underground
5   And a steep bank paved with flagstones
Leads down to a lintel in the earthwork.
And there he stood, studying what next,
Between a stone cairn and a marble plaque
To the dead of our late wars.
10 Other wars and words were in my mind,
Another last look taken upon earth –
Roads shining after rain
Like uphill rivers – so that I all but
Wept for his loneliness.
15   He loosed the girdle then
Off his scarecrow rags, called for his girls to fetch
River water for him, find a place
Where overhanging grass combed long and green
And dip their pitchers there. So off they went
20 And came with overbrimming vessels back
To pour a last libation and to wash
Their dear departing father, hand and foot,
Prepare his linen garment and do all
According to the custom for the dead.

25 And when all was done, and the daughters waiting,
There came a noise like water rising fast
Far underground, then a low blast and rush
As if some holy name were breathed on air,
A sound that when they heard it made the girls
30 Cry out, and made blind Oedipus
Gather them in his arms. 'My children,' he said –
And the rest of us felt that we were his then too –
'Today is the day that ends your father's life.
The burden I have been to myself and you
35 Is lifted. And yet it was eased by love.
Now you must do without me and relearn
The meaning of that word by remembering.'

Then the waterfall of sound behind him grew
Into an overwhelming cavern-voice
Shouting shouts that came from all directions: 40
'You there. What are you waiting for? You keep
Us waiting. It's time to move. Come on.'

And now he was a stranger. He groped in air
As the daughters went to him, heads on his breast,
And he found and kissed their brows, instructing them   45
One final time: they were to turn and go
And (these were his words exactly) not look upon
Things that were not for seeing, nor listen to
Things not for hearing.
        And what he said to them   50
We took again as meant for all of us,
So turned away together when he turned
Away, with the king accompanying him.

But after a few steps I and other ones
Halted to look back. He was gone from sight: 55
That much I could see, and against the sky
The king had his arm up shielding his two eyes
As if from some brilliant light or blinding dread.
Next he was on his knees, head bowed to earth
In homage to those gods who dwell in it,   60
Then up again with his arms spread out to honour
The gods on high, like a windlass being turned
By every power above him and below,
Raised out knowledge into knowledge, sole
Witness of what passed.   65
        No god had galloped
His thunder chariot, no hurricane
Had swept the hill. Call me mad, if you like,
Or gullible, but that man surely went
In step with a guide he trusted down to where   70
Light has gone out but the door stands open.

Testimony: The Ajax Incident

'Lamps had gone out, the late sentries dozed,
When something just came over him. He rose
And rigged for action, lifted down
His two-edged slashing sword, a bedside weapon
5   He kept like a second bedmate, then slipped outside
Far more nimbly than you'd have expected
For a man his size, with that night-mirroring
Blade in hand, aloft. Anything
I said meant nothing to him, mere
10   Wife-babble, ignored the same as ever,
Even though this time there was no attack
Being sounded, no command.

                 Then he was back,
In through the tent door like a conquering drover
15   With his captive on a rope: bull calf, heifer,
Milk cows, rams and ewes, the very sheepdogs.
How long he'd rampaged through their pens and paddocks
Or why he was herding them I couldn't tell
Until the butchering started. I can still
20   Hear the slosh of innards, piss and muck.
Some he beheaded with a single stroke
Down through the neck bone, some he wrestled flat,
Legs and belly up, and cut their throats,
For all the spurted dung and kicks and horn-toss.
25   Some that he tied and tortured like prisoners
Slit by slit, hamstring and lip and ear,
Just bled to death, hoofs beating at a chair.
At last there came a lull, then a tirade
Against those chiefs he thought he'd left for dead
30   On the floor behind him, once comrades, men of honour,

But now reviled; he stood by the tent door
Bellowing hate and havoc and their names.
Then, bloody-spoored and raving, in he comes,
Returning to his senses bit by bit,
35   And starts to butt the tent-pole, going quiet
As he climbs and slips and struggles through a mess
Of entrails splattered and opened carcasses.

And so for a long while he just lay there dumb,
Dragging his nails and fingers for a comb
Through his slathered hair, breathing like a beast   40
Slack-mouthed and winded. But came round at last,
Risen off all fours to overbear,
Turning on me to explain the massacre,
So I told him what I think he knew he'd done.

Then Ajax raised his voice in lamentation,   45
At bay now and in disproof of his rule
That warriors didn't weep, they weren't old women –
But soon his head-back, harrowing wail
Turned to the long deep moaning of a bull.

Slumped, slow motioned, he is in there still,   50
Ensconced on a pile of slaughtered meat and offal,
Lowing to himself. Something gathers head
And is going to happen. We must pay him heed.
Nothing is over, only overdue.
A friend should go to him. One, friends, of you.'   55

To the Poets of St Andrews

ATTRIBUTED TO ARTHUR JOHNSTON

As when in Lusitania once the legions
Stood under halted standards by Lima River
And refused to wade across the water north
To make war on the clans because the clans
5   Had spread a rumour that Lethe flowed to Ocean
By way of those clear, gravel-chattering fords
And silent bends, one veteran commander
(To show this was no bourne of forgetfulness)
Splashed into the shallows and kept going
10 Under his campaign gear, his spear-shaft firm
As his grasp on memory when he'd got across
And started to call back name after Roman name
Of his sweltering comrades,
So I
15 Who instead of spear-shaft grasp my crummock
And step wet from a ferry south of Forth
Recall your poets' names, in wind-borne Latin
Ut in Lusitania olim miles.

The Apple Orchard

RAINER MARIA RILKE

Come just after the sun has gone down, watch
This deepening of green in the evening sward:
Is it not as if we'd long since garnered
And stored within ourselves a something which

From feeling and from feeling recollected,   5
From new hope and half-forgotten joys
And from an inner dark infused with these,
Issues in thoughts as ripe as windfalls scattered

Here under trees like trees in a Dürer woodcut –
Pendent, pruned, the husbandry of years   10
Gravid in them until the fruit appears –
Ready to serve, replete with patience, rooted

In the knowledge that no matter how above
Measure or expectation, all must be
Harvested and yielded, when a long life willingly   15
Cleaves to what's willed and grows in mute resolve.

After the Fire

RAINER MARIA RILKE

Early autumn morning hesitated,
Shying at newness, an emptiness behind
Scorched linden trees still crowding in around
The moorland house, now just one more wallstead

5   Where youngsters gathered up from god knows where
Hunted and yelled and ran wild in a pack.
Yet all of them fell silent when he appeared,
The son of the place, and with a long forked stick

Dragged an out-of-shape old can or kettle
10   From under hot, half burnt-away house-beams;
And then, like one with a doubtful tale to tell,
Turned to the others present, at great pains

To make them realise what had stood so.
For now that it was gone, it all seemed
15   Far stranger: more fantastical than Pharaoh.
And he was changed: a foreigner among them.

Roman Campagna

RAINER MARIA RILKE

Out of the sluggish, clogged-up city, which
Would rather sleep on, undisturbed, and dream
Of its soaring baths, the road to the fever marsh –
The Appian tomb-road – heads past each last farm

And farmhouse, out under the malign   5
Gaze of windows that fasten on its back,
Unnerving it, driving it, ram-stam, on
Until, imploring, out of breath, in panic

And with a quick look backwards, to make sure
The windows have stopped watching, it entrusts   10
Its emptiness to the skies. And as the far

Aqueducts come striding up, alerted,
The skies that have absorbed its emptiness
Now substitute their own. Which will outlast it.

The First Step

CONSTANTINE P. CAVAFY

The poet Eumenis, a young beginner,
complained one day to Theocritus:
'For two years I've been writing and rewriting
and a single eclogue's all I have to show,
5   my one finished work. I'm at my wit's end.
I see how steep the stair of poetry is,
how high it reaches, yet here I am, no farther
than the first step. From where I stand
I know the climb will be too much for me.'
10   Theocritus answered him: 'That kind of talk
is disallowed, an affront to poetry:
to stand on the first step should make you proud.
You should be happy with the work you've done.
It is no small thing to have come this far.
15   Achieving this much is already glory,
for negligible as this first step seems
it elevates you to a different plane.
If you've come this far, it means you must belong
by natural right in the city of ideas.
20   And to be admitted there as a citizen
is no easy or no ordinary thing.
No dubious character has ever fooled
the legislators in that agora.
It is no small thing to have come this far.
25   Achieving this much is already glory.'

Dionysos in Procession CONSTANTINE P. CAVAFY

The artist Damon (who's to equal him
in the Peloponnese?) completes his Parian
marble 'Dionysos in Procession'.
First comes the god, all power and glory, striding;
Intemperance next, and staggering by his side   5
Intoxication, pouring out the red
for satyrs, from an amphora twined with ivy.
Then Sweetwine, lazy-eyed, a little wobbly
but dainty on his pins, and then the trio,
Carouser and Musician and High Doh,   10
who bear the sacred torch and guard the flame.
Then Ritual, last, the most demure among them.
Damon adds a finishing touch. But as he works
his fee comes more and more into his thoughts:
three talents, no small sum, his proper due   15
to be paid out by the King of Syracusae.
Add that to his savings, and he stands
in the front rank, well got, a man of substance.
He can even run for office – Damon! Hurrah! –
He too on the Council! He too in the Agora!   20

The Satrapy

CONSTANTINE P. CAVAFY

It's hard on you, born and raised as you were
for the noblest, most magnificent challenges,
that this frustrating destiny of yours
keeps blocking recognition and success.
5   Trivial things are forever in your way,
pointless small concerns, despondency.
And then the tragic day when you acquiesce
(the day you allow yourself to acquiesce)
and take the road, a client bound for Sousa,
10 to present yourself to King Artaxerxes –
who favours you with a place at court
and grants you satrapies and all the rest,
positions you don't want, but all the same
positions you accept in sheer despair.
15 Your soul seeks other things, repines for them:
the people's praise, and the Sophists',
that hard-won and most precious acclaim.
The Agora, the Theatre, the Laurels.
How could Artaxerxes give you these?
20 Where in the satrapy will you ever find the like?
And without them, how will you live? What sort of life?

Sculptor of Tyana

CONSTANTINE P. CAVAFY

As you'll have no doubt gathered, I'm no beginner.
These hands have gone through a fair amount of stone.
In my homeland, in Tyana, I'm counted famous.
Here too commission after commission
comes my way from senators, for statues.   5

                Let me show you
just a few. Take a close look at this Rhea,
primal, noble, the model of endurance.
And Pompey too, the work I've done on him. And Marius,
and the African Scipio. Then Aemilius Paulus.   10
Honest likenesses, truly my best efforts.
And here (unfinished, granted) is Patroklos.
And over there, beside those blocks and drums
of yellowish marble, that's Caesarion.

What preoccupies me just now is Poseidon.   15
For a good while I've been figuring how to shape
and fit the horses in. The entire group
has to surge above the waves, be so borne up
their hooves appear to skim each crest and whitecap.

Here, though, is my favourite in the workshop.   20
All of my tender care went into this.
On a warm summer day, when my reveries
were chasing the ideal, his form arose –
a dream I turned to stone in this young Hermes.

The Displeasure of Selefkides

CONSTANTINE P. CAVAFY

Demetrios Selefkides was displeased
to be informed a Ptolemy had arrived
in Italy in a lamentable state,
in rags, on foot, with just a handful of slaves.
5   Henceforth their dynasty would be the butt
of Rome's behind-backs laughter and snide jokes.
This Selefkides knows; knows they are little more
than houseboys in Rome now, now Rome decides
who keeps his throne, who loses, who succeeds.
10   Selefkides, yes, is aware of this,
but appearances, even so, should be kept up.
They should maintain a certain pomp and carriage,
not forget that they were, in spite of all, kings still;
and still did go (alas) by the name of kings.

15   That is why Selefkides was distressed
and offered Ptolemy sumptuous purple robes,
a glittering crown, diamond rings and gemstones,
a retinue of courtiers, liveried slaves
and a team of thoroughbreds, so he could appear
20   as any Ptolemy should appear in Rome:
an Alexandrian Greek monarch.

But Ptolemy, who had come to Rome to beg,
knew how it should be done and refused the offer.
There would be no flaunt or flourish. He approached
25   as if he were a nobody, in rags,
and boarded in the city with a tradesman.
Then came before the Senate, down on his luck,
a sad case and a beggarman in earnest.

'The rest I'll speak of to the ones below in Hades'

CONSTANTINE P. CAVAFY

'Yes,' said the proconsul, replacing the scroll,
'indeed the line is true. And beautiful.
Sophocles at his most philosophical.
We'll talk about a whole lot more down there
and be happy to be seen for what we are. 5
Here we're like sentries, watching anxiously,
guarding every locked-up hurt and secret,
but all we cover up here, day and night,
down there we'll let out, frankly and completely.'

'That is,' said the sophist, with a slow half-smile, 10
'if down there they ever talk about such things,
if they can be bothered with the like at all.'

Deor

ANONYMOUS

Weland the blade-winder   suffered woe.
That steadfast man   knew misery.
Sorrow and longing   walked beside him,
wintered in him,   kept wearing him down
5   after Nithad   hampered and restrained him,
lithe sinew-bonds   on the better man.
     That passed over,   this can too.

For Beadohilde   her brother's death
weighed less heavily   than her own heartsoreness
10   once it was clearly   understood
she was bearing a child.   Her ability
to think and decide   deserted her then.
     That passed over,   this can too.

We have heard tell   of Mathilde's laments,
15   the grief that afflicted   Geat's wife.
Her love was her bane,   it banished sleep.
     That passed over,   this can too.

For thirty winters –   it was common knowledge –
Theodric held   the Maerings' fort.
20   That passed over,   this can too.

Earmonric   had the mind of a wolf,
by all accounts   a cruel king,
lord of the far flung   Gothic outlands.
Everywhere men sat   shackled in sorrow,
25   expecting the worst,   wishing often
he and his kingdom   would be conquered.
     That passed over,   this can too.

A man sits mournful,   his mind in darkness,
so daunted in spirit   he deems himself
30   Ever after   fated to endure.
He may think then   how throughout this world
the Lord in his wisdom   often works change –
meting out honour,   ongoing fame
to many, to others   only their distress.

Of myself, this much   I have to say: 35
for a time I was poet   of the Heoden people,
dear to my lord.   Deor was my name.
For years I enjoyed   my duties as minstrel
and that lord's favour,   but now the freehold
and land titles   he bestowed upon me once   40
he has vested in Heorrenda,   master of verse-craft.
   That passed over,   this can too.

Charles IX to Ronsard ATTRIBUTED TO CHARLES IX

The art of verse, if its true worth were known,
Would be more highly valued than a throne.
We both wear crowns and crowns to both are due.
King, I inherit; poet, you bestow.
Your glory shines, self-born, by inspiration,
Mine, by virtue only of my station.
And no point asking gods to compensate me:
Ronsard's their darling, I their deputy.
You sweep the strings, air swoons, pure spirits soar,
The notes I play are dead weight in the ear.
Which gives you mastery and right of way
Even beyond the proudest tyrant's sway.

Actaeon

High burdened brow, the antlers that astound,
Arms that end now in two hardened feet,
His nifty haunches, pointed ears, and fleet
Four-legged run . . . In the pool he saw a crowned
Stag's head and heard something that groaned   5
When he tried to speak. And it was no human sweat
That steamed off him: he was like a beast in heat,
As if he'd prowled and stalked until he found

The grove, the grotto, and the bathing place
Of the goddess and her nymphs, as if he'd sought   10
That virgin nook deliberately, as if
His desires were hounds that had quickened pace
On Diana's scent before his own pack wrought
Her vengeance on him, at bay beneath the leaf-

Lit woodland. There his branchy antlers caught   15
When he faced the hounds
That couldn't know him as they bayed and fought
And tore out mouthfuls of hide and flesh and blood
From what he was, while his companions stood
Impatient for the kill, assessing wounds.   20

A Herbal

EUGÈNE GUILLEVIC

Everywhere plants
Flourish among graves,

Sinking their roots
In all the dynasties
5   Of the dead.

*

Was graveyard grass
In our place
Any different?

Different from ordinary
10   Field grass?

Remember how you wanted
The sound recordist
To make a loop,

Wildtrack of your feet
15   Through the wet
At the foot of a field?

*

Yet for all their lush
Compliant dialect
No way have plants here
20   Arrived at a settlement.

Not the mare's tail,
Not the broom or whins.

It must have to do
With the wind.

*

25   Not that the grass itself
Ever rests in peace.

It too takes issue,
Now sets its face

To the wind,
Now turns its back.   30

                    *

'See me?' it says.
'The wind

Has me well rehearsed
In the ways of the world.

Unstable is good.   35
Permission granted!

Go then, citizen
Of the wind.
Go with the flow.'

                    *

The bracken   40
Is less boastful.

It closes and curls back
On its secrets,

The best kept
Upon earth.   45

                    *

And, to be fair,
There is sun as well.

Nowhere else
Is there sun like here,

Morning sunshine   50
All day long.

Which is why the plants,
Even the bracken,

Are sometimes tempted
55   Into trust.

                   *

On sunlit tarmac,
On memories of the hearse

At walking pace
Between overgrown verges,

60   The dead here are borne
Towards the future.

                   *

When the funeral bell tolls
The grass is all a-tremble.

But only then.
65   Not every time any old bell

Rings.

                   *

Broom
Is like the disregarded
And company for them,

70   Shows them
They have to keep going,

That the whole thing's worth
The effort.

And sometimes
75   Like those same characters
When the weather's very good

Broom sings.

                   *

Never, in later days,
Would fruit

So taste of earth.
There was slate

In the blackberries,
A slatey sap.

    *

Run your hand into
The ditchback growth

And you'd grope roots,
Thick and thin.
But roots of what?

Once, one that we saw
Gave itself away,

The tail of a rat
We killed.

    *

We had enemies,
Though why we never knew.

Among them,
Nettles,

Malignant things, letting on
To be asleep.

    *

Enemies –
Part of a world

Nobody seemed able to explain
But that had to be
Put up with.

There would always be dock leaves
To cure the vicious stings.

    *

80

85

90

95

100

105

There were leaves on the trees
And growth on the headrigs

You could confess
Everything to.

110   Even your fears
Of the night,

Of people
Even.

*

What was better then

115   Than to crush a leaf or a herb
Between your palms,
Then wave it slowly, soothingly
Past your mouth and nose

And breathe?

*

120   If you know a bit
About the universe

It's because you've taken it in
Like that,

Looked as hard
125   As you look into yourself,

Into the rat hole,
Through the vetch and dock
That mantled it.

Because you've laid your cheek
130   Against the rush clump

And known soft stone to break
On the quarry floor.

*

Between heather and marigold,
Between sphagnum and buttercup,
Between dandelion and broom,   135
Between forget-me-not and honeysuckle,

As between clear blue and cloud,
Between haystack and sunset sky,
Between oak tree and slated roof,

I had my existence. I was there.   140
Me in place and the place in me.

                    *

Where can it be found again,
An elsewhere world, beyond

Maps and atlases,
Where all is woven into   145

And of itself, like a nest
Of crosshatched grass blades?

The Kite

GIOVANNI PASCOLI

There's something new in the sun to-day – but no,
It's something older, previous: at this distance even
I sense the violets starting to peep through

Beside the Convent of the Capuchins,
5   On the wood floor, between the stumps of oak
Where dead leaves shilly-shally in the wind.

A breath of mild air breathes, its gentle frolic
Cajoles hard clods, combs the yielding grass
Round country churches and in each green nook –

10   Air from another life and time and place,
Pale blue heavenly air that is supporting
A lift and waft of white wings on the breeze –

And yes, it is the kites! It is the kites! This morning
There's no school and we have come trooping out
15   Among the briar hedges and the hawthorn.

The hedges bristled, shivered, spiky, stripped,
But autumn lingered in red clumps of berries
And spring in a few flowers, still blooming white.

A robin hopped around the leafless branches.
20   In the ditch a lizard showed its darting head
Above dead leaves and vanished: a few quick scurries.

So now we take our stand, halt opposite
Urbino's windy hill: each scans the blue
And picks his spot to launch his long-tailed comet.

25   And there it hovers, flips, veers, dives askew,
Lifts again, goes with the wind until
It rises to loud cheers from us below.

It rises, and the hand is like a spool
Unspooling thread, the kite a thin-stemmed flower
30   Borne far away to flower again as windfall.

It rises and it carries ever higher
The longing in the breast and anxious feet
And gazing face and heart of the kite-flier.

Higher and higher until it's just a dot
Of brightness far, far up . . . But now a sudden   35
Crosswind and a scream . . . Whose scream was it?

My companions' voices rise to me unbidden
And familiar, the same old chorus
Of sweet and high and low. And there isn't one

Of you, my friends, that I don't recognise, and yes,   40
Of us all, you in particular, who droop your head
On your shoulder and avert your quiet face,

You, over whom I shed *my* tears and prayed,
You who were lucky to have seen the fallen
Only in the windfall of a kite.   45

You were very pale, I remember, but had grown
Red at the knees from kneeling on the floor –
All that praying in the flagstoned kitchen.

And ah, were you not lucky to cross over
With conviction in your eyes, and in your arms   50
The plaything that of all things was most dear.

Gently, I well know, when the time comes
We die with our childhood clasped close to our breast
Like a flower in bloom that closes and reforms

Its petals into itself. O you, so young, the youngest   55
Of my dead, I too will soon go down into the clay
Where you sleep calmly, on your own, at rest.

Better to arrive there breathless, like a boy
Who has been racing up a hill,
Flushed and hot and soft, a boy at play,   60

Better to arrive there with a full
Head of blond hair, which spread cold on the pillow
As your mother combed it, wavy and beautiful,

Combed it slowly so as not to hurt you.

August X

I know, St Lawrence, why so many stars
are burning, falling through the quiet air,
why such a great shedding down of tears
makes the vault of heaven sparkle sapphire.

5   A swallow was returning to her roof.
They killed her: she fell in a thorn hedge.
In her beak, an insect she was bearing off,
supper for her nestlings, still not fledged.

Now she lies there, as though upon a cross,
10   holding that morsel out to the far off sky
while her nest waits for her in the shadows,
chirping, faintly chirping, and more faintly.

A man too was returning to his nest:
they killed him: he said, I forgive,
15   and his open eyes preserved a scream of protest:
he was bringing two dolls home with him as gifts.

Now back there in the desolate home place
they wait for him, wait for him in vain
while he, overwhelmed and motionless,
20   holds the dolls out to the far-off heaven.

And you, High Heaven, infinite, immortal,
higher far than all the worlds serene,
you shower upon this dark Atom of Evil
a rain of stars, a brilliant inundation.

The Owl

GIOVANNI PASCOLI

Where was the moon? The sky
Was aswim with pearling dawn
And the almond tree and apple tree
Seemed to crane towards where it shone.
Then from a banked black cloud   5
Lightnings flickered and flew
As a voice came out of the wood:
To whoo . . .

A scatter of sparkling stars
In the milky misting light.   10
I could hear the sea's sad choirs.
Could hear the rustling thicket.
In my heart I felt a beat miss
Like a cry of loss, or its echo.
The sob dwindled into the distance: 15
To whoo . . .

Over all the moonlit heights
Wind trembled, sighed and shivered.
Cicadas finicky notes
Tuned up quick, quicksilvered.   20
(Chimes at invisible doors somewhere
Closed for good, perhaps, against you? . . .)
Then that banshee wail on the air:
To whoo . . .

The Fallen Oak GIOVANNI PASCOLI

Where once its shadow spread, the oak tree lies in state.
Its battle with the hurricanes is lost.
People say, Now I see the size of it.

Here and there inside its fallen crest
5   The small spring nests hang on in tattered bits.
People say, Now I see the good of it.

Everyone's happy, everyone's chopping at it,
Everyone goes home with his bundle of sticks.
Next thing, a cry on the air . . . A blackcap flits

10   Searching for something she won't find: her nest.

The Foxglove

GIOVANNI PASCOLI

I

They are seated, each gazing at the other,
One slim and fair, simple in her dress
And candid gaze, the other slim and darker . . .

Two modest artless eyes
Stare into the other two that blaze. 'And you never   5
Went back, ever?' 'Never' 'Or saw their faces

Again?' 'Never, no, again' 'But I, my dear,
Did go. Saw our white-veiled sisterhood
And relived our sweet times there, year after year,

Those brief sweet years the heart stores up for good.'   10
The other smiled. 'And do you still recall
That walled garden, with its bitter boxwood,

Its blackberries that ripened on the bramble,
Its junipers where the thrushes sang
And that mysterious corner with its tall   15

Fior di . . .' 'Flower, yes, of death.' 'But was there anything
True in the old belief that kept me wary
Of that sad flower, Rachele? For there was whispering

About it, that it oozed a kind of honey
Drugging the garden air, a drifting poison   20
That left the soul oblivious and drowsy.

Oh! that convent in the sky-blue mountains!'
As Maria speaks she places
A hand on her companion's

And they both sit, gazing into the distance.   25

II

They see. There rises in the intense
Blue of the Maytime sky their convent school
Plangent with litanies, redolent of incense.

They see. It's as if a scented phial
5   Perfumed their thoughts with gillyflower and rose,
And innocence and mystery swathed the soul.

Now there's a humming as forgotten melodies
Rise to their lips and, gently, very gently
Keyboards start to answer the touched keys.

10   Oh! what dear visitor smiled at you today
From behind the grille so that you came back
To the echoing dormitories, flushed and happy,

And on this day, when your high attack
On *Ave Maria* sounds loudest in the chorus,
15   All at once and who knows why, you break

Into tears! They both weep without cause
In the golden sunset. And now those schoolgirls play
In the garden, white dresses on the grass,

White-sailed chattering girls who occasionally
20   Come close, full-bloused and billowy.
Others stay back, reading works of piety.

A bit off from the ones who are at play,
There's a stalk with flowers, or better say with fingers –
Bloodied human fingers seemingly –

25   The secret life of it wafts forth and lingers.

III

'Maria!' 'Rachele!'. The hands of both are pressed
Together tighter still. In that moment they have seen
Their childhood, the dear world of the past.

Each from the pressure knows what the other one
Is feeling – memories, sad and pitiful   5
As the gradual fading of a farewell keen.

'Maria!' 'Rachele!'. The latter weeps. 'Farewell,'
She says to herself, then directs grave words
But not her dark eyes to Maria, 'I smelled,

Yes, I smelled that flower,' she murmured.   10
'I was on my own among the green rose-flies.
The scent of rose and gillyflower was carried

On the wind. In my heart, the ignis
Fatuus of a dream lit up the night
And at dawn, in my unconscious   15

Soul, went out. A night I won't forget,
Maria, ever. The air exhaled silence
And flashed with lightning. Cautiously, I stepped

Forward on tiptoe over lush embankments
Where long grass snared my feet. Why do you smile?   20
And "Come," I heard a voice announce

And "Come," it said again. I was beguiled
By a great sweetness, so great that, don't you see . . .?
(The other looks dismayed and her eyes have filled

With recognition as, trembling, she hears . . .) You die!'   25

The Dapple-Grey Mare

GIOVANNI PASCOLI

for Peter Fallon, with his hands on the reins

I

At La Torre farm silence reigned already.
By Rio Salto the poplars gave a sigh.
Big workhorses stabled in the farmyard
Nosed their feed and munched it, milled and hard.

5   In the farthest stall a wild one stood, a mare
Born among pine trees on a salty shore.
Sting of spray in her nostrils she remembers
And roaring of the sea in her pricked-up ears.

Beside her there, one elbow on the hay-rack,
10   My mother stood and very softly spoke:
'O little dapple-grey, my little mare,
You brought the one back who comes back no more,

You understood his words and horseman's ways.
He left a son, the first of my family's
15   Boys and girls, the eldest of the eight,
Who has never touched a bridle or a bit.

You who live exposed to the hurricane,
Be obedient to his small hand on the rein,
You with the salt-stung strand inside your heart,
20   Be obedient to this child, his horseman's word.'

II

The mare then turned her slender listening head
To my sad mother who still more sadly said,
'O little dapple-grey, my little mare,
Who brought the one back who comes back no more,

5   I know you loved and bore him on his path,
Out on your own there with him and his death.
And you, sprung from the wild woods, wind and wave,
You quelled the terror in your breast, stayed brave.

Between your cheeks you felt the bit go loose.
You took care to slow down and mind your pace   10
As you drew him gently on, to give him ease
In his agony, and let the end be peace.'

The slender long head with its pricked-up ears
Bent to my mother then. She spoke through tears:
'O little dapple-grey, my little mare,   15
You brought the one back who comes back no more.

Two words at least he must have, O, cried out
Words that you understand but can't repeat,
You with your legs looped in the dangling reins,
And in your eyes the muzzle-flash reflections.   20

With the echoing of gunshot in your ears
You kept on going beneath tall poplar trees.
You brought him back as the sun blazed on its pyre
That he might speak his words and we might hear.'

The mare's long proud head was all attention.   25
My mother clasped her arms around her mane:
'O little dapple-grey, my little mare,
You carried back the one who comes no more,

The one who won't return to me again.
You were good, but cannot speak – not now or then.   30
Poor thing, you cannot; others do not dare.
But you must tell the one thing I must hear.'

   III

'You saw the man, you saw the murderer.
His features linger on behind your stare.
Who is it? Who is he? When I say a name,
With God's help, give a sign if he's to blame.'

The horses now no longer munched their feed.   5
They slept and dreamt the whiteness of the road.
They didn't stomp the straw with heavy hooves.
They slept and dreamt of turning wheels in grooves.

In that deep silence my mother raised a finger.
She spoke a name . . . A great neigh rang in answer.   10

Du Bellay in Rome

JOACHIM DU BELLAY

You who arrive to look for Rome in Rome
And can in Rome no Rome you know discover:
These palaces and arches ivied over
And ancient walls are Rome, now Rome's a name.

5 Here see Rome's overbearing overcome –
Rome, who brought the world beneath her power
And held sway, robbed of sway: see and consider
Rome the prey of all-consuming time.

And yet this Rome is Rome's one monument.
10 Rome alone could conquer Rome. And the one element
Of constancy in Rome is the ongoing

Seaward rush of Tiber. O world of flux
Where time destroys what's steady as the rocks
And what resists time is what's ever flowing.

'Wind fierce to-night'

ANONYMOUS

Wind fierce to-night.
Mane of the sea whipped white.
I am not afraid. No ravening Norse
On course through quiet waters.

'Pent under high tree canopy'   ANONYMOUS

Pent under high tree canopy,
A blackbird, listen, sings for me,
Above my little book's ruled quires
I hear the wild birds jubilant.

5   From a shrub covert, shadow-mantled
A cuckoo's clear sing-song delights me.
O at the last, the Lord protect me!
How well I write beneath the wood.

'Towards Ireland a grey eye'

ANONYMOUS

Towards Ireland a grey eye
Will look back but not see
Ever again
The men of Ireland or her women.

'Birdsong from a willow tree'

ANONYMOUS

Birdsong from a willow tree.
Whet-note music, clear, airy;
Inky treble, yellow bill –
Blackbird, practising his scale.

Brothers

LAOISEACH MAC AN BHAIRD

You who opt for English ways
And crop your curls, your crowning glory,
You, my handsome specimen,
Are no true son of Donncha's.

If you were, you would not switch   5
To modes in favour with the English;
You, the flower of Fódla's land,
Would never end up barbered.

A full head of long, fair hair
Is not for you; it is your brother   10
Who scorns the foreigners' close cut.
The pair of you are opposites.

Eoghan Bán won't ape their ways,
Eoghan beloved of noble ladies
Is enemy to English fads   15
And lives beyond the pale of fashion.

Eoghan Bán is not like you.
Breeches aren't a thing he values.
A clout will do him for a cloak.
Leggings he won't wear, nor greatcoat.   20

He hates the thought of jewelled spurs
Flashing on his feet and footwear,
And stockings of the English sort,
And being all prinked up and whiskered.

He's Donncha's true son, for sure.   25
He won't be seen with a rapier
Angled like an awl, out arseways,
As he swanks it to the meeting place.

Sashes worked with threads of gold
And high stiff collars out of Holland   30
Are not for him, nor satin scarves
That sweep the ground, nor gold rings even.

He has no conceit in feather beds,
Would rather stretch himself on rushes,
35   Dwell in a bothy than a bawn,
And make the branch his battlement.

Horsemen in the mouth of a glen,
A savage dash, kernes skirmishing –
This man is in his element
40   Taking on the foreigner.

But you are not like Eoghan Bán.
You're a laughing stock on stepping stones
With your dainty foot: a sad disgrace,
You who opt for English ways.

The Drowned Blackbird
SÉAMAS DALL MAC CUARTA

Lovely daughter of Conn O'Neill,
    You are in shock. Sleep a long sleep.
After the loss of what was dearest,
    Don't let your people hear you weep.

The song of the quick-quick flitting bird   5
    Has fled, sweet girl, left you forlorn.
Always what's dearest is endangered
    So bear up now, no beating of hands.

Instead of keens and beating hands
    Be silent, girl, as dew in air.   10
Lovely daughter of Conn O'Neill,
    The bird is dead, don't shed a tear.

Child of that high-born kingly Ulster line,
Show what you're made of, don't let yourself go wild
Even though the loveliest bird in the leaf-and-branch scrim   15
Is drowned, washed white in whitewash: water and lime.

The Fisherman

MARIO LUZI

People arrive by water, unspeaking ones
keeping close to the hulls of the anchored ships,
startling at the bump as they heave to.

                           Early summer breathes
5   soft and low, wafts the curtains, caresses
grass, lightly stirs the hair.
It's sunrise, it is the hour
when nets are lifted, the hour of tremulous light,
its hesitant, uncertain brightening
10   from house to house as it conjures voids
and visions that abscond – look –
over the trees and beyond the hedges.

A time suspended between what is hidden
and what stands open, when it seems
15   the real is not inside us, but in some oracle
or miracle about to reveal itself, a time
that dupes men – and any hope it inspires
can be hope only for a sign or wonder.

My mood detaches me, makes strange
20   shades by the water's edge
and on the wet sand: I keep watching them
behind those spars and stunted poplar trees.

Forgive me, it is a mark of the human
to search out, as I do, what is close to us,
25   humble and real, in hidden places –
there and nowhere else. I crane my neck
to follow with anxious eyes the fisherman
who comes over to the breakwater and hauls
from the sea what the sea allows,
30   a few gifts from its never-ending turmoil.

We have already told how Sweeney, son of Colman Cuar and king §1
of Dal-Arie, went astray when he flew out of the battle. This story
tells the why and the wherefore of his fits and trips, why he of all
men was subject to such frenzies; and it also tells what happened
to him afterwards.

There was a certain Ronan Finn in Ireland, a holy and §2
distinguished cleric. He was ascetic and pious, an active missionary,
a real Christian soldier. He was a worthy servant of God, one who
punished his body for the good of his soul, a shield against vice
and the devil's attacks, a gentle, genial, busy man.

One time when Sweeney was king of Dal-Arie, Ronan was there §3
marking out a church called Killaney. Sweeney was in a place
where he heard the clink of Ronan's bell as he was marking out
the site, so he asked his people what the sound was.
  – It is Ronan Finn, son of Bearach, they said. He is marking
out a church in your territory and what you hear is the ringing
of his bell.
  Sweeney was suddenly angered and rushed away to hunt the
cleric from the church. Eorann, his wife, a daughter of Conn of
Ciannacht, tried to hold him back and snatched at the fringe
of his crimson cloak, but the silver cloak-fastener broke at the
shoulder and sprang across the room. She got the cloak all right
but Sweeney had bolted, stark naked, and soon landed with Ronan.

He found the cleric glorifying the King of heaven and earth, §4
in full voice in front of his psalter, a beautiful illuminated book.
Sweeney grabbed the book and flung it into the cold depths of
a lake nearby, where it sank without trace. Then he took hold
of Ronan and was dragging him out through the church when he
heard a cry of alarm. The call came from a servant of Congal
Claon's who had come with orders from Congal to summon
Sweeney to battle at Moira. He gave a full report of the business
and Sweeney went off directly with the servant, leaving the cleric
distressed at the loss of his psalter and smarting from such contempt
and abuse.

§5   A day and a night passed and then an otter rose out of the lake
     with the psalter and brought it to Ronan, completely unharmed.
     Ronan gave thanks to God for that miracle, and cursed Sweeney,
     saying:

§6   Sweeney has trespassed upon me,
     abused me sacrilegiously
     and laid violent hands upon me
     to drag me with him from Killaney.

     When Sweeney heard my bell ringing
     he came all of a sudden hurtling,
     raving and raging wild against me
     to drive me off and banish me.

     Insult like that – being thrown
     off the ground I'd marked and chosen –
     was too grievous to endure;
     so God inclined unto my prayer.

     My hand was locked in Sweeney's hand
     until he heard a loud command:
     he was called to Moira, bid to join
     battle with Donal on the plain.

     And so I offered thanks and praise
     for the grace of my release,
     that unpredictable off-chance
     of marching orders from the prince.

     From far off he approached the field
     that drove his mind and senses wild.
     He shall roam Ireland, mad and bare.
     He shall find death on the point of a spear.

     The psalter that he grabbed and tore
     from me and cast into deep water –
     Christ brought it back without a spot.
     The psalter stayed immaculate.

     A day and a night in brimming waters,
     my speckled book was none the worse!
     Through the will of God the Son
     an otter gave me it again.

This psalter that he profaned
I bequeath with a malediction:
that it bode evil for Colman's race
the day this psalter meets their eyes.

Bare to the world, here came Sweeney
to harass and to harrow me:
therefore, it is God's decree
bare to the world he'll always be.

Eorann, daughter of Conn of Ciannacht,
tried to hold him by his cloak.
Eorann has my blessing for this
but Sweeney lives under my curse.

After that, Ronan came to Moira to make peace between Donal,   §7
son of Aodh, and Congal Claon, son of Scannlan, but he did not
succeed. Nevertheless, the cleric's presence was taken as a seal
and guarantee of the rules of the battle; they made agreements
that no killing would be allowed except between those hours
they had set for beginning and ending the fight each day. Sweeney,
however, would continually violate every peace and truce which
the cleric had ratified, slaying a man each day before the sides
were engaged and slaying another each evening when the combat
was finished. Then, on the day fixed for the great battle, Sweeney
was in the field before everyone else.

He was dressed like this: §8
next his white skin, the shimmer of silk;
and his satin girdle around him;
and his tunic, that reward of service
and gift of fealty from Congal,
was like this –
crimson, close-woven,
bordered in gemstones and gold,
a rustle of sashes and loops,
the studded silver gleaming,
the slashed hem embroidered in points.
He had an iron-shod spear in each hand,
a shield of mottled horn on his back,
a gold-hilted sword at his side.

§9   He marched out like that until he encountered Ronan with eight psalmists from his community. They were blessing the armies, sprinkling them with holy water, and they sprinkled Sweeney with the rest. Sweeney thought they had done it just to mock him, so he lifted one of his spears, hurled it, and killed one of Ronan's psalmists in a single cast. He made another throw with the second spear at the cleric himself, so that it pierced the bell that hung from his neck, and the shaft sprang off into the air. Ronan burst out:

§10   My curse fall on Sweeney
for his great offence.
his smooth spear profaned
my bell's holiness,

Cracked bell hoarding grace
since the first saint rang it –
it will curse you to the trees,
bird-brain among branches.

Just as the spear-shaft broke
and sprang into the air
may the mad spasms strike
you, Sweeney, forever.

My fosterling lies slain,
your spear-point has been reddened:
to finish off this bargain
you shall die at spear-point.

Should the steadfast tribe of Owen
try to oppose me,
Uradhran and Telle
will visit them with decay.

Uradhran and Telle
have visited them with decay.
Until time dies away
my curse attend you.

My blessing upon Eorann
that she flourish and grow lovely.
Through everlasting pain
my curse fall on Sweeney.

There were three great shouts as the herded armies clashed and
roared out their war cries like stags. When Sweeney heard these
howls and echoes assumed into the travelling clouds and amplified
through the vaults of space, he looked up and was possessed by
a dark rending energy. §11

His brain convulsed,
his mind split open.
Vertigo, hysteria, lurchings
and launchings came over him,
he staggered and flapped desperately,
he was revolted by the thought of known places
and dreamed strange migrations.
His fingers stiffened,
his feet scuttled and flurried,
his heart was startled,
his senses were mesmerised,
his sight was bent,
the weapons fell from his hands
and he levitated in a frantic cumbersome motion
like a bird of the air.
And Ronan's curse was fulfilled.

His feet skimmed over the grasses so lightly he never unsettled
a dewdrop and all that day he was a hurtling visitant of plain and
field, bare mountain and bog, thicket and marshland, and there was
no hill or hollow, no plantation or forest in Ireland that he did not
appear in that day; until he reached Ros Bearaigh in Glen Arkin,
where he hid in a yew tree in the glen. §12

Donal, son of Aodh, won the battle that day. A kinsman of Sweeney's
called Aongus the Stout survived and came fleeing with a band of his
people into Glen Arkin. They were wondering about Sweeney because
they had not seen him alive after the fight and he had not been
counted among the casualties. They were discussing this and deciding
that Ronan's curse had something to do with it when Sweeney spoke
out of the yew. §13

Soldiers, come here.
You are from Dal-Arie,
and the man you are looking for
roosts in his tree. §14

The life God grants me now
is bare and strait;
I am haggard, womanless,
and cut off from music.

So I am here at Ros Bearaigh.
Ronan has brought me low,
God has exiled me from myself –
soldiers, forget the man you knew.

§15   When the men heard Sweeney's recitation they knew him at once
and tried to persuade him to trust them. He said he never would,
and as they closed round the tree, he launched himself nimbly and
lightly and flew to Kilreagan in Tyrconnell, where he perched on
the old tree by the church.

    It turned out that Donal, son of Aodh, and his army were there
after the battle, and when they saw the madman lighting in the tree,
a crowd of them ringed and besieged it. They began shouting out
guesses about the creature in the branches; one would say it was
a woman, another that it was a man, until Donal himself recognised
him and said:

    – It is Sweeney, the king of Dal-Arie, the man that Ronan
cursed on the day of the battle. That is a good man up there, he said,
and if he wanted wealth and store he would be welcome to them,
if only he would trust us. I am upset that Congal's people are
reduced to this, for he and I had strong ties before we faced the
battle. But then, Sweeney was warned by Colmcille when he went
over with Congal to ask the king of Scotland for an army to field
against me. Then Donal uttered the lay:

§16   Sweeney, what has happened here?
Sweeney, who led hosts to war
and was the flower among them all
at Moira on that day of battle!

To see you flushed after a feast,
poppy in the gold of harvest!
Hair like shavings or like down,
your natural and perfect crown.

To see your handsome person go
was morning after a fall of snow.

The blue and crystal of your eyes
shone like deepening windswept ice.

Surefooted, elegant, except
you stumbled in the path of kingship,
you were a blooded swordsman, quick
to sense a chance and quick to strike.

Colmcille promised you, good son,
sovereignty and salvation:
how eagerly you strutted forth
blessed by that voice of heaven and earth.

Truthful seer, Colmcille
prophesied in this oracle:
All crossed the sea and here you stand
who'll never all return from Ireland.

Find the answer to his riddle
at Moira on the field of battle,
a gout of blood on a shining blade,
Congal Claon among the dead.

When Sweeney heard the shouts of the soldiers and the big noise   §17
of the army, he rose out of the tree towards the dark clouds and
ranged far over mountains and territories.

A long time he went faring all through Ireland,
poking his way into hard rocky clefts,
shouldering through ivy bushes,
unsettling falls of pebbles in narrow defiles,
wading estuaries,
breasting summits,
trekking through glens,
until he found the pleasures of Glen Bolcain.

That place is a natural asylum where all the madmen of Ireland
used to assemble once their year in madness was complete.

Glen Bolcain is like this:
it has four gaps to the wind,
pleasant woods, clean-banked wells,
cold springs and clear sandy streams

where green-topped watercress and languid brooklime
philander over the surface.
It is nature's pantry
with its sorrels, its wood-sorrels,
its berries, its wild garlic,
its black sloes and its brown acorns.

The madmen would beat each other for the pick of its watercresses
and for the beds on its banks.

§18   Sweeney stayed a long time in that glen until one night he was
cooped up in the top of a tall ivy-grown hawthorn. He could
hardly endure it, for every time he twisted or turned, the thorny
twigs would flail him so that he was prickled and cut and bleeding
all over. He changed from that station to another one, a clump of
thick briars with a single young blackthorn standing up out
of the thorny bed, and he settled in the top of the blackthorn.
But it was too slender. It wobbled and bent so that Sweeney fell
heavily through the thicket and ended up on the ground like
a man in a bloodbath. Then he gathered himself up, exhausted
and beaten, and came out of the thicket, saying:
       – It is hard to bear this life after the pleasant times I knew.
And it has been like this a year to the night last night!
            Then he spoke this poem:

§19   A year until last night
I have lived among dark trees,
between the flood and ebb-tide,
going cold and naked

with no pillow for my head,
no human company
and, so help me, God,
no spear and no sword.

No sweet talk with women.
Instead, I pine
for cresses, for the clean
pickings of brooklime.

No surge of royal blood,
camped here in solitude;
no glory flames the wood,
no friends, no music.

Tell the truth: a hard lot.
And no shirking this fate;
no sleep, no respite,
no hope for a long time.

No house, humming full,
no men, loud with good will,
nobody to call me king,
no drink or banqueting.

A great gulf yawns now
between me and that retinue,
between craziness and reason.
Scavenging through the glen

on my mad royal visit:
no pomp or king's circuit
but wild scuttles in the wood.
Heavenly saints! O Holy God!

No skilled musicians' cunning,
no soft discoursing women,
no open-handed giving;
my doom to be a long dying.

Far other than tonight,
far different my plight
the times when with firm hand
I ruled over a good land.

Prospering, smiled upon,
curbing some mighty steed,
I rode high, on the full tide
of good luck and kingship.

That tide has come and gone
and spewed me up in Glen Bolcain,
Disabled now, outcast
for the way I sold my Christ,

fallen almost through death's door,
drained out, spiked and torn,
under a hard-twigged bush,
the brown, jaggy hawthorn.

Our sorrows were multiplied
that Tuesday when Congal fell.
Our dead made a great harvest,
our remnant, a last swathe.

This has been my plight.
Fallen from noble heights,
grieving and astray,
a year until last night.

§20   He remained in that state in Glen Bolcain until at last he mustered
his strength and flew to Cloonkill on the borders of Bannagh and
Tyrconnell. That night he went to the edge of the well for a drink
of water and a bite of watercress and after that he went into the
old tree by the church. That was a very bad night for Sweeney.
There was a terrible storm and he despaired, saying:
    – It is a pity I wasn't killed at Moira instead of having to put up
with hardship like this.
    Then he said this poem:

§21   Tonight the snow is cold.
I was at the end of my tether
but hunger and bother
are endless.

Look at me, broken
and down-at-heel,
Sweeney from Rasharkin.
Look at me now,

always shifting,
making fresh pads,
and always at night.
At times I am afraid.

In the grip of dread
I would launch and sail
beyond the known seas.
I am the madman of Glen Bolcain,

wind-scourged, stripped
like a winter tree
clad in black frost
and frozen snow.

Hard grey branches
have torn my hands,
the skin of my feet
is in strips from briars

and the pain of frostbite
has put me astray,
from Slemish to Slieve Gullion,
from Slieve Gullion to Cooley.

I went raving with grief
on the top of Croagh Patrick,
from Glen Bolcain to Islay,
from Kintyre to Mourne.

I woke at dawn
with a fasting spittle:
then at Cloonkill, a bunch of cress,
then at Kilnoo, the cuckoo flower.

I wish I lived safe
and sound in Rasharkin
and not here, heartbroken,
in my bare pelt, at bay in the snow.

Sweeney kept going until he reached the church at Swim-Two-Birds   §22
on the Shannon, which is now called Cloonburren; he arrived there
on a Friday, to be exact. The clerics of the church were singing
nones, women were beating flax and one was giving birth to a child.
    – It is unseemly, said Sweeney, for the women to violate the
Lord's fast day. That woman beating the flax reminds me of our
beating at Moira.
    Then he heard the vesper bell ringing and said:
    – It would be sweeter to listen to the notes of the cuckoos
on the banks of the Bann than to the whinge of this bell tonight.
    Then he uttered the poem:

I perched for rest and imagined   §23
cuckoos calling across water,
the Bann cuckoo, calling sweeter
than church bells that whinge and grind.

Friday is the wrong day, woman,
for you to give birth to a son,

the day when Mad Sweeney fasts
for love of God, in penitence.

Do not just discount me. Listen.
At Moira my tribe was beaten,
beetled, heckled, hammered down,
like flax being scutched by these women.

From the crag of Lough Diolar
up to Derry Colmcille
I saw the great swans and heard their calls
sweetly rebuking wars and battles.

On solitary cliffs, a stag
bells and makes the whole glen shake
and re-echo. I am ravished.
Unearthly sweetness shakes my breast.

O Christ, the loving and the sinless,
hear my prayer, attend, O Christ,
and let nothing separate us.
Blend me forever in your sweetness.

§24   The next day Sweeney went on to St Derville's church, west of Erris,
where he fed on watercress and drank the water that was in the
church. The night was tempestuous, and he was shaken with grief
at his misery and deprivation. He was also homesick for Dal-Arie
and spoke these verses:

§25   I pined the whole night
in Derville's chapel
for Dal-Arie
and peopled the dark

with a thousand ghosts.
My dream restored me:
the army lay at Drumfree
and I came into my kingdom,

camped with my troop,
back with Faolchu and Congal
for our night at Drumduff.
Taunters, will-o'-the-wisps,

who saw me brought to heel
at Moira, you crowd my head
and fade away
and leave me to the night.

Sweeney wandered Ireland for all of the next seven years until §26
one night he arrived back in Glen Bolcain. That was his ark and
his Eden, where he would go to ground and would only leave when
terror struck. He stayed there that night and the next morning
Lynchseachan arrived looking for him. Some say Lynchseachan
was a half-brother of Sweeney's, some say he was a foster-brother,
but whichever he was, he was deeply concerned for Sweeney and
brought him back three times out of his madness.

 This time Lynchseachan was after him in the glen and found
his footprints on the bank of the stream where Sweeney would go
to eat watercress. He also followed the trail of snapped branches
where Sweeney had shifted from tree to tree. But he did not catch up
that day, so he went into a deserted house in the glen and lay down,
fatigued by all his trailing and scouting. Soon he was in a deep sleep.

 Then Sweeney, following the tracks of his tracker, was led to
the house and stood listening to the snores of Lynchseachan; and
consequently he came out with this poem:

I dare not sink down, snore and fall §27
fast asleep like the man at the wall,
I who never batted an eye
during the seven years since Moira.

God of Heaven! Why did I go
battling out that famous Tuesday
to end up changed into Mad Sweeney,
roosting alone up in the ivy?

From the well at Druim Crib, watercress
supplies my bit and sup at terce;
its juices that have greened my chin
are Sweeney's markings and his birth-stain.

And the manhunt is an expiation.
Mad Sweeney is on the run
and sleeps curled up beneath a rag
under the shadow of Slieve League –

long cut off from the happy time
when I lived apart, an honoured name;
long exiled from those rushy hillsides,
far from my home among the reeds.

I give thanks to the King above
whose harshness only proves His love
which was outraged by my offence
and shaped my new shape for my sins –

shivering; glimpsed against the sky,
a waif alarmed out of the ivy.
Going drenched in teems of rain,
crouching under thunderstorms.

Though I still have life, haunting deep
in the yew glen, climbing mountain slopes,
I would swop places with Congal Claon,
stretched on his back among the slain.

My life is steady lamentation.
The roof above my head has gone.
I am doomed to rags, starved and mad,
brought to this by the power of God.

It was sheer madness to imagine
any life outside Glen Bolcain –
Glen Bolcain, my pillow and heart's ease,
my Eden thick with apple trees.

What does he know, the man at the wall,
how Sweeney managed since his downfall?
Going stooped through the long grass.
A sup of water. Watercress.

Summering where herons stalk.
Wintering out among wolf-packs.
Plumed with twigs that green and fall.
What does he know, the man at the wall?

I who once camped among mad friends
in Bolcain, happy glen of winds
and wind-borne echoes, live miserable
beyond the dreams of the man at the wall.

After that poem he arrived, on the following night, at a mill owned §28
by Lynchseachan. The caretaker of the mill was Lynchseachan's
mother-in-law, an old woman called Lonnog, daughter of Dubh
Dithribh. When Sweeney went in to see her she gave him a few
scraps to eat and so, for a long time, he kept coming back to the mill.

One day when Lynchseachan was out trailing him, he caught sight
of Sweeney by the mill-stream, and went to speak to the old woman.

– Has Sweeney come to the mill? said Lynchseachan.

– He was here last night, said the woman.

Lynchseachan then disguised himself as his mother-in-law and
sat on in the mill after she had gone, until Sweeney arrived that night.
But when Sweeney saw the eyes under the shawl, he recognised
Lynchseachan and at once sprang out of his reach and up through
the skylight, saying:

– This is a pitiful jaunt you are on, Lynchseachan, hunting me
from every place I love in Ireland. Don't you know Ronan has left
me with the fears of a bird, so I cannot trust you? I am exasperated
at the way you are constantly after me.

And he made this poem:

Lynchseachan, you are a bother. §29
Leave me alone, give me peace.
Is it not enough that Ronan doomed me
to live furtive and suspicious?

When I let fly that fatal spear
at Ronan in the heat of battle
it split his holy breastplate open,
it made a dent in his cleric's bell.

When I nailed him in the battle
with that magnificent spear-cast,
– Let the freedom of the birds be yours!
was how he prayed, Ronan the priest.

And I rebounded off his prayer
up, up and up, flying through air
lighter and nimbler and far higher
than I would ever fly again.

To see me in my morning glory
that Tuesday morning, turn time back:
still in my mind's eye I march out
in rank, in step with my own folk.

But now, with my own two eyes I see
a thing that's more astonishing:
under the hood of a woman's shawl,
the weather eyes of Lynchseachan.

§30   – All you intend is to make me ridiculous, he said. Leave off,
harass me no more but go back to your own place and I will go on
to see Eorann.

§31   When Sweeney deserted the kingship, his wife had gone to live
with Guaire. There had been two kinsmen with equal rights to
the kingship Sweeney had abandoned, two grandsons of Scannlan's
called Guaire and Eochaidh. At that time, Eorann was with Guaire
and they had gone hunting through the Fews towards Edenterriff
in Cavan. His camp was near Glen Bolcain, on a plain in the
Armagh district.
      Sweeney landed on the lintel of Eorann's hut and spoke to her:
      – Do you remember, lady, the great love we shared when we
were together? Life is still a pleasure to you but not to me.
      And this exchange ensued between them:

§32   SWEENEY
Restless as wingbeats
of memory, I hover
above you, and your bed
still warm from your lover.

Remember when you played
the promise-game with me?
Sun and moon would have died
if ever you lost your Sweeney!

But you have broken trust,
unmade it like a bed –
not mine in the dawn frost
but yours, that he invaded.

EORANN
Welcome here, my crazy dote,
my first and last and favourite!
I'm easy now, and yet I wasted
at the cruel news of your being bested.

SWEENEY
There's more welcome for the prince
who preens for you and struts
to those amorous banquets
where Sweeney feasted once.

EORANN
All the same, I would prefer
a hollow tree and Sweeney bare –
that sweetest game we used to play –
to banqueting with him today.

I tell you, Sweeney, if I were given
the pick of all in earth and Ireland,
I'd rather go with you, live sinless
and sup on water and watercress.

SWEENEY
But cold and hard as stone
lies Sweeney's path
through the beds of Lisardowlin.
There I go to earth

in panic, starved and bare,
a rickle of skin and bones.
I am yours no longer.
And you are another man's.

EORANN
My poor tormented lunatic!
When I see you like this it makes me sick,
your cheek gone pale, your skin all scars,
ripped and scored by thorns and briars.

SWEENEY
And yet I hold no grudge,
my gentle one.
Christ ordained my bondage
and exhaustion.

EORANN
I wish we could fly away together,
be rolling stones, birds of a feather:

I'd swoop to pleasure you in flight
and huddle close on the roost at night.

SWEENEY
I have gone north and south.
One night I was in the Mournes.
I have wandered as far as the Bann mouth
and Kilsooney.

§33 They had no sooner finished than the army swept into the camp
from every side, and as usual, he was away in panic, never stopping
until twilight, when he arrived at Ros Bearaigh – that church where
he first halted after the battle of Moira – and again he went into
the yew tree of the church. Murtagh McEarca was erenach of the
church at the time and his wife was passing the yew when by chance
she caught sight of the madman. Recognising Sweeney, she said:
  – Come down out of the yew. I know you are king of Dal-Arie,
and there is nobody here but myself, a woman on her own.
  That is what she said, though she hoped to beguile him somehow
into a trap and catch him.
  – Indeed I shall not come down, said Sweeney, for Lynchseachan
and his wife might come upon me. But am I not hard to recognise
nowadays?
  And he uttered these stanzas:

§34 Only your hawk eye
could pick me out
who was cock of the walk once
in Dal-Arie –

the talk of Ireland
for style and appearance.
Since the shock of battle
I'm a ghost of myself.

So, good woman, mind
your husband and your house.
I cannot stay. We shall meet
again on Judgement Day.

§35 He cleared the tree lightly and nimbly and went on his way until
he reached the old tree in Rasharkin, which was one of the three
hide-outs he had in his own country, the others being at Teach

mic Ninnedha and Cluan Creamha. He lodged undiscovered there for six weeks in the yew tree but he was detected in the end and the nobles of Dal-Arie held a meeting to decide who should go to apprehend him. Lynchseachan was the unanimous choice and he agreed to go.

Off he went to the tree and there was Sweeney, perched on a branch above him.

– It is a pity, Sweeney, he said, that you ended up like this, like any bird of the air, without food or drink or clothes, you that went in silk and satin and rode foreign steeds in their matchless harness. Do you remember your train, the lovely gentle women, the many young men and their hounds, the retinue of craftsmen? Do you remember the assemblies under your sway? Do you remember the cups and goblets and carved horns that flowed with pleasant heady drink? It is a pity to find you like any poor bird flitting from one waste ground to the next.

– Stop now, said Sweeney, it was my destiny. But have you any news for me about my country?

– I have indeed, said Lynchseachan, for your father is dead.

– That is a seizure, he said.

– Your mother is dead too, said the young man.

– There'll be pity from nobody now, he said.

– And your brother, said Lynchseachan.

– My side bleeds for that, said Sweeney.

– Your daughter is dead, said Lynchseachan.

– The heart's needle is an only daughter, said Sweeney.

– And your son who used to call you Daddy, said Lynchseachan.

– Indeed, he said, that is the drop that fells me to the ground.

After that, Sweeney and Lynchseachan made up this poem between them:

LYNCHSEACHAN §36
Sweeney from the high mountains,
blooded swordsman, veteran:
for the sake of Christ, your judge and saviour,
speak to me, your foster-brother.

If you hear me, listen. Listen,
my royal lord, my great prince,
for I bring, as gently as I can,
the bad news from your native ground.

You left behind a dead kingdom
and that is why I had to come
with tidings of a dead brother,
a father dead, a dead mother.

SWEENEY
If my gentle mother's dead, I face
a harder exile from my place;
yet she had cooled in love of me
and love that's cooled is worse than pity.

The son whose father's lately dead
kicks the trace and lives unbridled.
His pain's a branch bowed down with nuts.
A dead brother is a wounded side.

LYNCHSEACHAN
Things that the world already knows
I still must break to you as news:
thin as you are, and starved, your wife
pined after you, and died of grief.

SWEENEY
A household when the wife is gone,
a boat that's rudderless in storm;
it is pens of feathers next the skin;
a widower at his bleak kindling.

LYNCHSEACHAN
Sorrow accumulates: heartbreak,
keens and wailings fill the air.
but all of that's like a fist round smoke
now that you have lost your sister.

SWEENEY
No common wisdom I might invoke
can stanch the wound from such a stroke.
A sister's love is still, unselfish,
like sunlight mild upon a ditch.

LYNCHSEACHAN
Our north is colder than it was,
calves are kept in from their cows

since your daughter and sister's son,
who both loved you, were stricken down.

SWEENEY
My faithful hound, my faithful nephew –
no bribe could buy their love of me.
But you've unstitched the rent of sorrow.
The heart's needle is an only daughter.

LYNCHSEACHAN
I have to tell what I would keep back.
It wounds me to the very quick!
In Dal-Arie, everyone
laments the death of your son.

SWEENEY
This is the news that daunts all men.
This is the thing that brings us down –
the loss, the wound in memory,
the death of him who called me *Daddy*.

This is a blow I cannot stand.
Here resistance has to end.
You are the beater, I the bird
frightened and driven out of covert.

LYNCHSEACHAN
Sweeney, now you are in my hands,
I tell you I can heal these wounds.
None of your family's in the grave.
All your people are alive.

Calm yourself. Come to. Rest.
Come home east. Forget the west.
Admit, Sweeney, you have come too far
from where your heart's affections are.

Woods and forests and wild deer –
things like these delight you more
than sleeping in your eastern dun
on a bed of feather-down.

Near a quick mill-pond, your perch
on a dark green holly branch

means more now than any feast
among the brightest and the best.

Harp music in the breasting hills
would not soothe you: you would still
strain to hear from the oak-wood
the brown stag belling to the herd.

Swifter than the wind in glens,
once the figure of a champion,
now a legend, and a madman –
your exile's over, Sweeney. Come.

§37   When Sweeney heard the news of his only son he fell from the yew
tree and Lynchseachan caught him and put manacles on him.
Then he told him that all his people were alive, and escorted him
back to the assembled nobles of Dal-Arie. They produced locks
and fetters in which they shackled Sweeney and left him under
Lynchseachan's supervision for the next six weeks. During that
time the nobles of the province kept visiting him, and at the end
of it, his sense and memory came back to him and he felt himself
restored to his old shape and manner. So they took the tackle
off him and he was back to his former self, the man they had
known as king.
     After that, Sweeney was quartered in Lynchseachan's bedroom.
Then harvest time came round and one day Lynchseachan went
with his people to reap. Sweeney, shut in the bedroom, was left
in the care of the mill-hag, who was warned not to speak to him.
All the same, she did speak to him, asking him to relate some of
his adventures when he was in his state of madness.
     – A curse on your mouth, hag, said Sweeney, for your talk is
dangerous. God will not allow me to go mad again.
     – It was your insult to Ronan that put you mad, said the hag.
     – This is hateful, he said, to have to put up with your treachery
and trickery.
     – It is no treachery, only the truth.
     And Sweeney said:

§38   SWEENEY
Hag, did you come here from your mill
to spring me over wood and hill?
Is it to be a woman's ploy
and treachery to send me astray?

THE HAG

Sweeney, your sorrows are well known,
but I am not the treacherous one:
the miracles of holy Ronan
maddened and drove you among madmen.

SWEENEY

If I were king and I wish I were
again the king who held sway here,
instead of the banquet and ale-mug
I'd give you a fist on the mouth, hag.

– Now listen, woman, he said, if you only knew the hard times §39
I have been through. Many's the dreadful leap I have leaped from
hill and fort and land and valley.
　　– For God's sake, said the hag, let me see one of those leaps
now. Show me how you did it when you were off in your madness.
　　With that, he bounded over the bed-rail and lit on the end of
the bench.
　　– Sure I could do that leap myself, said the hag, and she did it.
　　Then Sweeney took another leap out through the skylight of
the lodge.
　　– I could do that too, said the hag, and leaped it, there and then.
　　Anyhow, this is the way it ended up: Sweeney went lifting over
five cantreds of Dal-Arie that day until he arrived at Gleann na
n-Eachtach in Feegile and she was on his heels the whole way.
When he took a rest there, in the top of an ivy-bunch, the hag
perched on another tree beside him.
　　It was the end of the harvest season and Sweeney heard a
hunting-call from a company in the skirts of the wood.
　　– This will be the outcry of the Ui Faolain coming to kill me,
he said. I slew their king at Moira and this host is out to avenge him.
　　He heard the stag bellowing and he made a poem in which he
praised aloud all the trees of Ireland, and rehearsed some of his
own hardships and sorrows, saying:

Suddenly this bleating §40
and belling in the glen!
The little timorous stag
like a scared musician

startles my heartstrings
with high homesick refrains –

deer on my lost mountains,
flocks out on the plain.

The bushy leafy oak tree
is highest in the wood,
the forking shoots of hazel
hide sweet hazel-nuts.

The alder is my darling,
all thornless in the gap,
some milk of human kindness
coursing in its sap.

The blackthorn is a jaggy creel
stippled with dark sloes;
green watercress in thatch on wells
where the drinking blackbird goes.

Sweetest of the leafy stalks,
the vetches strew the pathway;
the oyster-grass is my delight,
and the wild strawberry.

Low-set clumps of apple trees
drum down fruit when shaken;
scarlet berries clot like blood
on mountain rowan.

Briars curl in sideways,
arch a stickle back,
draw blood and curl up innocent
to sneak the next attack.

The yew tree in each churchyard
wraps night in its dark hood.
Ivy is a shadowy
genius of the wood.

Holly rears its windbreak,
a door in winter's face;
life-blood on a spear-shaft
darkens the grain of ash.

Birch tree, smooth and blessed,
delicious to the breeze,
high twigs plait and crown it
the queen of trees.

The aspen pales
and whispers, hesitates:
a thousand frightened scuts
race in its leaves.

But what disturbs me most
in the leafy wood
is the to and fro and to and fro
of an oak rod.

Ronan was dishonoured,
he rang his cleric's bell:
my spasm and outrage
brought curse and miracle.

And noble Congal's armour,
his tunic edged in gold,
swathed me in doomed glory
with omens in each fold.

His lovely tunic marked me
in the middle of the rout,
the host pursuing, shouting:
– The one in the gold coat!

Get him, take him live or dead,
every man fall to.
Draw and quarter, pike
and spit him, none will blame you.

Still the horsemen followed
across the north of Down,
my back escaping nimbly
from every javelin thrown.

As if I had been cast
by a spearsman, I flew high,
my course a whisper in the air,
a breeze flicking through ivy.

I overtook the startled fawn,
kept step with his fleet step,
I caught, I rode him lightly –
from peak to peak we leapt,

mountain after mountain,
a high demented spree
from Inishowen south,
and south, as far as Galtee.

From Galtee up to Liffey
I was swept along and driven
on through bitter twilight
to the slopes of Benn Bulben.

And that was the first night
of my long restless vigil:
my last night at rest,
the eve of Congal's battle.

And then Glen Bolcain was my lair,
my earth and den;
I've scaled and strained against those slopes
by star and moon.

I wouldn't swop a lonely hut
in that dear glen
for a world of moorland acres
on a russet mountain.

Its water flashing like wet grass,
its wind so keen,
its tall brooklime, its watercress
the greenest green.

I love the ancient ivy tree,
the pale-leafed sallow,
the birth's sibilant melody,
the solemn yew.

And you, Lynchseachan, can try
disguise, deceit;
come in the mask and shawl of night,
I won't be caught.

You managed it the first time
with your litany of the dead:
father, mother, daughter, son,
brother, wife – you lied

but if you want your say again,
then be ready
to face the heights and crags of Mourne
to follow me.

I would live happy
in an ivy bush
high in some twisted tree
and never come out.

The skylarks rising
into their high space
send me pitching and tripping
over stumps on the moor

and my hurry flushes
the turtle-dove.
I overtake it,
my plumage rushing,

am startled then
by the startled woodcock
or a blackbird's sudden
volubility.

Think of my alarms,
my coming to earth
where the fox still
gnaws at the bones,

my wild career
as the wolf from the wood
goes tearing ahead
and I lift towards the mountain,

the bark of foxes
echoing below me,
the wolves behind me
howling and rending –

their vapoury tongues
their low-slung speed
shaken off like nightmare
at the foot of the slope.

If I show my heels
I am hobbled by guilt.
I am a sheep
without a fold

who sleeps his sound sleep
in the old tree at Kilnoo,
dreaming back the good days
with Congal in Antrim.

A starry frost will come
dropping on the pools
and I'll be out
on unsheltered hills:

herons calling
in cold Glenelly,
flocks of birds quickly
coming and going.

I prefer the scurry
and song of blackbirds
to the usual blather
of men and women.

I prefer the squeal of badgers
in their sett
to the hullabaloo
of the morning hunt.

I prefer the re-
echoing belling of a stag
among the peaks
to that terrible horn.

Those unharnessed runners
from glen to glen!
Nobody tames
that royal blood,

each one aloof
on its rightful summit,
antlered, watchful.
Imagine them,

the stag of high Slieve Felim,
the stag of the steep Fews,
the stag of Duhallow, the stag of Orrery,
the fierce stag of Killarney.

The stag of Islandmagee, Larne's stag,
the stag of Moylinny,
the stag of Cooley, the stag of Cunghill,
the stag of the two-peaked Burren.

The mother of this herd
is old and grey,
The stags that follow her
are branchy, many-tined.

I would be cloaked in the grey
sanctuary of her head,
I would roost among
her mazy antlers

and would be lofted into
this thicket of horns
on the stag that lows at me
over the glen.

I am Sweeney, the whinger,
the scuttler in the valley.
But call me, instead,
Peak-pate, Stag-head.

The springs I always liked
were the fountain at Dunmall
and the spring-well on Knocklayde
that tasted pure and cool.

Forever mendicant,
my rags all frayed and scanty,
high in the mountains
like a crazed, frost-bitten sentry

I find no bed, no quarter,
no easy place in the sun –
not even in this reddening
covert of tall fern.

My only rest: eternal
sleep in holy ground
when Moling's earth lets fall
its dark balm on my wound.

But now that sudden bleating
and belling in the glen!
I am a timorous stag
feathered by Ronan Finn.

§41   After that poem, Sweeney went on from Feegile through Bannagh,
Benevenagh and Maghera but he could not shake off the hag until
he reached Dunseverick in Ulster. There he leaped from the summit
of the fort, down a sheer drop, coaxing the hag to follow. She leaped
quickly after him but fell on the cliff of Dunseverick, where she was
smashed to pieces and scattered into the sea. That is how she got her
end on Sweeney's trail.

§42   Then Sweeney said:
        – From now on, I won't tarry in Dal-Arie because Lynchseachan
would have my life to avenge the hag's.
        So he proceeded to Roscommon in Connacht, where he alighted
on the bank of the well and treated himself to watercress and water.
But when a woman came out of the erenach's house, he panicked
and fled, and she gathered the watercress from the stream. Sweeney
watched her from his tree and greatly lamented the theft of his patch
of cress, saying:
        – It is a shame that you are taking my watercress. If only you
knew my plight, how I am unpitied by tribesman or kinsman, how
I am no longer a guest in any house on the ridge of the world.
Watercress is my wealth, water is my wine, and hard bare trees and
soft tree bowers are my friends. Even if you left that cress, you would
not be left wanting; but if you take it, you are taking the bite from
my mouth.
        And he made this poem:

§43   Woman, picking the watercress
and scooping up my drink of water,

were you to leave them as my due
you would still be none the poorer.

Woman, have consideration!
We two go two different ways:
I perch out among tree-tops,
you lodge here in a friendly house.

Woman, have consideration.
Think of me in the sharp wind,
forgotten, past consideration,
without a cloak to wrap me in.

Woman, you cannot start to know
sorrows Sweeney has forgotten:
how friends were so long denied him
he killed his gift for friendship even.

Fugitive, deserted, mocked
by memories of my days as king,
no longer called to head the troop
when warriors are mustering,

no longer the guest of honour
at tables anywhere in Ireland,
ranging like a mad pilgrim
over rock-peaks on the mountain.

The harper who harped me to rest,
where is his soothing music now?
My people too, my kith and kin,
where did their affection go?

In my heyday, on horseback,
I rode high into my own:
now memory's an unbroken horse
that rears and suddenly throws me down.

Over starlit moors and plains,
woman taking my watercress,
to his cold and lonely station
the shadow of that Sweeney goes

with watercresses for his herds
and cold water for his mead,
bushes for companions,
the naked hillside for his bed.

Hugging these, my cold comforts,
ever hungering after cress,
above the bare plain of Emly
I hear cries of the wild geese,

and still bowed to my hard yoke,
still a bag of skin and bone,
I reel as if a blow hit me
and fly off at the cry of a heron

to land in Dairbre, maybe,
in spring, when days are on the turn,
to scare away again by twilight
westward, into the Mournes.

Gazing down at clean gravel,
to lean out over a cool well,
drink a mouthful of sunlit water
and gather cress by the handful –

even this you would pluck from me,
lean pickings that have thinned my blood
and chilled me on the cold uplands,
hunkering low when winds spring up.

Morning wind is the coldest wind,
it flays me of my rags, it freezes –
the very memory leaves me speechless,
woman, picking the watercress.

WOMAN
Sweeney, be merciful to me.
Leave retribution to the Lord.
Judge not and you won't be judged.
Triumph and bless. Do not be hard.

SWEENEY
Then here is justice, fair and even,
from my high court in the yew:

if you leave the cress for me,
I shall leave my rags in lieu.

I have no place to lay my head.
Human love has failed me. So
let me swop my sins for cress,
let me make a scapegoat of you.

Your greed has left me hungering.
Therefore, may all you robbed me of
come between you and good luck
and leave you hungering for love.

As you snatched cress, may you be snatched
by the foraging, blue-coated Norse.
And live eaten by remorse.
And cursing God that our paths crossed.

He stayed in Roscommon that night and the next day he went on §44
to Slieve Aughty, from there to the pleasant slopes of Slemish, then
on to the high peaks of Slieve Bloom, and from there to Inishmurray.
After that, he stayed six weeks in a cave that belonged to Donnan
on the island of Eig off the west of Scotland. From there he went on
to Ailsa Craig, where he spent another six weeks, and when he finally
left there he bade the place farewell and bewailed his state, like this:

Without bed or board §45
I face dark days
in frozen lairs
and wind-driven snow.

Ice scoured by winds.
Watery shadows from weak sun.
Shelter from the one tree
on a plateau.

Haunting deerpaths,
enduring rain,
first-footing the grey
frosted grass.

I climb towards the pass
and the stag's belling

rings off the wood,
surf-noise rises

where I go, heartbroken
and worn out,
sharp-haunched Sweeney,
raving and moaning.

The sough of the winter night,
my feet packing the hailstones
as I pad the dappled
banks of Mourne

or lie, unslept, in a wet bed
on the hills by Lough Erne,
tensed for first light
and an early start.

Skimming the waves
at Dunseverick,
listening to billows
at Dun Rodairce,

hurtling from that great wave
to the wave running
in tidal Barrow,
one night in hard Dun Cernan,

the next among the wild flowers
of Benn Boirne;
and then a stone pillow
on the screes of Croagh Patrick.

I shift restlessly
on the plain of Boroma,
from Benn Iughoine
to Benn Boghaine.

Then that woman
interfered,
disturbed me
and affronted me

and made off with
the bite from my mouth.
It is retribution
and it is constant.

I gather cress
in delicious bunches,
four round handfuls
in Glen Bolcain,

and then I unpick
the shy bog-berry,
then drink water
from Ronan's well.

My nails are bent,
my loins weak,
my feet bleeding,
my thighs bare –

and I'll be overtaken
by a stubborn band
of Ulstermen
faring through Scotland.

But to have ended up
lamenting here
on Ailsa Craig.
A hard station!

Ailsa Craig,
the seagulls' home,
God knows it is
hard lodgings.

Ailsa Craig,
bell-shaped rock,
reaching sky-high,
snout in the sea –

it hard-beaked,
me seasoned and scraggy:
we mated like a couple
of hard-shanked cranes.

I tread the slop
and foam of beds,
unlooked for,
penitential,

and imagine treelines
far away
a banked-up, soothing
wooded haze,

not like the swung
depths and swells
of that nightmare-black
lough in Mourne.

I need woods
for consolation,
some grove in Meath –
or the space of Ossory.

Or Ulster in harvest.
Strangford, shimmering.
Or a summer visit
to green Tyrone.

At Lammas I migrate
to the pools of Teltown,
pass the springtime fishing
bends of the Shannon.

I often get as far
as my old domain,
those groomed armies,
those stern hillsides.

§46   Then Sweeney left Ailsa Craig and flew over the stormy maw of
the sea to the land of the Britons. He passed their royal stronghold
on his right and discovered a great wood where he could hear
wailing and lamentation. Sometimes it was a great moan of anguish,
sometimes an exhausted sigh. The moaner turned out to be another
madman astray in the wood. Sweeney approached him.
    – Who are you, friend? Sweeney asked.
    – A madman, said he.

– In that case, you are a friend indeed. I am a madman myself, said Sweeney. Why don't you join up with me?

– I would, the other man said, except that I am in dread of the king or the king's retinue capturing me, and I am not sure that you are not one of them.

– I am no such thing, said Sweeney, and since you can trust me, tell me your name.

– They call me the Man of the Wood, said the madman.

Then Sweeney spoke this verse and the Man of the Wood answered as follows:

SWEENEY   §47
What happened, Man of the Wood,
to make you whinge
and hobble like this? Why did
your mind unhinge?

MAN
Caution and fear of the king
have silenced me.
I made a tombstone of my tongue
to keep my story.

I am the Man of the Wood.
I was famous
in battles once. Now I hide
among bushes.

SWEENEY
I come from the Bush myself.
I am Sweeney,
son of Colman. Like yourself,
outcast, shifty.

After that, they did confide in each other and shared their life stories.   §48
Sweeney said to the madman:

– Tell me about yourself.

– I am a landowner's son, said the mad Briton, a native of this country, and my name is Alan.

– Tell me, Sweeney asked, what made you mad?

– It is simple. Once upon a time there were two kings in this country, struggling for the kingship. Their names were Eochaidh and Cuagu. Eochaidh was the better king and I am one of his people.

Anyhow, the issue was to be decided at a great muster where there was to be a battle. I laid solemn obligations on each of my chief's people that none was to come to the battle unless he was arrayed in silk. I did this so that they would be magnificent, outstanding beyond the others in pomp and panoply. But, for doing that, the hosts cursed me with three howls of malediction that sent me astray and frightened, the way you see me.

§49 In the same way he asked Sweeney what drove him to madness.
– The words of Ronan, said Sweeney. At the battle of Moira he cursed me in front of the armies so that I sprang out of the battle and have been wandering and fleeing ever since.
– Sweeney, said Alan, since we have trusted each other, let us now be guardians to each other.

Whoever of us is the first to hear
the cry of a heron from a lough's blue-green waters
or the clear note of a cormorant
or the flight of a woodcock off a branch
or the wheep of a plover disturbed in its sleep
or the crackle of feet in withered branches,
or whoever of us is the first to see
the shadow of a bird above the wood,
let him warn the other.
Let us move always
with the breadth of two trees between us.
And if one of us hears any of these things
or anything like them,
let both of us scatter immediately.

§50 So they went about like that for a year. At the end of the year Alan said to Sweeney:
– Today is the day we must part, for the end of my life has come, and I will go where I am destined to meet my death.
– How will you die? Sweeney asked.
– That is simple, Alan said. I will proceed now to the waterfall at Doovey, where a blast of wind will unbalance me and pitch me into the waterfall, so that I'll be drowned. Afterwards, I will be buried in the churchyard of a saint. And I'll go to heaven. And now, Sweeney, said Alan, tell me what your own fate will be.
Sweeney told him what this story goes on to tell and they parted. The Briton set out for the waterfall and when he reached it he was drowned in it.

Then Sweeney came to Ireland, reaching the plain of Moylinny, in §51
Antrim, as the evening was drawing on. When he realised where he
was, he said:

– This was always a good plain, and I was here once with a good
man. That was Scannlan's son, my friend Congal Claon. One day
here I said to Congal that I wanted to go to another lord and master
because the rewards I got from him were too small. To persuade me
to stay with him, Congal immediately gave me a hundred and fifty
lovely horses, and his own brown steed into the bargain; and a
hundred and fifty flashing swords, hafted in tusks; fifty servants and
fifty servant girls; a tunic made of cloth-of gold, and a magnificent
girdle of chequered silk.

Then Sweeney recited this poem:

Now my bare skin feels §52
night falling on Moylinny,
the plain where Congal lived.
Now in my memory

I see Congal and me
riding across the plain
deep in conversation,
headed for Drum Lurgan.

I am saying to the king:
– The services I give
are not being rewarded.
And I threaten I will leave.

What does the king do then?
He gives me in their hundreds
horses, bridles, swords, foreign
captives, girl attendants.

And my great chestnut steed,
the best that grazed or galloped,
his cloth-of-gold tunic,
his girdle of silk plaits.

So what plain matches this plain?
Is it the plain of Meath
or the plain of Airgeadros
or Moyfevin with its crosses?

Moylurg or Moyfea,
the lovely plain of Connacht,
the Liffey banks, Bannside,
or the plain of Muirhevna?

I have seen all of them,
north, south, east and west,
but never saw the equal
of this ground in Antrim.

§53   When he had made that poem Sweeney came on to Glen Bolcain,
where he went wandering freely until he met with a madwoman.
He shied and ran away from her, yet divining somehow that she too
was simple-minded, he stopped in his tracks and turned to her.
With that, she shied and ran away from him.
    – Alas, God, Sweeney said, life is a misery. I scare away from her
and she scares away from me. And in Glen Bolcain, of all places!
    Then he began:

§54   Whoever stirs up enmity
should never have been born;
may every bitter man and woman
be barred at the gate of heaven.

If three conspire and combine,
one will backbite or complain
as I complain, going torn
by briar and sharp blackthorn.

First, madwoman flees from man.
Then, it's something stranger even:
barefoot, in his bare skin,
the man is running from the woman.

In November, wild ducks fly.
From those dark evenings until May
let us forage, nest and hide
in ivy in the brown-floored wood

and hear behind the late birds' song
sounds of water in Glen Bolcain,
its streams, all hurry, hush and jabber,
its islands in the forking rivers,

its hazel trees and holly bowers,
its leaves, its acorns, its briars,
its nuts, its sharp-tasting sloes,
all its cool-fleshed winter-berries:

and under trees, its hounds coursing,
its dappled antlered stags belling,
its water's endless, endless fall –
sounds of water in Glen Bolcain.

After that, Sweeney went to the house where his wife, Eorann, was   §55
lodging with her retinue of maidservants. He stood at the outer
door of the house and spoke to his former queen:
    – Here you are, Eorann, laid in the lap of luxury, and still there
is no lap for me to lie in.
    – That is how it is, Eorann said, but come in.
    – Indeed I will not, said Sweeney, in case the army traps me in
the house.
    – Well, said the woman, it seems your mind has not got any
better, and since you don't want to stop with us, why don't you go
away and leave us in peace? There are people here who knew you
when you were in your right mind; it would be an embarrassment
if they were to see you like this.
    – Isn't that terrible? said Sweeney. Now I know it. It is fatal
to trust a woman. And I was generous to this one. She is spurning
me now but I would have been the man of the moment if I had
come back that day when I slew Oilill Caedach, the king of
Ui Faolain.
    And with that he said:

Any man a woman falls for,   §56
however handsome, should beware.
Sweeney is the living proof,
he was cast off by his love.

And any trusting man must stay
on guard against their treachery:
betrayal such as mine by Eorann
is second nature in a woman.

Gullible, open-handed,
straightforward and wide-eyed,

I gave my steeds and herds away,
filled her pastures in a day.

In the thick of fighting men
I could more than hold my own:
when the battle cry was sounded
I handled thirty single-handed.

It was Congal's right to ask for
a warrior to champion Ulster:
– Who among you will take on
the fighter king of Ui Faolain?

Oilill was a berserk giant,
a shield and spear in either hand,
so overbearing in his stride
for a while our ranks were daunted.

But when I spoke at Congal's side
it was not to whinge or backslide:
– Though Oilill is their strongest bastion,
I will hold the line against him.

I left him shortened by a head
and left the torso, overjoyed,
and left five other princes dead
before I stopped to wipe my blade.

§57 With that, Sweeney rose lightly and stealthily and went hopping
airily from peak to peak, from one hill to the next, until he reached
Mourne in the south of Ulster. He rested there, saying:
 – This is a good place for a madman, but it is no place for corn
or milk or food. And though it is a lovely, lofty station, it is still
uncomfortable and uneasy. There is no shelter here from the storm
or the shower.
 And then he uttered these words:

§58 The Mournes are cold tonight,
my quarters are desolate:
no milk or honey in this land
of snowdrift and gusting wind.

And my bed is cold at night
up here on the naked summit.

In a sharp-branched holly tree
I cower and shiver and waste away.

The pools are ice, frost hardens on me.
I shake myself and then break free,
coming alive like a fanned ember
in stormwinds sweeping north from Leinster,

and dreaming, when the summer dies
round Hallowe'en and All Hallows,
of another move to my old ground –
the clear well-waters of Glen Bolcain.

Astray no more then east or west,
blizzards whipping my bare face,
not shivering in some drifted den,
a starved, pinched, raving madman,

but sheltered in that lovely arbour,
my winter haven and my harbour,
my refuge from the bare heath,
my royal fort, my king's rath.

Every night I glean and raid
and comb the floor of the oak wood.
My hands work into leaf and rind,
old roots, old windfalls on the ground,

they rake through matted watercress
and grope among the bog-berries,
cool brooklime, sorrel and damp moss,
wild garlic and wild raspberries,

apples, hazel-nuts and acorns,
the haws of sharp, jaggy hawthorns,
the blackberries, the floating weed,
the whole store of the oak wood.

Keep me here, Christ, far away
from open ground and flat country.
Let me suffer the cold of glens.
I dread the cold space of the plains.

§59   The next morning Sweeney started again. He passed Moyfevin and the clear, green-wavering Shannon; he passed the inviting slopes of Aughty, the spreading pastures of Loughrea, the delightful banks of the River Suck, and landed on the shores of broad Lough Ree. He spent that night in the fork of Bile Tiobradain, which was one of his favourite hide-outs in the country. It was Creegaille, in the east of Connacht.

     Great sorrow and misery descended on him and he said:

     – Indeed I have suffered great trouble and distress. It was cold in the Mournes last night and it is no better tonight in the fork of Bile Tiobradain.

§60   It was snowing that night, and as fast as the snow fell, it was frozen. So he said:

     – I have endured purgatories since the feathers grew on me. And still there is no respite. I realise, he said, that even if it were to mean my death, it would be better to trust my people than to endure these woes forever.

     Then he recited the poem, proclaiming aloud his woes:

§61   Almighty God, I deserved this,
my cut feet, my drained face,
winnowed by a sheer wind
and miserable in my mind.

Last night I lay in Mourne
plastered in wet; cold rain poured.
Tonight, in torment, in Glasgally
I am crucified in the fork of a tree.

I who endured unflinchingly
through long nights and long days
since the feathers penned my frame
foresee nothing but the same.

Hard weather has withered me,
blizzards have buried me.
As I wince here in cutting wind
Glen Bolcain's heather haunts my mind.

Unsettled, panicky, astray,
I course over the whole country

from River Liffey to Lower Bann,
from Bannside to the banks of Lagan;

then over Rathmore to Roscommon,
and fields that lie around Cruachan,
above Moylurg's level plain
and the brow of bushy Fews Mountain.

Or else I make a tough migration
to the Knockmealdown mountains;
or from Glasgally, a long glide
eastward to a Louth hillside.

All this is hard to thole, Lord!
Still without bed or board,
crouching to graze on cress,
drinking cold water from rivers.

Alarmed out of the autumn wood,
whipped by whins, flecked with blood,
running wild among wolf-packs,
shying away with the red stag.

Son of God, have mercy on us!
Never to hear a human voice!
To sleep naked every night
up there in the highest thickets,

to have lost my proper shape and looks,
a mad scuttler on mountain peaks,
a derelict doomed to loneliness:
Son of God, have mercy on us!

– All the same, Sweeney said, even if Donal, son of Aodh, were §62
to kill me, I will still go to Dal-Arie and trust to the mercy of
my own people. If the mill-hag had not duped me into that bout
of leaping, I would still be sane enough.

Then a glimmer of reason came back to him and he set out for §63
his own country, ready to settle there and entrust himself to the
people.
   Ronan heard of Sweeney's return to his senses and his decision
to go back among his own, and cried out:

– I beseech you, Lord, that the persecutor come not near the church to torment it again; I beseech you, do not relent in your vengeance or ease his affliction until he is sundered body from soul in his death-swoon. Remember that you struck him for an example, a warning to tyrants that you and your people were sacred and not to be lightly dishonoured or outraged.

§64   God answered Ronan's prayer. When Sweeney was out on the uplands of the Fews he halted, stock still: a strange apparition rose before him at midnight. Bleeding headless torsos and disembodied heads – five scraggy, goat-bearded heads – screamed and bounced this way and that over the road. When he got among them, they were talking to each other.

    – He is a madman, said the first head.
    – A madman from Ulster, said the second.
    – Follow him well, said the third.
    – May the pursuit be long, said the fourth.
    – Until he reaches the sea, said the fifth.

    They rose in a flock, coming for him, but he soared away in front, skimming from thicket to thicket; and no matter how wide the glen that opened before him, he bounded from edge to edge, from the top of one hill to the top of the next.

§65   The heads were pursuing him,
lolling and baying,
snapping and yelping,
whining and squealing.

They nosed at his calves and his thighs,
they breathed on his shoulder,
they nuzzled the back of his neck,
they went bumping off tree-trunks and rock-face,
they spouted and plunged like a waterfall,
until he gave them the slip and escaped
in a swirling tongue of low cloud.

§66   He had lost them, goat-head and dog-head and the whole terrifying pack he had sensed there. But his previous wandering and flying were nothing compared with what he suffered now, for he was startled into a fit which lasted six weeks until he perched one night in the top of a tree, on the summit of Slieve Eidhneach. In the morning he began lamenting:

My dark night has come round again.
The world goes on but I return
to haunt myself. I freeze and burn.
I am the bare figure of pain.

Frost crystals and the level ice,
the scourging snow, the male-voiced storm,
they all perform my requiem.
My hearth goes cold, my fire dies.

Are there still some who call me prince?
The King of Kings, the Lord of All
revoked my title, worked my downfall,
unhoused, unwived me for my sins.

Why did He spare my life at Moira?
Why did He grudge me death in battle?
Why ordained the hag of the mill
His hound of heaven and my fury?

The mill-hag's millstone round my neck!
Hell roast her soul! She dragged me down
when I leaped up in agitation.
I fell for that old witch's trick.

Then Lynchseachan was in full cry,
a bloodhound never off my trail.
I fell for his lies too and fell
among captors out of the tree.

They made me face the love I'd lost.
They tied me up and carried me
back to the house. The mockery!
I overheard their victory feast

yet gradually grew self-possessed,
for there were decent people there,
and gaming and constant laughter.
My mind was knitting up at last

but soon unravelled into nightmare.
I was for the high jump once more.
The mill-hag spun her web and swore
her innocence. I leaped for her

and leaped beyond the bounds of sense.
She challenged me a second time.
We kept in step like words in rhyme.
I set the pace and led the dance –

I cleared the skylight and the roof,
I flew away beyond the fortress
but she hung on. Through smooth and rough
I raised the wind and led the chase.

We coursed all over Ireland then.
I was the wind and she was smoke.
I was the prow and she the wake.
I was the earth and she the moon.

But always look before you leap!
Though she was fit for bog and hill,
Dunseverick gave her the spill.
She followed me down off the top

of the fort and spread-eagled
her bitch's body in the air.
I trod the water, watching her
hit the rocks. And I was glad

to see her float in smithereens.
A crew of devils made a corpse
of her and buried it. Cursed
be the ground that housed her bones.

One night I walked across the Fews –
the hills were dark, the starlight dead –
when suddenly five severed heads,
five lantern ghouls, appeared and rose

like bats from hell, surrounding me.
Then a head spoke – another shock!
– This is the Ulster lunatic.
Let us drive him into the sea!

I went like an arrow from a bow.
My feet disdained that upland ground.
Goat-head and dog-head cursed but found
me impossible to follow.

I have deserved all this:
night-vigils, terror,
flittings across water,
women's cried-out eyes.

One time during his wild career Sweeney left Slieve Lougher and   §68
landed in Feegile. He stayed there for a year among the clear streams
and branches of the wood, eating red holly-berries and dark brown
acorns, and drinking from the River Feegile. At the end of that time,
deep grief and sorrow settled over him because of his terrible life;
so he came out with this short poem:

Look at Sweeney now, alas!   §69
His body mortified and numb,
unconsoled, sleepless
in the rough blast of the storm.

From Slieve Lougher I came
to the border marches of Feegile,
my diet still the usual
ivy-berries and oak-mast.

I spent a whole year on the mountain
enduring my transformation,
dabbing, dabbing like a bird
at the holly-berry's crimson.

My grief is raw and constant.
Tonight all my strength is gone.
Who has more cause to lament
than Mad Sweeney of Glen Bolcain?

One day Sweeney went to Drum Iarann in Connacht where he stole   §70
some watercress and drank from a green-flecked well. A cleric
came out of the church, full of indignation and resentment, calling
Sweeney a well-fed, contented madman, and reproaching him where
he cowered in the yew tree:

CLERIC   §71
Aren't you the contented one?
You eat my watercress,
then you perch in the yew tree
beside my little house.

SWEENEY

Contented's not the word!
I am so terrified,
so panicky, so haunted
I dare not bat an eyelid.

The flight of a small wren
scares me as much, bell-man,
as a great expedition
out to hunt me down.

Were you in my place, monk,
and I in yours, think:
would you enjoy being mad?
Would you be contented?

§72   Once when Sweeney was rambling and raking through Connacht he
ended up in Alternan in Tireragh. A community of holy people had
made their home there, and it was a lovely valley, with a turbulent
river shooting down the cliff; trees fruited and blossomed on the
cliff-face; there were sheltering ivies and heavy-topped orchards,
there were wild deer and hares and fat swine; and sleek seals, that
used to sleep on the cliff, having come in from the ocean beyond.
Sweeney coveted the place mightily and sang its praises aloud in this
poem:

§73   Sainted cliff at Alternan,
nut grove, hazel-wood!
Cold quick sweeps of water
fall down the cliff-side.

Ivies green and thicken there,
its oak-mast is precious.
Fruited branches nod and bend
from heavy-headed apple trees.

Badgers make their setts there
and swift hares have their form;
and seals' heads swim the ocean,
cobbling the running foam.

And by the waterfall, Colman's son,
Ronan of Drumgesh's victim,

haggard, spent, frost-bitten Sweeney,
is sleeping at the foot of a tree.

At last Sweeney arrived where Moling lived, the place that is known   §74
as St Mullins. Just then, Moling was addressing himself to Kevin's
psalter and reading from it to his students. Sweeney presented himself
at the brink of the well and began to eat watercress.
    – Aren't you the early bird? said the cleric; and continued, with
Sweeney answering, as follows:

MOLING   §75
So, you would steal a march on us,
up and breakfasting so early!

SWEENEY
Not so very early, priest.
Terce has come in Rome already.

MOLING
And what knowledge has a fool
about the hour of terce in Rome?

SWEENEY
The Lord makes me His oracle
from sunrise till sun's going down.

MOLING
Then speak to us of hidden things,
give us tidings of the Lord.

SWEENEY
Not I. But if you are Moling,
you are gifted with the Word.

MOLING
Mad as you are, you are sharp-witted.
How do you know my face and name?

SWEENEY
In my days astray I rested
in this enclosure many a time.

MOLING
But Sweeney, son of Colman Cuar,
why won't you settle in one place?

SWEENEY
The resting place that I prefer
is life in everlasting peace.

MOLING
God help you then. Do you not dread
the slippery brim of hell's wide mouth?

SWEENEY
My one affliction is that God
denies me all repose on earth.

MOLING
Come closer then. Come here and share
whatever morsels you would like.

SWEENEY
There are worse things, priest, than hunger.
Imagine living without a cloak.

MOLING
Then you are welcome to my smock,
welcome to my cowl as well.

SWEENEY
Sometimes memory brings back
times it hurts me to recall.

MOLING
Are you Sweeney, the bogey-man,
escaped out of the fight at Moira?

SWEENEY
I am the early bird, the one
who scavenges, if I am Sweeney.

MOLING
You're mad and sly and know my name
and recognised me. How is that?

SWEENEY
In this enclosure time after time
I've watched you from an airy hide-out.

MOLING
Look at this leaf of Kevin's book,
the coilings on this psalter's page.

SWEENEY
The yew leaf coils around my nook
deep in Glen Bolcain's foliage.

MOLING
This churchyard, this whole flush of colour,
is there no pleasure here for you?

SWEENEY
My pleasure is great and other:
the hosting that day at Moira.

MOLING
I will sing Mass and make a hush
of high celebration.

SWEENEY
Leaping from an ivy bush
is a higher calling even.

MOLING
My ministry is only toil,
the weak and strong exhaust me so.

SWEENEY
I toil to a bed up on the chill
steeps of Benevenagh.

MOLING
When your end comes, is it to be
death by water, in holy ground?

SWEENEY
It will be early when I die.
One of your herds will make the wound.

§76 – You are more than welcome here, Sweeney, said Moling, for you are fated to live and die here. You shall leave the history of your adventures with us and receive a Christian burial in a churchyard. Therefore, said Moling, no matter how far you range over Ireland, day by day, I bind you to return to me every evening so that I may record your story.

§77 All during the next year the madman kept coming back to Moling. One day he would go to Inishbofin in west Connacht, another day to lovely Assaroe. Some days he would view the clean lines of Slemish, some days he would be shivering on the Mournes. But wherever he went, every night he would be back for vespers at St Mullins.

Moling ordered his cook to leave aside some of each day's milking for Sweeney's supper. This cook's name was Muirghil and she was married to a swine-herd of Moling's called Mongan. Anyhow, Sweeney's supper was like this: she would sink her heel to the ankle in the nearest cow-dung and fill the hole to the brim with new milk. Then Sweeney would sneak into the deserted corner of the milking yard and lap it up.

§78 One night there was a row between Muirghil and another woman, in the course of which the woman said:
– If you do not prefer your husband, it is a pity you cannot take up with some other man than the looney you have been meeting all year.
The herd's sister was within earshot and listening but she said nothing until the next morning. Then when she saw Muirghil going to leave the milk in the cow-dung beside the hedge where Sweeney roosted, she came in to her brother and said:
– Are you a man at all? Your wife's in the hedge yonder with another man.
Jealousy shook him like a brainstorm. He got up in a sudden fury, seized a spear from a rack in the house, and made for the madman. Sweeney was down swilling the milk out of the cow-dung with his side exposed towards the herd, who let go at him with the spear. It went into Sweeney at the nipple of his left breast, went through him, and broke his back.
There is another story. Some say the herd had hidden a deer's horn at the spot where Sweeney drank from the cow-dung and that Sweeney fell and killed himself on the point of it.

Enna McBracken was ringing the bell for prime at the door of the §79
churchyard and saw what had happened. He spoke this poem:

This is sad, herd, this was deliberate, §80
outrageous, sickening and sinful.
Whoever struck here will live to regret
killing the king, the saint, the holy fool.

What good did you expect to come of it?
Repentance will be denied you at your death.
Your soul will go howling to the devil,
your body draw an unabsolved last breath.

But I expect to be with him in heaven,
united in a single strain of prayer.
The soul of the true guest is sped by psalms
on the lips of a fasting, chanting choir.

My heart is breaking with pity for him.
He was a man of fame and high birth.
He was a king, he was a madman.
His grave will be a hallowing of earth.

Enna went back and told Moling that Sweeney had been killed by §81
his swineherd Mongan. Immediately, Moling and his community
came along to where Sweeney lay and Sweeney repented and made
his confession to Moling. He received Christ's body and thanked
God for having received it and after that was anointed by the clerics.

SWEENEY §83
There was a time when I preferred
the turtle-dove's soft jubilation
as it flitted round a pool
to the murmur of conversation.

There was a time when I preferred
the blackbird singing on the hill
and the stag loud against the storm
to the clinking tongue of this bell.

There was a time when I preferred
the mountain grouse crying at dawn
to the voice and closeness
of a beautiful woman.

There was a time when I preferred
wolf-packs yelping and howling
to the sheepish voice of a cleric
bleating out plainsong.

You are welcome to pledge healths
and carouse in your drinking dens;
I will dip and steal water
from a well with my open palm.

You are welcome to that cloistered hush
of your students' conversation;
I will study the pure chant
of hounds baying in Glen Bolcain.

You are welcome to your salt meat
and fresh meat in feasting-houses;
I will live content elsewhere
on tufts of green watercress.

The herd's sharp spear wounded me
and passed clean through my body.
Ah Christ, who disposed all things, why
was I not killed at Moira?

Of all the innocent lairs I made
the length and breadth of Ireland
I remember an open bed
above the lough in Mourne.

Of all the innocent lairs I made
the length and breadth of Ireland
I remember bedding down
above the wood in Glen Bolcain.

To You, Christ, I give thanks
for Your Body in communion.
Whatever evil I have done
in this world, I repent.

§84   Then Sweeney's death-swoon came over him and Moling, attended
by his clerics, rose up and each of them placed a stone on Sweeney's
grave.

– The man who is buried here was cherished indeed, said Moling. How happy we were when we walked and talked along this path. And how I loved to watch him yonder at the well. It is called the Madman's Well because he would often eat its watercress and drink its water, and so it is named after him. And every other place he used to haunt will be cherished, too.

And then Moling said:

I am standing beside Sweeney's grave §85
remembering him. Wherever he
loved and nested and removed to
will always be dear to me.

Because Sweeney loved Glen Bolcain,
I learned to love it, too. He'll miss
all the fresh streams tumbling down,
all the beds of watercress.

He would drink his sup of water from
the well beyond that we have called
The Madman's Well; and now his name
keeps brimming in its sandy cold.

I waited long but knew he'd come.
I welcomed, sped him as a guest.
With holy viaticum
I limed him for the Holy Ghost.

Because Mad Sweeney was a pilgrim
to the lip of every well
and every green-banked, cress-topped stream,
their water's his memorial.

Now, if it be the will of God,
rise, Sweeney, take this guiding hand
that has to lay you in the sod
and draw the dark blinds of the ground.

I ask a blessing, by Sweeney's grave.
His memory rises in my breast.
His soul roosts in the tree of love.
His body sinks in its clay nest.

§86   After that, Sweeney rose out of his swoon. Moling took him by the
       hand and both went towards the door of the church. When they
       reached the door Sweeney leaned his shoulders against the jamb
       and breathed a loud sigh. His spirit fled to heaven and his body
       was given an honourable burial by Moling.

§87   These have been some of the stories about the adventures of
       Sweeney, son of Colman Cuar, king of Dal-Arie.

The Cure at Troy

SOPHOCLES

in memory of Robert Fitzgerald
poet and translator
1910–1985

O look, look in the mirror,
O look in your distress;
Life remains a blessing
Although you cannot bless.

O stand, stand at the window
As the tears scald and start;
You shall love your crooked neighbour
With your crooked heart.

W. H. Auden

CHARACTERS

ODYSSEUS
NEOPTOLEMUS
PHILOCTETES

CHORUS
Attendants to NEOPTOLEMUS, *at least three:*
CHORUS LEADER
SENTRY
MERCHANT (*in disguise*)

HERCULES (*in person of* CHORUS LEADER)

A sea shore. Spacious fetch of sea-light. Upstage right (from
audience's point of view) rocks piled, cliff-face, grass tufts,
stunted bushes. A cave mouth/archway visible up there, with
small acting area at that level. A sort of strewn pathway, coming
downstage, forking towards acting area. Access to cave mouth
possible from this point. Access to second entrance of cave is

offstage, right. If a volcano can be suggested in background,
all the better but it should not be overemphasised.
   CHORUS *discovered, boulder-still, wrapped in shawls. All three*
in series stir and move, as it were seabirds stretching and unstiffening.
The prologue can be divided between the three voices. By the end
of the prologue, CHORUS LEADER *has positioned herself where*
she will speak as HERCULES *at the end of the play.*

CHORUS
Philoctetes.
            Hercules.
                        Odysseus.

Heroes. Victims. Gods and human beings.
5   All throwing shapes, every one of them
       Convinced he's in the right, all of them glad
       To repeat themselves and their every last mistake,
       No matter what.

                        People so deep into
10   Their own self-pity self-pity buoys them up.
       People so staunch and true, they're fixated,
       Shining with self-regard like polished stones.
       And their whole life spent admiring themselves
       For their own long-suffering.
15   Licking their wounds
       And flashing them around like decorations.
       I hate it, I always hated it, and I am
       A part of it myself.

                        And a part of you,
20   For my part is the chorus, and the chorus
       Is more or less a borderline between
       The you and the me and the it of it.

                        Between
       The gods' and human beings' sense of things.

25   And that's the borderline that poetry
       Operates on too, always in between
       What you would like to happen and what will –
       Whether you like it or not.

Poetry
Allowed the god to speak. It was the voice   30
Of reality and justice. The voice of Hercules
That Philoctetes is going to have to hear
When the stone cracks open and the lava flows.
But we'll come to that.
                          For now, remember this: 35
Every time the crater on Lemnos Island
Starts to erupt, what Philoctetes sees
Is a blaze he started years and years ago
Under Hercules' funeral pyre.

The god's mind lights up his mind every time.   40

Volcanic effects. Lurid flame-trembles, commotions and eruptions.
   Then, a gradual, brightened stillness. The CHORUS *are now*
positioned as lookouts attending the entry of ODYSSEUS *and*
NEOPTOLEMUS.

Enter NEOPTOLEMUS *and* ODYSSEUS.

ODYSSEUS
Yes.
     This is the place.
                          This strand.
This is Lemnos all right.
                          Not a creature!   45

And here we are then, Neoptolemus,
You and me.
               Greeks with a job to do –
But neither of us nearly half the man
Your father was.   50
               Achilles had nobility.
                          Achilles stood
Head and shoulders above everybody.

Yes. I left Philoctetes here.
                          Marooned him – but   55
Only because I had been ordered to.
I did it, all the same. I am the one
That dumped him, him and his cankered foot –
Or what had been a foot before it rotted

60   And ate itself with ulcers.
                                 It was awful.
       We couldn't even get peace at the altar
       Without him breaking out in these howling fits,
       And slabbering and cursing.
65   He was putting us on edge.
       He couldn't be stopped.

                   Everybody's nerves were getting raw.

       Anyway.
                   That was then.
70   The thing is different now entirely – so
       Go canny.
                                 One false move.
       And everything is wrecked.

       Somewhere here he has a sort of den,
75   An open-ended shelter that gets sun
       In the wintertime and in the summer
       Has a breeze that cools him.
       And down a bit there, over to the left –
       Unless the spring's dried up, you should see water.

80   Go very easy now.
                   Study the lie of the land
       And then we'll plan the moves.

       I can see the whole thing in my head,
       So all you'll need to do is listen
85   And do the things I tell you.

       NEOPTOLEMUS
       Odysseus. For sure, sir. This is it.
       This cave is the one that you remember.

       ODYSSEUS
       Whereabouts? I can't see any cave.

       NEOPTOLEMUS
       Up here, above you. But there's no sign of him.

       ODYSSEUS
90   Take care he's not inside there, dozing.

NEOPTOLEMUS
There's a pile of old leaves that somebody slept on.

ODYSSEUS
And is that it? No other signs of life?

NEOPTOLEMUS
No: wait. There's a mug or something, very rough,
Hagged out of a log. And bits of kindling.

ODYSSEUS
All his earthly goods.   95

NEOPTOLEMUS
                          Aww! Look at this.
Aw! Rotten, rotten stuff. Bandage-rags.
Nothing but old dry pus and dirty clouts.

ODYSSEUS
That's it. That's him:
                          So he has to be around.   100
With a foot like his, he'll not be travelling far.
                          Out scavenging, likely,
Poking for things to eat, or maybe out
Gathering herbs to try to get relief.
Anyway, he's going to be back,   105
                          And something tells me, soon –
So get your lookout posted. We can take no risks.
I am the marked man here.
                          Of all the Greeks,
I am the one that Philoctetes wants.   110

NEOPTOLEMUS
This man here's

Exit ATTENDANT.

                          a watchman you can trust.
But you're going to have to tell me more
About these moves you're planning. What's going on?

ODYSSEUS
Neoptolemus. There's a noble streak in you   115
And you're a strong man.

Truly your father's son.

But you're going to have to tell me more.

Force isn't going to work.

120   So, if parts of this brief seem puzzling to you,
Just remember: you're here to serve a cause.

NEOPTOLEMUS
What are the orders?

ODYSSEUS
You're going to have to work out some way, you, you,
Of getting round Philoctetes with a story.

125   He'll ask you who you are and where you're from
And you'll say, Achilles' son, which will be true.
And that you're on your voyage back from Troy,
Heading home in a rage against the Greeks.
And you can make the rage look natural if you say

130   You were insulted.

You'll tell him
How the Greeks begged and coaxed you to join up
And leave your native place because you –

you and only you –

135   Were the man they absolutely needed.

Troy could not be taken without you.

Well then. You land at Troy. You naturally
Expect to be presented with the arms
Your father bore. You are Achilles' son.

140   But Odysseus is the man who bears those arms.
Odysseus tricked you. Odysseus this and that!
You can let loose at me for all you're worth.
The worse it is the better you'll please me.
If I am not the lowest of the low

145   By the time you're finished, the Greek cause is doomed.
For the old story actually is true:
Without you, Troy cannot be taken.

We need you.
To commandeer the bow from Philoctetes.

150   And always remember this:

you are the only one

That can approach him. You weren't sworn in
On the first expedition, you didn't sail
Under oath to anybody. Your slate is clean.
But if I was challenged, I could not deny   155
Any of that. And if he recognised me
And had his bow with him, I would be dead.
And you'd be dead for associating with me.
So the trick you're going to have to turn is this:
                    Sweet talk him and relieve him   160
Of a bow and arrows that are actually miraculous.

But, of course, son, I know what you are like.
I know all this goes against the grain
And you hate it. You're a very honest lad,
But, all the same, even you have to enjoy   165
Coming out ahead.
                    Do it my way, this once.
All right, you'll be ashamed
                        but that won't last.
And once you're over it,   170
                    you'll have the whole rest of your life
To be good and true and incorruptible.

NEOPTOLEMUS
I hate hearing you say this
                    and I hate more
The thought of having to do it.   175
                      It goes against
All I was ever brought up to believe.
It's really low behaviour.
                 Why could we not
Go at him, man to man? If he's so badly lamed   180
He'd never be a match for two of us.

We're Greeks, so, all right, we do our duty.
I don't think I could bear being called a traitor.
But in all honesty I have to say
I'd rather fail and keep my self-respect   185
Than win by cheating.

ODYSSEUS
               Neoptolemus,
As long as you're alive

your father's never going to be dead.
190 And in my day, I was the same as you.
I'd lift my hand before I'd use my brains.
But experience has taught me: the very people
That go mad at the slightest show of force
Will be eating from your hand if you take them right
195 And tell the story so as to suit just them.

NEOPTOLEMUS
Which boils down to a policy of lies.

ODYSSEUS
Arguments wouldn't work, no more than force.

NEOPTOLEMUS
So just how dangerous is this famous bow?

ODYSSEUS
The arrows never miss and always kill.

NEOPTOLEMUS
200 But if you go at him close in, hand to hand?

ODYSSEUS
Combat is out. We have to use the head here. I've told you.

NEOPTOLEMUS
You don't think lying undermines your life?

ODYSSEUS
Not if it will save life, and save the day.

NEOPTOLEMUS
You can look me in the eye and still say that?

ODYSSEUS
205 Scruples are self-indulgence at this stage.

NEOPTOLEMUS
So what stage is it? Why must he go to Troy?

ODYSSEUS
We need his weapons if we're to take the town.

NEOPTOLEMUS
You said without me Troy would not be taken.

ODYSSEUS
But not without his weapons.
                              Nor the weapons without you.   210

NEOPTOLEMUS
Well then.
          So be it.
                    The weapons are our target.

ODYSSEUS
And once you have them, you'll have triumphed twice.

NEOPTOLEMUS
In what way twice?   215
                    Is this more double-talk?

ODYSSEUS
You'll be praised for courage first.
                                    Then for farsightedness.

NEOPTOLEMUS
Duplicity! Complicity!
                      All right.   220
                                I'll do it.

ODYSSEUS
Do you remember everything I told you?

NEOPTOLEMUS
I have said I am going to do it.
                                Trust me.

ODYSSEUS
So. Well. What you do now is wait for him.   225
I'm going to have to leave in case he sees me.
And I'll take that watchman with me.
                                    But one last thing.
If I think you are being held up for what seems
A dangerously long time, I'll send the man back.   230
He'll be dressed up like a ship's captain, you know,
All innocence and full of sailor-talk,

But you'll be fit to read between the lines
For the message, whatever the message is.

235   Well, if there's nothing else,
I'm away to the ship. It's in your hands now.
Hermes that guides the go-betweens and dealers
Be your protector, and Athene too,
My own best patron.

Exit ODYSSEUS.

CHORUS
240   What are the likes of us to do?
We're here and we're supposed to help you,
But we're in a maze.
We're strangers and this place is strange.
We're on shifting sand. It is all sea-change.
245   Clear one minute. Next minute, haze.
But you are blessed with special insight,
So tell us, son.
Give us our instructions.

NEOPTOLEMUS
Be very careful as you go.
250   Keep on the lookout for the creature,
But watch me too
In case I signal.

CHORUS
We'll do that. Don't you worry, sir.
That's what we are here for.
255   But what about this wild man on the loose?
Is his head away? Is he dangerous?
Does he live in a den or a house?

NEOPTOLEMUS
His shake-down is up there
In a sort of roofed-in place under the rocks.

CHORUS
260   And where is he?

NEOPTOLEMUS
Out scavenging, somewhere near.
His old gifts as an archer

Stand him in good stead.
But all the same, it's sad.
Him, the master bowman, the great name,   265
Dragging himself through bushes after game.
Festering inside and out.
Contrary, hard and proud.

CHORUS
It's a pity of him too
Afflicted like that,   270
Him and that terrible foot.
And not a one to talk to.
Like the last man left alive.
How does the being survive?

Human beings suffer   275
But not to this extent:
You would wonder if it's meant.
Why him more than another?
What is the sense of it?

Out in the open always,   280
Behaving like a savage.
Nothing but squeals and laments.
Nothing left but his instincts.
Howling wild like a wolf.

NEOPTOLEMUS
In one way, it does make sense.   285
It all had to happen – the snake-bite at the shrine.
And everything that happened since.

Fate works in its own time.
                        If he had sailed then
Troy would have fallen too soon.   290
                        But this is now.

PHILOCTETES *begins to cry out, offstage.*

CHORUS
Quiet. Wheesht!

NEOPTOLEMUS
This is the hour of the bow!

Listen to that . . .

295   He is in awful pain.

That squeal
Must be every time he drags his foot.

CHORUS
Watch out. Get ready.

NEOPTOLEMUS
How?

CHORUS
300   Think of your plan.
This is not some shepherd in a book
With his Pan pipes and his shepherd's crook.
This is a danger-man.
That shouting's desperate and it's violent.
305   He sounds provoked.

He maybe saw the boat.

Enter PHILOCTETES.

PHILOCTETES
What's this? Who is this here? How did you land?
What brought you to a deserted island?
Tell us who you are and where you come from.
310   Your clothes look Greek and that warms my heart
But I need to hear your voices.
I know I look like a wild animal
But don't let that scare you.

Don't treat me
315   Like an untouchable.

What I am
Is what I was made into by the traitors.
Do the friendly human thing and speak.

NEOPTOLEMUS
All right.
320   I can tell you this:

What warms your heart
Warms ours.

We are Greeks.

PHILOCTETES
Ohh! Hearing you talk,
                            just hearing you   325
And seeing you –
                you have no idea
How much that means.
                            But who was it sent you?
Was it only chance?   330
                    Or was there purpose to it?
Did a wind blow you off course?
Tell me what happened and who you are.

NEOPTOLEMUS
The whole story is very short and simple.
My home-ground is the island of Scyros   335
And I am heading for its wave-lashed shores.
My name is Neoptolemus. Achilles was my father.

PHILOCTETES
Then you are one lucky son, and a lucky sailor
To be heading for that home. But where are you coming from?

NEOPTOLEMUS
The walls of Troy. We hoisted sail at Troy.   340

PHILOCTETES
What's that you say? You must have been with us.
Did you not sail with the original Greek force?

NEOPTOLEMUS
Do you mean to say that you sailed with that force?

PHILOCTETES
Och! Och! Och ho!
                    Child, do you not know me?   345

NEOPTOLEMUS
How could I know a man I never saw?

PHILOCTETES
And you haven't even heard my name . . . ?
Och ho!
        Or heard about the way that I'm afflicted?

350 Never. I have no notion
                    what all this is about.

PHILOCTETES
Gods curse it!
            But it's me the gods have cursed.
They've let my name and story be wiped out.
355 The real offenders have got away with it
And I'm still here, rotting like a leper.
Tell me, son. Achilles was your father.
Did you ever maybe hear him mentioning
A man who had inherited a bow –
360 The actual bow and arrows that belonged
To Hercules, and that Hercules gave him?
Did you never hear, son, about Philoctetes?
About the snake-bite he got at a shrine
When the first fleet was voyaging to Troy?
365 And then the way he broke out with a sore
And was marooned on the commander's orders?
Let me tell you, son, the way they abandoned me.
The sea and the sea-swell had me all worn out
So I dozed and fell asleep under a rock
370 Down on the shore.
                    And there and then, just like that,
They headed off.
                And they were delighted.
                                And the only thing
375 They left me was a bundle of old rags.
Some day I want them all to waken up
The way I did that day. Imagine, son.
The bay all empty. The ships all disappeared.
Absolute loneliness. Nothing there except
380 The beat of the waves and the beat of my raw wound.

But I had to keep alive. Crawling and twisting
To get myself down for a drink of water.
Think of what that was like in the wintertime,
When the water got iced over. And then I'd have to
385 Gather sticks and break them,
                            and every day
Start a fire from scratch, out of two flints.
Terrible times.

                             I managed to come through
But I never healed.   390
                                  My whole life has been
Just one long cruel parody.

This island is a nowhere. Nobody
Would ever put in here. There's nothing.
Nothing to attract a lookout's eye.   395
Nobody in his right mind would come near it.
And the rare ones that ever did turn up
Landed by accident, against their will.
They would take pity on me, naturally.
Share out their supplies and give me clothes.   400
But not a one of them would ever, ever
Take me on board with them to ship me home.
                        Every day has been a weeping wound
For ten years now. Ten years' misery and starvation –
That's all my service ever got for me.   405
That's what I have to thank Odysseus for
And Menelaus and Agamemnon.
                            Gods curse them all!
I ask for the retribution I deserve.
I solemnly beseech the gods to strike   410
The sons of Atreus in retaliation.

CHORUS
I know the way those people must have felt
When they landed here and saw you.

NEOPTOLEMUS
And I know from experience, Philoctetes,
That this has the ring of truth. I know   415
What Odysseus and that whole crowd are like.

PHILOCTETES
                             How is that?
Have you a score to settle with them too?

NEOPTOLEMUS
I'll choke them all some day with my two bare hands
And let them know that Scyros is a match   420
For Sparta and Mycenae put together.

PHILOCTETES
More power to you, child!
                              But what brought you here
If you're so desperate to be after them?

NEOPTOLEMUS
425 I'll tell you – though you of all men know
What it's like when you've been humiliated.
Still, humiliate me was what they did.
After my father died, there came a day . . .

PHILOCTETES
Achilles died?
430   Achilles?
                              How? What happened?

NEOPTOLEMUS
Human enemies did not slay Achilles.
It was the great god Apollo.

PHILOCTETES
No shame, in that event, on either side . . .
435 Your father, dead. I'm heartbroken for him.

NEOPTOLEMUS
You have heartbreak enough, Philoctetes,
Without starting to take on another man's.

PHILOCTETES
You're right.
           You are right.
440   So keep on with the story.

NEOPTOLEMUS
My father's foster-father and Odysseus
Landed from Troy in a freshly rigged-out boat.
They had crucial information, they maintained,
And to this day I cannot be sure
445 If it was lies or the truth.
                              What they said
Was this:
           With Achilles gone,
I was the destined one, the only man
450 Who could ever take the citadel of Troy.

So, naturally, I went straight into action.
There was the Greek cause, and –
                              inevitably –
There was my father.
                    I wanted to see   455
My father's body before they buried him.
And behind all that, maybe there was the lure
Of being the one who would take the citadel.

Well. After two days' good sailing,
We disembarked on the shore at Sigeum   460
And it was a great moment.
                          The whole army
Gathered to salute me, everybody declared
It was just like seeing Achilles in the flesh,
Alive again.   465
            But Achilles was a corpse.
I mourned him. I took my last look at him
And then went to the sons of Atreus
As friends of mine, for how could they not be?
I made the formal claim for my father's armour   470
And whatever else was due to me. But they
Violated every law and custom
And said, yes, I could have the personal effects,
But Achilles' arms were being worn already
By another man. By Laertes' son, in fact,   475
Odysseus himself. And that put me wild.
I raved and cried, then I asked them simply, why?
Why were the weapons not reserved for me?
So who pipes up but Odysseus himself
And says because he was present on the spot   480
And saved the arms and saved my father's body,
He was entitled.
                And that put me wilder still.
I had a fit. I savaged him to his face
And insulted him and cursed him. But he comes up –   485
Not out of control, but definitely provoked –
And he says to me,
                  'We bore the brunt, not you.
When you should have been with us, you went missing.
So rant and rave your fill, but you will never   490
Be seen in your famous armour on Scyros Island.'

That was enough. There was nothing else to do
But turn round for home, humiliated
By the lowest of the low.

495   But Odysseus
In the end is less responsible
Than the ones who held command.
People in high office are bound to rule
By the force of their example. Bad actions come
500   From being badly influenced. What you see
Is what you do yourself.
                            Anyway.
That's all I have to say. But you'll understand
Why I consider anyone a friend
505   That suffered at the hands of that alliance.

CHORUS
I asked the ground to open under them,
Menelaus and Agamemnon,
When they demeaned this man.

They robbed him of his father's arms. But worse:
510   They robbed him of dignity. He lost face.
He was openly insulted by Odysseus.

I asked Earth herself, the mother of Zeus,
The mistress of the bull-killing lions,
Native of gold Pactolus, spirit of mountains.

PHILOCTETES
515   Well, there's nothing I can teach you
You don't know already. Odysseus
Is contemptible and plausible and dangerous.
And always was. But what about Ajax?
I am astonished Ajax made no moves.
520   Did he take no hand at all?

NEOPTOLEMUS
Ajax, friend, had died before this started.
If he had been alive, the arms were mine.

PHILOCTETES
Say that again, child. Ajax is dead and gone?

NEOPTOLEMUS
Ajax has gone away out of the light.

PHILOCTETES

And the ones that never should have seen the light   525
Are thriving still.

NEOPTOLEMUS
                                        They are.
The whole seed, breed and generation of them.
The biggest names in the Greek army now.

PHILOCTETES

But there was one good influence. One good man.   530
Nestor. My friend, old Nestor of Pylos.
What has become of him?

NEOPTOLEMUS
                                        He's losing ground.
His son, Antilochus, was a casualty
And that weakened Nestor's own position.   535

PHILOCTETES

This is terrible news. Of all people,
Those two are the last I'd want to think of
Being dead. But they are the ones, of course.
And the one man that does deserve to die –
Odysseus – Odysseus walks free.   540

NEOPTOLEMUS

Odysseus can outfox most opposition.
But long runs the fox that isn't caught at last.

PHILOCTETES

Gods! I forgot! Patroclus. Where was Patroclus
When you needed him? Where was your father's friend?

NEOPTOLEMUS

Philoctetes. Let me educate you   545
In one short sentence. War has an appetite
For human goodness but it won't touch the bad.

PHILOCTETES

I'm not going to contradict you there. No,
                                        But there was a certain
Gifted, sharp-tongued, useless nobody –   550

NEOPTOLEMUS
You mean Odysseus?

PHILOCTETES
                              No. Not him.
But a man you couldn't bear to listen to
And therefore the man you had to listen to
555   Incessantly. I mean Thersites.

NEOPTOLEMUS
I didn't see him. But I know he's still alive.

PHILOCTETES
Of course. Of course. What else could you expect?
The gods do grant immunity, you see,
To everybody except the true and the just.
560   The more of a plague you are, and the crueller,
The better your chances of being turned away
From the doors of death. Whose side are gods on?
What are human beings to make of them?
How am I to keep on praising gods
565   If they keep disappointing me, and never
Match the good on my side with their good?

NEOPTOLEMUS
One thing's certain in all this. I intend
To get very far away from that crew camped at Troy.
Once sharks and tramps start being in charge,
570   All ordinary decency is gone.
In future, the rocks and backwardness
Of my old home will mean far more to me . . .
Which is why I'm bound for Scyros. I have to go
Back down to the ship now. I am sorry,
575   Philoctetes, but I must say goodbye.
I hope the gods relent and your sores get cured.
We have to head on. Goodbye again, my friend.

PHILOCTETES
Are you going away again as soon as this?

NEOPTOLEMUS
We are. The minute the weather's right.
580   We have to be standing by for speedy boarding.

PHILOCTETES

No. Wait, son. Listen. And when I ask
What I am asking of you now, remember
Your own father and mother.
You know how your heart lifts when you think of home?
Well, think of what it's like to be me here,   585
Always homesick, abandoned every time.
Take me with you. As a passenger.
The state I'm in, I know I'm the last thing
A crew would want on board. But, do it, son,
Even so. Make yourself go through with it.   590
Generous people should follow their instincts.
Saying no is not your natural way
And even if you do, you'll suffer for it.
So go with your impulse, take me to Oeta,
And you'll be proud, and people will be proud   595
Of you.
              You could do it all in a day.
One single day. You can stow me anywhere.
The hold. The stern. Up under the prow.
Wherever I'm the least bother to the men.   600
Come on now, son. It's in you to do this.
You're not going to leave a wounded man behind.
I'm on my knees to you, look, and me not fit
To move hardly. I'm lamed for life. I'm done.

Take me out of here. Take me home with you   605
To your place, or somewhere in Euboea.
It'll be easy from there to get to Oeta,
And the Trachinian Hills and the Sperchius,
The River Sperchius, flowing away there still.
And my father too.   610
              So long ago, my father.
But I am afraid, not any more.
                        Time
After time, when they would sail away,
I would send word. But my predicament   615
Was the last thing on their minds. So probably
He never got my news. Or else he's dead.
But you'll take my message this time, and take me
As well.
              Life is shaky. Never, son, forget   620
How risky and slippy things are in this world.

Walk easy when the jug's full, and don't ever
Take your luck for granted. Count your blessings
And always be ready to pity other people.

CHORUS
625   Pity him, sir, do.
The man's at breaking point.
Imagine he was your friend.
And you didn't take him then?
It would cry out to heaven.

630   You have it in for the sons of Atreus,
So now's your chance to thwart them.
Take Philoctetes home
In your speedy ship. Do justice
And upset them – all at once.

NEOPTOLEMUS
635   Be sure this just isn't all loose talk.
Take care that you aren't going to change your tune
When he's stinking up the boat, and your stomach's turning.

CHORUS
Trust us. We're not going to renege.

NEOPTOLEMUS
If that's the case, then, I'll not have it said
640   I ever stopped a stranger being helped.
                                    But we have to get a move on.
He's welcome, he's in with us, so get him ready
And we'll be off, to wherever the gods grant
Safe passage and plain sailing.

PHILOCTETES
645   This is a happy day! And you, son dear,
And all of you, how will I ever manage
To pay you back? Friends! Friends,
We have to go, but before we go, I want
To kiss this ground . . . Take one last farewell
650   Of a home where I never was at home.
You have to realise the way I lived.
Many's another would have given up.
For most people, one glimpse of the life here

Would have been enough. But I was fit for it.
I matched necessity. I passed the test.   655

CHORUS
Hold on a moment. There are two people here.
The one from the ship I recognise, but not
The other one. We should see what they want.

Enter MERCHANT *(in disguise).*

MERCHANT
Son of Achilles, I was told of your whereabouts
By the watchman at the boat.   660
                              Lucky for you
That we landed here at all, in fact.
                                        Pure chance.
Anyhow, I'm a skipper with a fleet
Of merchant vessels, coming back from Troy.   665
And when I heard from your sailors you were captain
I thought the right thing was to get in touch
Before I sailed – for your own good, that is,
And maybe do myself a good turn too.
                              Who knows?   670
Let me just say, then:
There are certain things you should be aware of.
The Greeks have plans for you, and some of them
Are going ahead already as we speak.

NEOPTOLEMUS
A good deed should be rewarded, friend,   675
So you'll be treated right. I'll see to that.
But what's your news exactly? What are these moves?

MERCHANT
Old Phoenix and two sons of Theseus
Are on the high seas after you.

NEOPTOLEMUS
Why this time? To snatch me or negotiate?   680

MERCHANT
I've no idea. I'm telling you all I know.

NEOPTOLEMUS
But why are Phoenix and those two young fellows
In such a hurry to please the leadership?

MERCHANT
This is it . . . But you have to realise
685 This is what you are actually up against.

NEOPTOLEMUS
And why not Odysseus this time too?
Was he too scared to volunteer? I can't believe it!

MERCHANT
Odysseus? Oh, he was gone already
When I set sail. He and Tydeus' son
690 Were away after another, different man.

NEOPTOLEMUS
So what about this other man? What sent
Odysseus after him? Who is he?

MERCHANT
Oh! He's himself, somewhere . . .
                                    But you tell me,
695 And keep your voice down when you do: who's this?

NEOPTOLEMUS
This, friend, is the famous Philoctetes.

MERCHANT
That's that, then. End of questions. Time to go.
Get yourself on board and get as far
Away from this island as you ever can.

PHILOCTETES
700 What's he saying there? What bad is this man
Trying to put into your head about me?

NEOPTOLEMUS
I can make no sense of it myself. But
Whatever it is, he'll have to speak it out,
In the open, to you, to me, and everyone.

MERCHANT

Son of Achilles, don't report me. Don't   705
Get me into trouble with the army.
I'm only a trader and have to trade
In whatever's going. Like information.

NEOPTOLEMUS

Look. This man and I are two fast friends.
Both of us have our knife in that Atreus clan.   710
But you have come to me as a friend as well,
So keep nothing back, from me *or* from him.

MERCHANT

Well. For your own good, you should watch yourself.

NEOPTOLEMUS

I can watch myself.

MERCHANT

                        All right, then.   715
Here is the story as I understand it.
Odysseus and the other captain sailed
In pursuit of Philoctetes here.
They have sworn to take him into custody
One way or another. If they can't   720
Manage to soft-soap him, they'll use force.
Odysseus declared all this in public.
He was far more overbearing than the other.

NEOPTOLEMUS

But they did their dirty work on Philoctetes
Years ago, so what's possessed them now?   725
Why do they all of a sudden want him back?
Fear of the gods? Remorse? I wouldn't think it.

MERCHANT

I can see I have to start at the beginning
And get this whole thing clear, once and for all.
                                        All right.   730
First, you should know about a soothsayer
Called Helenus.
                A Trojan.
                            One of Priam's sons.
So Odysseus organises a night raid   735

And with all his usual old dirty dodges
He captures this Helenus and shows him off
In front of the Greek army. But Helenus
Can more than hold his own. He prophesies
740 And the gist of his prophecy concerns
This man.
                    He tells the Greeks
That unless they can coax Philoctetes
To leave this island – of his own accord –
745 They are never going to take the town of Troy.

Well, that was what got Odysseus interested.
His line was simple: he would bring Philoctetes
And make a show of him among the ranks.
If he came willingly, then well and good.
750 If not, no matter. He would still be forced to come.
And Odysseus makes a vow of this and says,
'You can take the head off me,' he says,
'Cut off my head,
                    if I don't deliver Philoctetes.'
755 So, young man. That's it. And if you have sense,
You'll mind yourself – whatever about him –
And make tracks out of here.

PHILOCTETES
                    Oh! Desperate! Desperate!
Incredible that he could even imagine it,
760 Think that he could ever talk me back among them.
There's about as much chance of that as of me
Rising from the dead.

MERCHANT
                    Well, whatever.
I'm away back now to the ship.
                              The pair of you
765 Are in the lap of the gods.
                              I wish you well.

Exit MERCHANT.

PHILOCTETES
Can you believe this, child? Odysseus
Thinks it possible he can cajole me

Into a ship, and back to face the Greeks.   770
I'd sooner meet the snake that poisoned me.
I'd sooner its forked tongue any day than his.
He has the neck for anything, nothing
Is sacrosanct, he'll say and do the worst.
I know him, and I know he will be here.   775
                                        So, set sail.
Get as much ocean as you can between
Him and us. It's action stations now!

NEOPTOLEMUS
We need the wind behind us. We can't move
Till it changes in our favour.   780

PHILOCTETES
Everything has to favour any move
Out of harm's way.

NEOPTOLEMUS
                        True enough.
But what's against us is also against them.

PHILOCTETES
It'll be for them, one way or another.   785
You can never blow a pirate off his course.

NEOPTOLEMUS
All right. We will go now. But first, think:
Is there anything here you really need?

PHILOCTETES
                        Only one thing.
Not much, but still essential.   790

NEOPTOLEMUS
Something we wouldn't have on board the ship?

PHILOCTETES
I've got this store of herbs put by, for when
The sore gets bad. They ease the pain a bit.

NEOPTOLEMUS
Bring them with you, then, and whatever else.

PHILOCTETES

795   The only other thing would be the arrows
I might have dropped.

                      Nobody else must ever
Lay hands on them.

NEOPTOLEMUS

                 And that, in your hands there:

800   Is that the bow?

PHILOCTETES

                   This is the bow.
I inherited this from Hercules
When his body burned on the funeral pyre
And his name became a god's.

NEOPTOLEMUS

805   The bow
Is like a god itself.

               I feel this urge
To touch it.

         For its virtue.

810   Venerate it.
Can I hold it in my hands?

PHILOCTETES

              If you can't hold it, child,
Then who else can? From now on, what's mine is yours.

NEOPTOLEMUS

I want to take it but I don't want to
815   Go beyond the bounds of what is allowed.

PHILOCTETES

You are allowed, son. Your natural reverence
Gives you the right. You've brought back sunlight here.
You've lit the world and now I'm fit to see
A way home to my father and my friends.
820   I was under the heel of enemies
But you raised me up above them.
You of all men have the right to hold
Philoctetes' bow. What's mine is yours.
You gave to me, I give to you . . .

The bow is proffered, elevated and held significantly between them.

You and you alone can tell the world   825
You touched this weapon, and the reason why
Is the reason I got it from Hercules
In the first place: generous behaviour.

NEOPTOLEMUS
There's a whole economy of kindness
Possible in the world; befriend a friend   830
And the chance of it's increased and multiplied.
Come on now. Check the cave.

PHILOCTETES
                                    But you come too.
I am hardly fit.

Exit PHILOCTETES *and* NEOPTOLEMUS *up to cave.*

CHORUS
You've heard the famous tale   835
Of Ixion on his wheel:
When he wanted Zeus' wife
Zeus punished him for life
And bent him like a hoop.

Ixion courted fate   840
And had to suffer for it.
But Philoctetes, no.
He didn't seduce or kill.
He was just and dutiful.

Think what that man came through.   845
What did he ever do
To be cursed with his abscess,
Crippled and deserted,
Doomed in a wilderness?

When he could bear no more,   850
The pain kept on. His sore
Made him squeal and scream
For somebody to come.
But nobody ever came.

855   He crept round like an infant.
       He wept. And when he hunted
       For herbs to soothe the foot,
       The foot wept as he dragged it.
       His trail was blood and matter.

860   But when an infant creeps
       And hurts himself and weeps,
       The helping hand is there.
       For Philoctetes, never:
       His echo was his neighbour.

865   No cultivated ground,
       No field where crops abound,
       No milled grain or bread.
       Only what he could kill
       With his great bowman's skill.

870   But now it is farewell
       To the thicket and the pool.
       Now it's wine in the bowl.
       Set out in his father's house –
       To give thanks and to bless.

875   With Neoptolemus
       He will voyage to where
       He knows each well and river,
       And Hercules' pyre
       Blazed once upon the hills.

       NEOPTOLEMUS *and* PHILOCTETES *come out of the cave.*
       NEOPTOLEMUS *gets down to a lower level.* PHILOCTETES *arrested*
       higher up, gradually rocking a little and supported on the bow.

       NEOPTOLEMUS
880   All right.
                    We'd better go.
                                    What's wrong with you?

       PHILOCTETES
       Ahhhhhhhhh. Ahhhhhhhhh. Hohohohohoh.

       NEOPTOLEMUS
       What is this anyway?

PHILOCTETES
Nothing.   885
          Nothing's wrong.
                    You keep going.

NEOPTOLEMUS
Is it the ulcer? Is it going to start?

PHILOCTETES
I don't think so.
          No harm.   890
                    You keep going.
Oh gods! O holy gods! Oh! Ohhhhh! Ohhhhhhh!

NEOPTOLEMUS
What are we going to do? You're in awful pain.

PHILOCTETES
This is the end, son.
                    This ruins everything.   895
I'm being cut open! Can you not do anything?
It's coming now. It's coming.
                    Oh! Ah! AHHHHHHH!
Get your sword, son. Take the sword to me.
Cut off that foot.   900
          Destroy it.
                    Give me peace.
Quick, quick, quick, do something!
                    I want to die.

A silence.

NEOPTOLEMUS
Philoctetes. What has come over you?   905
What is this turn? Can you still hear me?

PHILOCTETES
You know . . .

NEOPTOLEMUS
          Know what?

PHILOCTETES
                    All these spasms of mine . . .

NEOPTOLEMUS

910 What about them?

PHILOCTETES

                    I can't go on. I'm done.

NEOPTOLEMUS

You were at the limit. At the breaking point.

PHILOCTETES

There are no words for it. Only pity.

                                        Pity.

NEOPTOLEMUS

915 But what am I going to do?

PHILOCTETES

Whatever you do, don't leave. Don't let me
Scare you.

                    This thing comes over me.

                                        One minute

920 It's nowhere and the next I'm squalling.

NEOPTOLEMUS

This is terrible. There must be something
I could do. Can I not give you a hand?
Would it not help you just to hold on to me?

PHILOCTETES

No! No! Don't touch me. But you can hold the bow.

925 You'll have to guard it till this turn is over.
The pain will run its course, and once it eases
I'll go straight to sleep. Out like a light.
That'll mean I'm on the mend, so let me sleep.
But if any of them land when I'm like that,

930 I bind you in the sight of all the gods:
Never part with this bow. Willingly
Or unwillingly. That will be fatal. Fatal
For you, and for me that's in your power.
Do you understand?

NEOPTOLEMUS

                    Easy, Philoctetes. Rely on me.

935 No other hands will ever touch this bow
But yours and mine. Trust fate. Give it over.

PHILOCTETES
Here is the bow for you. Here are the arrows.
Dangerous weapons. And dangerous because
They tempt the gods to be jealous of your luck.   940
So say a prayer that you'll come through this better
Than I did, and the man that gave them to me.

NEOPTOLEMUS
I will pray for that.
                    But I also pray
That the gods' intentions and our destination   945
Won't be at odds, and they speed us on our journey.

PHILOCTETES
O son, take care I am not a stumbling block
To this prayer of yours. I'm all blood again.
I'm open deeper than ever. It's pouring out.
It's here again. Circling for a kill.   950
Why me? Gods curse this foot.

                              Oh. Ahhhhhh.
No, wait. Don't go. Don't let me scare you.
Shout instead. Shout hard. Shout their names.
Odysseus. Agamemnon. Menelaus.   955
I'll be the death of them. Let me smite them all.
O son, my body's burning.
                          Could you not
Carry me up to the crater of Lemnos
And burn me right?   960
                  What I did for Hercules
You should do for me.
                      Throw me into the fire
And keep the bow.
                  Are you there, son?   965
                                  Say something.
Where are you?

NEOPTOLEMUS
            I'm here. I'm here.
                          But I'm useless.
I know it's desperate.   970

PHILOCTETES
As long as you are there, that does me good.
And it's going to go soon, all of a sudden,
Just the way it came.

NEOPTOLEMUS
                              We're staying with you.
Don't worry about that.

PHILOCTETES
                              You're going to stay?

NEOPTOLEMUS
I promise.

PHILOCTETES
                    Promise. What use is promise?
Swear it to me.
                    But no. Swear nothing.
                                             Son,
I am astray. What am I saying?

NEOPTOLEMUS
I tell you, Philoctetes, I am bound
To you, and bound to take you.

PHILOCTETES
                                        So. Give me your hand.

NEOPTOLEMUS
Gladly. Here. We are well and truly pledged.

PHILOCTETES
Good. Good. Now the way is open.

NEOPTOLEMUS
                                        What way? Where?

PHILOCTETES
Up there. Into the sky world. High beyond.

NEOPTOLEMUS
He's raving now again. What do you see?

PHILOCTETES
Let me go. Don't touch me. Stay away!

NEOPTOLEMUS
I will. But you stay calm.
                   That's right. Stretch out.

PHILOCTETES
From now on, I am going to belong
Entirely to the earth. Be earth's for the taking.   995
I'll lie on top here first, and then lie under.

NEOPTOLEMUS
This man's bound to sleep now, very soon.
He's sweated out, the head is down, and his whole
Body is exhausted.
                 The flux has stopped,   1000
There's hardly any issue from his foot.
We should leave him quiet, friends, to get some rest.

(If there is to be an interval, it occurs now.)

CHORUS
Sleep is the god-sent cure.
Deep-reaching, painless, sure.
Its touch is certain.   1005
The light of paradise
Creeps into sleepers' eyes
As through a curtain.

But you, sir, must wake up.
Don't let this moment slip.   1010
Hold off no longer.
Now that the coast is clear
You have to do and dare.
You were never stronger.

NEOPTOLEMUS
Obviously now we could steal away with the bow.   1015
That would be easy. But easy and meaningless. No.
It's to this wounded man the triumph has to be due.
He has earned it. The oracle said it. I see it all now.
Without him the cause will be shamed and our victory hollow.

CHORUS

1020 Oracles are devious,
Beyond the likes of us.
We don't inquire too deep.
And we keep our voices down,
For sick men have been known
1025 To hear things in their sleep.

Take care. Chances like this
You can't afford to miss.
Even a fool can see
There's trouble brewing.
1030 So move. Immediately.

The man is at death's door.
You couldn't ask for more.
The winds are for us.
Before the birds can scare
1035 Wise huntsmen draw the snare
And the noose closes.

NEOPTOLEMUS

Quiet. This is nonsense. Give it over.
There's a flicker in the eyes there. His head's moving.

PHILOCTETES

The light.
1040   Sunlight.
                    And you still here, my friends.
I never thought I'd waken up like this.
I never thought you'd stand your ground with me.
I didn't think you'd have the heart for it.
1045 It was different, I tell you, the first time here.
But, Neoptolemus, you are no betrayer.
You're no Odysseus, and couldn't be.
You have it in you from both sides, straight and true
By nature. You made light of everything,
1050 The reeks and roars and the whole mess of me.
But that's all over now. So, help me up.
Put me on my feet here. Stand me straight
And once I'm steadied right, then everybody
Can go down to the boat, and all set sail.

NEOPTOLEMUS

This is more than I expected. It's great   1055
You've come round again, that you're alive
And out of danger.
                    Up you get!
Or if you'd rather, we could carry you.
These men are fit for that. Whatever you like.   1060

PHILOCTETES

That's a real friend's thought. And since you thought it,
Lift me, you yourself. Don't bother them.
They'll all be sickened of me soon enough
Once we're on board.

NEOPTOLEMUS

                    So. On your feet, then.   1065
Get yourself together.

PHILOCTETES

                    All right. All right.
                                        I'll be
Into my stride in no time.

NEOPTOLEMUS

What's to become of me now anyway?   1070

PHILOCTETES

What's to become of who?
                        What is it, child?

NEOPTOLEMUS

I'm all throughother.
                    This isn't me.
                                        I'm sorry.   1075

PHILOCTETES

What has upset you now? Don't be afflicted.

NEOPTOLEMUS

I'm an affliction to myself, that's all I am.

PHILOCTETES

Have you changed your mind? Can you not face the thing?
Does having to ship with me disgust you that much?

NEOPTOLEMUS

1080   It's more like self-disgust. No. One false move,
One move that's not your own, and everything
Goes to the bad.

PHILOCTETES

                    This is not you. Who, son,
Was ever more like himself or them before him?

NEOPTOLEMUS

1085   I'll be seen for what I am.
                              I just can't face it.

PHILOCTETES

Face what? What false move? What do you mean?

NEOPTOLEMUS

Zeus, you must help me now. There's no way out.
If I tell or if I don't tell, it's still disgrace.

PHILOCTETES

1090   Unless I'm wrong, I think – but no – not him –
I think he's for sailing on without me!

NEOPTOLEMUS

Oh no. I won't be leaving you. And more's the pity.
We'll both rue that.

PHILOCTETES

                    There's no sense in this.

NEOPTOLEMUS

1095   There is sense in it all right, Philoctetes.
The real story is this: you will be sailing,
Sailing to Troy to connect up with the Greeks.

PHILOCTETES

What?
        What?
1100   What sort of talk is this?

NEOPTOLEMUS

Quiet. Hold on. Listen.
                    There's a meaning to it.

PHILOCTETES
Meaning? What meaning? How could there be meaning?

NEOPTOLEMUS
I have to take you from this plight you're in.
You have to go with me and level Troy.   1105

PHILOCTETES
Never.
      Never.
            That will never happen.

NEOPTOLEMUS
None of us can dictate the shape of things.
It's all laid out. I'm not the one to blame.   1110

PHILOCTETES
You're as two-faced as the rest. Why did you do it?
Who are you?
           Give me back my bow.

NEOPTOLEMUS
I cannot.
       There's a cause, a plan, big moves,   1115
And I'm a part of them. I'm under orders.

PHILOCTETES
Burnt bones!
      Sears and blisters!
               There was more left
Of Hercules on the pyre than's left of me.   1120
The salamanders have me. I'm scorched to nothing.

I kneeled to him. How can he bear to do it?
Steal the bow and leave me as good as dead?
And still not say a word. Not meet my eye.
Hard little two-faced crab. He knows. He knows   1125
He's reneging on doing the right thing.

What will I do? What's left here now but me
And the place itself? The island's all there is
That'll stand to me. If I turn and leave,
The cliffs and caves and bays will still be there   1130
When I come back. If I shout for sympathy

To animals and birds, they'll answer me.
There's more nature in their dens and nests
Than there is in you, you sacrilegious
1135 Heartbreaking little coward.
                              But the man you tricked
Was never the man you came to snatch away.
You'll be showing off a phantom to the Greeks
And your big name and fame will always be
1140 Hollow to the core.
                    You faced nothing here.
You overpowered a cripple without weapons,
And even then, you did it underhand.

O son, be yourself again. This isn't you.
1145 Give me the bow.
                              Still nothing.
He's condemning me to a death by hunger.
I'm going to be a ghost before my time.
                              The birds and brutes
1150 I slaughtered with the bow, they're closing in.
I can see their beaks and muzzles crowding up
Both ends of the cave. They'll pick me clean.
My life for theirs, eye and tooth and claw.
                              Look at him there!
1155 Any kind of trust is a mistake!

Oh, but, son, you don't want to believe
That's how it is. Change things back again
And change your mind. My tongue could hardly bear
To curse you after all I felt for you.

CHORUS
1160 Why are we listening to this now, sir? Are we
On our way or not? What are you thinking?

NEOPTOLEMUS
I can't help it. There's something in me he touched
From the very start. I can't just cut him off.

PHILOCTETES
The gods have their eyes on him and that's why
1165 He can't get off the hook. He knows all this
Solidarity with the Greeks is sham.

The only real thing is the thing he lives for:
                              his own self-respect.

NEOPTOLEMUS
How did I end up here? Why did I go
Behind backs ever?   1170

PHILOCTETES
                        You did it because
You had agreed to do it. Somebody else
Rehearsed you. It has to be. There's nothing low
Or crooked in you at all. Come on, child.
Give me the bow.   1175

NEOPTOLEMUS
                        Well, friends, where are we now?

NEOPTOLEMUS *moves,* PHILOCTETES *reaches, the body language
and handling of the bow suggest that their original mutual rite of
exchange will now be repeated. It is a slightly somnambulant
movement, which* ODYSSEUS *interrupts, coming between them
suddenly, his back to* PHILOCTETES.

ODYSSEUS
Now who's the bow for, Neoptolemus?
Hand it over! A traitor can't expect
To carry weapons.

PHILOCTETES
                        Odysseus! That voice!   1180
It has to be.

ODYSSEUS
                                    Odysseus
That was and is!

PHILOCTETES
                        And when else but now?
Hangmen and betrayers never show   1185
Till the moment's ripe.

ODYSSEUS
                        That I don't deny.

PHILOCTETES
Return my bow, now, boy. You nearly did.

ODYSSEUS
He nearly did but now he never will,
1190 And you have your marching orders. Understand:
The bow goes, and you with it, with these men.

PHILOCTETES
Are you going to herd me like a wild animal?

ODYSSEUS
That's up to you. Everybody else
Wants you to come back of your own free will.

PHILOCTETES
1195 Ground of my island, be with me here and now.
And Vulcan, lord of forge-fire, volcano god,
Scorch the earth and brand the hills of Lemnos
With the mark of my ordeal at his hands.

ODYSSEUS
My hands, Philoctetes, are in the hands
1200 Of Zeus. Zeus and his thunderbolts
Rule Vulcan even. Zeus is the Lord of Lemnos.

PHILOCTETES
Anything that comes out of your mouth
Just turns to dirt. Don't foul the name of Zeus.
No god could stoop as low as Odysseus.

ODYSSEUS
1205 What do gods care? It's what they say that matters
And they say you'll march.

PHILOCTETES
                                        I say not.

ODYSSEUS
Say what you like, but you'll obey and move.

PHILOCTETES
Like a slave in chains. Oh, weep for the free man
1210 That's broken here.

ODYSSEUS

No. Wrong. The free man here
Is being raised up. These are his first steps
Towards Troy and triumph.

PHILOCTETES

Never. Not while earth
Is under me and the rocks above.   1215

ODYSSEUS
What blather's this?

PHILOCTETES

I can throw myself
From any cliff or headland on this island.

ODYSSEUS
There! Get him by the arms. He's asking for it.

PHILOCTETES
Odysseus, you have taken everything I ever had and was. The best
years of my life, my means of self-defence, my freedom, the use
of my two hands. Everything that made me my own self, you've
stripped away. And now you're going to take my second self.
This boy. He's your accomplice but he was my friend. With you
he does what he is told, with me he did what his nature told him.
I made him free, you only fouled him up. Look at him there,
he can't look me in the eye, he knows he's contaminated.
My body may be corrupting but with him it is the mind, and you
did that. You spread death-in-life. I am like a lost soul bound
for Hades, being led away out of the house of life and light and
friendship.   1220
    I curse you. I have cursed you always. It changes nothing.
I'm chaff and you're the flail. I'm beaten to nothing. I'm gone
out of mind now like a man that's dead.
    So why, why are you tearing me up out of the grave? Has the
bad smell left me? Will you not start vomiting all over the altar
now again? Will I not make you get sick into the holy vessels
this time? That was your excuse, don't you forget. That was why
you dumped me.
    But the wheel is turning, the scales are tilting back. Justice is
going to waken up at last. The gods were only biding time and
the time has gone. It wasn't love of me that brought you to
this island, there's a shape to this that's bigger than you could know.

Your eye's so jaundiced, you can't see the balance shifting and
weighing down against you – but I see it and my heart is singing.
I'd give the whole agony of my life just to see you cut down in the
end, and your tongue ripped out of you like a bleeding ox-tongue.

CHORUS
This is terrible talk. I always heard
1225 Suffering made people compassionate,
But it's only made him harder.

ODYSSEUS
                              There's plenty
I could tell him, and tell about him,
If there was time. But I'll say only this:
1230 My aim has always been to get things done
By being adaptable. If I'm dealing with
Plain-spoken, honest people, they'll find me
As honest and plain-spoken as they come.
My main concern is to keep things moving on
1235 In the right direction.
                              But in this case, no.
Not any more.
                    I give up.
                              Let him go.
1240 He's welcome to his island. All we need
Is Philoctetes' bow. Not him. Don't forget
I am the bender of as great a bow
Myself. And don't forget Teucer either.
You're only another archer among archers.
1245 And since you're so worried about who's going to be
The Lord of Lemnos, you be it yourself.
You should have been the Lord of Fallen Troy
But that's an honour fallen now to me.

PHILOCTETES
You of all of them!

ODYSSEUS
1250   Enough said. Time to move!

PHILOCTETES
Son of Achilles, are you going to go
Without one word still? Don't deny yourself.

ODYSSEUS
Ignore him, Neoptolemus. The thing's
Ruined if you start shilly-shallying.

PHILOCTETES
And what about the rest of you?   1255
Where's your pity now? Are you all just yes-men?

CHORUS
When the captain speaks, the crew has to obey.

NEOPTOLEMUS
Whether it's shilly-shallying or not,
What you'll do is wait here to the last
When all the prayers and thanksgivings are over   1260
And the boat's rigged out.
                                    Maybe he'll come round
And see the sense of moving with us yet.
I'm away on with Odysseus.
                                    You hear?   1265
Be ready and be listening for the shout.

Exit ODYSSEUS *and* NEOPTOLEMUS.

PHILOCTETES
I am going to die here,
I'm going to die of hunger,
That's what's going to happen.
Trapped among fallen rocks   1270
In the bare mouth of a cave.
Watching clouds and birds
Blowing across the sky.
No bow any more.
Slow death by exposure.   1275

CHORUS
You walked yourself into it. Don't protest and lament
As if at this stage your whole predicament
Was unavoidable. It is not Odysseus
But your own self you have to blame for this.

PHILOCTETES
Some animals in a trap   1280
Eat their own legs off

In order to escape.
I'd like to see him caught
And so stuck and smashed up
1285   He couldn't do even that.

CHORUS
We had no hand in whatever scheme he laid
So listen to us: don't contradict a god.
I sense that there's some overarching fate
You must obey. I say this in all friendship.

PHILOCTETES
1290   He'll be sitting laughing at me,
Sitting watching the sea
Somewhere, him and the bow.
Turning it over and over,
Trying it out in his hands,
1295   Testing the weight and the lift.
I loved the feel of it,
Its grip and give, and the grain
That was seasoned with my sweat.
When I held it, I had a hold
1300   On the crossbeam of the world.
I was the wind and the trees
And the pillar of Hercules.
But now he's sitting with it,
Laughing and turning it over.
1305   Great gods, be just!
I am mocked and accursed
And I hate that man for ever.

CHORUS
If you seek justice, you should deal justly always.
You should govern your tongue and present a true case.
1310   For don't forget: Odysseus was commanded.
There was nothing personal in what he did.

PHILOCTETES
I'll soon be tainted meat
For scavengers to pick at.
The shining eyes and claws
1315   Of all the hunted creatures
Are sharpening for a kill:

Crows and wolves and vultures
And every animal
That was my victim ever.
I'm at their mercy now.   1320
This is the last stand
And I haven't an arrow even.
All I've left is a wound.

CHORUS
Your wound is what you feed on, Philoctetes.
I say it again in friendship and say this: 1325
Stop eating yourself up with hate and come with us.

PHILOCTETES
I can feel your sympathy,
And did feel it all along.
But now leave me alone.
Once bitten is hard-bitten.   1330
Stop this torturing me.

CHORUS
What torture?

PHILOCTETES
            All talk of Troy and me, me
That was stabbed in the back, going back ever.

CHORUS
For your own good you have to.   1335

PHILOCTETES
                        For my own good,
For the last time, leave me alone!

CHORUS
                            All right.
All right.
        Goodbye.   1340
                You are on your own.
We're back to the rowing benches and the rowing.

PHILOCTETES
No. Wait.
        Not yet.
                Are you away for good?   1345

CHORUS
Easy.
        Take it easy.

PHILOCTETES
                        No! Hold on still!

CHORUS
What's wrong? What is it now?

PHILOCTETES
1350   The foot! The foot!
Being left with that, left on my own again.

CHORUS
                        What do you want?
Are you for coming with us now or are you not?

PHILOCTETES
The sore has me astray. I can't think right.

CHORUS
1355 But listen to yourself.
                        You want to come.

PHILOCTETES
Never. No. No matter how I'm besieged.
I'll be my own Troy. The Greeks will never take me.
But, friends, still, friends, there is one last thing.

CHORUS
1360   What is it?

PHILOCTETES
Have you not a sword for me? Or an axe?
                                    Or something?

CHORUS
What for?

PHILOCTETES
                What for? What do you think for?
1365 For foot and head and hand. For the relief
Of cutting myself off. I want away.

CHORUS
How away?

PHILOCTETES
Away to the house of death.
To my father, sitting waiting there
Under the clay roof. I'll come back in to him   1370
Out of the light, out of his memory
Of the day I left.
                                   We'll be on the riverbank
Again, and see the Greeks arriving
And me setting out for Troy,   1375
                         in all good faith.

CHORUS
Setting-out time is here for us anyhow.
But maybe not.
                    There's something holding these two.

Enter NEOPTOLEMUS *and* ODYSSEUS.

ODYSSEUS
What has you so worked up? Why can we not   1380
Just rise and go? What's on your mind?

NEOPTOLEMUS
I did a wrong thing and I have to right it.

ODYSSEUS
What was that?

NEOPTOLEMUS
                    I did this whole thing your way.

ODYSSEUS
We were Greeks with a job to do, and we did it.   1385

NEOPTOLEMUS
I behaved like a born liar.

ODYSSEUS
                    But it worked!
It worked, so what about it?

NEOPTOLEMUS

                              Not for me.
1390   And I'm not leaving till the thing's put right.

ODYSSEUS
It's the bow. You're having second thoughts.

NEOPTOLEMUS

                                    What else?

ODYSSEUS
You mean you're going to just give it back?

NEOPTOLEMUS
The scales will even out when the bow's restored.

ODYSSEUS
1395   Act your age. Be reasonable. Use your head.

NEOPTOLEMUS
Since when did the use of reason rule out truth?

ODYSSEUS
Neoptolemus: am I hearing right?

NEOPTOLEMUS
Oh yes. Loud and clear, and more and more.

ODYSSEUS
I'd have been better then not hearing you.

NEOPTOLEMUS
1400   Too bad. Too late.

ODYSSEUS
                         Oh, not too late at all.
There's one last barrier you'll not get past.

NEOPTOLEMUS
What's that?

ODYSSEUS
                    The will of the Greek people,
1405   And me here as their representative.

NEOPTOLEMUS
What kind of talk is that? You're capable,
Odysseus, and resourceful. But you have no values.

ODYSSEUS
And where's the value in your carry-on?

NEOPTOLEMUS
Candour before canniness. Doing the right thing
And not just saying it.   1410

ODYSSEUS
                        What's so right about
Reneging on your Greek commission?
You're under my command here. Don't you forget it.

NEOPTOLEMUS
The commands that I am hearing overrule
You and all you stand for.   1415

ODYSSEUS
                        And what about
The Greeks? Have they no jurisdiction left?

NEOPTOLEMUS
The jurisdiction I am under here
Is justice herself. She isn't only Greek.

ODYSSEUS
You've turned yourself into a Trojan, lad,   1420
And that will have consequences.

NEOPTOLEMUS
                        So let them come.

ODYSSEUS
(*Reaching for his sword*)
Do you see where this hand is now?

NEOPTOLEMUS
                        Do you see mine?

ODYSSEUS
Right! What I've seen and heard here, I'll report.   1425
You won't get off with this. I'm going back

To outline all the charges.
                                    You were right
When you said you did a wrong thing here.

Exit ODYSSEUS.

NEOPTOLEMUS
1430   Philoctetes!
Philoctetes! Come out here. Where are you?

Enter PHILOCTETES, *at the cave mouth.*

PHILOCTETES
What's all this now?
                                Have you not done enough
Damage already?

NEOPTOLEMUS
1435   Listen. Listen to me.

PHILOCTETES
I listened to you once and I believed you.
But never again.

NEOPTOLEMUS
                        Do you deny
The possibility of a change of heart?

PHILOCTETES
1440   Once was enough. You slithered in like this,
All sincerity till you got the bow.

NEOPTOLEMUS
Things are different now. I ask again:
Are you going to stay here saying no for ever
Or do you come in with us?

PHILOCTETES
1445   I'll never join,
So you can save your breath.

NEOPTOLEMUS
                        That is your last word?

PHILOCTETES
Utterly. No more.

NEOPTOLEMUS
        In that case, I give up.
Reluctantly, regretfully, give up.   1450

PHILOCTETES
What sort of a surrender do you want?
How do you think I could believe you ever,
That told me lies and then when I relented
Opened the trapdoor under me? Gods curse you
And the traitors that you're in with.   1455

NEOPTOLEMUS
                    Curse no more.
I have the bow for you.
            Look. Take it.
                Here!

PHILOCTETES
Where's the ambush? This I do not believe.   1460

NEOPTOLEMUS
I swear by the name of Zeus, the almighty god.

PHILOCTETES
Swear, oh, you'll swear! It's only words to you.

NEOPTOLEMUS
It is more than words.
            Hold your hand out.
                  Take it.   1465

PHILOCTETES *comes down. Pause and momentary mutual clasp
to recall original pledging. Enter* ODYSSEUS.

ODYSSEUS
As the gods are my witness, as both of you are Greeks,
In my capacity as your commander,
I forbid the handover of this weapon.
Whether Achilles' son wants it or not,
You are under orders, Philoctetes,   1470
To join the force at Troy.

PHILOCTETES

                    And you are in range at last.

He aims the bow.

NEOPTOLEMUS
No, Philoctetes, no!
                    Hold off. Don't.
1475   Don't!

PHILOCTETES
Let go. How dare you, son?
                    Let go!

NEOPTOLEMUS
                              You can't.

Exit ODYSSEUS.

PHILOCTETES
He was mine for the taking and you saved him. Why?

NEOPTOLEMUS
1480   It would have been the end of both of us.

PHILOCTETES
Commander, he said. One of the big names.
Big talk only, when all was said and done.

NEOPTOLEMUS
Forget about him. You have the bow
And my slate's clean again. The air is cleared.

PHILOCTETES
1485   Entirely.
                    You are back to your old self,
Your father's son.

NEOPTOLEMUS
It does me good to hear that.
                                    It gives me hope
1490   You might credit what I'm going to tell you.
You know it already anyhow. You know
Human beings have to bear up and face
Whatever's meant to be. There's a courage

And dignity in ordinary people
That can be breathtaking. But you're the opposite.   1495
Your courage has gone wild, you're like a brute
That can only foam at the mouth. You aren't
Bearing up, you are bearing down. Anybody
That ever tries to help you just gets savaged.
You're a wounded man in terrible need of healing   1500
But when your friends try, all you do is snarl
Like some animal protecting cubs.
So listen now to me, Philoctetes,
And brand this into your skull.

                         You're a sick man.   1505
The snake-bite at the shrine was from a god,
But the gods send remedies, and they expect
Obedience then as well.

                 You are to come
Of your own free will to the town of Troy.   1510
Asclepius, the healer, you remember,
He'll be there with his sons, and they'll cure you.
Then you're to take your bow and go with me
Into the front line and win the city.

All this must come to pass. A soothsayer,   1515
And a Trojan soothsayer at that, has foretold it.
This is the summer of the fall of Troy.
It'll be talked about for ever and you're to be
The hero that was healed and then went on
To heal the wound of the Trojan war itself.   1520

PHILOCTETES
You're making me see things in such brilliant light
I can't bear it. I've been in the afterlife
For ten years now, ten years of being gone
And being forgotten. Even you, my son,
Won't bring me back. The past is bearable,   1525
The past's only a scar, but the future –
Never. Never again can I see myself
Eye to eye with the sons of Atreus.

What's happened to you, son? This makes no sense.
These people defiled your father's memory   1530
And gave his armour to Odysseus.
Why are you arguing a case for them?

Forget them, and remember what you said
You'd do for me. You made a promise
1535 To take me with you when you were going home
To Scyros. And that's what you must do.
Otherwise, you'll be tainted with their guilt
Just by association.

NEOPTOLEMUS
                              I can see that.
1540 But even so, the signs are that the gods
Want you to go to Troy, and me with you.

PHILOCTETES
How can you bear to take their side like that?

NEOPTOLEMUS
It's not their side.
                              It's what our fates involve.

PHILOCTETES
1545 This is real turncoat talk. Have you no shame?

NEOPTOLEMUS
What's the shame in working for a good thing?

PHILOCTETES
But good for who? Me or my enemies?

NEOPTOLEMUS
Am I your friend or not?

PHILOCTETES
                              I thought you were.

NEOPTOLEMUS
1550 Stop just licking your wounds. Start seeing things.

PHILOCTETES
There's danger in all this somewhere. I can sense it.

NEOPTOLEMUS
The danger is you'll break if you don't bend,
So I give up. From now on, you can live
With every consequence of your decision.

PHILOCTETES
Whatever's been laid out, I'm ready for it.   1555
But there's consequence to your own endeavours:
You gave your word – you pledged with your hand
And promised you'd take me home.
                                        So do that now.
Restore your good name. Bury the name of Troy.   1560

NEOPTOLEMUS
I gave my word. I pledged it with my hand.
My life was an open door that started closing
The minute I landed here. But maybe now
It could open back again. So. We go.

PHILOCTETES
                                        We go?   1565

NEOPTOLEMUS
Gather yourself. Come on.

PHILOCTETES
                            I can't believe it.

NEOPTOLEMUS
The Greeks.
            No, wait.
                        The Greeks'll be after us.   1570

PHILOCTETES
Forget them. You'll be safe.

NEOPTOLEMUS
                            But the country won't be.

PHILOCTETES
I'll be in your country.

NEOPTOLEMUS
                            And what good's that?

PHILOCTETES
Hercules' bow!   1575

NEOPTOLEMUS
                    The bow. We have it still.

PHILOCTETES
Hercules' bow is miraculous
And will save us every time.

NEOPTOLEMUS
                              Then so be it.
1580   This time your farewell is farewell for good.

PHILOCTETES *repeats some part of his original rite of departure.*
Perhaps he raises both arms, perhaps prostrates himself. A silence
then, music perhaps also. Then an eerie, soundless (at first) flash
and flame; mountain-rumble far off; an air of danger, settling into
a kind of threatened, pre-thunder stillness. Darker stage, a kind of
purpled twilight. CHORUS *in spotlight, positioned as at end of*
prologue.

CHORUS
Human beings suffer,
They torture one another,
They get hurt and get hard.
No poem or play or song
1585   Can fully right a wrong
Inflicted and endured.

The innocent in gaols
Beat on their bars together.
A hunger-striker's father
1590   Stands in the graveyard dumb.
The police widow in veils
Faints at the funeral home.

History says, *Don't hope*
On this side of the grave.
1595   But then, once in a lifetime
The longed-for tidal wave
Of justice can rise up,
And hope and history rhyme.

So hope for a great sea-change
1600   On the far side of revenge.
Believe that a further shore
Is reachable from here.
Believe in miracles
And cures and healing wells.

Call miracle self-healing: 1605
The utter, self-revealing
Double-take of feeling.
If there's fire on the mountain
Or lightning and storm
And a god speaks from the sky   1610

That means someone is hearing
The outcry and the birth-cry
Of new life at its term.

The full thunderclap and eruption-effects occur. Then a lingering,
wavering aftermath of half-light. Brilliant spots find PHILOCTETES
and CHORUS.

PHILOCTETES
(Crying out)
Hercules:
        I saw him in the fire.   1615
Hercules
        was shining in the air.
I heard the voice of Hercules in my head.

CHORUS
(Ritually clamant, as HERCULES)
I have opened the closed road
Between the living and the dead   1620
To make the right road clear to you.
This is the voice of Hercules now.

Here on earth my labours were
The stepping-stones to upper air:
Lives that suffer and come right   1625
Are backlit by immortal light.

So let my mind light up your mind.
You must see straight and turn around.
You must complete your oath-bound course.
You cannot yet return to Scyros.   1630

Go, Philoctetes, with this boy,
Go and be cured and capture Troy.
Asclepius will make you whole,
Relieve your body and your soul.

1635   Go, with your bow. Conclude the sore
        And cruel stalemate of our war.
        Win by fair combat. But know to shun
        Reprisal killings when that's done.

        Then take just spoils and sail at last
1640   Out of the bad dream of your past.
        Make sacrifice. Burn spoils to me.
        Shoot arrows in my memory.

        And, Neoptolemus, you must be
        His twin in arms and archery.
1645   Marauding lions on that shore,
        Troy's nemesis and last nightmare.

        But when the city's being sacked
        Preserve the shrines. Show gods respect.
        Reverence for the gods survives
1650   Our individual mortal lives.

        PHILOCTETES
        Something told me this was going to happen.
        Something told me the channels were going to open.
        It's as if a thing I knew and had forgotten
        Came back completely clear. I can see
1655   The cure at Troy. All that you say
        Is like a dream to me and I obey.

        NEOPTOLEMUS
        And so will I.

        CHORUS
                    Then go, immediately.
        The winds are blowing and the tides are high.

        PHILOCTETES
        (In a sort of daze, on all fours perhaps, or clasping an upright
        support: knocked out, flattened)
1660   But I can't believe I'm going. My head's light at the thought of a
        different ground and a different sky. I'll never get over Lemnos;
        this island's going to be the keel under me and the ballast inside me.
        I'm like a fossil that's being carried away, I'm nothing but cave
        stones and damp walls and an old mush of dead leaves. The sound
        of waves in draughty passages. A cliff that's wet with spray on a

winter's morning. I feel like the sixth sense of the world. I feel I'm
a part of what was always meant to happen, and is happening now
at last. Come on, my friends.

CHORUS
Now it's high watermark
And floodtide in the heart
And time to go.
The sea-nymphs in the spray
Will be the chorus now.   1665
What's left to say?

Suspect too much sweet talk
But never close your mind.
It was a fortunate wind
That blew me here. I leave   1670
Half-ready to believe
That a crippled trust might walk

And the half-true rhyme is love.

The Midnight Verdict

OVID / BRIAN MERRIMAN

for Jean and Peter

Orpheus and Eurydice

OVID

Orpheus called for Hymen and Hymen came
Robed in saffron like a saffron flame
Leaping across tremendous airy zones
To reach the land of the Ciconians.
5   So Hymen did attend the rites, but no
Good luck or cheer or salutations, no
Auspicious outcome was to come of that.
Instead, the torch he carried smoked and spat
And no matter how he fanned it wouldn't flare.
10 His eyes kept watering. And a worse disaster
Than could have been predicted came to pass
For as the bride went roaming through the grass
With all her naiads round her, she fell down.
A snake had bit her ankle. She was gone.

15 Orpheus mourned her in the world above,
Raving and astray, until his love
Compelled him down among the very shades.
He dared to venture on the Stygian roads
Among those shadow people, the many, many
20 Ghosts of the dead, to find Persephone
And the lord who rules the dismal land of Hades;
Then plucked the lyre-gut for its melodies
And sang in harmony: 'O founded powers
Who rule the underearth, this life of ours,
25 This mortal life we live in upper air
Will be returned to you. To you, therefore,
We may speak the whole truth and speak it out
As I do now, directly: I have not
Transgressed your gloomy borders just to see
30 The sights of Tartarus, nor to tie all three
Of the three-necked monster's snake-snarled necks in one.
I crossed into your jurisdiction
Because my wife is here. The snake she stepped on

Poisoned her and cut her off too soon
And though I have tried to suffer on my own   35
And outlive loss, in the end Love won.
Whether or not you underpowers feel
The force of this god, Love, I cannot tell,
But surely he prevails down here as well
Unless that ancient story about hell   40
And its lord and a ravaged girl's not true.
Was it not Love that bound the two of you?
I pray you, therefore, by the extent of these
Scaresome voids and mist-veiled silences,
Unweave the woven fate Eurydice   45
Endured too soon. All of humanity
Is in your power, your kingdom is our home.
We may put off the day but it will come.
Sooner or later, the last house on the road
Will be this immemorial abode.   50
This is the throne-room of the universe.
Allow Eurydice her unlived years
And when she will have lived them, she'll be yours
Inalienably. I desire on sufferance
And want my wife. But if the fates pronounce   55
Against this privilege, then you can take
Credit for two deaths. I shall not go back.'

As Orpheus played and pleaded, the bodiless
Hordes of the dead wept for him. Tantalus
Was so bewitched he let the next wave fill   60
And fall without reaching. Ixion's wheel
Stood spellbound. The vultures' beaks held off
Above Tityos' liver. The obsessive
Water-riddlers heard and did not move.
And Sisyphus, you dozed upon your rock   65
Which stood dazed also. A tear then wet the cheek
Of each of the Eumenides, the one
And only time: song had made them human
And made the lord of Hades and his lady
Relent as well. They called Eurydice   70
Who limped out from among the newly dead
As eager as the day when she'd been wed
To Orpheus. But there was one term set:
Until he left Avernus, he was not
To look back, or the gift would be in vain.   75

They took the pathway up a steep incline
That kept on rising higher, through a grim
Silence and thick mist, and they had come
Close to the rim of earth when Orpheus –
80   Anxious for her, wild to see her face –
Turned his head to look and she was gone
Immediately, forever, back and down.

He reached his arms out, desperate to hold
And be held on to, but his arms just filled
85   With insubstantial air. She died again,
Bridal and doomed, but still did not complain
Against her husband – as indeed how could she
Complain about being loved so totally?
Instead, as she slipped away, she called out dear
90   And desperate farewells he strained to hear.

The second death stunned Orpheus. He stood
Disconsolate, beyond himself, dumbfounded
Like the man who turned to stone because he'd seen
Hercules lead Cerberus on a chain
95   Leashed to his middle neck; or like that pair
Petrified to two rocks underwater
In the riverlands of lda – Olenos
And Lethea, uxorious sinners.
Pleading and pleading to be let across
100 The Styx again, he sat for seven days
Fasting and filthy on the bank, but Charon
Would not allow it. So he travelled on
Accusing the cruel gods until he found
A way back to his mountainous home ground
105 In Rhodope.

            The sun passed through the house
Of Pisces three times then, and Orpheus
Withdrew and turned away from loving women –
Perhaps because there only could be one
110 Eurydice, or because the shock of loss
Had changed his very nature. Nonetheless,
Many women loved him and, denied
Or not, adored. But now the only bride
For Orpheus was going to be a boy

And Thracians learned from him, who still enjoy
Plucking those spring flowers bright and early.

The Midnight Verdict   BRIAN MERRIMAN

ONE

I used to wade through heavy dews
On the riverbank, in the grassy meadows,
Beside the woods, in a glen apart
As the morning light lit sky and heart
And sky and heart kept growing lighter   5
At the sight of Graney's clear lough water.
The lift of the mountains there! Their brows
Shining and stern in serried rows!
My withered heart would start to quicken,
Everything small in me, hardbitten,   10
Everything hurt and needy and shrewd
Lifted its eyes to the top of the wood
Past flocks of ducks on a glassy bay
And a swan there too in all her glory;
Jumping fish in the heady light   15
And the perch's belly flashing white.
The sheen of the lough, the grumble and roar
Of the blue-black waves as they rolled ashore.
There'd be chirruping birds from tree to tree
And leaping deer in the woods nearby,   20
Sounding of horns, the dashing crowd
As the hounds gave tongue and Reynard fled.

Yesterday morning the sky was clear,
The sun flamed up in the house of Cancer
With the night behind it, fit to take on   25
The work of the day that had to be done.
Leafy branches were all around me,
Shooting grasses and growths abounded;
There were green plants climbing and worts and weeds
That would gladden your mind and clear your head.   30
I was tired out, dead sleepy and slack,
So I lay at my length on the flat of my back
With my head well propped, my limbs at ease
In a nest in a ditch beside the trees.

35   The minute I closed my eyes, I drowsed.
My lids were locked, I couldn't be roused.
I was hidden from flies, felt safe and sound
When a nightmare swarmed and gathered around,
Battered me, flattened me, dragged me down
40   Through weltering sleep and left me stunned.
But my rest was short for next there comes
A sound from the ground like the roll of drums,
A wind from the north, a furious rout
And the lough in a sulphurous thunderlight.
45   And then comes looming into view
And steering towards me along the bay
This hefty menacing dangerwoman,
Bony and huge, a terrible hallion.
Her height, I'd say, to the nearest measure,
50   Was six or seven yards or more,
With a swatch of her shawl all muck and japs
Streeling behind in the puddly gaps.
It was awe-inspiring just to see her,
So hatchet-faced and scarred and sour –
55   With her ganting gums and her mouth in a twist
She'd have put the wind up man or beast.
And Lord of Fates! Her hand was a vise
Clamped on a towering staff or mace
With a spike on top and a flange of brass
60   That indicated her bailiff's powers.

Her words were grim when she got started.
'Get up,' she said, 'and on your feet!
What do you think gives you the right
To shun the crowds and the sitting court?
65   A court of justice, truly founded,
And not the usual rigged charade,
But a fair and clement court of women
Of the gentlest stock and regimen
The Irish race should be grateful always
70   For a bench that's so composed and wise
And in session now, two days and a night,
In the spacious fort on Graney Height.

Their king, moreover, has taken to heart
The state of the country; he feels its hurt
75   As if it were his own, and the whole

Of his entourage are aghast as well.
It's goodbye to freedom and ancient right,
To honest dealing and leadership:
The ground ripped off and nothing put back,
Weeds in the field once crop is stacked.   80
With the best of the people leaving the land,
Graft has the under- and upper hand.
Just line your pockets, a wink and a nod,
And to hell with the poor! Their backs are broad.

Alas for the plight of the underclass   85
And the system's victims who seek redress:
Their one recourse is the licensed robber
With his legalese and his fancy slabber.
Lawyers corrupt, their standards gone,
Favouritism the way it's done,   90
The bar disgraced, truth compromised,
Nothing but kick-backs, bribes and lies.

To add to which, the whole assembly
Decreed on the Bible this very day:
The youth has failed, declined, gone fallow –   95
Bad news and bad marks, sir, for you.
In living memory, with birth rates fallen
And marriage in Ireland on the wane,
The country's life has been dissipated,
Pillage and death have combined to waste it.   100
Blame arrogant kings, blame emigration,
But it's you and your spunkless generation.
You're a source blocked off that won't refill.
You have failed your women, one and all.

Think of the way they're made and moulded,   105
The flush and zest in their flesh and blood –
Those easy ladies half on offer
And the big strait-laced ones, all ignored.
Why aren't they all consoled and gravid,
In full proud sail with their breasts in bud?   110
Say but the word and the clustered fruit
Will be piled like windfalls round your feet.

So the meeting pondered the country's crisis
And the best opinions agreed on this:

115 That one of their own should be deputed
To come back here to adjudicate.
Then Aoibheall rises, as Munster's guardian
And Craglee's peerless fairy queen
And offers to leave the fairy palace
120 And go to Thomond to hear the case.
And, honest princess, she makes a promise
To come down hard on the law's abuse.
Might without right to be defeated
And right as right reinstated straight.
125 So hereinafter, greasing the palm
Of pimp or madam or sycophant
Won't work or avail, for it's not an inch
Now that Her Grace is boss of the bench.
Already at Feakle the court's in session
130 That you must answer. The pressure's on
For you to appear. So move. And fast.
Move or I'll make you move, you bast—.'

With that she crooked her staff in my cape
And hooked me behind and hauled me up
135 And we went like hell over glen and hill
To Moinmoy Church, by the gable wall.

And there (I am sure) lit torches showed
A handsome, grand, well-built abode,
A stately, steadfast, glittering space,
140 Accessible and commodious.
And I saw a lovely vision woman
Ensconced on the bench of law and freedom,
And saw her fierce, fleet guard of honour
Rank upon rank in throngs around her.
145 I saw then too rooms filling full,
Crowding with women from wall to wall,
And saw this other heavenly beauty
With her lazy eye, on her dignity,
Seductive, pouting, with curling locks,
150 Biding her time in the witness box.
Her hair spilled down, loosed tress on tress,
And a hurt expression marked her face;
She was full of fight, with a glinting eye,
Hot on the boil, ill-set and angry –
155 Yet for all her spasms, she couldn't speak

For her hefts and huffing had made her weak.
She looked like death or a living death wish
She was so cried out; but straight as a rush,
She stood to the fore as a witness stands
Flailing and wailing and wringing hands.   160
And she kept it up; she raved and screeched
Till sighing restored her powers of speech.
Then her downlook went, her colour rose,
She dried her eyes and commenced as follows:

'A thousand welcomes! And bless Your Highness!   165
Aoibheall of Crag, our prophetess!
Our daylight's light, our moon forever,
Our hope of life when the weeping's over!
O head of all the hosted sisters,
Thomond can thole no more! Assist us!   170
My cause, my case, the reason why
My plea's prolonged so endlessly
Until I'm raving and round the twist
Like a maenad whirled in a swirl of mist –
The reason why is the unattached   175
And unprovided for, unmatched
Women I know, like flowers in a bed
Nobody's dibbled or mulched or weeded
Or trimmed or watered or ever tended;
So here they are, unhusbanded,   180
Unasked, untouched, beyond conception –
And, needless to say, I'm no exception.
I'm scorched and tossed, a sorry case
Of nerves and drives and neediness,
Depressed, obsessed, awake at night,   185
Unused, unsoothed, disconsolate,
A throbbing ache, a dumb discord,
My mind and bed like a kneading board.
O Warden of the Crag, incline!
Observe the plight of Ireland's women,   190
For if things go on like this, then fuck it!
The men will have to be abducted!'

TWO

Bathed in an aura of morning light,
Her Grace on the bench got up to her feet;
Beautiful, youthful, full of poise,
She cleared her throat and raised her voice,
5   Then clenched her fists with definite menace
And ordered the bailiff to call for silence.
The court complied; they sat entranced
As her lovely fluent lips pronounced:

'To my mind, girl, you've stated your case
10   With point and force. You deserve redress.
So I here enact a law for women:
Unmated men turned twenty-one
To be sought, pursued, and hunted down,
Tied to this tree beside the headstone,
15   Their vests stripped off, their jackets ripped,
Their backs and asses scourged and whipped.
But the long-in-the-tooth and the dry-in-marrow,
The ones whose harrow-pins won't harrow,
Who pen the pent and lock away
20   The ram that's rampant in their body,
Keeping in hand what should go the rounds
And fencing off the pleasure grounds –
Their nemesis I leave to you
Whose hearths they'd neither fan nor blow.
25   Dear natural sexual women, think!
Consult your gender, mind and instinct.
Take cognisance. Co-operate.
For I here invest you with the right
(To be exercised to the breaking point)
30   And powers of violent punishment.

Yet who gives a damn in the end of all
For them and their dribbling stroup and fall?
With forks collapsed and the feeling gone,
Their hardest part is a pubic bone.
35   So let them connive, sing dumb and smile
If ever a young man rings their bell
For it seems to me that the best solution
For men past making a contribution
Is not to resent their conjugal plight

But stand by their wives when they put it about,   40
Facilitate their womanly drives
And lend their name when the baby arrives.
And that, for the moment, will have to do.
I'm on the circuit, and overdue
In another part of Munster. So: 45
My verdict's short because I go.
But I'll be back, and God help then
Recalcitrant, male-bonded men.'

She stopped, but still her starry gaze
Transfixed me in a kind of daze   50
I couldn't shake off. My head went light,
I suffered cramps and a fainting fit.
The whole earth seemed to tilt and swing,
My two ears sang from the tongue-lashing
And then the awful targe who'd brought me,   55
The plank-armed bailiff, reached and caught me
Up by the ears and scruff of the neck
And dragged me struggling into the dock.
Where next comes skipping, clapping hands,
The lass who had aired her love-demands   60
And says to my face, 'You hardened chaw,
I've waited long, now I'll curry you raw!
You've had your warnings, you cold-rifed blirt.
But now you're caught in a woman's court
And nobody's here to plead your case.   65
Where is the credit you've earned with us?
Is there anyone here your action's eased?
One that your input's roused or pleased?
Observe him closely, Madam Judge.
From head to toe, he's your average   70
Passable male – no paragon
But nothing a woman wouldn't take on.
Unshapely, yes, and off the plumb,
But with all his kit of tools about him.
A shade whey-faced and pale and wan,   75
But what about it? There's bone and brawn.
For it's him and his likes with their humps and stoops
Can shoulder doors and flutter the coops;
As long as a man is randy and game,
Who gives a damn if he's bandy or lame?   80

So why is he single? Some secret wound
Or problem back in the family background?
And him the quality's darling boy,
All smiles and friends with everybody,
85 Playing his tunes, on sprees and batters
With his intellectual and social betters.
Wining and dining, day in, day out –
The creep, I can see why they think he's great!
A star bucklepper, the very man
90 You'd be apt to nickname 'merry man',
But the kind of man I would sweep away,
The virgin merry, going grey.
It bothers me deeply. I've come to hate
His plausible, capable, charming note
95 And his beaming, bland, unfurrowed forehead:
Thirty years old, and never bedded.

So hear me now, long-suffering judge!
My own long hurt and ingrown grudge
Have me desolated. I hereby claim
100 A woman's right to punish him.
And you, dear women, you must assist.
So rope him, Una, and all the rest –
Anna, Maura – take hold and bind him.
Double twist his arms behind him.
105 Remember all the sentence called for
And execute it to the letter.
Maeve and Sive and Sheila! Maureen!
Knot the rope till it tears the skin.
Let Mr Brian take what we give,
110 Let him have it. Flay him alive
And don't draw back when you're drawing blood.
Test all of your whips against his manhood.
Cut deep. No mercy. Make him squeal.
Leave him in strips from head to heel
115 Until every single mother's son
In the land of Ireland learns the lesson.

And it only seems both right and fitting
To note the date of this special sitting
So calm your nerves and start computing:
120 A thousand minus a hundred and ten –

Take what that gives you, double it, then
Your product's the year.' She'd lifted her pen
And her hand was poised to ratify
The fate that was looking me straight in the eye.
She was writing it down, the household guard   125
Sat at attention, staring hard
As I stared back. Then my dreaming ceased
And I started up, awake, released.

The Death of Orpheus
OVID

The songs of Orpheus held the woods entranced.
The animals were hushed, the field-stones danced
Until a band of crazed Ciconian women,
A maenad band dressed up in wild beasts' skins,
Spied him from a hilltop with his lyre.   5
As he tuned his voice to it and cocked his ear,
One of them whose hair streamed in the breeze
Began to shout, 'Look, look, it's Orpheus,
Orpheus the misogynist,' and flung
Her staff straight at the bard's mouth while he sang.   10
But the staff being twined with leaves just left a bruise
And did no injury. So another throws
A stone that his singing spellbinds in the air,
Making it drop like a shamed petitioner
At his affronted feet. But even so,   15
There could be no stop to the violence now.
The furies were unleashed. And his magic note
That should have stalled their weapons was drowned out
By blaring horns and drums, beatings and yells
And the pandemonium of those bacchanals   20
So that at last his red blood wet the rocks.
But first the maenads ripped apart the snakes
And the flocks of birds he'd charmed out of the sky
And the dreambound beasts that formed his retinue.
Orpheus then, torn by their blood-filled nails,   25
Was like an owl in daytime when it falls
Prey to the hawks of light; or a stag that stands
In the amphitheatre early, before the hounds
Have savaged it to pieces on the sand.
They circled him, still using as their weapons   30

Staffs they had twined with leaves and tipped with cones
That were never meant for duty such as this.
Some pelted him with clods, some stripped the branches
To scourge him raw, some stoned him with flintstones.
35 But as their frenzy peaked, they chanced upon
Far deadlier implements.

Near at hand
Oxen in yokes pulled ploughshares through the ground
And sturdy farmers sweated as they dug –
40 Only to flee across their drills and rigs
When they saw the horde advancing. They downed tools
So there for the taking on the empty fields
Lay hoes and heavy mattocks and long spades.
The oxen lowered their horns, the squealing maenads
45 Cut them to pieces, then turned to rend the bard,
Committing sacrilege when they ignored
His hands stretched out to plead and the extreme
Pitch of his song that now for the first time
Failed to enchant. And so, alas, the breath
50 Of life streamed out of him, out of that mouth
Whose songs had tamed the beasts and made stones dance,
And was blown away on the indiscriminate winds.
For Orpheus then the birds in cheeping flocks,
The animals in packs, the flint-veined rocks
55 And woods that had listened, straining every leaf,
Wept and kept weeping. For it seemed as if
The trees were mourners tearing at their hair
As the leaves streamed off them and the branch went bare.
And rivers too, they say, rose up in floods
60 Of their own tears, and all the nymphs and naiads
Went dishevelled in drab mourning gowns.
Meanwhile, the poet's mangled flesh and bones
Lay scattered and exposed. But his head and lyre
Were saved by miracle: the Hebrus River
65 Rose for them, ran with them, bore them out midstream
Where the lyre trembled and the dead mouth swam
Lapping the ripples that lipped the muddy shore
And a fluent humming sadness filled the air.
As they rode the current downstream, they were swept
70 On out to sea off Lesbos and washed up
On the strand there, unprotected. Then a snake

Unleashed itself like a slick whip to attack
The head in its tangled web of sopping locks
But Phoebus intervened. Just as its bite
Gaped at its widest, it solidified.   75
The jaws' hinge hardened and the open yawn
Of the empty vicious mouth was set in stone.

The poet's shade fled underneath the earth
Past landmarks that he recognised, down paths
He'd travelled on the first time, desperately   80
Scouring the blessed fields for Eurydice.
And when he found her, wound her in his arms
And moved with her, and she with him, two forms
Of the one love, restored and mutual –
For Orpheus now walks free, is free to fall   85
Out of step, into step, follow, go in front
And look behind him to his heart's content.

But Bacchus was unwilling to forget
The atrocities against his sacred poet,
So, there and then, in a web of roots, he wound   90
And bound the offending women to the ground.
However deftly they would try to go,
Earth's grip and traction clutched them from below.
They felt it latch them, load them heel and toe.
And, as a caught bird struggles to get free   95
From a cunningly set snare, but still can only
Tighten the mesh around its feet still tighter
The more it strains its wings and frets and flutters,
So each of the landlogged women heaved and hauled
In vain, in agony, as the roots took hold   100
And bark began to thicken the smooth skin.
It gripped them and crept up above their knees.
They struggled like a storm in storm-tossed trees.
Then, as each finger twigged and toe dug in,
Arms turned to oak boughs, thighs to oak, oak leaves   105
Matted their breasts and camouflaged their moves
So that you couldn't tell if the whole strange growth
Were a wood or women in distress or both.

Laments

JAN KOCHANOWSKI

Lament 1

All Heraclitus' tears, all threnodies
And plaintive dirges of Simonides,
All keens and slow airs in the world, all griefs,
Wrung hands, wet eyes, laments and epitaphs,
5   All, all assemble, come from every quarter,
Help me to mourn my small girl, my dear daughter,
Whom cruel Death tore up with such wild force
Out of my life, it left me no recourse.
So the snake, when he finds a hidden nest
10   Of fledgling nightingales, rears and strikes fast
Repeatedly, while the poor mother bird
Tries to distract him with a fierce, absurd
Fluttering – but in vain! The venomous tongue
Darts, and she must retreat on ruffled wing.
15   'You weep in vain,' my friends will say. But then,
What is not vain, by God, in lives of men?
All is in vain! We play at blind man's buff
Until hard edges break into our path.
Man's life is error. Where, then, is relief?
20   In shedding tears or wrestling down my grief?

Lament 2

If my vocation had been children's rhymes
And my true art the one that mimes and calms
The rhythm of the cradle, then my verse
Might have made dandling songs for the wet nurse
5   To sing to her new charge until at last
Its tears would stop and its small woes be past!
Such jingles would have been of much more use
Than what misfortune forces me to choose:
To weep on a small daughter's grave, to keen
10   Her loss to Pluto's dark hard-hearted queen.
Admittedly, my choice was never free:
The lullaby, to a grown man like me,

Seemed far too childish; now the epitaph
Looms like a cliff above some wild and rough
Shore, where I'm cast by fate and where I sing   15
Oblivious to my fame, to everything
Except my grief. And I, who never wrote
To court a living ear, have tuned my note
To appease the dead; in vain, alas! One rule
Applies to all, for man is Fortune's fool.   20
O cruel, unjust law! How can you be
So implacable, so hard, Persephone!
Why did you have to snatch away my small
Girl who had hardly learned to live at all,
Who never came to full bloom in the light   25
Before her eyes closed underneath your night?
I wish she had not seen the world – for what
True sense of it could she, a child, have got?
She saw her birth and death; and then she fled
And turned hearts full of love to hearts of lead.   30

Lament 3

You've scorned me, then – dear apple of my eye,
My heiress! For how could I satisfy
You, my dear you, with such small inheritance?
How could it equal the deservingness
Of all your early reason, all your grace: 5
Your future virtues shone out of your face!
Your words, your curtsies, your young lady's pose –
How weighed down I am now without all those!
For you, my comfort, you will never more
Come back to warm my old heart to its core!   10
What can I do, then? what else do, except
Follow whatever way your light foot stepped?
There, Heaven grant it, at my journey's end,
Your slender arms will reach and gird me round.

Lament 4

Ungodly Death, my eyes have been defiled
By having had to watch my best loved child
Die! Watch you like a robber stalk the house

And shake the green fruit from her parents' boughs.
5   Not that at any age, had she survived,
     Could her sad father easily have outlived
     The memory of having watched her die;
     But even so, I cannot think that I
     Could ever be, at any later date,
10   More stricken by despair, more desolate!
     She, had God granted her a few more years,
     She could have spared my eyes these scalding tears;
     And I could have lived on far more at peace
     So that the stern gaze of Persephone's
15   Obliterating eyes might have searched my heart
     And found no hurt there equal to this hurt.
     But no, all's changed; for when a father's eyes
     See what Niobe saw, he petrifies.

     Lament 5

     Just as an olive seedling, when it tries
     To grow up like the big trees towards the skies
     And sprouts out of the ground, a single stalk,
     A slender, leafless, twigless, living stick;
5   And which, if lopped by the swift sickle's blade
     As it weeds out thorns and nettles, starts to fade
     And, sapped of natural strength, cut off, forlorn,
     Drops by the tree from whose seed it was born –
     So was my dearest Ursula's demise.
10   Growing before her parents' caring eyes,
     She'd barely risen above ground when Death
     Felled the dear child with his infectious breath
     At our very feet. Hard-eyed Persephone,
     Were all those tears of no avail to me?

     Lament 6

     My Slavic Sappho, little poet-heiress,
     Ghost owner of my goods, even my rarest
     Treasure: the lute! How well you did deserve
     This one bequest! With what sheer wit and verve
5   You fitted words together, song by song,
     And, never tiring, hummed them all day long

Like a nightingale that sings, small and alone,
Among green leaves, from dusk to early dawn.
Oh, you fell silent much too soon! The fright
That sudden death gave you put you to flight, 10
My tiny warbling one! You did not fill
My ears with songs enough, and yet I still
Pay with my tears for those few that I heard.
Even in death you sang, my lovely bird:
'Dear mother, kiss me, I'll no more be able 15
To do my tasks or sit here at your table;
I must give back my keys and go away,
Never return to where my parents stay.'
This was her last word, her last song, and I
Can only echo it in fond goodbye: 20
Her mother's heart, since she endured such sweet
Shocks of farewell, has nearly ceased to beat.

Lament 7

Pathetic garments that my girl once wore
    But cannot anymore!
The sight of them still haunts me everywhere
    And feeds my great despair.
They miss her body's warmth; and so do I: 5
    All I can do is cry.
Eternal, iron slumbers now possess
    My child: each flowered dress,
Smooth ribbon, gold-clasped belt her mother bought –
    Their worth is set at nought. 10
You were not meant, my daughter, to be led
    To that last, stone-cold bed
By your poor mother! She had promised more
    Than what your four planks store:
The shroud she herself sewed, the earthen clod 15
    I set down at your head.
O sealed oak chest, dark lid, board walls that hide
    The dowry and the bride!

Lament 8

The void that fills my house is so immense
Now that my girl has gone. It baffles sense:
We all are here, yet no one is, I feel;
The flight of one small soul has tipped the scale.
5   You talked for all of us, you sang for all,
You played in every nook and cubbyhole.
You never would have made your mother brood
Nor father think too much for his own good;
The house was carefree. Everybody laughed.
10   You held us in your arms: our hearts would lift.
Now emptiness reigns here; the house is still;
Nobody ever laughs nor ever will.
All your old haunts have turned to haunts of pain,
And every heart is hankering in vain.

Lament 9

I'd buy you, Wisdom, with all of the world's gold –
But is there any truth in what we're told
About your power to purge our human thought
Of all its dread, and raise up the distraught
5   Spirit to heaven, to the highest sphere
Where angels dwell beyond distress and fear?
You see mere trifles in all human things;
Mourning and mirth are two extended wings
On which you bring us equanimity,
10   Yourself unmoved by Death, calm, changeless, free.
For you, the rich man is the one who owns
No more than what's enough – no precious stones,
Or land, or rents; you see through to the truth,
The misery beneath the gilded roof;
15   But if poor people heed your sober voice,
You do not grudge the poor their simple joys.
To think that I have spent my life in one
Long climb towards your threshold! All delusion!
Wisdom for me was castles in the air;
20   I'm hurled, like all the rest, from the topmost stair.

Lament 10

Ursula, my sweet girl, where did you go?
Is it a place or country that we know?
Or were you borne above the highest sphere
To dwell and sing among the cherub choir?
Have you flown into Paradise? Or soared   5
To the Islands of the Blest? Are you aboard
With Charon, scooping water while he steers,
And does that drink inure you to my tears?
Clad in grey feathers of a nightingale,
No longer human, do you fill some vale   10
With plaintive song? Or must you still remain
In Purgatory, as if the slightest stain
Of sin could have defiled your soul? Did it return
To where you were (my woe) before being born?
Wherever you may be – if you exist –   15
Take pity on my grief. O presence missed,
Comfort me, haunt me; you whom I have lost,
Come back again, be shadow, dream, or ghost.

Lament 11

'Virtue's a trifle!' – stricken Brutus swore.
A trifle, yes, it is, and nothing more!
Did works of piety ever mitigate
Our destined pain? Did good once counter fate?
Some enemy, indifferent to all   5
Our mortal fault or merit, plots our fall.
Where his breath blows, we cannot flee or hide:
Just and unjust are brought down side by side.
Yet still we, in our arrogance, pretend
To higher faculties that comprehend   10
God's mysteries; we climb to heaven, try
To fathom its designs, but our mind's eye
Proves far too weak! The meanings it divines
Are not meant to be read – fleet dreams, not signs . . .
Grief, what do you intend? Am I to be   15
Robbed first of joy, then equanimity?

Lament 12

I think no father ever doted more
Upon a child or mourned a child's loss more;
Nor was there ever child whose virtues could
Make both its parents feel such gratitude.
5   Obedient, never wilful or morose,
Eager to babble, sing, even compose
Rhymes of her own, a girl who knew just how
To bear herself and make a proper bow,
She was good-mannered, wise, sweet-natured, neat,
10   Courteous, modest, lively and discreet;
She would put off taking supper every night
Until she'd said her prayers, and said them right;
And would not sleep or feel the house was safe
Until she'd asked the good God to ward off
15   Everything bad. She would hurry to the door
To welcome me back home; there was no chore
She would avoid, keen always to compete,
To outrun servants on her tiny feet.
And all that from a thirty-month-old child!
20   Her young and slender frame could not uphold
Such a rich wreath of virtues: their bright crown
Imposed so heavily, she was brought down
Much before harvest. Little ear of grain,
Before your time, I sow you once again
25   In the sad earth – and it is not just you
That I am burying, but my own hope too:
For you will never, never sprout nor bloom
Again, to light my eyes' unending gloom.

Lament 13

Sweet girl, I wish that you had either never
Been born or never died! For you to sever
All your attachments, take such early leave –
What else, what else can I do now but grieve?
5   You were like one of those recurrent dreams
About a crock of gold, fool's gold that gleams
And tempts our greed, but when we wake at dawn,
Our hands are empty and the gleam is gone.
Dear daughter, this you did in your own way:

Your light appeared to me but would not stay.   10
It was as if you wanted to destroy
My very soul by robbing all its joy.
The shock of sudden death tore it in two:
One half stayed grieving, one half fled with you.
Here is your epitaph. Stonecutters, hone   15
The chisels sharp and cut the words in stone:
'Ursula Kochanowski lies beneath,
Her father's joy that slipped his loving hands.
Learn from this grave the ways of careless Death:
The green shoot is mown down – the ripe crop stands.'   20

Lament 14

Where is that gate for grief which, long ago,
Let Orpheus enter the dark realm below
In search of his lost love? My loss is such
That I would go as far and do as much
Where Charon poles the flood, while his boat moves   5
Thronged with pale shades he lands in cypress groves.
And you, my lovely lute, do not desert
Your singer now: now we must both assert
Our rights before stern Pluto, soften him
With songs and tears until his own eyes swim   10
And he relents, and lets my dear girl go
And come to my embrace, and end my woe.
Which won't mean he'll have lost her – we're all his!
(If fruit's not ripe, you wait until it is.)
Yet is this god so heartless that he can   15
Turn a deaf ear to a despairing man?
If that is so, earth won't see me again.
I'll yield my own soul, find peace and remain.

Lament 15

Golden-haired Erato, your sweet-stringed lute
Soothes what is grievous, cures the sharpest hurt,
So cure me too! I'll turn, if I'm not healed,
Into a marble pillar in a field,
A monument to pain, a standing stone   5
That weeps and bleeds like living flesh and bone.

But why rehearse the fate of Niobe?
What human grief can match her misery?
Niobe, mother most unfortunate
10 (If Fortune can be blamed for evil fate
More than our Folly): where have they gone, where are
The seven girls and seven boys you bore?
I see their fourteen graves; and you, poor thing,
Incorrigibly proud, still challenging
15 The gods themselves – you dash against each tomb,
Too late to shield your dead brood from their doom.
Thus flowers, when mown by a sickle's blade
Or flattened by a downpour, wilt and fade.
What hope keeps you alive? Is it not clear
20 That death alone can conquer your despair?
Diana, Phoebus, take revenge! Allow
Your flighted arrows and unerring bow
To strike her for her fault, if not in rage,
Out of compassion, to spare her her old age!
25 But how you were to strike, who could have known?
You turned proud Niobe into a stone,
A deathless marble, standing on the top
Of Sipylus. Her running wounds won't stop
Tormenting her: the rock sheds crystal-clear
30 Tears that flow down in streams where birds and deer
Gather to drink; but she, forever chained
On rocky heights, defies the howling wind.
This tomb keeps no corpse; this corpse keeps no tomb:
Here the room's tenant is the tenant's room.

Lament 16

No end to misery; my own
Has chilled me to the marrowbone;
I must forgo my rhyme and lute:
        My soul is mute.

5 Am I alive? asleep? It seems
My head's a haunted house for dreams
That first delude my inner eye,
        Then fade and die.

O error of our minds! Insane
Conceit of men! We feel no pain,
Then straight presume our reason proof
      Against all grief.   10

In plenty we praise poverty;
In pleasure, sorrow seems to be
Easy to bear; each living breath   15
      Makes light of Death.

But when the Parcae cease to spin
Their thread, when sorrows enter in,
When Death knocks at the door, at last
      We stand aghast.   20

Cicero, silver tongue, please tell
Why exile's tears afflict you still;
Did you not claim: 'The world's my home,
      And not just Rome'?

Why do you mourn your lovely girl?   25
Did you not say your dearest pearl
Was clear conscience? Doesn't your woe
      Prove that untrue?

Only the godless – you have said –
Fear death; then what about your dread,   30
When threats were Antony's rewards
      For your bold words?

Your logic, O angelic pen,
Compelling to the minds of men,
Rings hollow when your soul, like mine,   35
      Cries out in pain.

Man is not stone; his wounds run deep;
His joys are like a scar on top;
And once it's touched, that buried ache
      Throbs wide awake.   40

Time, father of forgetfulness,
Stronger than reason and no less
Potent than faith; heal, heal my heart
      That's torn apart.

Lament 17

That the Lord's hand could destroy
In one stroke all my joy!
My soul, sick and oppressed,
Scarce stirs inside my breast.

5   Whether I watch the sun
Rising or going down,
Always the same dull ache
Keeps my poor heart awake.

Will nothing stop my cry!
10   Despair like mine won't die.
I'll cry on as I cried:
When God strikes, men can't hide.

You may abjure the sword,
Or never dare to board
15   A ship; yet, near or far,
Grief finds out where you are.

Unknown, withdrawn, my life
Was ruled by this belief:
Modesty is the gate
20   That locks out envy, hate.

But God knows where to touch:
Our prudence can't help much.
My best plans went amiss:
His blow shattered my bliss.

25   Reason, once adequate
To weigh and arbitrate
What God and life allow,
Is no help to me now.

It duly plays its part,
30   Tries to persuade my heart
To overcome its pain:
But all this is in vain.

Philosophers who claim:
'Loss? Loss is a mere name,

No more. Laugh at your lot!' –   35
They just tighten the knot.

My ear attends and hears
Calm Reason mocking tears,
Yet tears in my own eyes
Prove such words blatant lies.   40

If my soul's wounded, I
Can do nothing but cry;
False comfort only sears
My heart and brings new tears.

O bitter placebo!   45
My tortured mind says No
To mockeries that rend it.
It wants a cure to mend it.

Therefore my tears flow on,
For there are things beyond   50
Calm Reason's power to cope:
God is my only hope.

Lament 18

My Lord, each of us is your wilful child:
        By happiness beguiled,
        Entranced by earthly joys,
He soon forgets you and heeds not your voice.

We fail to see how much your Grace attends   5
        Our welfare; which soon ends
        When your infinite Good
Is not repaid with infinite gratitude.

Rein us in, Lord, before vain pleasure blinds
        Our supercilious minds!   10
        Remind them of your cause
If not with blessings, then at least with blows!

Yet punish us as loving fathers do:
        Your wrath would burn us through;
        We'd vanish without trace   15
Like snow when warmed by the sun's piercing rays.

Oh, let your hand not crush those in discord
    With you, Eternal Lord;
    You hurt us to the core
20   With your mere frown: we could not withstand more.

Though fools claim you have never been man's friend,
    Sooner the world may end
    Than you shall ever scorn
A rebel soul, when broken and forlorn.

25   Great are my sins before you, Lord; yet still
    Your mercy and goodwill
    Would not let evil reign.
Have pity, Lord, on my despair and pain!

Lament 19, or: A Dream

Through the long night, grief kept me wide awake;
My body was worn out, my mind all ache
And restlessness. The dark was growing pale
Before sleep touched my brow with its black veil.
5   Then, at that instant (was I lulled by charms?),
I saw my mother, holding in her arms
My Ursula, my never lovelier
Daughter, in white nightgown, gold-curled hair,
Rose-petal skin, eyes bright as a new day –
10   Just like those mornings when she'd come to say
Her prayers for me. I stared and stared, until
My mother spoke: 'Are you asleep, or ill
With sorrow, son?' At which, my own deep sigh
Seemed to have wakened me; but presently
15   She spoke again: 'Your cry! Your cry, my dear,
Disturbed my distant shore and brought me here;
Each moan of yours, each bitter tear you shed
Has reached the hidden chambers of the dead.
Here is your girl: look at her smiling face
20   And be consoled. Take heart. Although your case
Is hard in the extreme, although you are
In torment, mind and body, every hour,
Be comforted. Why make yourself heartsick?
Why is your mind a burning candlewick
25   Wasting itself ? You think the dead are gone,

Extinct forever, banished from the sun?
You are mistaken: there, the lives we live
Are far more glorious. There we are alive
Beyond the flesh. The dust returns to dust,
But spirit is divine, a gift that must   30
Return to its Giver. Trust and understand
This mystery: she sits at God's right hand.
You cannot see her as she is – your sight
Is mortal and sees things in mortal light –
But now your daughter shines, a morning star   35
Among angelic spirits. You who are
So desolate, know that she prays for you
And for her mother – as she used to do
When she was still a child learning to speak.
To you her life may have seemed short and bleak,   40
She may have missed the pleasures adults know –
But what are pleasures when they end in woe?
The more you have, the faster your life moves
Towards the loss of it. Your own case proves
This beyond doubt. Your daughter brought you joy   45
But could that match the pangs that now destroy
All your tranquillity? It never could,
So recollect yourself. This desolate mood
Is natural when your child is in the grave,
But how would she be better off alive?   50
What did she lose? Not true peace or delight.
She freed herself from things that devastate
Our life on earth with heartbreak and despair,
Things that weigh down the cross that humans bear
And haunt their moments of felicity   55
With deep foreboding and anxiety.
So why do you keep crying? My God, son,
What is there to regret? That no man won
Her dowry and her heart, then made her years
One long declension into strife and tears?   60
That her body wasn't torn by labour pains?
That her experience was, is and remains
Virginal, that she got release before
She learned if birth or death mark women more?
Earthly boundaries limit earthly joys –   65
Heavenly joys are boundless. Paradise
Exists forever, crystalline, secure.

There happiness is absolute and pure;
There tragedy, disease, death have no place;
70 There tears are wiped away from every face.
We live our endless lives in endless bliss.
We know the cause of each thing that exists.
Our Sun will never set; our days don't end,
The dark and fear of night never descend
75 Upon our realm, where we unceasingly
Witness our Maker in His majesty.
You mortals cannot see Him. Still, dear son,
Turn your thoughts toward Him, try to live on
Consoled by changeless heaven's certainty.
80 You've learned how futile earthly love can be,
Heed now the other, heavenly love's voice!
The truth is: your girl made a better choice.
Thus, sailors making for the open sea
Will head back towards the haven when they see
85 Dark clouds above; while others, who keep going,
Are wrecked on blind reefs when the gale starts blowing
And drowned and lost; lucky the few who are
Cast up on shore safe, clinging to some spar!
Had she outlived the Sibyl, her one fate
90 Would still be death. So why prolong that wait
For what was certain anyhow? She chose
Departure over waiting, chose to close
The door early and cut life's sorrows short.
Some lose their parents and have no resort
95 But orphanages; some are married off
In haste and lose their fortune and young life
To God knows what impostor; others still,
Abducted and made slaves of, tread the mill
In some wild heathen enclave, stooped and lame,
100 Praying for death to come and end their shame.
These threats are threats your child no longer faces.
Her life on earth was happy, an oasis
Of small protected joys, a heaven-sent
Interlude, short-lived but innocent.
105 It was for her, my son, things turned out best,
So dry your tears. Believe. Take comfort. Rest.
Weigh up your losses, ponder each mistake,
Yet never overlook what is at stake:
Your peace of mind, your equanimity!

However robbed of these you seem to be,   110
However little of a help they are
Be your own master. Every evil star
Shines with impunity and as of right:
No matter how it hurts, we must abide,
We must obey. That burden's placed upon   115
Each one of us, so why then feel, my son,
You have been singled out? She was mortal too,
And lived as long as she was destined to.
You think not long enough? But even so,
You cannot alter it, and who can know   120
How living on for just a few more hours
Would have been better? The Lord's ways are not ours.
Our task is simply to accord with them.
Tears cannot call back souls who are called home.
For how can we on earth adjudicate   125
Fairly upon what seems unfair in fate?
Prone to see things in the worst light, mankind
Can hardly recognise or bear in mind
The fortunate things. And yet proud Fortune's ways
Are not to be contested. Sing in praise   130
Of loss even, in praise of all that's left
That might have gone instead down Death's dark shaft.
You must accept, although your wound's still raw,
The rule and sway of universal law
And fill your heart with new peace, banish pain: 135
Whatever is not loss should be called gain.
What profit have you reaped for all that cost,
That foolishly, irretrievably lost
Time you spend poring over books, those years
Of study that still leave you in arrears?   140
By now your grafting should have yielded fruit:
Windfalls of wisdom, comfort, resolute
Self-mastery. When others were in pain,
You've helped them over it, time and again;
Now, master, you will have to heal yourself.   145
Time is the cure for everything, but if
Somebody has such faith in his own power
Of healing, should he wait another hour?
Yet what is time's great remedy? The wax
And wane of things, and nothing more; the flux   150
Of new events, now painful, now serene;

He who has grasped this accepts what has been
And what will be with equal steadfastness,
Resigned to suffer, glad to suffer less.
155   Bear humanly the human lot. There is –
Never forget – one Lord of blight and bliss.'
She vanished, and I woke, uncertain what
I had just seen: was this a dream or not?

Beowulf

ANONYMOUS

in memory of Ted Hughes

So. The Spear-Danes in days gone by
and the kings who ruled them had courage and greatness.
We have heard of those princes' heroic campaigns.

There was Shield Sheafson, scourge of many tribes,
5   a wrecker of mead-benches, rampaging among foes.
This terror of the hall-troops had come far.
A foundling to start with, he would flourish later on
as his powers waxed and his worth was proved.
In the end each clan on the outlying coasts
10   beyond the whale-road had to yield to him
and begin to pay tribute. That was one good king.

Afterwards a boy-child was born to Shield,
a cub in the yard, a comfort sent
by God to that nation. He knew what they had tholed,
15   the long times and troubles they'd come through
without a leader; so the Lord of Life,
the glorious Almighty, made this man renowned.
Shield had fathered a famous son:
Beow's name was known through the north.
20   And a young prince must be prudent like that,
giving freely while his father lives
so that afterwards in age when fighting starts
steadfast companions will stand by him
and hold the line. Behaviour that's admired
25   is the path to power among people everywhere.

Shield was still thriving when his time came
and he crossed over into the Lord's keeping.
His warrior band did what he bade them
when he laid down the law among the Danes:
30   they shouldered him out to the sea's flood,
the chief they revered who had long ruled them.
A ring-whorled prow rode in the harbour,
ice-clad, outbound, a craft for a prince.
They stretched their beloved lord in his boat,

The Danes have legends about their warrior kings. The most famous was Shield Sheafson, who founded the ruling house.

Shield's funeral.

35   laid out by the mast, amidships,
the great ring-giver. Far-fetched treasures
were piled upon him, and precious gear.
I never heard before of a ship so well furbished
with battle tackle, bladed weapons
40   and coats of mail. The massed treasure
was loaded on top of him: it would travel far
on out into the ocean's sway.
They decked his body no less bountifully
with offerings than those first ones did
45   who cast him away when he was a child
and launched him alone out over the waves.
And they set a gold standard up
high above his head and let him drift
to wind and tide, bewailing him
50   and mourning their loss. No man can tell,
no wise man in hall or weathered veteran
knows for certain who salvaged that load.

Then it fell to Beow to keep the forts.   Shield's heirs:
He was well regarded and ruled the Danes   his son Beow
55   for a long time after his father took leave   succeeded by
of his life on earth. And then his heir,   Halfdane,
the great Halfdane, held sway   Halfdane by
for as long as he lived, their elder and warlord. Hrothgar.
He was four times a father, this fighter prince:
60   one by one they entered the world,
Heorogar, Hrothgar, the good Halga
and a daughter, I have heard, who was Onela's queen,
a balm in bed to the battle-scarred Swede.

The fortunes of war favoured Hrothgar.   King Hrothgar
65   Friends and kinsmen flocked to his ranks,   builds Heorot
young followers, a force that grew   Hall.
to be a mighty army. So his mind turned
to hall-building: he handed down orders
for men to work on a great mead-hall
70   meant to be a wonder of the world forever;
it would be his throne-room and there he would dispense
his God-given goods to young and old –
but not the common land or people's lives.
Far and wide through the world, I have heard,

75 orders for work to adorn that wallstead
    were sent to many peoples. And soon it stood there,
    finished and ready, in full view,
    the hall of halls. Heorot was the name
    he had settled on it, whose utterance was law.
80 Nor did he renege, but doled out rings
    and torques at the table. The hall towered,
    its gables wide and high and awaiting
    a barbarous burning. That doom abided,
    but in time it would come: the killer instinct
85 unleashed among in-laws, the blood-lust rampant.

    Then a powerful demon, a prowler through the dark,   Heorot is
    nursed a hard grievance. It harrowed him   threatened.
    to hear the din of the loud banquet
    every day in the hall, the harp being struck
90 and the clear song of a skilled poet
    telling with mastery of man's beginnings,
    how the Almighty had made the earth
    a gleaming plain girdled with waters;
    in His splendour He set the sun and the moon
95 to be earth's lamplight, lanterns for men,
    and filled the broad lap of the world
    with branches and leaves; and quickened life
    in every other thing that moved.

    So times were pleasant for the people there   Grendel, a monster
100 until finally one, a fiend out of hell,   descended from
    began to work his evil in the world.   'Cain's clan',
    Grendel was the name of this grim demon   begins to prowl.
    haunting the marches, marauding round the heath
    and the desolate fens; he had dwelt for a time
105 in misery among the banished monsters,
    Cain's clan, whom the Creator had outlawed
    and condemned as outcasts. For the killing of Abel
    the Eternal Lord had exacted a price:
    Cain got no good from committing that murder
110 because the Almighty made him anathema
    and out of the curse of his exile there sprang
    ogres and elves and evil phantoms
    and the giants too who strove with God
    time and again until He gave them their reward.

115 So, after nightfall, Grendel set out
for the lofty house, to see how the Ring-Danes
were settling into it after their drink,
and there he came upon them, a company of the best
asleep from their feasting, insensible to pain
120 and human sorrow. Suddenly then
the God-cursed brute was creating havoc:
greedy and grim, he grabbed thirty men
from their resting places and rushed to his lair,
flushed up and inflamed from the raid,
125 blundering back with the butchered corpses.

Then as dawn brightened and the day broke
Grendel's powers of destruction were plain:
their wassail was over, they wept to heaven
and mourned under morning. Their mighty prince,
130 the storied leader, sat stricken and helpless,
humiliated by the loss of his guard,
bewildered and stunned, staring aghast
at the demon's trail, in deep distress.
He was numb with grief, but got no respite
135 for one night later merciless Grendel
struck again with more gruesome murders.
Malignant by nature, he never showed remorse.
It was easy then to meet with a man
shifting himself to a safer distance
140 to bed in the bothies, for who could be blind
to the evidence of his eyes, the obviousness
of that hall-watcher's hate? Whoever escaped
kept a weather-eye open and moved away.

So Grendel ruled in defiance of right,
145 one against all, until the greatest house
in the world stood empty, a deserted wallstead.
For twelve winters, seasons of woe,
the lord of the Shieldings suffered under
his load of sorrow; and so, before long,
150 the news was known over the whole world.
Sad lays were sung about the beset king,
the vicious raids and ravages of Grendel,
his long and unrelenting feud,
nothing but war; how he would never

Grendel attacks
Heorot.

King Hrothgar's
distress and
helplessness.

155 parley or make peace with any Dane
     nor stop his death-dealing nor pay the death-price.
     No counsellor could ever expect
     fair reparation from those rabid hands.
     All were endangered; young and old
160 were hunted down by that dark death-shadow
     who lurked and swooped in the long nights
     on the misty moors; nobody knows
     where these reavers from hell roam on their errands.

     So Grendel waged his lonely war,
165 inflicting constant cruelties on the people,
     atrocious hurt. He took over Heorot,
     haunted the glittering hall after dark,
     but the throne itself, the treasure-seat,
     he was kept from approaching; he was the Lord's outcast.

170 These were hard times, heart-breaking   The Danes, hard-
     for the prince of the Shieldings; powerful counsellors,   pressed, turn for
     the highest in the land, would lend advice,   help to heathen
     plotting how best the bold defenders   gods.
     might resist and beat off sudden attacks.
175 Sometimes at pagan shrines they vowed
     offerings to idols, swore oaths
     that the killer of souls might come to their aid
     and save the people. That was their way,
     their heathenish hope; deep in their hearts
180 they remembered hell. The Almighty Judge
     of good deeds and bad, the Lord God,
     Head of the Heavens and High King of the World,
     was unknown to them. Oh, cursed is he
     who in time of trouble has to thrust his soul
185 in the fire's embrace, forfeiting help;
     he has nowhere to turn. But blessed is he
     who after death can approach the Lord
     and find friendship in the Father's embrace.

     So that troubled time continued, woe
190 that never stopped, steady affliction
     for Halfdane's son, too hard an ordeal.
     There was panic after dark, people endured
     raids in the night, riven by the terror.

When he heard about Grendel, Hygelac's thane
195　was on home ground, over in Geatland.
There was no one else like him alive.
In his day, he was the mightiest man on earth,
high-born and powerful. He ordered a boat
that would ply the waves. He announced his plan:
200　to sail the swan's road and search out that king,
the famous prince who needed defenders.
Nobody tried to keep him from going,
no elder denied him, dear as he was to them.
Instead, they inspected omens and spurred
205　his ambition to go, whilst he moved about
like the leader he was, enlisting men,
the best he could find; with fourteen others
the warrior boarded the boat as captain,
a canny pilot along coast and currents.

210　Time went by, the boat was on water,
in close under the cliffs.
Men climbed eagerly up the gangplank,
sand churned in surf, warriors loaded
a cargo of weapons, shining war-gear
215　in the vessel's hold, then heaved out,
away with a will in their wood-wreathed ship.
Over the waves, with the wind behind her
and foam at her neck, she flew like a bird
until her curved prow had covered the distance
220　and on the following day, at the due hour,
those seafarers sighted land,
sunlit cliffs, sheer crags
and looming headlands, the landfall they sought.
It was the end of their voyage and the Geats vaulted
225　over the side, out on to the sand,
and moored their ship. There was a clash of mail
and a thresh of gear. They thanked God
for that easy crossing on a calm sea.

When the watchman on the wall, the Shieldings' lookout
230　whose job it was to guard the sea-cliffs,
saw shields glittering on the gangplank
and battle-equipment being unloaded
he had to find out who and what
the arrivals were. So he rode to the shore,

At the court of
King Hygelac,
a Geat warrior
prepares to help
Hrothgar.

The hero and his
troop sail from the
land of the Geats.

The Danish coast-
guard challenges
the outsiders.

235 this horseman of Hrothgar's, and challenged them
in formal terms, flourishing his spear:

'What kind of men are you who arrive
rigged out for combat in coats of mail,
sailing here over the sea-lanes
240 in your steep-hulled boat? I have been stationed
as lookout on this coast for a long time.
My job is to watch the waves for raiders,
any danger to the Danish shore.
Never before has a force under arms
245 disembarked so openly – not bothering to ask
if the sentries allowed them safe passage
or the clan had consented. Nor have I seen
a mightier man-at-arms on this earth
than the one standing here: unless I am mistaken,
250 he is truly noble. This is no mere
hanger-on in a hero's armour.
So now, before you fare inland
as interlopers, I have to be informed
about who you are and where you hail from.
255 Outsiders from across the water,
I say it again: the sooner you tell
where you come from and why, the better.'

The leader of the troop unlocked his word-hoard;
the distinguished one delivered this answer:
260 'We belong by birth to the Geat people
and owe allegiance to Lord Hygelac.
In his day, my father was a famous man,
a noble warrior-lord named Ecgtheow.
He outlasted many a long winter
265 and went on his way. All over the world
men wise in counsel continue to remember him.
We come in good faith to find your lord
and nation's shield, the son of Halfdane.
Give us the right advice and direction.
270 We have arrived here on a great errand
to the lord of the Danes, and I believe therefore
there should be nothing hidden or withheld between us.
So tell us if what we have heard is true
about this threat, whatever it is,
275 this danger abroad in the dark nights,

The Geat hero
announces himself
and explains his
mission.

this corpse-maker mongering death
in the Shieldings' country. I come to proffer
my wholehearted help and counsel.
I can show the wise Hrothgar a way
280   to defeat his enemy and find respite –
if any respite is to reach him, ever.
I can calm the turmoil and terror in his mind.
Otherwise, he must endure woes
and live with grief for as long as his hall
285   stands at the horizon, on its high ground.'

Undaunted, sitting astride his horse,
the coast-guard answered, 'Anyone with gumption
and a sharp mind will take the measure
of two things: what's said and what's done.
290   I believe what you have told me: that you are a troop
loyal to our king. So come ahead
with your arms and your gear, and I will guide you.
What's more, I'll order my own comrades
on their word of honour to watch your boat
295   down there on the strand – keep her safe
in her fresh tar, until the time comes
for her curved prow to preen on the waves
and bear this hero back to Geatland.
May one so valiant and venturesome
300   come unharmed through the clash of battle.'

So they went on their way. The ship rode the water,
broad-beamed, bound by its hawser
and anchored fast. Boar-shapes flashed
above their cheek-guards, the brightly forged
305   work of goldsmiths, watching over
those stern-faced men. They marched in step,
hurrying on till the timbered hall
rose before them, radiant with gold.
Nobody on earth knew of another
310   building like it. Majesty lodged there,
its light shone over many lands.
So their gallant escort guided them
to that dazzling stronghold and indicated
the shortest way to it; then the noble warrior
315   wheeled on his horse and spoke these words:

> The coast-guard
> allows the Geats to
> pass.

'It is time for me to go. May the Almighty
Father keep you and in His kindness
watch over your exploits. I'm away to the sea,
back on alert against enemy raiders.'

320 It was a paved track, a path that kept them   They arrive at
in marching order. Their mail-shirts glinted,   Heorot.
hard and hand-linked; the high-gloss iron
of their armour rang. So they duly arrived
in their grim war-graith and gear at the hall,
325 and, weary from the sea, stacked wide shields
of the toughest hardwood against the wall,
then collapsed on the benches; battle-dress
and weapons clashed. They collected their spears
in a seafarers' stook, a stand of greyish
330 tapering ash. And the troops themselves
were as good as their weapons.
                               Then a proud warrior
questioned the men concerning their origins:
'Where do you come from, carrying these
decorated shields and shirts of mail,
335 these cheek-hinged helmets and javelins?
I am Hrothgar's herald and officer.
I have never seen so impressive or large
an assembly of strangers. Stoutness of heart,
bravery not banishment, must have brought you to Hrothgar.'

340 The man whose name was known for courage,   Beowulf
the Geat leader, resolute in his helmet,   announces his
answered in return: 'We are retainers   name.
from Hygelac's band. Beowulf is my name.
If your lord and master, the most renowned
345 son of Halfdane, will hear me out
and graciously allow me to greet him in person,
I am ready and willing to report my errand.'

Wulfgar replied, a Wendel chief   Formalities are
renowned as a warrior, well known for his wisdom   observed.
350 and the temper of his mind: 'I will take this message,
in accordance with your wish, to our noble king,
our dear lord, friend of the Danes,
the giver of rings. I will go and ask him

about your coming here, then hurry back
355 with whatever reply it pleases him to give.'

With that he turned to where Hrothgar sat,
an old man among retainers;
the valiant follower stood four-square
in front of his king: he knew the courtesies.
360 Wulfgar addressed his dear lord:
'People from Geatland have put ashore.
They have sailed far over the wide sea.
They call the chief in charge of their band
by the name of Beowulf. They beg, my lord,
365 an audience with you, exchange of words
and formal greeting. Most gracious Hrothgar,
do not refuse them, but grant them a reply.
From their arms and appointment, they appear well born
and worthy of respect, especially the one
370 who has led them this far: he is formidable indeed.'

Hrothgar, protector of Shieldings, replied: Hrothgar recognises
'I used to know him when he was a young boy.   Beowulf's name
His father before him was called Ecgtheow.   and approves his
Hrethel the Geat gave Ecgtheow   arrival.
375 his daughter in marriage. This man is their son,
here to follow up an old friendship.
A crew of seamen who sailed for me once
with a gift-cargo across to Geatland
returned with marvellous tales about him:
380 a thane, they declared, with the strength of thirty
in the grip of each hand. Now Holy God
has, in His goodness, guided him here
to the West-Danes, to defend us from Grendel.
This is my hope; and for his heroism
385 I will recompense him with a rich treasure.
Go immediately, bid him and the Geats
he has in attendance to assemble and enter.
Say, moreover, when you speak to them,
they are welcome to Denmark.'
                                        At the door of the hall,
390 Wulfgar duly delivered the message:
'My lord, the conquering king of the Danes,
bids me announce that he knows your ancestry;

also that he welcomes you here to Heorot
and salutes your arrival from across the sea.
395 You are free now to move forward
to meet Hrothgar, in helmets and armour,
but shields must stay here and spears be stacked
until the outcome of the audience is clear.'

The hero arose, surrounded closely
400 by his powerful thanes. A party remained
under orders to keep watch on the arms;
the rest proceeded, led by their prince
under Heorot's roof. And standing on the hearth
in webbed links that the smith had woven,
405 the fine-forged mesh of his gleaming mail-shirt,
resolute in his helmet, Beowulf spoke:
'Greetings to Hrothgar. I am Hygelac's kinsman,
one of his hall-troop. When I was younger,
I had great triumphs. Then news of Grendel,
410 hard to ignore, reached me at home:
sailors brought stories of the plight you suffer
in this legendary hall, how it lies deserted,
empty and useless once the evening light
hides itself under heaven's dome.
415 So every elder and experienced councilman
among my people supported my resolve
to come here to you, King Hrothgar,
because all knew of my awesome strength.
They had seen me boltered in the blood of enemies
420 when I battled and bound five beasts,
raided a troll-nest and in the night-sea
slaughtered sea-brutes. I have suffered extremes
and avenged the Geats (their enemies brought it
upon themselves, I devastated them).
425 Now I mean to be a match for Grendel,
settle the outcome in single combat.
And so, my request, O king of Bright-Danes,
dear prince of the Shieldings, friend of the people
and their ring of defence, my one request
430 is that you won't refuse me, who have come this far,
the privilege of purifying Heorot,
with my own men to help me, and nobody else.
I have heard moreover that the monster scorns

> Beowulf enters
> Heorot. He gives
> an account of his
> heroic exploits.

> He declares he will
> fight Grendel.

in his reckless way to use weapons;
435   therefore, to heighten Hygelac's fame
and gladden his heart, I hereby renounce
sword and the shelter of the broad shield,
the heavy war-board: hand-to-hand
is how it will be, a life-and-death
440   fight with the fiend. Whichever one death fells
must deem it a just judgement by God.
If Grendel wins, it will be a gruesome day;
he will glut himself on the Geats in the war-hall,
swoop without fear on that flower of manhood
445   as on others before. Then my face won't be there
to be covered in death: he will carry me away
as he goes to ground, gorged and bloodied;
he will run gloating with my raw corpse
and feed on it alone, in a cruel frenzy,
450   fouling his moor-nest. No need then
to lament for long or lay out my body:
if the battle takes me, send back
this breast-webbing that Weland fashioned
and Hrethel gave me, to Lord Hygelac.
455   Fate goes ever as fate must.'

Hrothgar, the helmet of Shieldings, spoke:
'Beowulf, my friend, you have travelled here
to favour us with help and to fight for us.
There was a feud one time, begun by your father.

Hrothgar recollects
a friendship and
tells of Grendel's
raids.

460   With his own hands he had killed Heatholaf,
who was a Wulfing; so war was looming
and his people, in fear of it, forced him to leave.
He came away then over rolling waves
to the South-Danes here, the sons of honour.
465   I was then in the first flush of kingship,
establishing my sway over all the rich strongholds
of this heroic land. Heorogar,
my older brother and the better man,
also a son of Halfdane's, had died.
470   Finally I healed the feud by paying:
I shipped a treasure-trove to the Wulfings
and Ecgtheow acknowledged me with oaths of allegiance.

'It bothers me to have to burden anyone
with all the grief Grendel has caused

475 and the havoc he has wreaked upon us in Heorot,
our humiliations. My household-guard
are on the wane, fate sweeps them away
into Grendel's clutches –

but God can easily
halt these raids and harrowing attacks!

480 'Time and again, when the goblets passed
and seasoned fighters got flushed with beer
they would pledge themselves to protect Heorot
and wait for Grendel with whetted swords.
But when dawn broke and day crept in
485 over each empty, blood-spattered bench,
the floor of the mead-hall where they had feasted
would be slick with slaughter. And so they died,
faithful retainers, and my following dwindled.

'Now take your place at the table, relish
490 the triumph of heroes to your heart's content.'

Then a bench was cleared in that banquet hall   A feast in Heorot.
so the Geats could have room to be together
and the party sat, proud in their bearing,
strong and stalwart. An attendant stood by
495 with a decorated pitcher, pouring bright
helpings of mead. And the minstrel sang,
filling Heorot with his head-clearing voice,
gladdening that great rally of Geats and Danes.

From where he crouched at the king's feet,   Unferth strikes a
500 Unferth, a son of Ecglaf's, spoke   discordant note.
contrary words. Beowulf's coming,
his sea-braving, made him sick with envy:
he could not brook or abide the fact
that anyone else alive under heaven
505 might enjoy greater regard than he did: Unferth's version
'Are you the Beowulf who took on Breca   of a swimming
in a swimming match on the open sea,   contest.
risking the water just to prove that you could win?
It was sheer vanity made you venture out
510 on the main deep. And no matter who tried,
friend or foe, to deflect the pair of you,
neither would back down: the sea-test obsessed you.

You waded in, embracing water,
taking its measure, mastering currents,
515 riding on the swell. The ocean swayed,
winter went wild in the waves, but you vied
for seven nights; and then he outswam you,
came ashore the stronger contender.
He was cast up safe and sound one morning
520 among the Heathoreams, then made his way
to where he belonged in Bronding country,
home again, sure of his ground
in strongroom and bawn. So Breca made good
his boast upon you and was proved right.
525 No matter, therefore, how you may have fared
in every bout and battle until now,
this time you'll be worsted; no one has ever
outlasted an entire night against Grendel.'

Beowulf, Ecgtheow's son, replied:
530 'Well, friend Unferth, you have had your say
about Breca and me. But it was mostly beer
that was doing the talking. The truth is this:
when the going was heavy in those high waves,
I was the strongest swimmer of all.
535 We'd been children together and we grew up
daring ourselves to outdo each other,
boasting and urging each other to risk
our lives on the sea. And so it turned out.
Each of us swam holding a sword,
540 a naked, hard-proofed blade for protection
against the whale-beasts. But Breca could never
move out farther or faster from me
than I could manage to move from him.
Shoulder to shoulder, we struggled on
545 for five nights, until the long flow
and pitch of the waves, the perishing cold,
night falling and winds from the north
drove us apart. The deep boiled up
and its wallowing sent the sea-brutes wild.
550 My armour helped me to hold out;
my hard-ringed chain-mail, hand-forged and linked,
a fine, close-fitting filigree of gold,
kept me safe when some ocean creature

Beowulf corrects
Unferth.

pulled me to the bottom. Pinioned fast
555 and swathed in its grip, I was granted one
final chance: my sword plunged
and the ordeal was over. Through my own hands,
the fury of battle had finished off the sea-beast.

'Time and again, foul things attacked me,
560 lurking and stalking, but I lashed out,
gave as good as I got with my sword.
My flesh was not for feasting on,
there would be no monsters gnawing and gloating
over their banquet at the bottom of the sea.
565 Instead, in the morning, mangled and sleeping
the sleep of the sword, they slopped and floated
like the ocean's leavings. From now on
sailors would be safe, the deep-sea raids
were over for good. Light came from the east,
570 bright guarantee of God, and the waves
went quiet; I could see headlands
and buffeted cliffs. Often, for undaunted courage,
fate spares the man it has not already marked.
However it occurred, my sword had killed
575 nine sea-monsters. Such night-dangers
and hard ordeals I have never heard of
nor of a man more desolate in surging waves.
But worn out as I was, I survived,
came through with my life. The ocean lifted
580 and laid me ashore, I landed safe
on the coast of Finland.
                              Now I cannot recall
any fight you entered, Unferth,
that bears comparison. I don't boast when I say
that neither you nor Breca were ever much
585 celebrated for swordsmanship
or for facing danger on the field of battle.
You killed your own kith and kin,
so for all your cleverness and quick tongue,
you will suffer damnation in the depths of hell.
590 The fact is, Unferth, if you were truly
as keen or courageous as you claim to be
Grendel would never have got away with
such unchecked atrocity, attacks on your king,

Beowulf tells of his
ordeal in the sea.

Unferth rebuked.
Beowulf reaffirms
his determination
to defeat Grendel.

havoc in Heorot and horrors everywhere.
595 But he knows he need never be in dread
of your blade making a mizzle of his blood
or of vengeance arriving ever from this quarter –
from the Victory-Shieldings, the shoulderers of the spear.
He knows he can trample down you Danes
600 to his heart's content, humiliate and murder
without fear of reprisal. But he will find me different.
I will show him how Geats shape to kill
in the heat of battle. Then whoever wants to
may go bravely to mead, when morning light,
605 scarfed in sun-dazzle, shines forth from the south
and brings another daybreak to the world.'

Then the grey-haired treasure-giver was glad;   Wealhtheow,
far-famed in battle, the prince of Bright-Danes   Hrothgar's queen,
and keeper of his people counted on Beowulf,   graces the banquet.
610 on the warrior's steadfastness and his word.
So the laughter started, the din got louder
and the crowd was happy. Wealhtheow came in,
Hrothgar's queen, observing the courtesies.
Adorned in her gold, she graciously saluted
615 the men in hall, then handed the cup
first to Hrothgar, their homeland's guardian,
urging him to drink deep and enjoy it
because he was dear to them. And he drank it down
like the warlord he was, with festive cheer.
620 So the Helming woman went on her rounds,
queenly and dignified, decked out in rings,
offering the goblet to all ranks,
treating the household and the assembled troop
until it was Beowulf's turn to take it from her hand.
625 With measured words she welcomed the Geat
and thanked God for granting her wish
that a deliverer she could believe in would arrive
to ease their afflictions. He accepted the cup,
a daunting man, dangerous in action
630 and eager for it always. He addressed Wealhtheow;
Beowulf, son of Ecgtheow, said:

'I had a fixed purpose when I put to sea.   Beowulf's formal
As I sat in the boat with my band of men,   boast.
I meant to perform to the uttermost

635 what your people wanted or perish in the attempt,
in the fiend's clutches. And I shall fulfil that purpose,
prove myself with a proud deed
or meet my death here in the mead-hall.'

This formal boast by Beowulf the Geat
640 pleased the lady well and she went to sit
by Hrothgar, regal and arrayed with gold.

Then it was like old times in the echoing hall,   Hrothgar leaves
proud talk and the people happy,   Heorot in
loud and excited; until soon enough   Beowulf's keeping.
645 Halfdane's heir had to be away
to his night's rest. He realised
that the demon was going to descend on the hall,
that he had plotted all day, from dawn-light
until darkness gathered again over the world
650 and stealthy night-shapes came stealing forth
under the cloud-murk. The company stood
as the two leaders took leave of each other:
Hrothgar wished Beowulf health and good luck,
named him hall-warden and announced as follows:
655 'Never, since my hand could hold a shield
have I entrusted or given control
of the Danes' hall to anyone but you.
Ward and guard it, for it is the greatest of houses.
Be on your mettle now, keep in mind your fame,
660 beware of the enemy. There's nothing you wish for
that won't be yours if you win through alive.'

Hrothgar departed then with his house-guard.
The lord of the Shieldings, their shelter in war,
left the mead-hall to lie with Wealhtheow,
665 his queen and bedmate. The King of Glory
(as people learned) had posted a lookout
who was a match for Grendel, a guard against monsters,
special protection to the Danish prince.
And the Geat placed complete trust
670 in his strength of limb and the Lord's favour.
He began to remove his iron breast-mail,
took off the helmet and handed his attendant
the patterned sword, a smith's masterpiece,
ordering him to keep the equipment guarded.

675	And before he bedded down, Beowulf,
	that prince of goodness, proudly asserted:
	'When it comes to fighting, I count myself
	as dangerous any day as Grendel.
	So it won't be a cutting edge I'll wield
680	to mow him down, easily as I might.
	He has no idea of the arts of war,
	of shield or sword-play, although he does possess
	a wild strength. No weapons, therefore,
	for either this night: unarmed he shall face me
685	if face me he dares. And may the Divine Lord
	in His wisdom grant the glory of victory
	to whichever side He sees fit.'

Beowulf renounces the use of weapons.

	Then down the brave man lay with his bolster
	under his head and his whole company
690	of sea-rovers at rest beside him.
	None of them expected he would ever see
	his homeland again or get back
	to his native place and the people who reared him.
	They knew too well the way it was before,
695	how often the Danes had fallen prey
	to death in the mead-hall. But the Lord was weaving
	a victory on His war-loom for the Weather-Geats.
	Through the strength of one they all prevailed;
	they would crush their enemy and come through
700	in triumph and gladness. The truth is clear:
	Almighty God rules over mankind
	and always has.
	Then out of the night
	came the shadow-stalker, stealthy and swift;
	the hall-guards were slack, asleep at their posts,
705	all except one; it was widely understood
	that as long as God disallowed it,
	the fiend could not bear them to his shadow-bourne.
	One man, however, was in fighting mood,
	awake and on edge, spoiling for action.

The Geats await Grendel's attack.

710	In off the moors, down through the mist bands
	God-cursed Grendel came greedily loping.
	The bane of the race of men roamed forth,
	hunting for a prey in the high hall.
	Under the cloud-murk he moved towards it

Grendel strikes.

715   until it shone above him, a sheer keep
         of fortified gold. Nor was that the first time
         he had scouted the grounds of Hrothgar's dwelling –
         although never in his life, before or since,
         did he find harder fortune or hall-defenders.
720   Spurned and joyless, he journeyed on ahead
         and arrived at the bawn. The iron-braced door
         turned on its hinge when his hands touched it.
         Then his rage boiled over, he ripped open
         the mouth of the building, maddening for blood,
725   pacing the length of the patterned floor
         with his loathsome tread, while a baleful light,
         flame more than light, flared from his eyes.
         He saw many men in the mansion, sleeping,
         a ranked company of kinsmen and warriors
730   quartered together. And his glee was demonic,
         picturing the mayhem: before morning
         he would rip life from limb and devour them,
         feed on their flesh; but his fate that night
         was due to change, his days of ravening
735   had come to an end.

                     Mighty and canny,   *A Geat warrior*
         Hygelac's kinsman was keenly watching   *perishes.*
         for the first move the monster would make.
         Nor did the creature keep him waiting
         but struck suddenly and started in;
740   he grabbed and mauled a man on his bench,
         bit into his bone-lappings, bolted down his blood
         and gorged on him in lumps, leaving the body
         utterly lifeless, eaten up
         hand and foot. Venturing closer,
745   his talon was raised to attack Beowulf
         where he lay on the bed; he was bearing in
         with open claw when the alert hero's
         comeback and armlock forestalled him utterly.
         The captain of evil discovered himself   *Beowulf's fight*
750   in a handgrip harder than anything   *with Grendel.*
         he had ever encountered in any man
         on the face of the earth. Every bone in his body
         quailed and recoiled, but he could not escape.
         He was desperate to flee to his den and hide
755   with the devil's litter, for in all his days

he had never been clamped or cornered like this.
Then Hygelac's trusty retainer recalled
his bedtime speech, sprang to his feet
and got a firm hold. Fingers were bursting,
760   the monster back-tracking, the man overpowering.
The dread of the land was desperate to escape,
to take a roundabout road and flee
to his lair in the fens. The latching power
in his fingers weakened; it was the worst trip
765   the terror-monger had taken to Heorot.
And now the timbers trembled and sang,
a hall-session that harrowed every Dane
inside the stockade: stumbling in fury,
the two contenders crashed through the building.
770   The hall clattered and hammered, but somehow
survived the onslaught and kept standing:
it was handsomely structured, a sturdy frame
braced with the best of blacksmith's work
inside and out. The story goes
775   that as the pair struggled, mead-benches were smashed
and sprung off the floor, gold fittings and all.
Before then, no Shielding elder would believe
there was any power or person upon earth
capable of wrecking their horn-rigged hall
780   unless the burning embrace of a fire
engulf it in flame. Then an extraordinary
wail arose, and bewildering fear
came over the Danes. Everyone felt it
who heard that cry as it echoed off the wall,
785   a God-cursed scream and strain of catastrophe,
the howl of the loser, the lament of the hell-serf
keening his wound. He was overwhelmed,
manacled tight by the man who of all men
was foremost and strongest in the days of this life.

790   But the earl-troop's leader was not inclined   Beowulf's thanes
to allow his caller to depart alive: defend him.
he did not consider that life of much account
to anyone anywhere. Time and again,
Beowulf's warriors worked to defend
795   their lord's life, laying about them
as best they could with their ancestral blades.
Stalwart in action, they kept striking out

on every side, seeking to cut
straight to the soul. When they joined the struggle
800 there was something they could not have known at the time,
that no blade on earth, no blacksmith's art
could ever damage their demon opponent.
He had conjured the harm from the cutting edge
of every weapon. But his going away
805 out of this world and the days of his life
would be agony to him, and his alien spirit
would travel far into fiends' keeping.

Then he who had harrowed the hearts of men
with pain and affliction in former times
810 and had given offence also to God
found that his bodily powers failed him.
Hygelac's kinsman kept him helplessly
locked in a handgrip. As long as either lived,
he was hateful to the other. The monster's whole
815 body was in pain, a tremendous wound
appeared on his shoulder. Sinews split
and the bone-lappings burst. Beowulf was granted
the glory of winning; Grendel was driven
under the fen-banks, fatally hurt,
820 to his desolate lair. His days were numbered,
the end of his life was coming over him,
he knew it for certain; and one bloody clash
had fulfilled the dearest wishes of the Danes.
The man who had lately landed among them,
825 proud and sure, had purged the hall,
kept it from harm; he was happy with his nightwork
and the courage he had shown. The Geat captain
had boldly fulfilled his boast to the Danes:
he had healed and relieved a huge distress,
830 unremitting humiliations,
the hard fate they'd been forced to undergo,
no small affliction. Clear proof of this
could be seen in the hand the hero displayed
high up near the roof: the whole of Grendel's
835 shoulder and arm, his awesome grasp.

Then morning came and many a warrior
gathered, as I've heard, around the gift-hall,
clan-chiefs flocking from far and near

Grendel is defeated,
Beowulf fulfils his
boast.

The morning after:
relief and rejoicings.

down wide-ranging roads, wondering greatly
840   at the monster's footprints. His fatal departure
was regretted by no-one who witnessed his trail,
the ignominious marks of his flight
where he'd skulked away, exhausted in spirit
and beaten in battle, bloodying the path,
845   hauling his doom to the demons' mere.
The bloodshot water wallowed and surged,
there were loathsome upthrows and overturnings
of waves and gore and wound-slurry.
With his death upon him, he had dived deep
850   into his marsh-den, drowned out his life
and his heathen soul: hell claimed him there.

Then away they rode, the old retainers
with many a young man following after,
a troop on horseback, in high spirits
855   on their bay steeds. Beowulf's doings
were praised over and over again.
Nowhere, they said, north or south
between the two seas or under the tall sky
on the broad earth was there anyone better
860   to raise a shield or to rule a kingdom.
Yet there was no laying of blame on their lord,
the noble Hrothgar; he was a good king.

At times the war-band broke into a gallop,
letting their chestnut horses race
865   wherever they found the going good
on those well-known tracks. Meanwhile, a thane   *Hrothgar's minstrel*
of the king's household, a carrier of tales,   *sings about*
a traditional singer deeply schooled   *Beowulf.*
in the lore of the past, linked a new theme
870   to a strict metre. The man started
to recite with skill, rehearsing Beowulf's
triumphs and feats in well-fashioned lines,
entwining his words.
                He told what he'd heard
repeated in songs about Sigemund's exploits,   *The tale of*
875   all of those many feats and marvels,   *Sigemund, the*
the struggles and wanderings of Waels's son,   *dragon-slayer.*
things unknown to anyone   *Appropriate for*
except to Fitela, feuds and foul doings   *Beowulf, who has*
                                  defeated Grendel.

confided by uncle to nephew when he felt
880 the urge to speak of them: always they had been
partners in the fight, friends in need.
They killed giants, their conquering swords
had brought them down.

                       After his death
Sigemund's glory   grew and grew
885 *because of his courage   when he killed the dragon,*
the guardian of the hoard.   Under grey stone
he had dared to enter   all by himself
to face the worst   without Fitela.
But it came to pass   that his sword plunged
890 *right through   those radiant scales*
and drove into the wall.   The dragon died of it.
His daring had given him   total possession
of the treasure hoard,   his to dispose of
however he liked.   He loaded a boat:
895 *Waels's son   weighted her hold*
with dazzling spoils.   The hot dragon melted.

Sigemund's name   was known everywhere.
He was utterly valiant   and venturesome,
a fence round his fighters   and flourished therefore
900 *after King Heremod's   prowess declined*
and his campaigns slowed down.   The king was betrayed,
ambushed in Jutland,   overpowered
and done away with.   The waves of his grief
had beaten him down,   made him a burden,
905 *a source of anxiety   to his own nobles:*
that expedition   was often condemned
in those earlier times   by experienced men,
men who relied   on his lordship for redress,
who presumed that the part   of a prince was to thrive
910 *on his father's throne   and defend the nation,*
the Shielding land   where they lived and belonged,
its holdings and strongholds.   Such was Beowulf
in the affection of his friends   and of everyone alive.
But evil entered   into Heremod.

King Heremod remembered and contrasted with Beowulf.

915 Meanwhile, the Danes kept racing their mounts
down sandy lanes. The light of day
broke and kept brightening. Bands of retainers

galloped in excitement to the gabled hall
to see the marvel; and the king himself,
920   guardian of the ring-hoard, goodness in person,
walked in majesty from the women's quarters
with a numerous train, attended by his queen
and her crowd of maidens, across to the mead-hall.

When Hrothgar arrived at the hall, he spoke,
925   standing on the steps, under the steep eaves,
gazing at the roofwork and Grendel's talon:
'First and foremost, let the Almighty Father
be thanked for this sight. I suffered a long
harrowing by Grendel. But the Heavenly Shepherd
930   can work His wonders always and everywhere.
Not long since, it seemed I would never
be granted the slightest solace or relief
from any of my burdens: the best of houses
glittered and reeked and ran with blood.
935   This one worry outweighed all others –
a constant distress to counsellors entrusted
with defending the people's forts from assault
by monsters and demons. But now a man,
with the Lord's assistance, has accomplished something
940   none of us could manage before now
for all our efforts. Whoever she was
who brought forth this flower of manhood,
if she is still alive, that woman can say
that in her labour the Lord of Ages
945   bestowed a grace on her. So now, Beowulf,
I adopt you in my heart as a dear son.
Nourish and maintain this new connection,
you noblest of men; there'll be nothing you'll want for,
no worldly goods that won't be yours.
950   I have often honoured smaller achievements,
recognised warriors not nearly as worthy,
lavished rewards on the less deserving.
But you have made yourself immortal
by your glorious action. May the God of Ages
955   continue to keep and requite you well.'

Beowulf, son of Ecgtheow, spoke:
'We have gone through with a glorious endeavour
and been much favoured in this fight we dared

King Hrothgar
gives thanks
for the relief of
Heorot and adopts
Beowulf 'in his
heart'.

Beowulf's account
of the fight.

against the unknown. Nevertheless,
960 if you could have seen the monster himself
where he lay beaten, I would have been better pleased.
My plan was to pounce, pin him down
in a tight grip and grapple him to death –
have him panting for life, powerless and clasped
965 in my bare hands, his body in thrall.
But I couldn't stop him from slipping my hold.
The Lord allowed it, my lock on him
wasn't strong enough, he struggled fiercely
and broke and ran. Yet he bought his freedom
970 at a high price, for he left his hand
and arm and shoulder to show he had been here,
a cold comfort for having come among us.
And now he won't be long for this world.
He has done his worst but the wound will end him.
975 He is hasped and hooped and hirpling with pain,
limping and looped in it. Like a man outlawed
for wickedness, he must await
the mighty judgement of God in majesty.'

There was less tampering and big talk then   The trophy:
980 from Unferth the boaster, less of his blather   Grendel's shoulder
as the hall-thanes eyed the awful proof   and claw.
of the hero's prowess, the splayed hand
up under the eaves. Every nail,
claw-scale and spur, every spike
985 and welt on the hand of that heathen brute
was like barbed steel. Everybody said
there was no honed iron hard enough
to pierce him through, no time-proofed blade
that could cut his brutal, blood-caked claw.

990 Then the order was given for all hands   The damaged hall
to help to refurbish Heorot immediately: repaired.
men and women thronging the wine-hall,
getting it ready. Gold thread shone
in the wall-hangings, woven scenes
995 that attracted and held the eye's attention.
But iron-braced as the inside of it had been,
that bright room lay in ruins now.
The very doors had been dragged from their hinges.
Only the roof remained unscathed

1000 by the time the guilt-fouled fiend turned tail
in despair of his life. But death is not easily
escaped from by anyone:
all of us with souls, earth-dwellers
and children of men, must make our way
1005 to a destination already ordained
where the body, after the banqueting,
sleeps on its deathbed.
                              Then the due time arrived   A victory feast.
for Halfdane's son to proceed to the hall.
The king himself would sit down to feast.
1010 No group ever gathered in greater numbers
or better order around their ring-giver.
The benches filled with famous men
who fell to with relish; round upon round
of mead was passed; those powerful kinsmen,
1015 Hrothgar and Hrothulf, were in high spirits
in the raftered hall. Inside Heorot
there was nothing but friendship. The Shielding nation
was not yet familiar with feud and betrayal.

Then Halfdane's son presented Beowulf   Victory gifts
1020 with a gold standard as a victory gift,   presented to
an embroidered banner; also breast-mail   Beowulf.
and a helmet; and a sword carried high,
that was both precious object and token of honour.
So Beowulf drank his drink, at ease;
1025 it was hardly a shame to be showered with such gifts
in front of the hall-troops. There haven't been many
moments, I am sure, when men exchanged
four such treasures at so friendly a sitting.
An embossed ridge, a band lapped with wire
1030 arched over the helmet: head-protection
to keep the keen-ground cutting edge
from damaging it when danger threatened
and the man was battling behind his shield.
Next the king ordered eight horses
1035 with gold bridles to be brought through the yard
into the hall. The harness of one
included a saddle of sumptuous design,
the battle-seat where the son of Halfdane
rode when he wished to join the sword-play:

wherever the killing and carnage were the worst,
he would be to the fore, fighting hard.
Then the Danish prince, descendant of Ing,
handed over both the arms and the horses,
urging Beowulf to use them well.

1045 And so their leader, the lord and guard
of coffer and strongroom, with customary grace
bestowed upon Beowulf both sets of gifts.
A fair witness can see how well each one behaved.

The chieftain went on to reward the others:

The other Geats
are rewarded.

1050 each man on the bench who had sailed with Beowulf
and risked the voyage received a bounty,
some treasured possession. And compensation,
a price in gold, was settled for the Geat
Grendel had cruelly killed earlier –
1055 as he would have killed more, had not mindful God
and one man's daring prevented that doom.
Past and present, God's will prevails.
Hence, understanding is always best
and a prudent mind. Whoever remains
1060 for long here in this earthly life
will enjoy and endure more than enough.

They sang then and played to please the hero,
words and music for their warrior prince,
harp tunes and tales of adventure:

Another
performance by
the minstrel.

1065 there were high times on the hall benches
and the king's poet performed his part
with the saga of Finn and his sons, unfolding
the tale of the fierce attack in Friesland
where Hnaef, king of the Danes, met death.

1070 *Hildeburh*
            had little cause
to credit the Jutes:
            son and brother,
she lost them both
            on the battlefield.
She, bereft
            and blameless, they
foredoomed, cut down
            and spear-gored. She,

Hildeburh, a
Danish princess
married to the
Frisian King Finn,
loses her son
(unnamed here)
and her brother
Hnaef in a fight at
Finn's hall.

1075 *the woman in shock,*
                    waylaid by grief,
      Hoc's daughter –
                    how could she not
      lament her fate
                    when morning came
      and the light broke
                    on her murdered dears?
      And so farewell
                    delight on earth,
1080 *war carried away*
                    Finn's troop of thanes,
      all but a few.
                    How then could Finn
      hold the line
                    or fight on
      to the end with Hengest,
                    how save
      the rump of his force
                    from that enemy chief?
1085 *So a truce was offered*
                    as follows: first
      separate quarters
                    to be cleared for the Danes,
      hall and throne
                    to be shared with the Frisians.
      Then, second:
                    every day
      at the dole-out of gifts
                    Finn, son of Focwald,
1090 *should honour the Danes,*
                    bestow with an even
      hand to Hengest
                    and Hengest's men
      the wrought-gold rings,
                    bounty to match
      the measure he gave
                    his own Frisians –
      to keep morale
                    in the beer-hall high
1095 *both sides then*
                    sealed their agreement.

The Danish attack
is bloody but
indecisive. Hnaef
is killed, Hengest
takes charge and
makes a truce
with Finn and the
Frisians.

With oaths to Hengest

        Finn swore

openly, solemnly,

        that the battle survivors

would be guaranteed

        honour and status.

No infringement

        by word or deed,

1100 no provocation

        would be permitted.

Their own ring-giver

        after all

was dead and gone,

        they were leaderless,

in forced allegiance

        to his murderer.

So if any Frisian

        stirred up bad blood

1105 with insinuations

        or taunts about this,

the blade of the sword

        would arbitrate it.

A funeral pyre

        was then prepared,

effulgent gold

        brought out from the hoard.

The pride and prince

        of the Shieldings lay

1110 awaiting the flame.

        Everywhere

there were blood-plastered

        coats of mail.

The pyre was heaped

        with boar-shaped helmets

forged in gold,

        with the gashed corpses

of well-born Danes –

        many had fallen.

1115 Then Hildeburh

        ordered her own

son's body

        be burnt with Hnaef's,

The Danish survivors to be quartered and given parity of treatment with the Frisians and their allies, the Jutes.

The bodies of the slain burnt on the pyre.

the flesh on his bones

              to sputter and blaze

beside his uncle's.

              The woman wailed

and sang keens,

              the warrior went up.

1120 *Carcass flame*

              swirled and fumed,

they stood round the burial

              mound and howled

as heads melted,

              crusted gashes

spattered and ran

              bloody matter.

The glutton element

              flamed and consumed

1125 *the dead of both sides.*

              Their great days were gone.

Warriors scattered

              to homes and forts

all over Friesland,

              fewer now, feeling

loss of friends.

              Hengest stayed,

lived out that whole

              resentful, blood-sullen

1130 *winter with Finn,*

              homesick and helpless.

No ring-whorled prow

              could up then

and away on the sea.

              Wind and water

raged with storms,

              wave and shingle

were shackled in ice

              until another year

1135 *appeared in the yard*

              as it does to this day,

the seasons constant,

              the wonder of light

coming over us.

              Then winter was gone,

The Danes, homesick and resentful, spend a winter in exile.

Spring comes.

earth's lap grew lovely,
                longing woke
in the cooped-up exile
                for a voyage home –
but more for vengeance,
                some way of bringing
things to a head:
                his sword arm hankered
to greet the Jutes.
                So he did not balk
once Hunlafing
                placed on his lap
Dazzle-the-Duel,
                the best sword of all,
whose edges Jutes
                knew only too well.
Thus, blood was spilled,
                the gallant Finn
slain in his home
                after Guthlaf and Oslaf
back from their voyage
                made old accusation:
the brutal ambush,
                the fate they had suffered,
all blamed on Finn.
                The wildness in them
had to brim over.
                The hall ran red
with blood of enemies.
                Finn was cut down,
the queen brought away
                and everything
the Shieldings could find
                inside Finn's walls –
the Frisian king's
                gold collars and gemstones –
swept off to the ship.
                Over sea-lanes then
back to Daneland
                the warrior troop
bore that lady home.

Danish warriors
spur themselves
to renew the feud.
Finn is killed,
his stronghold
looted, his widow
Hildeburh carried
back to Denmark.

1140

1145

1150

1155

The poem was over,
the poet had performed, a pleasant murmur
1160 started on the benches, stewards did the rounds
with wine in splendid jugs, and Wealhtheow came to sit
in her gold crown between two good men,
uncle and nephew, each one of whom
still trusted the other; and the forthright Unferth,
1165 admired by all for his mind and courage
although under a cloud for killing his brothers,
reclined near the king.

The queen spoke:
'Enjoy this drink, my most generous lord;
raise up your goblet, entertain the Geats
1170 duly and gently, discourse with them,
be open-handed, happy and fond.
Relish their company, but recollect as well
all of the boons that have been bestowed on you.
The bright court of Heorot has been cleansed
1175 and now the word is that you want to adopt
this warrior as a son. So, while you may,
bask in your fortune, and then bequeath
kingdom and nation to your kith and kin,
before your decease. I am certain of Hrothulf.
1180 He is noble and will use the young ones well.
He will not let you down. Should you die before him,
he will treat our children truly and fairly.
He will honour, I am sure, our two sons,
repay them in kind when he recollects
1185 all the good things we gave him once,
the favour and respect he found in his childhood.'

She turned then to the bench where her boys sat,
Hrethric and Hrothmund, with other nobles' sons,
all the youth together; and that good man,
1190 Beowulf the Geat, sat between the brothers.

The cup was carried to him, kind words
spoken in welcome and a wealth of wrought gold
graciously bestowed: two arm bangles,
a mail-shirt and rings, and the most resplendent
1195 torque of gold I ever heard tell of
anywhere on earth or under heaven.
There was no hoard like it since Hama snatched

Gifts presented,
including a torque:
Beowulf will
present it in due
course to King
Hygelac, who will
die wearing it.

the Brosings' neck-chain and bore it away
with its gems and settings to his shining fort,
1200 away from Eormenric's wiles and hatred,
and thereby ensured his eternal reward.
Hygelac the Geat, grandson of Swerting,
wore this neck-ring on his last raid;
at bay under his banner, he defended the booty,
1205 treasure he had won. Fate swept him away
because of his proud need to provoke
a feud with the Frisians. He fell beneath his shield,
in the same gem-crusted, kingly gear
he had worn when he crossed the frothing wave-vat.
1210 So the dead king fell into Frankish hands.
They took his breast-mail, also his neck-torque,
and punier warriors plundered the slain
when the carnage ended; Geat corpses
covered the field.

Applause filled the hall.
1215 Then Wealhtheow pronounced in the presence of the company:
'Take delight in this torque, dear Beowulf,
wear it for luck and wear also this mail
from our people's armoury: may you prosper in them!
Be acclaimed for strength, for kindly guidance
1220 to these two boys, and your bounty will be sure.
You have won renown: you are known to all men
far and near, now and forever.
Your sway is wide as the wind's home,
as the sea around cliffs. And so, my prince,
1225 I wish you a lifetime's luck and blessings
to enjoy this treasure. Treat my sons
with tender care, be strong and kind.
Here each comrade is true to the other,
loyal to lord, loving in spirit.
1230 The thanes have one purpose, the people are ready:
having drunk and pledged, the ranks do as I bid.'

She moved then to her place. Men were drinking wine   Bedtime in Heorot.
at that rare feast; how could they know fate,
the grim shape of things to come,
1235 the threat looming over many thanes
as night approached and King Hrothgar prepared
to retire to his quarters? Retainers in great numbers

were posted on guard as so often in the past.
Benches were pushed back, bedding gear and bolsters
1240 spread across the floor, and one man
lay down to his rest, already marked for death.
At their heads they placed their polished timber
battle-shields; and on the bench above them,
each man's kit was kept to hand:
1245 a towering war-helmet, webbed mail-shirt
and great-shafted spear. It was their habit
always and everywhere to be ready for action,
at home or in the camp, in whatever case
and at whatever time the need arose
1250 to rally round their lord. They were a right people.

They went to sleep. And one paid dearly   Another threat
for his night's ease, as had happened to them often,   is lurking in the
ever since Grendel occupied the gold-hall,   night.
committing evil until the end came,
1255 death after his crimes. Then it became clear,
obvious to everyone once the fight was over,
that an avenger lurked and was still alive,
grimly biding time. Grendel's mother,
monstrous hell-bride, brooded on her wrongs.
1260 She had been forced down into fearful waters,
the cold depths, after Cain had killed
his father's son, felled his own
brother with a sword. Branded an outlaw,
marked by having murdered, he moved into the wilds,
1265 shunned company and joy. And from Cain there sprang
misbegotten spirits, among them Grendel,
the banished and accursed, due to come to grips
with that watcher in Heorot waiting to do battle.
The monster wrenched and wrestled with him
1270 but Beowulf was mindful of his mighty strength,
the wondrous gifts God had showered on him:
he relied for help on the Lord of All,
on His care and favour. So he overcame the foe,
brought down the hell-brute. Broken and bowed,
1275 outcast from all sweetness, the enemy of mankind
made for his death-den. But now his mother
had sallied forth on a savage journey,
grief-racked and ravenous, desperate for revenge.

She came to Heorot. There, inside the hall,

Grendel's mother
attacks.

1280 Danes lay asleep, earls who would soon endure
a great reversal, once Grendel's mother
attacked and entered. Her onslaught was less
only by as much as an amazon warrior's
strength is less than an armed man's
1285 when the hefted sword, its hammered edge
and gleaming blade slathered in blood,
razes the sturdy boar-ridge off a helmet.
Then in the hall, hard-honed swords
were grabbed from the bench, many a broad shield
1290 lifted and braced; there was little thought of helmets
or woven mail when they woke in terror.

The hell-dam was in panic, desperate to get out,
in mortal terror the moment she was found.
She had pounced and taken one of the retainers
1295 in a tight hold, then headed for the fen.
To Hrothgar, this man was the most beloved
of the friends he trusted between the two seas.
She had done away with a great warrior,
ambushed him at rest.   Beowulf was elsewhere.
1300 Earlier, after the award of the treasure,
the Geat had been given another lodging.
There was uproar in Heorot. She had snatched their trophy,
Grendel's bloodied hand. It was a fresh blow
to the afflicted bawn. The bargain was hard,
1305 both parties having to pay
with the lives of friends. And the old lord,
the grey-haired warrior, was heartsore and weary
when he heard the news: his highest-placed adviser,
his dearest companion, was dead and gone.
1310 Beowulf was quickly brought to the chamber:

Beowulf is
summoned.

the winner of fights, the arch-warrior,
came first-footing in with his fellow troops
to where the king in his wisdom waited,
still wondering whether Almighty God
1315 would ever turn the tide of his misfortunes.
So Beowulf entered with his band in attendance
and the wooden floor-boards banged and rang
as he advanced, hurrying to address

the prince of the Ingwins, asking if he'd rested
1320 since the urgent summons had come as a surprise.

Then Hrothgar, the Shieldings' helmet, spoke:
'Rest? What is rest? Sorrow has returned.
Alas for the Danes! Aeschere is dead.
He was Yrmenlaf's elder brother
1325 and a soul-mate to me, a true mentor,
my right-hand man when the ranks clashed
and our boar-crests had to take a battering
in the line of action. Aeschere was everything
the world admires in a wise man and a friend.
1330 Then this roaming killer came in a fury
and slaughtered him in Heorot. Where she is hiding,
glutting on the corpse and glorying in her escape,
I cannot tell; she has taken up the feud
because of last night, when you killed Grendel,
1335 wrestled and racked him in ruinous combat
since for too long he had terrorised us
with his depredations. He died in battle,
paid with his life; and now this powerful
other one arrives, this force for evil
1340 driven to avenge her kinsman's death.
Or so it seems to thanes in their grief,
in the anguish every thane endures
at the loss of a ring-giver, now that the hand
that bestowed so richly has been stilled in death.

1345 'I have heard it said by my people in hall,
counsellors who live in the upland country,
that they have seen two such creatures
prowling the moors, huge marauders
from some other world. One of these things,
1350 as far as anyone ever can discern,
looks like a woman; the other, warped
in the shape of a man, moves beyond the pale
bigger than any man, an unnatural birth
called Grendel by country people
1355 in former days. They are fatherless creatures,
and their whole ancestry is hidden in a past
of demons and ghosts. They dwell apart
among wolves on the hills, on windswept crags
and treacherous keshes, where cold streams

Hrothgar laments
the death of his
counsellor. He
knows Grendel's
mother must
avenge her son.

The country
people's tales
about the
monsters.

1360 pour down the mountain and disappear
under mist and moorland.
                              A few miles from here   The haunted mere.
a frost-stiffened wood waits and keeps watch
above a mere; the overhanging bank
is a maze of tree-roots mirrored in its surface.
1365 At night there, something uncanny happens:
the water burns. And the mere bottom
has never been sounded by the sons of men.
On its bank, the heather-stepper halts:
the hart in flight from pursuing hounds
1370 will turn to face them with firm-set horns
and die in the wood rather than dive
beneath its surface. That is no good place.
When wind blows up and stormy weather
makes clouds scud and the skies weep,
1375 out of its depths a dirty surge
is pitched towards the heavens. Now help depends
again on you and on you alone.
The gap of danger where the demon waits
is still unknown to you. Seek it if you dare.
1380 I will compensate you for settling the feud
as I did the last time with lavish wealth,
coffers of coiled gold, if you come back.'

Beowulf, son of Ecgtheow, spoke: Beowulf bolsters
'Wise sir, do not grieve. It is always better   Hrothgar's
1385 to avenge dear ones than to indulge in mourning.   courage. He
For every one of us, living in this world   proclaims the
means waiting for our end. Let whoever can   heroic code that
win glory before death. When a warrior is gone,   guides their lives.
that will be his best and only bulwark.
1390 So arise, my lord, and let us immediately
set forth on the trail of this troll-dam.
I guarantee you: she will not get away,
not to dens under ground nor upland groves
nor the ocean floor. She'll have nowhere to flee to.
1395 Endure your troubles to-day. Bear up
and be the man I expect you to be.'

With that the old lord sprang to his feet
and praised God for Beowulf's pledge.
Then a bit and halter were brought for his horse

1400 with the plaited mane. The wise king mounted
the royal saddle and rode out in style
with a force of shield-bearers. The forest paths
were marked all over with the monster's tracks,
her trail on the ground wherever she had gone
1405 across the dark moors, dragging away
the body of that thane, Hrothgar's best
counsellor and overseer of the country.
So the noble prince proceeded undismayed
up fells and screes, along narrow footpaths
1410 and ways where they were forced into single file,
ledges on cliffs above lairs of water-monsters.
He went in front with a few men,
good judges of the lie of the land,
and suddenly discovered the dismal wood,
1415 mountain trees growing out at an angle
above grey stones: the bloodshot water
surged underneath. It was a sore blow
to all of the Danes, friends of the Shieldings,
a hurt to each and every one
1420 of that noble company when they came upon
Aeschere's head at the foot of the cliff.

Everybody gazed as the hot gore
kept wallowing up and an urgent war-horn
repeated its notes: the whole party
1425 sat down to watch. The water was infested
with all kinds of reptiles. There were writhing sea-dragons
and monsters slouching on slopes by the cliff,
serpents and wild things such as those that often
surface at dawn to roam the sail-road
1430 and doom the voyage. Down they plunged,
lashing in anger at the loud call
of the battle-bugle. An arrow from the bow
of the Geat chief got one of them
as he surged to the surface: the seasoned shaft
1435 stuck deep in his flank and his freedom in the water
got less and less. It was his last swim.
He was swiftly overwhelmed in the shallows,
prodded by barbed boar-spears,
cornered, beaten, pulled up on the bank,
1440 a strange lake-birth, a loathsome catch

men gazed at in awe.
                          Beowulf got ready,   Beowulf arms for
donned his war-gear, indifferent to death;   the underwater
his mighty, hand-forged, fine-webbed mail   fight.
would soon meet with the menace underwater.
1445   It would keep the bone-cage of his body safe:
no enemy's clasp could crush him in it,
no vicious armlock choke his life out.
To guard his head he had a glittering helmet
that was due to be muddied on the mere bottom
1450   and blurred in the upswirl. It was of beaten gold,
princely headgear hooped and hasped
by a weapon-smith who had worked wonders
in days gone by and adorned it with boar-shapes;
since then it had resisted every sword.
1455   And another item lent by Unferth
at that moment of need was of no small importance:
the brehon handed him a hilted weapon,
a rare and ancient sword named Hrunting.
The iron blade with its ill-boding patterns
1460   had been tempered in blood. It had never failed
the hand of anyone who hefted it in battle,
anyone who had fought and faced the worst
in the gap of danger. This was not the first time
it had been called to perform heroic feats.

1465   When he lent that blade to the better swordsman,
Unferth, the strong-built son of Ecglaf,
could hardly have remembered the ranting speech
he had made in his cups. He was not man enough
to face the turmoil of a fight under water
1470   and the risk to his life. So there he lost
fame and repute. It was different for the other
rigged out in his gear, ready to do battle.

Beowulf, son of Ecgtheow, spoke: Beowulf takes his
'Wisest of kings, now that I have come   leave.
1475   to the point of action, I ask you to recall
what we said earlier: that you, son of Halfdane
and gold-friend to retainers, that you, if I should fall
and suffer death while serving your cause,
would act like a father to me afterwards.
1480   If this combat kills me, take care

of my young company, my comrades in arms.
And be sure also, my beloved Hrothgar,
to send Hygelac the treasures I received.
Let the lord of the Geats gaze on that gold,
1485   let Hrethel's son take note of it and see
that I found a ring-giver of rare magnificence
and enjoyed the good of his generosity.
And Unferth is to have what I inherited:
to that far-famed man I bequeath my own
1490   sharp-honed, wave-sheened wonderblade.
With Hrunting I shall gain glory or die.'

After these words, the prince of the Weather-Geats
was impatient to be away and plunged suddenly:
without more ado, he dived into the heaving
1495   depths of the lake. It was the best part of a day
before he could see the solid bottom.

Quickly the one who haunted those waters,
who had scavenged and gone her gluttonous rounds
for a hundred seasons, sensed a human
1500   observing her outlandish lair from above.
So she lunged and clutched and managed to catch him
in her brutal grip; but his body, for all that,
remained unscathed: the mesh of the chain-mail
saved him on the outside. Her savage talons
1505   failed to rip the web of his warshirt.
Then once she touched bottom, that wolfish swimmer
carried the ring-mailed prince to her court
so that for all his courage he could never use
the weapons he carried; and a bewildering horde
1510   came at him from the depths, droves of sea-beasts
who attacked with tusks and tore at his chain-mail
in a ghastly onslaught. The gallant man
could see he had entered some hellish turn-hole
and yet the water did not work against him
1515   because the hall-roofing held off
the force of the current; then he saw firelight,
a gleam and flare-up, a glimmer of brightness.

The hero observed that swamp-thing from hell,
the tarn-hag in all her terrible strength,
1520   then heaved his war-sword and swung his arm:

Beowulf is
captured by
Grendel's mother.

the decorated blade came down ringing
and singing on her head. But he soon found
his battle-torch extinguished: the shining blade
refused to bite. It spared her and failed

₁₅₂₅ the man in his need. It had gone through many
hand-to-hand fights, had hewed the armour
and helmets of the doomed, but here at last
the fabulous powers of that heirloom failed.

His sword fails to
do damage.

Hygelac's kinsman kept thinking about

₁₅₃₀ his name and fame: he never lost heart.
Then, in a fury, he flung his sword away.
The keen, inlaid, worm-loop-patterned steel
was hurled to the ground: he would have to rely
on the might of his arm. So must a man do

₁₅₃₅ who intends to gain enduring glory
in a combat. Life doesn't cost him a thought.
Then the prince of War-Geats, warming to this fight
with Grendel's mother, gripped her shoulder
and laid about him in a battle frenzy:

₁₅₄₀ he pitched his killer opponent to the floor
but she rose quickly and retaliated,
grappled him tightly in her grim embrace.
The sure-footed fighter felt daunted,
the strongest of warriors stumbled and fell.

₁₅₄₅ So she pounced upon him and pulled out
a broad, whetted knife: now she would avenge
her only child. But the mesh of chain-mail
on Beowulf's shoulder shielded his life,
turned the edge and tip of the blade.

₁₅₅₀ The son of Ecgtheow would have surely perished
and the Geats lost their warrior under the wide earth
had the strong links and locks of his war-gear
not helped to save him: holy God
decided the victory. It was easy for the Lord,

₁₅₅₅ the Ruler of Heaven, to redress the balance
once Beowulf got back up on his feet.

He fights back
with his bare
hands.

Then he saw a blade that boded well,
a sword in her armoury, an ancient heirloom
from the days of the giants, an ideal weapon,

₁₅₆₀ one that any warrior would envy,
but so huge and heavy of itself

Beowulf discovers
a mighty sword
and slays his
opponent.

only Beowulf could wield it in a battle.
So the Shieldings' hero, hard-pressed and enraged,
took a firm hold of the hilt and swung
1565 the blade in an arc, a resolute blow
that bit deep into her neck-bone
and severed it entirely, toppling the doomed
house of her flesh; she fell to the floor.
The sword dripped blood, the swordsman was elated.

1570 A light appeared and the place brightened
the way the sky does when heaven's candle
is shining brightly. He inspected the vault:
with sword held high, its hilt raised
to guard and threaten, Hygelac's thane
1575 scouted by the wall in Grendel's wake.
Now the weapon was to prove its worth.
The warrior determined to take revenge
for every gross act Grendel had committed –
and not only for that one occasion
1580 when he'd come to slaughter the sleeping troops,
fifteen of Hrothgar's house-guards
surprised on their benches and ruthlessly devoured,
and as many again carried away,
a brutal plunder. Beowulf in his fury
1585 now settled that score: he saw the monster
in his resting place, war-weary and wrecked,
a lifeless corpse, a casualty
of the battle in Heorot. The body gaped
at the stroke dealt to it after death:
1590 Beowulf cut the corpse's head off.

He proceeds to behead Grendel's corpse.

Immediately the counsellors keeping a lookout
with Hrothgar, watching the lake water,
saw a heave-up and surge of waves
and blood in the backwash. They bowed grey heads,
1595 spoke in their sage, experienced way
about the good warrior, how they never again
expected to see that prince returning
in triumph to their king. It was clear to many
that the wolf of the deep had destroyed him forever.

Forebodings of those on the shore.

1600 The ninth hour of the day arrived.
The brave Shieldings abandoned the cliff-top

and the king went home; but sick at heart,
staring at the mere, the strangers held on.
They wished, without hope, to behold their lord,
1605 Beowulf himself.
                     Meanwhile, the sword   The sword blade
began to wilt into gory icicles,   melts.
to slather and thaw. It was a wonderful thing,
the way it all melted as ice melts
when the Father eases the fetters off the frost
1610 and unravels the water-ropes. He who wields power
over time and tide: He is the true Lord.

The Geat captain saw treasure in abundance   Beowulf returns
but carried no spoils from those quarters   with the sword's
except for the head and the inlaid hilt   hilt and Grendel's
1615 embossed with jewels; its blade had melted   head.
and the scrollwork on it burnt, so scalding was the blood
of the poisonous fiend who had perished there.
Then away he swam, the one who had survived
the fall of his enemies, flailing to the surface.
1620 The wide water, the waves and pools
were no longer infested once the wandering fiend
let go of her life and this unreliable world.
The seafarers' leader made for land,
resolutely swimming, delighted with his prize,
1625 the mighty load he was lugging to the surface.
His thanes advanced in a troop to meet him,
thanking God and taking great delight
in seeing their prince back safe and sound.
Quickly the hero's helmet and mail-shirt
1630 were loosed and unlaced. The lake settled,
clouds darkened above the bloodshot depths.

With high hearts they headed away
along footpaths and trails through the fields,
roads that they knew, each of them wrestling
1635 with the head they were carrying from the lakeside cliff,
men kingly in their courage and capable
of difficult work. It was a task for four
to hoist Grendel's head on a spear
and bear it under strain to the bright hall.
1640 But soon enough they neared the place,
fourteen Geats in fine fettle,

striding across the outlying ground
in a delighted throng around their leader.

In he came then, the thanes' commander,
the arch-warrior, to address Hrothgar:
his courage was proven, his glory was secure.
Grendel's head was hauled by the hair,
dragged across the floor where the people were drinking,
a horror for both queen and company to behold.
1650 They stared in awe. It was an astonishing sight.

Beowulf, son of Ecgtheow, spoke:
'So, son of Halfdane, prince of the Shieldings,
we are glad to bring this booty from the lake.
It is a token of triumph and we tender it to you.
1655 I barely survived the battle under water.
It was hard-fought, a desperate affair
that could have gone badly; if God had not helped me,
the outcome would have been quick and fatal.
Although Hrunting is hard-edged,
1660 I could never bring it to bear in battle.
But the Lord of Men allowed me to behold –
for He often helps the unbefriended –
an ancient sword shining on the wall,
a weapon made for giants, there for the wielding.
1665 Then my moment came in the combat and I struck
the dwellers in that den. Next thing the damascened
sword blade melted; it bloated and it burned
in their rushing blood. I have wrested the hilt
from the enemies' hand, avenged the evil
1670 done to the Danes; it is what was due.
And this I pledge, O prince of the Shieldings:
you can sleep secure with your company of troops
in Heorot Hall. Never need you fear
for a single thane of your sept or nation,
1675 young warriors or old, that laying waste of life
that you and your people endured of yore.'

Then the gold hilt was handed over
to the old lord, a relic from long ago
for the venerable ruler. That rare smithwork
1680 was passed on to the prince of the Danes
when those devils perished; once death removed

He displays
Grendel's head in
Heorot.

A brief account of
the fight.

Beowulf presents
the sword-hilt to
Hrothgar.

that murdering, guilt-steeped, God-cursed fiend,
eliminating his unholy life
and his mother's as well, it was willed to that king
1685 who of all the lavish gift-lords of the north
was the best regarded between the two seas.

Hrothgar spoke; he examined the hilt,
that relic of old times. It was engraved all over
and showed how war first came into the world
1690 and the flood destroyed the tribe of giants.
They suffered a terrible severance from the Lord;
the Almighty made the waters rise,
drowned them in the deluge for retribution.
In pure gold inlay on the sword-guards
1695 there were rune-markings correctly incised,
stating and recording for whom the sword
had been first made and ornamented
with its scrollworked hilt. Then everyone hushed
as the son of Halfdane spoke this wisdom.
1700 'A protector of his people, pledged to uphold   Hrothgar's address
truth and justice and to respect tradition,   to Beowulf.
is entitled to affirm that this man
was born to distinction. Beowulf, my friend,
your fame has gone far and wide,
1705 you are known everywhere. In all things you are even-tempered,
prudent and resolute. So I stand firm by the promise of friendship
we exchanged before. Forever you will be
your people's mainstay and your own warriors'
helping hand.
                    Heremod was different,   He contrasts
1710 the way he behaved to Ecgwala's sons.   Beowulf with King
His rise in the world brought little joy   Heremod.
to the Danish people, only death and destruction.
He vented his rage on men he caroused with,
killed his own comrades, a pariah king
1715 who cut himself off from his own kind,
even though Almighty God had made him
eminent and powerful and marked him from the start
for a happy life. But a change happened,
he grew bloodthirsty, gave no more rings
1720 to honour the Danes. He suffered in the end
for having plagued his people for so long:

his life lost happiness.
                    So learn from this
and understand true values. I who tell you
have wintered into wisdom.
                    It is a great wonder

1725 how Almighty God in His magnificence
favours our race with rank and scope
and the gift of wisdom; His sway is wide.
Sometimes He allows the mind of a man
of distinguished birth to follow its bent,

1730 grants him fulfilment and felicity on earth
and forts to command in his own country.
He permits him to lord it in many lands
until the man in his unthinkingness
forgets that it will ever end for him.

1735 He indulges his desires; illness and old age
mean nothing to him; his mind is untroubled
by envy or malice or the thought of enemies
with their hate-honed swords. The whole world
conforms to his will, he is kept from the worst

1740 until an element of overweening
enters him and takes hold
while the soul's guard, its sentry, drowses,
grown too distracted. A killer stalks him,
an archer who draws a deadly bow.

1745 And then the man is hit in the heart,
the arrow flies beneath his defences,
the devious promptings of the demon start.
His old possessions seem paltry to him now.
He covets and resents; dishonours custom

1750 and bestows no gold; and because of good things
that the Heavenly Powers gave him in the past
he ignores the shape of things to come.
Then finally the end arrives
when the body he was lent collapses and falls

1755 prey to its death; ancestral possessions
and the goods he hoarded are inherited by another
who lets them go with a liberal hand.

'O flower of warriors, beware of that trap.
Choose, dear Beowulf, the better part,

Hrothgar's
discourse on the
dangers of power.

1760 eternal rewards. Do not give way to pride.
For a brief while your strength is in bloom
but it fades quickly; and soon there will follow
illness or the sword to lay you low,
or a sudden fire or surge of water

1765 or jabbing blade or javelin from the air
or repellent age. Your piercing eye
will dim and darken; and death will arrive,
dear warrior, to sweep you away.

'Just so I ruled the Ring-Danes' country
1770 for fifty years, defended them in wartime
with spear and sword against constant assaults
by many tribes: I came to believe
my enemies had faded from the face of the earth.
Still, what happened was a hard reversal

1775 from bliss to grief. Grendel struck
after lying in wait. He laid waste to the land
and from that moment my mind was in dread
of his depredations. So I praise God
in His heavenly glory that I lived to behold

1780 this head dripping blood and that after such harrowing
I can look upon it in triumph at last.
Take your place, then, with pride and pleasure
and move to the feast. To-morrow morning
our treasure will be shared and showered upon you.'

1785 The Geat was elated and gladly obeyed
the old man's bidding; he sat on the bench.
And soon all was restored, the same as before.
Happiness came back, the hall was thronged,
and a banquet set forth; black night fell

1790 and covered them in darkness.
                                   Then the company rose
for the old campaigner: the grey-haired prince
was ready for bed. And a need for rest
came over the brave shield-bearing Geat.
He was a weary seafarer, far from home,

1795 so immediately a house-guard guided him out,
one whose office entailed looking after
whatever a thane on the road in those days
might need or require. It was noble courtesy.

Beowulf is exhorted
to be mindful of the
fragility of life.

No life is immune to
danger: Hrothgar's
experience proves it.

A feast. The
warriors rest.

That great heart rested. The hall towered,
1800 gold-shingled and gabled, and the guest slept in it
until the black raven with raucous glee
announced heaven's joy, and a hurry of brightness
overran the shadows. Warriors rose quickly,
impatient to be off: their own country
1805 was beckoning the nobles; and the bold voyager
longed to be aboard his distant boat.
Then that stalwart fighter ordered Hrunting
to be brought to Unferth, and bade Unferth
take the sword and thanked him for lending it.
1810 He said he had found it a friend in battle
and a powerful help; he put no blame
on the blade's cutting edge. He was a considerate man.

And there the warriors stood in their war-gear,   Beowulf and his
eager to go, while their honoured lord   band prepare to
1815 approached the platform where the other sat.   depart.
The undaunted hero addressed Hrothgar.
Beowulf, son of Ecgtheow, spoke:
'Now we who crossed the wide sea
have to inform you that we feel a desire
1820 to return to Hygelac. Here we have been welcomed
and thoroughly entertained. You have treated us well.
If there is any favour on earth I can perform
beyond deeds of arms I have done already,
anything that would merit your affections more,
1825 I shall act, my lord, with alacrity.
If ever I hear from across the ocean
that people on your borders are threatening battle
as attackers have done from time to time,
I shall land with a thousand thanes at my back
1830 to help your cause. Hygelac may be young
to rule a nation, but this much I know
about the king of the Geats: he will come to my aid
and want to support me by word and action
in your hour of need, when honour dictates
1835 that I raise a hedge of spears around you.
Then if Hrethric should think about travelling
as a king's son to the court of the Geats,
he will find many friends. Foreign places
yield more to one who is himself worth meeting.'

1840   Hrothgar spoke and answered him:
       'The Lord in His wisdom sent you those words
       and they came from the heart. I have never heard
       so young a man make truer observations.
       You are strong in body and mature in mind,
1845   impressive in speech. If it should come to pass
       that Hrethel's descendant dies beneath a spear,
       if deadly battle or the sword blade or disease
       fells the prince who guards your people
       and you are still alive, then I firmly believe
1850   the seafaring Geats won't find a man
       worthier of acclaim as their king and defender
       than you, if only you would undertake
       the lordship of your homeland. My liking for you
       deepens with time, dear Beowulf.
1855   What you have done is to draw two peoples,
       the Geat nation and us neighbouring Danes,
       into shared peace and a pact of friendship
       in spite of hatreds we have harboured in the past.
       For as long as I rule this far-flung land
1860   treasures will change hands and each side will treat
       the other with gifts; across the gannet's bath,
       over the broad sea, whorled prows will bring
       presents and tokens. I know your people
       are beyond reproach in every respect,
1865   steadfast in the old way with friend or foe.'

       Then the earls' defender furnished the hero
       with twelve treasures and told him to set out,
       sail with those gifts safely home
       to the people he loved, but to return promptly.
1870   And so the good and grey-haired Dane,
       that high-born king, kissed Beowulf
       and embraced his neck, then broke down
       in sudden tears. Two forebodings
       disturbed him in his wisdom, but one was stronger:
1875   nevermore would they meet each other
       face to face. And such was his affection
       that he could not help being overcome:
       his fondness for the man was so deep-founded,
       it warmed his heart and wound the heartstrings

Hrothgar declares
that Beowulf is fit
to be king of the
Geats.

Gifts presented,
farewells taken.

1880   tight in his breast.
The embrace ended
and Beowulf, glorious in his gold regalia,
stepped the green earth. Straining at anchor
and ready for boarding, his boat awaited him.
So they went on their journey, and Hrothgar's generosity
1885   was praised repeatedly. He was a peerless king
until old age sapped his strength and did him
mortal harm, as it has done so many.

Down to the waves then, dressed in the web
of their chain-mail and warshirts the young men marched
1890   in high spirits. The coast-guard spied them,
thanes setting forth, the same as before.

The Geats march back to the shore.

His salute this time from the top of the cliff
was far from unmannerly; he galloped to meet them
and as they took ship in their shining gear,
1895   he said how welcome they would be in Geatland.
Then the broad hull was beached on the sand
to be cargoed with treasure, horses and war-gear.
The curved prow motioned; the mast stood high
above Hrothgar's riches in the loaded hold.

1900   The guard who had watched the boat was given
a sword with gold fittings and in future days
that present would make him a respected man
at his place on the mead-bench.
Then the keel plunged
and shook in the sea; and they sailed from Denmark.

1905   Right away the mast was rigged with its sea-shawl;
sail-ropes were tightened, timbers drummed

They sail from Denmark.

and stiff winds kept the wave-crosser
skimming ahead; as she heaved forward,
her foamy neck was fleet and buoyant,
1910   a lapped prow loping over currents,
until finally the Geats caught sight of coastline
and familiar cliffs. The keel reared up,
wind lifted it home, it hit on the land.

The harbour guard came hurrying out
1915   to the rolling water: he had watched the offing
long and hard, on the lookout for those friends.

They arrive at Hygelac's stronghold.

With the anchor cables, he moored their craft
right where it had beached, in case a backwash
might catch the hull and carry it away.
1920 Then he ordered the prince's treasure-trove
to be carried ashore. It was a short step
from there to where Hrethel's son and heir,
Hygelac the gold-giver, makes his home
on a secure cliff, in the company of retainers.

1925 The building was magnificent, the king majestic,
ensconced in his hall; and although Hygd, his queen,
was young, a few short years at court,
her mind was thoughtful and her manners sure.
Haereth's daughter behaved generously
1930 and stinted nothing when she distributed
bounty to the Geats.
                    Great Queen Modthryth
perpetrated terrible wrongs.
If any retainer ever made bold
to look her in the face, if an eye not her lord's
1935 stared at her directly during daylight,
the outcome was sealed: he was kept bound
in hand-tightened shackles, racked, tortured
until doom was pronounced – death by the sword,
slash of blade, blood-gush and death qualms
1940 in an evil display. Even a queen
outstanding in beauty must not overstep like that.
A queen should weave peace, not punish the innocent
with loss of life for imagined insults.
But Hemming's kinsman put a halt to her ways
1945 and drinkers round the table had another tale:
she was less of a bane to people's lives,
less cruel-minded, after she was married
to the brave Offa, a bride arrayed
in her gold finery, given away
1950 by a caring father, ferried to her young prince
over dim seas. In days to come
she would grace the throne and grow famous
for her good deeds and conduct of life,
her high devotion to the hero king
1955 who was the best king, it has been said,
between the two seas or anywhere else

Queen Hygd
introduced. The
story of Queen
Modthryth, Hygd's
opposite, is told by
the poet.

on the face of the earth. Offa was honoured
far and wide for his generous ways,
his fighting spirit and his far-seeing

1960   defence of his homeland; from him there sprang Eomer,
Garmund's grandson, kinsman of Hemming,
his warriors' mainstay and master of the field.

Heroic Beowulf and his band of men
crossed the wide strand, striding along

1965   the sandy foreshore; the sun shone,
the world's candle warmed them from the south
as they hastened to where, as they had heard,
the young king, Ongentheow's killer
and his people's protector, was dispensing rings

1970   inside his bawn. Beowulf's return
was reported to Hygelac as soon as possible,
news that the captain was now in the enclosure,
his battle-brother back from the fray
alive and well, walking to the hall.

1975   Room was quickly made, on the king's orders,
and the troops filed across the cleared floor.

After Hygelac had offered greetings
to his loyal thane in lofty speech,
he and his kinsman, that hale survivor,

1980   sat face to face. Haereth's daughter
moved about with the mead-jug in her hand,
taking care of the company, filling the cups
that warriors held out. Then Hygelac began
to put courteous questions to his old comrade

1985   in the high hall. He hankered to know
every tale the Sea-Geats had to tell.

'How did you fare on your foreign voyage,
dear Beowulf, when you abruptly decided
to sail away across the salt water

1990   and fight at Heorot? Did you help Hrothgar
much in the end? Could you ease the prince
of his well-known troubles? Your undertaking
cast my spirits down, I dreaded the outcome
of your expedition and pleaded with you

1995   long and hard to leave the killer be,
let the South-Danes settle their own

Beowulf and
his troop are
welcomed in
Hygelac's hall.

Hygelac questions
Beowulf.

blood-feud with Grendel. So God be thanked
I am granted this sight of you, safe and sound.'

Beowulf, son of Ecgtheow, spoke:

Beowulf tells what
happened in the
land of the Danes.

2000 'What happened, Lord Hygelac, is hardly a secret
any more among men in this world –
myself and Grendel coming to grips
on the very spot where he visited destruction
on the Victory-Shieldings and violated
2005 life and limb, losses I avenged
so no earthly offspring of Grendel's
need ever boast of that bout before dawn,
no matter how long the last of his evil
family survives.
                    When I first landed
2010 I hastened to the ring-hall and saluted Hrothgar.
Once he discovered why I had come
the son of Halfdane sent me immediately
to sit with his own sons on the bench.
It was a happy gathering. In my whole life
2015 I have never seen mead enjoyed more
in any hall on earth. Sometimes the queen
herself appeared, peace-pledge between nations,
to hearten the young ones and hand out
a torque to a warrior, then take her place.
2020 Sometimes Hrothgar's daughter distributed
ale to older ranks, in order on the benches:
I heard the company call her Freawaru
as she made her rounds, presenting men
with the gem-studded bowl, young bride-to-be
2025 to the gracious Ingeld, in her gold-trimmed attire.
The friend of the Shieldings favours her betrothal:
the guardian of the kingdom sees good in it
and hopes this woman will heal old wounds
and grievous feuds.

He foresees the
grim consequence
of a proposed
marriage.

                    But generally the spear
2030 is prompt to retaliate when a prince is killed,
no matter how admirable the bride may be.

'Think how the Heathobards will be bound to feel,
their lord, Ingeld, and his loyal thanes,
when he walks in with that woman to the feast:

2035 Danes are at the table, being entertained,
honoured guests in glittering regalia,
burnished ring-mail that was their hosts' birthright,
looted when the Heathobards could no longer wield
their weapons in the shield-clash, when they went down
2040 with their beloved comrades and forfeited their lives.
Then an old spearman will speak while they are drinking,
having glimpsed some heirloom that brings alive
memories of the massacre; his mood will darken
and heart-stricken, in the stress of his emotion,
2045 he will begin to test a young man's temper
and stir up trouble, starting like this:
'Now, my friend, don't you recognise
your father's sword, his favourite weapon,
the one he wore when he went out in his war-mask
2050 to face the Danes on that final day?

After Wethergeld died and his men were doomed
the Shieldings quickly claimed the field,
and now here's a son of one or other
of those same killers coming through our hall
2055 overbearing us, mouthing boasts,
and rigged in armour that by right is yours.'
And so he keeps on, recalling and accusing,
working things up with bitter words
until one of the lady's retainers lies
2060 spattered in blood, split open
on his father's account. The killer knows
the lie of the land and escapes with his life.
Then on both sides the oath-bound lords
will break the peace, a passionate hate
2065 will build up in Ingeld and love for his bride
will falter in him as the feud rankles.
I therefore suspect the good faith of the Heathobards,
the truth of their friendship and the trustworthiness
of their alliance with the Danes.
But now, my lord,
2070 I shall carry on with my account of Grendel,
the whole story of everything that happened
in the hand-to-hand fight.
After heaven's gem
had gone mildly to earth, that maddened spirit,

When the Danes
appear at Freawaru's
wedding, their hosts,
the Heathobards,
will be stirred to
avenge an old
defeat.

The tale of the
fight with Grendel
resumed.

the terror of those twilights, came to attack us
2075 where we stood guard, still safe inside the hall.
There deadly violence came down on Handscio
and he fell as fate ordained, the first to perish,
rigged out for the combat. A comrade from our ranks
had come to grief in Grendel's maw:
2080 he ate up the entire body.
There was blood on his teeth, he was bloated and furious,
all roused up, yet still unready
to leave the hall empty-handed;
renowned for his might, he matched himself against me,
2085 wildly reaching. He had this roomy pouch,
a strange accoutrement, intricately strung
and hung at the ready, a rare patchwork
of devilishly fitted dragon-skins.
I had done him no wrong, yet the raging demon
2090 wanted to cram me and many another
into this bag – but it was not to be
once I got to my feet in a blind fury.
It would take too long to tell how I repaid
the terror of the land for every life he took
2095 and so won credit for you, my king,
and for all your people. And although he got away
to enjoy life's sweetness for a while longer,
his right hand stayed behind him in Heorot,
evidence of his miserable overthrow
2100 as he dived into murk on the mere bottom.

'I got lavish rewards from the lord of the Danes
for my part in the battle, beaten gold
and much else, once morning came
and we took our places at the banquet table.
2105 There was singing and excitement: an old reciter,
a carrier of stories, recalled the early days.
At times some hero made the timbered harp
tremble with sweetness, or related true
and tragic happenings; at times the king
2110 gave the proper turn to some fantastic tale,
or a battle-scarred veteran, bowed with age,
would begin to remember the martial deeds
of his youth and prime and be overcome
as the past welled up in his wintry heart.

Beowulf recalls the
feast in Heorot.

'We were happy there the whole day long
and enjoyed our time until another night
descended upon us. Then suddenly
the vehement mother avenged her son   He tells about
and wreaked destruction. Death had robbed her,   Grendel's mother.
Geats had slain Grendel, so his ghastly dam
struck back and with bare-faced defiance
laid a man low. Thus life departed
from the sage Aeschere, an elder wise in counsel.
But afterwards, on the morning following,
the Danes could not burn the dead body
nor lay the remains of the man they loved
on his funeral pyre. She had fled with the corpse
and taken refuge beneath torrents on the mountain.
It was a hard blow for Hrothgar to bear,
harder than any he had undergone before.
And so the heartsore king beseeched me
in your royal name to take my chances
underwater, to win glory
and prove my worth. He promised me rewards.
Hence, as is well known, I went to my encounter
with the terror-monger at the bottom of the tarn.
For a while it was hand-to-hand between us,
then blood went curling along the currents
and I beheaded Grendel's mother in the hall
with a mighty sword. I barely managed
to escape with my life; my time had not yet come.
But Halfdane's heir, the shelter of those earls,
again endowed me with gifts in abundance.

'Thus the king acted with due custom.
I was paid and recompensed completely,
given full measure and the freedom to choose
from Hrothgar's treasures by Hrothgar himself.
These, King Hygelac, I am happy to present
to you as gifts. It is still upon your grace
that all favour depends. I have few kinsmen
who are close, my king, except for your kind self.'
Then he ordered the boar-framed standard to be brought,
the battle-topping helmet, the mail-shirt grey as hoar-frost
and the precious war-sword; and proceeded with his speech.
'When Hrothgar presented this war-gear to me

2115
2120
2125
2130
2135
2140
2145
2150
2155

he instructed me, my lord, to give you some account
of why it signifies his special favour.
He said it had belonged to his older brother,
King Heorogar, who had long kept it,
2160 but that Heorogar had never bequeathed it
to his son Heoroweard, that worthy scion,
loyal as he was.
                    Enjoy it well.'

I heard four horses were handed over next.
Beowulf bestowed four bay steeds
2165 to go with the armour, swift gallopers,
all alike. So ought a kinsman act,
instead of plotting and planning in secret
to bring people to grief, or conspiring to arrange
the death of comrades. The warrior king
2170 was uncle to Beowulf and honoured by his nephew:
each was concerned for the other's good.

I heard he presented Hygd with a gorget,
the priceless torque that the prince's daughter,
Wealhtheow, had given him; and three horses,
2175 supple creatures, brilliantly saddled.
The bright necklace would be luminous on Hygd's breast.

Thus Beowulf bore himself with valour;
he was formidable in battle yet behaved with honour
and took no advantage; never cut down
2180 a comrade who was drunk, kept his temper
and, warrior that he was, watched and controlled
his God-sent strength and his outstanding
natural powers. He had been poorly regarded
for a long time, was taken by the Geats
2185 for less than he was worth: and their lord too
had never much esteemed him in the mead-hall.
They firmly believed that he lacked force,
that the prince was a weakling; but presently
every affront to his deserving was reversed.

2190 The battle-famed king, bulwark of his earls,
ordered a gold-chased heirloom of Hrethel's
to be brought in; it was the best example
of a gem-studded sword in the Geat treasury.

Beowulf presents
Hygelac with the
treasures he has
won.

Beowulf's
exemplary life is
extolled.

Hygelac presents
Beowulf with a
sword and great
tracts of land.

This he laid on Beowulf's lap
2195   and then rewarded him with land as well,
seven thousand hides, and a hall and a throne.
Both owned land by birth in that country,
ancestral grounds; but the greater right
and sway were inherited by the higher born.

2200   A lot was to happen in later days
in the fury of battle. Hygelac fell
and the shelter of Heardred's shield proved useless
against the fierce aggression of the Shylfings:
ruthless swordsmen, seasoned campaigners,
2205   they came against him and his conquering nation,
and with cruel force cut him down
so that afterwards
                    the wide kingdom
reverted to Beowulf. He ruled it well
for fifty winters, grew old and wise
2210   as warden of the land
                    until one began
to dominate the dark, a dragon on the prowl
from the steep vaults of a stone-roofed barrow
where he guarded a hoard; there was a hidden passage,
unknown to men, but someone managed
2215   to enter by it and interfere
with the heathen trove. He had handled and removed
a gem-studded goblet; it gained him nothing,
though with a thief's wiles he had outwitted
the sleeping dragon; that drove him into rage,
2220   as the people of that country would soon discover.

The intruder who broached the dragon's treasure
and moved him to wrath had never meant to.
It was desperation on the part of a slave
fleeing the heavy hand of some master,
2225   guilt-ridden and on the run,
going to ground. But he soon began
to shake with terror; .... in shock
the wretch ....
.... panicked and ran
2230   away with the precious ....
metalwork. There were many other

Time passes. Beowulf rules the Geats for fifty years.

A dragon awakes. An accidental theft provokes his wrath.

heirlooms heaped inside the earth-house,
because long ago, with deliberate care,
somebody now forgotten
2235 had buried the riches of a high-born race
in this ancient cache. Death had come
and taken them all in times gone by
and the only one left to tell their tale,
the last of their line, could look forward to nothing
2240 but the same fate for himself: he foresaw that his joy
in the treasure would be brief.
                              A newly constructed
barrow stood waiting, on a wide headland
close to the waves, its entryway secured.
Into it the keeper of the hoard had carried
2245 all the goods and golden ware
worth preserving. His words were few:
'Now, earth, hold what earls once held
and heroes can no more; it was mined from you first
by honourable men. My own people
2250 have been ruined in war; one by one
they went down to death, looked their last
on sweet life in the hall. I am left with nobody
to bear a sword or burnish plated goblets,
put a sheen on the cup. The companies have departed.
2255 The hard helmet, hasped with gold,
will be stripped of its hoops; and the helmet-shiner
who should polish the metal of the war-mask sleeps;
the coat of mail that came through all fights,
through shield-collapse and cut of sword,
2260 decays with the warrior. Nor may webbed mail
range far and wide on the warlord's back
beside his mustered troops. No trembling harp,
no tuned timber, no tumbling hawk
swerving through the hall, no swift horse
2265 pawing the courtyard. Pillage and slaughter
have emptied the earth of entire peoples.'
And so he mourned as he moved about the world,
deserted and alone, lamenting his unhappiness
day and night, until death's flood
2270 brimmed up in his heart.
                              Then an old harrower of the dark
happened to find the hoard open,

Long ago, a hoard
was hidden in the
earth-house by the
last survivor of a
forgotten race.

the burning one who hunts out barrows,
the slick-skinned dragon, threatening the night sky
with streamers of fire. People on the farms

2275   are in dread of him. He is driven to hunt out
hoards under ground, to guard heathen gold
through age-long vigils, though to little avail.
For three centuries, this scourge of the people
had stood guard on that stoutly protected

2280   underground treasury, until the intruder
unleashed its fury; he hurried to his lord
with the gold-plated cup and made his plea
to be reinstated. Then the vault was rifled,
the ring-hoard robbed, and the wretched man

2285   had his request granted. His master gazed
on that find from the past for the first time.

When the dragon awoke, trouble flared again.
He rippled down the rock, writhing with anger
when he saw the footprints of the prowler who had stolen

2290   too close to his dreaming head.
So may a man not marked by fate
easily escape exile and woe
by the grace of God.
            The hoard-guardian
scorched the ground as he scoured and hunted

2295   for the trespasser who had troubled his sleep.
Hot and savage, he kept circling and circling
the outside of the mound. No man appeared
in that desert waste, but he worked himself up
by imagining battle; then back in he'd go

2300   in search of the cup, only to discover
signs that someone had stumbled upon
the golden treasures. So the guardian of the mound,
the hoard-watcher, waited for the gloaming
with fierce impatience; his pent-up fury

2305   at the loss of the vessel made him long to hit back
and lash out in flames. Then, to his delight,
the day waned and he could wait no longer
behind the wall, but hurtled forth
in a fiery blaze. The first to suffer

2310   were the people on the land, but before long
it was their treasure-giver who would come to grief.

The dragon nests
in the barrow and
guards the gold.

The dragon in
turmoil.

The dragon began to belch out flames
and burn bright homesteads; there was a hot glow
that scared everyone, for the vile sky-winger
2315 would leave nothing alive in his wake.
Everywhere the havoc he wrought was in evidence.
Far and near, the Geat nation
bore the brunt of his brutal assaults
and virulent hate. Then back to the hoard
2320 he would dart before daybreak, to hide in his den.
He had swinged the land, swathed it in flame,
in fire and burning, and now he felt secure
in the vaults of his barrow; but his trust was unavailing.

The dragon wreaks
havoc on the
Geats.

Then Beowulf was given bad news
2325 a hard truth: his own home,
the best of buildings, had been burnt to a cinder,
the throne-room of the Geats. It threw the hero
into deep anguish and darkened his mood:
the wise man thought he must have thwarted
2330 ancient ordinance of the eternal Lord,
broken His commandment. His mind was in turmoil,
unaccustomed anxiety and gloom
confused his brain; the fire-dragon
had rased the coastal region and reduced
2335 forts and earthworks to dust and ashes,
so the war-king planned and plotted his revenge.
The warriors' protector, prince of the hall-troop,
ordered a marvellous all-iron shield
from his smithy works. He well knew
2340 that linden boards would let him down
and timber burn. After many trials,
he was destined to face the end of his days
in this mortal world; as was the dragon,
for all his long leasehold on the treasure.

Beowulf's ominous
feelings about the
dragon

2345 Yet the prince of the rings was too proud
to line up with a large army
against the sky-plague. He had scant regard
for the dragon as a threat, no dread at all
of its courage or strength, for he had kept going
2350 often in the past, through perils and ordeals
of every sort, after he had purged

Beowulf's pride
and prowess
sustain him.

Hrothgar's hall, triumphed in Heorot
and beaten Grendel. He outgrappled the monster
and his evil kin.

One of his cruellest
2355   hand-to-hand encounters had happened
when Hygelac, king of the Geats, was killed
in Friesland: the people's friend and lord,
Hrethel's son, slaked a sword blade's
thirst for blood. But Beowulf's prodigious
2360   gifts as a swimmer guaranteed his safety:
he arrived at the shore, shouldering thirty
battle-dresses, the booty he had won.
There was little for the Hetware to be happy about
as they shielded their faces and fighting on the ground
2365   began in earnest. With Beowulf against them,
few could hope to return home.

Across the wide sea, desolate and alone,
the son of Ecgtheow swam back to his people.
There Hygd offered him throne and authority
2370   as lord of the ring-hoard: with Hygelac dead,
she had no belief in her son's ability
to defend their homeland against foreign invaders.
Yet there was no way the weakened nation
could get Beowulf to give in and agree
2375   to be elevated over Heardred as his lord
or to undertake the office of kingship.
But he did provide support for the prince,
honoured and minded him until he matured
as the ruler of Geatland.

Then over sea-roads
2380   exiles arrived, sons of Ohthere.
They had rebelled against the best of all
the sea-kings in Sweden, the one who held sway
in the Shylfing nation, their renowned prince,
lord of the mead-hall. That marked the end
2385   for Hygelac's son: his hospitality
was mortally rewarded with wounds from a sword.
Heardred lay slaughtered and Onela returned
to the land of Sweden, leaving Beowulf
to ascend the throne, to sit in majesty
2390   and rule over the Geats. He was a good king.

A flashback:
Hygelac's death,
Beowulf's rear-
guard action and
escape across the
sea.

Beowulf acts as
counsellor to
Hygelac's heir,
Heardred.

Heardred is
implicated in
Swedish feuds
and slain.

In days to come, he contrived to avenge
the fall of his prince; he befriended Eadgils
when Eadgils was friendless, aiding his cause
with weapons and warriors over the wide sea,
2395 sending him men. The feud was settled
on a comfortless campaign when he killed Onela.

And so the son of Ecgtheow had survived
every extreme, excelling himself
in daring and in danger, until the day arrived
2400 when he had to come face to face with the dragon.
The lord of the Geats took eleven comrades
and went in a rage to reconnoitre.
By then he had discovered the cause of the affliction
being visited on the people. The precious cup
2405 had come to him from the hand of the finder,
the one who had started all this strife
and was now added as a thirteenth to their number.
They press-ganged and compelled this poor creature
to be their guide. Against his will
2410 he led them to the earth-vault he alone knew,
an underground barrow near the sea-billows
and heaving waves, heaped inside
with exquisite metalwork. The one who stood guard
was dangerous and watchful, warden of that trove
2415 buried under earth: no easy bargain
would be made in that place by any man.

The veteran king sat down on the cliff-top.
He wished good luck to the Geats who had shared
his hearth and his gold. He was sad at heart,
2420 unsettled yet ready, sensing his death.
His fate hovered near, unknowable but certain:
it would soon claim his coffered soul,
part life from limb. Before long
the prince's spirit would spin free from his body.

2425 Beowulf, son of Ecgtheow, spoke:
'Many a skirmish I survived when I was young
and many times of war: I remember them well.
At seven, I was fostered out by my father,
left in the charge of my people's lord.
2430 King Hrethel kept me and took care of me,

Beowulf inherits
the kingship,
settles the feuding.

The day of
reckoning:
Beowulf and his
troop reconnoitre.

Beowulf's
forebodings.

He recalls his early
days as a ward
at King Hrethel's
court.

was open-handed, behaved like a kinsman.
While I was his ward, he treated me no worse
as a wean about the place than one of his own boys,
Herebeald and Haethcyn, or my own Hygelac.

2435 For the eldest, Herebeald, an unexpected
deathbed was laid out, through a brother's doing,
when Haethcyn bent his horn-tipped bow
and loosed the arrow that destroyed his life.
He shot wide and buried a shaft

2440 in the flesh and blood of his own brother.
That offence was beyond redress, a wrongfooting
of the heart's affections; for who could avenge
the prince's life or pay his death-price?
It was like the misery felt by an old man

2445 who has lived to see his son's body
swing on the gallows. He begins to keen
and weep for his boy, watching the raven
gloat where he hangs: he can be of no help.
The wisdom of age is worthless to him.

2450 Morning after morning, he wakes to remember
that his child is gone; he has no interest
in living on until another heir
is born in the hall, now that his first-born
has entered death's dominion forever.

2455 He gazes sorrowfully at his son's dwelling,
the banquet hall bereft of all delight,
the windswept hearthstone; the horsemen are sleeping,
the warriors under ground; what was is no more.
No tunes from the harp, no cheer raised in the yard.

2460 Alone with his longing, he lies down on his bed
and sings a lament; everything seems too large,
the steadings and the fields.
                              Such was the feeling
of loss endured by the lord of the Geats
after Herebeald's death. He was helplessly placed

2465 to set to rights the wrong committed,
could not punish the killer in accordance with the law
of the blood-feud, although he felt no love for him.
Heartsore, wearied, he turned away
from life's joys, chose God's light

2470 and departed, leaving buildings and lands
to his sons, as a man of substance will.

An accidental
killing and its sad
consequences for
Hrethel.

Hrethel's loss
reflected in 'The
Father's Lament'.

'Then over the wide sea Swedes and Geats
battled and feuded and fought without quarter.
Hostilities broke out when Hrethel died.

2475 Ongentheow's sons were unrelenting,
refusing to make peace, campaigning violently
from coast to coast, constantly setting up
terrible ambushes around Hreasnahill.
My own kith and kin avenged

2480 these evil events, as everybody knows,
but the price was high: one of them paid
with his life. Haethcyn, lord of the Geats,
met his fate there and fell in the battle.
Then, as I have heard, Hygelac's sword

2485 was raised in the morning against Ongentheow,
his brother's killer. When Eofor cleft
the old Swede's helmet, halved it open,
he fell, death-pale: his feud-calloused hand
could not stave off the fatal stroke.

2490 'The treasures that Hygelac lavished on me
I paid for when I fought, as fortune allowed me,
with my glittering sword. He gave me land
and the security land brings, so he had no call
to go looking for some lesser champion,

2495 some mercenary from among the Gifthas
or the Spear-Danes or the men of Sweden.
I marched ahead of him, always there
at the front of the line; and I shall fight like that
for as long as I live, as long as this sword

2500 shall last, which has stood me in good stead
late and soon, ever since I killed
Dayraven the Frank in front of the two armies.
He brought back no looted breastplate
to the Frisian king, but fell in battle,

2505 their standard-bearer, high-born and brave.
No sword blade sent him to his death,
my bare hands stilled his heartbeats
and wrecked the bone-house. Now blade and hand,
sword and sword-stroke, will assay the hoard.'

2510 Beowulf spoke, made a formal boast
for the last time: 'I risked my life
often when I was young. Now I am old,

Beowulf continues
his account of
wars between the
Geats and the
Swedes.

The Swedish king,
Ongentheow,
dies at the hands
of Eofor, one of
Hygelac's thanes.

Beowulf recalls
his proud days in
Hygelac's retinue.

Beowulf's last
boast.

but as king of the people I shall pursue this fight
for the glory of winning, if the evil one will only
2515   abandon his earth-fort and face me in the open.'

Then he addressed each dear companion
one final time, those fighters in their helmets,
resolute and high-born: 'I would rather not
use a weapon if I knew another way
2520   to grapple with the dragon and make good my boast
as I did against Grendel in days gone by.
But I shall be meeting molten venom
in the fire he breathes, so I go forth
in mail-shirt and shield. I won't shift a foot
2525   when I meet the cave-guard: what occurs on the wall
between the two of us will turn out as fate,
overseer of men, decides. I am resolved.
I scorn further words against this sky-borne foe.

'Men at arms, remain here on the barrow,
2530   safe in your armour, to see which one of us
is better in the end at bearing wounds
in a deadly fray. This fight is not yours,
nor is it up to any man except me
to measure his strength against the monster
2535   or to prove his worth. I shall win the gold
by my courage, or else mortal combat,
doom of battle, will bear your lord away.'

Then he drew himself up beside his shield.
The fabled warrior in his warshirt and helmet
2540   trusted in his own strength entirely
and went under the crag. No coward path.

Hard by the rock-face that hale veteran,   Beowulf fights the
a good man who had gone repeatedly   dragon.
into combat and danger and come through,
2545   saw a stone arch and a gushing stream
that burst from the barrow, blazing and wafting
a deadly heat. It would be hard to survive
unscathed near the hoard, to hold firm
against the dragon in those flaming depths.
2550   Then he gave a shout. The lord of the Geats
unburdened his breast and broke out

in a storm of anger. Under grey stone
his voice challenged and resounded clearly.
Hate was ignited. The hoard-guard recognised
2555 a human voice, the time was over
for peace and parleying. Pouring forth
in a hot battle-fume, the breath of the monster
burst from the rock. There was a rumble under ground.
Down there in the barrow, Beowulf the warrior
2560 lifted his shield: the outlandish thing
writhed and convulsed and viciously
turned on the king, whose keen-edged sword,
an heirloom inherited by ancient right,
was already in his hand. Roused to a fury,
2565 each antagonist struck terror in the other.
Unyielding, the lord of his people loomed
by his tall shield, sure of his ground,
while the serpent looped and unleashed itself.
Swaddled in flames, it came gliding and flexing
2570 and racing towards its fate. Yet his shield defended
the renowned leader's life and limb
for a shorter time than he meant it to:
that final day was the first time
when Beowulf fought and fate denied him
2575 glory in battle. So the king of the Geats
raised his hand and struck hard
at the enamelled scales, but scarcely cut through:
the blade flashed and slashed yet the blow
was far less powerful than the hard-pressed king
2580 had need of at that moment. The mound-keeper
went into a spasm and spouted deadly flames:
when he felt the stroke, battle-fire
billowed and spewed. Beowulf was foiled
of a glorious victory. The glittering sword,   Beowulf's sword
2585 infallible before that day,   fails him.
failed when he unsheathed it, as it never should have.
For the son of Ecgtheow, it was no easy thing
to have to give ground like that and go
unwillingly to inhabit another home
2590 in a place beyond; so every man must yield
the leasehold of his days.

Before long
the fierce contenders clashed again.

The hoard-guard took heart, inhaled and swelled up
and got a new wind; he who had once ruled
2595   was furled in fire and had to face the worst.
No help or backing was to be had then   All but one of
from his high-born comrades; that hand-picked troop Beowulf's band
broke ranks and ran for their lives   withdraw to
to the safety of the wood. But within one heart   safety.
2600   sorrow welled up: in a man of worth
the claims of kinship cannot be denied.

His name was Wiglaf, a son of Weohstan's,   Wiglaf stands by
a well-regarded Shylfing warrior   his lord.
related to Aelfhere. When he saw his lord
2605   tormented by the heat of his scalding helmet,
he remembered the bountiful gifts bestowed on him,
how well he lived among the Waegmundings,
the freehold he inherited from his father before him.
He could not hold back: one hand brandished
2610   the yellow-timbered shield, the other drew his sword –
an ancient blade that was said to have belonged
to Eanmund, the son of Ohthere, the one
Weohstan had slain when he was an exile without friends.
He carried the arms to the victim's kinfolk,   The deeds of
2615   the burnished helmet, the webbed chain-mail   Wiglaf's father,
and that relic of the giants. But Onela returned   Weohstan,
the weapons to him, rewarded Weohstan   recalled.
with Eanmund's war-gear. He ignored the blood-feud,
the fact that Eanmund was his brother's son.

2620   Weohstan kept that war-gear for a lifetime,
the sword and the mail-shirt, until it was the son's turn
to follow his father and perform his part.
Then, in old age, at the end of his days
among the Weather-Geats, he bequeathed to Wiglaf
2625   innumerable weapons.
                         And now the youth
was to enter the line of battle with his lord,
his first time to be tested as a fighter.
His spirit did not break and the ancestral blade
would keep its edge, as the dragon discovered
2630   as soon as they came together in the combat.

Sad at heart, addressing his companions,
Wiglaf spoke wise and fluent words:
'I remember that time when mead was flowing,
how we pledged loyalty to our lord in the hall,
2635 promised our ring-giver we would be worth our price,
make good the gift of the war-gear,
those swords and helmets, as and when
his need required it. He picked us out
from the army deliberately, honoured us and judged us
2640 fit for this action, made me these lavish gifts –
and all because he considered us the best
of his arms-bearing thanes. And now, although
he wanted this challenge to be one he'd face
by himself alone – the shepherd of our land,
2645 a man unequalled in the quest for glory
and a name for daring – now the day has come
when this lord we serve needs sound men
to give him their support. Let us go to him,
help our leader through the hot flame
2650 and dread of the fire. As God is my witness,
I would rather my body were robed in the same
burning blaze as my gold-giver's body
than go back home bearing arms.
That is unthinkable, unless we have first
2655 slain the foe and defended the life
of the prince of the Weather-Geats. I well know
the things he has done for us deserve better.
Should he alone be left exposed
to fall in battle? We must bond together,
2660 shield and helmet, mail-shirt and sword.'
Then he waded the dangerous reek and went
under arms to his lord, saying only:
'Go on, dear Beowulf, do everything
you said you would when you were still young
2665 and vowed you would never let your name and fame
be dimmed while you lived. Your deeds are famous,
so stay resolute, my lord, defend your life now
with the whole of your strength. I shall stand by you.'

After those words, a wildness rose
2670 in the dragon again and drove it to attack,
heaving up fire, hunting for enemies,

Wiglaf's speech to
the shirkers.

Wiglaf goes to
Beowulf's aid.

The dragon attacks
again.

the humans it loathed. Flames lapped the shield,
charred it to the boss, and the body armour
on the young warrior was useless to him.
2675 But Wiglaf did well under the wide rim
Beowulf shared with him once his own had shattered
in sparks and ashes.

Inspired again
by the thought of glory, the war-king threw
his whole strength behind a sword-stroke
2680 and connected with the skull. And Naegling snapped.   Another setback.
Beowulf's ancient iron-grey sword
let him down in the fight. It was never his fortune
to be helped in combat by the cutting edge
of weapons made of iron. When he wielded a sword,
2685 no matter how blooded and hard-edged the blade
his hand was too strong, the stroke he dealt
(I have heard) would ruin it. He could reap no advantage.

Then the bane of that people, the fire-breathing dragon,   The dragon's third
was mad to attack for a third time.   onslaught. He
2690 When a chance came, he caught the hero   draws blood.
in a rush of flame and clamped sharp fangs
into his neck. Beowulf's body
ran wet with his life-blood: it came welling out.

Next thing, they say, the noble son of Weohstan   Wiglaf gets past
2695 saw the king in danger at his side   the flames and
and displayed his inborn bravery and strength.   strikes.
He left the head alone, but his fighting hand
was burned when he came to his kinsman's aid.
He lunged at the enemy lower down
2700 so that his decorated sword sank into its belly
and the flames grew weaker.

Once again the king   Beowulf delivers
gathered his strength and drew a stabbing knife   the fatal wound.
he carried on his belt, sharpened for battle.
He stuck it deep into the dragon's flank.
2705 Beowulf dealt it a deadly wound.
They had killed the enemy, courage quelled his life;
that pair of kinsmen, partners in nobility,
had destroyed the foe. So every man should act,
be at hand when needed; but now, for the king,
2710 this would be the last of his many labours

and triumphs in the world.
                          Then the wound
dealt by the ground-burner earlier began
to scald and swell; Beowulf discovered
deadly poison suppurating inside him,
2715   surges of nausea, and so, in his wisdom,
the prince realised his state and struggled
towards a seat on the rampart. He steadied his gaze
on those gigantic stones, saw how the earthwork
was braced with arches built over columns.
2720   And now that thane unequalled for goodness
with his own hands washed his lord's wounds,
swabbed the weary prince with water,
bathed him clean, unbuckled his helmet.

Beowulf spoke: in spite of his wounds,
2725   mortal wounds, he still spoke
for he well knew his days in the world
had been lived out to the end: his allotted time
was drawing to a close, death was very near.

'Now is the time when I would have wanted
2730   to bestow this armour on my own son,
had it been my fortune to have fathered an heir
and live on in his flesh. For fifty years
I ruled this nation. No king
of any neighbouring clan would dare
2735   face me with troops, none had the power
to intimidate me. I took what came,
cared for and stood by things in my keeping,
never fomented quarrels, never
swore to a lie. All this consoles me,
2740   doomed as I am and sickening for death;
because of my right ways, the Ruler of mankind
need never blame me when the breath leaves my body
for murder of kinsmen. Go now quickly,
dearest Wiglaf, under the grey stone
2745   where the dragon is laid out, lost to his treasure;
hurry to feast your eyes on the hoard.
Away you go: I want to examine
that ancient gold, gaze my fill
on those garnered jewels; my going will be easier

*Beowulf senses
that he is near
death.*

*He thinks back on
his life.*

*He bids Wiglaf to
inspect the hoard
and return with
a portion of the
treasure.*

2750   for having seen the treasure, a less troubled letting-go
    of the life and lordship I have long maintained.'

    And so, I have heard, the son of Weohstan
    quickly obeyed the command of his languishing
    war-weary lord; he went in his chain-mail
2755   under the rock-piled roof of the barrow,
    exulting in his triumph, and saw beyond the seat
    a treasure-trove of astonishing richness,
    wall-hangings that were a wonder to behold,
    glittering gold spread across the ground,
2760   the old dawn-scorching serpent's den
    packed with goblets and vessels from the past,
    tarnished and corroding. Rusty helmets
    all eaten away. Armbands everywhere,
    artfully wrought. How easily treasure
2765   buried in the ground, gold hidden
    however skilfully, can escape from any man!

    And he saw too a standard, entirely of gold,
    hanging high over the hoard,
    a masterpiece of filigree; it glowed with light
2770   so he could make out the ground at his feet
    and inspect the valuables. Of the dragon there was no
    remaining sign: the sword had despatched him.
    Then, the story goes, a certain man
    plundered the hoard in that immemorial howe,
2775   filled his arms with flagons and plates,
    anything he wanted; and took the standard also,
    most brilliant of banners.
                    Already the blade
    of the old king's sharp killing-sword
    had done its worst: the one who had for long
2780   minded the hoard, hovering over gold,
    unleashing fire, surging forth
    midnight after midnight, had been mown down.

    Wiglaf went quickly, keen to get back,
    excited by the treasure. Anxiety weighed
2785   on his brave heart – he was hoping he would find
    the leader of the Geats alive where he had left him
    helpless, earlier, on the open ground.

Wiglaf enters the
dragon's barrow.

He returns with
treasure.

So he came to the place, carrying the treasure,
and found his lord bleeding profusely,
2790   his life at an end; again he began
to swab his body. The beginnings of an utterance
broke out from the king's breast-cage.
The old lord gazed sadly at the gold.

'To the everlasting Lord of All,
2795   to the King of Glory, I give thanks
that I behold this treasure here in front of me,
that I have been allowed to leave my people
so well endowed on the day I die.
Now that I have bartered my last breath
2800   to own this fortune, it is up to you
to look after their needs. I can hold out no longer.
Order my troop to construct a barrow
on a headland on the coast, after my pyre has cooled.
It will loom on the horizon at Hronesness
2805   and be a reminder among my people –
so that in coming times crews under sail
will call it Beowulf's Barrow, as they steer
ships across the wide and shrouded waters.'

Then the king in his great-heartedness unclasped
2810   the collar of gold from his neck and gave it
to the young thane, telling him to use
it and the warshirt and the gilded helmet well.

'You are the last of us, the only one left
of the Waegmundings. Fate swept us away,
2815   sent my whole brave high-born clan
to their final doom. Now I must follow them.'
That was the warrior's last word.
He had no more to confide. The furious heat
of the pyre would assail him. His soul fled from his breast
2820   to its destined place among the steadfast ones.

It was hard then on the young hero,
having to watch the one he held so dear
there on the ground, going through
his death agony. The dragon from underearth,
2825   his nightmarish destroyer, lay destroyed as well,
utterly without life. No longer would his snakefolds

> Beowulf gives thanks and orders the construction of a barrow to commemorate him.

> Beowulf's last words.

> The dragon too has been destroyed.

ply themselves to safeguard hidden gold.
Hard-edged blades, hammered out
and keenly filed, had finished him
2830   so that the sky-roamer lay there rigid,
brought low beside the treasure-lodge.

Never again would he glitter and glide
and show himself off in midnight air,
exulting in his riches: he fell to earth
2835   through the battle-strength in Beowulf's arm.
There were few, indeed, as far as I have heard,
big and brave as they may have been,
few who would have held out if they had had to face
the outpourings of that poison-breather
2840   or gone foraging on the ring-hall floor
and found the deep barrow-dweller
on guard and awake.
                              The treasure had been won,
bought and paid for by Beowulf's death.
Both had reached the end of the road
2845   through the life they had been lent.

                              Before long   The battle-dodgers
the battle-dodgers abandoned the wood,   come back.
the ones who had let down their lord earlier,
the tail-turners, ten of them together.
When he needed them most, they had made off.
2850   Now they were ashamed and came behind shields,
in their battle-outfits, to where the old man lay.
They watched Wiglaf, sitting worn out,
a comrade shoulder to shoulder with his lord,
trying in vain to bring him round with water.
2855   Much as he wanted to, there was no way
he could preserve his lord's life on earth
or alter in the least the Almighty's will.
What God judged right would rule what happened
to every man, as it does to this day.

2860   Then a stern rebuke was bound to come
from the young warrior to the ones who had been cowards.
Wiglaf, son of Weohstan, spoke
disdainfully and in disappointment: Wiglaf rebukes
'Anyone ready to admit the truth   them.

2865 will surely realise that the lord of men
who showered you with gifts and gave you the armour
you are standing in – when he would distribute
helmets and mail-shirts to men on the mead-benches,
a prince treating his thanes in hall
2870 to the best he could find, far or near –
was throwing weapons uselessly away.
It would be a sad waste when the war broke out.
Beowulf had little cause to brag
about his armed guard; yet God who ordains
2875 who wins or loses allowed him to strike
with his own blade when bravery was needed.
There was little I could do to protect his life
in the heat of the fray, yet I found new strength
welling up when I went to help him.
2880 Then my sword connected and the deadly assaults
of our foe grew weaker, the fire coursed
less strongly from his head. But when the worst happened
too few rallied around the prince.

So it is goodbye now to all you know and love
2885 on your home ground, the open-handedness,
the giving of war-swords. Every one of you   He predicts that
with freeholds of land, our whole nation,   enemies will now
will be dispossessed, once princes from beyond   attack the Geats.
get tidings of how you turned and fled
2890 and disgraced yourselves. A warrior will sooner
die than live a life of shame.'

Then he ordered the outcome of the fight to be reported
to those camped on the ridge, that crowd of retainers
who had sat all morning, sad at heart,
2895 shield-bearers wondering about
the man they loved: would this day be his last
or would he return? He told the truth
and did not balk, the rider who bore
news to the cliff-top. He addressed them all: A messenger tells
2900 'Now the people's pride and love,   the people that
the lord of the Geats, is laid on his deathbed,   Beowulf is dead.
brought down by the dragon's attack.
Beside him lies the bane of his life,
dead from knife-wounds. There was no way
2905 Beowulf could manage to get the better

of the monster with his sword. Wiglaf sits
at Beowulf's side, the son of Weohstan,
the living warrior watching by the dead,
keeping weary vigil, holding a wake

2910   for the loved and the loathed.

                        Now war is looming
over our nation, soon it will be known
to Franks and Frisians, far and wide,
that the king is gone. Hostility has been great
among the Franks since Hygelac sailed forth

2915   at the head of a war-fleet into Friesland:
there the Hetware harried and attacked
and overwhelmed him with great odds.
The leader in his war-gear was laid low,
fell amongst followers; that lord did not favour

2920   his company with spoils. The Merovingian king
has been an enemy to us ever since.

  'Nor do I expect peace or pact-keeping
of any sort from the Swedes. Remember:
at Ravenswood, Ongentheow

2925   slaughtered Haethcyn, Hrethel's son,
when the Geat people in their arrogance
first attacked the fierce Shylfings.
The return blow was quickly struck
by Ohthere's father. Old and terrible,

2930   he felled the sea-king and saved his own
aged wife, the mother of Onela
and of Ohthere, bereft of her gold rings.
Then he kept hard on the heels of the foe
and drove them, leaderless, lucky to get away,

2935   in a desperate rout into Ravenswood.
His army surrounded the weary remnant
where they nursed their wounds; all through the night
he howled threats at those huddled survivors,
promised to axe their bodies open

2940   when dawn broke, dangle them from gallows
to feed the birds. But at first light
when their spirits were lowest, relief arrived.
They heard the sound of Hygelac's horn,
his trumpet calling as he came to find them,

2945   the hero in pursuit, at hand with troops.

*He foresees wars
with the Franks
and the Frisians.*

*The Swedes too
will strike to avenge
the slaughter of
Ongentheow.*

*Ongentheow's last
engagement at
Ravenswood: he
cornered a Geatish
force.*

*Hygelac relieved
the besieged Geats.*

'The bloody swathe that Swedes and Geats
cut through each other was everywhere.
No one could miss their murderous feuding.
Then the old man made his move,
2950 pulled back, barred his people in:
Ongentheow withdrew to higher ground.

Ongentheow
withdrew.

Hygelac's pride and prowess as a fighter
were known to the earl; he had no confidence
that he could hold out against that horde of seamen,
2955 defend wife and the ones he loved
from the shock of the attack. He retreated for shelter
behind the earthwall. Then Hygelac swooped
on the Swedes at bay, his banners swarmed
into their refuge, his Geat forces
2960 drove forward to destroy the camp.
There in his grey hairs, Ongentheow
was cornered, ringed around with swords.
And it came to pass that the king's fate
was in Eofor's hands, and in his alone.

The Swedish king
fought for his life.
He survived a
blow from Wulf,
hit back, but was
killed by Wulf's
brother, Eofor.

2965 Wulf, son of Wonred, went for him in anger,
split him open so that blood came spurting
from under his hair. The old hero
still did not flinch, but parried fast,
hit back with a harder stroke:
2970 the king turned and took him on.
Then Wonred's son, the brave Wulf,
could land no blow against the aged lord.
Ongentheow divided his helmet
so that he buckled and bowed his bloodied head
2975 and dropped to the ground. But his doom held off.
Though he was cut deep, he recovered again.

'With his brother down, the undaunted Eofor,
Hygelac's thane, hefted his sword
and smashed murderously at the massive helmet
2980 past the lifted shield. And the king collapsed,
the shepherd of people was sheared of life.

'Many then hurried to help Wulf,
bandaged and lifted him, now that they were left
masters of the blood-soaked battleground.
2985 One warrior stripped the other,
looted Ongentheow's iron mail-coat,

his hard sword-hilt, his helmet too,
and carried the graith to King Hygelac;
he accepted the prize, promised fairly

The victorious
Geats returned
home.

2990 that reward would come, and kept his word.
For their bravery in action, when they arrived home
Eofor and Wulf were overloaded
by Hrethel's son, Hygelac the Geat,
with gifts of land and linked rings
2995 that were worth a fortune. They had won glory,
so there was no gainsaying his generosity.
And he gave Eofor his only daughter
to bide at home with him, an honour and a bond.

'So this bad blood between us and the Swedes,

The messenger
predicts that the
Swedes will soon
retaliate.

3000 this vicious feud, I am convinced,
is bound to revive; they will cross our borders
and attack in force when they find out
that Beowulf is dead. In days gone by
when our warriors fell and we were undefended
3005 he kept our coffers and our kingdom safe.
He worked for the people, but as well as that
he behaved like a hero.
                          We must hurry now

With Beowulf
gone, a tragic
future awaits.

to take a last look at the king
and launch him, lord and lavisher of rings,
3010 on the funeral road. His royal pyre
will melt no small amount of gold:
heaped there in a hoard, it was bought at heavy cost,
and that pile of rings he paid for at the end
with his own life will go up with the flame,
3015 be furled in fire: treasure no follower
will wear in his memory, nor lovely woman
link and attach as a torque around her neck –
but often, repeatedly, in the path of exile
they shall walk bereft, bowed under woe,
3020 now that their leader's laugh is silenced,
high spirits quenched. Many a spear
dawn-cold to the touch will be taken down
and waved on high; the swept harp
won't waken warriors, but the raven winging
3025 darkly over the doomed will have news,
tidings for the eagle of how he hoked and ate,
how the wolf and he made short work of the dead.'

Such was the drift of the dire report
that gallant man delivered. He got little wrong
3030   in what he told and predicted.
                                    The whole troop
rose in tears, then took their way
to the uncanny scene under Earnaness.
There, on the sand, where his soul had left him,
they found him at rest, their ring-giver   The Geats find the
3035   from days gone by. The great man   two bodies.
had breathed his last. Beowulf the king
had indeed met with a marvellous death.

But what they saw first was far stranger:
the serpent on the ground, gruesome and vile,
3040   lying facing him. The fire-dragon
was scaresomely burnt, scorched all colours.
From head to tail, his entire length
was fifty feet. He had shimmered forth
on the night air once, then winged back
3045   down to his den; but death owned him now,
he would never enter his earth-gallery again.
Beside him stood pitchers and piled-up dishes,
silent flagons, precious swords
eaten through with rust, ranged as they had been
3050   while they waited their thousand winters under ground.
That huge cache, gold inherited
from an ancient race, was under a spell –
which meant no one was ever permitted
to enter the ring-hall unless God Himself,
3055   mankind's Keeper, True King of Triumphs,
allowed some person pleasing to Him –
and in His eyes worthy – to open the hoard.

What came about brought to nothing
the hopes of the one who had wrongly hidden
3060   riches under the rock-face. First the dragon slew
that man among men, who in turn made fierce amends
and settled the feud. Famous for his deeds
a warrior may be, but it remains a mystery
where his life will end, when he may no longer
3065   dwell in the mead-hall among his own.
So it was with Beowulf, when he faced the cruelty

and cunning of the mound-guard. He himself was ignorant
of how his departure from the world would happen.
The high-born chiefs who had buried the treasure
3070 declared it until doomsday so accursed
that whoever robbed it would be guilty of wrong
and grimly punished for their transgression,
hasped in hell-bonds in heathen shrines.
Yet Beowulf's gaze at the gold treasure
3075 when he first saw it had not been selfish.

Wiglaf, son of Weohstan, spoke: Wiglaf ponders
'Often when one man follows his own will   Beowulf's fate.
many are hurt. This happened to us.
Nothing we advised could ever convince
3080 the prince we loved, our land's guardian,
not to vex the custodian of the gold,
let him lie where he was long accustomed,
lurk there under earth until the end of the world.
He held to his high destiny. The hoard is laid bare,
3085 but at a grave cost; it was too cruel a fate
that forced the king to that encounter.
I have been inside and seen everything
amassed in the vault. I managed to enter
although no great welcome awaited me
3090 under the earthwall. I quickly gathered up
a huge pile of the priceless treasures
handpicked from the hoard and carried them here
where the king could see them. He was still himself,
alive, aware, and in spite of his weakness
3095 he had many requests. He wanted me to greet you   He reports
and order the building of a barrow that would crown   Beowulf's last
the site of his pyre, serve as his memorial,   wishes.
in a commanding position, since of all men
to have lived and thrived and lorded it on earth
3100 his worth and due as a warrior were the greatest.
Now let us again go quickly
and feast our eyes on that amazing fortune
heaped under the wall. I will show the way
and take you close to those coffers packed with rings
3105 and bars of gold. Let a bier be made
and got ready quickly when we come out
and then let us bring the body of our lord,

the man we loved, to where he will lodge
for a long time in the care of the Almighty.'

3110   Then Weohstan's son, stalwart to the end,
had orders given to owners of dwellings,
many people of importance in the land,
to fetch wood from far and wide
for the good man's pyre.
                          'Now shall flame consume

3115   our leader in battle, the blaze darken
round him who stood his ground in the steel-hail,
when the arrow-storm shot from bowstrings
pelted the shield-wall. The shaft hit home.
Feather-fledged, it finned the barb in flight.'

3120   Next the wise son of Weohstan
called from among the king's thanes
a group of seven: he selected the best
and entered with them, the eighth of their number,
under the God-cursed roof; one raised

3125   a lighted torch and led the way.
No lots were cast for who should loot the hoard
for it was obvious to them that every bit of it
lay unprotected within the vault,
there for the taking. It was no trouble

3130   to hurry to work and haul out
the priceless store. They pitched the dragon
over the clifftop, let tide's flow
and backwash take the treasure-minder.
Then coiled gold was loaded on a cart

3135   in great abundance, and the grey-haired leader,
the prince on his bier, borne to Hronesness.

    The Geat people built a pyre for Beowulf,
stacked and decked it until it stood four-square,
hung with helmets, heavy war-shields

3140   and shining armour, just as he had ordered.
Then his warriors laid him in the middle of it,
mourning a lord far-famed and beloved.
On a height they kindled the hugest of all
funeral fires; fumes of woodsmoke

3145   billowed darkly up, the blaze roared
and drowned out their weeping, wind died down

Wiglaf gives orders
for the building of
a funeral pyre.

He goes with seven
thanes to remove
the treasure from
the hoard.

Beowulf's funeral.

and flames wrought havoc in the hot bone-house,
burning it to the core. They were disconsolate
and wailed aloud for their lord's decease.

3150 A Geat woman too sang out in grief;   A Geat woman's
with hair bound up, she unburdened herself   dread.
of her worst fears, a wild litany
of nightmare and lament: her nation invaded,
enemies on the rampage, bodies in piles,

3155 slavery and abasement. Heaven swallowed the smoke.
Then the Geat people began to construct   Beowulf's barrow.
a mound on a headland, high and imposing,
a marker that sailors could see from far away,
and in ten days they had done the work.

3160 It was their hero's memorial; what remained from the fire
they housed inside it, behind a wall
as worthy of him as their workmanship could make it.
And they buried torques in the barrow, and jewels
and a trove of such things as trespassing men

3165 had once dared to drag from the hoard.
They let the ground keep that ancestral treasure,
gold under gravel, gone to earth,
as useless to men now as it ever was.
Then twelve warriors rode around the tomb,

3170 chieftain's sons, champions in battle,
all of them distraught, chanting in dirges,   His people lament.
mourning his loss as a man and a king.
They extolled his heroic nature and exploits
and gave thanks for his greatness; which was the proper thing,

3175 for a man should praise a prince whom he holds dear
and cherish his memory when that moment comes
when he has to be convoyed from his bodily home.
So the Geat people, his hearth companions,
sorrowed for the lord who had been laid low.

3180 They said that of all the kings upon the earth
he was the man most gracious and fair-minded,
kindest to his people and keenest to win fame.

Diary of One Who Vanished

I

I startled this young gypsy girl
Lightfooted as a deer,
Black ringlets on her mushroom breast,
Her eyes like the night air,
Two eyes that cut deep into me   5
As she slipped behind a tree,
Two eyes that haunt and follow me
All the long
             long day.

II

That dark gypsy lass
Keeps coming to the townland:
Why is she still out there?
Why is she still out there?
What brings her near the place?   5

My heart, be still and wait.
Pray God grant me respite
And pray that praying helps
Or my plight is helpless.

III

Glow-worms in the gloaming
Glimmer through their dances,
In the twilit hay-field
A lonely figure wanders.

Keep away. Leave me be   5
For I won't be tempted.
Why do I see so clear
Mother broken hearted?

Now the moon is setting,
10   Country shadows darken:
Someone stands stock still
Beyond there, past the gable.

Two eyes like hot coals
Are glowing in the night.
15   God Almighty, O dear
God Almighty, help me!
Send me Your light.

IV

Now small scaldies twitter
And chirrup in their nest.
I have lain awake all night
As if on thistles.

5   Now it is break of day,
The east fills up with dawn.
I have lain awake all night
On a bed of thorn!

V

Ploughing makes me weary,
I got so little sleep
And when I did get sleep
Dreaming of her woke me.

VI

Top it up, my oxen team,
And plough it straight and take the strain.
Don't look near the boor-tree hedge,
Just top it up and plough it down.
5   Ploughshare bumps off ground that's hard
And everything is skid and kick.
Flutter of a headscarf frill,
Shadow-dapple, hide-and-seek.

Who's out there
                    haunting me
I want her
                    turned to stone.
Throbbing head.
                    Molten lead
Is pouring through
                    my burning mind.

VII

My plough-pin is broken.
I'll have to stop and mend it.
So, oxen, stand your ground,
Soon all will work again.

Over there I'll cut one
From that boor-tree bower.
Who can escape his fate?
Fate comes upon its hour.

VIII

You oxen, don't be sad.
Don't be afraid to look.
Don't be afraid, I say.
I'll come back from the wood.
Dark-haired Zefka stands there
In the deep boor-tree shade.
Night-sparkle from a fire
The brilliance of her gaze.
Don't be afraid, I say.
Even though she is there –

Shifting shape –
                    I'll resist
Her hide-
          and-seek allure.

IX

'Johnny, you are welcome
Underneath the greenwood.
What star kept you on course,
Well and truly guided?

5   'Johnny, you are welcome!
What are you afraid of?
You are pale, you are scared.
Are you scared of me, love?'

'Scared? Why should I scare from
10   You or from anyone?
I'm here to cut and wedge
And whittle sharp a pin.'

'O Johnny, there's no need
To whittle and sharpen.
15   I'll sing. Listen now.
Hear my gypsy song now.'

THREE WOMEN (*off-stage in low voices*)

Then she joined her hands
Singing her sad hurt
And the notes she sang
20   *Ravished his young heart.*

X

God Almighty, hidden from us,
Why did You give gypsies life?
Coming, going, toing, froing,
Moved along and hunted off.

5   'Can you hear larks, Johnny,
The skylarks rising there?'

THREE WOMEN

And the notes she sang
Ravished his young heart.

'Sit and rest, be happy
Beside a gypsy girl.   10

'God almighty, God of mercy,
Grant, grant me this
Before I leave this world:
Let me near life,
Let me know it.'   15

THREE WOMEN

And the notes she sang
Ravished his sad heart.

'Still you stand there staring,
Silent as a statue.
Do I scare you that much?   20
What has happened to you?
Move beside me closer.
Why are you so distant?
Is it just my colour?
Does that still disturb you?   25
My face and hands and arms
Are burnt dark in the sun
But parts I'll let you see
The sunlight's never seen.'

THREE WOMEN

She opened her blouse,   30
She showed her unsunned self,

His young blood was rising,

His young blood was rising.

    XI

Fragrance fills the woodland,
Wind-swayed wheat is ripe.
'Now, Johnny, I'll show you
How sunburnt gypsies sleep.'
With that she broke a branch   5
And laid it on a stone:

'There now, my bed is made,'
She lightly said, and laughed.
'Earth is my pillow,
10   The sky my counterpane.
I keep my dew-cold fingers
Warm-buried in my lap.'
In her skirt she lay
Bare on the barren ground
15   And for sad virtue's sake
He wept with a sad heart.

XII

Dappled woodland light,
Spring well chill and bright,
Eyes like stars at night,
Open knees so white.
5   Four things death itself won't cover,
Unforgettable forever.

XIII

[*Piano solo: Andante*]

XIV

Sun and sunlight heighten,
Shadows shorten.
Who, O who can bring back
All I have forfeited?

XV

Move, you tawny oxen!
What are you looking at?
Could it be you're waiting
To let my secret out?
5   Try it and you'll see
The flogging I'll give you.
Just you try, my oxen,
Then see what will happen!

Now I dread my summons,
The noonday angelus   10
That calls me home, alas,
To meet my mother's eyes.

XVI

How did this happen me?
Can I live to bear it?
And take this girl to wife?
And rear a gypsy brat?
Gypsies all around me,   5
Father, mother? Never!

O find a millstone quickly!
Throw me in the millrace!
Even skylarks singing
Unearthly melodies   10
Cannot ease this sadness
Or bring joy to my days.

XVII

Who can escape his fate?
Fate comes upon its hour.
Evenings now I hurry
To the boor-tree bower.
What is it leads me there?   5
Looking for strawberries . . .
Tiny leaves prinked open.
Taste of felicity!

XVIII

Night-time, night-time, night-time
Cannot come soon enough,
Dark night in Zefka's bed,
The small hours of love.
Roosters, I'll wring your necks   5
If you don't stop crowing.
Roosters, your cry at dawn

Is beyond enduring –
Interrupting love's
10   Deep dream and yearning.
With her in my arms
I defy the morning.

XIX

Magpie, sorrow's magpie
Rising up suddenly,
Did you rob my sister's
Washing on wash day?
5   What if she should ever
Find who the real thief was?
She would abhor me,
All of my lies to her.

Holy God, Holy God,
10   What has come over me?
Everything's up-ended. God,
What has happened to me?

I kick against myself
Like a horse that's spancelled.
15   Prayers pour through my mind like
Sand down through an hourglass.

XX

Now she's in full bloom
How she ti- ti- tightens dresses!
Now her time has come
Look how bri- bri- bright-eyed she is!

XXI

Father, what made you think
My match could be arranged?
Father, you little knew
What sort of son you'd raised.
5   As the night follows day
Punishment's sure to come.

Father, my fate is clear,
Cannot be escaped from.

XXII

Fare you well, my townland,
Fare you well, my people.
Nothing matters here now.
I embrace my exile.
So farewell, father dear,   5
And farewell, my mother.
Fare you well, sister dear,
Farewell, my little flower.
Pardon me, don't blame me,
Take my hand and kiss it.   10
There'll be no returning.
To find my life, I lose it.
Destiny directs me.
Life's doorway stands open.
Zefka waits and calls me,   15
Nursing our first-born son.

The Burial at Thebes

SOPHOCLES

for Marianne McDonald

CHARACTERS

ANTIGONE

ISMENE
her sister

CHORUS
of Theban elders

CREON
King of Thebes

GUARD

HAEMON
Creon's son

TIRESIAS

MESSENGER

EURYDICE
Creon's wife

The scene is Thebes, in front of CREON's *palace, just as the dawn
is breaking.* ANTIGONE *and* ISMENE *enter hastily.*

ANTIGONE
Ismene, quick, come here!
What's to become of us?
Why are we always the ones?

There's nothing, sister, nothing
Zeus hasn't put us through
Just because we are who we are –
The daughters of Oedipus.
And because we are his daughters
We took what came, Ismene,

5

In public and in private,   10
Hurt and humiliation –
But this I cannot take.

No, wait.
              Here's what has happened.
There's a general order issued   15
And again it hits us hardest.
The ones we love, it says,
Are enemies of the state.
To be considered traitors –

ISMENE
How so?   20

ANTIGONE
Have you not heard?

ISMENE
What I heard was enough.
Our two brothers are dead,
The Argos troops withdrawn
And the pair of us left to cope.   25
But what's next, I don't know.

ANTIGONE
That's why I stayed outside.
The walls in there have ears.
This is for your ears only.

ISMENE
What is it? You have me scared.   30

ANTIGONE
And right you are to be scared.
Creon has made a law.
Eteocles will be buried
As a soldier, with full honours,
So he's gone home to the dead.   35
But not Polyneices.
Polyneices is denied
Any burial at all.

Word has come down from Creon.
40 There's to be no laying to rest,
No mourning, and the corpse
Is to be publicly dishonoured.
His body's to be dumped,
Disposed of like a carcass,
45 Left for the birds to feed on.
If you so much as throw him
The common handful of clay
You'll have committed a crime.

This is law and order
50 In the land of good King Creon.
This is his edict for you
And for me, Ismene, for me.
And he's coming to announce it.
'Whoever breaks this law,
55 I'll hunt them down,' he says.
'I'll have them stoned to death,' he says.

                            I say,
He has put it to us.
                            I say
60 It's a test you're facing,
Whether you are who you are,
And true to all you belong to,
Or –

ISMENE
Antigone . . .
65   Antigone,
What do you mean, a test?
If things have gone this far
What is there I can do?

ANTIGONE
You can help me do one thing.

ISMENE
70 And what thing is that?

ANTIGONE
His body . . . Help me to lift
And lay your brother's body.

ISMENE
And bury him, no matter . . .?

ANTIGONE
Are we sister, sister, brother?
Or traitor, coward, coward?   75

ISMENE
But what about Creon's order?

ANTIGONE
What are Creon's rights
When it comes to me and mine?

ISMENE
Easy now, my sister.
Think this through for a minute.   80
Think of the line we come from:
We're the children of Oedipus –
Daughters of the man
Who fathered us on his mother –
The king they drove from their city.   85
No matter he didn't know.
No matter it was Oedipus
Brought his own crimes to light
And then reached into his eyes
And tore them out of their sockets –   90
Still they drove him out.
Oedipus had to perish.
And then his wife, the mother
Who bared her breasts for him
In the child-bed and the bride-bed,   95
She hanged herself in a noose.

And now this last thing happens.
The family curse comes back
And brother slaughters brother –
The two of them, dead in a day.   100

Are you and I to be next?
How do you think they see us?
How do you think we'd fare
If we went against the order?
Two women on our own   105

Faced with a death decree –
Women, defying Creon?
It's not a woman's place.
We're weak where they are strong.
110 Whether it's this or worse,
We must do as we're told.

In the land of the living, sister,
The laws of the land obtain –
And the dead know that as well.
115 The dead will have to forgive me.
I'll be ruled by Creon's word.
Anything else is madness.

ANTIGONE
You and the laws of the land!
Sister, let me tell you:
120 From now on, and no matter
How your mind may change,
I'll never accept your help.
I will bury him myself.
And if death comes, so be it.
125 There'll be a glory in it.
I'll go down to the underworld
Hand in hand with a brother.
And I'll go with my head held high.
The gods will be proud of me.

130 The land of the living, sister,
Is neither here nor there.
We enter it and we leave it.
The dead in the land of the dead
Are the ones you'll be with longest.
135 And how are you going to face them,
Ismene, if you dishonour
Their laws and the gods' law?

ISMENE
Dishonour them I do not.
But nor am I strong enough
140 To defy the laws of the land.

ANTIGONE
Live, then; and live with your choice.
I am going to bury his body.

ISMENE
I fear for you, Antigone.

ANTIGONE
Better fear for yourself.

ISMENE
Oh stop! This must never get out.   145

ANTIGONE
No. No. Broadcast it.
Your cover-ups sicken me.
I have nothing to hide
From the powers that see all.
I am doing what has to be done.   150

ISMENE
What are you, Antigone?
Hot-headed or cold-blooded?
This thing cannot be done.

ANTIGONE
But it still has to be tried.

ISMENE
You're mad. And you are doomed.   155

ANTIGONE
Here and now, Ismene,
I hate you for saying that.
And our dead are going to hate you.
Call me mad if you like
But leave me alone to do it.   160
If Creon has me killed,
Where's the disgrace in that?
The disgrace would be to avoid it.

Exit ANTIGONE.

Nothing's going to stop you.

165 But nothing's going to stop
The ones that love you, sister,
From keeping on loving you

Exit ISMENE.

Enter CHORUS *of Theban Elders.*

CHORUS
Glory be to brightness, to the gleaming sun,
Shining guardian of our seven gates.
170 Burn away the darkness, dawn on Thebes,
Dazzle the city you have saved from destruction.

Argos is defeated, the army beaten back,
                         All their brilliant shields
Smashed into shards and smithereens.

175 Like a golden eagle, the enemy came swooping,
Like an eagle screaming down the sky,
Hoping to set fire to the seven towers.
But the dragon of Thebes had grown teeth.
We overwhelmed him on the walls
180 And Zeus blasted his overbearing.

A god of war stiffened our will
And locked our arms, so the line held.

Glory be to brightness, to the gleaming sun.

Seven guardians at our seven gates
185 Bore the brunt and broke the charge.
                    Our attackers
Were struck down and stripped of their armour.
Their spears and helmets are the spoils of war.
We have hung their shields among the trophies.

190 But Polyneices and Eteocles:
The only trophies they took at Thebes
Were each other's deaths. Their doom was sealed.
Their banners flew, the battle raged
And they fell together, their father's sons.

Glory be to brightness, to the gleaming sun.   195

Glory be to Victory. I can feel her wings
                    Fanning the air.
The joy in my eyes is like the joy in hers
Dazzling the city she has saved from destruction.

Race the chariots and run to the temples.   200
Drum the earth from early until late.
Give glory to the god of the dance.
Let Dionysus burn away the dark!
Glory be to brightness, to the gleaming world.

Enter CREON *with his guards.*

King Creon. All hail to Creon.   205
He's a new king but he's right
For this city at this moment.
Now we will know what's what,
Why he has sent for us
To be privy to his thinking.   210

CREON
Gentlemen. We have entered calmer waters.
Our ship of state was very nearly wrecked
But the gods have kept her safe.
                         So, friends, well done.
You from the start have been a loyal crew.   215
You stood by Oedipus when he was at the helm
And when his sons stepped in to take his place
You stood by them as well. But now they're gone,
Two brothers badged red with each other's blood,
And I, as next of kin to those dead and doomed,   220
I'm next in line. The throne has come to me.

Until a man has passed this test of office
And proved himself in the exercise of power,
He can't be truly known – for what he is, I mean,
In his heart and mind and capabilities.   225
Worst is the man who has all the good advice
And then, because his nerve fails, fails to act
In accordance with it, as a leader ought to.
                         And equally to blame

230 Is anyone who puts the personal
Above the overall thing, puts friend
Or family first. But rest assured:
My nerve's not going to fail, and there's no threat
That's going to stop me acting, ever,
235 In the interests of all citizens. Nor would I,
Ever, have anything to do
With my country's enemy. For the patriot,
Personal loyalty always must give way
To patriotic duty.
240   Solidarity, friends,
Is what we need. The whole crew must close ranks.
The safety of our state depends upon it.
Our trust. Our friendships. Our security.
Good order in the city. And our greatness.

245 Understand therefore that I intend
To make good what I say by what I do.
And hear this first. This ordinance is binding.

Concerning the sons of Oedipus:
Eteocles, who fell in our defence,
250 Eteocles will be buried with full honours
As a hero of his country.
                      But his brother
Polyneices, an exile who came back
To visit us with fire and sword, a traitor,
255 An anti-Theban Theban prepared to kill
His countrymen in war, and desecrate
The shrines of his country's gods, hear this
About Polyneices:
                      He is forbidden
260 Any ceremonial whatsoever.
No mourning, no interment, no observance
Of any of the rites. Hereby he is adjudged
A carcass for the dogs and birds to feed on.
And nobody, let it be understood,
265 Nobody is to treat him otherwise
Than as the obscenity he was and is.

This is where I stand when it comes to Thebes:
Never to grant traitors and subversives

Equal footing with loyal citizens,
But to honour patriots in life and death.   270

CHORUS
Loud and clear, King Creon,
You have laid down the law.
You exercise the power.
Your regulations hold
For the living and dead.   275

CREON
And that is why I regard you from now on
As agents of the law.

CHORUS
                              Younger men
Would be better for that job.

CREON
                              I don't mean   280
You should do work on the ground. Naturally
I have guards out there already as we speak.

CHORUS
Then why do you call us 'agents of the law'?

CREON
I mean you're not to lend the least support
To anyone who'd go against the order.   285

CHORUS
                              But who'd do that?
Who would choose to be dead?

CREON
Death, yes, it would be. But you never know.
There's always money lurking and I never
Underestimate the lure of money.   290

Enter GUARD.

GUARD
Sir, I wouldn't exactly say I was panting to get here. Far from it.
As a matter of fact, I was more for turning back. I was over a barrel.
One part of me was saying, 'Only a loony would walk himself into

this,' and another part was saying, 'You'd be a bigger loony not to
get to Creon first.' It was, 'You take the high road, I'll take the low
road,' then, 'What's your hurry?', then, 'Get a move on.' But when
all was said and done there was only one thing for it: get here, get it
out and get it over, no matter what. So here I am, the old dog for the
hard road. What will be, says I, will be.

CREON
What has got you into this state, guard?

GUARD
First off, boss, you must know I'm in the clear. I didn't do the thing,
I didn't see who did it and so, in fairness, I shouldn't be blamed for it.

CREON
Why do you need such fences and defences?
295 Your news is hardly all that desperate.

GUARD
Desperate enough to panic me, your honour.

CREON
Then get it out, man, as you say yourself,
And get it over.

GUARD
Well, here's what it is. The corpse. Somebody has as good as buried
it. Somebody's after attending to it right. Casting the earth on it and
all the rest.

CREON
300 What are you saying? What man would dare do this?

GUARD
That, for the life of me, I cannot tell. There wasn't so much as
a scrape left on the ground. No sign of pick-work or that class of
thing. No rut-marks from a wheel. Nothing but the land, the old
hard scrabble. Whoever did it was a mystery man entirely. When the
sentry showed us this morning, we were stunned. The corpse had
actually gone and disappeared. But then it turned out it was only
hidden, under this coat of dust. As if somebody had treated it,
you know, just to be on the safe side. Somebody observing all
the customs.

There were no tears in the flesh, so it couldn't have been wild
animals or the dogs.

And then the row broke out, everybody shouting, one man blaming
the next and ready to fight to prove his innocence. We'd have put
our hands in fire to clear ourselves. Swearing by this and that that
we'd neither done the deed nor knew who did it. And then, when
we'd more or less calmed down, one man speaks up and panics us
again. And what he stated was the obvious: you would have to be
told, the thing could be hid no longer. So that was agreed and I was
the lucky man. I drew the short straw and that, sir, is why I'm here.
The one that's never welcome, the bearer of bad news.

CHORUS
Creon, sir, I cannot help but think
The gods have had a hand in this somewhere.   305

CREON
Enough. Don't anger me. Your age, my friend,
Still doesn't give you rights to talk such nonsense.
The gods, you think, are going to attend
To this particular corpse? Preposterous.
Did they hide him under clay for his religion?   310
For coming to burn their colonnaded temples?
For attacking a city under their protection?
The gods, you think, will side with the likes of him?
Here's something else for you to think about.
For a good while now I have had reports   315
Of disaffected elements at work here,
A certain poisonous minority
Unready to admit the rule of law
And my law in particular.
                         I know   320
These people and how they operate.
                         Maybe they are not
The actual perpetrators, but they possess
The money and the means to bribe their way.
Money has a long and sinister reach.   325
It slips into the system, changes hands
And starts to eat away at the foundations
Of everything we stand for.
                         Money brings down leaders,
Warps minds and generally corrupts   330

People and institutions. But in this case
Whoever took the bribe will pay the price.
                        You then: listen to this
For this is my solemn vow: if you do not
335   Apprehend, arrest and bring before me
The one who interred the corpse, I'll hang you out
And have you so racked and ripped and pulled apart
You'll be pleading to be dead. You'll discover then
What interest your kind of money earns.

GUARD

340   Can I say a word or am I just dismissed?

CREON

Dismissed. That's it. You and your news disturb me.

GUARD

Your conscience is what's doing the disturbing.

CREON

Watch out, guard. You're overstepping here.

GUARD

It's that mystery man who has you really bothered.

CREON

345   I warn you. You have far too much to say.

GUARD

                        But I didn't do it.

CREON

Oh yes, you did. The minute you smelt money.

GUARD

What's happening here, Creon, is that the judge
Has misjudged everything.

CREON

350   And what I'm telling you
Is this: unless you expose the guilty party to me,
You'll rue the day you bought into this plot.

Exit CREON.

GUARD
O yes, of course, expose him! Bring him in.
But be that as may be, this much is sure:
Yours truly won't be back here in a hurry.   355

Exit GUARD.

CHORUS
Among the many wonders of the world
Where is the equal of this creature, man?
First he was shivering on the shore in skins,
Or paddling a dug-out, terrified of drowning.
Then he took up oars, put tackle on a mast   360
And steered himself by the stars through gales.

Once upon a time from the womb of earth
The gods were born and he bowed down
To worship them. He worked the land,
Stubbed the forests and harnessed stallions.   365
His furrows cropped, he feasted his eyes
On hay and herds as far as the horizon.

The wind is no more swift or mysterious
Than his mind and words; he has mastered thinking,
Roofed his house against hail and rain   370
And worked out laws for living together.

Home-maker, thought-taker, measure of all things,
He can heal with herbs and read the heavens.
Nothing seems beyond him, except death.
Death he can defy but not defeat.   375
          When he yields to his gods,
When truth is the treadle of his loom
And justice the shuttle, he'll be shown respect –
The city will reward him. But if he once

Oversteps the limits set by the city,   380
If he tramps down right or starts to treat the law
Wilfully, as his own word,
Then let this wonder of the world remember:
He'll have put himself beyond the pale.
When he comes begging we will turn our backs.   385

Enter GUARD, *leading* ANTIGONE.

Now what has happened? Is this
The gods at work?
Antigone, child of doom,
Have you gone and broken the law?

GUARD

390   This is the one. We caught her at it,
Attending to the corpse. Where's Creon gone?

CHORUS

Creon knows when he's needed. He's coming now.

Enter CREON.

CREON

Needed? Why am I needed?

GUARD

                          King Creon. Sir.
395   There's no such thing as an oath that can't be broken.
Circumstances change and your mind changes.
After the going-over you gave me here
I swore I was off for good. But every now and then
The thing you'd hardly let yourself imagine
400   Actually happens. So here I am again.
And here's the one that was covering up the corpse.
I was on to her in a flash: my prisoner
And mine alone. No need to draw lots this time,
I can tell you.
405   And now, sir, she is yours.
It's up to you to judge her and convict her –
And let me go. I deserve to be discharged.
My job is done.

CREON

               How did you come on her?

GUARD

410   At her work, for all to see, interring Polyneices.

CREON

And you stand over this? This is the truth?

GUARD

I saw her burying the body you said
Nobody was to bury. Will that do?

CREON

How was she observed and caught? Describe it.

GUARD

Oh, I'll describe it. Gladly. After your tongue-lashing   415
I went back and joined the watch, and told them
We were all marked men. So we did what we could do.
Approached the corpse again and cleaned it down
And peeled away the clothes. It was going off
So we stationed ourselves at points around the hill –   420
Out of the wind, you know, because of the smell.
Every man on guard, watching the other man,
And all the while there's a fireball of a sun
Going up and up the sky until at midday
You could hardly bear it. The ground was like a grid-iron . . .   425

And then what happens? A whirlwind. Out of nowhere.
Leaves whipped off trees. Flying sand and dust.
The plain below us disappeared, and the path up,
And the hills on the horizon – like the sky was
Vomiting black air. So we closed our eyes   430
And braced ourselves for whatever plague it was
The gods were sending.
                              But then it clears
And this one's standing, crying her eyes out.
She sees the bare corpse and lets out a screech   435
And starts to curse whoever did the deed.
She was like a wild bird round an empty nest.
She lifted dust in her hands and let it fall.
Poured the water three times from her urn,
Performed the entire ceremony   440
Exactly as it's meant to be performed.
And she showed no signs of panic when we trapped her,
Denied no thing she was accused of doing
Then or earlier.
                    But here's what's strange: 445
I felt a sadness coming over me.
It's one thing to be let off the hook yourself,

Another thing to land your friends in trouble.
But if I don't watch out for myself, who will?

CREON

450   You there, studying the ground: hold up your head
And tell us: is this true?

ANTIGONE

                    True. I admit it.

CREON (*to* GUARD)
All right. You're in the clear. Back to your post. Go on.

Exit GUARD.
                   You then. Tell me
455   And be quick about it: did you or did you not
Know that the proclamation forbade all this?

ANTIGONE
I did know. How could I not? Everybody knew.

CREON
And still you dared to disobey the law?

ANTIGONE
I disobeyed because the law was not
460   The law of Zeus nor the law ordained
By Justice, Justice dwelling deep
Among the gods of the dead. What they decree
Is immemorial and binding for us all.
The proclamation had your force behind it
465   But it was mortal force, and I, another mortal,
Chose to disregard it. I abide
By statutes utter and immutable –
Unwritten, original, god-given laws.

Was I going to humour you, or honour gods?
470   Sooner or later I'll die anyhow
And sooner may be better in my case:
This death sentence is almost a relief.
If I had to live and suffer in the knowledge
That Polyneices was lying above ground
475   Insulted and defiled, that would be worse
Than having to suffer any penalty

Or punishment of yours.
You think I'm just a reckless woman, but –
Never, Creon, forget:
You yourself could be the reckless one.   480

CHORUS
This wildness in her comes from Oedipus.
She gets it from her father. She won't relent.

CREON
We'll wait and see. The bigger the resistance
The bigger the collapse.
                          The hardest forged iron   485
Snaps the quickest. Wild she may well be
But even the wildest horses can be broken
If they're reined and bitted right.
When she defied the general order
Antigone had already gone too far,   490
But flaunting that defiance in my face
Puts her beyond the pale. Who does she think
She is? The man in charge?
                          Have I to be
The woman of the house and take her orders?   495
She has brought death sentences upon herself
And on her sister –
                   Yes, yes, yes,
Ismene is involved in this thing too.
The pair of them, my own sister's daughters,   500
In it, up to the hilt. But neither seed nor breed
Will save them now.
                   Get Ismene out here.
She was inside in the house a while ago,
Raving, out of her mind.   505
                       That's how guilt
Affects some people. They simply break
And everything comes out.
                        But the barefaced ones,
The ones who defy you when they're found out,   510
They're worse again.

ANTIGONE
                   Will it be enough for you
To see me executed?

CREON

More than enough.

ANTIGONE

515   Then why don't you do it quickly?
Me having to speak to you
Or you to me is only torture now.
I never did a nobler thing than bury
My brother Polyneices. And if these men
520   Weren't so afraid to sound unpatriotic
They'd say the same. But you are king
And because you're king you won't be contradicted.

CREON

So you know something no one else in Thebes knows?

ANTIGONE

They know it too. They're just afraid to say it.

CREON

525   But you're so high and mighty you've no qualms.

ANTIGONE

None. There's no shame in burying a brother.

CREON

Your brother Eteocles also died in the war.

ANTIGONE

My father's and my mother's son, yes, dead.

CREON

– And dishonoured, when you honour Polyneices.

ANTIGONE

530   The dead aren't going to begrudge the dead.

CREON

So wrongdoers and the ones wronged fare the same?

ANTIGONE

Polyneices was no common criminal.

CREON

He terrorised us. Eteocles stood by us.

ANTIGONE
Religion dictates the burial of the dead.

CREON
Dictates the same for loyal and disloyal?   535

ANTIGONE
Who knows what loyalty is in the underworld?

CREON
Even there, I'd know my enemy.

ANTIGONE
And I would know my friend. Where I assist
With love, you set at odds.

CREON
Go then and love your fill in the underworld.   540
No woman will dictate the law to me.

ISMENE *is brought in.*

CHORUS
Ismene, look, in tears!
For her sister. For herself.

CREON
You bloodsucker.
The pair of you at me like a pair of leeches!   545
Two vipers spitting venom at the throne.
Speak, you, now. You helped her, didn't you?

ISMENE
I helped her, yes, if I'm allowed to say so
And now I stand with her to take what comes.

ANTIGONE
I don't allow this.   550
            We cut our ties.

ISMENE
But I am with you now.

ANTIGONE
Too late, my sister.
The dead and Hades know who did this deed.

ISMENE
555 Antigone, don't rob me of all honour.
Let me die with you and act right by the dead.

ANTIGONE
You can't just pluck your honour off a bush
You didn't plant. You forfeited your right.

ISMENE
If Antigone dies, how will I keep on living?

ANTIGONE
560 Ask Creon, since he means so much to you.

ISMENE
What good does it do you, twisting the knife like this?

ANTIGONE
I can't help it, dear heart. It hurts me too.

ISMENE
But even at this stage, can I not do something?

ANTIGONE
You can save yourself. That is my honest wish.

ISMENE
565 And be forever shamed in my own eyes?

ANTIGONE
You made a choice, you bear the consequence.

ISMENE
I was against your choice and made it clear.

ANTIGONE
One world stood by you, one stood by me.

ISMENE
Different worlds, both equally offended.

ANTIGONE

Take heart, Ismene: you are still alive   570
But I have long gone over to the dead.

CREON

This one was her father's daughter always,
Headstrong from the start.
But I never thought to see it in Ismene.

ISMENE

You think, Creon, when you drive us to the edge   575
We won't go over?

CREON

                              You went over long ago,
The minute you took up with this one here.

ISMENE

My sister is the mainstay of my life.

CREON

Your sister was . . . There's no 'is' any more.   580

ISMENE

You mean you'd kill your own son's bride-to-be?

CREON

I would and will. He has other fields to plough.

ISMENE

He loves her utterly. For him, there is no one else.

CREON

No son of mine will take a condemned wife.

ISMENE

O poor, poor Haemon! To have you for a father!   585

CREON

You and your marriage talk. Too late for that.

CHORUS

Do you mean, sir, you'll rob Haemon of this woman?

CREON

Death will rob him first.

CHORUS

But the sentence –
590   Has the sentence been decided?

CREON

It has, by me,
And I, remember, have your acclamation.
Get her away from here. And the other one.
Women were never meant for this assembly.
595   From now on they'll be kept in place again
And better be.

Yes, keep an eye on them.
Once the end's in sight they all get desperate.
Even the bravest will make a run for it.

ANTIGONE *and* ISMENE *are led out.*

CHORUS
600   Whoever has been spared the worst is lucky.
When high gods shake a house
That family is going to feel the blow
Generation after generation.
It starts like an undulation underwater,
605   A surge that hauls black sand up off the bottom,
Then turns itself into a tidal current
Lashing the shingle and shaking promontories.

I see the sorrows of this ancient house
Break on the inmates and keep breaking on them
610   Like foaming wave on wave across a strand.
They stagger to their feet and struggle on
But the gods do not relent, the living fall
Where the dead fell in their day
Generation after generation.

615   And now a light that seemed about to glow,
A hope for the house of Oedipus, has died.
Dust cast upon a corpse extinguished it.
Bloodstained dust. A defiant spirit.
The fury and backlash of overbearing words.

620   O Zeus on high, beyond all human reach,
Nothing outwits you and nothing ever will.

You cannot be lulled by sleep or slowed by time.
O dazzle on Olympus, O power made light!
Now and forever your law is manifest:
No windfall or good fortune comes to mortals   625
That isn't paid for in the coin of pain.

Here is what happens: hope and mad ambition
Are many a time fulfilled for many a man;
But just as often they are will-o'-the-wisps
That'll send him wild-eyed into fire and flood.   630
Well has it been said: the man obsessed
Is a man blindfolded, walking towards the worst.
Our luck is little more than a short reprieve
That the gods allow.

                But look, there's Haemon.   635

Be easy with him, sir.
Allow a youngest son to say his say.
He'll be beyond himself. He'll have gone wild.
He'll know his father doomed his bride to death.

Enter HAEMON.

CREON
Unlike you gentlemen, I don't possess   640
Clairvoyant powers. I prefer to wait
And hear what Haemon has to say himself.

Haemon, son, the judgement I pronounced
Is what the law requires. Are you coming here
To rant and rage against me, or are we still   645
Father dear and father's son, as ever?

HAEMON
Yes, father. Father's son . . . I do rely
On your wisdom and experience and would want
No match or marriage to displace you ever.

CREON
That's how it is and how it should be, Haemon.   650
It's right for the son to heed his father's judgement.
                It's what all men pray for,
Children who will show a due respect,

Who will make their father's enemies
655 Their enemies, and his friends their friends.
Nothing gives an enemy more pleasure
Than to see you let down by the child you've reared:
That is a bitter pill to have to swallow.
Don't, Haemon, lose your wits over a woman.
660 You're wild for her, but the minute you have had her
There and then your comfort turns cold comfort.
Nothing's worse than marrying yourself
To a woman that's no good. Nothing cuts as deep
As when the one who's closest turns against you.
665 That's why I say: have nothing to do with her.
If she needs a husband, let Hades find her one,
For of this you can be certain: I won't be making
A liar of myself in front of the city.
She, and she alone, defied the order
670 Openly and deliberately, so she shall perish.

Her and her brother and her sacred family bonds!
Let her beseech Zeus to her heart's content:
My family too have bonds they need to honour.
They must observe the discipline I expect
675 From every citizen. The city has to see
The standards of a public man reflected
In his private conduct. He has to be a man
Ready to abide by his own orders,
A comrade you'd depend on in a battle.
680 When discipline goes, self-discipline goes as well
And once that happens cities, homes and armies
Collapse, inevitably. Failure of rule
Is the most destructive thing. Obedience
And respect must be instilled. And that is why
685 No woman here is going to be allowed
To walk all over us. Otherwise, as men
We'll be disgraced. We won't deserve the name.

CHORUS
Well, we are old men, so perhaps our judgement's shaky,
But what you're saying seems to make good sense.

HAEMON
690 The use of reason, father . . . The gods
Have given us the use of reason.

But do we use it right? Do I? Do you?
It's hard to know, but this much I can tell you:
When you hear things you'd rather not be hearing
You get worked up. So therefore people shield you. 695
But not me, father. I hear everything
Or overhear it. And all that's talked about
In this city now is Antigone.
People are heartbroken for her. What,
They're asking, did she do so wrong? What deserves 700
A punishment like this? As far as they're concerned,
She should be honoured – a woman who rebelled!
Rebelled when her brother's corpse was being thrown
To the carrion crows. *She was heroic!*
That's what's being said behind closed doors. 705

Believe me, father, nothing means more to me
Than you and your good name. What else could?
Father/son, son/father – that regard
Is natural and mutual.
                              For your own sake, then, 710
I ask you: reconsider. Nobody,
Nobody can be sure they're always right.
The ones who are fullest of themselves that way
Are the emptiest vessels. There's no shame
In taking good advice. 715
                              It's a sign of wisdom.
                              If a river floods
The trees on the bank that bend to it survive.
If a skipper doesn't slacken sail in storm
His whole crew ends up clinging to the keel. 720
So. Swallow pride and anger. Allow yourself
To change.

I'm young, I know, but I offer you this thought:
All of us would like to have been born
Infallible, but since we know we weren't, 725
It's better to attend to those who speak
In honesty and good faith, and learn from them.

CHORUS
You should take good note, Creon, of Haemon's words
And he of yours. Both of you say sound things.

CREON

730 So a man of my age, you are telling me,
Must take instruction from a man of his?

HAEMON

Only if it is the right instruction.
The rightness is what matters, not the age.

CREON

Rightness? What rightness? Aren't you against the law?

HAEMON

735 I am not, and I don't want you to be.

CREON

But isn't that why Antigone's a danger?

HAEMON

People here in Thebes don't seem to think so.

CREON

Do my orders come from Thebes and from the people?

HAEMON

Can you hear yourself? What age do you sound now?

CREON

740 Who's to take charge? The ruler or the ruled?

HAEMON

There's no city that belongs in single hands.

CREON

Rulers, I thought, were meant to be in charge.

HAEMON

Where you should be in charge is in a desert.

CREON

Listen to him. He's on the woman's side.

HAEMON

745 Are you a woman? I'm on your side, father.

CREON
On my side, but always going against me?

HAEMON
Not against *you*. Against your going wrong.

CREON
Am I wrong to wield the powers vested in me?

HAEMON
Do they give you rights to disregard the gods?

CREON
Son, you're pathetic. You give in to a woman.   750

HAEMON
But to nothing that's forbidden or wrong.

CREON
Everything you say is on her behalf.

HAEMON
And yours and mine and the gods' under the earth.

CREON
You'll never marry her while she draws breath.

HAEMON
Then she'll have to die, and she won't die on her own.   755

CREON
Has it come to this? Is this an open threat?

HAEMON
It's my resolution. Read it as you wish.

CREON
You'll rue the day you took it on yourself
To lecture me. You're a real know-nothing.

HAEMON
If you weren't my father, father –   760

CREON
                        That's enough.
The woman has you round her little finger.

HAEMON

Shutting me up still doesn't make you right.

CREON

By all the gods that look down from Olympus,
765 I'm telling you you'll pay a heavy price
For this disrespect.
                        Bring her out here.
Bring her out and do away with her
So that her groom can watch the deed being done.

HAEMON

770 Never. And never, father, again
Will you set eyes on me. You are deranged.
Let whoever can abide you watch her die.

Exit HAEMON.

CHORUS

King Creon – a younger man like that,
Out of control – he could do anything.

CREON

775 He can do what he likes, do his worst or his best.
It won't affect the fate of those two women.

CHORUS

Two, you say? Have you condemned them both?

CREON

No, you are right. One didn't lift a finger.

CHORUS

But Antigone. You've actually considered
780 How you're going to put Antigone to death?

CREON

Up in the rocks, up where nobody goes,
There's a steep path that leads higher, to a cave.
She'll be put in there and food put in with her –
To ward off any blood-guilt from the city.
785 And once she's in, take stones and wall her up.
And let her pray then to her heart's content
To her god of death. After all her Hades talk,
It'll be her chance to see if he can save her.

Exit CREON.

CHORUS
Love that can't be withstood,
Love that scatters fortunes,   790
Love like a green fern shading
The cheek of a sleeping girl.
Love like spume off a wave
Or turf-smoke in the air,
Love, you wield your power   795
Over mortal and immortal
And you put them mad.

Love leads the good astray,
Plays havoc in heart and home;
You, love, here and now   800
In this tormented house
Are letting madness loose.
The naked gaze of a bride
Breeds desire and danger.
Eternal, sexual, smiling,   805
The goddess Aphrodite
Is irresistible.
Love mounts to the throne with law.

ANTIGONE *is led in under guard.*

But the law and all it stands for
Cannot hold back my tears.   810
Antigone, you are a bride,
Being given away to death.

ANTIGONE
Given away to death!
Remember this, citizens.
I am linked on Hades' arm,   815
I am taking my last look,
My last walk in the light.
Soon the sun will go out
On a silent, starless shore
And Hades will step aside.   820
He will give me to Acheron,
Lord of the pitch-black lake,

And that bridegroom's cold hand
Will take my hand in the dark.

CHORUS

825 Steadfast Antigone,
Never before did Death
Open his stone door
To one so radiant.
You would not live a lie.
830 Vindicated, lauded,
Age and disease outwitted,
You go with head held high.

ANTIGONE

I am like Niobe,
Niobe turned to stone
835 In the thawing snow and rain,
A rock that weeps forever
Like ivy in a shower
Sluicing down the ridge
Of high Mount Sipylus.

CHORUS

840 Niobe was immortal,
Sky-born, far beyond us,
For we are born of the earth.
But someone as glorious
In life and in death as you
845 Can also seem immortal.

ANTIGONE

Stop. Enough. Don't mock.
Wait, at least, till I'm gone.
I am still in life, but I dread
To leave our groves and springs.
850 O fortunate men of Thebes,
O my Thebes of the chariots,
Farewell. I am going away
Under my rock-piled roof.
No mourner waits at the mound.
855 I'll be shut in my halfway house,
Unwept by those alive,
Unwelcomed as yet by the dead.

CHORUS
Ah, child, you were carried away
But now you are halted and hauled
Before implacable Justice,   860
Paying, perhaps, in your life
For the past life of your father.

ANTIGONE
There. You have hit home.
Over and over again
Because I am who I am   865
I retrace that fatal line
And the ghastly love I sprang from.
My father weds his mother.
He mounts her. Me and mine,
His half-sisters and brothers,   870
Are born in their sullied bed.
These are the stricken dead
I go to meet in Hades.

CHORUS
You go because you were noble.
Nobility mitigates   875
The offence you gave; but power
And everyone who wields it
Will brook no opposition.
You were headstrong and self-willed
And now you suffer for it.   880

ANTIGONE
No flinching then at fate.
No wedding guests. No wake.
I close my eye on the sun.
I turn my back on the light.

Enter CREON.

CREON
If people had the chance to keen themselves   885
Before they died, they'd weep and wail forever.
She has had her say.
                    Get her ready and march.
March to the rock vault, wall her in and leave.

890 After that it'll be up to her to choose.
She can live there under dry stone, or can die.
There's no blood on my hands here. It was she
Who put herself beyond the pale. She is to blame
For every blackout stone they pile up round her.

ANTIGONE

895 Stone of my wedding chamber, stone of my tomb,
Stone of my prison roof and prison floor,
Behind you and beyond you stand the dead.
They are my people and they're waiting for me
And when they see me coming down the road
900 They'll hurry out to meet me, all of them.
My father and my mother first, and then
Eteocles, my brother – every one
As dear to me as when I washed and dressed
And laid them out.
905   But Polyneices,
When I did the same for you, when I did
What people know in their hearts of hearts
Was right, I was doomed for it.

Not for a husband, not even for a son
910 Would I have broken the law.
Another husband I could always find
And have other sons by him if one were lost.
But with my father gone, and my mother gone,
Where can I find another brother, ever?
915 When I disobeyed Creon, I obeyed this law.
It is a law of life.
But all Creon can see is a crazy girl
He must get rid of.
        Have I offended gods?
920 Do the gods have no regard for what I did?
Where can I turn if they have turned away?
The right observance put me in the wrong:
And if that is the gods' verdict, so be it.
But if the wrong was laid upon me wrongly
925 By these unjust ones, then let their penalty
Be no less than the one they've doomed me to.

CHORUS
She's still unreconciled, as driven as ever.

CREON

The quicker then they move her on, the better.

ANTIGONE

This man's words are as cold as death itself.

CREON

They are meant to be. Meant to destroy your hope.   930
The sentence stands. The law will take its course.

ANTIGONE

Now gods of Thebes, look down.
Through my native streets and fields
I'm being marched away.
And never, you men of Thebes,   935
Forget what you saw today:
The daughter of Oedipus,
The last of his royal house
Condemned. And condemned for what?
For practising devotion,   940
For a reverence that was right.

ANTIGONE *is led out.*

CHORUS

Danae too was walled up in the dark,
Princess daughter imprisoned by her father,
Barred and bolted in a tower of brass.

Then molten Zeus, a battering ray of light,   945
(O flash and cloud-burst! Blossom-stripping shower!)
Ungirdled and dishevelled her with gold.

Fate finds strange ways to fulfil its ends.
Not military power nor the power of money,
Not battlements of stone nor black-hulled fleets   950

Can fend off fate or keep its force at bay.
Blood under maenads' nails, on the mountain path,
Cries on the wind, weeping heard in the palace.

Whoever has been spared the worst is lucky.

Enter TIRESIAS, *blind, led by a boy.*

TIRESIAS

955 My lord, my countrymen, I know you're there.
We have been going the roads, the pair of us
Going by the one same pair of eyes.
The man that's blinded always needs a guide.

CREON

Tiresias, you venerable man:
960 What news have you brought for me this time?

TIRESIAS

News that you would be as well to heed.

CREON

When did I not, prophetic father, heed you?

TIRESIAS

And isn't that why your ship has stayed on course?

CREON

You kept me right. I know it. In my bones.

TIRESIAS

965 Then know this: where you are standing now
Is a cliff edge, and there's cold wind blowing.

CREON

Why do you always put that shiver through me?

TIRESIAS

Because I have the power to see and warn.
I know things once I sit in that stone chair
970 And the birds begin to skirl above my head.
But never in all my years have I heard anything
Like the screams and screeches that I heard this day.
There was no meaning to them. I knew by the whirl of wings
And the rips and spits of blood the birds were mad.

975 I was afraid, so once the blaze was lit
On the altar stone I brought my offerings,
But the fire had no effect. It wouldn't take
And none of the bits would burn.
                                        Slime,
980 Slime was what I got instead of flame.

Matter oozing out from near the bone.
The fat stayed raw and wept into the ash.
Everywhere there was this spattered gall
From the burst gall-bladder. Slurry, smoke and dirt . . .
Some deep fault caused that. The boy here saw it   985
And I rely on him as much as you
On me . . .
             There was no sign to be read.
                              The rite had failed.

Because of you, Creon. You and your headstrongness.   990

That body lying out there decomposing
Is where the pollution starts. The dogs and birds
Are at it day and night, spreading reek and rot
On every altar stone and temple step, and the gods
Are revolted. That's why we have this plague,   995
That's why my birds in flight
Aren't making sense. They're feeding on his flesh.

Consider well, my son. All men make mistakes.
But mistakes don't have to be forever,
They can be admitted and atoned for.   1000
It's the overbearing man who is to blame.
Pull back. Yield to the dead. Don't stab a ghost.
What can you win when you only wound a corpse?
I have your good at heart, and have good advice.
The easiest thing for you would be to take it.   1005

CREON
Why am I standing out here like a target?
Why is every arrow aimed at me?
                              You, Tiresias,
You and your whole fortune-telling tribe
Have bled me white. But not anymore.   1010
Whoever wants can cross your palm with silver
But they still won't get that body under ground.
None of your pollution talk scares me.
Not if Zeus himself were to send his eagle
To eat that rotten flesh and shit it down,   1015
Not even that would put me back on my word.
Nothing done on earth can defile the gods.
But even the wisest man on earth, old man,

Has been corrupted the minute he's prepared
1020   To come up with false prophecy for bribes.

TIRESIAS
It is an insult to call me a false prophet.

CREON
All of you so-called seers have your price.

TIRESIAS
Rulers too have a name for being corrupt.

CREON
Do you realise you are talking to your king?

TIRESIAS
1025   A king my words once helped to save the city.

CREON
Your second sight has been well warped since then.

TIRESIAS
My second sight scares me and should scare you.

CREON
Scare me then, but don't expect a bribe.
The decisions that I take aren't up for sale.

TIRESIAS
1030   Then listen, Creon, and listen carefully.
The sun won't ride his chariot round the sky
Very much longer before flesh of your flesh
Will answer, corpse for corpse, for your enactments.
This is what you'll get for thrusting down
1035   A daughter of the sunlight to the shades.
You have buried her alive, and among the living
You have forbidden burial of one dead,
One who belongs by right to the gods below.
You have violated their prerogatives.
1040   No earthly power, no god in upper air
Exerts authority over the dead.
Henceforth, therefore, there lie in wait for you
The inexorable ones, the Furies who destroy.
Then tell me, when the lamentation starts,

When woman-wail and man-howl rake your walls, 1045
Tell me I've been bribed. And tell me it again
When enemy cities rise to avenge each corpse
You left dishonoured on the battlefield.
They turned to filth, remember, and the crows
Puddled and poked in it and would fly back 1050
To foul each city with droppings of its dead.
I am not the target. I am the archer.
My shafts are tipped with truth and they stick deep.
Come, boy, take me home. Let him affront
Somebody younger now, and learn to control 1055
His tongue, and see things in truer light.

Exit TIRESIAS *and boy.*

CHORUS
He's gone, my lord, but his words won't go away.
Never, in all my days, was that man wrong.
When he warned the city, the city knew to listen.

CREON
I know. I listened too. And learned from him. 1060
I hate a climb-down, but something's gathering head.

CHORUS
Now, of all times, you must heed advice.

CREON
What's to be done? Tell me and I'll do it.

CHORUS
Set the girl free from behind the rocks
And make a burial mound for her brother's corpse. 1065

CREON
You want me to renege?

CHORUS
Immediately, in case the gods strike first.

CREON
It goes against the grain. But I am beaten.
Fate has the upper hand.

CHORUS

1070   Do it then, and do it yourself, quickly.

CREON
Right.
            All hands get a move on, here and now.
The judgement is reversed. Take your crowbars,
Take picks up to the hill. I walled her in
1075   And therefore I'll be there to bring her out.
In my heart of hearts I know what must be done.
Until we breathe our last breath we should keep
The established law.

Exit CREON *with attendants.*

CHORUS
Call up the god of Thebes,
1080   Son of thundering Zeus,
Fleet foot and open hand.

We who live where Cadmus
Sowed the dragon's teeth
Call on you, Dionysus –

1085   Vine-man, pine-god, prince
Of the ivy bunch and wine cup,
We glory in your names.

From Delphi's high-faced cliff,
From the sunk Castalian spring,
1090   From hillsides of ripe grapes

Come brilliantly to Thebes,
Thebes where the bright bolt struck
And begot you on Semele.

Now plague has struck your birthplace.
1095   O Dionysus, appear
With men and maenads headlong

And dance the world to rights.
Be sunlight from Parnassus
Adazzle on the gulf,

Be the necklace-fire of stars,   1100
The cauterising lightning.
Bewilder us with good.

We who live where Cadmus
Sowed the dragon's teeth
We call on you, Dionysus.   1105

Enter MESSENGER.

MESSENGER
Old neighbours, elder citizens, you don't need me
To tell you about life. You've seen it all.
Nobody can predict what lies ahead.
Take our own man, Creon. Creon saved us,
Saved the country, and there he was, strong king,   1110
Strong head of family, the man in charge.
And now it's all been lost. He might as well
Be dead, for when you lose your happiness,
You lose your life.
            You can dwell in state,   1115
Have all the pomp and trappings of success,
But if you can't enjoy them in your heart,
What does it mean? If your joy in life's destroyed,
You're left with a mirage. Shadows and ash.

CHORUS
Is this more bad news for the royal house?   1120

MESSENGER
Dead. They are dead. And the living bear the guilt.

CHORUS
Who was killed? Who did the killing? Quick!

MESSENGER
Haemon was killed –

CHORUS
            By himself or Creon?

MESSENGER
By himself. For the blood on Creon's hands.   1125

CHORUS
Tiresias, mighty seer, it has come to pass!

MESSENGER
We must make sense of it as best we can.

CHORUS
Eurydice!
                    The queen, look, on her way.
1130   Distracted. She must have heard the news.

Enter EURYDICE.

EURYDICE
I am in dread. My hand was on the latch
Of the little gate into the temple shrine . . .
Then I heard keening in the house and fainted.
O citizens, there's not any of you here
1135   Knows better than I what wailing like that means.
I know what to expect. Just say what happened.

MESSENGER
I can tell you the whole thing, ma'am.
Right from the start I was at your husband's side,
All of us climbing the hill. And sure enough
1140   It was still there, Polyneices' corpse,
Or what the dogs had left of it. So we prayed
To the goddess of the crossroads and to Hades
To hold their anger back and to ignore
The pitilessness of that desecration.
1145   Then we washed the remains in purifying water,
Gathered sticks and made enough of a fire
To burn him decently. And as was right,
We piled his home ground over him at last.

Then on we went, right up to the cave mouth,
1150   And deep in that unholy vault we hear
Such terrible howling we have to send for Creon.
And when Creon comes, he howls himself and he knows.
'O hide me, hide me from myself,' he cries,
'For I face the saddest door I ever faced.
1155   I hear my son's voice in there. Come on,'
He shouts, 'Tumble the stones, break through
And look and tell me. Tell me if it's Haemon.'

So we broke the stone wall down
And saw into the gallery. Antigone was there,
Hanging by her neck from a linen noose, 1160
And Haemon on his knees beside her
With his arms around her waist, imploring
The underworld, lamenting his dead bride
And shouting execrations against Creon.

But Creon couldn't help himself and went 1165
With open arms to the boy and started pleading,
Calling him 'son', saying he'd had a fit
And to watch himself. But Haemon spat in his face
And made a quick lunge with his two-edged sword
And would have got him if Creon hadn't dodged. 1170
Then before we knew where we were, he had turned
The sword on himself and buried the blade half-way
Into his own side. And as he fell
His arms still clung to the girl and blood came spurting
Out of his mouth all over her white cheek . . . 1175
That was the kiss he gave his bride-to-be.
A wedding witnessed in the halls of death.
One to teach us living witnesses
The mortal cost of ill-judged words and deeds.

EURYDICE *makes her exit.*

CHORUS
But not a word from her. I wish there'd been 1180
A cry at least or a sigh or a single tear.

MESSENGER
                                        Maybe now
She needs her privacy inside the house.
Maybe she can't give vent to grief in public.
I hope that's why. I too am afraid. 1185

CHORUS
That silence is a danger in itself.

MESSENGER
She shouldn't be going in there unattended.

Exit MESSENGER.

CHORUS
Look. Stand back. It's the king
Coming to bury his own.
1190 How did the likes of us
Foresee this and not him?

Enter CREON, *with* HAEMON's *body.*

CREON
Make way for your king of wrong.
Wrong-headed on the throne,
Wrong-headed in the home,
1195 Wrong-footed by the heavens.
And you, dear son, dead son,
I was wrong to deny you.

CHORUS
Too late, alas, you have learned.

CREON
The hammer-blow of justice
1200 Has caught me and brought me low.
I am under the wheels of the world.
Smashed to bits by a god.

Enter MESSENGER.

MESSENGER
My lord, you come bowed down with grief enough,
But you must brace yourself to suffer more.

CREON
1205 What can be worse than worst?
What else has happened now?

MESSENGER
The one who brought your son into the world
Has taken leave of it. Your queen's life-blood
Is on the palace floor.

CREON
1210 The god of death is greedy
He has set his hounds upon me

And they are merciless.
Say again the news of the queen.

The corpse of EURYDICE *is revealed.*

CHORUS
It doesn't need to be said.
It cannot be kept hidden.   1215

CREON
Mother. And child. Both.
I have wived and fathered death.

MESSENGER
She stabbed herself in front of the house altar.
The sword was two-edged, and so was her grief
For her two sons, for Megareus killed in the war   1220
Defending Thebes, and Haemon who killed himself.
But then as the dark stole down over her eyes,
She called you death-dealer and cursed your name.

CREON
Why doesn't somebody take
A two-edged sword to me?   1225
The dark is on me too.
I'm at bay in guilt and grief.

MESSENGER
Death-dealer, she said, because you and your doings
Felled her children.

CREON
And then she raised her hand   1230
To do the deed?

MESSENGER
When she'd listened to how Haemon stabbed himself
She went and took your own sword from its scabbard
And buried it in her heart.

CREON
Let every verdict be pronounced   1235
Against me. She was guiltless.
It was my hand on the hilt,

My hand that drove the blade.
Take me out of your sight.
1240   I am nothing any more.
Forget me. Treat me as nothing.
From now on I don't exist.

CHORUS
This is right, if right can ever come
From wrongs like yours. This is good.
1245   When the worst has to be faced, the best thing is
To face it quickly.

CREON
The quicker it comes, the better.
I want to hurry death.
I want to be free of the dread
1250   Of wakening in the morning.
Waking up to myself.
All I pray for now
Is the dawn of my last day.

CHORUS
Bear with the present.
1255   The future is cloth waiting to be cut.

CREON
All that I want
I have prayed for in my prayer.

CHORUS
You have prayed enough.
There is no protection.
1260   Fate must take its course.
Humans must endure.

CREON
Take me, hide me, blindfold me from these dead
And keep your distance. Everything I touched
I have destroyed. There's nobody I can turn to,
1265   Nowhere I can go. My recklessness and pride
I paid for in the end. The blow came quick.

Exit CREON.

CHORUS
Wise conduct is the way.
Always rule by the gods and reverence them.
Those who overbear will be brought to grief.
Fate will flail them on its winnowing floor   1270
And in due season teach them to be wise.

The Testament of Cresseid & Seven Fables

ROBERT HENRYSON

The Testament of Cresseid

A gloomy time, a poem full of hurt
Should correspond and be equivalent.
Just so it was when I began my work
On this retelling, and the weather went
5   From close to frosty, as Aries, mid-Lent,
Made showers of hail from the north descend
In a great cold I barely could withstand.

Still, there I stood, inside my oratory
When Titan had withdrawn his beams of light
10   And draped and sealed the brightness of the day,
And lovely Venus, beauty of the night,
Had risen up and toward the true west set
Her golden face, direct in opposition
To the god Phoebus, straight descending down.

15   Beyond the glass her beams broke out so fair
I could see away on every side of me.
The northern wind had purified the air
And hunted the cloud-cover off the sky.
The frost froze hard, the blast came bitterly
20   From the pole-star, whistling loud and shrill,
And forced me to remove against my will.

I had placed my trust in Venus, as love's queen
To whom one time I vowed obedience,
That she should sprig my fallow heart with green;
25   And there and then, with humble reverence,
I thought to pray her high magnificence,
But hindered by that freezing arctic air
Returned into my chamber to the fire.

Though love is hot, yet in an older man
30   It kindles not so soon as in the young:
Their blood burns furiously in every vein

But in the old the blaze is lapsed so long
It needs an outer fire to burn and bring
The spark to life – as I myself know well:
Remedies, when the urge dies, can avail.   35

I stacked the fire and got warm at the hearth,
Then took a drink to soothe and lift my spirit
And arm myself against the bitter north.
To pass the time and kill the winter night
I chose a book – and was soon absorbed in it –   40
Written by Chaucer, the great and glorious,
About fair Cresseid and worthy Troilus.

And there I found that after Diomede
Had won that lady in her radiance
Troilus was driven nearly mad   45
And wept sore and lost colour and then, once
He had despaired his fill, would recommence
As memory and hope revived again.
Thus whiles he lived in joy and whiles in pain.

She had promised him and this was his consoling.   50
He trusted her to come to Troy once more
Which he desired more than any thing
Because she was his only paramour.
But when he saw the day and the due hour
Of her return go past, a heavy weight   55
Of care and woe oppressed his broken heart.

No need here to rehearse the man's distress
Since worthy Chaucer in that selfsame book
Has told his troubles in beguiling verse
And pleasant style, whoever cares to look.   60
It was a different volume that I took
To keep myself awake, in which I found
Cresseid's most miserable and fated end.

Who knows if all that Chaucer wrote was true?
Nor do I know if this second version   65
Was genuine, or maybe something new
Invented by a poet, some narration
Framed so as to include the lamentation
And woeful fall of passionate Cresseid,
What she would endure and how she died.   70

When Diomede had sated his desire
And oversated it on this fair lady
He sought fresh satisfactions with another
And sent Cresseid a banishment decree
To bind and bar her from his company.
She went distracted then and would ramble
And be, as men will say, available.

O fair Cresseid, the flower and paragon
Of Troy and Greece, how could it be your fate
To let yourself be dragged down as a woman
And sullied so by lustful appetite
To go among the Greeks early and late
So obviously, like any common pickup?
When I recollect your fall, I want to weep.

And yet whatever men may think or say
Contemptuously about your quick compliance
I will excuse to what extent I may
Your womanhood, wisdom and loveliness
Which the whim of fortune put to such distress –
No guilt for it to be attributed
To you, bad-mouthed by noxious gossip.

Then fair Cresseid, completely destitute,
Bereft of comfort and all consolation,
Friendless and unprotected, managed out
By stealth and in disguise beyond the town
A mile or two and crossed beyond the line
To a splendid mansion in the Greek-held quarter,
The residence of Calchas, her old father.

When he saw her there, he enquired why
She had returned. 'From the moment Diomede
Had his pleasure,' she answered desperately,
'He began to tire of me and have no need.'
'There is nothing here to weep for,' Calchas said,
'It could be all has turned out for the best.
You are welcome, daughter dear, my dearest guest.'

Old Calchas, as the law required then
Of temple-keepers, was a temple-priest,
Servant of Venus and Cupid, her young son,

Keeper of their precincts where, distressed,
Cresseid would go, heart heavy in her breast,   110
To hide from public notice and to pray.
And then it happened on a certain day

When custom called for general devotion
And sacrifice was due, the people went
Devoutly to the temple before noon;   115
But still Cresseid stayed firm in her intent
To avoid the sanctuary and not present
Herself in public, to keep her secret safe,
Not let them guess her prince had cast her off.

She moved instead into a cell, in private,   120
Where she might weep for what had come to pass.
Behind her back she closed the door and barred it,
Then hurriedly fell down on her bare knees,
Crying all the while, berating Venus
And Cupid angrily, in words like these: 125
'Why, alas, did I ever sacrifice

To you, you gods, who once divinely promised
That I would be the flower of love in Troy?
I have been demeaned into an outcast,
Translated and betrayed out of my joy.   130
Who's now to guide, accompany or stand by
Me, set at odds and made so odious
To Diomede and noble Troilus?

O false Cupid, none is to blame but you,
You and your mother, who is love's blind goddess.   135
You gave me to believe and I trusted you
That the seed of love was sown in my face
And would grow greener through your constant grace.
But now, alas, that seed with frost is killed
And I from lovers banished forth and exiled.'   140

When this was said, her spirits ebbed away
In a fainting fit and into dream she fell
So that it seemed she heard from where she lay
Cupid the King ringing a silver bell
That filled men's ears from heaven down to hell.   145
At which sound before Cupid there appear
The seven planets, descending from their spheres.

They of all things brought into creation
Have power to rule through their great influence
150   Wind and weather and the course of fortune,
And Saturn, being first up to pronounce,
Treated Cupid with no great reverence
But crabbedly, with cramped look and demeanour,
Behaved in his churlish, rough, thick-witted manner.

155   With rucked and wrinkled face, a lyre like lead,
His chattering teeth sent shivers through his chin,
His eyes were droopy, holes sunk in his head,
His lips were blue, his cheek hollow and thin,
And from his nose there streamed a steady nose-run.
160   And lo too, and behold! Down from his hair
Hung icicles as long as any spear.

Around his belt, his hoary lank locks lay
Tousled and messed and tinselled with the frost.
His cloak and suit were of a gloomy grey,
165   Like faded flags they flapped on him and tossed.
He held a hefty bow in his strong grasp,
A sheaf of cruel arrows in his sash
With hailstone heads and feather-flights of ice.

Then Jupiter, so amiable, so handsome,
170   God of all stars in the firmament
And nurse of all potential and creation,
The son of Saturn but far different:
Fine-featured face, his forehead radiant,
A garland on his head, a lovely spray
175   Woven of flowers that made it seem like May.

His voice was clear, his crystal eyes were keen,
His fair hair had the shine of golden wire,
His cloak and suit were of a glorious green
With gilt appliqué hems on every gore.
180   A gallant sword strapped to his waist he wore
And in his right hand held a sharpened spear
To keep us safe and ward off Saturn's anger.

Next after him came Mars, the god of ire,
Of strife and of debate and all dissension,
185   To quarrel and attack as quick as wildfire,

In armour dressed, helmet and habergeon.
He flaunted at his hip a dangerous falchion
As rusty as the sword he held aloft,
And raged, grimaced, rampaged and bawled and scoffed.

Shaking this sword, before Cupid he comes,   190
Red in the face and glowering balefully.
Like a boar that whets its tusks, he grinds and fumes
And foams at the mouth, making spittle fly.
Brawling, spoiling, keeping himself angry,
He blows coarse, constant blasts upon a horn   195
That has rocked this world with war to its foundation.

Then Phoebus fair, lantern and lamp of light,
Tender nurse of flourishing and fruiting,
Of man and beast; the banisher of night;
By influence and motion cause and spring   200
Of life in the world and every earthly thing;
Without whose comfort, all that has been brought
Into being needs must die and count for naught.

As king in state, he rode his chariot,
The one that Phaeton had once driven off course.   205
The brightness of his countenance when not
Shielded would hurt the eyes of onlookers.
The golden coach, with its gleaming fiery rays,
Four harnessed steeds, each differently coloured,
Drew through the spheres and never slowed or tired.   210

The first was his sorrel, his mane as red as a rose,
Eous his name, the east his element.
The second was the steed called Ethios,
Whitish and pale, inclined to the ascendant.
The third was Peros, hot-blooded and ardent.   215
The fourth, a black steed named Philogeus,
Rolls Phoebus down into the western seas.

Venus attended too, that lovely goddess,
There to plead her son's case, and to make
Her own complaint, dressed with a certain feyness,   220
Half of her costume green, half sable black,
Her golden hair combed, parted and drawn back;
But in her face great variance seemed to be,
Inconstant now, now faithful absolutely.

225 For all her smiling, she was a deceiver.
Her insinuating becks and glances
Could change all of a sudden and reveal her
Serpent anger, in the spit and hiss
Of language that was truly venomous.
230 Her changeableness was there for all to see:
A tear in one, a smile in the other eye.

Betokening this: that bodily desire
Which Venus has it in her power to rule
Is sweet at times, at times bitter and sour,
235 Unstable always, ever variable,
Its pleasures sad, joys unreliable,
Now hot, now cold, now blithe, now full of woe,
Now green in leaf, now withered on the bough.

Then, with his book in hand, came Mercury,
240 So eloquent, adept in rhetoric,
With stylish terms and sweet delivery,
Ready to record in pen and ink,
Composing, singing, setting tune and lyric.
His hood was red, a thing of frills and scallops
245 Worn above his crown like an old-time poet's.

Boxes he bore with fine electuaries
And sugared syrups, aids for the digestion,
Spices belonging to apothecaries
And many other wholesome sweet confections.
250 Clad in scarlet, doctor of medicine,
Gowned and well furred – as such a one should be –
A good and honest man who did not lie.

Next after him came Lady Cynthia,
Last of all and swiftest in her sphere,
255 Darkling and in double-horned regalia
As in the night she likes best to appear –
Blue-grey like lead, a colour that's unclear
Since all her light she borrows from her brother
Titan, her single source. She has no other.

260 Her gown was grey with patterned spots of black
And on her breast a painting of a peasant
Bearing a bunch of thorn sticks on his back,

The theft of which still foiled his climb to heaven.
And so from among themselves, that group of seven
Gods chose Mercury with one assent   265
To be the spokesman in their parliament.

Whoever had been there and interested
To hear his speech, so well turned and precise,
Would have learnt the art of rhetoric, how to put
A weighty meaning in a brief address.   270
Doffing his cap to Cupid, he requests
To know why they'd been summoned there in session
And Cupid promptly made his accusation.

'Whoever', he began, 'blasphemes the name
Of his own god, in either word or deed,   275
To all gods offers insult and brings shame
And deserves hard punishment upon that head.
I say this because yon miserable Cresseid
Who thanks to me was once the flower of love
Offered me and my mother stark reproof,   280

Saying I was the cause of her misfortune;
And furthermore she called my mother Venus
A blind goddess, thus slandering love's queen
In terms defaming and injurious.
So for her life unchaste and lecherous   285
She whom I favoured more than any other
Would lay the blame on me and on my mother.

And since you seven all participate
In power divine and knowledge, you are owed
Due recompense; the slight to your estate   290
Should be, I think, most painfully repaid.
There never was such violence done to gods.
So as much for you as for myself I say,
Come lend a hand: revenge! That is my plea.'

Mercury answered Cupid, 'Royal sir,   295
This counsel I would give your majesty:
Rest your case with the highest planet here.
Let him, with her who's lowest in degree,
Decide how painful Cresseid's fate should be –
Saturn and Lady Cynthia, I mean.'   300
'I am content,' he said, 'I agree to them.'

Thus they passed sentence, Saturn and the Moon,
After due process of deliberation:
Since the injury that Cresseid had done
305   Cupid and Venus was manifest and blatant
She would live in painful torment from then on,
By lovers be despised, abominable,
Beyond the pale, diseased, incurable.

This grievous sentence Saturn took charge of,
310   And coming down to where sad Cresseid lay
He placed upon her head a frosty tipstaff
And spoke as follows in his legal way:
'Your great good looks and your delightful beauty,
Your hot blood and your golden hair also
315   Henceforth forevermore I disallow you.

Your mirth I hereby change to melancholy
Which is the mother of all downcastness,
Your moisture and your heat to cold and dry,
Your lust, presumption and your giddiness
320   To great disease; your pomp and show and riches
To fatal need; and you will suffer
Penury extreme and die a beggar.'

O cruel Saturn, ill-natured and angry,
Your doom is hard and too malicious.
325   Why to fair Cresseid won't you show mercy
Who was so loving, kind and courteous?
Withdraw your sentence and be gracious –
Who never have been: it shows in what you did,
A vengeful sentence passed on fair Cresseid.

330   Then Cynthia, when Saturn moved away,
Left her seat and descended down below
And read decrees on Cresseid where she lay
Spelling out the last word of the law:
'I hereby of your body's heat deprive you
335   And for your sickness there shall be no cure,
Your days to come days solely to endure.

Your eyes so bright and crystal I make bloodshot,
Your voice so clear, unpleasing, grating, hoarse.
Your healthy skin I blacken, blotch and spot.

With livid lumps I cover your fair face.   340
Go where you will, all men will flee the place.
From house to house you'll travel thus, a leper
Begging your way, bearing a cup and clapper.'

When this dark dream, this terrifying vision
Concluded, Cresseid, released, awoke   345
And all that sitting court and convocation
Vanished away. Then up she rose and took
A polished looking glass where she could look
And when she saw her face in it so ruined
God knows if she was not heartsore and stunned.   350

Bitterly weeping, 'Lo, what it means', said she,
'To contradict and aggravate and rouse
Our ill-set gods. Look and take note of me.
My blasphemy is paid for now, alas.
I leave behind all earthly happiness.   355
Alas the day! Alas the time and tide
I ever remonstrated with a god!'

When this was said, a child came from the hall
To notify Cresseid supper awaited.
He knocked first at the door, then gave the call: 360
'Madam, make haste. Your father bids. You're needed.
He is amazed you lie so long prostrated.
He says you spend too long at your devotions,
That the gods well know your prayers and petitions.'

'Fair child,' she said, 'go to my father dear   365
And pray him come to speak with me anon.'
And so he did and 'Daughter,' exclaimed, 'what cheer?'
'Father,' she cried, 'alas, my mirth is gone!'
'How so?' he asked, and she told there and then
What I have told, the vengeance and redress   370
Cupid had exacted for her trespass.

He looked upon her ugly leprous face,
Fair until then as any lily flower.
Wringing his hands, he cried and cried alas
That he had lived to see that woeful hour   375
For well he knew that there would be no cure
For her disease, which doubled his own grief.
And so between them there was pain enough.

Together they lamented long, and then
380 'Father,' said Cresseid, 'I cannot bear
To be recognised, so let me go unknown
To yon leper house beyond the town, and there
Keep me in food and charitable care
And I will live. All happiness on earth
385 Has left me now, I take my fated path.'

For her then, in her cloak and beaver hat,
With cup and clapper, very stealthily
He opened secret gates and let her out,
Conveying her unseen by anybody
390 To a village about half a mile away;
Left her there in the leper colony
And sent in victuals to her every day.

Some knew her well, and others not at all
Because of her appearance, so deformed,
395 Her face all covered over with black boils,
Her colour pale, her lovely skin ringwormed.
Still, they assumed from grief so mildly borne
And yet so cruel, she was of noble kin
And with better will, therefore, they took her in.

400 The daylight died and Phoebus went to rest.
Black nightclouds spread out over the whole sky.
Cresseid, God knows, must have been a stricken guest
As she viewed her plate and pallet in dismay.
Eat or drink she would not, but made ready
405 For bed in a dark corner where she went
To weep alone, and utter this lament.

CRESSEID'S LAMENT

'O sop of sorrow, sunk and steeped in care!
O poor Cresseid! Now and for evermore
Delight on earth is gone, and all your joy.
There is no salve can heal or soothe your sore.
5 Your spirit flags that was flushed up before.
Your fate will doom you, destiny destroy.
Your bliss is banished and fresh fears annoy.
God send me under earth, down through death's door
Where no one's heard the name of Greece or Troy.

'Where is your chamber's cushioned chair and screen   10
And handsome bed and hand-embroidered linen?
The wine and spice, the supper that you supped on?
Where are the cups of gold and silver sheen,
The sweetmeats and the saffron sauce, the clean
Platters they were seasoned and served up on?   15
Your goodly raiment and many a stately gown,
Your shawl of lawn pinned up with its gold pin?
It's as if it never was, your high renown.

'Where is your garden full of herb and spray
And Flora's flowers, which she so pleasantly   20
Planted in every cranny where they sprang,
And where most blithely in the month of May
You'd walk and wade the dew at break of day
And hear the thrush and blackbird at their song
And go with ladies, carolling along,   25
And see the knights beribboned *cap-à-pie*,
Arrayed in ranks to crowd the royal throng.

'Your name and fame that held the world in thrall,
Your triumphs there, the flower among them all,
Fate overturned. Those days won't come again.   30
Your high estate is in decline and fall
So make this leper's hut your banquet hall
And make your bed up now in this straw pen.
For the choice wines and dishes you had then
Take mouldy bread, sour cider and pear-gall.   35
Make do with cup and clapper. They remain.

'My voice once clear from courtly carolling
With ladies whom I used to meet to sing
Is like a rook's, grown husky, hoarse and raucous.
I who once moved attractively, excelling   40
And acknowledged in my beauty, now must hang
My head and turn aside my deformed face.
Nobody wants to see my changed appearance.
Lodged among leper folk, in grief past telling,
I sigh a sore and desolate, Alas!   45

'O ladies fair of Troy and Greece, attend
To my sad state which none may comprehend,
My fickle fortune, lost felicity,

My great distress that no man may amend.
50 Beware in time, the end draws close, attend
And in your mind a mirror make of me.
Remember well what I am now, for ye
For all your strength may come to the same end
Or worse again, if any worse may be.

55 'Your beauty's nothing but a flower that fades,
Nothing your honoured name and famous praise
But mouthfuls of air in other people's ears.
The rot will fester in your cheek's red rose.
Remember and take cognisance: my woes
60 Bear witness to a world that's full of tears.
All wealth on earth is wind that flits and veers;
Beware therefore in time. The hour draws close
And fate is fickle when she plies the shears.'

And so she pleaded her sad destiny
65 And couldn't sleep for weeping out the night,
But all in vain – her grief and painful cry
Could neither remedy nor mend her plight.
A leper woman rose, went to her side
And 'Why', she said, 'do you kick against the wall
70 To destroy yourself and do no good at all?

'Your weeping only doubles all you suffer.
Make virtue of necessity. For my sake,
Go and learn to wave and clap your clapper
And live the life required of leper folk.'
75 There was no help, so out with them she took
Her way from place to place, till cold and hunger
Compelled her to become an utter beggar.

At that same time the garrison of Troy
Led by their chieftain, worthy Troilus,
80 Had beaten down, by war and jeopardy,
The Grecian knights. The rout was marvellous
So back to Troy, triumphant, glorious
In victory, right royally they rode
Past where Cresseid with lepers made abode.

85 Seeing that company, they cried as one
And shook their cups immediately and prayed,

'Good lords, for the love of God in heaven,
Spare us your alms, our lepers' livelihood.'
Then noble Troilus to their cry paid heed
And pitied them and passed by near the place   90
Where Cresseid sat, not knowing who she was.

Upon him then she cast up both her eyes
And at a glance it came into his thought
That he some time before had seen her face.
But she was in such state he knew her not;   95
Yet still into his mind her look had brought
The features and the amorous sweet glancing
Of fair Cresseid, one time his own, his darling.

No wonder then if in his mind he promptly
Received the likeness of her – this is why: 100
The image of a thing by chance may be
So deeply printed in the memory
That it deludes what's in the outer eye,
Presenting a form similar and twinned
To that which had been shaped within the mind.   105

A spark of love then sprang into his heart
And kindled his whole body in a fire.
A fever fit, hot tremblings and a sweat
Came over him: he was ready to expire.
The shield upon his shoulder made him tire.   110
Quickly and often his countenance changed hue
But neither, even so, the other knew.

For knightly piety and in remembrance
Of fair Cresseid, a girdle he took out,
A purse of gold and many shining gemstones,   115
And threw them down into Cresseid's skirt,
Then rode away and didn't speak a word,
Pensive in heart, until he reached the town
And often for great grief almost fell down.

The lepers, to make sure the alms were doled   120
Equally among them, pressed together
Around Cresseid, but when they saw the gold
Each in secret whispered to the other,
'Yon lord has more affection for this leper

125 Than for the rest of us, whatever be
The sense of it. Look at this charity.'

'Yon lord,' she said, 'who is he, can you tell,
Who has shown us such great charity?'
'Yes,' said a leper man, 'I know him well,
130 Sir Troilus it is, high-born and free.'
When Cresseid understood that it was he,
A stun of pain, a stroke sharper than steel,
Went through her heart and to the ground she fell.

When she came to, she sighed sore and bewailed
135 Her woeful plight, and cried in desolation
'Now is my heart with gusts of grief assailed,
Swaddled in sadness, wretched and undone.'
Often she fainted before she quietened,
And in her fainting fits kept crying thus:
140 'O false Cresseid and true knight Troilus!

Your love, your loyalty, your noble ways
I took small notice of when I was happy,
Giddy and loose in loving as I was
And fixed upon the fickle wheel so high.
145 The love I vowed, the faith I plighted you
Were fickle in themselves and frivolous:
O false Cresseid and true knight Troilus!

For love of me you kept desire reined in,
Honourable and chaste in your behaviour.
150 Defender and protector of all women
You always were, their good names' guarantor.
But I with my hot flesh, my mind a fetor,
Was lustful, passionate and lecherous:
Fie, false Cresseid! O true knight Troilus!

155 Lovers beware and take good heed to whom
You give your love, for whom you suffer pain.
I tell you there are few enough among them
To be trusted to give true love back again.
Make proof, your effort will be proved in vain.
160 Therefore I urge you, take them as you find,
For their constancy's like weathercocks in wind.

Because I know in my own self how quick
I am to change, to snap like glass in two,
Because I assume that others are alike
Faithless, inconstant, light, I counsel you: 165
Though some be sound, I warrant they are few.
Who finds truth in his lady, let him praise her.
I myself will be my own accuser.'

When this was said, with paper she sat down
And made her testament as hereunder: 170
'I here commit my bodily remains
For earthworms and for toads to break and enter.
My cup and clapper, the ornaments I wore,
And all my gold the leper folk shall have
To pay for my interment and my grave.   175

This royal ring, set with this ruby red,
Which Troilus sent me for a love token,
I leave to him again when I am dead
To make my death and suffering known to him.
Thus I briefly end and make conclusion: 180
I leave my spirit to stray by paths and springs
With Diana in her wildwood wanderings.

O you have belt and brooch, both, Diomede,
That Troilus gave me for a sign and sealing
Of his true love,' and with those words she died.   185
Then soon a leper man took off the ring
And buried her. There was no tarrying.
Forthwith to Troilus the ring he carried
And made report of how Cresseid had died.

When he had listened to the whole story   190
Of her ordeal, her keen, her testament,
And how she ended in such poverty,
He swooned for grief and fell down in a faint.
The sorrow in his breast could scarce be pent.
Sighing hard, 'I can do', he said, 'no more.   195
She was untrue and woe is me therefore.'

Some said he made a tomb of marble grey
And wrote her name on it and an inscription
In golden letters, above where she lay

200   Inside her grave. These were the words set down:
       'Lo, fair ladies, Cresseid of Troy town,
       Accounted once the flower of womanhood,
       Of late a leper, under this stone lies dead.'

       Now, worthy women, in this short narration
205   Made in your honour and for your instruction,
       For charity, I urge you and I caution:
       Do not pollute your love with false deception.
       Bear in mind the final quick declension
       Of fair Cresseid, as I have told it here.
210   Since she is dead, I speak of her no more.

Seven Fables

THE PROLOGUE

       The fables told by poets in old times
       Are by no means all grounded upon truth
       Yet their attractive style, their craft and themes
       Still make for pleasant listening; and with
5   Good cause, since they, from the beginning,
       Aimed to reprove man's whole wrong way of living
       Under the figure of another thing.

       Just as through a hard unyielding ground,
       If it is laboured with real diligence,
10   The flowers will spring and young shoots of green corn,
       Wholesome and good for human sustenance,
       So sweetly edifying moral lessons
       Spring from the well-worked plot of poetry
       For those who have ears to hear and eyes to see.

15   The shell upon the nut, though hard and tough,
       Holds the kernel and is still delightful.
       Just so there lies a doctrine of great worth
       And fruitfulness beneath a made-up fable.
       And scholars say it is most profitable
20   To mix the merry in with graver matter:
       It makes the spirit lift and time go quicker.

Furthermore, a bow that's always bent
Goes weak and gives and loses all its spring.
The same is true of minds always intent
On earnest thought and constant studying.   25
To alleviate what's sad by adding something
Cheerful is good; Aesop expressed it thus:
Dulcius arrident seria picta iocis.

Which author's Latin, masters, by your leave,
Submitting myself here to your correction,   30
I would convert to mother tongue and prove
Equal to the task of a translation –
Not out of vain presumption of my own,
But at the invitation of a lord
Whose name it is not needful to record.   35

In homely language and rough turns of speech
I have to write, for always eloquence
And rhetoric remained beyond my reach.
Therefore I humbly pray your reverence
That if you find here through my negligence   40
Anything much shortened – or protracted –
By your good will and good grace you'll correct it.

My author in his fables records how
Wild animals spoke sense and understood,
Debated point for point, could argue too,   45
Propound a syllogism and conclude;
He shows by example and similitude
How often humans in their own behaviour
Resemble the wild animals in nature.

No wonder that a man grows like a beast!   50
Loving each carnal and each foul delight
Until no shame can hold or halt his lust,
He soon indulges every appetite
Which through repetition and bad habit
Roots in the mind so ineradicably   55
He is transformed: then bestiality.

This scholar, Aesop, as I have been telling,
Composed in verse of elegance and weight
A coded book, for he was unwilling
That readers high or low should underrate   60

His art; and first of a cock he wrote,
Hunting for food, that found a brilliant stone.
His is the fable you shall hear anon.

THE COCK AND THE JASPER

A cock one time, with feathers pert and bright,
Canty and bold, although he was dirt poor,
Rose and flew to a dunghill at first light,
An early bird, already to the fore,
5   Scraping away, when next thing in the stour
He finds this gemstone under dust and ashes,
Swept out by chance with sweepings from the house.

Giddy young ones, with their minds on nothing
But swanking in the street and being seen
10   Have little interest in their besoming.
They birl the brush to make the floor look clean.
So precious items dropped are very often
Swept from the doorstep out into the yard.
Something like that, in this case, had occurred.

15   He marvels at the stone and then says he,
'O jewel rare, O rich and noble thing,
I may have found you, but you're not for me.
You are a gemstone for a lord or king.
For you to be interred here in the dung
20   Is a great pity, down in the muck and mould,
And you so lovely and worth so much gold.

'And a pity I should find you, who could never
Make clear hues like yours more sheer and clear
Nor prove your great worth any worthier:
25   Little about you gives me heart or cheer.
Let great lords cherish you and hold you dear.
Lesser things are better fit to tempt me,
Like corn or hogwash when my gizzard's empty.

'I'd rather be here scraping with my nails
30   In dust and dirt for dear life, hunting food –
The dregs and dross and little worms and snails
Or any grub at all that does me good –
I'd rather them than gems by the cartload.

While you, for your part, are uninterested
In anything that I desire or need.   35

'You don't have corn, and corn is what I covet.
Your colour calms the eye and feeds the sight
But colour's never going to feed my gullet.
I'm foraging from morning until night
And on the lookout always. But that's it!   40
How can I live on looks? It's food I need,
Not cooked or even hot: I'd eat dry bread.

'But where, gemstone, should be your habitation?
Where should you dwell but in a royal tower?
Where should you sit but on a royal crown   45
Exalted and installed in honour there?
Arise, Sir Jasper, fairest of the fair,
Shake off this filth and go where you should be.
I was not meant for you, nor you for me.'

Leaving the jewel lying on the ground,   50
This cock went foraging upon his way.
But when or how or by whom it was found
I have no sure report, so cannot say.
But the inner point and import and idea
Behind the fable in the original   55
I shall rehearse in plain and homely style.

MORALITAS

The properties of this fair gem are seven:
First, as to colour, it is marvellous,
Like fire partly, partly like the heaven.
It makes a man strong and victorious,   60
Preserves him too when things turn dangerous.
Whoever has this stone, good luck will favour:
No need for him to fear the fire or water.

This noble jasper, with its changing hue,
Signifies true wisdom and true learning   65
Perfected by the exercise of virtue
And far excelling any earthly thing.
This is what inclines men to good living
And makes them glad to strive, and fit to conquer
Every vice and spiritual danger.   70

Who's to be wealthy, kind, courageous?
Who is immune to chance and misadventure?
Who can take charge in home, town-hall or palace
And be a know-nothing? No one, for sure.
75   Knowledge is the wealth that will endure,
That rain won't ruin, nor moth nor rust devour.
To man's soul it is sustenance forever.

This cock, so obsessed with ordinary corn
He scorned a jasper, may in his ignorance
80   Be likened to a fool, who will scoff and scorn
At learning; impervious, thick, a dunce,
He takes a scunner at wise arguments,
The same as a sow that snotters in her gruel,
And spurns pearls in the trough, preferring swill.

85   Ignoramuses are the enemy
Of knowledge and of learning, and possess
No understanding of a thing so worthy,
So noble it is past all earthly price.
The luckiest man is one who spends his days
90   In study of the knowledge of the good:
A man like that fulfils his every need.

But now, alas, this jewel is lost and hid;
No one looks for it, no one pursues
The study of it. We make our wealth our god
95   And turn our souls to paupers, gain to lose.
But talk of this is like the wind that blows.
Therefore I conclude. I have said my say.
Look for the jewel who will, for there it lay.

THE TWO MICE

Aesop tells a tale – Aesop, my author –
Of two mice who were sisters fair and fond.
The elder had a town-house in a borough.
The younger dwelt up country, near at hand
5   And by herself, at times on whinny ground,
At times in corn crops, living hand to mouth
Beyond the pale and off the land, by stealth

This country mouse, when winter came, endured
Cold and hunger and extreme distress.
The other mouse, in town, sat on a board   10
With guild members, an independent burgess,
Exempt from tax, from port and market cess,
Free to go roaming wherever she liked best
Among the cheese and meal, in bin and chest.

One time, well-fed and lightsome on her feet,   15
She thought about her sister on the land
And wondered how she fared, what kind of state
She lived in, in the greenwood out beyond.
So, barefoot and alone, with staff in hand,
Like a poor pilgrim she set out from the town   20
To seek her sister, over dale and down.

Through many wild and lonesome ways she goes,
By moss and moor, by bank and bush and briar,
Calling across the fallow land and furrows,
'Come out to me, my own sweet sister dear!   25
Just give one cheep.' With that the mouse could hear
And knew the voice, since it's in our nature
To recognise our own, and came to meet her.

If you had seen, Lord God! the high excitement
That overcame those sisters when they met,   30
The way the sighs passed back and forth between them,
The way they laughed and then for gladness wept!
They sweetly kissed, they held each other tight
And kept this up until they both grew calm,
Then went indoors together, arm in arm.   35

It was, as I have heard, a simple hut
Made expertly of foggage and of fern,
On stone supports sunk into earth upright,
The jambs set close, the lintel near the ground,
And into it they went and there remained.   40
No fire burned for them nor candle bright
For shady rooms best suit the fly-by-night.

When they were lodged and settled, these poor mice,
The younger sister to the pantry hurries
And brings out nuts and peas instead of spice.   45

Without being there, who'll say how good it was?
The burgess then gets haughty and pretentious,
And asks her sister, 'Is this how you eat?'
'Why,' she replies, 'is there something wrong with it?'

50   'No, by my soul, it's just so ordinary!'
'Madam,' she said, 'you are the more to blame.
When we were born I heard my mother say
The womb we both came out of was the same.
I'm true to her example and good name
55   And to my father's, to their frugal ways.
We own no lands or grounds or properties.'

'Please,' the reply came, 'let me be excused.
My tastes and this rough diet are at odds.
I live a lady's life now and am used
60   To tender meat; it's what my system needs.
These withered peas and nuts and shells and pods
Will break my teeth and hurt me in the stomach,
Now that I know what standards to expect.'

'Well, well, my sister,' says the country mouse,
65   'If you would like, and seeing that you're here,
You're welcome to the free run of the house
And food and drink. Stay on for the year!
It'll warm my heart to keep you and to share.
Our friendship matters more than middling food.
70   Who sniffs at cooking when the company's good?

'Delicacies pall, and fancy dishes,
When they are served up by a scowling face.
A sweetness in the giver's more delicious.
Fine sauces don't make up for lack of grace.
75   A modicum suffices, we do with less
When the carver carves from the goodness of his heart.
A sour-faced host can blink the best cook's art.'

In spite of all this well-disposed advice
The burgess was in no mood to be humoured.
80   She knit her brows above two glowering eyes,
No matter what choice pickings she was offered
Until, at last, she half-sighed and half-sneered,
'Sister, for a country mouse, this stuff
You've laid on makes a spread and is good enough.

'Give over this place, be my visitor   85
Come where I live, and learn when you're my guest
How my Good Friday's better than your Easter.
My dish-lickings more luscious than your feast.
My quarters are among the very safest.
Of cat or trap or trip I have no dread.'   90
'All right,' says sister, and they take the road.

Under cover, through clumps of corn and weed,
Keeping themselves hidden, on they creep.
The elder acts as guide and stays ahead.
The younger follows close and minds her step.   95
By night they make a run, by day they sleep,
Until one morning, when the lark was singing,
They reached the town and thankfully went in.

With none to greet or give them time of day,
The town mouse led on and they made their entry   100
To a residence not far along the way.
Next thing they stood inside a well-stocked pantry
With cheese and butter stacked on shelves, great plenty
Of red meat and hung game, fish fresh and salt,
Sacks full of groats, milled corn and meal and malt.   105

Later, when they felt the urge to dine,
They washed their hands and sat, but said no grace.
There was every course a cook's art could design,
Roast beef and mutton relished slice by slice,
A meal fit for a lord. But they were mice   110
And showed it when they drank not wine but water,
Yet could hardly have enjoyed their banquet better.

Taunting and cajoling all at once,
The elder mouse enquired of her guest
Whether she thought there was real difference   115
Between that chamber and her sorry nest.
'Yes, ma'am,' said she, 'but how long will this last?'
'Forever, I expect, and even longer.'
'In that case, it's a safe house,' said the younger.

The town mouse, for their pleasure, produced more: 120
Groats on a plate and meal piled in a pan,
And didn't stay her hand, you can be sure,

When she doled the oatcakes out and served a scone
Of best white baker's bread instead of brawn,
125   Then stole a tall white candle from a chest
As a final touch, to give the meal more taste.

And so they revelled on and raised a cry,
And shouted 'Hail, Yule, hail!' and made merry.
Yet often care comes on the heels of joy
130   And trouble after great prosperity.
Thus, as they sat in all their jollity,
The steward comes along swinging his keys,
Opens the door and finds them at their ease.

They didn't wait to wash, as I imagine,
135   But rushed and raced and sped off desperately;
The burgess had a hole and in she went,
Her sister no such place of sanctuary.
To see that mouse in panic was great pity,
In dread, bewildered, cornered and astray
140   So that she swooned and nearly passed away.

But God had willed and worked a happy outcome:
The hard-pressed steward could not afford to bide.
He hadn't time to harry or to hunt them
But hurried on, and left the room-door wide.
145   The burgess watched him make his way outside,
Then scooted from her hole and cried on high,
'How are you, sister? Where? Just cheep for me!'

Sure she was doomed, and terrified to die,
This country mouse lay on the ground prostrate.
150   Her heart beat fast, she was like somebody
Shaken by fever, trembling hand and foot,
And when her sister found her in this state
For very pity she broke down in tears,
Then spoke these words, sweet honey to her ears:

155   'Why do you cower like this, dear sister? Rise!
Return to table. Come. The danger's past.'
The other answered in a stricken voice,
'I cannot eat, I am so sore aghast.
I'd rather do Lent's forty days of fast
160   On cabbage water, gnawing peas and beans,
Than feast with you here in such dread conditions.'

Still, being soothed so sweetly, she got up
And went to table where again they sat,
But hardly had they time to drink one cup
When in comes Hunter Gib, our jolly cat,   165
And bids good day. The burgess ups with that
And speedy as the spark from flint makes off.
His nibs then takes the other by the scruff.

From foot to foot he chased her to and fro,
Whiles up, whiles down, as quick as any kid,   170
Whiles letting her go free beneath the straw,
Whiles playing blind man's buff with her, shut-eyed.
And thus he kept that poor mouse in great dread,
Until by lucky chance, at the last call,
She slipped between the hangings and the wall.   175

Then up in haste behind the tapestry
She climbed so high that Gilbert couldn't get her
And hung there by the claws most capably
Till he was gone; and when her mood was better
And she could move with no cat to upset her   180
Down she came on the town mouse, shouting out,
'Sister, farewell. Your feast I set at nought.

'Your spread is spoiled, your cream in curds from worry.
Your goose is good, your sauce as sour as gall,
Your second helpings sure to make you sorry,   185
Mishaps still sure to haunt you and befall.
I thank that curtain and partition-wall
For guarding me against yon cruel beast.
Save me, Almighty God, from such a feast.

'If I were back on home ground, I would stay,   190
Never, for weal or woe, come forth again.'
With that she took her leave and went her way,
Now through the corn, now on the open plain,
Glad to be on the loose and given rein
To gambol and be giddy on the moor.   195
What then became of her I can't be sure,

Though I have heard she made it to her nest
That was as warm as wool, if small and strait,
Packed snugly from back wall to chimney breast

200   With peas and nuts and beans and rye and wheat.
      When she inclined, she had enough to eat
      In peace and quiet there, amidst her store,
      But to her sister's house she went no more.

MORALITAS

      Friends, you will find, if only you'll take heed,
205   This fable masks a good morality.
      As vetches are mixed in with wholesome seed
      So intermingled is adversity
      With joy on earth, and no class is free
      Of trouble or their share of tribulation,
210   But the discontented ones especially,
      Climbers with a craving for possessions.

      Blessed be simple life lived free of dread;
      And blessed be a frugal decency.
      Whoever has enough is not in need,
215   No matter how reduced his portion be.
      Abundance, comfort, blind prosperity
      Often prove the last and worst illusion:
      So to be safe, not sorry in this country
      Content yourself with just a few possessions.

220   O self-indulgent man, glutton for food,
      Worshipper of your own pampered belly,
      Be on your guard! Beware and take good heed:
      Cat prowls and you're the mouse in that cat's eye.
      Your feast and fashion are no guarantee
225   Of peace of mind, sweet thought in quiet sessions.
      For happiness on earth, therefore, I say,
      Content yourself with just a few possessions.

      Friend, your own fireside, though flame be dead,
      Is still the warmest and the place to be;
230   And Solomon's wise words you will have read,
      'Under heaven there is no better way
      To happiness than living virtuously.'
      Wherefore I end with this reassertion:
      To live on earth and know the greatest joy,
235   Content yourself with just a few possessions.

It was in that sweet season, middle June,
When Phoebus with his fair beams shining bright
Had dried the dew off every dale and down
And clad the land in raiment made of light:
One morning as the sun climbed to its height   5
I rose and cast all sloth and sleep aside
And wandered on my own out to a wood.

Sweet was the smell of flowers, white and red,
The singing of the birds a sheer delight.
Broad boughs were in full bloom above my head.   10
Rich herbs and herbage flourished at my feet.
All pleasure and all plenty seemed to meet
In fragrances and birdsong in that place.
And the mild morning made me more rejoice.

Red roses blossoming on twig and bush,   15
The primrose and the violet, purplish-blue:
The jubilating blackbird and the thrush
Were paradise on earth to listen to.
The banks and braes in bloom made a fine show.
And scented herbs and the small birds crying –   20
All these things in contention, sweetly vying.

To keep myself out of the burning sun,
I lay among sweet-smelling flowers, at ease
Beneath a hawthorn tree in shadows green,
Then covered up my head and closed my eyes.   25
I fell asleep beneath those balmy boughs
And dreamt I saw come towards me through the wood
The handsomest man I ever had encountered.

His gown was made of cloth as white as milk,
His outer cloak of camlet, murky purple,   30
His hood of scarlet, bordered well with silk
Hanging down like hackles to his girdle.
His bonnet round, in the old-fashioned style.
Beard white; eyes wide and grey; a head of hair
That curled and lay in locks upon each shoulder.   35

He carried in his hand a roll of paper.
A swan's-quill pen stuck out behind his ear.
An inkhorn, a neat gilt pen container
And silken pouch hung from the belt he wore.
40 Thus was he tackled trimly in his gear,
Of stature large, imposing countenance.
Then up to where I lay he made advance

Saying, 'God bless you, son', and I was glad
Of those warm words and of his company.
45 I greeted him respectfully and said,
'Welcome, father', and as he sat by me
Went on, 'My good master, may I kindly
Ask who you are, your profession and your name,
Why you come here, and where you call your home?'

50 'My son,' said he, 'I am a well-born man.
None will deny my native place is Rome –
And I got my early schooling in that town.
I studied civil law there a long time
And now forever heaven is my home.
55 My name is Aesop: works that I have written
Are known and conned by many a learned man.'

'O master Aesop, poet laureate,
God knows you are most welcome here to me
For are you not the very one who wrote
60 Those fables, which are make-believe, maybe,
But full of wisdom and morality?'
'Fair son,' said he, 'I am that selfsame man.'
God knows indeed my heart was happy then.

'Aesop,' I said, 'my master venerable,
65 Grant, I pray, this most heartfelt petition:
Deign to tell me, please, a well-turned fable
Leading to a good moral conclusion.'
He shook his head and answered, 'Ah, my son,
What good is it to tell a made-up tale
70 When holy preachers preach to no avail?

'In this world now, it seems that few or none
Hear the word of God with due devotion.
Their ears are deaf, their hearts as hard as stone.

Sin is blatant, flaunts without correction,
And earthbound instinct drags the pure heart down.   75
The world's so rotted, bletted, cankered black,
My tales are told to small or no effect.'

'Yet, gentle sir,' said I, 'I would request –
Not to disrespect your reservation –
That you would frame a tale around a beast,   80
A fable with a moral, a narration
That might contribute to my education,
Something worth remembering.' 'Well, I shall,'
Said Aesop, and proceeded with this tale:

                              *

A hunting lion, tired from his run,   85
Needing to catch his breath and have a rest
Lay warming breast and belly in the sun
Under a tree in a pleasant forest.
Next thing a troop of mice skips from their nest,
Nifty and nimble, dancing briskly round,   90
And step-dance two or three times on the lion.

He lay so still the mice were not afraid,
But advanced, retired, jigged and reeled apace,
Some plucking at the whiskers of his beard,
Some bold enough to scratch him in the face,   95
Lightsome and blithe, the merriest of mice,
Till the noble lion woke at last and pounced
And clamped down on the one who led the dance.

She gave a cry, and the rest all cried, aghast,
And scattered and hid hurriedly wherever.   100
The leader in the lion's paw held fast
Laments 'Alas, alas', and weeps in terror.
'O woe me,' she wails, 'I'm a prisoner,
And must face trial now for my offence.
My life and death hang trembling in the balance.'   105

The lion spoke then to that stricken mouse,
'You miserable, despicable, mean thing,
Overly familiar and presumptuous,
Treating my person as your dancing ring:
Do you not know I am both lord and king   110

Of all the beasts?' 'Yes,' said the mouse, 'I do,
But you lay so quiet there, I mistook you.

'So, my lord, I beseech your majesty
To hear my plea and attend in patience.
115 Take good account first of my poverty
And then consider your magnificence.
Consider too how simple negligence –
A thing not done with malice or presumption –
Should sooner receive gracious remission.

120 'We'd had our fill, enjoyed in great abundance
The proper dues and needs of our condition;
The pleasant season prompted us to dance
And sport ourselves in our own natural fashion.
You lay so still, had such a dead expression,
125 We thought, by my soul, that you were dead indeed.
Why else would we have danced upon your head?'

'This is a false excuse,' the lion said,
'And will not in the least, be warned, avail.
Supposing that I had indeed been dead
130 And what you'd found was a stuffed animal,
A straw lion, my skin alone, then still
You should have been in awe and kneeling down
Because it bore the imprint of my person.

'Your crime is such you have no defence.
135 What you've committed is *lèse-majesté*.
There is no case, you have no arguments
To absolve yourself or those accessory.
Wherefore your disgraceful doom shall be
To suffer death, as is decreed for treason –
140 And mount the gallows, struggling and squealing.'

'Ah no, my lord, I beseech your royal grace
As crowned head of the beasts to moderate
Your anger: let your fit of fury pass,
Let mercy change your mind, be temperate.
145 Your honour has been injured, I admit,
And I deserve the sentence you decree –
Unless you relent, my lord, and pardon me.

'In every judge, mercy and compassion
Should act as learned friends and counsellors.
Justice is cruelty when mercy's wanting   150
As the highest, holiest law we know allows.
When rigour won't relent and sits and glowers
Who will believe the bench impartial? None
Or very few, unless there is compassion.

'When it comes to martial honour too you know   155
The value of a victory depends
Upon the strength of the opponent, how
Fiercely he fights or manfully defends.
What praise or honour, when the battle ends,
Is due to one whose foe would not or could not   160
Stand to and meet and match him in the fight?

'To kill and then devour a thousand mice –
What's manly about that in a great lion?
The weaker the defeated is, the less
Enhanced is a strong conqueror's renown.   165
It will demean and mar your reputation
To kill a mouse whose one defence was free
Reliance on your excellency's mercy.

'Moreover, it's below your majesty
Whose diet day by day is so delicious   170
To soil your teeth and lips by eating me.
My blood would turn your stomach and cause illness.
There is infection in the meat of mice
To which lions, in particular, are prone,
Used as they are to noble venison.   175

'My life's of little value, my death less.
Yet if I live, who knows, it could happen
I'd help your highness in a chance distress,
For often one who seems in no condition
To rescue some imperilled lord from prison   180
Will prove to be the only one who can.
Which case, if fortune failed, could be your own.'

When this was said, the lion reconsidered.
His anger was assuaged, he heeded reason,
And letting mercy moderate his hard   185
Pronouncement, granted the mouse remission,

Opened his paw and dropped her. She fell down,
Then reached her two hands heavenward and cried,
'Almighty God reward you for this deed.'

190   When she was gone, the lion went to hunt
Since he never gathered food but lived on prey,
Killing both wild and tame, as was his wont,
Spreading terror over the whole country
Until at last the people found a way
195   To trap this cruel lion. From hemp cord
They wove strong nets and set them in the road

The lion used when he was on the prowl,
Stretching them tight across from tree to tree;
Then lined up in the wood to await the kill.
200   The hounds and horns create a wild melee.
Along the road the lion starts to flee,
Trips on the net, gets tangled head and foot,
And for all his strength and struggle, can't get out.

He turned and twisted, gave a hideous roar,
205   Strained, contorted, kicked this way and that,
But all to no avail. His reign was over.
The more he turned, the tighter drew the net,
The purchase of the ropes being so complete
On every part of him; and thus forlorn,
210   He ceased his struggle and began to mourn.

'O crippled lion, lying here so low,
Where is the power of your magnificence
Of which earth's animals all stood in awe
And feared to look upon your countenance?
215   No hope or help, no succour or defence
Are left to me. Alas, I am tied down
In sturdy bonds and certain to be slain.

'There's nobody to right my wrongs and wreak
Vengeance for me, none to respect my crown.
220   Who'll help me now? Come to my aid and break
These bonds, release me from this prison?'
The minute he had made this lamentation
It so happened the little mouse came by
And overheard the lion's grievous cry.

And suddenly it came into her mind   225
This was the lion who had pardoned her,
Saying, 'I'd be unnatural and unkind
Not to repay in some small part the favour
You graciously did me', and so she called her
Companions loud and long, repeatedly,   230
To come and help, which they did immediately.

'Look,' said the mouse, 'this is that same lion
Who pardoned me when I was in his power.
Now here he lies, heartbroken, making moan
Like a prisoner tied up inside a tower.   235
Unless we help, he cannot hope for succour.
But one good turn deserves another, so,
Do we free him?' 'Sister,' they said, 'we do.'

They took no knife, their teeth were sharp enough –
To watch them at their work was a great wonder: 240
It didn't matter that the ropes were tough,
They went for them, top, bottom, over, under,
Bit bindings till the net just fell asunder,
Then bade him rise. He sprang immediately
Up on his feet with thanks; and went his way.   245

The lion is at large now, out of danger,
Loosed and delivered, set at liberty
By little beasts, possessed of little power,
Because, as you have heard, he showed them pity.
'Master,' I asked, 'does a morality   250
Attach to this fable?' 'Yes,' he said, 'a good one.'
'Please,' I said then, 'share it, in conclusion.'

MORALITAS

This mighty lion, to my way of thinking,
May signify a prince or emperor
Or any potentate – say a crowned king –   255
Who should be a sure guide and governor
Of his nation, rule and administer
Justice in the land, but whose control
Slips as dull sloth and lust possess his soul.

The pleasant sheltered forest, calm and leafy,   260
With its birdsong and delightful flowers

Stands for the world and its prosperity
Where sorrows stalk and shadow empty pleasures.
Just as the rose fades, faced with the cold winter's
265 Frost and wet, so does the world play false
To those flushed up with lustful self-indulgence.

These little mice are the common people,
Thoughtless, wilful, without discipline,
Who, seeing princes and their lords neglectful
270 Of justice and its proper execution
Have no fear of rising in rebellion
And disobeying, since the dread is gone
That kept them subject to their sovereign.

By means of this fable then Your Worships
275 May take into consideration pity,
Learn sometimes to pardon great relapse
And mitigate your cruelty with mercy,
For it often chances a man of low degree
Will give back as he got according as
280 His lord to him was merciful or harsh.

Who knows how soon a lord of high renown,
But slovenly, degraded, carnal, vain,
Will suffer ruin and be overthrown
By Fortune, that false mistress and the main
285 Decider of the fates of unjust men:
She leads them a mad dance, she makes them blind
To falls they should have reckoned on beforehand.

Those countrymen who set and stretched the net
Which made the lion captive – they resemble
290 Resentful men, the wronged who watch and wait,
Hurt carved into their hearts as into marble.
No need for more expounding on this gospel.
Kings and lords should know and catch my drift.
The world supplies enough examples of it.

295 Having pronounced thus, Aesop said, 'My son,
I beseech you and all men to pray
That this country be kept clear of treason,
Justice reign, and those in authority
Stay loyal to their sovereign night and day.'

And with these words he vanished and I woke,   300
Then homeward through the wood my journey took.

THE PREACHING OF THE SWALLOW

God's great wisdom and his marvellous workings,
The deep insight of the Omnipotent,
Are in themselves so perfect and discerning
They far excel our merely human judgement,
All things for Him being ever present,   5
As they are now and at all times shall be
In the full sight of His divinity.

Because our soul, imprisoned in the body,
Is bound and fettered by the sensual
We may not clearly understand or see   10
God as he is, or things celestial.
Our murky, gross, death-bound material
Blindfolds the operation of the spirit
Like a prisoner shut in darkness and chained up.

In his *Metaphysics* Aristotle says   15
The soul of man resembles a bat's eye,
The bat that hides daylong from the sun's rays,
Then in the gloaming ventures forth to fly –
Her eyes are weak, the sun she must not see.
Soul's vision too is faulty and unsure,   20
Missing true things manifest in Nature.

For God is in His power infinite,
Man's soul feeble, diminutively small,
Weak in understanding and unfit
To comprehend the One who contains all.   25
None should presume by their own natural
Reason to unravel the Trinity.
They should have firm faith and let reason be.

Nevertheless we may gain comprehension
Of God Almighty and learn from His creatures   30
That He is just, good, wise and most benign.
Take, for example, the loveliness of flowers,
Their rich, sweet smells, the pleasure of their colours,

Some green, some blue, some purple, white and red –
35   Their variety the gift of His Godhead.

The firmament, star-stippled sheer and clear,
From east to west rolling round and round;
Every planet in its proper sphere
And motion making harmony and sound;
40   The fire, the air, the water and the ground –
They should suffice to demonstrate to us
The intelligence of God in all his works.

Consider well the fish that swim the sea,
Consider too the beasts that dwell on land,
45   Birds in their strength and beauty as they fly
Cleaving the air with large or small wingspan,
Consider then His last creation, man
Made in His image and similitude:
By these we know that God is just and good.

50   He created all things for man's benefit,
For his subsistence and his preservation
Upon the earth, beneath it and above it,
In weight, in number and correct proportion;
Differentiating time and every season
55   To our advantage and convenience –
As is daily evident from experience.

Summer comes in his garment green and cheerful,
Every hem and pleating flounced with flowers,
Which Flora, queen and goddess bountiful,
60   Has lent that lord for his due season's hours,
And Phoebus with his golden beams and glamours
And heat and moisture hazing from the sky
Has decked and dyed with colours pleasantly.

Next then warm autumn when the goddess Ceres
65   Heaps the barn floors high with her abundance,
And Bacchus, god of wine, replenishes
Her casks for her in Italy and France
With heady wines and liquors that entrance;
And the plenty of the season fills that horn
70   Of plenty never filled with wheat or corn.

Then gloomy winter, when stern Aeolus,
God of the wind, with his bleak northern blasts
Tears open, rends and rips into small pieces
The green and glorious garment summer sports.
Now fairest flowers must fade and fall to frosts 75
And the nearly perished songbirds modulate
Their sweet notes to lament the snow and sleet.

The dales are flooded deep with dirty puddles,
Hills and hedges covered with hoar frost,
The sheltering bough is stripped and shrinks and shudders 80
In cruel winds as winter does its worst.
All creatures of the wild withdraw perforce
From blasted farmlands to hole up and cower
Against the cold in burrow, den or lair.

Then when winter's gone there comes the spring – 85
Summer's secretary, bearing his seal –
When columbine peeps out after hiding
Her fearful head beneath the frosty field.
The thrushes and the blackbirds sing their fill.
The lark on high, soaring far up yonder, 90
Is seen again, and other little songsters.

That same season, one mild and pleasant morning,
Delighted that the bitter blasts were gone,
I walked in woods to see the flowers blooming
And hear the thrush and songbirds at their song, 95
And as I walked and looked and wandered on
Enjoyed the prospect of the vernal soil
Ready for seed, in good heart, fresh and fertile.

Free and easy like that, on I go,
Happy watching labourers at their tasks, 100
Some digging ditches, some behind the plough,
Some in full stride, sowing the seed broadcast,
The harrow hopping off the ground they'd paced.
For one who loved the corn crop, it was joy
To see them at their work there, late and early. 105

Then as I stood beneath a bank to rest,
Heartened and elated by the scene,
There swooped into the hedge in sudden haste
And quickly lit and roosted on the green

110　　Leaves of the hawthorn bush that was my screen
　　　　A flock of small birds, everywhere at once,
　　　　Innumerable, amazing, marvellous.

　　　　Among them next I heard a swallow cry
　　　　From where she perched on the top branch of the thorn,
115　　'You birds there on your branches, hear, O hear me,
　　　　And be instructed; understand and learn.
　　　　When dangers loom or when perils threaten
　　　　The wise course is to foresee and take care:
　　　　Plan, make provision, think, forestall and store.'

120　　The lark laughed and then answered, 'Lady Swallow,
　　　　What have you seen that's making you afraid?'
　　　　'Do you see', she said, 'yon fellow with his plough
　　　　Sowing – look – hemp and lint, broadcasting seed?
　　　　In no time at all the lint will braird
125　　And when it's grown that churl will make a net
　　　　And already plots to snare us under it.

　　　　'So my advice is this: when he is gone
　　　　This evening we descend and with our claws
　　　　Scrape every seed out of the earth and then
130　　Eat it immediately, for if it grows
　　　　We'll surely rue the day – and with good cause.
　　　　Thus straightway we shall remedy our case
　　　　Since the one who takes precautions suffers less.

　　　　'For scholars say it is not sufficient
135　　To consider only things that you can see,
　　　　Prudence being an inner discipline
　　　　That causes one to look ahead and be
　　　　Aware what good or evil end is likely,
　　　　Which course of action better guarantees
140　　Our safety in the last analysis.'

　　　　The lark laughed at the swallow then for scorn
　　　　And said she fished before she'd found a net –
　　　　'The baby's easy dressed before it's born.
　　　　What grows is never all that has been set;
145　　It's time enough to bend and bare the neck
　　　　When the blow is aimed; most fated's like to fall.'
　　　　And so they scorned the swallow, one and all.

Despising thus her salutary lesson
The birds departed in a sudden flurry;
Some whirled across the fields in quick commotion,   150
Some to the greenwood in a panicked hurry.
Left on my own then, out there in the country,
I took my staff and headed back for home
In wonderment, as in a waking dream.

Time passed, then came the pleasant month of June   155
When seeds that had been sown earlier
Grew high round corncrakes craking out their tune
And hiding places of the leaping hare.
So again one morning l went roving where
I found that same hedge and green hawthorn tree   160
Which held those birds I've spoken of already.

And as I stood there, by the strangest chance,
Those same birds you have heard me talk about –
Maybe because it was one of their haunts,
A safer, maybe, or a lonelier spot –   165
They lighted down and when they had alit
The swallow cheeped, still harping on her theme:
'Woe to the one who won't beware in time.

'You birds, so blinded and so negligent,
Unmindful of your own prosperity,   170
Lift up your eyes, see clearly what has happened:
Look at the lint now growing on yon lea.
That is the stuff I argued once that we
Should uproot, while it was seed, from the earth.
Now it's a crop, young stalks, a sprouting braird.   175

'While it's still tender, immature, and small,
Go, stop it growing. Pull it up this minute.
It makes my heart beat fast and my flesh crawl,
It gives me nightmares just to think of it.'
The other birds then cried out and protested   180
And told the swallow: 'That lint will do us good.
Is linseed not our little fledglings' food?

'When the flax is grown and the seed-pods ripe
We'll feast and take our fill then of the seed,
And sing and swing on it and peep and pipe.   185
Who cares about the farmer?' 'So be it,'

The swallow said. 'But I am sore afraid
You'll find things bitter that now seem so sweet
When you're scorched and skewered on yon fellow's spit.

190   'The owner of that lint field is a fowler,
A stealthy hunter, full of craft and guile,
We'll all be prey for him, birds of a feather,
Unless we watch and match him, wile for wile.
Our kith and kin he has been wont to kill:
195   He spilled their blood for sport, most casually.
God and his holy cross save and preserve me.'

These little birds who hardly gave a thought
To dangers that might fall by misadventure
Ignored the swallow; they set her words at nought
200   As they rose up and flew away together,
Some to the wood, some to the heather moor.
Noontime was approaching; I took my staff
And bearing all in mind I headed off.

The flax grew ripe, the farmer pulled it green,
205   Combed and dressed the seed-heads, stooked the beets,
Then buried it and steeped it in the burn,
Spread and dried it, beetled the stalks to bits,
And scutched and heckled all to tow in plaits.
His wife then spun a linen thread from it
210   Which the fowler took and wove into a net.

The winter came, the freezing wind did blow,
Green woods wilted in the weltering wet,
Hoar frosts hardened over hill and hollow,
Glens and gullies were slippery with sleet.
215   The frail and famished birds fell off their feet –
Useless to try to shelter on bare boughs,
So they hied them to the haggard and outhouses.

Some to the barn, some to the stacks of corn
Fly for shelter and settle themselves in.
220   The fowler sees them coming and has sworn
He'll catch and make them pay for pilfering.
He spreads his nets and in preparation
Clears a space, shovels the surface snow off,
Then tops it level with a layer of chaff.

The small birds saw the chaff and were distracted.   225
Believing it was corn they lighted down.
The net was the last thing they suspected.
They set to work to scrape and grub for grain
With no thought of the fowler's cunning plan.
The swallow on a little branch nearby,   230
Fearing a trick, shouted this warning cry:

'Scrape in that chaff until your nails are bleeding,
You're won't find any corn, no matter what.
Do you think yon churl's the sort who would be feeding
Birds out of pity? No, that chaff is bait.   235
I'm warning you, away, or you'll get caught.
The nets are set and ready for their prey.
Beware in time therefore, or rue the day.

'Only a fool is going to risk life
And honour on a useless enterprise;   240
Only a fool persists when he's warned off
And continues to ignore all good advice.
Only a fool fails to take cognisance
Of what the future holds and thinks the present
Forever stable, safe and permanent.'   245

These little birds, half-dead from hunger now
And foraging for dear life for their food,
Paid no heed to the preaching of the swallow
Although their grubbing did them little good.
That was the moment when she understood   250
Their foolish hearts and minds were obdurate
And as she fled the fowler drew his net.

Alas, it was heartbreaking then to see him
Butcher those little songbirds out of hand
And hear, when they understood their hour had come,   255
How grievously they sang their last and mourned.
Some he hit with his stick and left there stunned,
Some he beheaded, on some he broke the neck,
Some he just stuffed alive into his sack.

And when the swallow saw that they were dead,   260
'Behold', she said, 'the fate that often follows
Those who won't take counsel or pay heed
To words of prudent men or wisest scholars.

Three times and more I warned them of the perils.
265 Now they are dead. I am saddened and heartsore.'
She flew off and I saw her then no more.

MORALITAS

Lo, worthy people, that noble scholar Aesop,
A poet worthy to be laureate,
When he relaxed from more exacting work
270 Wrote this fable and other fables like it
Which at this moment serve to educate
And edify, because they have a meaning
That furthers good and accords with reason.

This tenant churl, this mean ignoble peasant
275 Sowing chaff, making small birds his prey,
He is the fiend in exile from high heaven,
An angel cast down by the deity,
Ever unrelenting and unweary,
Apt to poison man's thought and his soul
280 Which Christ redeemed most dearly for us all.

And when the soul (figured as seed in earth)
Yields to the flesh and sensual temptation,
Then wickedness begins to bloom and braird
As mortal sin, which issues in damnation.
285 Reason is thus blindfolded by passion
And carnal lust springs green and takes deep root
Daily and deliciously through habit.

Thus practised and confirmed, habituated,
Sin ripens and all shame is cast aside.
290 The fiend cross-weaves and webs his cruel net
And lurks in secret under pleasure's bed.
Then on the field he sows chaff far and wide –
Lusts of the flesh, insubstantial, empty,
Will-o'-the-wisps and vacuous vanity.

295 These hungry birds stand for those poor wretches
Grubbing in the world for goods and gain,
Busy rooting round for earthly riches
Which, like the chaff, are insubstantial, vain,
Of no real value, fleeting, false, a bane –

As dust whipped up and whisked before the wind   300
Flung in poor wretches' faces makes them blind.

This swallow, who escaped free from the snare,
May signify in turn the holy preacher
Warning his flock to watch and still beware
The wicked fiend, our cruel fowler-netter –   305
Devious, unsleeping, vigilant, ever
Ready as wretches scrape in the world's chaff
To draw the net and spit them on his gaff.

Alas what grief, what weeping and what woes
There will be when the body's reft from soul.   310
Down to the worms' kitchen body goes,
Soul to the fire, to everlasting dole.
What help's your chaff then, will your goods console
When Lucifer has you captured in his sack
And brought to hell, to hang there by the neck?   315

To keep these nets in mind and not lose sight
But stay on guard against this chaff, you must
Beware most when you are most fortunate
For in this world no thing is made to last;
No man knows how his own lot has been cast,   320
How long he'll live, what destination he
Is going to for all eternity.

Therefore let us pray while we're alive
For these four things: the first is to shun sin;
The second is to cease from war and strife;   325
The third to practise charity and love;
The fourth, and the most crucial, is to win
Heavenly bliss, and hence our lives to hallow.
And so concludes the preaching of the swallow.

THE FOX, THE WOLF AND THE CARTER

Once upon a time, in a wilderness
(According to the author of my tale)
There lived a wolf, a reiver ravenous
Round field and fold, freebooting in great style,
Killing, culling, plundering at will,   5

Showing no fear or favour: he rampaged.
The strong weren't spared. The weaker ones were savaged.

One day when he was on his usual hunt
He chanced to meet a fox upon the way.
10   But fox had spied him and as was his wont
Dissembled. Acted scared. Bowed. Bade good day.
'Well met,' said he, 'friend wolf.' Then down he lay
And wolf falls for it, reaches out his hand
And says, 'Sir fox! Come now. Stop cringing. Stand!

15   'Where have you been these ages from my sight?
We must link up. You be my agent. Be
My hen-snatcher, my roost-raider by night.
Creep into coops. Go on a fowling spree.'
'O sir,' said fox, 'that's not a job for me.
20   You know what happens. The minute I appear,
There's panic in each henhouse, pen and byre.'

'No,' cries the wolf. 'Not so. For you can creep
Low on your knees and nab hens by the head,
Can make a sudden tackle on a sheep,
25   Then shake and rake and rack him till he's dead.'
'Sir,' says the fox, 'you know my coat is red
And so well watched, in spite of all my cunning
There's not a beast now doesn't see me coming.'

'Still,' said the wolf, 'by brakes and braes you wend
30   And slink along and steal up on your prey.'
'Sir,' said the fox, 'you know how these things end.
They catch my scent downwind from far away
And scatter fast and leave me in dismay.
They could be lying sleeping in a field
35   But once I'm close they're off. It puts me wild.'

'But', cried the wolf, 'you can come down upwind.
For every trick they work you have a wile.'
'Sir,' said the fox, 'no beast that isn't blind
But could escape from me by many a mile.
40   How can I fend when all my old schemes fail?
These pointed ears! These two grey eyes! I'm known
Before I'm seen at all. My cover's gone.'

'Oh,' cried the wolf, 'I fear you tell a lie.
You weave and dodge to keep your secrets safe.
You beat about the bush. You're far too sly.   45
But nothing you can say will put me off.
Lies and false trails won't give you the last laugh
So listen well to what I'm saying to you:
Do what you're bid. Obey before you're made to.'

'Sir,' said the fox, 'it's Lent, you understand,   50
And I can't fish. I dare not wet my feet.
I'm starved for a stickleback, for here on land
There's not a thing that you or I can eat.
But when Easter comes, when red meat and white meat
Fall off the bone, when kid and lamb and hen   55
Turn on the spits, I'll be your agent then.'

'So,' said the wolf in rage, 'you think you can
Get round me still? Am I wet behind the ears?
I'm far too old for all this carry-on.
Where do you think I've been these thirty years?'   60
'Sir,' said the fox, 'for God's sake, calm your fears.
You're so far wrong, you don't make any sense:
I could hang myself to prove my innocence.

'But now I see how foolish I have been.
No man should ever argue with his boss.   65
I was playing games. In no way did I mean
To give offence. So please, sir, don't be cross.
I'm at your service now and will take orders
At any time, wherever, night or day.'
'Well,' cried the wolf, 'I like well what you say,   70

'But even so, you'll have to swear an oath
To be true to me and put me always first.'
'Fie,' cried the fox, 'what's this? You doubt my faith?
Your suspicions are an insult. I protest!
And yet, all right, to set your mind at rest   75
I swear by Jupiter, on pain of death,
I'll keep my word to you while I draw breath.'

With that a carter with his cart and creels
Came rattling along, and fox took note.
A whiff of herring hit him in the nostrils   80
And he whispers to the wolf, 'Can you smell that?

It's herring that your man has in that cart
So my advice is this: we study ways
To lay in fish to tide us through fast days.

85 'Now I'm your agent, I have to find supplies
But you don't have two brass pence to rub together,
And if I begged and went down on my knees
On all fours here before him in the gutter
Yon gobshite wouldn't hand one herring over.
90 But still, no matter, wait a while and see:
I'll put one over on him presently.

'The thing is this: if we're to rip him off
You'll have to lend a hand and take a chance
For the man who's not prepared to make a move
95 To help himself I must discountenance.
I intend to go to work now all at once.
All you need do is walk behind the cart
And lift the herring. Thus each will play his part.'

With that he made a far, free-ranging detour,
100 Then stretched out in the middle of the road
Pretending to be dead, and making sure
He looked it, that the whites of his eyes showed
Like one who'd perished there for want of food.
His tongue lolled out a hand's breadth from his head
105 As he lay stiff and still. Perfectly dead.

The carter found the fox and he was glad,
Boasting to himself what he would do:
'At the next stop, I'll have the fellow flayed
And fox-skin mittens cut.' Then heel and toe
110 He danced a dance as lightsome as a doe
As if he'd heard a piper playing reels.
Then paused and gazed and hunkered on his heels.

'Here lies', he said, 'the devil in the ditch.
I've never seen the like of it before.
115 Some mongrel mangled you and made dispatch
And sank you in that sleep where you don't snore.
So, Sir Fox, you are all the welcomer.
Some housewife's curse, some malison, I fear,
For raiding roosts has lighted on you here.

'No pedlar's going to purchase you. Your pelt   120
Won't make him gloves or trimmings or a purse.
I'm going to keep a hold of it myself
And cut and sew it into hand-warmers.
It won't be shipped across the sea to Flanders.'
And there and then he grabbed the fox's heels   125
And landed him high up among the creels.

Then cheerfully he takes the horse's head.
The wily fox takes heed and has begun
To bite the plug and loosen and unload
Herring from the creel-mouth, one by one,   130
A shoal of them, a fish-slide pouring down.
The wolf keeps close and gathers them at speed.
The carter sings 'Halloo' right long and loud.

But at a burn he turns and looks about.
The fox leaps clear and legs it from the creels.   135
The carter would have hit a deadly clout
But fox has shown a clean pair of heels
And headed for his den. Then carter howls:
'A gutting I'll give you, a herring-treat,
A second helping that you'll not forget.'   140

'Be damned,' the fox said, 'for we'll never meet.
I heard you planning how you'd use my skin.
Your hands will never feel those mittens' heat.
God's curse you, hellion, you and all your kin.
Go sell your goods. I won't be in the bargain.   145
Sell herring at the highest price you can –
Whatever herring's left. Farewell, fishman!'

The carter shook with anger where he stood.
'It serves me right,' he said, 'I missed the cur.
I should have had a staff of seasoned wood   150
To hammer him and break his sleekit shoulder.'
With that he faced the ditch and vaulted over
And hacked himself a staff and dressed it clean,
A heavy, hard, straight stick of holly green.

Off went the fox then to his boss accomplice   155
And found him by the herring, standing guard.
'Sir,' said the fox, 'can I not pierce defences

Stylishly and well? It is always hard
To keep a brave man from his just reward.'
160 The wolf agreed. He said, 'I do confess
You're ever capable and brave and wise.

'But what', he went on, 'was that idiot shouting
When he hunted you and howled and shook his fist?'
'Sir,' said the fox, 'his words are worth repeating.
165 A herring treat, he mocked me, I had missed.
A second helping that I'd never taste.'
'And was there such a treat?' 'There was. I'd caught it
But it weighed too much and nearly tore my teeth out.

'But truly, boss, if we could land that catch
170 It would see us through our forty days of fast.'
Then wolf said, 'I will risk it. We must fetch
That Lent-food here. My strong teeth can lay waste
To herring-bone and basket-work, I trust.'
'Indeed,' the fox replied, 'I often wished
175 For your bite and brawn to help me raise that fish.

'It's like a side of salmon, more or less,
Shiny as a partridge eye, and luscious –
Worth more than all those herring on the grass,
Three times as tasty, three times more precious.'
180 'Then,' cried the wolf, 'advise me on my course.'
'Sir,' said the fox, 'keep strictly to my plan
And all being well, we will outwit our man.

'First you must make a far, free-ranging detour,
Then stretch down in the middle of the road
185 With head and feet and tail out, making sure
Your tongue is lolling and your two eyes closed.
Then find a hard support to hold your head
And ignoring every threat that may appear,
Stay motionless until the coof comes near.

190 'And though you see a staff, continue quiet.
Don't move a muscle and don't be afraid.
Keep eyes tight closed as though they'd been put out.
Don't shrink at knee or neck or foot or head.
That carter clown will imagine you are dead
195 And quickly lug and lift you by the heels
As he did me, and fling you on the creels.'

'But wait,' the wolf says, 'for as sure as God
I'll be too weighty for the coof to lift.'
'Sir,' said the fox, 'he is a hefty bawd.
One heave and you'll be high and dry aloft. 200
But this much I can guarantee you: if
You haul that herring safely out of there,
You needn't fish again till Lent next year.

I now say *in principio* and pray
A blessing on your body, head to toe, 205
Which means henceforth you travel on your way
Protected against death. God speed you. Go!'
Up springs the wolf then and away out through
The gaps and gates, detouring to avoid
The fishman coming up along the road. 210

He makes a sturdy pillow of a stone,
Then stretches out his four feet and his head,
Lets his tongue loll and settles himself down,
Just as the fox instructed, to feign dead.
He's over any fear he might have had. 215
The only thing he thinks is 'herring-treat'.
The last thing on his mind is fox-deceit.

Along the carter comes then, riding high
Now that the load is lighter, in a rage
That fox had fooled him and had got away, 220
Mad to get his own back. At which stage
The wolf comes into view, at his old dodge,
Stiffly stretched in the middle of the road.
The carter (you'll have guessed) jumps off the load.

Under his breath he swears, 'I was tricked once. 225
Be damned if I am going to be again.
The hammering I'll give you in your bones
Your friend should have been given first time round.'
With that he lifts the holly in his hand
And comes down with such force upon his head 230
The wolf convulsed and very nearly died.

Three blows he bore before he found his feet
And though he still was strong enough to flee
The blows had blinded him: he had been hit
So hard he hardly saw the light of day. 235

The fox, who watched it all from where he lay,
Laughed long and loud at wolf-who-would-be-boss
Brought to his knees, two-double, in collapse.

Thus one who's not content with what's enough
240 But covets all deserves to forfeit all.
The fox, when he saw the sad rout of the wolf,
Thought 'Herring-treat!' and then 'A bellyful!'
It takes, you will agree, both neck and skill
To teach a boss what's honour among thieves.
245 The fox secures his herring-hoard and leaves.

The wolf was lucky to escape alive.
He had been so unmercifully beaten
He limped and could no longer roam nor reive.
The fox slipped off downwind back to his den,
250 Glad to have duped his master and the man:
The one was missing herring from his creels,
The other losing ground, blood to the heels.

MORALITAS

This story happens to contain a moral
Which in conclusion I must underline.
255 The fox may be compared unto the World,
The robber wolf most definitely to Man
And the fish-carter to Death, our mortal bane,
Since all that lives in nature has to die –
On earth or under earth, in sea or sky.

260 Man has the world as servant; and the world
Makes him forget that one day he'll be dead.
It sets his mind on wealth, it turns his head,
So in my tale the herring means this greed
For goods and gain the wolf exhibited.
265 Greed and plunder, war and devastation
Are still the wolf's rampage in every nation.

The fox with plausibility and guile
Gulled the wolf into false security.
Just so the world gulls people for a while.
270 They credit their newfound prosperity
Only to see it lost as suddenly.

They burgle time and fill their sack with things
But death will dog their heels and cut their hamstrings.

The drive to own possessions makes men blind.
Avarice rampant is renamed success.   275
But they forget the carter comes behind
To spoil the sport and void what they invest.
The hollow of the wave follows the crest.
I therefore counsel all concerned: remember
Carter, fox and wolf, and what they stand for.   280

THE FOX, THE WOLF AND THE FARMER

In olden days, as Aesop has recorded,
There was a farmer wont to speed the plough.
Early rising ever was his habit
And so, come ploughing time, he rose to go
Early afield to open the first furrow,   5
His farmhand with him, leading out the oxen.
He blessed himself and them, and started in.

The farmhand shouted, 'Top it up! Come on!
Pull straight, my pets!' Then flailed them hard and sore.
The team was fresh and young and barely broken,   10
So hard to rein they wrecked the new-ploughed score.
The farmer let a sudden angry roar,
Stoned them, threw down the pattle of the plough.
'The wolf', he yelled, 'can have the lot of you.'

But yet the wolf was nearer than he knew   15
For he lay with Mr Fox in a bush nearby,
A thicket at the far end of the furrow,
And heard the vow. Fox laughed in quick reply:
'Now there's an offer', he told wolf, 'which I
Consider good.' 'I promise you,' wolf answered,   20
'I'll make yon royal clown stand by his word.'

Finally the oxen settled down.
Then, later on, the two men unyoked them.
The farmer with his team set off for home.
The wolf straightway limped out and came loping   25
Into their path to work his stratagem.

The farmer saw him, couldn't but take fright,
And thought to turn the beasts and make retreat.

'Where are you going with this stolen stock,'
30 The wolf laid claim, 'for none of them are yours?'
The man, although now thrown into panic,
Faces the wolf and deliberately answers,
'Sir, by my soul, all of these oxen-steers
Are mine. I am puzzled that you stop me.
35 For never once did I offend you. Truly.'

The wolf said, 'Fellow, did you not just now
Donate them to me as you ploughed yon bank?
And is there any finer deed, I ask you,
Than a free deed of gift? You forfeit thanks
40 By stalling. Better liberal with your halfpence
Than forced in the end to part with fatted stock.
Generosity not from the heart is mock.'

'Sir,' said the farmer, 'a man may speak in fury
And then gainsay himself once he's considered.
45 If I say I'll steal, does it make a thief of me?
Do promises like that have to be honoured?
Did I sign documents? Or give my word?
What writ or witness do you have to show?
Do not, sir, seek to rob me. Go to law.'

50 'Clown,' said the wolf, 'a lord, if he is honest
And lives in fear of shame and of reproof,
His word alone will be his seal of trust.
Fie on the man we can't believe or have
Respect for. You're contriving to deceive,
55 And without honesty, the proverbs say,
Other virtues are flimsy as a fly.'

'Sir,' said the farmer, 'remember this one thing.
An honest man's not tricked by a half-truth.
I may say and gainsay, I am no king,
60 But where's the witness you can put on oath?'
Then said the wolf, 'Let you take him on good faith.
Lawrence,' he calls, 'come here out of that covert,
And say exactly what you saw and heard.'

Lawrence came lurking – he never loved the light –
And soon appeared before them in that place.   65
The man saw nothing in the sight to laugh at.
'Lawrence,' said wolf, 'you must decide this case,
The truth of which we'll demonstrate with ease.
I call for honest witness: in his wrath,
What gift did this man promise I would have?'   70

'Sir,' said the fox, 'a final verdict now
Would be premature and unduly hasty,
But if you would submit, the pair of you,
To what I rule in perpetuity
I'll do my best to judge the case as fairly   75
As can be done.' 'Well,' said the wolf, 'agreed.'
And the man said, 'Yes, again agreed.'

Both then made their allegations frankly,
Both sets of pleas set forth by them complete.
'Though I act as judge in friendship, you must be   80
Bound', said Lawrence, 'to accept my verdict
However it may strike you, sour or sweet.'
The wolf stretched out his foot, the man his hand,
And swore on the fox's tail their pact would stand.

The fox then took the man off to one side   85
And, 'Friend,' he said, 'you're landed in a mess.
This wolf won't let you off a single oxhide
And while I myself would wish to lend assistance
I am very loath to act against my conscience.
You'll spoil your case if you make your own defence.   90
This can't be won without some real expense.

'You see how bribes work best to get men through
And how, for gifts, the crooked path will straighten?
Sometimes a hen will save a man a cow.
All are not holy who hoist their hands to heaven.'   95
'Sir,' said the man, 'you shall have six or seven
Of the very fattest hens out of my flock.
There'll be enough left if you leave the cock.'

'Now I am a judge,' said the fox and laughed,
'Bribes should not divert me from doing right.   100
Yet hens and capons I may well bear off

For God is gone to sleep, at least this night.
Such carry-on is petty in his sight.
These hens', he said, 'will make your case secure.
105 No man draws hawk to hand without a lure.'

With these things settled, Lawrence took his leave,
Then went immediately to see the wolf
And there in private plucked him by the sleeve.
'Are you in earnest', he asks, 'as a plaintiff?
110 No, by my soul, you can't be. It's a laugh.'
'What, Lawrence, do you mean?' the wolf replied.
'You heard yourself the promise that he made.'

'The promise, is it, the man made at the plough?
Is that what you would base your case upon?'
115 Half-mocking like this Lawrence gave a laugh
And 'Sir, by the rood,' says he, 'your head is gone.
Devil an oxtail are you going to win!
And tricking a poor man? Who has no defence?
How could I bear to have that on my conscience?

120 'But I've consulted with the soul,' said he,
'And we agreed upon this covenant:
You cancel all your claims and set him free
And you'll be given, whole into your hand,
A cheese unparalleled in all the land.
125 He says it weighs a stone and maybe more.
It's summer cheese. Fresh. Nothing lovelier.'

'So you're advising this is what I do –
Accept the cheese so that clown can go free?'
'Yes, by my soul, and were I counsel for you
130 It's what I would advise professionally.
For even pushed to its extremity
Your case won't win a turnip in return.
Nor do I, sir, intend my soul to burn.'

'Well,' said the wolf, 'it goes against the grain
135 That for a cheese this fellow's off the hook.'
'Sir,' said the fox, 'you ought not to complain
For, by my soul, you are the one at fault.'
'Then,' said the wolf, 'I'm finished with the plot;
But I'd like to see this cheese you boast about.'
140 'Sir,' said the fox, 'he told me where it's kept.'

Then hand in hand they go on to a hill.
The farmer to his farmhouse takes his way,
Glad to have eluded their ill will,
And stands guard by his door till break of day.
So let us turn to the others now as they   145
Proceed through lonely woods, two footsore prowlers
From bush to bush well into the small hours.

All through the long night Lawrence wracks his wits
How he might pacify the wolf by guile.
His promise of the cheese he now regrets   150
But in the end he hits upon a wile
So satisfactory he has to smile.
'This is blind man's buff,' wolf says, 'my friend.
We hunt all night, but not a thing we find.'

'Sir,' said the fox, 'we are all but there.   155
Stop worrying and you shall see it soon.'
They hurried on until they reached a manor.
Like a new penny shone the full round moon.
Then to a draw-well these two gents are come
Where a bucket hung at each end of the rope.   160
As the one went down the other was cranked up.

The moon's reflection shone deep in the well.
'Sir,' said the fox, 'for once you'll find me true.
Now don't you see the cheese there, visible,
White as a turnip, round as a seal, although   165
He hung it deep to keep it hid from view?
For this cheese, sir, believe me, is a thing
Would make a gift for any lord or king.'

'Ah,' said the wolf, 'if I could have yon cheese
Out high and dry in its entirety   170
I'd let yon clown off everything he owes.
What good's a dumb ox team? I set him free.
Yon cheese is more the fare for men like me.
Lawrence,' he cried, 'into that bucket, quick,
And I will hold on here, then wind you back.'   175

Quickly, dexterously the fox leaps in.
The other stays to keep hold of the handle.
'It's so immense,' says fox, 'it has me beaten.
My toes won't grip, I've torn off every nail.

180 You'll have to help me up. Such a huge haul!
Get into that other bucket and descend
This minute to me here and lend a hand.'

Nimbly then the idiot leapt in
Which made, of course, the other bucket rise.
185 The fox was hoisted up, the wolf wound down.
And as they pass wolf furiously cries,
'Why is my bucket falling while yours flies?'
'Sir,' said the fox, 'it's thus with Fortune ever,
If she lets one soar, she's like to sink another.'

190 Down to the bottom then the wolf shot past
While Lawrence lands on top, a happy fox
Leaving the wolf in water to the waist.
To tell who rescued him, I'm at a loss.
The text ends here. There is no further gloss.
195 Except that men may find morality
In this narration, fable though it be.

MORALITAS

This wolf I liken to a wicked man,
Oppressor of the poor, a callous bully,
Involving them in every quarrel he can,
200 Extortionate, harsh, and full of cruelty.
And fox is devil in the allegory,
Inveigling into viciousness the man
He would lead to ruin on his lock and chain.

The farmer may be classed a godly man
205 With whom the fiend finds fault (as scholars warn),
Waylaying him at all times with temptation.
The hens are works from firm faith bred and born.
Where such things sprout, evil is spurned and turned
Back on the evildoer once again,
210 Who ends up an embittered, angry man.

The lonely woods where the wolf was hoodwinked
Are corrupting riches all men long to get
But fail to see they're trash, not worth a trinket,
For riches may be called the Devil's Net
215 Which Satan has for sinners stretched and set.

Without a special grace, indulgent man
Can never be absolved of sins of Mammon.

The cheese may be denoted covetousness,
Ever in full bloom in many an eye.
Cursed be the well that incubates that vice   220
For all it is is fraud and fantasy,
Driving men wild into the buttery
That drags and draws them down to burning hell –
Christ keep all Christians from that wicked well.

THE TOAD AND THE MOUSE

Upon a time, as Aesop makes report,
A little mouse came to a riverside.
She couldn't wade, her mouse-shanks were so short,
She couldn't swim, she had no horse to ride,
So willy-nilly there she had to bide   5
And to and fro beside that river deep
She ran and cried with many a piteous *peep*.

'Help, help me over,' cried the poor wee mouse,
'For love of God, someone, across this stream.'
With that a toad, in water nearby, rose   10
(For toads by nature nimbly duck and swim),
And showed her head to mount the bank and come
Croaking ashore, then gave her greetings thus:
'Good morning! And what brings you here, Miss Mouse?'

'The corn', she said, 'in yon field, do you see it?   15
The ripened oats, the barley, peas and wheat?
I'm hungry and I'd love to get to it
But the water here's too wide, so here I sit
And on this side get not a thing to eat
But hard nuts that I have to gnaw and bore.   20
Over beyond, I'd feast on better fare.

'I have no boat, there is no ferryman,
And if there were, I have no coin to pay.'
'Sister,' said toad, 'would you stop worrying.
Do what I tell you and I shall find a way   25
Without horse, bridge or boat or any ferry

To get you over safely, never fear –
And not wet once a whisker or a hair.'

'I greatly wonder', said the little mouse,
30   'How you can, without fin or feather, float.
This river is so deep and dangerous
I think you'd drown as soon as you'd wade out.
Tell me, therefore, what is the gift or secret
You own to bring you over this dark flood?'
35   And thus in explanation spoke the toad:

'With my two feet for oars, webbed and broad,
I row the stream,' she said, 'and quietly pull,
And though it's deep and dangerous to wade,
I swim it to and fro at my own will
40   And cannot sink, because my open gill
Vents and voids the water I breathe in.
So truly, I am not afraid to drown.'

The mouse gazed up into her furrowed face,
Her wrinkled cheeks, her ridged lips like a lid
45   Hasped shut on her hoarse voice, her hanging brows,
Her lanky wobbly legs and wattled hide;
Then, taken aback, she faced the toad and cried,
'If I know any physiognomy,
The signs on you are of untruth and envy.

50   'For scholars say the main inclination
Of a man's thought will usually proceed
According to the corporal complexion,
The good or evil prompting in the blood.
A thrawn feature means a nature twisted.
55   The Latin tag affords a proof of this –
Mores, it says, are mirrored in the face.'

'No,' said the toad, 'that proverb isn't true,
For what looks good is often a false showing.
The bilberry may have a dreary hue
60   But will be picked while primrose is left growing.
The face may fail to be the heart's true token.
Therefore I find this judgement still applies:
'You shouldn't judge a man just by his face.'

'Unwholesome as I am to look upon,
It's not my fault. Why should people blame me?   65
Were I as fair as lovely Absalom,
I won't have been the cause of my own beauty.
This difference in form and quality
God Almighty has caused Mother Nature
To print and inset into every creature.   70

'Some people's faces may shine eagerly,
Their tongues be silken, their manner sweet and douce,
Yet they are insubstantial inwardly,
Deceitful, unreliable and false.'
'Let be your preaching,' cried the hungry mouse.   75
'Just make it clear to me how you intend
To guide me over to that bank beyond.'

'You know,' the toad said, 'whenever people need
To help themselves, they should think resourcefully.
Go therefore, take a double twine of thread   80
And bind your leg to mine and knot it firmly.
I'll teach you how to swim – no, no, don't worry –
As well as I.' 'As you?' replied the mouse.
'To play that game could prove most dangerous.

'I have my freedom, hope for help, but why   85
Should I be bound? Bad cess then to us both!
For I might lose both life and liberty
And then who's going to compensate that loss –
Unless you swear to me by life and death
To bring me safe and sound to the other side   90
Without cheating.' 'I'll do it,' said the toad

And rolled her eyes to heaven and gave a cry,
'O Jupiter, god and king of nature,
This oath I swear in truth to you, that I
Will bring this little mouse across the water.'   95
The oath was made. The mouse, who knew no better
Than to trust the fork-tongued falsehoods of this toad,
Took thread and bound her leg as she was bid.

Then both in step, they leapt into the stream,
But in their minds it was a different case.   100
The mouse's one thought was to float and swim.

To drown the mouse the toad had set her face
And when they reached midstream, started to press
Downward on her, with every ounce of force,
105 And mercilessly tried to sink the mouse.

Perceiving this, the mouse cried in dismay,
'Traitor to God! False witness! Perjurer!
Just now you swore by life and death that I
Would be ferried safe and sound across the water.'
110 But when she realised this was a matter
Of do or die, she scrambled hard to swim
And on the toad's back fought to cling and climb.

The fear of death had made her that much stronger.
In self-defence she fought with might and main.
115 The mouse strained up, the toad pressed down upon her,
Now to, now fro, now sunk, now safe again.
And so this poor mouse, plunged in such great pain,
Struggled as long as breath was in her breast
Till in the end she called out for a priest.

120 As they were battling on like this, a kite
Roosting upon a branch nearby took heed
And before they knew what happened made a strike
And clenched his claw between them round the thread,
Then swept them to the bank with all good speed,
125 Pleased with his prey, repeating his kite-call,
Then loosed them both and made a cruel kill.

That butcher disembowelled them with his bill,
Flayed them, stripped the skin off inside out
Like taking off a sock, but, guts and all,
130 They could no more than whet his appetite.
Then, having thus decided their debate,
He rose from the field, I hear, and off he flew.
Ask whoever saw if this be true.

MORALITAS

Now, my brother, if you pay attention
135 And study this last fable, you will see
How honeyed words that hide a false intention
Surpass all else in pure malignity,
So when you choose your friends, beware, be canny

For you'd better wheel a barrow full of stones
And bear the brunt and sweat it out all day   140
Than associate with bad companions.

A kindly face can mask maliciousness
And often brings the innocent to grief.
It's better to think twice, act cautious,
Suspect all blandishment, suspend belief.   145
Silken tongues are snares for the naif:
Fledged and barbed like arrows, they can wound.
So, brother, best beware and have no truck with
A crooked, double-dealing, two-faced friend.

I warn you also, it is a great mistake   150
To bind yourself when you're at large and free,
Since once you're bound, your very life's at stake,
You will have forfeited your liberty.
Brother, this simple warning take from me,
Remember it and learn it like your lessons: 155
Better be banished to live on lonely lea
Than associate with bad companions.

Attend to this: and I have more to tell
About the meanings these beasts represent.
The toad, at home in water, is natural   160
Man in this world, in his mortal element,
Aswim in sorrow, doomed to discontent:
Now high, now low, whiles lifted up, whiles down,
Always in peril, liable to drown.

Now sorrowful, now singing like a bird   165
Free betimes, betimes a captive spirit;
Now sound of health, now laid out in the morgue;
Now poor as Job, now lavish and elated;
Now in old rags, now rakishly outfitted,
Now a fed fish and now a famished hound;   170
Now Fortune's wheel and now the hard low ground.

This little mouse, tied up here by the shin
May signify the soul of man indeed,
Trapped in flesh and locked in body's prison.
Till death arrives to cut the living thread   175
Soul must be vigilant, must stand in dread

Of carnal lust that lures and tempts it down
And presses, pulls, loads, drags until it drown.

The water is the world, a turbulence
180   Of surging woe and waves of tribulation
Through which the soul and body must advance,
Distinct and different in their inclination:
Soul pushes up, the body presses down.
Soul's whole desire is to be borne across
185   Out of this world to heaven, into bliss.

The kite is death, that comes suddenly
Out of the blue to conclude the battle.
Therefore be on guard and always ready
For human life is shaky, fragile, mortal.
190   And you, my friend, fortify soul's castle
With good deeds, since there's no telling when
Death will attack you: morning, evening, noon.

Adieu then, friend, and if anyone enquires
About this fable I hasten to conclude,
195   Say it's to be continued by the friars
As an example or similitude.
And now, dear Christ, who died upon the rood,
Saviour of life and soul, grant that we pass
Happily through death in a state of grace.

The Last Walk

I. *Ploughing*

In the field, where there's a reddish look
And shine off the trained vines, where from hedgerows
Morning mist appears to rise like smoke,

They are ploughing. One drives slow oxen with a slow
Ploughman's word; one sows; one grubs the furrows   5
Patiently with his hoe.

Alert to this, the sparrow rejoices,
Spying all from the prickly mulberry tree;
And the robin – you can hear him from the hedges,
His notes like gold coins jingled for pure glee.   10

II. *From Above*

The skylark spirals upwards out of sight
Into the dawn, singing from above
A house where smoke scrolls up, then melts in light.

From above, his distant lark's eye watches white
Oxen in pairs criss-cross the field and leave   5
Broad acres ploughed, each furrow dark and straight.

In the black damp field, the turned, share-brightened ground
Shines in the sun like sunlight in a mirror.
Harvest and sheaves are on the farmer's mind,
A cuckoo's call re-echoes in his ear.   10

III. *Hens*

The old housewife, more spirited than us,
Won't lose heart at the falling of the leaves:
Her yard is full of jubilating roosters;

And often in the morning when it's peaceful
She hears the cackle of the laying hens.   5
The granary's plumped. Wine sings in the barrel.

COMMENTARY 640–2 | 485

Around her in the evening, pensive-eyed
Young girls in flower shuck the maize and sing
Rounds and refrains, while unruly boys collide
10   At their horseplay in the husks, crackling and snapping.

iv. *Washerwomen*

Out in a field half-fallow and half-furrowed,
A plough is standing, no oxen-team in sight,
Forgotten looking, half-hid in a mist-cloud.

From the mill-pond comes the wet slapping and surge
5   And rhythmic rinsings of the washerwomen,
Each splish-splash keeping time with their sing-song dirge:

The wind is blowing, the bush is snowing,
You've not come back to your native heath:
When you went, you left me sorrowing
10   Like a plough left out in a fallow field.

v. *Two Boys*

The two get to their feet, one stiff and numb,
The other serious; the first one lifts
His straw skep with a slow deliberation

And into the other's wicker creel lets fall
5   Bit by bit the jackpot of dried dung,
Then the winner goes, weighed down yet nimble still.

The loser sits, tries another throw
With hazel nuts, scatters, gathers them up
And says (is the big elm listening now?)
10   So maybe then he can say he's out of luck.

vi. *The Iron Road*

Between embankments where dairy cattle graze
Peacefully, the railway's straight brown track
Runs with the lines that gleam into the distance.

In the pearly sky, identical and upright
5   Poles wired to poles run parallel to the lines
And diminish in perspective out of sight.

What are these growls and rumblings now that rise
To a crescendo, then fade like a woman's keen?
At times the tight-strung wires will tune the noise,
A querulous immense harp swept by wind.   10

vii. *Feast Day in the Distance*

The signs are of a feast day in the distance:
A steady tremulous ringing haunts the air
As from behind a veil of forgetfulness.

There as the bells boom hollow waves of sound
Old men on the road bare white heads   5
And fix their lowered eyes upon the ground.

But when the quiet sky quivers and flares
Children's eyes then open to their widest.
They whoop at fireworks sputtering in the air.
Mother clasps them to her fragrant breast.   10

viii. *That Day*

After their chatter and bickering on the breeze
The swallows left the balconies of the priest's
House that stood off among the elm trees.

What whispering the rose-red tower heard
That day, or was it the shrieking swifts   5
Impatient with their fretting baby birds?

Now in the midday silence, what I hear
Is a chair inside being knocked against;
The rustle of a dress; and at the window there
A woman's face, beautiful and intense.   10

ix. *Noon*

At the Pergola Inn they're doing a brisk business.
The place is full of shouting, buzz, dull bumps.
Now and then flames leap in the smoking fireplace.

In the doorway, through a waft of kitchen odours,
A beggarman is muttering, Things were once   5
Different for the thrushes and the hunters.

Oh that, he says, was a happy time, as noon
Chimes out from the village's slow bells,
And all around, from far off campaniles
10   A wave of joy goes sweeping through the town.

x. *Since Early Morning*

Water, race and roar. Shake, mill-wheel, and pour.
Hood, rotate round the ringing apparatus.
Feed-slot, let the grain flow from the hopper

And dust, let fly. In the shadow of the hedge
5   The donkey stands; beside the rushing sluice.
Since early morning he has waited there, on edge.

His ears twitch, he turns around to look
For it's time now for things to go ahead
Calmly, as they knead, roll out the dough and bake
10   Until you sit there steaming, crisp-crusted wholegrain bread.

xi. *Carter*

O carter coming at your quiet pace
From the dark mountains, trudging through the night
Under beetling cliffs, on arched and airy bridges,

What did the howling north wind have to tell
5   As it echoed through the caves and the ravines?
But you were sleeping on top of your load of charcoal.

Then gradually there gathered on the road
A storm blast that came whistling and whirling,
But you were dreaming up there on your load
10   Of Christmastime and the pipes skirling.

xii. *In a Huddle*

The wobbly crossing gate shuts with a creak
And the road is blocked. In a huddle by the fence
Neighbour women, hard at the usual talk:

About so and so who could be whoever's twin.
5   About wine that costs the earth and isn't worth it.
This government; this latest bad infection.

About the little one; the big one nearly twenty;
About the pig that feeds but doesn't thrive.
As the black train goes clanging past them
Their gaze is far away and meditative.   10

XIII. *The Dog*

We, while the world goes turning on its axis,
We live our surly lives, endure the stress
While world turns and more slowly turns than us.

As when a heavy cart lumbers and moves
Past a cottage, and the old spavined horse   5
Pounds the ground with his sluggish hooves,

A dog will break from bushes like the wind.
While he races out, gives chase, barks long and hard,
Slowly, slowly the cart leaves him behind.
He runs back in, goes snuffling round the yard.   10

XIV. *O Princess!*

Your mother bore the perfect housekeeper
When she bore you: on bushes by the roadside
Your laundry whitens and you couldn't be happier.

Soon it will be the holiday, so everyone
Is asking for clean linen from the chest,   5
The lavender-scented one you keep it in.

Your parents are happy for you; and your brothers.
And the minute you decide the time has come,
O princess with arms white as alabaster,
He'll bear you across the doorstep of his home.   10

XV. *She Calls You*

That night your ageing parents (do you hear?)
Mother calls, steam curls from the black pot,
The little ones are fighting for the sheer

Love of a fight. Be strict, then, and take over,
Here check a cheeky hand, there quieten a shout,   5
And that way keep the little flock in order

Until you're settled, after all that pother,
Sharing a bite with your chastened family),
That night your parents, growing old together
10   Beneath the sheets, endure their piety.

    XVI. *O Vain Dream!*

By the hearth, where myrtle crackles in the blaze,
I'm either nodding off or sitting with you,
Nibbling at my chicory and lettuce.

When the storm-blast swoops and the night wind blows
5   I bring a forkful of sweet-smelling hay
To fodder my companionable cows.

And then I go upstairs with you – vain dream!
But now the brushwood blooms with cyclamen,
The student shakes off sloth and blows a film
10   Of dust off his long neglected lexicon:

The blackbird's warbling and the snipe is drumming
And I, in my native tongue, return to versing.

In tears as he speaks, Aeneas loosens out sail
And gives the whole fleet its head, so now at last
They ride ashore on the waves at Euboean Cumae.
There they turn round the ships to face out to sea.
Anchors bite deep, craft are held fast, curved   5
Sterns cushion on sand, prows frill the beach.
Now a band of young hotbloods vaults quickly out
On to the shore of Italia, some after flint
For the seedling fire it hides in its veins,
Some crashing through woodland thickets, the haunts   10
Of wild beasts, pointing amazed at new rivers.
But Aeneas, devoted as ever, has taken the road
Up towards a fort, the high seat of Apollo,
Then on to a place apart, a vast scaresome cavern,
The Sibyl's deep-hidden retreat. There the god breathes   15
Into her, overwhelmingly, knowledge and vision,
Opening her eyes to the future. Before long
They pass through the golden precincts and groves
Of Diana, the goddess of crossroads.

And now they pause on that hill where Dedalus,   20
At the end of his flight, first fluttered to earth:
He had risked himself to the sky, away and afloat
To the north, through the cold air, unprecedented,
Rowing with wings – which he then dedicated
To you, Phoebus Apollo, there on the spot   25
Where he landed, and built in your honour
A mighty temple, the doors of it decorated
With scenes in relief.
                        First the death of Androgeos.
Then the stricken Athenians, doomed to deliver   30
Seven grown-up sons for sacrifice every year.
There too stood the empty urn, from which
Only now the fatal lots had been drawn.
On the opposite leaf, the land of Knossos
Rising out of the sea: here was the horn-cruel bull   35
With Pasiphaë under him (a congress
Her cunning arranged), whence would be born
The Minotaur, crossbreed and offspring

Of abominable desire.
40   Also shown:
The bewildering, intricate maze –
Never got through until Dedalus, out of pity
For infatuated Ariadne,
Guided a prince's blind footsteps
45   With a payout of thread, past every wrong turn
And every dead end he himself had devised
And constructed.
                          In which grand design
You too would figure significantly,
50   Icarus, had sorrow allowed it. Twice
Dedalus tried to model your fall in gold, twice
His hands, the hands of a father, failed him.

The Trojans would have kept standing, fascinated
By all on display, except that just then Achates,
55   Who'd been sent on ahead, came back accompanied
By the Sibyl, Deiphobe, daughter of Glaucus, priestess
Of Diana and Phoebus. Who addressed the prince:
'This is no time to be standing staring here.
It would be better now to pick out for sacrifice
60   Seven bullocks from a herd that has not been yoked,
And an equal number of properly chosen ewes.'
Having spoken these words to Aeneas (whose men
Are quick to obey her instructions) the priestess
Summons the Trojans into her high inner sanctum.

65   At Cumae, behind the broad cliff, an enormous cave
Has been quarried: a hundred entrances, a hundred
Wide-open mouths lead in, and out of them scramble
A hundred echoing voices, the Sibyl's responses.
They arrived at that threshold and the vestal cried,
70   'Now! Now you must ask what your fate is. The god
Is here with us! Apollo!' Her countenance suddenly
Paled and convulsed, hair got dishevelled,
Breast was aheave, heart beating wilder and wilder.
Before their eyes she grows tall, something not mortal
75   Enters, she is changed by the breath of the god
Breathing through her. 'Aeneas of Troy,' she demands,
'Your vows and your prayers, why do you wait? Pray,
For until you have prayed, the jaws of this cavern

Won't echo or open.' And there she fell silent.
The hardy Trojans feel a cold shiver go through them,   80
Their prince from the depths of his heart beseeches
The god:

      'Phoebus, you always had pity for Troy
And her troubles, it was you who steadied
Paris's aim and directed the arrow   85
Into Achilles, you who were pilot
As I entered sea after sea, skirting the coasts
Of distant land masses, remotest Massylia,
The sandbanked Syrtian gulfs. Here then at last
We set foot on Italia that seemed for so long   90
The unreachable: henceforth let Trojan ill fortune
Be a thing of the past. For now, all you gods
And goddesses, you to whom Troy's name and fame
Gave affront, divine law constrains you
To spare us, the last of its relicts. And you,   95
Seeress most holy, to whom the future lies open,
Grant what I ask (no more in the end than my fate
Has assigned): home ground for my people
In Latium, refuge for our wandering gods
And all Troy ever held sacred. Then to Phoebus   100
Apollo, and Diana, I will set up a temple
In solid marble and inaugurate feast days
In the god's honour. And for you, O all gracious one,
A sanctuary will be established, a vault
Where I shall preserve divinations from lots   105
And oracles you'll have vouchsafed to my people;
And in your service I shall ordain chosen men.
Yet one thing I ask of you: not to inscribe
Your visions in verse on the leaves
In case they go frolicking off   110
In the wind. Chant them yourself, I beseech you.'
So saying, Aeneas fell silent.

               Meanwhile the Sibyl,
Resisting possession, storms through the cavern,
In the throes of her struggle with Phoebus   115
Apollo. But the more she froths at the mouth
And contorts, the more he controls her, commands her
And makes her his creature. Then of their own accord
Those hundred vast tunnel-mouths gape and give vent
To the prophetess's responses: 120

'O you who survived,
In the end, the sea's dangers (though worse still await
On the land), you and your Trojans will come
Into your own in Lavinium: have no fear of that.
125   But the day is one you will rue. I see wars,
Atrocious wars, and the Tiber surging with blood.
A second Simois river, a second Xanthus,
A second enemy camp lie ahead. And already
In Latium a second Achilles comes forth, he too
130   The son of a goddess. Nor will Trojans ever be free
Of Juno's harassments, while you, without allies,
Dependent, will go through Italia petitioning
Cities and peoples. And again the cause of such pain
And disaster for Trojans will be as before: a bride
135   Culled in a host country, an outlander groom.
But whatever disasters befall, do not flinch.
Go all the bolder to face them, follow your fate
To the limit. A road will open to safety
From the last place you would expect: a city of Greeks.'

140   Thus from her innermost shrine the Sibyl of Cumae
Chanted menacing riddles and made the cave echo
With sayings where truths and enigmas were twined
Inextricably, while Apollo reined in her spasms
And curbed her, or sank the spurs in her ribs.

145   Then as her fit passed away and her raving went quiet,
Heroic Aeneas began: 'No ordeal, O Sibyl, no new
Test can dismay me, for I have foreseen
And foresuffered all. But one thing I pray for
Especially: since here the gate opens, they say,
150   To the King of the Underworld's realms, and here
In these shadowy marshes the Acheron floods
To the surface, vouchsafe me one look,
One face-to-face meeting with my dear father.
Point out the road, open the holy doors wide.
155   On these shoulders I bore him through flames
And a thousand enemy spears. In the thick of fighting
I saved him, and he was at my side then
On all my sea-crossings, battling tempests and tides,
A man in old age, worn out, not meant for duress.
160   He too it was who half-prayed and half-ordered me

To make this approach, to find and petition you.
Wherefore have pity, O most gracious one,
On a son and a father, for you have the power,
You whom Hecate named mistress of wooded Avernus.
If Orpheus could call back the shade of a wife   165
By trusting and tuning the strings of his Thracian lyre,
If Pollux could win back a brother by taking the road
Repeatedly in and out of the land of the dead,
If Theseus and Hercules too . . . But why speak of them?
I myself am of highest birth, a descendant of Jove.'   170

He was praying like that and holding on to the altar
When the Sibyl started to speak: 'Blood relation
Of gods, Trojan, son of Anchises,
It is easy to descend into Avernus.
Death's dark door stands open day and night.   175
But to retrace your steps and get back to upper air,
That is the task, that is the undertaking.
Only a few have prevailed, sons of gods
Whom Jupiter favoured, or heroes exalted to glory
By their own worth. At the centre it is all forest   180
And a ring of dark waters, the river Cocytus, furls
And flows round it. Still, if love so torments you,
If your need to be ferried twice across the Styx
And twice to explore that deep dark abyss
Is so overwhelming, if you will and must go   185
That far, understand what else you must do.
Hid in the thick of a tree is a golden bough,
Gold to the tips of its leaves and the base of its stem,
Sacred (tradition declares) to the queen of that place.
It is safe there, roofed in by forests, in the pathless   190
Shadowy valleys. No one is ever allowed
Down to earth's hidden places unless he has first
Plucked this sprout of fledged gold from its tree
And handed it over to fair Proserpina
To whom it belongs, by decree, her own special gift.   195
And when it is plucked, a second one grows every time
In its place, golden again, emanating
That same sheen and shimmer. Therefore look up
And search deep, and as soon as you find it
Take hold of it boldly and duly. If fate has called you,   200
The bough will come away in your hand.

Otherwise, no strength you muster will break it,
Nor the hardest forged blade lop it off.

'But while you linger here on my doorstep,
205   Consulting and suing, sad news, alas,
Awaits: the body of one of your friends
Lies emptied of life, and his death pollutes
The whole fleet. Carry this man to a right
Resting place, lay him into his tomb,
210   Sacrifice herds of black sheep as your first
Votive offerings. Then and then only
Will you view the forests of Styx, those realms
Barred to the living.' She said these things,
Pressed her lips shut, and went silent.

215   Aeneas, his face sadder now, looking downcast,
Walked away from the cave, not sure what to think
Or expect. Trusty Achates walked at his side,
In step with his friend, apprehensive,
Intense, the give and take of their talk
220   Uncertain yet urgent: who, for example, might be
The dead comrade the Sibyl enjoined them
To bury? And then they saw him, Misenus,
On a dry stretch of beach – they came up and saw
The son of Aeolus, unfairly, peremptorily
225   Called to his death, this man unsurpassed
At rallying fighters, blaring the war call
On his bronze trumpet. Once he had been
Great Hector's comrade, standing by him in battle,
Unmistakable, known by his trumpet and spear.
230   Then after Achilles had savaged Hector to death
This staunchest of heroes, unwilling to join
A less worthy cause, chose to follow Aeneas.
But a mad moment came when the trumpeter blew
Resonant notes from a conch shell over the waves,
235   Intending to challenge the gods
To a musical contest. Triton was shaken
With envy (hard as it is to believe) and surged up
And drowned him in a sudden backwash of foam.

So the Trojans assembled and lifted their voices
240   In mourning, none louder, more devout than Aeneas;
Then, still in tears, they set to at once, eager

To follow the Sibyl's instruction, piling up logs,
Building an altar-pyre that rose toward the heavens.
High in the virgin forest, near dens of wild beasts,
Holm oaks echo the crack of their axes, spruce trees   245
Get felled, they hammer in wedges, split open
Beams of the ash and the tougher cross-grain of oak.
Big rowan trees crash and roll from the hilltop down.

As all this proceeded, Aeneas was to the fore,
Geared out like the rest, cheering everyone on.   250
But he kept gazing up at that high stretch of forest,
Sadly preoccupied, pondering things in his heart
Until a prayer rose to his lips and he said:
'If only that golden bough would show itself
On its tree in the deep forest den – for everything   255
The prophetess said about you, Misenus, was true,
Altogether too true!' And almost immediately
A pair of doves chanced down from the sky
In full view, and settled on the green grass;
In them the great hero knew his own mother's birds   260
And prayed and rejoiced: 'O, if a way can be found.
Be you my guides. Hold course through the air,
Lead on to the grove where that opulent bough
Overshadows the rich forest floor. And you,
O my goddess mother, do not abandon me   265
In this time of confusion.' With that he halted
To watch for what signs they might give, what place
They might make for. But the doves kept on going,
Now feeding, now flying ahead, at all times
Staying in view of the eyes that pursued them.   270

Then when they came to the fuming gorge at Avernus
They swept up through clear air and back down
To their chosen perch, a tree that was two trees
In one, green-leafed yet refulgent with gold.
Like mistletoe shining in cold winter woods,   275
Gripping its tree but not grafted, always in leaf,
Its yellowy berries in sprays curled round the bole –
Those flickering gold tendrils lit up the dark
Overhang of the oak and chimed in the breeze.
There and then Aeneas took hold of the bough   280
And although it resisted greedily tore it off,
Then carried it back to the Sibyl's cavern.

On the beach the Trojans were mourning
Misenus as sorely as ever, paying
285   Their last respects to the inert ash.
With resinous pinewood and cut-off sections of oak
They constructed first a huge pyre, dressing its flanks
With branches darkly in leaf, fencing the base
With funereal cypress, crowning all
290   With resplendent armour and weapons. Some heated
Water in bubbling vats above open fires, washed
And anointed the corpse, then raised the lament.
Next, when the weeping was over, they laid him out
On the ritual couch, his remains swathed in purple,
295   Familiar robes of the dead. Some stepped in
To lift high the great bier – a grievous observance –
And with eyes averted, as ancestral custom required,
Touched a blazing torch to the base of the pyre.
Gifts of food, piled offerings, incense, and bowls
300   Brimming over with oil went up in the flames.
Then when the fire had died, collapsing to ash,
They poured wine on his parched dust; and Corynaeus
Collected the bones in a bronze urn and sealed them.
Three times he moved round the company, sprinkling
305   Clean water for purification, asperging men lightly
From an olive branch, dewy with promise; then gave
The farewell. And under a high airy hill
Aeneas reared a magnificent tomb
Hung with the dead man's equipment, his oar
310   And his trumpet, so the hill is now called
Misenus, a name that will live down the ages.
Once this was done, Aeneas quickly proceeded
To follow the Sibyl's instructions. There was a cave,
A deep rough-walled cleft, stone jaws agape
315   Above a dark lake, with the lake and a grove
For protection and shelter. No creature of air
Could wing its way safely over that water,
Such were the noxious fumes spewing up
From the murky chasm into the vault of the heavens.
320   (The Greeks therefore called it Avernus, 'place
Without birds').
                    The first thing the priestess did here
Was line up four black heifers, pour libations of wine
On their foreheads, clip off the bristles that sprouted

Between their horns and commence sacrifice,   325
Offering them on the flames, all the while praying
Her clamorous prayers to Hecate, she who has power
Under the earth and above it. Others draw blades,
Catching warm blood in vessels. Aeneas himself
With a stroke of his sword, to honour Dark Night   330
And her sister, the Earth, slays a black-fleeced lamb,
And to honour you, Proserpina, a heifer,
Infertile. Then for the King of the Underworld
He illumines the dark, consecrating an altar
Where he burns whole carcasses and pours   335
Sluggish oil on the glowing entrails of bulls.
But all of a sudden, between the first glimmer
And full rise of the sun, the ground at their feet
Starts rumbling and shaking, the wooded heights
Are atremble, and in the uncanny light what they hear   340
Sounds like the howling of dogs as Hecate approaches.
'Out from here,' the seeress is shouting, 'out,
Anyone here not initiate – all such,
Depart from the grove. But not you, Aeneas:
Take you the sword from your scabbard, go ahead   345
On the road. Now will spirit be tested,
Now, now your courage must hold.' So saying, rapt
And unstoppable, she hurled herself into the mouth
Of the wide-open cave, and he, without fear,
Kept in step as she guided him forward.   350

Gods who rule over souls! Shades who subsist
In the silence! Chaos and Phlegethon, O you hushed
Nocturnal expanses, let assent be forthcoming
As I tell what's been given to tell, let assent be divine
As I unveil things profoundly beyond us,   355
Mysteries and truths buried under the earth.

On they went then in darkness, through the lonely
Shadowing night, a nowhere of deserted dwellings,
Dim phantasmal reaches where Pluto is king –
Like following a forest path by the hovering light   360
Of a moon that clouds and unclouds at Jupiter's whim,
While the colours of the world pall in the gloom.

In front of the house of the dead,
Between its dread jambs, is a courtyard where pain

365 And self-wounding thoughts have ensconced themselves.
     Here too are pallid diseases, the sorrows of age,
     Hunger that drives men to crime, agonies of the mind,
     Poverty that demeans – all of these haunting nightmares
     Have their beds in the niches. Death too, and sleep,
370 The brother of death, and terror, and guilty pleasures
     That memory battens on. Also close by that doorway:
     The iron cells of the Furies, death-dealing War
     And fanatical Violence, her viper-tresses astream
     In a bloodstained tangle of ribbons.
375   Right in the middle
     Stands an elm, copious, darkly aflutter, old branches
     Spread wide like arms, and here, it is said,
     False dreams come to roost, clinging together
     On the undersides of the leaves. At the gates,
380 Monstrosities brood in their pens, bewildering beasts
     Of every form and description: two-natured Centaurs
     And Scyllas, hundred-headed Briareus, the beast of Lerna,
     Loathsome and hissing, and fire-fanged Chimaera;
     Gorgons and Harpies too, and the looming menace
385 Of triple-framed Geryon. Faced with this rout,
     Aeneas is thrown into panic, pulls out his sword,
     Swings it round in defence, and had not his guide
     In her wisdom forewarned him
     That these were lives without substance, phantoms,
390 Apparitional forms, he would have charged
     And tried to draw blood from shadows.

     A road starts here that leads to Acheron river.
     Here too is the roiling abyss, heaving with mud,
     Venting a silty upsurge into Cocytus,
395 And beside these flowing streams and flooded wastes
     A ferryman keeps watch, surly, filthy and bedraggled
     Charon. His chin is bearded with unclean white shag;
     The eyes stand in his head and glow; a grimy cloak
     Flaps out from a knot tied at the shoulder.
400 All by himself he poles the boat, hoists sail
     And ferries dead souls in his rusted craft,
     Old but still a god, and in a god old age
     Is green and hardy.
                          Hereabouts a crowd
405 Came pouring to the banks, women and men,

And noble-minded heroes separated now
From their living flesh, young boys, unmarried girls,
And sons cremated before their fathers' eyes:
Continuous as the streaming leaves nipped off
By first frost in the autumn woods, or flocks of birds   410
Blown inland from the stormy ocean, when the year
Turns cold and drives them to migrate
To countries in the sun. There they stood, those souls,
Begging to be the first allowed across, stretching out
Arms that hankered towards the farther shore.   415
The stern boatman permits one group to board
And now another, but the rest he denies passage,
Driving them back, away from the sandy banks.

Amazed and then moved by all this press and pleading,
Aeneas asks his guide: 'What does it mean, O Sibyl,   420
This push to the riverbank? What do these souls desire?
What decides that one group is held back, another
Rowed across the muddy waters?'
                          'Son of Anchises,'
The venerable one replied, 'O true born son of heaven,   425
What you see here are the standing pools
Of Cocytus and the Stygian marsh.
These are the names invoked when gods swear oaths
They will never dare to break. That crowd in front of you
Died but were left unburied, with no help or hope.   430
The ferryman is Charon. The ones on board his craft
Are the buried. Not until bones have found a last
Resting place will shades be let across
These gurgling currents, their doom instead to wander
And haunt about the banks for a hundred years.   435
Then and then only are they again allowed
To approach the brink and waters that they long for.'

Aeneas stopped and stood there, lost in thought,
Comprehending, pity in his heart
At their misfortune, then caught sight of Leucaspis   440
And Orontes, who'd captained the Lycian fleet,
Downcast men, denied the rites of the dead:
On their journey out from Troy, a southern gale
Struck ship and crew in heavy seas, and both
Were swept away, overwhelmed in the turmoil.   445

And now there appears his helmsman, Palinurus,
Who not long since had pitched and tumbled off
The stern into open sea, as he held course
From Africa, eyes fixed upon the stars.
450   To whom Aeneas, once he recognised
His sad form in the congregating dark,
Spoke first: 'Which god snatched you from us,
Palinurus, and drowned you in the deep?
Tell, O tell what happened. Never until now
455   Did Apollo's oracle prove false, but this time
He deceived me: you would survive the waves,
He prophesied, and land safe on the shore
Of Italia. Is this how he keeps his word?'
But Palinurus answered, 'My captain, son
460   Of Anchises, the god Apollo's oracle
Did not play you false, nor did any god
Plunge me into the waves. What happened was this:
The steering oar I held and was in charge of
Snapped in a sudden gale and as I fell
465   I dragged it down with me. But I swear by Ocean
The fear I had for myself then was as nothing
To the fear I had for your ship.
Stripped of her tackle, her steersman overboard,
Would she not wallow and founder
470   In those mountainous seas? For three nights,
Through horizonless surge, a south wind
Hurled me and burled me. The fourth day at dawn,
I rose on a swell and got my first glimpse
Of Italia. Little by little then I was making headway,
475   Slugging towards land in my waterlogged clothes,
Getting a grip on the razor-backed ridges,
When savage locals appeared with drawn swords,
A pack who for want of knowing assumed
That I'd be rich pickings. Now surf keeps me dandled,
480   The shore winds loll me and roll me.

'You, therefore, you the unbowed, the unbroken,
I implore, by the cheerful light of the sky
And its breezes, by your father and your hopes
As the father of Iulus, get me away
485   From this place, put an end to my woes.
Either scatter the handful of earth

On my corpse, which you easily can
Once you're back in the harbour at Velia,
Or else – if there be a way, if your goddess-mother
Can direct you to one – for I believe you are bound   490
To enjoy the favour of heaven, prepared as you are
To face these vast waterways and set sail
On the Stygian marsh – reach out your hand
To one who is suffering, take me with you
Over the waves, so that in death at the least   495
I shall find a calm haven.'
                              That was his plea
To Aeneas, and this was the answer he got
From the Sibyl: 'What madness is this, Palinurus?
You who aren't even buried, what makes you think   500
You can look on the waters of Styx or the Furies'
Grim river? You have not been called to the bank.
Banish the thought that praying can ever affect
The edicts of gods. Your plight is a hard one,
But hear and remember my words: they should be   505
A comfort. What will happen is this:
Your bones will be reverenced; the sky
Will reveal signs and portents, in cities
On every side populations will know
To build you a tomb and observe solemn custom   510
With offerings year after year. And the place
For all time will bear the name Palinurus.'
These words lifted his heart and raised,
For a moment, his spirits. The thought
Of the land in his name makes him happy.   515

So now they resumed their journey and kept going
Until they were near the river, moving through
Silent woodland towards the bank, when Charon
From his boat out on the water spied them
And began to remonstrate, on the attack   520
Before they even spoke: 'You, whoever you are,
Approaching our river under arms, stop there,
Not one step farther, and say what brings you:
This is the country of the shades, of heavy-lidded
Night and sleep. It is a thing forbidden   525
To load the Stygian ferry with living bodies.
I rue the day I carried Hercules

And Theseus and Pirithous, sons of gods as they were,
Strongmen, invincibles. Hercules arrived
530 To chain up and restrain the hellmouth watchdog,
To steal him from the very throne of the king –
And did carry the panicked beast away. The others
Tried to abduct the queen from Pluto's bed.'
To which the soothsaying priestess made reply:
535 'Nothing like that is being plotted here. These arms
And weapons present you with no threat, so be calm.
Let the monster cave-dog howl his howl forever
And keep on terrifying bloodless shades,
Proserpina be her pure self behind her uncle's doors.
540 Aeneas of Troy, renowned for his right life
And warrior prowess, descends among the shades,
Down to death's deepest regions, to see his father.
If the sight of such devotedness won't move you,
You nevertheless must recognise this bough,'
545 And she shows the bough concealed by her cloak.
Charon quietens then, his bad temper subsides,
He says no more. It is long since he beheld
The holy proffer of that fateful branch. He turns
His dark barge round and steers for the shore.
550 Other souls ensconced on the long thwarts
He hurries off up gangways, then at once
Hands mighty Aeneas down into the vessel.
Under that weight the boat's plied timbers groan
And thick marsh water oozes through the leaks,
555 But in the end it is a safe crossing, and he lands
Soldier and soothsayer on slithery mud, knee-deep
In grey-green sedge.
                           Here Cerberus keeps watch,
Growling from three gullets, his brute bulk couched
560 In the cave, facing down all comers. But the Sibyl,
Seeing snake-hackles bristle on his necks,
Flings him a dumpling of soporific honey
And heavily drugged grain. The ravenous triple maw
Yawns open, snaffles the sop it has been thrown
565 Until next thing the enormous flanks go slack
And the inert form slumps to the cave floor.
Thus, with the watchdog sunk in a deep sleep,
Aeneas gains entry and is quick to put behind him
The bank of that river none comes back across.

At once a sound of crying fills the air, the high wails   570
And weeping of infant souls, little ones denied
Their share of sweet life, torn from the breast
On life's very doorstep. A dark day bore them off
And sank them in untimely death. Next to them
Are those condemned to death on false charges,   575
Although here they are assigned their proper verdicts
By a rightly chosen jury. Minos, the judge,
Presides and shakes the urn, convenes a panel
Of the silent dead, seeking to establish
Men's characters and crimes. Farther on   580
Is the dwelling place of those unhappy spirits
Who died by their own hand, simply driven
By life to a fierce rejection of the light.
How they long now for the open air above,
How willingly they would endure the lot   585
Of exhausted workers and the hard-wrought poor.
But their way is barred by laws of gods. The waste
And desolate marsh water laps round,
River Styx with its nine loops binds and bounds them.

Not far from here the fields called the Fields   590
Of Mourning stretch out in all directions.
On these plains, hidden on shadowy paths,
Secluded and embowered in myrtle groves,
Are those who suffered hard and cruel decline
In thrall to an unremitting love. Their griefs   595
Do not relent, not even in death. Here Aeneas saw
Among other lovers Phaedra and Procris,
And sad Eriphyle, pointing to the wounds
Dealt by her callous son. Evadne too,
And Pasiphaë. And moving in step with them   600
Laodamia, and Caeneus who in her time had known
Life as a man, though fate had now restored
The figure of the woman she once was.

Along with these, still nursing her raw wound,
Dido of Carthage strayed in the great forest.   605
As soon as the Trojan came close and made out
Her dimly wavering form among the shadows,
He was like one who sees or imagines he has seen
A new moon rising up among the clouds
On the first day of the month; there and then   610

He wept and spoke these loving, tender words:
'Unhappy Dido! So the news I got was true,
That you had left the world, had taken a sword
And bade your last farewell. Was I, O was I to blame
615 For your death? I swear by the stars, by the powers
Above and by any truth there may be under earth,
I embarked from your shore, my queen, unwillingly.
Orders from the gods, which compel me now
To travel among shades in this mouldering world,
620 This bottomless pit of night, dictated
Obedience then as well. How could I believe
My going would devastate you with such grief?
Stay a moment, don't slip out of our sight.
Is there someone you are trying to avoid?
625 These words I'm saying to you are the last
Fate will permit me, ever.'
                                    Pleading like this,
Tears welling up inside him, Aeneas tried
To placate her fiery spirit and soften
630 Her fierce gaze; but she, averting her face,
Her eyes fixed steadily on the ground, turned
And showed no sign of having heard, no more
Than if her features had been carved in flint
Or Parian marble. At length she swept away
635 And fled, implacable, into the dappling shadows
Of the grove, where Sychaeus, her husband
In another earlier time, feels for her pain
And reciprocates the love she bears him still;
While Aeneas, no less stricken by the injustice
640 Of her fate, gazes into the distance after her,
Gazes through tears, and pities her as she goes.

Then he braces himself for the journey still to come
And soon they arrive in the farthest outlying fields,
The hosting grounds of those renowned in war.
645 In one place Tydeus meets him, in another
Parthenopaeus, glorious in arms, and the bloodless
Shade of Adrastus; elsewhere the Trojan chieftains
Who fell in battle, much mourned in the world above.
And now he also moaned to see them
650 Thronging in such numbers: Glaucus, Medon
And Thersilochus, Antenor's three sons; Polyboetes,

The priest of Ceres; and Idaeus, still
The chariot driver, still dressed in his armour.
From right and left souls crowd and jostle close,
Eager for more than just a look at him; they want   655
His company, the joy of keeping in step, talking,
Learning why he has come. But the Greek captains
And the gleaming cohorts once led by Agamemnon
Cowered in panic when they saw Aeneas
Advance in dazzling armour through the gloom.   660
Some turned to flee as they had once to the ships,
Some raised a spectral cry that came to nothing,
Dying away as it left their gaping mouths.
And here Aeneas caught sight of Priam's son,
Deiphobus, mutilated in every part, his face   665
In shreds – his face and his two hands –
Ears torn from his head, and his nostrils
(A low dishonourable wounding, this)
His nostrils cut away: unrecognisable almost
As he shivered and shrank into himself to hide   670
The cruel laceration. Aeneas,
In a voice well known to him, spoke first, resolutely:
'Deiphobus, mightiest in the field, offspring
Of Teucer's ancient line, who was there capable
Of such mutilation? Who let themselves   675
Run so ruthlessly amok? The story I heard was this:
On the last night in Troy, you waded in Greek blood
Till you fell exhausted, fell like a dead man
On a heap of their slobbered corpses. That is why
I raised an empty tomb for you at Rhoetum,   680
On the shore, and with my three loud cries
Invoked your spirit. Your name now and your arms
Hallow that spot. But not you in the flesh, my friend,
Whom I could neither see as I embarked
Nor bury in home ground.'   685
                              Priam's son replied:
'And you, my friend, you left no thing undone.
You paid the right attention to Deiphobus,
Dead man and shade. It was my destiny
And the criminal, widowing schemes of my lady   690
Of Sparta wrecked and ruined me. What you see
Are the love bites she left me in remembrance
Of that last night, of all our city's nights

The most jubilant and most deluded. But this you know
695 Too well already, for how could you forget?
When the horse that was our fate came at a leap
On to the heights of Troy, big in the belly
With armed men, she was to the fore, involved
In the dance, contriving to lead our women
700 In the loud frenzy of the bacchanal.
Up she went to our citadel, in her hand
A torch conspicuously ablaze,
Signalling to the Greeks. And me then! Me
In my god-cursed marriage-bed, lying dead beat,
705 Far gone, giving in to sleep, sweet, welcoming,
Drowsy sleep, serene almost as death. Meanwhile,
My paragon of a bride had cleared the house
Of every weapon and even stolen the sword
From underneath my head; and now she opened doors
710 And called for Menelaus to come in, hoping, no doubt,
That this grand favour to her lover boy
Would blot out memories of old betrayals.
But why say more? They broke into the bedroom,
Ulysses with them, the insidious and malignant . . .
715 O gods, as my plea for vengeance is a just one. Gods!
Retaliate! Strike the Greeks with all due punishment.
But you, what of you? It is time I heard your story:
What turn of events has brought you here alive?
Do you come as a survivor, tempest-tossed,
720 Or at the gods' behest? What destiny hounds you
Down to these sunless, poor abodes, this land
Of troubles?'

        Dawn in her rose-flushed chariot
Had taken her airy drive up half the sky
725 As they talked together, and in all likelihood
They would have talked on for whatever time
Had been allotted, but that the Sibyl at Aeneas' side
Reproved him in a few brief words. 'Night, Aeneas,
Has begun to fall. We are wasting time lamenting.
730 This is the fork of the road, here it divides.
To the right, where it runs beneath the walls
Of mighty Pluto's fortress, that one we take
To Elysium; the one to the left sends evil-doers
To punishment in merciless Tartarus.'

Deiphobus   735
Then replied, 'Do not, high priestess, be angry.
I will be gone, will take my place with the rest, yield
Once more to the dark. But you, the glory of Troy, go,
Go you to a happier fate.'
                        He had said   740
His say, and as he spoke turned on his heel.

Aeneas suddenly looks back and sees
A broad-based fortress under a cliff to the left,
Set behind three rings of wall, encircled
By a hurtling torrent, a surge and rush of flame,   745
Rock-rumbling, thunder-flowing Phlegethon, the fiery
Bourne of Tartarus. A gate rears up in front,
Flanked by pillars of solid adamant, so massive
No human force, nor even the sky-gods' squadrons
Could dislodge them. There too stands an iron tower   750
And from its top Tisiphone the Fury
Oversees the entrance day and night, unsleeping
And on guard, her bloody dress hitched up.
Sounds of groaning could be heard inside, the savage
Application of the lash, the fling and scringe and drag   755
Of iron chains. Aeneas stopped short, petrified,
Taking in the turmoil and the shouting,
Then asked the Sibyl: 'What wrong-doing
Is being dealt with here? What punishments
Afflict the wrong-doers? What is this wailing   760
High upon the wind?'
                    And the prophetess
Answered him: 'Famed chieftain of the Trojans,
Know it is forbidden for the pure in spirit
To set foot on the god-cursed threshold. And yet   765
When Hecate gave me charge of Avernus' woods
She took me through this whole place and explained
The punishments gods impose. Rhadamanthus
Of Knossos rules here, unforgiving, castigating,
Hearing admissions of guilt and exacting   770
Confession from those self-deceiving souls
Who thought to hide wrongs done in the world above
And left them unatoned for till too late.
Vengeful Tisiphone keeps bearing down, a whiplash
Lapped and lithe in her right hand, in her left   775

A flail of writing snakes, scourging the guilty,
Summoning her ferocious claque of sisters.
Next comes a grinding scrunch and screech
Of hinges as the dread doors open
780 And you see what waits inside, the shape
And threat of the guard who haunts the threshold.
Farther in and more ruthless still, the Hydra lurks,
Monstrous, with her fifty gaping mouth-holes
And black gullets. And beyond, the sheer plunge
785 Of Tartarus down to the depths, to darkness, a drop
Twice as far beneath the earth as Olympus
Appears to soar above it.
                          In the bottom of the pit,
In the very lowest sump, felled by Jove's thunderbolt,
790 Earth's ancient sons, the Titans, writhe, abased.
Here too I saw the sons of Aloeus, giant twins
Who attempted to grapple with high heaven
And depose the Father of the Skies.
Salmoneus too I saw, paying dear
795 For having played at being Jupiter, wielding fire
And imitating the thunders of Olympus.
He rode in triumph through the Greek nations
And his own city in Elis, drawn by four horses
And flourishing a torch, assuming to himself
800 The honour due to gods. It was madness:
To think that the batter of bronze and the clatter
Of horses' hoofs could mimic Jupiter's
Absolute thunder and his scowling storms!
But the all-powerful Father – no fake lightning for him
805 From torches or smoky guttering pine-brands –
Hurled his bright bolt from behind the cloud murk
And blasted Salmoneus headlong down
In an overwhelming whirlwind. There as well
You'd see Tityos, foster-son of Earth,
810 The mother of all. Tityos, his body stretching out
Over nine whole acres while a huge, horrendous
Vulture puddles forever with hooked beak
In his liver and entrails teeming with raw pain.
It burrows deep below the breastbone, feeding
815 And foraging without respite, for the gnawed-at
Gut and gutstrings keep renewing.
                          And the Lapiths,

Ixion and Parothous, should I mention them?
Eternally menaced by a looming boulder, black
And eternally about to fall. Golden headrests   820
Gleam on their high banquet couches, a sumptuous
Royal feast is spread to tempt them; but nearby
The arch-Fury occupies her place, warding off
Hands that long to reach out to the meal, ever ready
To spring, with her lifted torch and terrifying yells.   825

'Also incarcerated, those who for a lifetime
Hated a brother, abused a parent, or ruined
The good name of a client; those who gloated
On wealth they'd secretly amassed and hoarded
And failed to share with kith and kin (they comprised   830
The biggest crowd); those killed as adulterers;
Those who broke oaths of loyalty to masters
In violent rebellions: all were confined there
Awaiting punishment. What that punishment would be,
What fault or fate entailed it, do not seek to know.   835
Some roll a massive boulder or hang spreadeagled,
Tied to the spokes of wheels. Theseus, unlucky soul,
Sits unmoving and will sit like that forever,
While Phlegyas, most stricken of all, cautions all,
A constant proof of what his voice proclaims   840
Loudly through the darkness: "Take warning by me;
Learn to do right; learn not to scorn the gods."
Here too was one who sold his country's freedom,
Leaving her in thrall to a tyrant lord;
Here one who would fix laws for a price and for a price   845
Unfix them; here another who forced a daughter
In her bed and into an abominable marriage.
All dared to commit great wrong and were fit
For what they dared. If I had a hundred tongues,
If I had a hundred mouths and an iron voice,   850
I could neither spell out the foul catalogue
Of those crimes nor name their punishments.'

Here Apollo's venerable priestess paused
Before continuing: 'But enough. Be quick. You must
Conclude your undertaking now. We both must hurry.   855
I see ramparts fashioned in Cyclopic foundries
And gates there in the arch in front of us
Where the powers that be require us to deposit

Proserpina's gift.' That said, they proceed in step
860 Along the dark of pathways, then hurry out
Across the open ground that fronts the doors.
Aeneas takes his stand in the entrance, purifies
His body with fresh water, and there and then
Plants the bough in the threshold.

865   With this ritual
Finally performed and honour done to the goddess,
They came into happy vistas and the green welcome
Of the Groves of the Fortunate Ones who dwell in joy.
Here a more spacious air sheds brightness
870 Over the land; they enjoy their own sun here
And their own stars – some at their exercises
On the grass, some competing in earnest, wrestling
On yellow sand; others are dancing dances
And singing songs, Orpheus among them
875 In his long musician's robe, keeping time,
Plucking his seven notes from the seven-stringed lyre
Now with his fingers, now with an ivory plectrum.
Here too were members of Teucer's ancient stock,
That noblest of families, magnificent heroes
880 Born in better days – Illus and Assaracus
And Dardanus who founded Troy. Aeneas gazed
In wonder at their armour and the chariots beside them
Standing idle, their spears struck tall in the ground
And their horses loosed out, free to graze the plain
885 Anywhere they liked. The pride they took when alive
In armour and chariots, the care they gave
To their glossy well-groomed teams, it is still the same
Now they have gone away under the earth. Others too
He sees on every side, feasting in lush meadows
890 Or singing songs together to Apollo
Deep in a laurel grove, where the Eridanus
Courses through on its way to the earth above.

Here was a band of those who suffered wounds
Fighting for their country; those who lived the pure life
895 Of the priest; those who were dedicated poets
And made songs fit for Apollo; others still
Whose discoveries improved our arts or ease, and those
Remembered for a life spent serving others –

All of them with headbands white as snow
Tied round their brows. These the Sibyl now addressed   900
As they bustled close around her, Musaeus
In particular, who stood out at the centre of the crowd,
The one looked up to, towering head and shoulders
Over them. 'Tell us, happy spirits,' she began,
'And you, the best of the poets, tell us   905
Where does Anchises lodge, in which quarter?
For his sake we have crossed the mighty waterways
To be here.' Her question the great hero answered
Briefly: 'None of us has one definite home place.
We haunt the shadowy woods, bed down on riverbanks,   910
On meadowland in earshot of running streams.
But you, if your heart is set upon it, climb this ridge
And I'll direct you soon on an easy path.' He spoke,
Walked on ahead and showed the fields of light.
Aeneas and the Sibyl came down the hill.   915
                            Elsewhere Anchises,
Fatherly and intent, was off in a deep green valley
Surveying and reviewing souls consigned there,
Those due to pass to the light of the upper world.
It so happened he was just then taking note   920
Of his whole posterity, the destinies and doings,
Traits and qualities of descendants dear to him,
But seeing Aeneas come wading through the grass
Towards him, he reached his two hands out
In eager joy, his eyes filled up with tears   925
And he gave a cry: 'At last! Are you here at last?
I always trusted that your sense of right
Would prevail and keep you going to the end.
And am I now allowed to see your face,
My son, and hear you talk, and talk to you myself?   930
This is what I imagined and looked forward to
As I counted the days; and my trust was not misplaced.
To think of the lands and the outlying seas
You have crossed, my son, to receive this welcome.
And after such dangers! I was afraid that Africa   935
Might be your undoing.' But Aeneas replied:
'Often and often, father, you would appear to me,
Your sad shade would appear, and that kept me going
To this end. My ships are anchored in the Tuscan sea.
Let me take your hand, my father, O let me, and do not   940

Hold back from my embrace.' And as he spoke he wept.
Three times he tried to reach arms round that neck.
Three times the form, reached for in vain, escaped
Like a breeze between his hands, a dream on wings.

945 Meanwhile, at the far end of a valley, Aeneas saw
A remote grove, bushy rustling thickets,
And the river Lethe somnolently flowing,
Lapping those peaceful haunts along its banks.
Here a hovering multitude, innumerable
950 Nations and gathered clans, kept the fields
Humming with life, like bees in meadows
On a clear summer day alighting on pied flowers
And wafting in mazy swarms around white lilies.
Aeneas startled at this unexpected sight
955 And in his bewilderment asked what was happening,
What was the river drifting past beyond them,
Who were the ones in such a populous throng
Beside it?
                    'Spirits,' Anchises answered,
960 'They are spirits destined to live a second life
In the body; they assemble here to drink
From the brimming Lethe, and its water
Heals their anxieties and obliterates
All trace of memory. For a long time now
965 I have looked forward to telling you about them,
Letting you see them face to face, but most of all
I wished to call the roll of my descendants, parade
My children's children, so you could all the more
Share my joy at your landfall in Italia.'

970 'Are we to believe then, father, there are souls
Who rise from here to the sky of the upper world
And re-enter the sluggish drag of the body?
What possesses the poor souls? Why this mad desire
To get back to the light?' 'To put you out of doubt,'
975 Anchises answers, 'I shall explain it straightaway.'
And point by point he then outlines the doctrine.

'To begin at the beginning: a nurturing inner spirit
Works to sustain sky, earth, the fields of ocean,
The moon's bright disc and Titan's star, the sun;
980 And mind, operative in every part, imbues

The massive whole, blending with world's body.
From which are born races of men and beasts,
Creatures that fly, and prodigies ocean breeds
Beneath the molten marble of its surface.
The seeds of life are strong sparks out of fire,   985
Their origin divine, so to that extent
They are immune to the heavy toll of the body,
Their quickness unaffected by the toil
Of human limbs and the mortal clothing
Of the flesh. It is from body   990
That fear and desire, grief and delight derive,
And in the darkness of its prison house
Those first pure elements are shut off and screened
From the light of heaven. Besides which, at the end
When life departs, they remain sadly infested   995
By every evil and every bodily ill,
For inevitably, in the course of time,
Many flaws mysteriously coalesce, hard set
And deep ingrained. Therefore souls are visited
With due chastisements and affliction, to atone   1000
For past offences. Some are hung racked
And raked by vacuous winds; for others, the stain
Is washed away beneath whirling torrents
Or burnt off in fire. Each of us suffers
The death we're due, then given the freedom   1005
Of broad Elysium – the few, that is, who'll dwell
In those blessèd fields until the end of time
When length of days will remove the deep-dyed taint,
Purify the aethereal sense and that sheer original stuff
Of fire and spirit. The rest, when they have trod   1010
Time's mill for a thousand years, the god commands
Wave upon wave into the Lethe river, so at that stage
Their memory is effaced and they go once more
To dwell beneath sky's dome and start again
To long for the old life of flesh and blood.'   1015

Anchises concluded and led his son
Accompanied by the Sibyl into the crowd,
Into the thick and buzzing throb of it,
Then took his stand on a height where he could inspect
The long, drawn-out procession and take note   1020
Of every face as it approached and passed.

'So now I will instruct you in what is to be,
The future glory of the Trojan race,
Descendants due to be born in Italia,
1025 Souls who in time will make our name illustrious –
I speak of them to reveal your destiny to you.
The lad you see there, who leans on his untipped spear,
Placed next and nearest to the light, he will be
The first to ascend to upper air, the first
1030 Of our people with mixed Italian blood.
He'll be known as Silvius, an Alban name,
And be the last of your children; when you are old
Your wife Lavinia will rear him in the woods
To be a king and to father kings our stock
1035 Will issue from and rule in Alba Longa.
Next to him stands Procas, pride and joy
Of the Trojan nation, then Capys and Numitor
And the one in whose name you will survive, Silvius
Aeneas, no less distinguished as a warrior than you
1040 And no less devoted, though he'll be waiting long
To rule in Alba. Look at them! Marvellous, strong
Young men, wearing their civic honours, oak wreaths
Like shadowy crowns. These, when you are gone,
Will build Nomentum and Gabii and the city of Fidena,
1045 Fortify hill towns, wall the citadels
Of Collatia, found Pometii, Bola and Cora
And Camp Inuus: unheard-of today, unsignified,
Their name and fame will come. And Romulus, yes,
Son of Mars, grandson of Numitor, whom Illia
1050 Is to bear, Romulus will stand firm by his grandfather.
Do you see how the twin plumes wave above his head,
How the Father of the gods has marked him out
With his own insignia for singular majesty?
Once he inaugurates the power of Rome,
1055 She in her glory will push an empire's bounds
To the ends of earth and harbour aspirations
High as heaven; seven hills she will girdle with a wall
Into a single city and be blessed with heroic sons.
She will be like Cybele with her crown of towers,
1060 The Great Mother borne in her chariot
Through the cities of Phrygia, happy and fulfilled
To have given birth to gods, grandchildren

By the score in her generous arms,
All of them sky-dwellers, tenants of the heights.

'Now look this way, take good note of this clan,   1065
Your own bloodline in Rome: there is Caesar
And the whole offspring of Iulus, destined one day
To issue forth beneath the dome of heaven.
This is he whose coming you've heard foretold
So often: Augustus Caesar, child of the divine one,   1070
Who will establish in Latium, in Saturn's old domain,
A second golden age. He will advance his empire
Beyond the Garamants and the Indians
To lands unseen beneath our constellations
Beyond the sun's path through the zodiac,   1075
Away where sky-braced Atlas pivots on his shoulder
The firmament, inlaid with glittering stars.
Already the Caspian kingdoms and Maeotia
Know of his coming and begin to tremble
At the oracles of their gods; the waters of the Nile   1080
Quail in alarm and roil through their seven mouths.
Not even Hercules pursued his labours over
So much of earth's surface, not when he stalked
And shot the bronze-toed deer, silenced the boar
In the woods of Erymanthus and left the air of Lerna   1085
Vibrating to his bowstring; not Bacchus either
Careering in triumph, the vine-reins in his grip,
Driving his tiger team down the heights of Nysa.
So why should we then hesitate to test
And prove our worth in action or be afraid   1090
To stake and stand our ground in Italia?

'But that one in the crown of olive sprays,
Offering sacrifice – that grey head
And grizzled beard I recognise as Numa's,
King of Rome, sprung from the humble town   1095
Of Cures, called from its poor land to wield high power
And frame the city's first system of laws.
To be succeeded next by Tullus, who will wreck
His country's peace, turn an easygoing people
Militant and drill an army long out of the field   1100
For victory. After him, that's Ancus, swaggering,
Too full of himself already, overly susceptible
To the wind of popularity in his sails.

And there, if you care to look, are the regal Tarquins
1105 And haughty Brutus, called Avenger, who'll arrange
The handover of the fasces – first consul
To be installed and given authority
As custodian of the pitiless axes.
Then as a father, when his sons foment their plot,
1110 He will decree their summary execution
In the fair name of liberty – stricken in this
No matter how future generations may comprehend it:
Love of country will prevail and the overwhelming
Desire for fame.

1115   'Now over there you see
The Decii and the Drusi, Torquatus who will behead
His son, and Camillus who'll recapture the standards.
But alas for that pair in their burnished armour,
Well-matched champions, twin souls in accord
1120 As long as they stay pent in this shadowland,
But once promoted to the light above
What mutual destruction they will wreak,
The internecine savagery and slaughter
Of a civil war: Caesar, the bride's father,
1125 Bearing down from the northern Alps,
Pompey, the husband, with his legions in formation
Advancing from the east. Do not, O my sons,
Inure yourselves to such dreadful consequence, do not
Bloody the bosom of your country with vicious,
1130 Valiant battle. And you, child of my blood,
Of the gods on high Olympus, be you the first
In clemency: rid your hands of those weapons.

'Yonder too is Mummius, conqueror
Of Corinth, who will ride his victor's chariot
1135 Up to the Capitol, a hero for having brought
Ruination on the Greeks. That other at his side
Will destroy Argos and Agamemnon's Mycenae,
Defeat descendants of arch-warrior Achilles,
Avenge his Trojan forebears and the rape
1140 Of Cassandra in Minerva's temple.
Next, great Cato, you, who could not sing your praise
Or, Cossus, yours? Or the family of the Gracchi;
Or those two Scipios, two warrior thunderbolts
Who will strike down bellicose Carthage; or Fabricius,

The indomitable and frugal; or you, Serranus,   1145
Sowing your furrowed fields? Nor is there a quick
Or easy way to scan the long line of the Fabii,
Down to the greatest, Fabius Maximus,
He who'll contrive to stall and thereby save our state.
Others, I have no doubt, with a more delicate touch   1150
Will beat bronze into breathing likenesses,
Conjure living features out of marble,
Argue cases more effectively, and with their compass
Plot the heavens' orbit and predict
The rising of the constellations. But you, Roman,   1155
Remember: to you will fall the exercise of power
Over the nations, and these will be your gifts –
To impose peace and justify your sway,
Spare those you conquer, crush those who overbear.'

Here Anchises paused; then, while they wondered   1160
At his words, continued: 'Look now, there goes
Marcellus, head and shoulders above all the rest,
Victorious in armour of the general he killed.
He will help Rome to stand firm while it bears the brunt
Of fierce invasion, he will ride high over   1165
Carthaginians and insurgent Gauls, then dedicate
Those rich, rare spoils won only twice before
To Father Quirinus.'
                        At which point Aeneas saw
A young man in step with Marcellus, arrayed   1170
In glittering arms, exceedingly handsome
But with lowered eyes, unhappy looking, so he asked,
'Who, father, is that companion at his side?
A son, or another of his great descendants?
What crowds and clamour follow him! What presence   1175
He has! But black night wreathes his brow
With dolorous shadow.'
                        Choking back his tears,
Anchises answered, 'Do not, O my son,
Seek foreknowledge of the heavy sorrow   1180
Your people will endure. Fate will allow the world
Only to glimpse him, then rob it of him quickly.
It's as if the gods decided the Roman people
Would be manifestly too powerful, were the gift
Of his life to last. How the city will re-echo   1185

Massed laments from the brave on the Field of Mars!
What a funeral procession, Tiber, you will witness
As you go flowing past the new built tomb!
No boy born from our Trojan stock will ever raise
1190   The hopes of his Latin ancestors so high
Nor the land of Romulus take such pride in a son.
Alas for his goodness! His antique loyalties!
His strong right arm unbeaten in the battle!
No foe would have faced and fought him and survived,
1195   Whether he marched on foot or sank his spurs
In the flanks of some foaming, lathering warhorse.
O son of pity! Alas that you cannot strike
Fate's cruel fetters off! For you are to be Marcellus . . .
Load my arms with lilies, let me scatter
1200   Purple flowers, let me lavish these gifts at least
On the soul of my inheritor and perform
My unavailing duty.'
                    And so
Far and wide in those fields, through regions of air,
1205   They go wandering at will, surveying all.
Then after Anchises has conducted Aeneas
Across the whole expanse, scene after scene,
And fired his mind with promise of future glory,
He tells of wars that will first have to be waged,
1210   Of the Laurentines and the town of King Latinus,
How he should face or flee each undertaking.

There are two gates of Sleep, one of which, they say,
Is made of horn and offers easy passage
To true visions; the other has a luminous, dense
1215   Ivory sheen, but through it, to the sky above,
The spirits of the dead send up false dreams.
Anchises, still guiding and discoursing,
Escorts his son and the Sibyl on their way
And lets them both out by the ivory gate.
1220   Aeneas hurries to the ships and rejoins his comrades,
Then sails, hugging the shore, to the port of Caietae.
Anchors are cast from the prow; sterns cushion on sand.

Fig. 1. 'Prayer' (from sixteenth-century French)

One of SH's earliest translations, published for the first time in this edition. (*Seamus Heaney Literary Papers [1963–2010]*, *National Library of Ireland, Dublin*)

Fig. 2. 'Colmcille the Scribe' (from eleventh-century Irish)

One of SH's later translations, published with revisions in *Human Chain* (2010). (*Seamus Heaney Literary Papers [1963–2010]*, *National Library of Ireland, Dublin*)

My hand is cramped from penwork.
My quill has a tapered point.
Its bird-mouth issues a blue-black
Beetle-sparkle of ink.

Wisdom keeps welling in streams
From my fine-drawn sallow hand.
Riverrun on the vellum
Of ink - from green-skinned holly.

My small runny pen keeps going
Through books, through thick and
thin
To enrich the scholars' holdings-
Penwork that cramps my hand.

COMMENTARY

The following notes reflect SH's work as reader and translator, as critic and author – as student and teacher in a school of poetry that never closes. In this Commentary, poem titles are numbered in square brackets for the purposes of cross-reference.

1940s

At primary school (Anahorish Primary School, 1944–51) a deferred scholarship gives SH 'an extra year of preparation for secondary school' (SS, 30). Master Barney Murphy gives SH his 'first lessons in Latin', as the poet recalls in *Station Island* (1984): 'the mists of all the mornings I set out/for Latin classes with him, face to face,/refreshed me. *Mensa, mensa, mensam*/sang in the air like a busy whetstone' (*SI*, 73). Murphy also makes 'a stab' at teaching SH Irish. Even though the student is 'so nervous', the teacher 'so abrupt and unclear', and the 'one-to-one sessions such an ordeal' (SS, 30), Latin and Irish begin to shape SH's imagination and it is no coincidence that translations from Latin and Irish bookend and punctuate his entire writing career.

1950s

At secondary school (St Columb's College, Derry, 1951–7) SH continues to study Latin and Irish and begins to learn French. 'Growing up as a Catholic in the age of the Latin mass,' Heaney reminisced in conversation with Lorna Hardwick, 'the Latin language had a hieratic foundational quality' and was 'a kind of a ratified sacred tongue'. SH reads 'Virgil, Livy, a little bit of Horace and so on' and is 'as they say, good at Latin' (Hardwick 2016, 00:27–01:05). In the prose poem 'Cloistered', SH remembers doing 'classics homework' (*ABVIa*, vii), how he found his 'foothold in a main verb in Livy' (*Stations*, 20).

SH's Latin teacher 'loved the language and had a feel for the literary qualities of the texts – especially Virgil' (SS, 296). SH 'sighed for his favourite Virgil in that 1950s classroom' (*ABVIa*, ix), the beginning of a lifelong interest in the *Aeneid* and a lifelong desire to honour the memory of Father McGlinchey that will bring him to translate Book VI. At St Columb's College SH's Catholic formation becomes 'more systematic' and for five years he takes 'a Latin Mass every morning' and 'an annual religious knowledge exam' (SS, 38).

SH's Irish teacher introduces him to Daniel Corkery's *The Hidden Ireland* (1925). 'Taken by the pathos of the scenario,' Heaney immediately sees himself 'an heir to the Irish speakers in the cabins, one of Eoghan Ruadh Ó Suilleabháin's and Aodhagán Ó Rathaille's "audience in posterity"' (*SS*, 41). SH's first translations from Irish are early Irish nature poems. In conversation with Sue Lawley, Heaney places himself 'in the tradition of the hermit poets' and describes his countryside cottage as 'a hermit's hut' (Heaney 1989b, 03:47–03:49; *SS*, 168).

SH's French teacher 'chalked up and belted out the sixteen vowel sounds' on SH's first day in St Columb's College, 'the whole class uttering the pure notes in concert: *ee, ay, eh, ah, aw, o, oo*'. SH would remember vividly that first French class as 'a completely bewildering forty minutes' that left him feeling 'suddenly very far from home' (*SS*,125–6). SH hears 'French spoken by French people' when he travels abroad for the first time in 1958 as he takes part in the Derry Diocesan Pilgrimage to Lourdes to serve as a stretcher-bearer (*SS*, 257–8).

At university (Queen's University Belfast, 1957–61) SH takes Latin and French, which he drops when he is admitted to an Honours degree in English Language and Literature. SH's interest in Latin and French, however, continues and his first few translations will be from Latin and French literature. In conversation with Robert Druce, SH states that, of Dante, he 'had looked at *The Divine Comedy* in translation as an undergraduate and had frankly not finished it' (Heaney 1995, 28:32–28:50). SH's relationship with Dante will change in the 1970s.

1960S

As he starts his academic career and begins publishing poems, SH is invited by Philip Hobsbaum, a lecturer at Queen's University Belfast and a poet, to join the Belfast Group poetry workshop. SH is 'incredibly pleased to be noticed' especially as he has 'absolutely no confidence as a writer' (Kinahan 1982, 407). However, 'intimidated by the practical criticism they were subjected to by his more polished colleagues', SH puts aside 'a good number of the poems' he submits to the Group (Crowder 2017, 95), including what evidence suggests is his first complete translation: 'To a Wine Jar', after the Latin of Horace.

In the second half of this decade SH publishes two collections of poems: *Death of a Naturalist* (1966), his first book, and *Door into* the *Dark* (1969). In fulfilment of the terms of the Somerset Maugham Award for his debut collection, SH spends the summer of 1969 abroad. While in the Basses-Pyrénées region of France, he sets out to translate Guillevic's earlier poetry but is unhappy with the result: 'I scraped at the "Les Rocs" of Carnac – but didn't altogether believe in the noise I was making' (Conroy 2009, 121). An invitation to speak at a conference in University College Dublin, marking the centenary of Guillevic's birth in 2007, will prompt SH to return to and translate the poetry of Guillevic [85], who is among the writers SH hosts at the Kilkenny Arts Week in 1976.

Around the end of the 1960s or in the early 1970s SH completes two translations from French: one he will never publish and the other he collects in *North* (1975).

[1] 'To a Wine Jar'

HORACE (65–8 BCE), CLASSICAL LATIN

First published in *Honest Ulsterman* (Spring 1994, 19–20) and reprinted posthumously in *Seamus Heaney and the Classics* (Harrison 2019, 245).
    Uncollected.

SH's complete translation of *Carmina* (*Odes*) 3.21. The text in this edition is drawn from *Seamus Heaney and the Classics* (2019).
    Dated 1965 in the typewritten sheets of the Belfast Group, this is SH's first complete translation, a relationship between translator and author that was to reach an international readership with 'Anything Can Happen' [57] (*DC*, 13), his 2001 translation of another ode, *Carmina* 1.34. For all the magnitude of that later work, SH admired the simplicity of life captured by the Latin writer: 'Horace says: *vivitur parvo bene*. You can live well on a little' (*SS*, 151). The use of the quatrain and the word 'pitcher' can also be found in 'Cana Revisited', a poem first published in the *Irish Times* (8 and 9 April 1966, 8) and then collected in *Door into the Dark* (*DD*, 20). The 'two joyous quatrains' (Parker 1993, 81) of 'Cana Revisited' reference the first miracle of Jesus narrated in the Gospel of John: the transformation of water into wine at a wedding in Cana. SH uses 'pitcher' also in 'Grotus and Coventina', a poem inspired by a visit to Hadrian's Wall where SH stood on ground sacred to the Romano-Celtic goddess Coventina (*HL*, 42).
    As Ruth Macklin notes, 'To a Wine Jar' 'is significant for a study of Heaney's Latin translations as it reveals the highly competent

student of Latin negotiating with the developing poet' (Sonzogni 2021, 194).

1970S

In this decade SH publishes three books of poems – *Wintering Out* (1972), *North* (1975) and *Field Work* (1979) – and embraces the creative potential of translation, completing versions from three languages: French, Irish and Italian. In 1970–1, SH is living in the USA as Visiting Lecturer at the University of California, Berkeley. While there, he is exposed to what he calls 'the impact of translation' for the first time, and experiences an awakening to what translation can do for literatures emerging from the margins of mainstream canons. A year after returning to Northern Ireland, SH remembers being read a poem by Czesław Miłosz, 'Incantation', which had been translated by the author and Robert Pinsky. This recollections opens one of the T. S. Eliot Memorial Lectures SH delivers at the University of Kent in 1986, significantly titled 'The Impact of Translation' and collected in his second volume of prose, *The Government of the Tongue* (1988): 'What translation has done over the last couple of decades', SH observes, 'is not only to introduce us to new literary traditions but also to link the new literary experience to a modern martyrology, a record of courage and sacrifice which elicits our unstinted admiration' (*GT*, 38). SH also notes how 'subtly, with a kind of hangdog intimation of desertion, poets in English have felt compelled to turn their gaze East and have been encouraged to concede that the locus of greatness is shifting away from their language' (*GT*, 38). SH will engage with Eastern European poetry, especially Polish (Anna Swir, Czesław Miłosz, Wisława Szymborska, Zbigniew Herbert, Stanisław Barańczak), and accept invitations to translate the poetry of two contemporary Romanian poets, Marin Sorescu, [10] to [15] and Ana Blandiana, [28] to [37]; a Czech song cycle, written by Ozef Kalda and set to music by Leoš Janáček, [51]; and poems by two giants of Russian poetry, Alexander Pushkin, [52] and [53], and Joseph Brodsky, [54] and [55].

SH's interest in French literature and in translation is kindled in 1968 when Faber & Faber publishes an anthology of Baudelaire's poems rendered into English by Robert Lowell, *The Voyage and Other Versions of Poems by Baudelaire*. Asked by Dennis O'Driscoll to discuss his relationship with Lowell's poetry, SH states that he was reading him 'all through the sixties' and 'constantly'. Lowell's collection of his own poetry translations, *Imitations,* published by Farrar, Straus and Cudahy in 1961 and by Faber in 1962 and including several poems by Baudelaire, was one of the 'books that were just part of the air we breathed'. SH also notes that Lowell 'was often favoured at The Group: Philip Hobsbaum inclined in particular to *Life Studies* and *Imitations*' and remembers 'his reading of the Victor Hugo piece from the latter, and Arthur Terry's reading – from that book – of Leopardi's "Saturday Night in the Village"' (*SS,* 217). Included in *Imitations* are poems by Rilke and Pasternak, whose work SH will also read in translation and translate. SH meets Lowell, forging a strong friendship, and another poet-translator, Joseph Brodsky, in 1972, a crucial year in his life and work.

SH's desire to safeguard his personal and poetic integrity sharpens and he decides to leave Belfast for Wicklow, in the countryside south of Dublin, surrendering the stability of an academic career for the uncertainty of freelance writing. 'The move I made in 1972 had, I know this clearly, nothing to do with the political situation,' SH explains in conversation with Charlie Rose, 'it had to do with an inner development, an inner necessity in myself as a writer as a poet to change my life' (Heaney 1996, 17:40–18:01).

Two exiled figures – a cursed pagan king, Sweeney, and a vilified Christian poet, Dante – enter SH's imagination, leading to a string of translations from Irish and Italian in the second half of this decade and to the publication of two books in the first half of the following. *Sweeney Astray* [7], SH's retelling of *Buile Suibhne,* is published in 1983; *Station Island,* his *Purgatory,* in 1984.

In a 1978 Raidió Teilifís Éireann (RTÉ) script titled 'The God in the Tree: Early Irish Nature Poetry' and included in his first book of essays, *Preoccupations* (1980), SH highlights the 'unique cleanliness of line' of this poetic genre and 'the tang and clarity of a pristine world full of woods and water and birdsong' it describes. As an example, noting also that early Irish nature poems have been 'translated often', SH offers an uncredited version of the iconic blackbird poem '*Int én bec*' ('The Blackbird of Belfast Lough'), which is actually his (*Preoccupations,* 181). This is the first of many poetry translations from Irish published during and after SH's lifetime.

After the Bloody Sunday massacre on 30 January 1972, SH's decision that year to leave the North is seen by some as breaking ranks, as a form of betrayal. With escalating violence, the British authorities imprison more and more IRA members – they regard themselves as prisoners of war and therefore entitled to various privileges not given to inmates of ordinary British prisons. When this is refused,

IRA prisoners begin hunger strikes in 1980, in which ten eventually die in 1981. The story of Ugolino in Dante's *Inferno*, locked in a tower with his children and left there to starve to death because of his political choices, provides SH with a narrative that enables him to address the ideological motives of the hunger strikers and the personal consequences of their actions.

Ugolino too can be seen to hunger-strike: in prison he refuses to eat his children even though they ask him to before dropping dead in front of him, one after the other, in one of the most harrowing scenes in Dante's *Inferno*. SH places his first translation from Dante's *Inferno* at the end of *Field Work* (1979), establishing an unsettling parallel with the opening poem where he describes the guilty pleasure derived from a meal of oysters. As Corrina Salvadori Lonergan notes, it is also an eerie reminder (*l.* 6: 'Like a famine victim') that hunger, in Ireland, inexorably evokes the Great Hunger, the Irish Potato Famine that in the years after 1845 killed about a million people (Lonergan 2020, 179; *FW*, 60).

[2] Prayer

GABRIELLE DE COIGNARD (*c.* 1550–1586/94), MIDDLE FRENCH

Unpublished.

This is SH's complete translation of '*La crainte de la mort incessamment me trouble*' (1594). The text in this edition is drawn from an undated typescript.

The materials related to *Wintering Out* housed in the Seamus Heaney Papers at Dublin's National Library of Ireland include an undated typescript translation titled 'Prayer' (MS 49,493/12 (107). The French original and a prose translation in English by Geoffrey Brereton can be found in Vol. 2 (*Sixteenth to Eighteenth Centuries*) of *The Penguin Book of French Verse*, published in 1958 when SH is a student at Queen's University Belfast, studying French (Brereton 1958, 116–17). A comparison between Brereton's prose translation and SH's verse translation seems to suggest that *The Penguin Book of French Verse* was SH's source, and it is likely that SH decided to translate it because of the 'familiar' title and subject matter.

The title, '*La crainte de la mort incessamment me trouble*', is the French translation of the Latin phrase '*Timor mortis conturbat me*' from the Catholic *Officium Defunctorum*, the Office of the Dead. In the third Nocturn of Matins we read: '*Peccantem me quotidie,*

et non pœnitentem, timor mortis conturbat me. Quia in inferno
nulla est redemptio, miserere mei, Deus, et salva me.' In English,
'Sinning daily, and not repenting, the fear of death disturbs me.
For there is no redemption in Hell, have mercy on me, o God, and
save me.' Gabrielle de Coignard is now regarded as 'one of the most
striking representatives of the rich body of women's devotional verse
in early modern France' – a 'female tradition', as Deborah Lesko
Baker remarks, that 'reaches back to the late twelfth century' (Baker
2015, 41, 43). The sonnet translated by SH is the confession of a
remorselessly sinful and death-fearing individual who pleads to God
that He be merciful on the day of the last judgement and rescue her
from falling into the abyss of eternal death. A less serious note can
also be detected in this poem, as the sinner reminds God that it is He
who clothes our soul in perishable flesh and bone and so he should
be merciful and forgiving *in hora mortis nostræ.*

According to Brian Cosgrove, SH's last words to his family, '*Noli
timere*', are 'related to a particular kind of fear – namely, fear of
death'. Cosgrove identifies what he refers to as the 'literary source'
in Matthew R. McDiarmid (1914–96), an English literature and
campaigning academic at Queen's University Belfast when SH was
a student there. McDiarmid 'gave some prominence to the poetry
of the so-called Scottish Chaucerians of the fifteenth/early sixteenth
century' (Cosgrove 2018, 400–1), including Robert Henryson,
whose work SH would translate, and William Dunbar. Dunbar's
most famous poem, 'Lament for the Makaris' ('I that in heill wes
and gladnes'), is 'a meditation on death and a dirge for the long line
of mediaeval Scots poets, famous in their time, who had faded into
obscurity by the late fifteenth century' (Howard 2013, 6). The poem,
as Cosgrove remarks, 'derives much of its power from the refrain
that concludes all twenty-five of the stanzas', a refrain that 'tolls like
a death-knell throughout the poem': *Timor mortis conturbat me.*
Cosgrove interprets Heaney's final *Noli timere* as 'nothing less than
a riposte to the sentiment expressed in Dunbar's insistent refrain; or,
more broadly, a rejection of the recurrent medieval preoccupation
with death (and transience) – as found, for example, in the tradition
of *memento mori*' (Cosgrove, 401).

The tragic death of his younger brother when SH is a teenager,
paired with his exposure to Catholic regulations and rituals, makes
SH sensitised to death. And the deaths, violent as well as natural,
of family members and of friends and acquaintances in both
Catholic and Protestant communities when SH is an adult reinforce

his familiarity with death and 'the black glacier/Of each funeral', as he writes in the opening section of 'Funeral Rites' (*North*, 7).

In a 'Letter to the Editor' published in the *Times Literary Supplement* shortly after SH's death, Ben Howard relays the disappearance of two Heaney poems, one of which was Dunbar-like in that SH used the *Timor mortis conturbat me* refrain. In 1984 SH gives a reading at Alfred University, New York, and is hosted by Carol Burdick. 'At the time,' says Howard, 'Seamus was suffering from a toothache, and for most of his reading he kept his palm pressed against his cheek. Early the following morning, he assuaged his pain by writing a piece of light verse, a self-ironic poem modelled after William Dunbar's "Lament for the Makaris". Each stanza ended with Dunbar's refrain: "*Timor mortis conturbat me*". As he was leaving, Seamus graciously thanked Carol Burdick for her hospitality and presented her with the handwritten manuscript.' For decades the poem 'hung near the woodstove in her country home' and 'when the ink began to fade', Burdick photocopied it and put it away for safe keeping. After Burdick's death in 2008, 'both the original and the photocopy were lost' and 'her family has no idea of where they might be' (Howard 2013, 6) – a story that echoes Dunbar's fears of death and oblivion.

Talking about teaching at Harvard, in conversation with Dennis O'Driscoll, SH states that he sees it as part of his job to introduce his Harvard students 'to poems from the fifteenth century onwards: sonnets, carols, songs, odes, elegies, the lot. William Dunbar, William Wordsworth, Wystan Auden. Irish poems too, of course, Yeats especially,' adding that he has made *The Norton Anthology of Poetry* 'a set text' (*SS*, 272). William Dunbar's 'Laments for the Makaris' is included in the anthology from the second, revised edition (1975: 72–4).

[3] The Digging Skeleton

CHARLES BAUDELAIRE (1821–1867), FRENCH

First published in *Fuse* (Nov. 1973, 34) and reprinted with minor revisions in the *Times Literary Supplement* (16 Aug. 1974, 880).
   Collected in *North* (17–18).

This is SH's complete translation of '*Le squelette laboureur*', a poem included in *Les Fleurs du Mal* (1857). The text in this edition is drawn from *North* (1975).

SH's translation is collected in *North*, a book 'concerned primarily with understanding imaginatively the North of Ireland in relation to the bloody, violent history of northern Europe'. The translation is thus 'informed by the emotional and moral pressures that lie behind much of the poetry that he wrote during the 1970s'. 'Like many of the lyrics in *Les Fleurs du Mal*, argues Donnelly, the poem 'has the appeal of the strange, the weird, the exotic, even the outrageous', and 'some of these characteristics appealed to Heaney as they had appealed to one of his most influential mentors, Robert Lowell' (Donnelly 2009, 246–7). In 1968 Faber had published the first UK edition of Robert Lowell's *The Voyage and Other Versions of Poems by Baudelaire* (1961), a book that SH would have undoubtedly noticed. SH follows an already long line of Baudelaire translators into English who had preceded Lowell and translated '*Le squelette laboureur*'. One of them, Roy Campbell, also a Faber author, translated this poem twice: the first and freer version is titled 'Overture'; the second and more literal version is titled 'The Skeleton Navvy', a title that evokes one of SH's original poems.

A 'creative surge' in May 1969 results in SH writing 'about forty poems' (*SS*, 147). One of them is titled 'Navvy', which was first published in that same year in the *Listener* (4 Sept., 311), reprinted in *Capella* 4 (April 1970, 26–7) and then collected with revisions in 1972 in *Wintering Out* (40). Adam Piette argues that SH 'has politicised Baudelaire's vision of a nightmare afterlife, making it describe the lives (and deaths) of those real labourers,' such as 'Irishmen sentenced to hard labour', 'the chain-gang', and 'the starving peasants during the Famine desperately digging for diseased potatoes'. The word 'gang', notes Piette, 'can also apply to the road-gangs and the railway-gangs of the navvies' (Piette 1991, 116) and to the labourer of SH's 'Navvy'. SH gives a place and a voice to this and other 'particular imagined or recalled human figures' usually excluded from poetry so that they carry – as they do in some poems in Part I of *Wintering Out*; as Baudelaire's digging skeleton does in *North* – 'historical and political themes' (Corcoran 1998, 30).

[4] Ugolino

DANTE (1265–1321), MEDIEVAL ITALIAN

First published in *Antaeus* (Spring 1979, 20–31) and *Lower Stumpf Lake Review* (Spring 1979, 6–7).
Collected in *Field Work* (60–3) and *Opened Ground* (187–90).

This is SH's abridged translation of *ll.* 124–39 from *Inferno*: Canto XXXII and *ll.* 1–90 from *Inferno*: Canto XXXIII. The text in this edition is drawn from *Opened Ground* (1998).

What draws SH to Dante and particularly to the *Inferno* is the sense of familiarity of the characters, figures readers can feel they have read of or seen, and how their stories are told with 'the urgency of a prison visit' as Osip Mandelstam describes 'Dante's encounters in the underworld with people' in his 'wonderful essay on Dante'. SH also admires 'the danger and sizzle of the political and religious situation' and at the same time how the 'chaos' and 'voltage' of the subject matter is 'envisaged stilly' by Dante (Heaney 1995, 28:50–30:38). The 'hatred, bestiality but also fatherly love' that 'coexist' in the story of Ugolino exemplify this intensity and are matched by SH in his rewriting (Lonergan 2020, 179).

Referring to what Nadine Gordimer has termed 'the Eden of creativity', SH argues that 'the creative act is witnessed by history'. However, even though the context of his 'Ugolino' includes the 'dirty protests' in the Maze prison, SH notes that such a 'contemporary parallel' is not necessary because 'the sine qua non is personal rapport and writerly excitement' (*SS*, 425). SH was 'so exhilarated by the whole marvel of Dante' that he was 'tempted to have a go at doing the complete *Inferno* – simply for its own imaginative splendour'. SH 'soldiered on for four hundred lines or so' with the help of prose translations in English ('consulting my Sinclair and my Singleton': *SS*, 425). However, he stopped after three cantos – [25], [26] and [27] – having realised that 'for a big job like that, you need a note that pays you back, if you know what I mean: you need to be making a music that doesn't just match the original but verifies something in yourself as well' (*SS*, 425–6). That note SH would find in *Buile Suibhne* and *Beowulf*, in Sophocles and in Virgil.

1980s

In this decade, alongside two books of poems, *Station Island* (1984) and *The Haw Lantern* (1987), and two books of prose, *Preoccupations* (1980) and *The Government of the Tongue* (1988), SH publishes numerous translations from Old and Middle Irish, Old and Middle English, Spanish, Romanian, Italian and Latin. He also works on two book translations that will be published in the following decade:

The Cure at Troy – his version of Sophocles' *Philoctetes*, and his award-winning translation of *Beowulf*.

SH's mother dies in 1984 and his father in 1986, leaving 'a colossal space, one which he has struggled to fill through poetry' (Parker 1993, 221). The death of his father gives new momentum to a schoolboy project that SH would finish days before his death: the complete translation of *Aeneid Book VI* [101], where Aeneas descends to the underworld in order to visit the spirit of his father Anchises. SH's version of that episode (*ll.* 98–148) is first published in *Translation* in 1989 (Fall, 197–201) and collected with revisions as the opening poem in *Seeing Things*, which comes out in 1991.

[5] 'The small bird' — [6] 'Look far. Cast'
ANONYMOUS (NINTH CENTURY), OLD IRISH

First published as a two-part poem titled 'After the Irish' on p. 5 of the Field Day Theatre Company programme for the premiere of Brian Friel's *Translations* at Derry's Guildhall on 23 September 1980, but clearly two separate translations: 'The small bird' is reprinted with revisions, including a new title – 'The Blackbird of Belfast Lough' – in 2001 (in *Garm Lu: A Canadian Celtic Arts Journal* (Earrach/Spring, 7); twice in 2003 (in *The Way You Say the World: A Celebration for Anne Stevenson*, compiled by John Lucas and Matt Simpson (Beeston: Shoestring Press, 64:1), and in the programme for the dedication of the Seamus Heaney Centre for Poetry, Queen's University Belfast, 3); in 2010 (in *The Penguin Book of Irish Poetry*, edited by Patrick Crotty with a Preface by SH, 40); and, with the original title and text, in 2014 (in *The Finest Music: Early Irish Poetry*, edited by Maurice Riordan, London: Faber & Faber, xxxii). 'Look far. Cast' is reprinted with revisions, including a new title, 'North-East', in 1982 (in *Harvard Advocate*, Summer, 40); 1994 (as a card published by the artist Henry Pearson in a limited edition of 100 copies); 2003 (in *The Way You Say the World*, 65:3); and 2009 (as a Gallery Press Christmas card).
Uncollected.

These are SH's complete translations of '*Int én bec*' and '*Fegaid uaib sair fo thuaid*'. The texts in this edition are both drawn from the Field Day Theatre Company programme for the premiere of Brian Friel's *Translations* (1980).

'The small bird' had appeared uncredited in an RTÉ script (1978) collected in *Preoccupations* (181) with the title 'The God in the Tree: Early Irish Nature Poetry' and reprinted – also uncredited, with the same title, and the Irish original – in Seán Mac Réamoinn's *The Pleasure of Gaelic Poetry* (25). At the end of his Robert Lowell Memorial Lecture at Boston University (Heaney 2008b), SH reads this version alongside other original and translated blackbird poems:

> The Blackbird of Belfast Lough
>
> The small bird
> chirp-chirruped:
> yellow neb,
> > a note-spurt.
> Blackbird over
> Lagan water.
> Clumps of yellow
> > whin-burst!

SH recited this translation in one of his last poetry readings, at the Irish Cultural Centre (Centre Culturel Irlandais) in Paris on 13 June 2013 (Heaney 2013a, 02:30–3:13).

Below is the second version of 'Look far. Cast', co-translated with Timothy O'Neill and used as the text for SH's Christmas card in 2009:

> North-East
>
> Look far, cast
> eyes northeast:
> reach of ocean
> > seething.
> Brilliant seal run.
> Flood tide risen.
> Hefted waters
> > shoaling.

These and other early Irish poems can be found in three popular and influential anthologies which SH could have readily accessed. Kenneth Hurlstone Jackson's *A Celtic Miscellany. Translations from the Celtic Literatures*, first published by Routledge & Kegan Paul in 1951 and republished by Penguin in a revised edition in 1971 (SS, 151–2; 321). Gerard Murphy's *Early Irish Lyrics: Eighth to Twelfth Century*, first published by Clarendon Press in 1956, reprinted by Four Courts Press in 1998 and again in 2007, the year when SH began a collaboration with the Irish calligrapher Timothy O'Neill, which would produce several co-translations. David Greene and Frank O'Connor's *A Golden Treasury of Irish Poetry. AD 600 to 1200* was published by Macmillan in 1967. The translations in prose or verse and the textual information in these and other anthologies – including Patrick Crotty's *Penguin Book of Irish Poetry* (2010), which contains a Preface by SH – would have appealed to SH as starting points for his own versions.

[7] Sweeney Astray

ANONYMOUS (TWELFTH CENTURY), MIDDLE IRISH

First published in Ireland by the Field Day Theatre Company in 1983 in an edition of 1,000 copies printed by Mount Salus Press; published in the USA by Farrar, Straus and Giroux in 1984, published in the UK by Faber & Faber in 1984. Revised edition – titled *Sweeney's Flight* and including the same 'Introduction' (87–8) and 'Notes and Acknowledgements' (89) to the 1984 edition as well as a new 'Preface' (vii–viii) and photographs by Rachel Giese – published in the UK by Faber & Faber and in the USA by Farrar, Straus and Giroux in 1992. Reset paperback edition with revisions, entitled *Sweeney Astray*, published by Faber & Faber in 2001.

SH published fourteen excerpts from the translation in progress. The first is 'An Extract from the Middle Irish Tale *Buile Shuibe* [*sic*]' (§§39–40) in *Grilled Flowers* (Fall/Winter 1976, 58–62), collected with revisions in *Sweeney Astray* (31–40; *SF*, 101–4; *TSH*, 157–64). The second is 'Sweeney Astray' (§40) in *Armadillo* 3 (1976, 20–4), collected with revisions in *Sweeney Astray* (32–40; *SF*, 102–4; *TSH*, 157–64). The third is 'From *Sweeney Astray*' (§40) in *Quest* (Jan./Feb. 1978, 46), collected with revisions in *Sweeney Astray* (32–40; *SF*, 102–4; *TSH*, 157–64). The fourth is 'Sweeney Astray' (§40) in *Pushcart Prize III: Best of the Small Presses*, edited by Bill Henderson and published by the Pushcart Press in 1978 (251–9; this contribution was nominated by *Armadillo*), collected in *Sweeney Astray* (32–40; *SF*, 102–4; *TSH*, 157–64). The fifth is 'Sweeney Praises the Trees' (§40) in *Celebration. A Salute to a Visiting Artist*, edited by Jim Fitzgerald and published by Veritas in 1979 (10–11); collected in *Sweeney Astray* (32–40; *SF*, 102–4; *TSH*, 157–64: this publication was a tribute by nineteen Irish poets to Pope John Paul II on the occasion of his visit to Ireland). The sixth is 'From Sweeney Astray' (§§17–23) in *Ploughshares* 6. 1 (1980, 111–17), collected with revisions in *Sweeney Astray* (11–17; *SF*, 94–6; *TSH*, 141–6). The seventh is 'Sweeney Praises the Trees' (§40), a card printed by Henry Pearson at the Kelly/Winterton Press in 1981 in an edition of 110 hand-numbered copies, collected with revisions in *Sweeney Astray* (32–40; *SF*, 102–4; *TSH*, 157–64). The eighth is 'Sweeney's Praise of Farannan' (§73) in *Harvard Advocate* (summer 1982, 40), collected with revisions in *Sweeney Astray* (66; *SF*, 114; *TSH*, 184–5).

The ninth is 'Sweeney's Lament in Mourne' (§58) in *Belfast Review* (Winter 1982, 27), collected with revisions in *Sweeney Astray* (56–7; *SF*, 110–11; *TSH*, 176–7). The tenth is 'Sweeney Astray' (§§1–17) in *Threshold* (Winter 1982, 35–40), collected in *Sweeney Astray* (3–12; *SF*, 91–4; *TSH*, 135–42). The eleventh is 'Sweeney's Lament' (§61) in the *Listener* (23–30 Dec. 1982, 38), collected with revisions in *Sweeney Astray* (58–9; *SF*, 111–12; *TSH*, 178–9). The twelfth is 'Sweeney's Praise of Farannan' (§73) in *Poems for Charles Causley*, edited by Michael Hanke and published by the Enitharmon Press in 1982 (16), collected with revisions in *Sweeney Astray* (66; *SF*, 114; *TSH*, 184–5). The thirteenth is 'Sweeney Praises the Trees' (§40) in *The Rattle Bag: An Anthology of Poetry*, selected by Seamus Heaney and Ted Hughes and published by Faber & Faber in 1982 (411–13), collected in *Sweeney Astray* (32–40; *SF*, 102–4; *TSH*, 157–64). The fourteenth is 'Sweeney and the Saint' (§§74–5) in a Christmas card in 1982, collected with revisions in *Sweeney Astray* (66–70; *SF*, 114–15; *TSH*, 185–7).

SH anthologised seven extracts from *Sweeney Astray*. 'Sweeney Praises the Trees' (§§39–40), 'Sweeney Astray' (§40), 'Sweeney's Lament on Ailsa Craig' (§45), 'Sweeney in Connacht' (§§70–3) and 'Sweeney's Last Poem' (§83) in *New Selected Poems 1966–1987* (1990, 132–45; *SA*, 31–40; *SF*, 101–4; *TSH*, 157–64; *SA*, 32–40; *SF*, 102–4; *TSH*, 157–64; *SA*, 44–8; *SF*, 103–4; *TSH*, 167–70; *SA*, 65–6; *SF*, 113–14; *TSH*, 183–5; and *SA*, 72–3; *SF*, 116–17; *TSH*, 189–90); 'Sweeney in Flight' (§§17–23; §§39–40; §§42–5; §§72–4; §§76–8; §§81–3; §84) in *Opened Ground* (1998, 191–208; *SA*, 11–17; *SF*, 95–6; *TSH*, 141–6; *SA*, 31–40; *SF*, 101–4; *TSH*, 157–64; *SA*, 40–8; *SF*, 104–7; *TSH*, 164–70; *SA*, 65–6; *SF*, 114; *TSH*, 184–5; *SA*, 70–1; *SF*, 115–16; *TSH*, 188; *SA*, 72–3; *SF*, 116; *TSH*, 189–90; *SA*, 74; *SF*, 116; *TSH*, 190–1), and 'Lynchseachan, you are a bother . . .' (§29) in *The Penguin Book of Irish Poetry*, edited by Patrick Crotty and published by Penguin in 2010 (85–6; *SA*, 21–2; *SF*, 98; *TSH*, 149–50).

Two extracts from *Sweeney Astray* have been published posthumously. 'The Man in the Wood' (§47), in *The Finest Music*, edited by Maurice Riordan and published by Faber & Faber (2014, 103; *SA*, 49; *SF*, 108; *TSH*, 171) and 'From Sweeney Astray' (§58) in *The Map and the Clock. A Laureate's Choice of the Poetry of Britain and Ireland*, edited by Carol Ann Duffy and Gillian Clarke and published by Faber & Faber in 2016 (28–9; *SA*, 56–7; *SF*, 110–11; *TSH*, 176–7).

This is SH's abridged translation of *Buile Suibhne*. For the 1984 US edition, the subtitle 'A Version from the Irish by Seamus Heaney' was added. The text in this edition is drawn from the Faber & Faber revised edition, *Sweeney's Flight* (1992).

SH based his translation on J. G. O'Keeffe's Irish Text Society edition but dropped fourteen stanzas: six from §16, seven from §40, and one from §43. He also excluded from his translation 'Section 82 and the first fifteen stanzas of Section 83' (*SF*, 89).

SH began working on this translation after making two life-changing decisions in 1972: to leave Belfast and the North, and to give up the stability of a permanent job and devote himself to full-time writing. This self-exiling move to a cottage in the countryside south of Dublin is noticed more for its political implications than as SH's renewed commitment to digging with a pen.

In conversation with Dennis O'Driscoll, SH explains that what got him 'interested in the Sweeney material were the short extracts that appear in Kenneth Hurlstone Jackson's *A Celtic Miscellany* and that prompted him to get his hands on the Early Irish Texts edition of the work, from which he then got the idea that he should translate it in its entirety when he went to Glanmore' (*SS*, 168; Jackson 1971, 73–5: 'Suibhne the Wild Man in the Forest' and 'Suibhne Praises the Garbh'; 180–1: 'The Cliff of Alternan'; 233–4: 'Maguire and McDermot'; 254: 'The Wild Man of the Woods' and 'The Wild Man's Life'; and 255: 'The Wild Man Comes to the Monastery'). And with 'the safety net of a job and a salary' now 'removed', SH was 'readier to contemplate spin-off work': the translation of *Buile Suibhne* could earn his keep 'in three or four different ways – as a book, of course, but also as a radio drama of some sort and maybe in a children's version, as an illustrated book for younger readers' (*SS*, 168).

Over a decade, however, will pass before SH publishes his translation (1983) and almost another decade before a revised version of *Sweeney Astray* is published (1992), prompted by the collaboration with a photographer that has led first to 'little acts of revision' and then to 'a new edition of the whole translation' (*SF*, vii). In between, SH is awarded the PEN Translation Prize (1985) for his retelling of *Buile Suibhne* (*SS*, xxvi). As Anne Clune points out, *Sweeney Astray* 'appears to have been a large undertaking, with interruptions along the way to completion'. Clune maintains that this translation held 'more personal significance' for SH than his other translations from Irish' (Clune 1996, 162).

SH opens his 'Introduction' with two important remarks. The first is that he has based his translation of *Buile Suibhne* 'on J. G. O'Keeffe's bilingual edition, which was published by the Irish Texts Society in 1913' (*SF*, 87). As Anne Clune explains, *Buile Suibhne* 'exists in three manuscript versions, two of them in the Royal Irish Academy and the third in the Royal Library in Brussels'. The text O'Keeffe used, she explains, 'came from the Stowe collection and was written in the sixteen-seventies by Daniel or David Ó Duignan'. Also,

'It is the longest of the three, and is bound with two other tales, the *Banquet of Dun na nGedh* and the *Battle of Magh Rath*, with which it forms an independent story cycle' (Clune 1996, 49–50).

The second is that SH is aware that Flann O'Brien – who gave 'the central character' of this story 'a second life, as hilarious as it was melancholy, when he made Sweeney part of the apparatus of his novel *At Swim-Two-Birds*' – and that 'other poets and scholars have continued to make translations of different sections of the verse'. SH then explains that even though Sweeney is not 'a given figure of myth or legend' but 'an historically situated character', he has been drawn to the 'literary imagination which fastened upon him' and embodied the 'tension between the newly dominant Christian ethos and the older, recalcitrant Celtic temperament' (*SF*, 87).

Moreover, SH argues that Sweeney can be seen as 'a figure of the artist, displaced, guilty, assuaging himself by his utterance' and *Buile Suibhne* as 'an aspect of the quarrel between free creative imagination and the constraints of religious, political, and domestic obligation' (*SA*, vi; *SF*, 87). But what 'first tempted' SH to try his hand at translating *Buile Suibhne* and gave him 'the encouragement to persist with stretches of less purely inspired quatrains' was 'the bareness and durability of the writing' and 'its double note of relish and penitence'.

The 'first impulse' for SH is 'to forage for the best lyric moments and to present them as poetic orphans, out of the context of the story': it is those points of 'poetic intensity', as he explains, that 'establish the work's highest artistic levels and offer the strongest invitations to the translator of verse'. However, as he will do with the least attractive passages in his last translation, *Aeneid Book VI*, SH felt he had 'to earn the right to do the high points by undertaking the whole thing' as the text he was 'dealing with' was, 'after all', a 'major work in the canon of medieval literature' (*SA*, vii; *SF*, 87).

SH's 'fundamental relation' with Sweeney, as he points out, was topographical. 'His kingdom,' he explains, 'lay in what is now south County Antrim and north County Down,' and 'for over thirty years' SH 'lived on the verges of that territory, in sight of some of Sweeney's places and in earshot of others – Slemish, Rasharkin, Benevenagh, Dunseverick, the Bann, the Roe, the Mournes'. As already noted, SH began work on this version when he moved to Wicklow, 'not all that far from Sweeney's final resting ground at St Mullins' (*SF*, 88).

SH also writes an essay on translating *Buile Suibhne* titled 'Earning a Rhyme' and based on a talk he has given at one of the weekly meetings of Boston University's Translation Seminar. Like the 'Introduction', his essay articulates two important points – one contextual and the other textual. First, SH discusses what he refers to as 'the conditions under which any Irish writer operates when he enters into the footsteps of the established translators' (Heaney 1989a, 13). SH names James Clarence Mangan, Samuel Ferguson, Douglas Hyde, Lady Charlotte Guest, Lady Augusta Gregory, Frank O'Connor and Thomas Kinsella, who 'sang to sustain a tradition that transcended their own personal literary ambitions' (Heaney 1989a, 13). And 'Any translator of a big Irish language work', he tells O'Driscoll, 'can't help but be aware of those predecessors.' Kinsella's 'example', SH adds, 'was very important' and SH 'went so far as to report to him' his 'intention of tackling Sweeney', getting 'his encouragement' which 'felt as much like permission as encouragement' (SS, 152).

Moreover, SH explains, 'The translation of a text from the Irish language by an Irish writer who speaks English is usually to be perceived in lights other than just those of the writer's own career and impulses.' The 'additional contexts', he says, are 'historical, cultural and political': as he puts it, 'a canonical literature in English creates the acoustic within which the translation is to be heard' (Heaney 1989a, 13–14). In the 'anxiety' of Northern Ireland in the late 1960s and early 1970s 'the abiding problem', SH explains, 'was to discover a properly literary activity which might contain a potentially public meaning,' and 'in writing the book which would eventually appear as Sweeney Astray', as he himself put it, SH 'persuaded myself that the problem had been given at least a temporary solution'. Namely, 'to offer an indigenous text that would not threaten a Unionist (after all, this was just a translation of an old tale, situated for much of the time in what is now county Antrim and county Down) and that would fortify a Nationalist (after all, this old tale tells us we belonged here always and that we still remain unextirpated)'. SH's goal was 'to deliver a work of imagination that could be read universally as the thing-in-itself' and 'would also sustain those extensions of meaning that our disastrously complicated predicament at home made both urgent and desirable' (Heaney 1989a, 15–16).

Second, SH discusses the 'actual process of working with a crib', focusing on 'the changes in approach to translation' that occurred between his first version and the '[second] published one, taken up after a period of seven years' (Heaney 1989a, 13). The 'energy' that was initially 'generated by hurry and boldness' was later 'gathered through the steadier, more lexically concentrated gaze at individual words'. And, 'Instead of the rhythmic principle being one of lanky, enjambed propulsion, the lines hurdling along for fear they might seize up, the unit of composition now became the quatrain itself, and the metrical pattern became more end-stopped and boxed-in' (Heaney 1989a, 18).

In addition to drawing lexical and structural inspiration from the English literary tradition and the Bible, and to keeping his eyes 'as much to the left, on the Irish, as to the right, on O'Keeffe's unnerving trot', SH was also drawn to Lowell's 'trick of heightening the sense by adding voltage to the diction and planting new metaphors into the circuit' and 'unabashed readiness to subdue the otherness of the original to his own autobiographical neediness'. SH began to inflate himself and his situation into Sweeney's, making analogies 'between the early medieval Ulsterman who rocketed out of the north, as a result of vehement squabbles there among the petty dynasties, and this poet from county Derry who had also come south for purposes of retreat and composure' (Heaney 1989a, 18).

'The association of fear, panic and exile with the thick of the forest,' Tim Smith remarks, is 'common' in Western literature and 'pervasive' in *Sweeney Astray*. Like Dante, Sweeney is 'astray in the wood' and 'unsettled, panicky, astray'. Sweeney is also forced 'to sleep naked every night up there in the highest thickets'. And 'all of this', Smith concludes, 'comes full circle' with SH's translation of *Aeneid Book VI*, in which he renders Virgil's '*silva*' as 'thicket' (Sonzogni 2021, 179). Henry Hart observes how 'St John of the Cross, Dante, and Sweeney merge for Heaney into a single persona' as 'voluntary or involuntary exiles' who 'join' SH as he 'journeys through his dark wood of Irish troubles'. It is 'through translation', Hart emphasises, that SH 'appropriates their masks, manipulating their medieval voices and texts so that they speak for his and his country's contemporary need for atonement' (Hart 1992, 144).

Ultimately, however, 'The true motivations of writing', SH argues, 'are much more inward, much more to do with freshets that start in good moments of intent concentration and hope.' The process of rewriting *Buile Suibhne* in English made SH fully aware of his approach to literary translation – 'or version-making or imitation or refraction or whatever one should call the linguistic carry-over that is mediated through a crib' – as 'an aesthetic activity'. As such, he explains, 'It has to do with form-feeling as much as with sense-giving,' and 'Unless the practitioner has the almost muscular sensation that rewards successful original composition, it is unlikely that results of the text-labour will have life of their own' (Heaney 1989a, 20).

It is no coincidence that 'The Faber edition of *Sweeney Astray*', as Stephen Regan points out, 'was published simultaneously with *Station Island* in 1984.' In addition to regarding and positing a translated and an original text as equals, the 'deliberate pairing of these volumes', argues Regan, was also 'a reminder that both are fundamentally concerned with pilgrimage and penance' and 'in ways that strongly impact' upon SH's 'consideration of the role of the poet'. Sweeney, Regan concludes, 'lives again in *Station Island*, spurring on the imagination' (Regan 2015, 337). Indeed, what SH refers to as the 'pay-off' for this translation is 'a group of poems in *Station Island* called "Sweeney Redivivus" where "Sweeney" is rhymed with "Heaney", autobiographically as well as phonetically' (*SS*, 153–4). SH 'always had a hope', as he puts it, 'to get as free as Sweeney' and to 'inhabit his voice or have his voice inhabit me' (*SS*, 236).

If equating SH with Sweeney 'on the grounds that they are both exiled Ulster poets, has elements of truth,' Dennell Downum argues, 'it also serves to suppress the genuine otherness of Sweeney's voice'. And if Sweeney has been 'useful' to SH in that it 'has helped to free him in important ways', Downum observes, it 'is not simply because his discourse is, in Bakhtin's terms, "internally persuasive" for the modern poet' and 'apt to be "affirmed through assimilation, tightly interwoven with [his] own word"'. As Downum suggests, Sweeney 'erupts' into SH's text 'as a revenant, a ghostly visitor from the past, literally estranged and a stranger in modern-day Ireland' (Downum 2009, 89; Bakhtin 1981, 345).

A similar voltage, personal and poetic, will surround the return of Virgil and Aeneas in SH's version of *Aeneid Book VI*. If strife and war make Sweeney and Aeneas more similar than different, there is a clear difference between SH's first and last book-length translations. The autobiographical correspondences SH tests in 'Sweeney Redivivus' (*SI*, 97–121) and in 'Route 110' (*HC*, 48–59) testify respectively to his attempted and achieved at-homeness – in poetry as much as in place.

The 'sense of place' that SH 'emphasises' in *Sweeney Astray*, according to Anne Clune, 'operates in contrast to the idea of personal displacement, of "inner exile",' which, as she puts it, is 'the lot of the twentieth-century artist in general and Heaney in particular'. Also, she notes, it 'contrasts with Sweeney's "easy sense of cultural affinity with both western Scotland and southern Ireland",' which, as SH puts it, is 'exemplary for all men and women in contemporary Ulster' (Clune 1996, 54; *SF*, 87). 'That indication of what is exemplary in *Buile Suibhne*,' she argues, accounts for SH's 'emphasis on the historical and political dimensions of the tale', as well as for his 'awareness that not much has changed' (Clune 1996, 54–5).

It has been claimed, as Clune notes, that SH 'chose Sweeney as an expression of his independence from Yeats' in the way that 'O'Brien chose Sweeney to define himself against Joyce'. But 'what has not been explained,' says Clune, is 'why either of them felt the need to choose this particular mythological figure' when, 'For either of the purposes stated, any character other than Cuchulain might have done' (Clune 1996, 59). Sweeney, Clune argues, 'encompasses both the continuity of human experience and its distinctiveness within particular cultures'. Consequently, 'aspects of this early literature are unique'. The writers who 'choose to revive or reinterpret it', she concludes, 'are not doing so only in order to find a mirror in which their own concerns are reflected, but also in order to perform that act of "cultural and political resistance and retrieval"' (Clune 1996, 60; *Preoccupations*, 141).

In 1980, when he participated in the inaugural edition of 'A Sense of Ireland', a major festival of Irish culture held in London, SH recited 'Sweeney Praises the Trees' (§40: *ll.* 9–56) from his translation in progress (*SF*, 102; Heaney 1980, 0:01–1:31). Asked by Gloria Hunniford why Ireland 'has produced so many excellent writers', SH states that 'It's partly because any society . . . has a need to define itself and to seek some kind of coherent image or sense of itself,' and the writers 'are expressing the incoherence and the need for coherence'. SH links 'the effulgence of poetry in the North' with 'the search to define the energies that are the blueprint of the place' (Heaney 1980, 2:00–3:19).

Brendan Kennelly suggests, 'What one remembers most about *Sweeney Astray* is the delicate, dramatic balance between pain and praise.' And, 'If there is anything in this work that balances the poetry of pain, it is the poetry of praise, and what is praised most beautifully and convincingly is the landscape of Ireland, its fields, meadows, hills, rivers, mountains, glens, the sea's eternal caress and threat' (Kennelly 1984; *BR*, 14).

[8] The Names of the Hare

ANONYMOUS (THIRTEENTH CENTURY), MIDDLE ENGLISH

First published in *Poetry Ireland Review* (Spring 1981, 8–9) and reprinted with revisions in *The Rattle Bag* (305–6): 'the grass-hopper'

(*l.* 35) becomes 'the grass-bounder'; 'the growth-cropper' (*l.* 38)
becomes 'the herb-cropper'; 'The stag that sprouts a leathery horn'
(*l.* 49) becomes 'The stag sprouting a suede horn'.

Collected in *Opened Ground* (209–11).

This is SH's complete translation of '*Les nouns de vn leure en
engleis*'. The text in this edition is drawn from *Opened Ground*
(1998).

At the end of 'Dame Sirith' – the earliest *fabliau* known in
English, written *c.* 1272–83 and preserved as MS Digby 86 in the
University of Oxford's Bodleian Library – there is 'a strange poem'
which is 'found only in this manuscript', is 'usually known as
"The Names of a Hare" (fol. 168 *r. col. ii*–fol. 168 *v. col. ii*)' and 'has
received very little discussion' (Sonzogni 2021, 80).

This poem – which has an incipit in Anglo-Norman French:
'*Les nouns de vn leure en engleis*' or 'The names of a hare in English'
– has 'no known source or close analogue'; it has a description of
itself as 'a prayer' ('on oreisoun', v. 8), and can be described as
'a series of charms or of curses' (Sonzogni 2021, 80).

There are two editions of the poem: one by Wright and Halliwell,
who include it in their *Reliquiae Antiquae* (Wright 1841, 133), and
one by A. C. S. Ross, who devotes to it one of the essays collected
in the *Proceedings of the Leeds Philosophical and Literary Society,
Literary and Historical Section* (Ross 1932). Neither, however,
appears to be SH's source, which Peter Whiteford has identified as a
book titled *The Leaping Hare*, co-authored by George Ewart Evans
and David Thomson, and published by Faber in 1972. Before the end
of the year this 'rare and remarkable book about every aspect of the
life and legend of the wild hare, in nature, poetry, folklore, history
and art', as it is described on Faber's website, was reviewed by SH in
The Listener.

SH opens his review with a personal account: 'I once spent a
whole sunlit afternoon lying on the earthworks of Maiden Castle
outside Dorchester, watching hares shifting about on a hillside
about a quarter of a mile away. The sense of being on an ancient
ground was perfectly complemented by a sense of being attended:
I retrieved a sense of the hare's numen, and although I was then only
vaguely aware of the magical associations that cluster around her,
I felt, as Lawrence felt about his snake, honoured.' SH's discussion
of 'a lovely book that is both exploratory of and rooted in this
sense of the hare's mystery' ends with a quotation from 'the Middle
English poem consisting of a litany of riddling names: The light-foot,

the sitter in the bracken,/The stag of the cabbages, the cropper of herbage,/The low-creeper, the sitter still' (Heaney 1972, 869).

[9] Song of the soul that delights in knowing God by faith

JOHN OF THE CROSS (1542–1591), EARLY MODERN SPANISH

First published in *Tenfold: Poems for Frances Horovitz* (1983, 9–10) with the title 'Song of the soul that delights in knowing God by faith'.

Collected with revisions as 'Station Island XI' in *Station Island* (89–91).

This is SH's complete translation of '*Cantar del alma que se huelga de conocer a Dios por fe*'. The text in this edition is drawn from *Station Island* (1984).

The text in *Station Island* consists of seventeen tercets. This edition of SH's translation does not include the first five tercets and the first line of the sixth as those lines are not part of the actual translation but an allegorical – 'the prisms of the kaleidoscope'; 'a marvellous lightship'; 'the zenith and glimpsed jewels of any gift/mistakenly abased' – yet personal explanation – 'a monk's face/that had spoken years ago from behind a grille/spoke again' – of what 'stirred' SH into translating John of the Cross (*SI*, 89).

There are two passages in SH's conversations with Dennis O'Driscoll that illuminate the genesis and purpose of this translation. In one, discussing the second priest introduced in the penultimate section of *Station Island*, SH explains: 'He was based on a Carmelite who gave a retreat during my last year in St Columb's. He didn't actually suggest I translate John of the Cross as penance, but he had indeed just come back from Spain and seemed to shine with inner light. And he *did* say to me, "Read poems as prayers"' (*SS*, 249). In the other, discussing his own faith, SH explains: 'In *Station Island*, I arranged for John of the Cross to help my unbelief by translating his "Song of the Soul that Knows God by Faith"' (*SS*, 234).

As Ross Woods notes, SH 'distances himself from the idea of writing or reading poetry as a form of religious epiphany and further proof of God's grandeur' (Sonzogni 2021, 290). There are two key images in the text. The dark night, which Henry Hart describes as 'a metaphor for the imagination which burns most intensely when darkened to the world' (Hart 1987, 3); and a fountain, for which SH offers two descriptions. The first is 'eternal' (*eterna*), a reference to God as a source of life that also echoes Dante: having completed her mission, Beatrice turns back to the eternal fountain of God (*Paradiso* XXXI 93: '*si tornò a l'etterna fontana*'). Maria Cristina Fumagalli adopted 'eternal' in the title she chose for her study of this translation, 'The Eternal Fountain of Poetic Imagination' (Fumagalli 1997b). The second is 'living' (*viva*), which conjures up *fons vivus*, the living spring evoked in the *Veni Creator Spiritus*, a ninth-century Pentecostal hymn in Latin SH was familiar with. Not to mention the wells SH could not be kept away from as a child, vividly described in 'Personal Helicon', the poem that ends his first book, *Death of a Naturalist* (*DN*, 44).

The source SH used for this translation is not certain – there are several English translations of the poetry of John of the Cross he could have drawn from. One can be singled out as of particular interest because it presents textual or contextual pointers: Roy Campbell's – the same Campbell whose poetry Faber once published and whose translation of Baudelaire's '*Le squelette laboureur*' may be among the sources of SH's 'The Digging Skeleton' [3].

Campbell and Heaney have hardly been linked. In his review of *Electric Light* for the *Guardian*, however, Robert Potts argues that reading SH's poetry and prose 'at times one is reminded of Roy Campbell's lines', especially to describe 'what is on offer': 'a quasi-pastoral, mostly secular Catholicism; a belief in and desire for transcendence' (Potts 2001, 8).

Their translations of '*Cantar del alma que se huelga de conocer a Dios por fe*' do present some similarities. The incipit, for example: both use 'How well I know that fountain' for '*Que bien se yo la fonte*'. Their versions of the refrain, '*Aunque es de noche*', are also similar: SH uses 'Although' throughout his translation whereas Campbell alternates 'Although' and 'Though'; and in the penultimate refrain, SH opts for 'Because' whereas Campbell chooses 'For' to translate '*porque*'. More interestingly, SH seems to adopt 'And they drink these waters' from Campbell's translation of '*Y de esta agua se hartan*', and for '*Y que cielos y tierra beben de ella*', which Campbell translates as 'And earth and heaven drink refreshments there', Heaney has 'Here the earth and heaven drink their fill'. And '*En este pan de vida*' is translated by SH and Campbell as 'Within this bread of life' and 'Within the bread of life'.

Campbell's translation, a dual-language volume titled *The Poems of St John of the Cross* and prefaced by M. C. D'Arcy, was published in London by the Harvill Press and in New York by Pantheon Books in 1951 and reprinted posthumously by Penguin in 1960. To save their marriage, Campbell and his wife had moved to Toledo, Spain, where Campbell discovered, studied and translated the poetry of John of the Cross. As Fumagalli notes, '*Cantar del alma que se huelga de conocer a Dios por fe*' 'is believed to be the first poem that the Carmelite monk wrote and it was composed in the hallucinatory silence of his cell in the prison of Toledo' (Fumagalli 1997b, 165). This setting would have appealed to SH's personal, political and poetic preoccupations throughout the 1970s and the 1980s.

[10] Fountains in the sea — [11] Angle — [12] The tear — [13] Old people in the shade — [14] The first words — [15] Proper names

MARIN SORESCU (1936–1996), ROMANIAN

First published in *The Biggest Egg in the World* (1987, 64–5; 69; 71–2; 76). 'The first words' and 'Proper names' are reprinted in *The Tree Clock* (1990, 21–2).
　　'The first words' is collected with revisions in *The Spirit Level* (38).

These are SH's complete translations of '*Fântâni în mare*', '*Unghi*, *Lacrima*', '*Bătrâni la umbră*', '*Primele cuvinte*' and '*Nume proprii*' (1982). The texts in this edition are drawn from *The Biggest Egg in the World* (1987) for 'Fountains in the sea', 'Angle', 'The tear', 'Old people in the shade' and 'Proper names'. The text of 'The first words' collected in *The Spirit Level* (1996) and in this edition has a variant: SH revises *l.* 9 from 'Up to fire and air and water and earth' to 'Up to water and earth and fire and air'.
　　In her Introduction to *The Biggest Egg in the World* – the second Bloodaxe anthology of Sorescu's poetry after *Selected Poems*, published in 1983 and translated by Michael Hamburger – Edna Longley explains that 'The book was conceived not only as a chronological follow up, but as a tribute to Marin Sorescu by English and Irish poets who know him personally.' Heaney meets Sorescu in the summer of 1981, when they are both on the programme of the international poetry festival in Morelia in Mexico, along with a number of other distinguished writers such as Jorge Luis Borges, Allen Ginsberg, Tadeusz Różewicz, Michael Hamburger and three future Nobel laureates: Octavio Paz, Günter Grass and Tomas Tranströmer (*SS*, xxv, 266–7).

Longley also notes that 'Fundamental to the project was the presence of Joanna Russell-Gebbett in Belfast.' She was 'a friend of Sorescu's to whom he had been sending poems for translation into English,' and 'All the poets except Michael Hamburger (who kept to his earlier practice) have based their readings on Joanna Russell-Gebbett's translations,' adding that 'They may also have received some marginal signals from what Hamburger calls "the recognition of Latin roots"' (Sorescu 1987, 11). Russell-Gebbett was introduced to Longley by John Fairleigh, a lecturer in Irish Studies at Queen's University Belfast who was Ireland's unofficial cultural ambassador to Romania and was involved in many cultural exchanges. Fairleigh would edit *Where the Tunnels Meet*, an anthology of contemporary Romanian poetry also published by Bloodaxe in 1996 to which SH contributed ten Ana Blandiana translations: [28] to [37].

For Alexandra Dumitrescu, Sorescu's and SH's 'cultural heritage and enterprises converge': 'Ireland during the Troubles and Romania during communism', she argues, were 'relatively small cultures haunted by big dreams delineated by violence' (Sonzogni 2021, 240, 245). For Irina Moga, their affinity is also poetic: 'their poems have a similar structure', she observes, and 'a misleading allure of poetic narratives that attracts the reader in the trap of metaphors' (Sonzogni 2021, 240).

SH's engagement with Sorescu's poetry extends beyond translation. In 1987 another Sorescu book was translated by an Irish poet and published in Ireland: Dedalus Press brought out *The Youth of Don Quixote*, John F. Dean's version of Sorescu's *Tineretea lui Don Quijote* (1968). SH includes this translation among his holiday reading suggestions for the *Sunday Tribune* (2 Aug. 1987, 6). In 1991 another anthology of Marin Sorescu's poetry in English translation comes out. *Hands Behind My Back: Selected Poems*, translated by Gabriela Dragnea, Stuart Friebert and Adriana Varga is published by Oberlin College Press with an introduction by SH (Sorescu 1991, 9–15). In conversations with Dennis O'Driscoll, SH says that he is 'glad to do a short introduction to a volume of his poems published in America' (*SS*, 307). SH also contributes a foreword (in Irish) to *Dánta deireadh saoil. Poemele Sfársítului*, an anthology of Sorescu's poetry in Irish translation, published in Dublin in 2000 by Coiscéim and translated by Aodh Ó Canainn and Anamaria Maior (Sorescu 2000, xi).

This decade is punctuated by poem-length and award-winning book-length translations from a staggering number of languages: classical Greek, Czech, Dutch, Old English, Irish, Latin, Polish, Romanian and Russian.

While passages from *Sweeney Astray* (1983) continue to be reprinted and new translations from Old, Middle and Modern Irish are published, a series of excerpts from Old English leads to the publication of SH's most famous translation, *Beowulf*, in 1999, ending a decade that had opened with the publication of SH's most quoted translation and the first from Greek, *The Cure at Troy* (1990). In between, SH brings out three other book-length translations: *The Midnight Verdict* (1993), a hybrid text from Latin and Irish; *Laments* (1995) from Polish, and *Diary of One Who Vanished* (1999) from Czech.

Halfway through this decade – which sees the publication of two books of poems: *Seeing Things* (1991) and *The Spirit Level* (1996); a book of essays: *The Redress of Poetry* (1995), SH's Oxford Lecture; and two anthologies: *The School Bag* (1997), co-edited with Ted Hughes, and *Opened Ground: Poems 1966–1996* (1998) – SH is awarded the Nobel Prize in Literature (1995). Two of SH's most important and influential friends die in this decade: Joseph Brodsky in 1996 and Ted Hughes in 1998.

[16] The Cure at Troy
A Version of Sophocles' *Philoctetes*
SOPHOCLES (*c.*496–406 BCE), CLASSICAL GREEK

Published in Northern Ireland by Field Day in 1990; published in the UK by Faber & Faber in association with Field Day in 1990; published with revisions in the USA by Farrar, Straus and Giroux in 1991.

SH published three extracts from *The Cure at Troy*. The first excerpt quickly became and remains to this day a herald of hope for a just and peaceful society. It is from the end of the play, where the Chorus talks about human suffering, justice, change and equality, and was reprinted several times: 'Excerpt from The Cure at Troy. A Version of Sophocles' Philoctetes' is included in *The Birmingham Six: An Appalling Vista*, edited by Oscar Gillian and published by Elo Press (1990, 66–9). 'A Chorus' is published with revisions in the *New York Times* (1 Jan. 1991, A29). This text presents two variants: 'jails' (*l.* 7) instead of 'gaols' (*TSH*, 250, *l.* 1587) and 'A police widow' (*l.* 11) instead of 'The police widow' (*CTb*, 77, *TSH*, 250, *l.* 1591). This version of the Chorus is identical to the typescript version housed at the National Library of Ireland in Dublin (MS 49,493/233–58): on p. 70 of this document SH typed 'jails' and 'A police widow' instead of 'The police widow'. In both the UK and US editions of the play, however, SH has reinstated 'The police widow'. 'Chorus from The Cure at Troy' features in *Arion: A Journal of Humanities and the Classics* (Spring 1991, 131–8). 'Chorus' is included as a single leaf insert in the programme for *The Cure at Troy,* directed by Derek Walcott at the Poetry Center of the 92nd Street YMCA, New York City, on 15 March 1993. 'From The Cure at Troy' is printed on linen scrolls by Queen's University Belfast in 1996. 'Chorus from The Cure at Troy' is part of the after-dinner speech delivered at the Atlantic Foundation's Irish Odyssey in 1997 and is printed by the Foundation for private circulation. The second excerpt consists of five passages from the beginning (I: Chorus; II: Philoctetes to Neoptolemus) and the end of the play (III: Philoctetes and Chorus; IV and VI: Chorus): 'Voices from Lemnos', in *Opened Ground: Poems 1966–1996* published by Faber & Faber in 1998 (*OG*, 327–32). The third excerpt is a Chorus (*CTb*, 37–9; *TSH*, 221–2, *ll.* 835–79): 'You've heard the famous tale', in SH's *Stone from Delphi: Poems with Classical References,* edited by Helen Vendler and published by the Arion Press in 2012 (52–3).

One excerpt was included posthumously in *100 Poems* (*ll.* 1581–86 and *ll.* 1593–1610; *100P*, 100–1; *CTb*, 77–8; *TSH*, 250–1; this version of the 'Chorus' ends with the addition of three lines: 'It means once in a lifetime/That justice can rise up/And hope and history rhyme.').

SH wrote two special texts about his version of Philoctetes: a note in the programme of Eton College's Double Edge Drama production of *The Cure at Troy* at the Edinburgh Fringe Festival in 1992; and an essay, 'Sweet talk and miracles: Notes on The Cure at Troy', for the American Repertory Theatre at Harvard University's Institute for Advanced Theatre Training in 1997.

This is SH's complete translation of Φιλοκτήτης (409 BCE) to which he added the subtitle 'A Version of Sophocles' *Philoctetes*'. The text in this edition is drawn from the Farrar, Straus and Giroux edition (1991).

'There are writings of mine', SH tells Dennis O'Driscoll, 'I'd think of as public in the megaphone sense of the term – things like the song I wrote after Bloody Sunday and the "Human beings suffer" chorus of *The Cure at Troy*' (*SS*, 385–6).

The message of the Chorus has found resonance in Ireland and beyond. SH's translation of *Philoctetes,* however, was 'slow to arrive' – 'ten years after *Translations,* six years after Tom Paulin's version of *Antigone* and Derek Mahon's version of Molière's *School for Husbands*' as SH notes – and when it did, it was 'a partial fulfilment of Brian Friel's hope that Field Day would induce the poets to have a go at work for the stage' (*SS*, 420).

'Understandably', Michael Parker observes, SH 'was anxious about how this new commission would be received, and conscious that for it to succeed the verse needed to pitch at a level and intensity that would match the power of the original, and yet not make excessive demands on a contemporary audience' (Parker 2017, 748). 'Personal friendships and cultural influences' – most notably Brian Friel in Ireland, Ted Hughes in the UK and Robert Fitzgerald in the USA (SH dedicates *The Cure at Troy* to him) – prompted SH 'to re-engage with Greek Literature from the early 1980s onwards' (Parker 2017, 747). For SH, however, 'the main attraction' would always rest with 'the material itself'. In this case, 'the way Sophocles explores the conflict experienced by the character Neoptolemus – the crunch that comes when the political solidarity required from him by the Greeks is at odds with the conduct he requires from himself if he's to maintain his self-respect'. It was a dilemma, SH explains, that 'was familiar to people on both sides of the political fence in Northern Ireland' who were 'living in a situation where to speak freely and truly on certain occasions would be regarded as letting down the side' (*SS*, 420).

'The goal of anyone writing a play', Matthew DeForrest argues, 'is to create a cast of characters universal enough to be able to evoke a feeling of sympathy from members of the audience while keeping them individual enough not to be labelled stock characters by reviewers.' SH, he maintains, set out 'to create a version of Sophocles' play which does not limit itself to the immediate events of the Trojan War' (DeForrest 1994, 126) – or, for that matter, to those in Northern Ireland, even though 'The Field Day Theatre Company in Derry, Northern Ireland', as Richard C. Jones III points out, 'has made the politics of translation central to its theatrical mission since its inception in 1980' (Jones 1997, 232). To allow for a 'broader view of the play', SH 'intentionally tips this balance in favour of the universal rather than the individual' (DeForrest 1994, 126), so that 'individuals and, by implication, cultures can advance in ethical consciousness' (Parker 2017, 775). SH's version of *Philoctetes* 'offers itself as a mirror and window' in and through which not only 'its audiences from the North and the Republic' but also from other parts of the world 'can catch glimpses of themselves, and insights into the ills afflicting them and their culture' (Parker 2017, 753).

As Patrick Crotty notes, Philoctetes' wound is 'emblematic of the trauma of Ulster's maimed and distrustful communities' (Crotty 2001, 204).

Parker, however, points out that the composition of *The Cure of Troy* coincides with '[m]omentous developments in global and local politics' coming to a head (Parker 2017, 748). SH is mindful of the challenges and consequences faced by political leaders committed to bringing about change in their society at home as well as abroad – and as far as South Africa, where a new government is committed to eradicating apartheid and ending white minority rule. In the 'Notes' for the programme that accompanied the production of *The Cure at Troy* by Eton College's Double Edge Drama for the Edinburgh Festival Fringe in 1992, SH reminds the audience that 'The first performances of this version of Sophocles' *Philoctetes* were given in Derry and Belfast in the autumn of 1990, not too long after the fall of the Berlin Wall, the collapse of the tyranny in Romania and the accession to power of the Havel government in Czechoslovakia.' And 'the sustained, selfless commitment to truth and justice' of Eastern European 'writers, painters and film-makers' has inspired SH to infuse his version of *Philoctetes* with 'art's ethical, spiritual and restorative potential' and 'its capacity to portray not just the world as it is, but as "it is wished-for"' (Parker 2017, 748–9). As Rosie Lavan puts it, *The Cure at Troy* has 'emerged in retrospect as a text that was ready for the future' (Harrison 2019, 58).

As he works on his version with these intentions in mind, SH relies on three English translations, each useful in its own way. 'A late-nineteenth-century crib', albeit stylistically 'a hash', was 'a godsend in that it gave the word order and the word-for-word meaning'. An 'old-fashioned', dual-language Loeb version in verse by Francis Storrs (1912) reflected 'the metrical shifts of the original Greek' and was 'full of pseudo-Shakespearean diction'. And David Grene's 'modern translation' in verse (1957) gave Sophocles a modern voice. Working 'line by line, in blank verse – except for the choruses, and a couple of prose paragraphs for a change of pitch', SH completes the translation 'relatively fast'. He starts it 'at the beginning of 1990', 'handed in a first draft in July' and 'by September' he is 'into rehearsals' (*SS*, 420–1).

SH's version of *Philoctetes* could have had an alternative epigraph to the eight lines (third and second last quatrains) from W. H. Auden's 'As I Walked Out One Evening' he used. The option SH considered – found in the Seamus Heaney Papers (1951–2004) housed at Emory University's Stuart A. Rose Manuscript, Archives and Rare Book

Library – was an excerpt from the ninth-century Irish of *Tecosca Cormaic*, transcribed by SH from Kuno Meyer's English translation, *The Instructions of King Cormac mac Airt* (1909):

'O Cormac, son of Conn,' said Carbery, 'I desire to know how I shall behave among the wise and the foolish, among friends and strangers, among the old and the young, among the innocent and the wicked.'
'Not hard to tell,' said Cormac.
'Be not too wise nor too foolish.
Be not too conceited nor too humble.
Be not too talkative nor too silent.
Be not too hard nor too feeble.
If you be too wise, they will expect too
    much of you.
If you be too foolish, you will be deceived.
If you be too conceited, you will be thought
    vexatious.
If you be too humble, you will be without
    honour.
If you be too talkative, you will not be heeded.
If you be too silent, you will not be regarded.
If you be too hard, you will be broken.
If you be too feeble, you will be crushed.'

Receiving *The Sunday Times* Award for Excellence in Writing in London on 28 April 1988, SH voiced his view that 'the British Government and sections of the British media' had 're-occupied their old positions on the high ground' and offered his plea 'for a renewed self-consciousness in the expression of just national concerns by the British media, an avoidance of the high ground, and an ongoing example of the free, self-regulating debate which has typically distinguished the British democratic process'. To channel his plea, SH turned to this 'piece of early Irish wisdom literature' – an Old Irish gnomic text in the form of a dialogue between 'the sagacious King Cormac' and 'the boyish Carbery' – for an alternative to 'Mediterranean culture' as 'the great source of the golden mean as a rule of behaviour'. These verses, SH argues, demonstrate that 'the middle way ran through Tara and Armagh as well' (Heaney 1988a: 9).

Some of the words spoken by Philoctetes in *The Cure at Troy* – 'Away to the house of death./To my father, sitting waiting there/ Under the clay roof' (*CTb*, 64; *TSH*, 241, *ll.* 1368–70) – return, in a slightly different form, at the beginning of 'The Blackbird of Glanmore': 'And lines I once translated/Come back: "I want away/To the house of death, to my father//Under the low clay roof"' (*DC*, 75, *ll.* 9–12).

[17] Miraculous Grass — [18] Mo Mhíle Stór

NUALA NÍ DHOMHNAILL (*b.* 1952), IRISH

First published in Nuala Ní Dhomhnaill's *Pharaoh's Daughter*, a collection of forty-five poems in Irish with facing translations by thirteen distinguished poets from Ireland, published by the Gallery Press in 1990 (33–5 and 49).
Uncollected.

These are SH's complete translations of '*Féar suaithinseach*' ('Miraculous Grass') and '*Mo mhíle stór*' ('My Dearest Lover') (1990). The texts in this edition are drawn from *Pharaoh's Daughter* (1990).
   Reviewing *Pharaoh's Daughter* for the *Times Literary Supplement*, Patricia Craig notes how each one of the thirteen translators, 'all poets, has found among the Irish language originals something peculiarly in keeping with his or her own predilection'. According to Craig, 'the metamorphosis, the branching-out, or shape-shifting, from Gaelic myth or folk-song to some less romantic or quirkier emblem of the present is a constant resource of Nuala Ní Dhomhnaill's poetry' (Craig 1991, 20).
   '*Féar suaithinseach*', the title poem in Ní Dhomhnaill's second collection, exemplifies Craig's comment as well as SH's motives for translation. As Angela Bourke remarks, the poem 'asserts that a culture which reduces female sexuality to a source of pollution and shame can invade a woman and deprive her of her essential integrity just as surely as if she had been raped' (Bourke 1993, 36). This description can be extended to some of SH's female protagonists in poems like 'Maighdean Mara' and 'Limbo' in *Wintering Out* (56–7, 58) and 'Punishment' and 'Strange Fruit' in *North* (30–1, 32). 'A very large portion of Ní Dhomhnaill's poems', Bo Almqvist maintains, 'are based on folktales and folk legends or contain allusions to oral narratives' (Almqvist 1990, 11) as are many poems by SH. Reading Ní Dhomhnaill's 'An Mhaighdean Mhara' alongside SH's 'Maighdean Mara' makes 'immediately obvious' not only their similar subject but also their distinctive ways of dealing with it –

'a couple of traits' reveal Ní Dhomhnaill's as 'undeniably southern as Heaney's is northern' (Almqvist 1990, 27).

Answering a question put to him by Dennis O'Driscoll about 'tenderness and empathy towards women' in his work and the perception of women in his poems as 'stereotypical and picturesque rather than living creatures', SH says that 'there's a picturesque setting, if you want to call it that, in poems like "Maighdean Mara" and "Shore Woman" in *Wintering Out*' – poems, SH glosses, that 'happen to be set in what is now Nuala Ní Dhomhnaill territory, both psychologically and geographically' (*SS*, 312–13).

SH wrote a poem 'to mark the presentation of the Parnell Stick by Seamus Heaney to Nuala Ní Dhomhnaill in the presence of Conor Cruise O'Brien, Guest of Honour', from whom Seamus Heaney had received it. 'The Stick' was published privately by Peter Fallon at the Gallery Press on 18 August 1998. When SH died, Ní Dhomhnaill wrote an elegy in Irish in memory of him, which she also translated into English. In the poem she compares SH's death to a tree fallen in the heart of a forest – 'the King of the Forest was felled' – and describes the poet as a piper who led the way – 'He piped us on and led us into the Promised Land' (Ní Dhomhnaill 2014, 163).

[19] Will Travel — [20] Exile's Return — [21] The Clay Pipes — [22] Lament

CATHAL Ó SEARCAIGH (*b.* 1956), IRISH

First published in Ó Searcaigh's selected poems, *Homecoming/An bealach 'na Bhaile – Selected Poems/Rogha Dánta*, edited by Gabriel Fitzmaurice and published by Cló Iar-Chonnachta in 1993 (81, 93, 199–201 and 209) and reprinted in Ó Searcaigh's *By the Hearth in Mín a' Leá*, translated by Frank Sewell, Seamus Heaney and Denise Blake and published by Arc Publications in 2006. 'The Clay Pipes', with photograph by Rachel Brown, was published in 1995 in Louisville by White Fields Press as broadside number 29 in the Heaven Poster Series. 'Lament', with a photograph by Kevin McKiernan, was printed in 1996 by Johnswood Press in Belfast as a broadside published by Coiscéim Feirste.

Uncollected.

These are SH's complete translations of '*Triall*', '*Pilleadh*', '*Na píopaí créafóige*' and '*Caoineadh: i gcuimhne mo mhathar*' (1993). The texts in this edition are drawn from *Homecoming/An bealach 'na Bhaile – Selected Poems/Rogha Dánta* (1993).

As Nobuaki Tochigi points out, 'since the late 1980s, translations from Irish to English have stimulated the general interest in literature written in the Irish language' (Tochigi 2000, 139). The publication of bilingual collections – most notably Nuala Ní Dhomhnaill's – and bilingual anthologies – especially *An Crann Faoi Bhláth/The Flowering Tree: Contemporary Irish Poetry with Verse Translations*, edited by Declan Kiberd and Gabriel Fitzmaurice – made Irish poetry accessible to a wider range of audiences. Ó Searcaigh's poetry, would 'add to those landmark works' (Tochigi 2000, 139). And like Ní Dhomhnaill's *Pharaoh's Daughter*, Ó Searcaigh's *Homecoming* is a selection of his poetry in Irish 'set together with English versions translated by leading Irish poets, among them Seamus Heaney' (Tochigi 2000, 139). The title of this book reflects the poet's 'return to his native Donegal after spending years going back and forth between Donegal and large cities in Britain and Ireland' (Tochigi 2000, 139) – a state of mind and a condition for writing that were familiar to SH.

Micheál Ó Conghaile, an Irish writer and the publisher at Clo Iar-Chonnachta, had invited Gabriel Fitzmaurice to select, translate and edit a collection of Ó Searcaigh's poetry. Fitzmaurice was to translate about half of the poems and was free to choose poets who would translate the rest. Ó Searcaigh himself picked SH and sent him a selection of poems from which to choose.

[23] The Midnight Verdict

OVID (43 BCE–CE 17/18), CLASSICAL LATIN
BRIAN MERRIMAN (*c.* 1747–1805), IRISH

Published in Ireland by the Gallery Press in 1993. This translation comprises three texts: 'Orpheus and Eurydice', SH's abridged version of Ovid's *Metamorphoses* Book X (*MV*, 15–19; *TSH*, 254–7); 'The Midnight Verdict', SH's abridged version of Merriman's '*Cúirt an Mheán Oíche*' (*MV*, 23–9; *TSH*, 257–65); and 'The Death of Orpheus', SH's abridged Ovid's *Metamorphoses* Book XI (*MV*, 39–42; *TSH*, 265–7). 'Orpheus and Eurydice' (Book X, 1–85) and 'Death of Orpheus' (Book XI, 1–84) are included in *After Ovid: New Metamorphoses*, edited by Michael Hofmann and James Lasdun and published by Faber & Faber in 1994 (222–5 and 226–9).

SH published six excerpts of this translation. The first in *Brangle, New Writing from the School of English* (Queen's University Belfast, 1993, 74–5, titled 'The Midnight Court'). The second in *Toward Harmony* (Dublin, Dedalus Press, 1993, 26, titled 'The Morning

Light'). The third in *Printer's Devil* (Issue D, summer 1994, 43–7, titled 'The Midnight Verdict'). The fourth in *The School Bag* (1997, 358–65, titled '*from* The Midnight Court'). The fifth in Crotty's *The Penguin Book of Irish Poetry* (2010, 325–7: 'The Midnight Verdict', One, *ll.* 93–192). The sixth in *Stone from Delphi* (2012, 66–73, 'Orpheus and Eurydice [after Ovid, *Metamorphoses*, X]' and 'The Death of Orpheus [after Ovid, *Metamorphoses*, XI]'). 'The Morning Light' is 'the opening passage, the scene-setting bit', as SH describes it, and is included in Pádraig Ó Canainn's anthology *Filíocht na nGael* (1938), which SH reads at school. In conversation with Dennis O'Driscoll, SH admits that it has been difficult to get to grips 'with even that much of the poem' at school 'simply because the Irish was too difficult [. . .] at that stage' (*SS*, 314).

These are SH's translations of *ll.* 1–85 from Book X and *ll.* 1–84 from Book XI of *Metamorphoses* (*c.*8 BCE) and of *ll.* 1–194 and an abridged version of *ll.* 855–1026 from '*Cúirt an Mheán Oíche*' ('The Midnight Court', *c.*1805). The text in this edition is drawn from the Gallery Press edition (1993). The Seamus Heaney Literary Papers housed at the National Library of Ireland contain a draft of this translation with the working title 'The Midnight Summons'.

'The three translations included here', writes SH in his 'Translator's Note', 'were all part of a single impulse' (*MV*, 11). The first translation, 'Orpheus and Eurydice', is made before SH prepares a lecture on '*Cúirt an Mheán Oíche*' for the Merriman Summer School. The second translation, 'The Midnight Verdict', is the result of SH's close reading of the Irish text. 'In order to get to closer grips with the original,' SH begins 'to put bits of the Irish into couplets' and then comes 'to think of the Merriman poem in relation to the story of Orpheus, and in particular the story of his death as related by Ovid' (*MV*, 11). This association leads to the third translation and gives SH 'the idea of juxtaposing the Irish poem (however drastically abridged) with the relevant passages of Ovid's *Metamorphoses*' (*MV*, 11). This triptych, as Eugene O'Brien observes, contributes to 'viewing Ireland within a classical and European perspective' (O'Brien 2004, 289).

In conversation with Dennis O'Driscoll, SH explains in more detail the genesis of this hybrid translation, which is the result of what he playfully refers to as 'a naughty intention'. As he has finished 'a version of the Orpheus and Eurydice story' that Michael Hofmann and James Lasdun asked him to do 'for their Ovid book', SH decides to 'go on and do the death of Orpheus, far more grievous material, and more sombre in the telling'. Once he gets under way, SH cannot help 'seeing the beleaguered Orpheus as a General Editor figure, being attacked not so much on the ground of a field as on the grounds of the Field Day Anthology' (*SS*, 313). SH alludes to the 'outrage and a debate about what was viewed as the alleged, deliberate marginalisation of Irish women writers' that followed the publication in 1991 of *The Field Day Anthology of Irish Writing,* edited by Seamus Deane, as Eileen Battersby writes in her *Irish Times* review of *The Field Day Anthology of Irish Writing,* Volumes IV and V: *Irish Women's Writing and Traditions* (Battersby 2002, 10).

SH explains that the episode in question begins with the women catching sight of Orpheus while he is playing his lyre: 'One of them whose hair streamed in the breeze/Began to shout, "Look, look, it's Orpheus,/Orpheus the misogynist"'. What happens next, as SH puts it, is 'the pursuit and dismemberment of the bard, until in the end the god proves unwilling to forget the atrocities committed against Orpheus and turns the women into trees'. Given that 'the general tenor of the Ovid fitted in with the women versus men theme in *The Midnight Court*,' and that he had 'other specifically literary reasons for linking the classical and the Irish material', it made sense 'to juxtapose the versions in a short book' (*SS*, 313–14).

'One major difference between Heaney's translation and those of others', as Ní Bhróithe Clements observes, is that SH 'produced a completely different work by translating only parts of Merriman's work and framing this translation within the story of Orpheus, at the point where Orpheus avoids women and becomes a misogynist' (Sonzogni 2021, 164). Another characteristic trait of this and all the other translations is that SH 'had a way of making the language that he used very peculiarly his,' Ní Bhróithe Clements points out, 'while also grounding his poetry in the language of his Ulster community' (Sonzogni 2021, 152). A telling example is Merriman's description of the large woman who rouses the poet to take him to court 'with dramatic, alliterative pairings or words connoting large and ugly physical features'. SH opts for 'more minimal physical descriptive words' but uses the word 'hallion' to ensure that 'the description belongs to his Ulster dialect of English' (Sonzogni 2021, 166).

SH's interest in Merriman makes him the subject of one of SH's lectures as Professor of Poetry at the University of Oxford. 'Orpheus in Ireland: On Brian Merriman's *The Midnight Court*', delivered on 21 October 1993, is included in *The Redress of Poetry* (38–62) and reprinted in *Southern Review* (July 1995, 786–806).

[24] After Liberation

JAKOBUS CORNELIS BLOEM (1887–1966), DUTCH

First published as 'part 3' of 'To a Dutch Potter in Ireland' in *Threepenny Review* (Spring 1993, 15); reprinted by itself in *Turning Tides: Modern Dutch & Flemish Verse in English Versions by Irish Poets*, edited by Peter van de Kamp, introduced by Theo D'Haen, and published by Story Line Press in 1994 (133); and reprinted as 'part 2' of 'To a Dutch Potter in Ireland' in *Poetry Ireland Review* (Autumn/Winter 1995, 62–4).

Collected with revisions as part 2 of 'To a Dutch Potter in Ireland' in *The Spirit Level* (3–4).

This is SH's complete translation of '*Na de bevrijding*' (1945). The text in this edition is drawn from *The Spirit Level* (1996).

SH describes Bloem's 'After Liberation' as a poem which is 'partly his act of thanksgiving for the ending of the war in Europe and partly an act of faith in the ultimate prevalence of life over death'. SH also notes that 'To a Dutch Potter in Ireland', the poem of which 'After Liberation' is part 2, gets 'written and published just as movement towards an IRA ceasefire was becoming perceptible' and 'there was a sense that our own "liberation" was imminent' (*SS*, 358).

As Heidi Thomson points out, 'the Second World War and its legacy in particular shaped a whole generation of Dutch poets' and Bloem's poem captures 'the spirit and the imagination of the Dutch after the liberation'. SH, Thomson notes, makes Bloem's poem 'part of a tribute to an artist who herself had been "translated", from the Netherlands to Ireland, and who now transforms the raw materials of her adopted environment, Bann clay, into another art form – pottery' (Sonzogni 2021, 40).

Asked about the poem dedicated to the Dutch potter, SH tells O'Driscoll that 'Sonja's father was actually shot by the Nazis as they retreated from the Netherlands at the end of the war'. SH recalls how one time when he visited her she talked about 'the savagery of that moment' but also about 'a marvellous thing that used to happen in her childhood, when the waters of the North Sea sometimes got luminous with plankton: she would go swimming and then come splashing out along the shore with the gleam of the stuff all over her body'. SH emphasises how Sonja 'was marked by the cruelty and evil of what happened to her father, but also by the beauty and marvel of what happened to her on that shore', which gave us 'a profound sense of what is at stake in the making of art' (*SS*, 357). 'To a Dutch Potter in Ireland' is thus 'a two-fold tribute': to Sonja Landweer, a war victim and survivor, and to J. C. Bloem, 'whose poem has become an iconic celebration of the Dutch liberation' (Sonzogni 2021, 41). And 'in both parts of the poem', Thomson argues, SH 'celebrates the survival of life and art over war', concluding that 'There is a strong sense that this is not only about the triumph of artistic expression but also about the human values of endurance, equanimity and decency' (Sonzogni 2021, 45).

'Yet', as Thomson remarks, 'there is a very dark undercurrent to Bloem's political thinking, which makes his patriotic fervour in "*Na de bevrijding*" sound hollow and opportunistic.' Bloem, explains Thomson, 'does not share Heaney's ethical integrity and humanity'. Bloem's fascism, 'long known about in Dutch literary circles', has been 'more often than not underplayed' because of 'the tranquil melancholy of his verse' (Sonzogni 2021, 40).

In the introduction to *Turning Tides. Modern Dutch & Flemish Verse in English Versions by Irish Poets*, Theo D'Haen states that Bloem owes his popularity to being 'an anti-Symbolist in his insistence on the everyday and the commonplace' (Van de Kamp 1994, xxxiv). This 'grounded quality', as Thomson observes, 'would have resonated with Heaney's own poetics' (Sonzogni 2021, 38).

This is the only translation from a language SH perceived to be 'exactly right' for his poetry after hearing *Death of a Naturalist* in Dutch (Heaney 2009b, 00:50:49–00:52:51).

[25] *Inferno*: Canto I — [26] *Inferno*: Canto II — [27] *Inferno*: Canto III

DANTE (1265–1321), MEDIEVAL ITALIAN

Inferno: Cantos I–III. Canto I, titled 'The Dark Wood' by SH, is first published in *Literature and the Art of Creation: Essays and Poems in Honour of A. Norman Jeffares*, edited by Robert Welch and Suheil Badi Bushrui and published by Colin Smythe in 1988 (247–51). Canto II is published first in *Dante's Inferno: Translations by Twenty Contemporary Poets*, edited by Daniel Halpern and published by the Ecco Press in 1993 (7–11) and reprinted with revisions in *Dante's Modern Afterlife: Reception and Response from Blake to Heaney*, edited by Nick Havely and published by Palgrave Macmillan in 1998 (261–4). Canto III: *ll.* 22–52, titled 'Inferno III', is first published in *Ploughshares* (Spring 1987, 64–9) and reprinted with revisions and with the title 'The Lost People' in *Confounded Language: New Poems by Nine Irish Writers*, edited with images by Noel Connor, published by Bloodaxe Books in 1991 (13); *ll.* 82–129, titled 'The Crossing', is first published in *Agenda* (Spring 1989, 5–31) and collected with revisions in *Seeing Things* (111–13). The complete translations of Cantos I–III are published in Daniel Halpern's *Dante's Inferno: Translations by Twenty Contemporary Poets* (1993; 3–15).

These are SH's complete translations of *Inferno*: Cantos I, II and III from *Commedia* (1306–21; published 1472). The texts in this edition are drawn from *Dante's Inferno: Translations by Twenty Contemporary Poets* (1993) for Cantos I and III and from *Dante's Modern Afterlife: Reception and Response from Blake to Heaney* (1998) for Canto II, with a further revision by SH of *l.* 137.

As Maria Cristina Fumagalli reports, SH translated the first three cantos of *Inferno* a decade before they were published, 'around 1982–3' (Fumagalli 1997a, 205). SH gave titles to his version of Canto I and the two sections of his version of Canto III: a clear indication that SH regarded his translations as original poems.

In conversation with Dennis O'Driscoll, SH reveals he has felt 'so exhilarated by the whole marvel of Dante' that he is 'tempted to have a go at doing the complete *Inferno* – simply for its own imaginative splendour'. SH, however, abandons the idea primarily because he 'couldn't gauge tone' and 'was at a loss about all the little particles strewn around the big nouns and verbs'. SH 'soldiered on for four hundred lines or so', with Sinclair's and Singleton's prose translations in English as reference. After doing the opening three cantos, SH realises that he is not achieving what he wants: 'to get a style going' that would be 'right for him and for the material'. SH does not manage to find the 'note that pays you back', 'you need to be making a music that doesn't just match the original but verifies something in yourself as well,' which will enable him to 'establish a measure that combined plain speaking with fluent movement' and 'match the shapes that the bright container of the terza rima contained' (*SS*, 425–6). SH translates Dante again, however, to mark the transition from one millennium to another, combining the rituals of pre-Christian Ireland with Dante's vision of a Christian Paradise in 'The Light of Heaven', SH's abridged translation of the *Commedia*'s final canto [67].

As Bernard O'Donoghue remarks, 'both directly in his poetic practice, and indirectly through his use of earlier Dante-influenced writers, Seamus Heaney's work shows and declares Dante to be an important presence' and 'the places where Heaney has incorporated Dante into his own poetry have often been noted' (Havely 1998, 242). SH himself, as Tim Smith observes, 'frequently acknowledged'

(Sonzogni 2021, 173) Dante's influence on his poetry, 'the generating power of the *Commedia*, its long reach into the first and deepest levels of the shaping spirit' (Heaney 1985, 7). SH finds in Dante's 'local intensity' a voltage, an *energeia* that he can 'translate to his personal, political and poetic world'. This, argues Smith, is 'typical of Heaney's translations in general' (Sonzogni 2021, 173): explorations of what Kevin Murphy describes as 'particular sites of anxiety or tension in his own circumstances' (Murphy 2016, 352).

The sources of SH's 'critical bearings from Dante', O'Donoghue points out, 'are at first glance distinct and mostly twofold': from Mandelstam and other East European writers on one hand, and on the other from 'various modernist writers in English, especially in the practice and theory of T. S. Eliot, from Yeats and to some extent Hopkins' (Havely 1998, 242). SH maintains that 'when poets turn to the great masters of the past, they turn to an image of their own creation, one which is likely to be a reflection of their own imaginative needs, their own artistic inclinations and procedures' (Heaney 1985, 5). The presence and influence of Dante is always daunting. As Maren Kraz notes, 'A poetic example can appeal to us through some particular common ground, but we may also envy it because it must always stay superior, unattainable and at a distance' (Kraz 2012, 14).

Heaney's critical engagement with Dante begins with two book reviews in 1980 and 1985 respectively: of C. H. Sisson's translation of Dante's *Divine Comedy* and of *Dante* by George Holmes for *Quarto* (IX, Aug. 1980, 14) and of Dante's *Divine Comedy* translated and illustrated by Tom Phillips for the *Sunday Tribune* (15 Sept. 1985, 16). More interventions followed over the years, including SH's inclusion of another translation of Dante into English, Ciaran Carson's Northern Irish version of the *Inferno*, among his books of the year selection for the *Sunday Tribune* (22 Dec. 2002, Artlife, 8).

[28] Do you remember the beach? — [29] The country
we come from — [30] Sometimes I dream —
[31] Maybe there's somebody dreaming me —
[32] It's snowing hostility — [33] The morning after
I die — [34] Inhabited by a song — [35] Loneliness —
[36] Hunt — [37] As if

ANA BLANDIANA (*b.* 1942), ROMANIAN

'Maybe there's somebody dreaming me', 'It's snowing enemy snow', and
'Inhabited by a song' were first published in *Lift Magazine* (April 1994,
133–5). 'As if', 'Loneliness' and 'Hunt' were first published, along with
'Maybe there's somebody dreaming me' and 'Inhabited by a song', in
Southern Review (July 1995, 468–71). These translations were reprinted
with revisions in *When the Tunnels Meet. Contemporary Romanian
Poetry*, edited by John Fairleigh and published by Bloodaxe Books in
1996 (26–32).

These are SH's complete translations of '*Îți aduci aminte plaja?*',
'*Despre țara din care venim*', '*Visez uneori trupul meu*', '*Poate că mă
visează cineva*', '*Ninge cu dușmănie*', '*În dimineața de după moarte*',
'*Locuită de-un cântec*', '*Singurătatea*', '*Vânătoarea*', and '*Ca și cum*'
(1972–1981). The texts in this edition are drawn from *When the
Tunnels Meet. Contemporary Romanian Poetry* (1996).

SH's versions, like all the translations in the Bloodaxe anthology,
are based upon literal translations by 'the Romanian novelist Simeon
Dumitrache and the young Irish poet Heather Brett' as well as by
Ștefania Hîrtopanu (Fairleigh 1996, 13).

Contextualising the renewed commitment of Irish poets and
Bloodaxe to making contemporary Romanian poetry accessible to
English-speaking audiences, the editor John Fairleigh points out that
'This island on the far side of Europe offered an identity beyond
the nightmarish present in the sense of a common racial inheritance
through the Celts who had settled the lands around the Black Sea as
early as the 3rd century BCE' (Fairleigh 1996, 11).

'After 1989, Romanian writers felt the urgent need to be heard
outside their borders, and there was a stampede of traducing [*sic*;
"translating"],' as Andrei Codrescu remarks. 'Well-respected writers,
whether pre- or post-1989,' he explains, 'felt that they had to be
read on the "outside", hoping for recognition that the increasingly
bitter internecine polemics made impossible.' Romanian poets within
the Romanian borders, as Codrescu puts it, 'condemned themselves

(and were condemned by the official ideologues) to provincialism'
(Codrescu 2007, 3).

SH's contribution to this new translation project comes in
versions of poems by Ana Blandiana, one of 'the best-known
Romanian poets of the second half of the twentieth century'. The
author of nearly 'fifty volumes of poetry, essays and fiction in
Romania and over forty volumes overseas [. . .] at seventy-eight
[she] continues to be an active and revered poet who takes part in
domestic and international literary events and actively supports
protests against corruption in Romania' (Sonzogni 2021, 230).
As with Sorescu, SH lends his voice to Blandiana in another 'gesture
of poetic recovery of a culture that seemed condemned to obscurity'
(Sonzogni 2021, 238). Dumitrescu proposes many reasons why
SH finds affinities with Blandiana's poetry. First, 'the musicality
of Blandiana's poems', which Dumitrescu describes as 'the telluric
rhythm of the hamitic Transylvanian space with its rolling hills, river
valleys, and eroded mountains,' is 'soothing through its offering
a grounding for the self' (Sonzogni 2021, 249). SH too found the
acoustics and visuals of his home ground a grounding factor for the
self as well as for this poetry. Blandiana's poems are also 'resounding
silent protests': a posture toward the injustices and wrongs in the
world SH adopted in some of his own poems. In Blandiana's poetry
one can find 'sustenance through difficult times – personal and
political', which also explains the timeless relevance and appeal of
SH's verse. And like Blandiana's and Sorescu's, SH's poetry inhabits
different 'realms simultaneously – aesthetic, emotional and political'
(Sonzogni 2021, 255) – creating an ideal for connection, empathy
and translation.

[38] Laments

JAN KOCHANOWSKI (1530–1584), MIDDLE POLISH

Published in the UK by Faber & Faber in 1995; published in the USA by
Farrar, Straus and Giroux in 1995; reprinted in Ireland by the Gallery
Press in 2009 with a preface by SH (9–12) as well as the original
epigraph in Latin (14) and Kochanowski's dedication to his daughter
in both Polish and English (15).

SH published some of the nineteen translated texts in *Poetry Review*
(summer 1995, 30–1, nos. 6, 7 and 8; *Laments*, 13–17; *TSH*, 270–2;
this issue also contains a note by SH on translating Kochanowski's
sonnets); in *Threepenny Review* (fall 1995, 13, no. 1); in *Times Literary
Supplement*, 6 Oct. 1995, 32, nos. 5 and 13; *Laments*, 11 and 27;

TSH, 270, 274–5); in *Graph* (second series, 1: 1995, 38–40, nos. 2, 3 and 4; *Laments*, 5–9, *TSH*, 268–70; this issue also contains a note by SH and his co-translator, Stanisław Barańczak); and in *Partisan Review* (3, 1995, 443–5, nos. 16 and 2; *Laments*, 35–7 and 5; *TSH*, 276–7 and 268–9).

This is SH's complete translation of *Treny* (1580), co-authored with Stanisław Barańczak. The text in this edition is drawn from the Faber & Faber edition (1995).

The 'imaginative affinities' (Kay 2012, 46) with Eastern European poets, especially with Polish poets Miłosz and Herbert, helped SH 'at crucial junctures in his career' (Quinn 2009, 104) as 'literary and moral exemplars' (Gwiazda 2016, 61) whose work SH admired for 'its inherent and enduring power, beauty, and truth' (Parker 2013, 831).

In the Introduction to the UK edition, Barańczak describes Kochanowski as 'the greatest poet of not just Poland but the entire Slavic world up to the beginning of the nineteenth century' (*Laments*, vii). Kochanowski's work, Barańczak remarks, 'encompasses the lows of our human desolation and doubt as well as the highs of our no less human fortitude and faith' (*Laments*, xvii). And it is through Kochanowski's work, Czesław Miłosz says, that the Polish language 'reached maturity' (Miłosz 1983, 60). As Piotr Blumczynski notes, 'Kochanowski's influence on the Polish poetic diction' has been compared to that of William Shakespeare, Ben Jonson and John Dryden on English letters' (Sonzogni 2021, 208).

Not only is *Treny* Kochanowski's 'most personal and dramatic' work (Barańczak 1995, 41), it is also his most controversial. On one hand, it 'represents a masterful deployment of the genre's convention, replete with classical references and echoes'. On the other, Kochanowski 'broke the decorum, and scandalised many of his contemporaries, by defiantly devoting not just one poem but an entire cycle to a most non-eminent person, his little daughter Ursula' (Sonzogni 2021, 210–11) and offering, as Miłosz observes, 'a highly subjective description of what a person who has lost a child lives through; a history of personal sorrow' (Miłosz 1983, 75–6).

The Gallery Press edition of these translations has three distinctive features. First, a preface by SH that describes the genesis and process of his collaborative translation with Stanisław Barańczak. Second, an epigraph in Latin from Cicero's *De Fato* ('*Fragmenta Huius Libri*' 3: 3–4): '*Tales sunt hominum mente quali pater ipse/Iuppiter auctiferas lustravist lumine terras*', ('The minds of men are such as the light/Wherewith the fruitful earth has been illuminated/By Father Jove himself', in Harry Rackham's 1942 Loeb translation). Third, Jan Kochanowski's heart-wrenching dedication to his late daughter Ursula, in Polish and in English translation.

In 1992 Barańczak's translation into Polish of a selection of Heaney's poems including 'Mid-Term Break' – where SH gives an account of losing his younger brother Christopher to a tragic road accident – paves the way for SH's translation into English of Kochanowksi's *Treny*.

In conversation with Dennis O'Driscoll, SH offers further details. In 'April or May of 1992, I was in the Barańczaks' house to meet the scholar and translator Clare Cavanagh,' SH says 'how susceptible' he had always been to poems 'about dead children', referring to Ben Jonson's 'On his first son' and John Crowe Ransom's 'Bells for John Whiteside's Daughter' as examples, and 'putting this down' to the 'accidental' death of his three-and-a-half-year-old brother. On that occasion, SH remembers 'a set of Polish poems about a dead child' sent to him years earlier by the poet and translator Adam Czerniawski (*SS*, 427) – an invitation to co-translate them SH declined (Sonzogni 2021, 218). 'The minute I mentioned them,' recalls SH, 'Clare and Stanisław began to talk about how good they were and how central to the Polish canon.' The university mail then delivers to SH 'this bundle of translations, accompanied by a suggestion that I might look them over and team up to produce the complete sequence in a book'. Months later, SH begins to engage with those translations 'while Stanisław delivered versions of the remaining poems'. Face-to-face sessions at Harvard, fax exchanges from Dublin, and 'on-the-spot dealings' in Poland – where Barańczak and SH launch an anthology of SH's poetry in Barańczak's translation – lead to the translation of the complete cycle (*SS*, 427). Magdalena Heydel has studied the correspondence between SH and Barańczak: more than thirty letters in which the two poet-translators discuss 'lexical and phraseological choices, syntactic and stylistic intricacies, and their significance for the meaning of the cycle and the relation of the English version to the Polish original'. What emerges from Heydel's study is a 'touching picture of their friendship and authentic joy in mutual work' that 'lay at the core of the project and gave it an immense creative energy' (Heydel 2022).

There are four other English translations of Kochanowski's *Treny*: George and Dorothea Prall Radin Noyes's in 1928, Michael Mikoś's in 1995, Adam Czerniawski's in 1996 (reprinted in 2001), and Barry Keane's in 2001 (reprinted in 2016). As Blumczynski

notes, Barańczak and SH's is 'the only collaborative translation'
(Sonzogni 2021, 220–1). Their translation, reviewed by Miłosz
as 'strong' (Miłosz 1996, 26), seeks 'to offer a self-contained,
autonomous collection, letting the poems speak for themselves'
(Sonzogni 2021, 225). The 'special affinity between the two poets' –
founded on 'complete respect and trust for each other's expertise
and judgement' (Heaney 1999b, 332) – created a relationship that
Helen Vendler defines as a 'shared congeniality' (Vendler 2015, [13]).
SH himself, discussing 'the question of co-translation', describes
his collaboration with Barańczak as a 'very satisfactory experience'
and his contribution as 'helping to make revisions' (Heaney 1999b,
332). This is 'a great testimony', Blumczynski emphasises, to SH's
'genuinely humble spirit' and to Barańczak's 'translational genius'
(Sonzogni 2021, 219).

[39] Lament for Timoleague

SEÁN Ó COILEÁIN (c. 1754–1817), IRISH

First published in *Recorder* (summer 1994, 52–4).
  Uncollected.

This is SH's complete translation of '*Machnamh an Duine
Dhoilíosaigh: Caoineadh Thigh Molaige*' (1813). The text in this
edition is drawn from *Recorder* (1994).
  Titled 'Elegy on the Ruins of Timoleague Abbey', this poem is
included in K. H. Jackson's *A Celtic Miscellany* (1951, 263–4), which
SH read for the first time in 1972 when he moved to the Dublin
countryside. The translation is dedicated to the Northern Irish writer
and broadcaster Benedict Kiely (1919–2007), who is among the
'writers and journalists and broadcasters associated with RTÉ' whom
SH feels 'at home with' in Dublin in the 1970s (*SS*, 152–3).
  Timoleague Friary was founded by the Franciscans in the late
thirteenth or early fourteenth century on the site of the ancient
monastery of St Molaga, Co. Cork, Ireland. In the mid-sixteenth
century the monks were expelled from Timoleague but some returned
and lived there intermittently until 1642, when the friary and the
town were burnt by English soldiers commanded by Lord Forbes.
The poem laments the destruction of the friary.
  'In the last decades of the fifteenth century,' as Margaret Smith
notes, 'the Franciscan friars of Timoleague presented a large codex
to their patron, Finghín Mac Carthaigh Riabhach, as a gift' (Smith

2016, 77). This codex, which is known today as the Book of Lismore, 'contained a diverse array of texts drawn from numerous sources and genres'.

[40] The Yellow Bittern

CATHAL BUÍ MAC GIOLLA GHUNNA (1680–1756), IRISH

First published in *Poetry Ireland Review* 50 (Summer 1996, 68–9) and reprinted in a special issue of *Ireland of the Welcomes* (Sept.–Oct. 1996, 31), 'New Irish Writing', edited by Derek Mahon; in *Austin Clarke Remembered*, edited by R. Dardis Clarke and published by the Bridge Press in 1996 (49–50; SH also wrote the 'Introduction', 9–11); in *The School Bag*, edited by SH and Ted Hughes and published by Faber & Faber in 1997 (349–51); and as a broadside in July 2002 by the Keogh-Notre Dame Centre, Dublin, to celebrate the Fourth Irish Seminar.
    Uncollected.

This is SH's complete translation of '*An Bonnán Buí*'. The text in this edition is drawn from the Keogh-Notre Dame Centre broadside (2002).
    This poem, which has been translated by other Irish poets including Thomas McDonagh, James Stephens, and Thomas Kinsella, is regarded as one of the best-known songs in the Irish tradition. It features in *The Poet and the Piper*, a studio album recorded by SH and the piper Liam O'Flynn in 2003 and released in the same year by Claddagh Records. The second piece of music selected by SH and played in his 19 November 1999 *Desert Island Discs* appearance is '*An Bonnán Buí*' sung by 'a namesake' of SH's, the Irish traditional singer Seosamh Ó hÉanaí (1919–84). As SH explains, this 'famous song' is sung in 'what is called in Irish the *Sean-nós*, which is the old way, the old traditional singing' (Heaney 1989, 8:28–8:52).
    Discussing the Irish-language curriculum at St Columb's College with Dennis O'Driscoll SH mentions 'an anthology called *Filíocht na nGael* that was used as textbook, adding that in some cases 'the Irish was too difficult' but singling out '*An Bonnán Buí*' as one of the texts students 'were fit for' (SS, 314).

[41] Raftery's Killeadan

ANTOINE Ó RAIFTEIRÍ (1779/84–1835), IRISH

First published in *Éire-Ireland* (fall/winter 1996, 9) and reprinted in
Force 10 (no. 9, 1998, 14–15, alongside [43]), and in *The Clifden
Anthology*, edited by Brendan Flynn and published by Colour Books
in 2002 (66–7).
  Uncollected.

This is SH's complete translation of '*Anois teacht an Earraigh:
Cill Aodáin*'. The text in this edition is drawn from *The Clifden
Anthology* (2002).
  In 1999 the readers of the *Irish Times* voted this poem among
Ireland's top fifty favourite poems. The translation is dedicated to the
Irish American librarian and scholar Michael J. Durkan (1930–96),
who worked with Rand Brandes on *Seamus Heaney: A Bibliography
1959–2003* (Brandes 2008a).
  Talking to Dennis O'Driscoll about Rosie Keenan, a childhood
neighbour and protagonist of the poem 'At the Wellhead' (*SL*, 65–6),
SH compares her to Raftery: 'Our Blind Rosie, like Blind Raftery,
"*ag seinm ceoil do phócaí folamh*" – "playing music to empty
pockets"' (*SS*, 366–7). This image evokes the scene described by
SH in the opening stanza (*ll.* 1–14) of the title poem in *District
and Circle*, where SH recalls 'walking down' to board his train
and hearing 'Tunes from a tin whistle underground' and then
encountering his 'watcher on the tiles' who stares 'In an unaccusing
look' as SH would 'trigger and untrigger a hot coin/Held at the
ready' (*DC*, 17).
  Mise Raiftearaí: An Fíodóir Focal, Tadhg Mac Dhonnagáin's
biography of Ó Raiftearaí, was published by Futa Fata in 2015 and
was awarded the Gradam Uí Shúilleabháin, the Irish Language Book
of the Year Award.

[42] I am Raftery

ANTOINE Ó RAIFTEIRÍ (1779/84–1835), IRISH

First published in *Merton Journal* (Advent 1996, 33) and reprinted as a
card on 13 December 1996 by the Deerfield Press to mark SH's poetry
reading at Deerfield Academy; and in *Rosebud* (summer 1997, 23).
  Uncollected.

This is SH's complete translation of '*Mise Raiftery an file*'. The text in this edition is drawn from *Rosebud* (1997).

In his keynote address to the Whiting Foundation for the 1998 Whiting Awards, SH quotes this poem in Irish and in his English translation, describing it 'one of the best-known poems about being in need of patronage' and 'a poem that every schoolchild used to know in Ireland' (Heaney 1998b).

John J. Ó Ríordáin quotes this poem in *The Music of What Happens. Celtic Spirituality* as 'so illustrative of that non-materialistic value system' of the old Gaelic world (Ó Ríordáin 1996, 69).

[43] A School of Poetry Closes

TADHG ÓG Ó HUIGINN (*c*. 1370–1448), EARLY MODERN IRISH

First published in *Force 10* (no. 9, 1998, 13, alongside [41]) and reprinted in *Kestrel* (spring, 1999, 62–3) and in *The Penguin Book of Irish Poetry* (Crotty 2010, 177–9). An excerpt from this translation (the last two quatrains) is included in *The School Bag* (1997, 495) with the title '*from* Lament for Fergal Rua'.

Uncollected.

This is SH's translation of *ll*. 1–32, 64–88 and 116–24 of '*Anocht sgaoilid na sgola*' (*c*. 1500). The text in this edition is drawn from *The Penguin Book of Irish Poetry* (2010).

SH ends his 1998 Whiting Foundation Keynote Address quoting this poem, which he describes as 'a beautiful [. . .] fifteenth-century bardic poem' written by a poet in memory of his brother and teacher. SH turns to this poem to emphasise how crucial to an individual is the knowledge that they are believed in by someone (Heaney 1998b). Ten years later SH will open his 2008 Robert Lowell Memorial Lecture at Boston University with this translation; this is a tribute to the school of poetry that has been meeting in room 222 at 236 Bay State Road in Boston where Lowell taught a poetry-writing class in which the students included George Starbuck, Anne Sexton and Sylvia Plath. SH recounts how the pupils of bardic schools of poetry would go to a school and spend from early fall to late spring learning 'off by heart the corpus of writing in the Irish language poetic tradition – genealogies, religious poetry, metrical forms'. The students 'were given exercises and the exercises were to be completed mentally: they composed these poems at night in the dark on their beds and then they presented them orally to the teacher'. SH then links the 'maintenance of the art' at Boston University to 'the Bardic commitments' and 'the deep affection' and 'the sense of belonging together' expressed in Ó hUiginn's poem (Heaney 2008b, 29:27–33:56).

SH read this translation at the funerals of Joseph Brodsky, Ted Hughes and Michael Hartnett (Connolly 2016, 184–5).

[44] Poet to Blacksmith

EOGHAN RUA Ó SÚILLEABHÁIN (1748–1784), IRISH

First published in 1997 by Pim Witteveen to celebrate the first twenty years of Hans van Eijk's private press, In de Bonnefant; reprinted in Louis de Paor's *Leabhar Sheáin Uí Thuama arna chur in eager*; published by Coiscéim, 1997 (1); and in *The Penguin Book of Irish Poetry* (Crotty 2010, 317).

Collected with revisions in *District and Circle* (25).

This is SH's complete translation of '*A Shéamais, déan dom*', Eoghan Rua Ó Súilleabháin's instructions to Séamus MacGearailt. The text in this edition is drawn from *District and Circle* (2006).

The work of a blacksmith is central to SH's idea of poetry as a craft that requires practice and perseverance to be executed as perfectly and as truthfully as possible.

In a melodrama staged in Bellaghy 'probably in 1959 or 1960' and based on *The Hearts of Down* – a novel about Betsy Gray who 'figures in the lore of the 1798 Rebellion in County Down as a kind of local Joan of Arc' – SH 'forged pikes for the United Irish insurgents on an anvil that Barney Devlin had supplied' (*SS*, 92).

Neighbour and blacksmith Barney Devlin (1920–2016) is the protagonist of an early and a late SH poem: 'The Forge', which contains the title-line of *Door into the Dark* (9), and 'Midnight Anvil', which follows this translation in *District and Circle* (26). Devlin 'had a part in that play too, although not, oddly enough, as a blacksmith' but 'lent the anvil and rehearsed me in the gentle art of making it sing'.

The play included a ballad that SH's friend the folk-singer David Hammond (1928–2008) used to sing where Betsy Gray 'appears in the last verse as the sister of the rebel leader, Harry Munro: "Then up came Munro's sister, she was all dressed in green,/With a sword by her side that was well-sharped and keen"' (*SS*, 92). This description echoes Eoghan Rua's in the poem SH translated: 'I see it well shaped from the anvil' (*l.* 10).

When SH signed the visitor's book at Devlin's forge he wrote. 'For Barney, old friend and good example of how to do good work and stay true. I'll maybe write a poem' – a dedication that encapsulates SH's view of what any artist should strive to achieve. Discussing the process and the purpose of writing poetry in conversation with George O'Brien at Georgetown University (1988), Heaney mentions a Middle English poem about 'brenwateres' (water-burning) blacksmiths (Heaney 1988b, 20:19–20:38).

[45] Colmcille the Scribe

ANONYMOUS (ELEVENTH CENTURY), MIDDLE IRISH

First published in *Recorder* (spring & fall 1997, 8–10, alongside [46]): reprinted with revisions in the *Irish Times* (7 June 1997, Weekend, 9, ahead of the feast day of St Colum Cille on 9 June, on the 1,400th anniversary of the saint's death); in *Trying The Line: A Volume of Tribute to Gillian Clarke*, edited by Menna Elfyn and published by Gomer Gomer Press in 1997 (38, titled 'Penworker'); in *Gazette of the Grolier Club* (spring 1999, 5); in *Kunapipi: Journal of Post-Colonial Writing*, 20. 3 (1998 [1999], 16) with 'Saint Brigid's Wish' [48]; and in Timothy O'Neill's *The Irish Hand: Scribes and their Manuscripts from the Earliest Times*, published by Cork University Press in 2014 (127).

Collected as Part 1 of 'Colum Cille Cecinit' in *Human Chain* (72).

This is SH's complete translation of '*Is scíth mo chrob ón scríbainn*'. The text in this edition is drawn from *Human Chain* (2010).

The Irish original and a prose translation of this poem – ascribed to Colum Cille, who died in 597 – are included in Gerard Murphy's *Early Irish Lyrics: Eighth to Twelfth Century* (Murphy 1956, 70–1), in Greene and O'Connor's *A Golden Treasury of Irish Poetry* (Greene 1967, 159–60) and in Patrick Crotty's *The Penguin Book of Irish Poetry* (Crotty 2010, 36–7), where it appears in Kuno Meyer's translation. This poem, titled 'The Scribe', features also in Maurice Riordan's *The Finest Music: Early Irish Lyrics* in the editor's own translation (Riordan 2014, 68).

A copy of 'Colmcille the Scribe' is enclosed with 'Saint Brigid's Wish' [48] in a fax SH sends to John Kinsella, who (as guest editor) had invited him to contribute to a post-colonial issue of *Kunapipi* – a tri-annual arts magazine featuring the new literatures written in English – devoted to 'Localities: Intercultural Poetics' (Heaney

1998a, 1). In another fax to Kinsella, SH asks him to 'add a comma at line 10 of Colmcille' (Heaney 1999a, 1).

As Timothy O'Neill notes, SH translates this early Irish poem 'to celebrate his enrolment as a member of the Royal Irish Academy and commissioned a presentation copy for the Academy in 1997 on the occasion of his admission' (O'Neill 2014, 127). SH's choice of author and this text – the other translation from the Irish is 'Saint Brigid's Wish' – is also linked to another important event in 1997: the 1,400th anniversary of Colmcille's death.

Thinking about his time as a scholar at St Columb's College, SH remembers that 'in the study hall' his hand 'was cold as a scribe's in winter,' as we read in 'Cloistered', one of the prose poems from *Stations* (20).

[46] The Glamoured

AODHAGÁN Ó RATHAILLE (*c*. 1675–1729), IRISH

First published in *Recorder* (Spring & Fall 1997, 8–10, alongside [45]); reprinted with revisions in *Index on Censorship. A Voice for the Persecuted* (Sept./Nov. 1998, 131–2, with a note on the aisling form in seventeenth- and eighteenth-century Irish-language poetry); in *Aquarius* (23/24, 1998, 15–16); in *The Poet and The Piper* (2003, track 7); in Crotty's *The Penguin Book of Irish Poetry* (2010, 276–7); and Carol Ann Duffy and Gillian Clarke's *The Map and the Clock* (2016, 171–2).
Uncollected.

This is SH's complete translation of '*Gile na gile*' ('Brightness of Brightness'). The text in this edition is drawn from *The Map and the Clock* (2016).

Asked about his attitude towards translation, SH tells Dennis O'Driscoll how at various times he had 'a different covenant with the original'. As an example, SH says that he 'couldn't imagine doing Ó Rathaille's "*Gile na Gile*" without trying to suggest something of the metrical drive' (*SS*, 218). SH's covenant with this poem entailed several revisions to arrive at the text included in this edition.

On the day of SH's passing (30 August 2013), Padraig Reidy, an *Index on Censorship* columnist, re-published SH's translation and commentary on the website of the magazine:

> 'The Glamoured' is my translation of *Gile na Gile*
> (literally Brightness of Brightness), one of the most
> famous Irish poems of the early eighteenth century.

It is a classic example of a genre known as the aisling (pronounced ashling) which was as characteristic of Irish language poetry in the late seventeenth and eighteenth centuries as rhymed satire was in England at the same time.

The aisling was in effect a mixture of samizdat and allegory, a form which mixed political message with passionate vision. After the devastations and repressions brought about by the armies of Oliver Cromwell and King William, the native Irish population became subject to the Penal Laws, a system of legislation as deliberately conceived as apartheid, enacted against them specifically as Catholics by the Irish parliament (representing the 'Protestant interest' which took control after William of Orange's victory over the forces of the Catholic Stuart king, James II, at the Battle of the Boyne). The native Irish aristocracy fled – and were ever afterwards known as The Wild Geese – and dreams of redress got transferred into poetry.

Politically, the aisling kept alive the hope of a Stuart restoration which would renew the fortunes of the native Irish. Symbolically, this was expressed in the ancient form of a dream encounter in which the poet meets a beautiful woman in some lonely place. This woman is at one and the same time an apparition of the spirit of Ireland and a muse figure who entrances him completely. She inevitably displays signs of grief and tells a story of how she is in thrall to some heretical foreign brute, but the poem usually ends with a promise – which history will not fulfil – of liberation in the form of a Stuart prince coming to her relief from beyond the seas.

As a corrected typescript of this translation housed at Emory University's Stuart A. Rose Library indicates, SH had initially used the literal translation of the Irish title, 'Brightness of Brightness', as the title of his version.

[47] Jesus and the Sparrows

ANONYMOUS (SEVENTH CENTURY), OLD IRISH

First published as a Christmas card by the Gallery Press in 1996;
republished in *Cordite Poetry Review* (1 July 1997) and in *Spirituality*
(July/Aug. 1997, 242).
   Uncollected.

This is SH's translation of *ll.* 1–32 from '*Imbu maccán cóic blíadnae*'.
The text in this edition is drawn from a revised version of the
translation SH sent to Maurice Riordan, who was compiling an
anthology of early Irish poetry, *The Finest Music* (Faber & Faber,
2014), to which he had invited SH to contribute.
   As Tony Burke explains, 'The Irish version of IGT [*Infancy
Gospel of Thomas*] is extant in a single manuscript of the 17th
century' (MS G 50, National Library of Ireland: Burke 2022).
In 1958 James Carney traced the text's origins to a translation from
around 700 CE, which is thus one of the earliest witnesses to IGT
(Carney 1958, 1–43). SH's translation echoes one of his early poems,
'Saint Francis and the Birds', collected in *Death of a Naturalist* (40).
   In 1976 the Heaney family settled in Dublin, at 191 Strand Road,
Sandymount. 'Starting in this happy year, 1976,' as Ashby Bland
Crowder notes, Seamus and Marie Heaney began sending bespoke
Christmas cards, a practice that they maintained over the years,
though the press of obligations sometimes led to gaps' (Crowder
2017, 34). The cards, privately printed by Peter Fallon at the Gallery
Press, are 'in a style reminiscent of his collections of poetry', as Freya
McClements points out, and feature 'an image from a favourite artist
– or his children's artwork – together with a line of text from a new
poem or other work in progress' (McClements 2017).
   The front of this Christmas card features a woodcut of – as SH
handwrote in the copy of this card housed at Emory University's
Stuart A. Rose Library – an 'aerodynamically challenged sparrow' by
Timothy Engelland (1950–2012).

[48] Saint Brigid's Wish

ATTRIBUTED TO ST BRIGID (438/452–524/526), MIDDLE IRISH

First published as 'Saint Brigid's Wish' in *Kunapipi: Journal of Post-Colonial Writing*, 20. 3 (1998 [1999], 16) with 'Colmcille the Scribe' [45].
Uncollected.

This is SH's abridged translation of four of the original seven quatrains of '*Robad maith lem corm-lind mór*'. The text in this edition is drawn from *Kunapipi: Journal of Post-Colonial Writing* (1998 [1999]).

The original text – from Manuscript XVII in the Burgundian Library, Brussels – was published and translated by Eugene O'Curry in his *Lectures on the Manuscript Materials of Ancient Irish History* (O'Curry 1878, 615–16).

A prose translation of this text is included in Kenneth Hurlstone Jackson's *A Celtic Miscellany: Translations from the Celtic Literatures*. The title given by Jackson is 'I Should Like to Have a Great Ale-Feast', the author 'unknown' and the date of composition 'tenth–eleventh century' (Jackson 1971, 284–5, 323). In his 'Notes' Jackson quotes David Greene's description of this text: 'A religious poet imagines himself as a tributary tenant of God, rendering the Irish legal dues of lodging and entertainment to his overlord and retinue' (citing Greene 1967, 150–3). Titled 'St Brigit's Housewarming', it is also included in Patrick Crotty's *The Penguin Book of Irish Verse* (26), where it appears in the editor's own translation (Crotty 2010, 26), which SH is very likely to have read while writing the Introduction to this anthology.

John J. Ó Ríordáin quotes this poem in *The Music of What Happens* as an example of 'the affinity and warm love-relationship between the people of this world and the otherworld'. Ó Ríordáin describes this poem as 'attributed to St Brigid' but the work of 'an anonymous tenth century poet who envisaged himself as God's vassal, and rejoices in the thought of fulfilling his legal obligations in relation to lodgings and entertainment for his over-lord and entourage'. The poem is also illustrative, Ó Ríordáin notes, 'of the Celtic Irish capacity to absorb ideas and images but rarely without adapting them to the native culture and environment', concluding that it is a 'refreshingly Irish presentation of the biblical heavenly banquet' (Ó Ríordáin 1996, 55).

In the version of this translation that SH faxed to Peter Fallon on 7 October 1997 and to John Kinsella (Heaney 1998a), the title has 'wishes', instead of 'wish', as published in *Kunapipi*. In *A Book of Saints and Wonders* (Gregory 1907), the title of the section in Book 1: 'Brigit, The Mary of the Gael' where this story is recounted, is plural: 'The Things Brigit wished for' (Gregory 1907, 7). In another fax to Kinsella (Heaney 1999a), SH reassures him that 'nobody will be worried whether or not the date is right for Brigid' and asks him to 'cut the question mark' (Heaney 1999a, 1).

In his guest-editor's introduction to 'this special poetry issue of *Kunapipi*' Kinsella explains that one of the 'prime concerns' was 'to challenge the colonial/post-colonial binary' and 'to bring into question both the discourse surrounding this construct and, indeed, the terminologies themselves'. These questions, Kinsella observes, 'are socio-political and linguistic, cultural and epistemological'. Kinsella also notes that when he sent letters of invitation to poets, he was 'surprised to find that many of recipients questioned the legitimacy of the term "post-colonial"' – a 'questioning', he notes, that 'came on a variety of levels'. The question of 'internal colonisations', he adds, 'was most frequently mentioned' (Kinsella 1999, vii).

In the fax sent to Kinsella in August 1998, SH says he doesn't 'have anything to hand at the moment except a couple of translations. At least they are pre-colonial' (Heaney 1998a, 1). The translations enclosed are 'Saint Brigid's Wishes' (revised to 'Saint Brigid's Wish' at proof stage) – and 'Colmcille the Scribe'. It is not surprising that SH contributes two translations from Irish – chronologically pre-colonial, as he says, but evidently post-colonial in the act of translation – related to prominent figures in Irish history, culture and literature, one female and one male. 'In the post-colonial phase of our criticism and cultural studies,' SH observes, 'we have heard much about "the other", but perhaps the moment of the through-other should now be proclaimed, if only because it seems to have arrived' and 'Translation, among other things, has seen to that' (*FK*, 379).

Describing the Mossbawn kitchen to Dennis O'Driscoll, SH mentions that on the walls there was 'a kind of little shrine picture, to commemorate the Eucharistic Congress in Dublin in 1932 – the three patron saints of Ireland on it, Patrick, Brigid and Colmcille' (*SS*, 11). St Brigid's Day or Imbolc, the Celtic feast of renewal and purification, is one of the eight special sacred days, holidays and festivals in Ireland, dating back to the old Celtic world. Beginning in 2023, Ireland will have a new public holiday on St Brigid's Day.

SH wrote two poems in which St Brigid's Day is mentioned – 'Crossings *xxx*' (*ST*, 88) and 'A Brigid's Girdle' (*SL*, 5) – and a poem where one of the miracles attributed to Brigid (hanging her cloak on a sunbeam) is associated with a different shrine as the poet recalls 'the new sweetness/In the early days' of his married life with Marie in Belfast – 'The Clothes Shrine' (*EL*, 27).

Talking about his surroundings and how they shaped his 'sense of place', SH describes them as 'the foundation for a marvellous or a magical view of the world, a foundation that sustained a diminished structure of lore and superstition and half-pagan, half-Christian thought and practice'. Among the examples he mentions are 'the green rushes' as a link to the 'beneficent spirit of St Brigid': they were 'cut in St Brigid's Eve, the first of February' and they were 'worked into Brigid's crosses that would deck the rooms and outhouses for the rest of the year'. One of SH's 'most cherished and in some ways mysterious memories,' as he puts it, 'is of an old neighbour of ours called Annie Devlin sitting in the middle of a floor strewn with green rushes, a kind of local Sybil, plaiting the rushes and plaiting all of us into that ritualized way of life' (*Preoccupations*, 133–4). Brigidine Annie Devlin – and her 'Overgrown/Back garden' resurface in 'Derry Derry Down', one of the poems in SH's last book (*HC*, 26).

[49] Elegy: The God of the Sea Greets Bran in the Land of the Waves

ANONYMOUS (SEVENTH–EIGHTH CENTURY), OLD IRISH

First published in the *New Yorker* (2 Aug. 1999, 48–9).
    Uncollected.

This is SH's translation of 32.1–12 [33]–[44] from *Caíni amra laisin m-Bran*. The text in this edition is drawn from the *New Yorker* (1999).

The complete chapter 32 of *Immram Brain* or *Voyage of Bran*, which consists of a prose section followed by twenty-eight quatrains: [33] to [60]; the chapter is included in Irish and in English translation in Murphy's *Early Irish Lyrics* among examples of 'otherworld poems' (Murphy 1956, 93–101).

In this text – which has the narrative impetus of a classical epic and the heroic voltage one finds in *Sweeney Astray* and in

Beowulf – an image stands out: the charioteer. SH weaves it into two autobiographical poems, one written before and one written after this translation. In 'The Toome Road', SH expresses his anger at the presence of a British military patrol outside the family farm (*FW*, 7) and in 'Chanson d'Aventure' he voices his frustration at the challenges of learning to walk again (*HC*, 14–16). In this text, the ocean deity Manannan is the charioteer and hurries to Bran and his crew to complain once again: what looks like a body of water to the intrepid voyagers appears as a flowery plain to him.

It is in May 1997, as Rowena Fowler points out, that SH sees the charioteer statue for the first time when he visits the Museum of Delphi. SH's 'five visits to Greece between 1995 and 2004', she remarks, 'fostered his awareness of a real country' with a 'documentary geography' (*FK*, 136) and 'a continuing history' (Harrison 2019, 47). Classical and Irish mythology coexist in this translation and anticipate the presence of another charioteer, Jupiter, in a poem SH comes to write in response to a terrorist event.

[50] Beowulf

ANONYMOUS (TENTH–ELEVENTH CENTURY), OLD ENGLISH

Published in the UK by Faber & Faber in 1999; published in the USA by Farrar, Straus and Giroux in 1999 with the title *Beowulf: A New Verse Translation*. A slightly different version of the translation, 'Beowulf' (*ll.* 1–3182), is included in the seventh, thoroughly revised edition of the *Norton Anthology of English Literature*, edited by M. H. Abrams and published by W. W. Norton & Co. in 1999 (32–99; *Beowulf*: 3–99). Published as a bilingual edition in the USA by W. W. Norton & Co. in 2000 and by Faber & Faber in 2007.

SH published fifteen excerpts from the translation in progress. The first is 'A Ship of Death' (*ll.* 26–52) in *Numbers* (autumn 1986, 96); collected with revisions in *The Haw Lantern* (as 'From the Land of the Unspoken', 20) and in *Beowulf* (3–4; *Beowulf BE*, 5; *TSH*, 285–6). The second is 'The Scop' (*ll.* 89–98) in *Causley at 70*, edited by Harry Chambers and published by Peterloo Poets in 1987 (70), collected with revisions in *Beowulf* (5; *BE*, 9; *TSH*, 287). The third is 'Sea Interlude, with Hero' (*ll.* 194–285) in *A Parcel of Poems for Ted Hughes on his Sixty-Fifth Birthday*, published for private distribution by Faber & Faber on 17 August 1995 (56–8), collected with revisions in *Beowulf* (8–11; *BE*, 15–21; *TSH*, 290–2). The fourth is 'Exile Runes' (*ll.* 1118–39) in the *London Review of Books* (21 Sept. 1995, 8), collected with revisions in *Beowulf* (37–8; *BE*, 77–9; *TSH*, 314–15). The fifth is 'Beowulf's Boat' (*ll.* 407–59) in *College Green* (Autumn 1995, [46–7]),

collected with revisions in *Beowulf* (15–16; *BE*, 29–33; *TSH*, 295–6).
The sixth is 'The Welcome to Denmark' (*ll*. 286–319), in *The Literary Man: Essays Presented to Donald W. Hannah*, edited by Karl-Heinz Wehstarp and published by Aarhus University Press in 1996 (7–8), collected with revisions in *Beowulf* (11–12; *BE*, 21–23; *TSH*, 292–3). The seventh is 'The Funeral of Beowulf' (*ll*. 3137–82) in the *Times Literary Supplement* (19 September 1997, 4), collected with revisions in *Beowulf* (98–9; *BE*, 211–13; *TSH*, 365–6). The eighth is 'The Last Survivor' (*ll*. 2242–70), in the *Times Literary Supplement* (14 Nov. 1997, 13), collected with revisions in *Beowulf* (10–11; *BE*, 153–5; *TSH*, 343). The ninth is 'A Sea-crossing' (*ll*. 194–228) in *River City* (Summer 1998, 117–18), collected with revisions in *Beowulf* (8–9; *BE*, 15–17; *TSH*, 290). The tenth, eleventh and twelfth are 'Paths to Power' (*ll*. 1–25), 'A Sea-crossing' (*ll*. 194–228) and 'The Return to Geatland' (*ll*. 1880–1924) in the *Sunday Times* (26 July 1998, Books, 6–7), collected with revisions in *Beowulf* (3, 8–9 and 60–2; *BE*, 3–5, 15–17 and 129–31; *TSH*, 285, 290 and 334–5; SH also contributes a 'Note' in which he discusses his translation). The thirteenth and fourteenth are 'Grendel Attacks Hrothgar's Hall' (*ll*. 86–163) and 'Beowulf's Departure from Denmark' (*ll*. 1880–1924), grouped as 'Selections from *Beowulf*', in *Agni*, 48 (1998, 1–3 and 4–5), collected with revisions in *Beowulf* (5–7 and 60–1; *BE*, 9–13 and 129–31; *TSH*, 287–9 and 334–5). The fifteenth is 'The Haunted Mere' (*ll*. 1310–79) in *Threepenny Review* (summer 1999, 8), collected with revisions in *Beowulf* (44–5; *BE*, 93–7; *TSH*, 319–21; the excerpt is introduced by the line: '*After the attack on Heorot Hall by Grendel's mother, King Hrothgar tells Beowulf about the monsters and their underwater den*').

SH published seven extracts after the complete translation came out. The first is 'Beowulf Fights with the Dragon' (*ll*. 2542–91; *Beowulf*, 80–1; *BE*, 173–5; *TSH*, 350–1) in the *New York Review of Books* (4 Nov. 1999, 8; the excerpt is part 2 of 3 under the title 'A New Beowulf', preceded by an introduction (part 1) and a commentary (part 3) based on SH's 'Introduction', *Beowulf*, xxii and xxiii, where SH also quotes *ll*. 2415–21, *Beowulf*, 76–7; *BE*, 163–5; *TSH*, 347, and *ll*. 2444–54 and *ll*. 2460–2, *Beowulf*, 77 and 78; *BE*, 165–7; *TSH*, 348). The second is 'A Skilled Poet' (*ll*. 87–98; *Beowulf*, 5; *BE*, 9; *TSH*, 287), a broadside for William Alfred, published with revisions in a limited edition of seventy-five numbered copies by Catherine McCanless at the Bow & Arrow Press, Adams House, Harvard University, in 1999. The third is 'A Light Appeared . . .' (*ll*. 1570–72; *Beowulf*, 51; *BE*, 109; *TSH*, 326), a Christmas card privately printed with revisions by Peter Fallon at the Gallery Press in 1999. The fourth is 'Then a powerful demon, a prowler through the dark' (*ll*. 86–98; *Beowulf*, 5; *BE*, 9; *TSH*, 287) reprinted by *Poems on the Underground* in 2000. The fifth is 'Beowulf' (*ll*. 1–490; *Beowulf*, 3–17; *BE*, 3–35; *TSH*, 285–97), in *American Poetry Review* (Jan./Feb. 2000, 21–8; SH's translation appears under the title:

'An Introduction and New Verse Translation', which also includes SH's comments under 'About this Translation'). The sixth is 'From *Beowulf*' (*ll.* 2510–859; *Beowulf*, 79–90; *BE*, 169–93; *TSH*, 349–58), in *Wizards. Stories of Mischief, Magic and Mayhem*, edited by Jennifer Schwamm Willis, New York: Thunder Mouth's Press, 2001, 135–47. The seventh is 'News of the Raven (adapted from *Beowulf*)' (*ll.* 2897–3027; *Beowulf*, 91–5; *BE*, 195–203; *TSH*, 359–62) in *Irish Writers Against War*, edited by Conor Kostick and Katherine Moore and published by O'Brien Press in 2003 (53–4).

Two excerpts appeared posthumously in *New Selected Poems 1988–2013* (*ll.* 1–163 and *ll.* 3137–82; *NSP2014*, 112–19; *Beowulf*, 3–7 and 98–9; *Beowulf BE*, 3–13 and 211–13; *TSH*, 285–89 and 365–6).

A revised typescript page showing SH's abandoned first attempt to translate the opening lines (*ll.* 1–31; *Beowulf*, 3–4; *BE*, 3–5; *TSH*, 285) of *Beowulf* is included in exhibition catalogue *Chapter and Verse: 1000 Years of English Literature*, edited by Chris Fletcher and published by British Library Publishing Division in 2000 (16).

Three poems inspired by translating *Beowulf* are included in *Electric Light* (2001), SH's first collections of poems to come out after the complete translation of *Beowulf* is published (1999). 'The Fragment', first published in *Harvard Review* (spring 1996, 12), is collected with revisions and the same title (57). 'An Image from *Beowulf*', first published in *A Writing Life: Celebrating Nadine Gordimer*, edited by Andries Walter Oliphant and published by Penguin Books (South Africa) in 1998 (121), is collected with revisions as 'The Border Campaign' (18). 'On First Looking Into Ted Hughes's *Birthday Letters*' (section 3 and 4), first published in *the New Yorker* (5 Oct. 1998, 64–5), is collected with revisions as 'On His Work in the English Tongue' (61).

Beowulf was issued in 1999 by Faber–Penguin Audiobooks, on two audio cassettes, duration approximately 135 minutes, abridged, and on CD; and in 2000 on cassette and CD by HighBridge Company as *Beowulf: The Original BBC Recording*.

This is SH's complete translation of *Beowulf*. The text in this edition is drawn from the Faber & Faber bilingual edition (2007).

In a two-part 'Introduction' (*Beowulf*, ix–xxx; *BE*, ix–xxxiv) SH offers an in-depth discussion of the original poem and of his translation. SH 'studied *Beowulf* and other Anglo-Saxon poems' as an undergraduate at Queen's University, developing 'not only a feel for the language, but a fondness for the melancholy and fortitude that characterised the poetry'. When the editors of *The Norton Anthology of English Literature* invited him to translate the poem in the mid-1980s, SH was 'tempted' to try his hand, driven by the 'strong desire to get back to the first stratum of the language and to "assay the hoard"' (*Beowulf*, xxii; *BE*, xxiv–xxv; *Beowulf*, 79; *BE*, 169; *TSH*, 349, *l.* 2509).

At a time when SH had begun teaching at Harvard and was opening his ear 'to the untethered music of some contemporary American poetry', the language of *Beowulf*, Old English, would provide 'a kind of aural antidote', as SH put it, 'a way of ensuring' that his 'linguistic anchor would stay lodged on the Anglo-Saxon sea-floor' (*Beowulf*, xxii; *BE*, xxv).

That initial connection, however, was dampened by hesitation as the task was 'labour-intensive' and 'scriptorium-slow', like a 'sixth-former at homework': an attempt that 'often' felt like 'trying to bring down a megalith with a toy hammer'. Consequently, 'what had been so attractive in the first place, the hand-built, rock-sure feel of the thing' made SH feel defeated: he 'turned to other work' and, unpursued by the commissioning editors, 'the project went into abeyance'. Yet SH had 'an instinct' concerning his own 'linguistic and literary origins' that made him 'reluctant to abandon the task'. SH considered *Beowulf* to be part of his 'voice-right' but persuading himself that he was 'born into its language', and that its language was born into him, 'took a while' (*Beowulf*, xxiii; *BE,* xxv–xxvi).

The issue of language expressed itself as 'consciousness' always 'pricking': an 'awareness of language-loss and cultural dispossession', as SH describes it, that first 'tempted' him 'into binary thinking about language' – English and Irish 'as adversarial tongues, as either/or conditions rather than both/ands' – that 'for a long time hampered the development of a more confident and creative way of dealing with the whole vexed question' of 'the relationship between nationality, language, history and literary tradition in Ireland' (*Beowulf*, xxiv; *BE*, xxvii). As Conor McCarthy remarks, 'notwithstanding the occasional misreading' that sees SH's translation of *Beowulf* 'as a continuation of cultural animosities, it's clear that in fact the translation is a gesture towards breaking down the barriers that are perceived to exist between Irish and English' (McCarthy 2008, 93). Translating *Beowulf*, SH can be seen to be both writing himself 'into the foundations of English literature' (McCarthy, 2008, 6) – he describes the poem as 'one of the foundation works of poetry in English' (*Beowulf*, ix; *BE*, ix) – and also writing those foundations into his own work.

The 'possibility of release from this kind of cultural determinism' (*Beowulf*, xxiv, where SH uses 'determination'; *BE*, xxvii), SH explains, manifested itself in his first arts year at Queen's University Belfast – where SH read the first half of *Beowulf* 'routinely and reluctantly, even in some cases resentfully' as it was 'prescribed for the final exam' (*SS*, 437) and where, above all, he was lectured on the history of the English language. That history in turn manifested itself as 'a kind of linguistic river of rivers issuing from a pristine Celto-British Land of Cockaigne, a riverrun of Finnegans Wakespeak pouring out of the cleft rock of some prepolitical, prelapsarian, ur-philological Big Rock Candy Mountain' (*Beowulf*, xxiv; *BE*, xxvii–xxviii)

This realisation had 'a wonderfully sweetening effect' on SH as 'The Irish/English duality, the Celtic/Saxon antithesis were momentarily collapsed' and 'in the resulting etymological eddy a gleam of recognition flashed through the synapses,' revealing 'an elsewhere of potential that seemed at the same time to be a somewhere being remembered' (*Beowulf*, xxv; *BE*, xxviii). Even though, as he told O'Driscoll, SH 'didn't, in truth, have any special fondness for *Beowulf*' before he 'started work on it' (*SS*, 436), translating the poem was the realisation of that potential – a legitimate and logical enactment of that revelation. 'The decision to accept Norton's invitation,' SH explains, 'was taken thirty-five years before the invitation was actually issued' but 'between one's sense of readiness to take on a subject and the actual inscription of the first lines, there is always a problematical hiatus' (*Beowulf*, xxvi; *BE*, xxix).

'The first approach by Norton had come around 1984 or 1985,' SH tells O'Driscoll, when he was contacted by 'an editor called John Benedict' who broached the idea of 'a commissioned translation'. SH 'prepared a draft of the first hundred lines or so, up to the point where the minstrel sings in the hall, and they seemed to like it all right, although they understandably wanted a bit more – something from the action sequences, from Beowulf's fight with Grendel, for example'. At that point, however, SH 'had no appetite to proceed further' and 'For various reasons, it was the spring of 1995 before I started on the job for a second time' (*SS*, 439). A note on the title page of a *Beowulf* typescript housed in the British Library indicates the precise date when the translation hiatus ended: 'Begun again at line 99 in Glanmore Cottage March 21 1995.'

In addition to recognising and claiming for himself the voice-right to translate *Beowulf*, SH was also drawn to the 'undeluded quality about the *Beowulf* poet's sense of the world' that 'gives his lines immense emotional credibility and allows him to make general observations about life which are too far grounded in experience and reticence to be called "moralising"' (*Beowulf*, xxiii; *BE*, xxxi).

SH found attractive the 'marked gravity and composure in the voice' as well as 'an attention, for example, to the details of protocol and correct behaviour' (*SS*, 441). These parts of the poem, SH explains, have 'the cadence and force of earned wisdom', combining 'cogency and verity' in the way the speech he heard 'as a youngster in the Scullion kitchen' did (*Beowulf*, xxviii; *BE*, xxxi–xxxii).

These familiar sounds have already nursed SH as he voices his 'hidden Ireland' in *Sweeney Astray* and will nurse his 'hidden Scotland' in *The Testament of Cresseid* (Homem 2001, 27; *SS*, 426). More than that, they will reverberate, as Bernard O'Donoghue notes, from 'the inspired first word' of the translation, 'So'– heightened 'by a portentous full-stop' – to render 'the notorious "Hwaet!" of the original's opening, usually translated by feeble exclamations like "Lo!")' (O'Donoghue 1999, 67). As Des O'Rawe suggests, even the choice of lines from 'The Settle Bed' as epigraph to the introductory essay that precedes his *Beowulf* translation – 'And now this is "an inheritance" –/Upright, rudimentary, unshiftably planked/ In the long ago, yet willable forward//Again and again and again' (*ST*, 28) – documents SH's 'creative relationship to the guttural music of Anglo-Saxon' (O'Rawe 2001, 180).

It is this at-homeness in language that ultimately creates a new original out of translation, liberating the poet from depending 'on glossaries in the different editions, and on cribs as well' – including 'the literal prose version' by E. T. Donaldson, which was included in *The Norton Anthology of English Literature* and which SH's translation 'was due to replace', and the version, 'again in prose', by Clark Hall and C. L. Wrenn, which SH used as a student (*SS*, 437). Indeed, SH's *Beowulf* is almost immediately regarded as a new book – so much so that in 1999 it is the recipient of the Whitbread Book of the Year, an award for which translations are not usually nominated (*SS*, 442–3).

Discussing *Beowulf*, O'Driscoll reminds SH that Terry Eagleton had referred to him as 'an erstwhile outsider' who had 'placed himself boldly at the *fons et origo*, claiming the tongue as always-already his own from the outset,' and to his translation as 'a marvellously sturdy, intricate reinvention' that represents 'the final, triumphant reversal of his cultural dispossession' (Eagleton 1999, 16). Stating that Eagleton's 'grand statement . . . made the right point,' SH tones it down with characteristic self-deprecation by suggesting that 'Instead of putting "The End" on the last page [he] could have finished by rewriting a line from the conclusion of

"Lycidas": "Fret no more, woeful Seamus, in the shadow of his language" (*SS*, 440).

This comment is deceivingly humorous: in fact, it reiterates SH's stance on his birthright to speak and write in English and illustrates the trials and tribulations underscoring his quest to become a *Beowulf* translator. To elucidate both his own particular position of poet-translator as well as, more generally, the position of any literary translator, SH turns to another Catholic Irish writer, James Joyce, who more than any other writer before or after him shook the foundation of the English language and with it its whole literary canon in an act of post-traumatic reaction.

In what appears to be, in *A Portrait of the Artist as A Young Man*, a trivial conversation over an ordinary object that some call a 'tundish' and others call a 'funnel' (Joyce 1916, 219–20; 297), Stephen Dedalus realises that 'his Dublin vernacular is related to the old English base' and thus 'discovers that his own linguistic rights to English are, as it were, prenatal'. If he may not be 'the true-born English man', SH explains, he is 'the new-born English speaker'. And it is 'at this moment', as SH emphasises, that he is also 'born as a writer, liberated from subject-people status, freed of the language question' (Heaney 1999c, 14). SH's linguistic and cultural experience of translating *Beowulf* is rooted in Stephen's realisation that 'his vernacular possessions are buried treasures' and that 'his own word-hoard is the artistic equivalent of a gold hoard' (Heaney 1999c, 14).

This precedent offers SH 'a way of talking about the liminal situation of the literary translator, the one standing at the frontier of a resonant original, in awe of its primacy, utterly persuaded, and yet called upon to utter a different yet equally persuasive version of it in his or her own words' (Heaney 1999c, 14). Stephen's 'transition from linguistic fret to linguistic offensive', therefore, illuminates the work of the literary translator who 'often suffers from what might be called the funnel complex – a self-doubt induced by the supreme undoubtingness of the original – and must overcome it through an assertion of his own tundish-based entitlement' (Heaney 1999c, 14). Revisiting and renewing his commitment to the translation of *Beowulf*, SH suggests that 'What the translator needs then is for a move to happen similar to Stephen's move from being daunted to being undaunted'. As an example, SH points to 'the origin' of his own 'translator-boldness': the word 'thole', which formed a part of his 'buried word-hoard' and 'possessed the kind of fetter-easing power' that SH 'eventually found described with such sweet accuracy by the *Beowulf* poet himself' (Heaney 1999c, 14).

SH maintained that 'Our language pays tribute to itself when tribute is exacted from it,' and 'It suggests that our value to ourselves as individuals or as a group or even as a species can be re-estimated and increased by dwelling upon the sum total of the experience stored in our word-hoard.' SH's *Beowulf* demonstrates that 'Our fret as investors in ourselves can be allayed when poetry recirculates the language's hidden wealth. This recirculation, SH concludes, is not only etymologically renovating, but psychologically and phenomenologically so as well' (Heaney 1999c, 16).

There is no doubt that *Beowulf* reveals not only SH's skills as a poet-translator but also how central translation is to the full expression of his identity, his language and his poetics. Indeed, Bernard O'Donoghue opens his review of *Beowulf* by observing that 'From early in his career [SH] has been recognised as a major critic as well as poet, in the great English tradition of artist/commentators from Sidney to Coleridge to Eliot,' but 'what has dawned on us more slowly is that he is also – to borrow a phrase used to describe Chaucer – a great translator' (O'Donoghue 1999, 67).

Alluding to the 'dazzle' and the 'solidity' of SH's translation, Robert Easting argues that 'perhaps the most remarkable thing is that so much of the translation does not call attention to itself,' but 'maintains the alliteration unobtrusively and moves the narrative along with quiet efficiency'. According to Easting, 'Such service to the poem and its readership is as it should be,' and 'we see one master respectfully acknowledging another' as SH 'does in all his translations.' For SH, Easting concludes, 'going back to *Beowulf* was a kind of homecoming,' and his translation 'proffers us the gift that fine art, in whatever medium, bestows': namely, 'that achieved *claritas*, that grateful sense of complexities coming into focus, that recognition of "illuminated rightness"' (*RP*, xvii; Sonzogni 2021, 74).

As Conor McCarthy observes, there is 'embedded' in *Beowulf* 'the possibility of the endurance of poetic creation beyond the transience of the suffering that spawns it' (McCarthy 2008, 120). 'The miraculous mix', as O'Donoghue describes it, of the poem's 'original spirit' and 'the master's voice-right', as well as the poem's 'substantial bearing on our modern condition', have enabled SH to enact that possibility 'with a power that will help to secure *Beowulf* in the academic canon for another generation' (O'Donoghue 1999, 67).

In 2000 SH visited Denmark and read from *Beowulf* at Lejre, believed to be the site of Hrothgar's Hall, and in 2001 took part in a three-day celebration of his work at Lincoln Center, New York, giving a reading of his translation of the poem in the Alice Tully Hall (*SS*, xxviii).

[51] Diary of One Who Vanished

OZEF KALDA (1871–1921), CZECH

Published in the UK by Faber & Faber in 1999; published in the USA by Farrar, Straus and Giroux in 2000. SH's 'Introduction' (*DOWV*, [5–6]) provides material for two notes: 'A Gate Left Open' (Joint programme for *Jane Eyre* and *Diary of One Who Vanished*, Eircom Dublin Theatre Festival '99, 4–16 Oct. 1999) and 'A Gate Left Open: On Translating the Songs of Janáček's *Journal d'un disparu*' (*Translation Ireland*, Dec. 1999, 1–2), which includes songs no. II and VI (*DOWV*, [10] and [14]; *TSH*, 367 and 368–9).

This is SH's complete translation of *Zápisník zmizelého* (1921). The text in this edition is drawn from the Faber & Faber edition (1999).

SH's version of this song cycle in twenty-two parts was commissioned by English National Opera (ENO) in partnership with the (British) National Theatre and other European companies. Only in the late 1990s was this work attributed to the Wallachian writer and railway official Ozef Kalda by Jan Mikeska, an amateur historian, and Jiří Demel, a literary scholar (Demel 1997, 93–6). As Alena Němcová observes, it is not certain whether this is Kalda's original work or an adaptation of folk poems that he had heard (Němcová 1998, 203). The Czech composer Leoš Janáček (1854–1928) set these texts to music in 1921 for tenor, alto, three female voices and piano. According to Stuart Young, this translation is unique in two respects: it is the only work that SH translated from Czech, and 'albeit the line between poetry and song may be a fine one, it is the only libretto that he translated' (Sonzogni 2021, 15).

Writing for the *New York Times*, Johanna Keller explains that when the tenor Ian Bostridge and Deborah Warner, the British director, were 'casting about for a translator' of a libretto for the 'Diary', Lucasta Miller, Bostridge's wife, suggested SH. Bostridge and Warner considered SH's sympathy towards its rural setting a perfect match. When they discovered that SH was incapacitated with a broken leg, they sent him a CD alongside a proposal. 'As I lay with my leg in plaster,' SH recalls, 'I listened to the cycle over and over on CD,' listening 'very acutely' to 'the Czech words'. SH also relied on a German and an English translation 'to get inside the sense, the syllable count, and the way the words and music fit together'. The first draft of the translation, SH admits, 'wasn't quite up to singability' but got him 'hooked', 'established in labour' (Keller 2001, 19). Michael Dervan points out how producing a singable translation is 'very risky' because 'writing songs is a rare art' and also because, as Stuart Young emphasises, 'it was evidently important' to SH 'to ensure that, shorn of the music, his verse had inherent "texture and lambency and staying power (*CP*, 23)"' (Dervan 2001, 39; Sonzogni 2021, 16). 'As is often the case with commissions of translations for the stage,' Stuart Young remarks, 'fine tuning occurred in the rehearsal room' (Sonzogni 2021, 32): 'the trading of rhymes and syllables', as SH puts it, 'the give of speech and the take of song' (*DOWV*, vi).

The childhood memories evoked by the rural setting of many of the poems in the song cycle intrigued SH into accepting to undertake an otherwise unusual work, even in the broader context of 'looking Eastwards' (Kay 2012, 18) to Eastern European poetics as a source of 'excitement and education' (*DOWV*, vi). 'There were things that immediately attracted me,' SH tells Keller and mentions 'the Gypsies coming to the district did have that kind of extra-ness about it, a kind of stealth'. Referring to the programme notes, SH says that 'it was as if a gate had been left open in the usual life, as if something might get in or get out' and 'the whole project had a delicious divertimento place in my life, a kind of experiment'. And 'with a self-effacing twinkle', as Keller puts it, SH says that he has been hired because he 'knew the word for plow' (Keller 2001, 19).

SH explains that 'It was this feeling of energy stalking the edge of the familiar' that he 'recognised immediately in the poems of *Diary of One Who Vanished*', and that he was 'pleased to discover that the poems had had a similar effect on Janáček'. 'The Wallachian dialect in which they were written woke echoes on the very floor of his memory', SH observes, and 'suddenly he was back within the acoustic of his own first country speech': the poems were 'a kind of time machine that transported the composer to a remembered place, the ground of pure potential where work begins in excitement before it begins in earnest'. Even though SH 'knew no Czech', he felt he 'knew enough' of the song-cycle's background to try his hand 'at making English versions'. For SH this process also meant 'a way too into Irish-English, since the vocabulary of the translation belongs as much in the country of the spancelled horse as in the concert room'. His gypsy girl, Zefka, comes to '"the townland" – a word not found in my *Shorter Oxford English Dictionary*, and a part of the land that has nothing to do with the town'. SH explains how the word itself 'was growing liminal', like '"boortree" and "scaldie" and even "spancel"', and the 'great pleasure' it gave him 'to let them loose for a flutter in the "shadowdapple, hide-and-seek" of greenwood and desire'. If the first draft of the translation was prepared 'by listening to the songs being sung in Czech', in the end SH says: 'I could only write for my own ear, which is partly tuned to the register of my original Co. Derry voice and partly to the demands of English verse-craft' (Heaney 1999d 1–2).

'And once you think twice about a local usage you have been displaced from it,' SH writes in his Oxford Lecture 'John Clare's Prog', 'your right to it has been contested by the official linguistic censor with whom another part of you is secretly in league' (*RP*, 63). As Stuart Young emphasises, the language SH uses in *Diary of One Who Vanished* 'ensures not only that the work sounds, as Heaney aspires for his translations, very "like a Heaney poem" but it also serves to capture the country-hearth speech and the once upon a time quality of the original' (Sonzogni 2021, 36). 'Inevitably, you want to be true to whatever makes you sound like yourself,' SH tells Keller, and 'You have to sound to yourself as if you had written it.' And SH's translation, says Keller, 'does have Mr Heaney's fingerprints all over it, in its straightforward depiction of the physical world and its delight in a local vocabulary and an enriched lexicon' (Keller 2001, 19).

The English National Opera production of Heaney's translation of *Diary of One Who Vanished* premiered at the Gaiety Theatre as part of the Dublin Theatre Festival in October 1999. It then played in Paris (MC93, in Bobigny) and London (Lyttelton Theatre), also in 1999; in Amsterdam (Stadsschouwburg) and Munich (Cuvilliés Theatre) in 2000; and in New York (John Jay College Theater) in 2001, as part of a three-day programme devoted to SH's work at the Lincoln Center. Reviewing 'Deborah Warner's intriguing production of Janacek's "Diary of One Who Vanished"' at the John Jay College Theater for The *New York Times*, Anthony Tommasini describes SH's version of Kalda's poems as 'pungent English verse that captures the rustic elegance of Janáček's music' (Tommasini 2001, B9).

[52] Arion — [53] The Civil Power

ALEXANDER PUSHKIN (1799–1837), RUSSIAN

'Arion' is first published in the *Times Literary Supplement* (15 Oct. 1999, 28); reprinted in *After Pushkin: Versions of the Poems of*

Alexander Sergeevich Pushkin by Contemporary Poets, edited and introduced by Elaine Feinstein and published by Carcanet Press for the Folio Society in 1999 (83); collected in *Electric Light* (2001, 72); and reprinted with revisions as a keepsake by Arion Press in 2002.

'The Civil Power' is first published in *Modern Poetry in Translation* (New Series 15, 1999, 174) and is uncollected.

These are SH's complete translations of 'Арион' (1827) and 'Мирская власть' (1836). The texts in this edition are drawn from the Arion Press keepsake (2002) for 'Arion' and from *Modern Poetry in Translation* (1999) for 'The Civil Power'.

On 10 June 1999, the bicentenary of Pushkin's birth 'was marked by a celebration opera and dinner held at St James's Palace, London, in the presence of HRH The Prince of Wales, Honorary President of The British Pushkin Bicentennial Trust'. The souvenir programme also contained a letter of support from Prince Charles, as he was then, in which he states that he had 'always had the greatest admiration for Pushkin'. 'The British Pushkin Bicentennial Trust was set up in 1994 to use this 200th anniversary year of his birth to increase understanding and awareness of Pushkin and his work in Britain. Five years of hard work have made possible the very many celebratory events which are now taking place: operas, concerts, a travelling exhibition starting at the Barbican this month and an exhibition at Kenwood, new publications, poetry readings, a puppet show, a new music commission, and much more.' Among the new publications, 'An anthology of new translations by major English-speaking poets, including Ted Hughes and Seamus Heaney, will be published by the Folio Society in the autumn' (Briggs 1999, 63–4).

As Stephanie Schwerter notes, SH's translation of 'Arion' was 'very much a "one-off job" he did for a volume of Pushkin translations edited by Elaine Feinstein', who 'personally provided for him' a literal translation. 'In contrast to Pushkin, who uses Greek myth to express an unambiguous political standpoint,' Schwerter remarks, SH 'engages with the Russian poem to explore the significance of artistic expression in times of social unrest'. Schwerter emphasises how SH, 'reflecting on his role as a writer', transforms 'Pushkin's public poem into private poetry'. Not concerned with 'establishing concrete political and historical parallels between Russia and Northern Ireland,' SH's 'interests lie rather in the discussion of the poet's moral duty in society' (Schwerter 2013, 65, 66–7).

The translation of 'Arion' finds its place among the 'many elegies both for personal friends and for poets who have been important to him' included in *Electric Light* (2001, 72). 'Marking their disappearance,' writes Helen Vendler in her review of the book for the *Irish Times*, SH 'the survivor, adapts (with nods to Eliot and – via Milton – Horace) Pushkin's poem in which Arion (saved from shipwreck by a dolphin) speaks a postlude' (Vendler 2001, 52). The Irish poet Gerry Murphy wrote a poem titled 'Pushkin's Arion' in response to SH's translation.

In the pseudo-ekphrastic poem 'The Civil Power', the scene at the crucifixion of Jesus is used by Pushkin to ask a series of questions aimed at denouncing the distinction between reality as it is and as it is portrayed and promoted by those in power. Even the death of Jesus on the cross is subject to ownership and interpretation. SH was of course very mindful of the political, social and cultural implications of faith on either side of the Protestant–Catholic divide. Significantly, the agreement that brought years of sectarian violence in Northern Ireland to an end was signed in 1998, the year before the publication of this translation, and on the day of the crucifixion, Good Friday. This Pushkin poem, in a sense, implies the tension that Miłosz would later describe and SH adopt: being 'stretched between contemplation of a motionless point and the command to participate actively in history' (*SS*, 260).

SH's decision to translate this poem is explained in its contents. Reflecting on the challenges of undertaking the translation of Sophocles' *Antigone* for the Abbey Theatre – 'there was an urgent political context, there was no writerly urge' – SH says that he 'was reading desultorily about the play' as 'again and again the old familiar topics came swimming up': 'individual conscience versus civil power, men versus women, the domestic versus the public sphere, the relevance of the action in times of crisis, in France, in Russia, in Poland, in Northern Ireland – of course, of course, of course' (Heaney 2005, 171).

While it is likely that the starting point of 'The Civil Power' is the same as for 'Arion' – a literal version prepared by Elaine Feinstein for her *After Pushkin* anthology – a different source can be suggested. One of the questions Dennis O'Driscoll puts to SH in the course of their conversations is whether Ted Hughes deepened SH's interest in foreign-language poetry. As O'Driscoll notes, Hughes 'had, after all, helped to initiate the Poetry International festivals in London' and was 'a friend of Daniel Weissbort – the poet, editor and translator with whom he co-edited the journal *Modern Poetry in Translation*'. In his reply SH tells O'Driscoll that he 'met Danny first' and that having Ted as a mutual friend made it 'that much readier' for them 'to be friends with each other' (*SS*, 298). It is plausible that Weissbort (if not Hughes) may have asked SH to translate a Pushkin poem for *Modern Poetry in Translation* as well. Weissbort and Hughes were among the translators featured in Carcanet's Pushkin anthology, along with Feinstein herself, an award-winning translator of Russian poetry as well as a biographer of, among others, Pushkin (*Pushkin*, 1998) and Hughes (*Ted Hughes: The Life of a Poet*, 2001).

In both translations SH has risen to the challenge of replicating 'the mixture of formal light-footedness and vernacular gumption that characterises Pushkin's Russian' (Heaney 1999c, 26).

[54] 'Imagine striking a match that night in the cave' — [55] Flight into Egypt

JOSEPH BRODSKY (1940–1996), RUSSIAN

Both translations are included in Joseph Brodsky's *Nativity Poems*, published by Farrar, Straus and Giroux in 2001 (79; 99, 101), and featured in the *New Yorker* on 18 December 2001 (69, 72), where 'Imagine striking a match that night in the cave' appears under the title 'Nativity Poem'. 'Flight into Egypt' is numbered (2) in both the book and the newspaper to distinguish SH's translation from Melissa Green's translation.

Uncollected.

These are SH's complete translations of Представь, чиркнув спичкой, тот вечер в пещере and Бегство в Египет (1992), which SH dated to 1989 and December 1995 respectively. The texts in this edition are both drawn from *Nativity Poems* (2001).

In his 2 April 2008 letter to Stephanie Schwerter, SH describes his translations as 'versifications of prose cribs supplied by Marina Brodsky' (Schwerter 2013, 59).

Brodsky's *Nativity Poems* is a bilingual anthology consisting of eighteen Russian poems followed by their English translations. The Russian originals were first published under the title *Рождественские стихи* [*Christmas Poems*] in *Nezavisimaya Gazeta* in 1992. Brodsky himself is one of the translators along with Melissa Green, Anthony Hecht, George L. Kline, Glyn Maxwell, Paul Muldoon, Alan Myers, Derek Walcott, Daniel Weissbort and Richard Wilbur. Heaney's 'Imagine striking a match that night in the cave' is the twelfth translation in the collection and 'Flight into Egypt' is the last. Brodsky wrote these poems over a period of thirty-three years,

1962–95. In the interview with Peter Vail that closes *Nativity Poems*, Brodsky states that since he 'took to writing poems seriously', he tried to compose one piece of work for every Christmas as 'a sort of birthday greeting' (Brodsky 2001, 103). As Schwerter points out, 'The poet explains his choice of topic with the fact that Christmas deals with the "calculation" of life and the existence of the individual.' Schwerter argues that 'The importance Brodsky attributes to the individual human being as well as the spiritual dimension of the *Nativity Poems* might have had some bearing on Heaney's interest in this collection of poetry' (Schwerter 2013, 59).

Brodsky's 'own metres and vowels' wake SH 'to a new sound in the early 70's'. SH first met Brodsky 'on his way from Moscow to Michigan, when he stopped for a couple of days in London during the 1972 Poetry International' (Heaney 1987, 63). SH's first impression of Brodsky 'was of a slight, somewhat nervous fellow about my own age, shooting the half-tentative, half-suspicious glances that any young poet shoots at a big-deal poetry reading' (*SS*, 376). SH also notes that there is something 'mysterious and enlivening' about Brodsky, who comes across as 'already marked for and propelled into history' (Heaney 1987, 63). SH quickly saw, as Jeffrey Meyers points out, that 'the artful and idealistic Brodsky commanded a formidable intelligence, erudition and intuition' and 'displayed an absolute belief in the supreme value of great art' (Meyers 2020, [1]). Their friendship blossomed, as Schwerter notes, 'when they were teaching in the US in the 1980s' (Schwerter 2013, 59).

In what is now a historic interview with the deported Chinese poet Bei Ling, who regarded Brodsky as one of the poets who concerned him the most, SH's describes Brodsky's poetry as 'very difficult' and 'very complicated' because 'very little of it is straightforward', adding that 'when it is, it can be devastating'. 'When you were in Joseph Brodsky's presence,' says SH, 'you felt you were close to a fountain of energy, first of all, and secondly, a fountain of truthfulness.' Brodsky, SH explains to Bei Ling, 'brought people to realise the joy of utterance in poetry' but 'most important – and this is why he mattered to poets – he never doubted for a moment that poetry was an essential part of the human equipment'. SH emphasises how 'something was always at stake for Brodsky' and 'the reality of poetry' was 'a matter of life and death' and so 'he changed the pressure, he increased the urgency' (Heaney 2000c, 7–8).

SH's critical engagement with Brodsky's poetics begins in 1986. SH's essay 'Heaney on Brodsky' features in the programme for

Seamus Heaney and Joseph Brodsky for the *Gate Theatre Readings* held on 6 October 1985 ([3]). Writing for the *Observer Review* (30 Nov. 1986, 2), SH references Brodsky's *Less Than One: Selected Essays* (1986). In 1987 Brodsky is awarded the Nobel Prize in Literature 'for an all-embracing authorship, imbued with clarity of thought and poetic intensity'. SH's reaction is captured in an essay titled 'Brodsky's Nobel: What the Applause Was About' published in the *New York Times Book Review* (8 Nov. 1987, 1, 63–5) and reprinted in part under the title 'Joseph Brodsky: Strong Poet Strong Man' in the *Irish Times Weekend* (11 June 1988, 5). 'Like other strong poets,' writes SH, 'Brodsky sets the reader's comfort below the poem's necessities' (Heaney 1987, 65).

When Brodsky died, SH wrote an elegy and an essay in his memory. Titled 'Audenesque', based on W. H. Auden's elegy for W. B. Yeats, and alluding to Brodsky's elegy for T. S. Eliot, the poem is published in the *Times Literary Supplement* (9 Feb. 1996, 11) and collected in *Electric Light* (2001, 64–6). Titled 'Secret Sharer: Seamus Heaney Remembers Joseph Brodsky', the essay is published in *Metre* (autumn 1996, 31–4). The last quatrain of 'Audenesque' summons Brodsky's personality and poetics: 'Dust-cake, still – see *Gilgamesh* –/Feed the dead. So be their guest./Do again what Auden said/Good poets do: bite, break their bread' (*EL*, 66).

2000S

In a decade when international terrorism shocks the world and illness forces SH to pause for one year, three books of poems – *Electric Light* (2001), *District and Circle* (2006) and *Human Chain* (2010) – and two book-length translations – *The Burial at Thebes* (2004) and *The Testament of Cresseid & Seven Fables* (2009) – are published. SH is also working on two more book-length translations that will come out after his death. Numerous poem-length translations – old ones and new ones from German, classical and modern Greek, Irish, Italian, Latin, Scottish Gaelic, Old and Middle English and French – continue to appear.

This decade brings SH the loss of one of the most important and influential figures for him, Czesław Miłosz (1911–2004), and the arrival of three granddaughters: Anna Rose (2006), Aibhín (2008) and Síofra (2010). SH dedicates new poems and translations to each.

[56] Eclogue IX

VIRGIL (70–19 BCE), CLASSICAL LATIN

First published in *Electric Light* (31–4).

This is SH's complete translation of '*Ecloga nona*'. The text in this edition is drawn from *Electric Light* (2001).

This eclogue, as Bernard O'Donoghue notes, is 'concerned with the hardships of country life' (Harrison 2019, 148). 'The roots of Heaney's interest in pastoral go back a long way,' O'Donoghue points out, 'and he has returned to the discussion of it in similar terms throughout his writing' to explore the tension between 'lyric utterance and social responsibility' (Harrison 2019, 147, 149). 'Heaney makes it plain in "Eclogues *In Extremis*",' O'Donoghue argues, 'that he finds that poem decidedly appropriate to the modern predicament: not only for himself but for other writers – MacNeice, the tragic Hungarian poet Miklos Radnoti, Michael Longley, and Czesław Miłosz' (Harrison 2019, 149). Virgil's poems '"establish a context" and provide the material with which the poet works rather than being an inherent part of his developing poetics' (Harrison 2019, 151).

In an interview with Rui Carvalho Homem (Homem 2001), SH offers a detailed and personal explanation for the genesis of this translation, locating it, as it were, in reading (as a student and as a teacher), in travelling (in Ireland and in Greece) and in writing (solicited and unsolicited poems). SH explains that he has read the *Eclogues* in translation when he was at school and again in a new translation (*The Eclogues of Virgil: A Translation*, by David Ferry and published in 1999 by Farrar, Straus and Giroux, SH's American publisher). 'This new encounter', says SH, 'awakened some kind of simple reader's delight' in him – a similar experience would inspire two other translations in response to the terrorist attack of 11 September: one from the Latin of Horace [57] and one from the German of Rilke [74].

Re-reading Virgil's *Eclogues* reminds SH 'of the beauty of these poems and their strangeness': impressions that return to him after travelling to Greece, writing 'a number of "Greek" sonnets', and seeing 'an actual goatherd in Arcadia', whom SH references in the opening sonnet as 'Subsisting beyond eclogue and translation' (*EL*, 38, 'Sonnets from Hellas', '1. Into Arcadia'). 'He was the real thing,' SH glosses, 'he wasn't in an eclogue, he was "in the forecourt of the filling station" with stinking goats; and yet there was a complete continuity between this twentieth-century creature and the literary figure you find in Theocritus.' An invitation 'to do an occasional poem for a volume of essays on John Millington Synge, whose antecedents had lived in Glanmore', and whose cottage in Glanmore was given to SH by Ann Saddlemyer, inspires SH to write 'Glanmore Eclogue': an autobiographical eclogue set in contemporary Ireland where 'a Wicklow farmer' complains to 'a cottage-renting poet' and Ann becomes Augusta, 'a kind of patroness'. It is the need to give this poem 'a bit more context' that prompts SH to translate Virgil's 'Eclogue IX', which precedes 'Glanmore Eclogue' in the collection (*EL*, 31–4 and 35–7). However, there is also 'a little secret, personal link' about this translation. When SH begins to publish poems while at university, he uses the pseudonym '*Incertus*', which means 'I'm not sure'. As SH tells Homem, 'Lycidas in the ninth eclogue of Virgil is a poet who says, well, "I'm not sure: I have done nothing yet/That Varius or Cinna would take note of".' SH also mentions Milton's *Lycidas* (1657), a poem that adopts the conventions of classical pastoral elegy and says, 'I'm not yet ready, but anyway, since this has happened, I have to get started.' While SH's main motive is 'to establish a context', there is also 'a kind of minimal literary self-referential quality in that translation' (Homem 2001, 25–6; *EL*, 33).

[57] Anything Can Happen

HORACE (65–8 BCE), CLASSICAL LATIN

First published in the *Irish Times* (17 Nov. 2001, Weekend 10) with the title 'Horace and the Thunder'); republished with revisions in the *Times Literary Supplement* (18 Jan. 2002, 40); in *Translation Ireland* (spring 2002, 8–11); in *Irish Pages* (1. 2, autumn/winter 2002/2003, 54); and in *Anything Can Happen: A Poem and an Essay by Seamus Heaney with Translations in Support of Art for Amnesty* (Dublin: TownHouse, 2004, 18); reprinted as a broadside with the title 'Horace and the Thunder' by Pressed Wafer to mark SH's reading at MIT, Cambridge, Mass., on 17 Oct. 2002.

Collected as 'Anything Can Happen' in *District and Circle* (13) and included posthumously in *New Selected Poems 1988–2013* (*NSP*2014, 148) and in *100 Poems* (*100P*, 142).

This is SH's translation of *ll.* 5–16 from *Carmina* 1.34. The text in this edition is drawn from *District and Circle* (2006).

SH 'produced' this adaptation 'in the aftermath of the September 11 attacks' (*SS*, 386). The McCabe Heaney Collection housed at the National Library of Ireland contains a manuscript and a typescript of this translation. The manuscript, titled 'Horace, Odes, 1, 34' and dedicated to Bernard and Jane McCabe, has a date, 29 September 2001, and a place, Bologna, which is known, like New York City, for its two towers, Garisenda and degli Asinelli – a poignant setting to get the translation under way. Seamus and Marie Heaney spent some time there with Bernard and Jane McCabe: a postcard Seamus sends to Barrie Cooke on 1 October 2001 – that year Cooke turned seventy – confirms it. This manuscript, undated and titled 'Out of the Blue', is clearly a revised version of the typescript.

SH quotes this translation for the first time in two public speeches in late 2001. The first speech is 'The Whole Thing: On the Good of Poetry', the address SH delivers in Dublin on 5 November 2001 as the Annual Distinguished Lecturer for the Department of International Health and Tropical Medicine, Royal College of Surgeons. The text of the lecture is published the following year (*Recorder*, spring 2002, 5–20). The second speech is 'Towers, Trees, Terrors: A Reverie in Urbino', the *Lectio Magistralis* SH delivers at the University of Urbino, Italy, on 23 November 2001 on the occasion of his graduation *honoris causa*. 'It was in Horace,' SH says, that he 'found the poem that held up most strongly and was the best for the reality of what we were feeling those days following the September 11 attacks on New York and Washington'. A poem, SH explains, 'about *terra tremens*, the opposite of *terra firma*'; a poem that is a 'match for reality: artistically, psychologically, even politically, it stands its ground' (Heaney 2007, 155). This version of the translation, published several years later, consists of three stanzas only: SH's own closing stanza is not included (Heaney 2007, 156).

In addition to changing the title from 'Out of the Blue' to 'Horace and the Thunder' to 'Anything Can Happen', and to reworking the final stanza in Horace's poem, SH continues to revisit the last line as the translation is published multiple times before he collects it in *District and Circle*: 'Telluric ash and fire-spores boil away' becomes 'Telluric ash and fire-spores darken day' then 'Smoke-furl and boiling ashes darken day' and then 'Telluric ash and fire-spores boil away'.

SH has given two in-depth and coeval explanations of how he came to do this translation: in conversation with Dennis O'Driscoll and in the Robert Lowell Memorial Lecture. As he tells O'Driscoll, 'the year before the 9/11 attacks' he had been brought to his senses when he read *Odes* 1.34 in David Ferry's complete translation. In the autumn of 2000 SH talked about this poem in a lecture at Harvard titled 'Bright Bolts', emphasising how shock and surprise are 'the *sine qua non* of a certain kind of terrific poetry' and juxtaposing it with Robert Graves's 'The White Goddess' – a work that ends with the poet hoping for the muse, 'Heedless of where the next bright bolt might fall'. Both Horace and Graves, SH explains, 'were writing about transformations caused by the "bright bolt" of terror'. In Graves, SH observes, 'it was a psychosomatic frisson, which he associated with the presence of the goddess'; in Horace, 'it came from the tremendous force of unexpected thunder and lightning which announced the power and presence of Jupiter'. And 'When the World Trade Center attacks happened,' SH realised that 'the shock-and-awe factor in the Horace poem matched' what he and 'everybody else was feeling'. SH's version, as he puts it, is 'partly an elegy' but is also 'meant "to warn"'. Remembering Ferry's translation, SH decides to translate the poem himself but 'disobeyed Horace' and 'beheaded the original poem', taking off the first stanza and doing 'something worse with an extra one at the end' (*SS*, 423–4; Heaney 2008b, 34:45–37:29).

'The poem's detached obliquity,' as Rachel Falconer observes, 'and the pointedly explicit nature of Heaney's prose commentary, are two complementary aspects of Heaney's ethically driven response to the international outbreak of violence at the start of the millennium' (Kean 2021, 136). In conversation with Dennis O'Driscoll, SH quotes a line from 'Mycenae Lookout', 'there is "No such thing/ as innocent/bystanding"' (*SL*, 30) to explain that 'during fourteen years in Harvard' he 'learned about being in America, how different it felt and they felt; and two occurrences particularly registered as a result: firstly the attack on the Twin Towers and secondly the Afghanistan and Iraq crackdowns'. SH states that 'You cannot distinguish between your condition as a creature of the times and your action as a scribbler' (*SS*, 409).

'Anything Can Happen', however, does what SH said Yeats's poetry does: 'take the brunt of public atrocity' (Heaney 1989b, 32:32–33:39).

[58] Summary

ANONYMOUS (NINTH CENTURY), OLD IRISH

First published in *Éire-Ireland* (spring/summer 2000, 88–9) and reprinted with revisions in *The Names Upon the Harp*, edited by Marie Heaney and published by Faber & Faber in 2000 (71).
    Uncollected.

This is SH's abridged translation (twelve quatrains) of *Cétemain cain cucht* (fourteen quatrains), which is included in both Kenneth Hurlstone Jackson's *A Celtic Miscellany* as an example of nature poems, with the title 'May Time' (Jackson 1971, 63–4), and in Gerard Murphy's *Early Irish Lyrics* as an example of the Finn-cycle poems, with the title 'May Day' (Murphy 1956, 156–9). In *The Names upon the Harp*, where the poem is reprinted, SH omitted four stanzas (*ll.* 13–26 and 37–43). The text in this edition is drawn from *Éire-Ireland* (2000).
    In conversation with Dennis O'Driscoll, SH revealed his intention to 'do some Irish-language translations' – 'one-off poems' that he had 'known and loved' – 'for pleasure and joy' and admitted to having come to like translation 'because it's a form of writing by proxy: you get the high of finishing something you don't have to start' (*SS*, 427).
    There are many summer poems in SH's work in verse, starting with 'A Midsummer', which was published in the *Irish Times* (13 Feb. 1971, 5) but has remained uncollected.

[59] Moling's Gloss

ANONYMOUS (TENTH CENTURY), MIDDLE IRISH

First published as the last text of 'Ten Glosses' in the *Guardian* (24 March 2001, Saturday Review, 12).
    Collected in *Electric Light* (56).

This is SH's complete translation of *Tan bím eter mo ṡruithe*, ascribed to Mo Ling of St Mullins, Co. Carlow, who died *c.*697, and is included in Murphy's *Early Irish Lyrics* among the monastic poems with the title 'All Things to All Men' (Murphy 1956, 32–3). The text in this edition is drawn from *Electric Light* (2001).
    A typescript note among the papers in the McCabe Heaney Collection at the National Library of Ireland confirms that Murphy's anthology was SH's source for this and other translations from the

Irish. SH's note describes the origin of this gloss: '*From a Middle Irish Commentary on the Old Irish Félire Óengusso, written in the tenth century, forming part of the entry for Moling's feast day on June 17.*//Gerard Murphy, *Early Irish Lyrics*'.

At the end of his peregrination, the exiled king and birdman Sweeney lands at St Mullins where his life also comes to an end. There, as we read in SH's translation of *Buile Suibhne* [7], 'Sweeney repented and made his confession to Moling' and 'received Christ's body and thanked God for having received it and after that was anointed by the clerics' and then 'his spirit fled to heaven and his body was given an honourable burial by Moling' (*SF*, 116–17).

[60] Colmcille's Derry — [61] The Monk's Tryst — [62] Gráinne's Words about Diarmait

ANONYMOUS (TWELFTH CENTURY/NINTH CENTURY/TWELFTH CENTURY), OLD AND MIDDLE IRISH

First published as poems no. 2, no. 3 and no. 4 respectively in a sequence with two previously published translations (1. 'The Blackbird of Belfast Lough' [5], and 5. 'North-East' [6]) under the title 'A Note Spurt: Five Poems from the Old Irish' in *The Way You Say the World: A Celebration for Anne Stevenson*, compiled by John Lucas and Matt Simpson and published by Shoestring Press in 2003 (64–5). All three translations are among the 'Seven Old Irish Poems' SH returned to and revisited with Timothy O'Neill between 2007 and 2009. O'Neill notes that no. 3 ('Colmcille's Derry' or 'Derry I cherish ever') 'was used on the 2008 Christmas card'; no. 5 ('The Monk's Tryst' or 'Sweet-toned bell') was 'worked out in 2007': and no. 6 ('Gráinne's Words about Diarmait' or 'One there is') 'got its final form in March 2008' (O'Neill 2013).

'Colmcille's Derry', with the Irish title '*Is aire charaim Doire*', is collected as part II of 'Colum Cille Cecinit', in *Human Chain* (72). 'The Monk's Tryst' and 'Gráinne's Words about Diarmait' are uncollected.

These are SH's complete translations of '*Is aire charaim Doire*', '*Clocán binn*', and '*Fil duine*', all three included in Murphy's *Early Irish Lyrics* among poems connected with the life of Colum Cille, monastic poems, and poems of the Finn-cycle, and titled respectively 'Derry', 'The Bell', and 'Gráinne speaks of Díarmait' (Murphy 1956, 68–9, 4–5, and 160–1). The texts in this edition are drawn from *The Way You Say the World: A Celebration for Anne Stevenson* (2003).

'Colmcille's Derry', titled 'He Remembers Derry', is included in Crotty's *The Penguin Book of Irish Poetry*, where it appears in the editor's own translation (Crotty 2010, 36).

SH re-translated these three poems with Timothy O'Neill (the first version is collected in *Human Chain* with a full stop instead of a colon at the end of *l*. 1 and a full stop instead of a comma at the end of *l*. 2):

No. 3:

Derry I cherish ever:
It is calm, it is clear,
Crowds of white angels on their rounds
At every corner.

No. 5:

Sweet-toned bell
Abrangle in the small hours gale:
Better it in community
Than out there, keeping company.

No. 6:

One there is
Beloved, delightful to my gaze
For whom, I'd trade the sunlit world
All, all of it, without regret.

The frequency and variety of versions from Irish suggests that SH was thinking about a collection of Irish translations.

[63] Pangur Bán

ANONYMOUS (NINTH CENTURY), OLD IRISH

First published in *Poetry* (April 2006, The Translation Issue, 3–4; SH accompanies the translation with a 'Translator's Note', 5) and reprinted in 'Mossbawn via Mantua: Ireland in/and Europe: Cross-Currents and Exchanges', in *Irish Studies in Europe*, edited by Werner Huber, Sandra Meyer, and Julia Novak and published by Wissenschaftlicher Verlag Trier in 2012 (26–7).

Uncollected.

This is SH's complete translation of *Messe ocus Pangur bán*, the poem that opens Murphy's *Early Irish Lyrics* (Murphy 1956, 2–3) and that, as SH puts it, 'pads naturally out of Irish and into the big-cat English of "The Tiger"' (Heaney 2006, 5). The text in this edition is drawn from *Poetry* (2006).

This poem is also included in Crotty's *The Penguin Book of Irish Poetry*, introduced by SH, where the poem appears in Paul Muldoon's translation, titled 'Myself and Pangur' (Crotty 2010, 16–17).

As SH explains, this text, 'found in a ninth-century manuscript belonging to the monastery of St Paul in Carinthia (southern Austria), was written in Irish and has often been translated'. In his 'Translator's Note' SH says that he knew by heart Robin Fowler's version, 'which keeps the rhymed and endstopped movement of the seven-syllable lines, but changes the packed, donnish/monkish style of the original into something more like a children's poem, employing an idiom at once wily and wilfully faux-naif'.

SH also says that he was invited to contribute to the 'Translation Issue' of *Poetry* and explains his reasons for choosing this text: 'Like many other early Irish lyrics – "The Blackbird of Belfast Lough", "The Scribe in the Woods", and various "season songs" by the hermit poets – "Pangur Bán" is a poem that Irish writers like to try their hand at.' SH's motive is not 'to outdo the previous versions, but simply to get a more exact and more intimate grip on the canonical goods'. SH humorously adds that 'A hangover helped': 'Not so much "tamed by *Miltown*" as dulled by Jameson', he 'applied' himself to 'the glossary and parallel text in the most recent edition of Gerard Murphy's *Early Irish Lyrics* (Four Courts Press, 1998)' and 'was happy to find' that he 'had enough Irish and enough insulation (thanks to Murphy's prose and whiskey's punch) to get started' (Heaney 2006, 5).

SH ends the opening address of a conference on cultural currents and exchanges between Ireland and Europe with his translation of 'a poem written by an Irish monk in ninth-century Europe' for which he provides two descriptions. First, he defines it as 'a diaspora poem' written 'by one of the first of those "rambling scholars", as Helen Waddell has called them, one of the peregrini far from his birthplace, deep in the learned language of Latin, but still very much at home in his native Irish language and in his newfound monastic life of study'. Then he says that it is a poem which 'affords a sense of novelty and freshness in relation to an old and familiar situation': the relationship 'between the monk and a cat called Pangur Bán who shares his cell'. SH highlights both 'the great technical intricacy' and 'the great intimacy and immediacy' of the original. He explains that he chose this poem in the hope that 'its theme of study rewarded and intellectual endeavour engaged upon as a pleasurable and profitable challenge will make a fitting end to my address and a fitting start to our conference' (Heaney 2012b, 26–7).

[64] Hallaig

SORLEY MACLEAN (1911–1996), SCOTTISH GAELIC

First published in a bilingual edition by Urras Shomhairle: The Sorley MacLean Trust in 2002 and reprinted in the *Guardian* alongside 'The Trance and the Translation', an edited version of the first Sorley MacLean Memorial Lecture delivered by Seamus Heaney at the Edinburgh International Book Festival on 15 August 2002 (30 Nov. 2002, 4, 6).

This is SH's complete translation of 'Hallaig' (1954). The text in this edition is drawn from the Sorley MacLean Trust edition (2002).

SH gets to 'know the poetry and the poet' on three different occasions in the 1970s. First, when he reads 'Iain Crichton Smith's translations of *Dàin do Eimhir*, published in 1971 by Jon Silkin in his Northern House Pamphlet series'; second, a couple of years later, when he meets MacLean and reads 'the English translations of poems he delivered in Gaelic at an event in the Abbey Theatre in Dublin' (Heaney 2002, 4); third, when he hosts the poet at the Kilkenny Arts Week in 1976 (*SS*, xxiv). The 'terrific directness' of Smith's translations and the 'bardic weirdness' of MacLean's voice have 'a hypnotic effect' on SH, which he describes as being 'led into an uncanny zone, somewhere between the land of heart's desire and a waste land created by history – a felt history that stretched from the Highland clearances to the Spanish civil war and the world war it ushered in' (Heaney 2002, 4).

SH explains that the poem he 'remembered best from MacLean's Abbey reading (and would eventually translate) was not one of the Eimhir poems' but one 'written later, in the 1950s': a poem 'haunted by the great absence that the Highland clearances represent in Scots Gaelic consciousness'. In his introduction to a volume of critical essays about the life and work of Sorley MacLean, SH says that hearing 'Hallaig' in the 'deep lamenting register of the Gaelic, extended and confirmed' his sense of MacLean 'as a major figure'. 'Hallaig' was 'the song of a man who had come through, a poem with all the lucidity and arbitrariness of a vision'. The poem, as SH puts it, 'rose like a mist over the ancestral ground in which this poet's tap-root is profoundly lodged' (Heaney 1986, 2). For SH 'Hallaig' is 'at once historical and hallucinatory, a poem in which the deserted homesteads of a little settlement on the Island of Raasay are repopulated by a vision of "a fair field full of folk"'. 'Hallaig', continues SH, 'arises out of MacLean's sense of belonging to a culture that is doomed but that he will never deny': it is 'as local as anything in Thomas Hardy and as lambent as Rilke's "Sonnets to Orpheus"' (Heaney 2002, 4) and 'belongs to the world of Eliot's "Marina"' (Heaney 1986, 2).

'As John MacInnes has pointed out,' says SH, 'the landscape of "Hallaig" is not just the topographical landscape of Raasay but a corner of the mythopoeic universe.' Still, Hallaig 'is an actual place, a ghost clachan north of Beinn na Lice on the poet's native island' (Heaney 2002, 4). SH describes the poem as 'set at twilight, in the Celtic twilight, in effect, at that time of day when the land of the living and the land of the dead become pervious to each other, when the deserted present becomes populous with past lives, when the modern conifers make way for the native birch and rowan, and when the birch and rowan in their turn metamorphose into a procession of girls walking together out of the 19th-century hills'. SH concludes his analysis stating that 'The poem tells us that in Hallaig there is something to protect' and 'goes on to show that it is indeed being protected, which is the reason for the uncanny joy a reader feels at the end' (Heaney 2002, 4).

Turning then to his own version, SH explains that 'it does not purport to equal, never mind replace the almost scriptural English that Sorley set down in place of his Gaelic poem'. SH's intention, as he puts it, was 'to catch something of the original trance in a verse translation', hoping that his English 'could do what Yeats wanted rhythm to do in poetry: prolong the moment of contemplation' (Heaney 2002, 4). SH was 'able to enter gradually' the original text, and on his own, partly because he had 'enough Irish to go word for word into the sense of the Gaelic'; partly because he had 'the cadences of it in my ear from hearing the poet read it'; and partly because he knew 'the kind of place the poem evokes – a setting of deserted wallsteads, houses with roofs fallen in and gardens and outgoings all overgrown with shrubs and nettles, the kind of thing you used to see everywhere in Ireland, in the south and west especially', like the 'ruined dwelling on land' that was very close to SH's own place in Derry (SS, 426).

SH evokes 'the saviour of Scots Gaelic poetry in modern times,' (SS, 363) in part 4 of a poem titled 'Would They Had Stay'd' and collected in *Electric Light*, where MacLean is described as 'A mirage' and 'A stag on a ridge/In the western desert above the burnt-out tanks' (*EL*, 69). In 2004 SH travelled to the east coast of Raasay to visit Hallaig – the setting and title of the poem that MacLean first published in the Gaelic literary periodical *Gairm* in 1954 to mark the hundredth anniversary of the last people being cleared from the township. As Alasdair Macrae explained, SH 'had been talking about wanting to walk to Hallaig for a long time'. SH 'had enormous respect and affection for Sorley, and he always admired the poem "Hallaig",' Macrae observed, and 'The loss of the people which was so important to Sorley, is a theme well-known in Ireland' (Ross 2004, 3).

[65] 'I sing of a maiden'

ANONYMOUS (FIFTEENTH CENTURY), MIDDLE ENGLISH

First published as a Christmas card by the Gallery Press in 2003 with a drawing of the nativity scene done by SH's daughter Catherine in 1976 when she was three years old.
   Uncollected.

This is SH's complete translation of '*I syng of a mayden*'. The text in this edition is drawn from the Gallery Press Christmas card (2003).
   This text is part of a collection of medieval lyrics that are now housed at the British Library (MS Sloane 2593, ff.10v–11). Considered one of the oldest surviving Christmas carols written in English, the poem celebrates the Virgin Mary and the Annunciation.
   'The translations with a straightforward religious theme do not involve Heaney's personal views, and he did not revise and re-present these poems,' Bland Crowder remarks. 'Nonetheless,' she glosses, 'they display his skill.' In this translation, she notes, SH 'combined lines with two hemistichs separated by a heavy caesura, in the manner of Old English versification' and skilfully transformed the Middle English poem into one easily available to a contemporary reader, even while drawing upon an even older form of English poetry' (Crowder 2017, 37).

[66] Cædmon's Hymn

CÆDMON (*fl. c.*657–684), OLD ENGLISH

First published in *Room to Rhyme* by the University of Dundee in May 2004 (24).

This is SH's complete translation of '*Nu scylun hergan/hefaenricaes Uard*'. The text in this edition is drawn from *Room to Rhyme* (2004).

As S. A. J. Bradley notes, 'The miracle by which Cædmon, an elderly and untutored lay-brother of the religious house at Whitby, mastered the traditional *ars poetica* of vernacular English and so became the first poet to adapt it to Christian subject-matter,' is narrated in Bede's *Historia Ecclesiastica* (Bk. IV, ch. 22) 'as part of his account of the reign of abbess Hilda'. Bradley also observes that 'The ancient vernacular poetry, which might well have been abandoned on account of its unredeemed worldliness or paganism, was successfully sanctified' (Bradley 1982, 3–4).

'If Cædmon's *Hymn* does indeed represent "probably the earliest extant Old English poem", as a recent edition of the *Norton Anthology of English Literature* [2000, I: 23] puts it,' Bruce Holsinger argues, 'this designation nevertheless invents this fragment of vernacular writing as the dawn of a tradition of specifically literary making.' The story of Cædmon's *Hymn*, he explains, 'can be understood as the "miracle that made literary history", in other words, only if we understand Cædmon's *Hymn* primarily as literature: as a putative point of origin for what we have come to know as English literary writing' (Holsinger 2007, 149). And the transmission of the poem referred to as 'Cædmon's *Hymn*' should be regarded as 'a small wonder in itself'. As Holsinger points out, 'its diverse appearance in Latin and Old English texts of Bede leaves its critics still unsettled on the basic question of whether what now survives was an oral poem later written down or a subsequent vernacular lyricisation of Bede's own Latin paraphrase' (Holsinger 2007, 151).

'The link between Heaney's contemporary task of crediting the "makers" and this medieval world quarried by his poetry to get it "pleasurably right" and "compellingly wise",' Joseph McGowan claims, 'shows up perhaps most clearly with an illumination of his continued allusive relationship to one of the most compelling characters from the Venerable Bede's *Ecclesiastical History of the English People*: Cædmon, the cow-herd turned poet' (McGowan 2002, 27).

McGowan notes how, 'Like Cædmon, Heaney grew up in a creaturely existence', and 'Like Cædmon, too, the gift of poetry brought him before an audience and enrolled him in that guild of scops and makars stretching from Cædmon forward.' McGowan also argues that 'Heaney's new translation of *Beowulf* may be seen in the context of the Cædmon story: as the culmination of a long association with a northern hoard of images, kennings, archaisms; as a quitting of an accumulated indebtedness to predecessors, including the *Beowulf* poet; as the shoring up of an ancient structure that it might suffice for a new generation of readers' (McGowan 2002, 36). According to McGowan, Heaney's *Beowulf* ought to be received as 'the work of a poet put in good stead by other poets such as Cædmon [. . .] and led naturally to the task by consequence of language and idiom', as 'the crowning of Heaney's long apprenticeship as scop' (McGowan 2002, 42).

Heaney's 'closest self-identification' (McGowan 2002, 36) with Cædmon is in a poem collected in *The Spirit Level*, 'Whitby-sur-Moyola' (Cædmon lived and cared for the livestock at the monastery of Streanaeshalch, later Whitby, in Yorkshire): 'Cædmon too I was lucky to have known,/Back *in situ* there with his full bucket/And armfuls of clean straw, the perfect yardman,/Unabsorbed in what he had to do/But doing it perfectly, and watching you./He had worked his angel stint. He was hard as nails/And all that time he'd been poeting with the harp/His real gift was the big ignorant roar/He could still let out of him, just bogging in/As if the sacred subjects were a herd/That had broken out and needed rounding up./I never saw him once with his hands joined/Unless it was a case of eyes to heaven/And the quick sniff and test of fingertips/After he'd passed them through a sick beast's water./Oh, Cædmon was the real thing all right' (*SL*, 41).

[67] The Light of Heaven

DANTE (1265–1321), MEDIEVAL ITALIAN

First published in *Between Poetry and Politics. Essays in Honour of Enda McDonagh*, edited by Linda Hogan and Barbara Fitzgerald (Dublin: Columba Press, 2004, 12–13).
    Uncollected.

This is SH's translation of *ll.* 49–145 from *Paradiso*: Canto XXXIII. The text in this edition is drawn from *Between Poetry and Politics. Essays in Honour of Enda McDonagh* (2004).

SH does not translate the theologically and linguistically complex prayer to the Virgin Mary that opens Dante's final canto of the *Commedia*. Lines from Dante's original (58–60 and 106–8) and from SH's translation (10–17) are included, respectively, as the epigraph, the opening eight lines and the closing two lines of 'A Dream of Solstice' (*Irish Times*, 21 Dec. 1999, 1, reprinted with revisions in *Kenyon Review* (winter 2001, 1–2), and in *Translation Ireland* (Dec. 2000/Jan. 2001, 22). The McCabe Heaney Collection housed at the National Library of Ireland contains a photocopy of this translation with an inscription to the McCabes, dated Christmas 2002.

On 5 January 2000 SH replied by fax to a 'pre-Christmas note' from John Kinsella 'about the *Kenyon Review*' and submitted 'A Dream of Solstice'. 'Will this work?,' SH asked, and then explained the genesis of the poem: 'The sun's rays enter Newgrange – 5000-year-old passage grave north of Dublin – on December 21 every year. A slot in the stone entrance, 70 feet away from the burial chamber at the core of the tumulus, admits the light . . . I translated the last 70 lines or so of the *Paradiso*, and then only used the nine or ten of them that appear in the following (2 pages)' (Heaney 2000a, 1).

SH was clearly at work on this translation while writing a commissioned poem about witnessing the last winter solstice of the millennium in Newgrange, one of Ireland's most significant prehistoric sites. Located in the Boyne River Valley in Co. Meath, inhabited and cultivated for five millennia, Newgrange became the site of megalithic tombs, small at first and then, mysteriously, enormous.

Heaney's imagination superimposes the divine light of Dante's *Paradiso* on the solar light of Newgrange's tomb (Guzzo 2021, 6). Every year on 21 December, the day of the winter solstice, a small group of people chosen by lot have the privilege of going into the tomb at 8.58 in the morning, when the rays of the rising sun enter through a hole in the ceiling into the tomb chamber, flooding it with light for seventeen minutes.

In 1999, asked by Sue Lawley who his favourite poet is, SH mentions Dante and explains his choice, comparing Dante with W. B. Yeats and in particular with how Yeats's poems can stand up to the occasion and the poet's 'inner energy takes the measure of the outer circumstances and wins a kind of freedom against it'. SH 'loves

Dante in that way too'. Dante, as SH puts it, 'is like the ultimate deterrent when you come to these discussions, he is the atom bomb that you bring out to deter all other discussions' (Heaney 1989b, 32:20–33:28).

As Dennison remarks, 'In *Envies and Identifications* Dante – who, where the poetics of adequacy are concerned, is mostly important as a refraction of Heaney's Mandelstam – is finally upheld for his ability to place himself in an historical world yet submit that world to scrutiny from a perspective beyond history, the way (like Miłosz) "he could accommodate the political and the transcendent"' (Dennison 2015, 119; Heaney 1985, 18). The timeless light of the sun on winter solstice accommodates Ireland's pre-Christian and Christian times and customs.

[68] Testimony: What Passed at Colonus

SOPHOCLES (*c*.496–*c*.406 BCE), CLASSICAL GREEK

First published in the *New York Review of Books* (7 Oct. 2004, 14). Uncollected.

This is SH's translation of *ll.* 1586–1666 from Οἰδίπου ἐπὶ Κολωνῷ. The text in this edition is drawn from the *New York Review of Books* (2004).

This translation is dedicated to one of SH's most influential friends: the Polish poet and Nobel Laureate Czesław Miłosz, who died on 14 August 2004.

A complete draft of this translation is ready on 18 August 2004, when SH faxes it to Maria Makuch ahead of Miłosz's funeral in Kraków's St Catherine Church on 27 August, which SH attended (Heaney 2004c, 1; *SS*, xxix). The last two lines (70–1) of that version are different from the version published in *The New York Review of Books* and reference the title of SH's second book of poems:

> Out of this world well readied, down to where
> The door into the dark is standing open.

While filming for RTÉ the award-winning documentary *Seamus Heaney: Out of the Marvellous*, Charlie McCarthy asks SH: 'Is there anything in your poems in any way useful as an epitaph?' SH's initial hesitation ('I think we'll leave that one, Charlie!') is challenged by McCarthy ('Really?') and after pausing SH singles out a passage from *Oedipus at Colonus* (*ll.* 1579–1674), which he explains as follows:

'I remember when Czesław Miłosz died, I translated a bit out of *Oedipus at Colonus*, where the old King is called by a mysterious voice to come up the hill and he disappears mysteriously into the ground, out of the ground, into the ground, and the Messenger tells the story and he says: "Wherever that man went, he went gratefully" – something like that. So, that is not an epitaph necessarily for a graveyard but it's the kind of epitaph that would work I think, would do' (Heaney 2009b, 0:43:00–0:44:12).

Noting that 'all the scriptural references in *Beowulf* are to the Old Testament', SH argues that 'The poet is more in sympathy with the tragic, waiting, unredeemed phase of things than with any transcendental promise.' For SH, 'Beowulf's mood as he gets ready to fight the dragon – who could be read as a projection of Beowulf's own chthonic wisdom refined in the crucible of experience – recalls the mood of other tragic heroes: Oedipus at Colonus, Lear at his "ripeness is all" extremity, Hamlet in the last illuminations of his "prophetic soul"' (*Beowulf BE*, xxii).

[69] Testimony: The Ajax Incident

SOPHOCLES (*c*.496–*c*.406 BCE), CLASSICAL GREEK

First published in the *Times Literary Supplement* (26 Nov. 2004, 3). Uncollected.

This is SH's translation of *ll.* 285–323/4 from Αἴας. The text in this edition is drawn from the *Times Literary Supplement* (2004).

In *Ajax*, as Marian McDonald remarks, Sophocles 'shows stubborn, if misguided heroes, whose indomitable wills have to be fulfilled' (Harrison 2019, 130–1). In *The Redress of Poetry* SH 'describes himself as searching for "an adequate response to the conditions in the world at a moment when the world [is] in crisis"', argues Elizabeth Lunday, and 'Mycenae Lookout' 'addresses a world polluted by violence at the moment after the violence stops' (*RP*, 191; Lunday 2008, 113). The passage from *Ajax* SH translates reflects those predicaments. 'Violence', Lunday notes, 'stains all it touches' (Lunday 2008, 116), and SH offers an uncompromising account of it not only as it boils up and over but also as it boils down and away. The surprise and shock of witnessing something that bursts violently into being and the consequences of it on all involved and affected as SH recorded them in 'Anything Can Happen', also inform 'Testimony: The Ajax Incident'. At the beginning of SH's

Horace translation, Jupiter waits 'for clouds to gather head/Before he hurls the lightning' (*ll.* 1–3); at the end of the Sophocles poem 'Something gathers head/And is going to happen' (*ll.* 52–3).

The narrative *energeia* and societal ethics of this passage evoke the emotions and actions described by SH in 'Mycenae Lookout', described by Neil Corcoran as a 'meditative version-translation, a literary gloss' on Aeschylus' *Agamemnon* (Corcoran 1998, 200). In that poem – written 'in direct reaction to the politics of Northern Ireland' and 'in particular, the IRA ceasefire that began on 31 August 1994' (Lunday 2008, 111), and first published in the *Times Literary Supplement* on 16 December 1994 (15; *SL,* 36) – SH 'forces us to recall Cassandra's violations, first by Ajax at the fall of Troy and then repeatedly by Agamemnon' (Lunday 2008, 117).

This translation exemplifies how, in 'freely adapting' a classical text, SH 'articulates what violence had silenced' (Lunday 2008, 116). It also reflects, as Sarah Broom remarks, 'his sudden recognition, after the 1994 ceasefire, of the degree to which the prolonged state of political tension had taken its toll on each individual' (Broom 1998, 72).

[70] The Burial at Thebes
Sophocles' *Antigone*

SOPHOCLES (*c.*496–*c.*406 BCE), CLASSICAL GREEK

Published in the UK by Faber & Faber in 2004; published in the USA, with the addition of SH's 'A Note on The Burial at Thebes', by Farrar, Straus and Giroux in 2004.

SH published four excerpts from the translation in progress. The first was published in the *New Yorker* (3 March 2003, 78), a poem titled 'Sophoclean', incorporated in the text spoken by the Chorus of the Theban Elders (*BTa,* 16–17; *TSH,* 389–90, *ll.* 356–89). The second was published in *Tin House Magazine* 6.1 (Fall 2004, 29–39) ahead of the American edition of the translation, released in November 2004, and consists of the opening dialogue between Antigone and Ismene followed by the words spoken by the Chorus of the Theban Elders when they enter for the first time (*BTa,* 1–9; *TSH,* 376–83, *ll.* 1–210). In the magazine's table of contents this excerpt is presented under 'Play', titled 'An Excerpt from "The Burial at Thebes. A Version of Sophocles' *Antigone*",' and is introduced by this narrative: '*What are Creon's rights when it comes to me and mine? The ancient question still matters.*' The question part of it comes from the play and is asked by Antigone (*BTa,* 4; *TSH,* 379, *ll.* 77–8). The third and the fourth excerpts are two Choruses: 'Among the many wonders of the world' (*BTa*, 16–17; *TSH*, 389–90, *ll.* 356–89) and 'Love that can't be withstood' (*BTa*, 36–7; *TSH*, 405, *ll.* 789–808), in *Stone from Delphi* (98–9).

This is SH's complete translation of Ἀντιγόνη (*c.*441 BCE) to which he added the subtitle 'Sophocles' *Antigone*'. The text in this edition is drawn from the Faber & Faber edition (2004) and reflects the subsequent changes 'marked for collation with Faber text' by SH in the final version of the Performance Script 'as played at Peacock/ Abbey [Theatre], April 2008' and housed at the National Library of Ireland in Dublin.

In the 'Note on The Burial at Thebes' included in the American edition of the play, SH explains that 'The invitation to translate *Antigone* for the Abbey [Theatre]'s centenary programme was an honour,' and that 'at first' he 'wasn't sure whether to accept' – 'How many *Antigones* could Irish theatre put up with?' SH asked himself, mindful of Conall Morrison's Middle Eastern adaptation and of Marianne McDonald's scholarly translation in addition to the other versions by Brendan Kennelly, Tom Paulin and Aidan Carl Mathews (*BTb*, 75).

SH reiterates his initial hesitation to accept the Abbey's invitation in a 2004 lecture devoted to the challenges and the issues that underscore translating a classic. 'At the beginning of 2003, the Abbey Theatre in Dublin invited me to do a version of *Antigone* for the centenary of the theatre,' he says, 'I was honoured and attracted, but unsure if I could take it on.' The play, he explains, 'had been translated and adapted so often, and had been co-opted into so many cultural and political arguments' that it 'had begun to feel less like a text from the theatrical repertoire and more like a pretext for debate, a work that was as much if not more at home in the seminar room than on the stage' – 'its heroine', SH glosses, 'could be adduced in the cause of liberation movements of many different kinds, in the cause of civil disobedience, of feminist resistance to the patriarchy, of prisoners of conscience, and even [. . .] of law and order reactions to all these things' (Heaney 2004d, 414–15).

These concerns are revisited again in a 2005 essay, where the focus is on what SH describes as 'Purchase on a language, a confidence amounting almost to a carelessness, a found pitch' (Heaney 2005, 171). 'The speeches of the chorus, for example,' SH notes, 'almost spoke themselves in an alliterating four-beat line, one that echoed very closely the metre of Anglo-Saxon poetry and that seemed right for the enunciation of proverbial wisdom and

the invocation of gods.' And 'the hymn to Victory, which is the
first utterance we hear from the Chorus,' SH explains, 'came out
as if it had been fetched up from the word-hoard of some Athenian
Cædmon' (Heaney 2004d, 425). As he explains also to Dennis
O'Driscoll, it was this 'different purchase' – 'an ongoing line-by-line,
hand-to-hand engagement with the material' – that also gave him
'more pleasure' in translating *Antigone* that he had experienced in
translating *Philoctetes* (*SS*, 422).

In all the discussions about his own *Antigone*, SH refers to three
factors that led to him accepting the invitation to translate this play.
The first was that W. B. Yeats 'had not done a version'. Yeats 'had
indeed made for the Abbey Theatre prose translations of Sophocles'
other two Theban plays, but with the exception of a few lines
entitled "From the *Antigone*" (included in his sequence "A Woman
Young and Old"), he had not put his trademark on this one'. The
second, which gave SH 'the poetic go-ahead', was an Irish simile.
'The sudden discovery of a note,' SH explains, 'that connected the
distressed heroine of Sophocles' tragedy in the fourth century BCE
and the author of the great eighteenth-century lament we know
by its Irish title, "*Caoineadh Airt Uí Laoghaire*" ["Lament for Art
O'Leary"].'

And the third was that 'Early in 2003, the situation that pertains
in Sophocles' play was being re-enacted in our own world.' As SH
put it, 'Just as Creon forced the citizens of Thebes into an either/
or situation in relation to Antigone, the Bush administration in the
White House was using the same tactic to forward its argument for
war on Iraq' (*BTb*, 76). SH elaborates on this: 'When the Abbey
asked me to do the *Antigone*,' he tells him. 'President Bush and his
secretary of defence were forcing not only their own electorate but
the nations of the world into an either/or situation with regard to
the tyrant of Baghdad' – so 'If you were not for state security to the
point that you were ready to bomb Iraq, you could be represented as
being in favour of terrorism'; and 'If you demurred at the linking of
Al Qaeda to the despotism of Saddam Hussein, you were revealing
yourself as unsound on important issues, soft on terrorism'; and
'If you demurred at the suspension of certain freedoms, you were
unpatriotic.' This context, SH explains, 'would have made it easy
to proceed with a treatment of Sophocles' play where Creon would
have been a cipher for President Bush and the relationship between
audience and action would have been knowing and predicated on the
assumption of political agreement'. SH also notes that 'to have gone
in this direction would have been reductive and demeaning, both of

Sophocles' art and of the huge responsibility the White House must bear for national security' (Heaney 2004d, 421–2). During rehearsals for the 2008 Peacock Theatre production of the play, SH excises Creon's prophetic warning as Antigone reports it in one of her early speeches: 'Whoever isn't for us/Is against us in this case' (*BTa,*3, *ll.*55–6). However, SH remarks, 'The issues of loyalty and disloyalty are real, both in the play and for the American legislature' (Heaney 2004d, 421–2).

As always, the most decisive factor was writerly: an immediate writerly urge was missing, SH admits, but 'all of a sudden it arrived' and 'Theme and tune coalesced.' SH 'remembered the opening lines of Eibhlín Dhubh Ní Chonaill's lament, an outburst of grief and anger from a woman whose husband had been cut down and left bleeding on the roadside in County Cork,' and the similarities with the fate of Polyneices, who was 'left outside the walls of Thebes, unburied, desecrated, picked at by the crows'. And what 'clinched it', as SH put it, was 'the drive and pitch of the Irish verse': in the 'three-beat line of Eibhlín Dhubh's keen' SH 'heard a note that the stricken Antigone might sound in the speedy, haunted opening movement of the play' (*BTb,* 77).

There is, however, another powerful connection between SH and *Antigone* – one that is so specific and at the same time so universal to make *The Burial of Thebes* arguably his most significant translation in personal, poetic and political terms.

'From beginning to end,' SH maintained, 'Sophocles' play centres on burial' (Heaney 2004d, 414). As he tells O'Driscoll, SH 'was glad when the phrase *The Burial at Thebes* came to mind, quite early on in the process' because 'the word "burial" pointed directly to one big anthropological concern that's central to the action' (*SS,* 422). O'Driscoll himself wittily asked SH what place he would consider for his 'final mould' – a 'nice question' SH confessed to considering and promptly answered as wittily (*SS,* 473–4).

One burial, however, was poignantly inscribed in the poet's memory and imagination since May 1981, when 'a gathering at once solemn and dangerous in the village of Toomebridge in Northern Ireland' – a placename, as SH explains, that 'comes from the Irish word *tuaim,* meaning, as you would expect, a burial mound' and that 'in the circumstances' was 'most appropriate'.

SH provides a detailed description of that event, and the connection between it and what goes down in Sophocles' *Antigone* becomes evident. The crowd 'gathered in the main street of the village', SH says, were there 'to meet a hearse that contained the body of a well-known Co. Derry figure, and once the hearse arrived they would accompany it back to a farmhouse on a bog road some six or seven miles away, where the body would be waked in traditional style by family and neighbours' – 'to observe custom', SH glosses, and 'to attend that part of the funeral rite known in Ireland as "the removal of the remains"'. SH then explains that 'before the remains of the deceased could be removed that evening from Toome, they had first to be removed from a prison some thirty or forty miles away'. And for that first leg of the journey, as SH points out, 'security forces deemed it necessary to take charge and to treat the body effectively as state property'. SH continues his detailed account of the facts, linking the local provenance of the story to the global attention it attracted. 'The living man had, after all, been in state custody as a terrorist and a murderer, a criminal lodged in Her Majesty's Prison at the Maze, better known in Northern Ireland as the H Blocks,' SH notes. 'He was a notorious figure in the eyes of Margaret Thatcher's government, but during the months of April and May 1981 he was the focus of the eyes of the world's media.'

The person in question was Francis Hughes (1956–81). SH 'did not know him personally' but 'knew and liked other members of his family': they were his neighbours and during the 1950s SH 'had walked the road to Mass with his sisters and had worked in summertime in the bog side by side with his father' – but 'his world' and SH's world had then grown 'far apart'. As SH says, 'For the last fifty-nine days of his life Francis Hughes had been on hunger strike, one of a group of IRA prisoners ready to make the ultimate sacrifice for what were known at the time as the five demands.' These demands, SH explains, 'constituted a claim by the prisoners to political status, a rejection of the demonizing terminology of criminal, murderer and terrorist, and an assertion of their rights to wear their own clothes, to abstain from penal labour and to associate freely within their own cell block.' The inflexibility of Margaret Thatcher and her government resulted, between 5 May and 30 August 1981, in the death of ten hunger strikers, followed by 'a steady issue of emaciated corpses from the gates of the prison and repeated processions of miles long funeral crowds through the gates of cemeteries'. SH refers to that time as 'a cruel time', particularly 'for those on the nationalist side of the Northern Ireland divide, all those who sought fundamental political change, who wanted to break the Unionist Party's monopoly on power, but who nevertheless did not think it an end worth killing for.' And 'It was possible for them, as for everyone else,' SH notes, 'to regard hunger strikes both as an exercise in *realpolitik* and an occasion of sacred drama.' This was the context, he concludes, 'in which the crowd of sympathisers waited for the hearse at Toomebridge, a crowd that naturally included family members, friends and neighbours in great numbers, and an even greater number of political supporters, enraged at the hijacking of the body'. SH's retelling of the events that led to Francis Hughes's death and burial climaxes with two Sophoclean questions about the body of the deceased: 'Who owned it? By what right did the steel ring of the defence forces close round the remains of one who was son, brother, comrade, neighbour, companion?'

And 'when the hearse with its police escort arrived on the village street,' SH narrates, 'the cordon that surrounded it was jostled in fury and indignation by the waiting crowd' – a surge of rage that was 'more than ideological'. While it 'did of course spring from political disaffection,' SH observes, 'it sprang also from a sense that something inviolate had been assailed by the state'. The 'nationalist collective', SH explains, 'felt that the police action was a deliberate assault on what the Irish language would call their *dúchas*', and quotes Brendan Devlin's description of it as 'inheritance, patrimony; native place or land; connection, affinity or attachment due to descent or long-standing; inherited instinct or natural tendency' and 'still vestigially present even in English-speaking Ulster in the late twentieth and early twenty-first centuries', adding that *dúchas* 'is all of these things' as well as 'the elevation of them to a kind of ideal of the spirit, an enduring value amid the change and the erosion of all human things'. SH ends his comparison between the events in Northern Ireland and the events in Ancient Greece, stating that 'If we wanted a set of words to describe the feelings that motivate the heroine of Sophocles' *Antigone*, we could hardly do better than that.' Antigone, the daughter of Oedipus, SH explains, is 'surely in thrall to patrimony, connection, affinity and attachment due to descent, to longstanding, to inherited instinct and natural tendency [. . .] for her all these things have been elevated to a kind of ideal of the spirit, an enduring value'. Despite the detailed description that builds up to it, SH's final point is striking: 'If we wanted, what's more, to find a confrontation that paralleled the confrontation between her and King Creon', he says, 'we could hardly do better than the incident on the street in Toomebridge that I've just recounted' (Heaney 2004d, 411–13; Ross 1986, 85).

The roots of SH's engagement with *Antigone*, however, date earlier than the 1981 events at Toomebridge. SH's first encounter with the play was 'in undergraduate lectures about the difference between Classical and Shakespearean tragedy' – 'all those old discussions of Greek plays in relation to Aristotle's *Poetics*,' SH recalls, 'much ado being made of the unities and the hero's flaw, the central importance of plot and the precise meaning of the word *catharsis*'. SH links 'that necessary early schooling' with Calvino's 'very first cheerful and slightly cheeky definition of a classic' as a book one finds oneself re-reading. SH's 'own re-reading' occurs 'in earnest' as a result of what happened in Derry on 4 October 1968. A civil rights march 'banned by the Unionist authorities was baton-charged by the Royal Ulster Constabulary' in what SH described as 'a nakedly repressive reaction' that 'set in motion a chain of events' that were 'still unfolding' when he undertook and completed his translation of *Antigone*. 'Other large protest meetings followed,' SH explains, including one in Belfast: 'basically a student march from Queen's University' where he was a lecturer. SH recalled 'sitting in the street, having been halted by a cordon of police who were there because the main city square had been occupied by a counter protest organised by the Reverend Ian Paisley'. Paisley's 'law and order bully-boys could call the tune', as SH puts it, 'and the police would fall into line and the rest of us could like it or lump it'. SH described the experience as 'humiliating and enraging' but there came a point when he 'had to act the academic Creon and restrain some students from making a charge at the police lines'. And among those SH restrained 'was a student who would go on to be the Antigone of that time in Northern Ireland, the passionate young protester Bernadette Devlin' (Heaney 2004d, 416).

SH contributed an article to the 23 October issue of the BBC's current affairs magazine *The Listener* in which he talked about that student march as well as 'the demands of the Northern Ireland Civil Rights Association for reform of the local government situation and an end to discrimination in the allocation of houses and jobs'. At the end of the article SH alluded to the song, 'Danny Boy', also known as 'The Londonderry Air'. Stating that for him and 'for many others – because of what we might call the *dúchas* factor – the song was better known as "The Derry Air",' SH concluded, with words that revealed his 'sympathy for the Antigone party', that 'The new Derry Air' sounded 'very much like "We Shall Overcome"' (Heaney 2004d, 417; Heaney 1968, 523). 'It was in that same issue of *The Listener*', SH reveals, 'that Antigone was finally sprung from her old place in the syllabus and took her place decisively in all future thinking about the developing political situation in Northern Ireland.'

Antigone and 'all she stands for,' SH explains, 'were invoked in an article of seminal importance by the writer and former diplomat Conor Cruise O'Brien'. At the time Cruise O'Brien was an academic in New York, where 'three years earlier, in December 1965,' he 'had been arrested for time he too had spent sitting down in the street in . . . "a highly respectable protest" outside the Induction Center in Manhattan' that was 'meant to obstruct the progress of recruitment for the war in Vietnam'. This man, SH notes, 'was now observing sit-downs by students in the north of his own country, highly aware of the righteousness of their cause and highly sensitive also to the ominousness of the situation' (Heaney 2004d, 417). Titled 'Views', O'Brien's 1968 article 'begins with a resumé of the plot of Sophocles' tragedy that emphasises how the consequences of Antigone's non-violent action emerge in acts of violence' – 'a cautionary tale for the febrile North' as Rosie Lavan describes it (Lavan 2020, 35). SH then turns to a later intervention by Cruise O'Brien where Cruise O'Brien says that 'Creon and Antigone are both part of our nature, inaccessible to advice and incapable of living at peace in the city,' and that 'Civil disobedience is non-violent, but everywhere attracts violence' (Cruise O'Brien 1974, 151). SH revisited these events and their implications at the New Yorker Festival in 2008 where he discussed 'History' and 'Homeland' in conversation with Paul Muldoon (Heaney 2008c, 0:23–06:01).

'Like many of the previous Irish versions of Sophocles' play,' as Kierstead and Perris observe, SH's translation 'openly invites us to compare the conflict in Thebes and the Troubles in Ireland.' However, 'What many previous analyses have missed or passed over,' they argue, 'is the extent to which *The Burial at Thebes* steps back from any simple equivalence between the Theban situation and the Irish one.' Indeed, Kierstead and Perris note, SH's translation 'at first seems to stress *dúchas* (kinship, belonging) as a simple counterpoint to the state' but 'in the end it serves as an entry-point for a universalist view of human relations' (Sonzogni 2021, 136).

In *The Burial at Thebes*, Kierstead and Perris conclude, SH 'pulled off a difficult act of poetic and cultural alchemy, emerging in the process not only as an unapologetic representative of the Irish tradition, but also as a universalist and a man of peace'. SH's version, as they put it, 'clearly has a place in a line of Irish Republican adaptations of Sophocles' *Antigone*, one which presents Antigone as a determined dissident against an occupying power'. His version, however, 'does more than that, multiplying references in a way that pushes the play away from the particular situation in Ireland and towards more universal concerns' (Sonzogni 2021, 151).

After all, SH himself, in a public Q&A at the Abbey Theatre on 27 April 2004, voiced the hope that his *Antigone* may deliver 'a more universal message' (Wilmer 2002, 242).

[71] To the Poets of St Andrews

ATTRIBUTED TO ARTHUR JOHNSTON (*c*. 1579–1641),
NEO-LATIN

First published in 2004 on one of a series of cards produced for the Poetry House, School of English, University of St Andrews, and reprinted in *The Book of St Andrews*, edited by Robert Crawford and published by Polygon in 2005 (11).
Uncollected.

This is SH's complete translation of *Ut in Lusitania olim miles*. The text in this edition is drawn from the Poetry House card (2004).

SH ascribes the original to Arthur Johnston, who wrote many works in Latin, most notably a translation of the Psalms, *Psalmorum Davidis paraphrasis poetica et canticorum evangelicorum*, and an anthology of contemporary Latin verse by Scottish poets, *Deliciae poetarum Scotorum huius aevi illustrium*, both published in 1637.

As Robert Crawford explains, SH read and liked several of Crawford's translations from the Latin of Johnston, which were published in the *Times Literary Supplement* and the *London Review of Books* and then collected in *Apollos of the North: Selected Poems of George Buchanan and Arthur Johnston* (2006). SH discussed the translations with Crawford and was 'particularly keen' on the poem titled 'To Robert Baron', which is 'partly about being stuck on an Aberdeenshire farm'. According to Crawford, 'that's why he pretended his poem "To the Poets of St Andrews" was connected to a Johnston poem and made up the Latin (no Johnston poem with those Latin words exists)' (Crawford 2019).

The actual source of this pseudo-translation is likely to be Portuguese legend based on different classical sources – from the Greek of Plato's *Republic* and Strabo's *Geography* to the Latin of Livy, Plutarch, Appian, and Florus – and to the Portuguese of João de Barros and Conde de Bernanos, where the story is enriched with a detail that is not present in the classical texts: the general calls the soldiers individually by their name ('*chamou os seus homens um a um, pelos seus nomes*'). According to the Polish philologist Krzysztof Tomasz Witczak, the locals may have used the legend of the Lethe to dissuade a Roman army from crossing the river and advancing their conquest (Witczak 2003, 355).

What matters is that the story has entered the folklore of Portugal, as witnessed by a tapestry that now hangs in the hall of the Grand Hotel Santa Luzia at Viana do Castelo, overlooking the mouth of the River Lima. It is the work of Almada Negreiros (1893–1970), an artist who worked alongside Fernando Pessoa in bringing Modernism to Portugal. The caption at the top of the tapestry recounts the story of Decimus Junius Brutus crossing the river and calling his soldiers by name to demonstrate that his memory is intact.

SH goes to Lusitania twice: in 2001, when he attends 'Identities: a European Poets' Meeting', a literary festival in Porto, and in 2004, when he represents Ireland at the 5th International Meetings of Poets, organised by the Department of Anglo-American Studies of the University of Coimbra, where SH was awarded an honorary degree. In his acceptance speech, titled 'Poetry Centres', SH recounts 'a story from the earliest history' of Portugal he was reminded of when he 'shared in the poetry reading [. . .] in that magical location on the site of the ancient Roman city at Conimbriga'. According to that story, when Roman legionaries 'engaged in wars against the Lusitani' reached the banks of the River Lima, 'the troops halted and refused to go any farther,' because, 'They had been led to believe that the Lima was a branch of the River Lethe, that it was the river of all forgetfulness, and that they would lose their minds and their memories if they entered its waters.' Their centurion, however, proves this to be unfounded. As SH puts it, 'he takes the initiative and marches out, chest deep, into the stream, splashing and swimming his way across, and arrives on the far bank, utterly drenched.' And once he is on the other side, his memory intact, the centurion 'resumes his customary stance of command' and 'with a clear voice and a clear mind' he 'calls to each of his men, name after Latin name'. And 'One by one they each enter and cross the river after him.' The 'good of this story', SH remarks, is that it reminds us of 'the fear that we will forget what we know' and of 'the need to be prepared to venture beyond the borders of what we know already' (Heaney 2004b, 635–7).

SH's familiarity with *Aeneid* Book VI is, of course, another powerful link with this story. 'For Heaney,' Rachel Falconer observes, 'the Lethean crossing offers the possibility of extracting oneself mentally from the trauma of military conflict.' As she notes, 'Two years before publishing *The Riverbank Field*, while on a visit to Portugal, he had come across the legend of a Roman legion crossing an actual River Lethe on their campaign to colonise Lusitania' (Falconer 2022, 154; Pretto 2020, 757–8). Falconer points out that Heaney's poem 'plays with two new possibilities that he would not have found in Virgil: one, that memory could be retained in crossing the Lethe, and two, that forgetfulness might be deployed strategically, by those attempting to escape military conflict'. And 'When he turns to Virgil's Lethe in 2006', SH 'gives a strongly positive valency to the idea of drinking forgetfulness from the mythical river' (Falconer 2022, 155). Falconer illustrates this point by quoting an interview with the poet Gerald Dawe, which was 'broadcast on RTÉ shortly after the publication of *The Riverbank Field*' and in which SH describes the Virgilian setting of the poem (Falconer 2022, 155). SH points out that 'when Aeneas gets down to the very end to the river of Lethe when he meets his father, it is in a beautiful riverbank situation on the broagh of the river'. And 'after a thousand years, they'll go over that river, they'll go through the River Lethe'; and 'They'll forget they were in the underworld, and they'll be reborn, up, under the dome of the sky again . . . So, there's that kind of transition: youth and age, age and youth . . . generations passing, generations arriving' (Heaney 2008d; Falconer 2022, 155).

As Falconer notes, in 'To the Poets of St Andrews', SH 'likens himself to the veteran commander', as he steps 'wet from a ferry south of Forth', bearing 'a poet's walking stick' instead of a weapon. 'Even in making the comparison,' Falconer concludes, SH's 'sympathies seem more inclined to the Lusitanian clans than the veteran commander' (Falconer 2022, 155).

The first time SH goes to Scotland, in 1973, is to attend a poetry event at the University of St Andrews, where he meets Norman MacCaig and Iain Crichton Smith (*SS*, xxiv) and where, in 2005, he is made a Doctor of Letters.

[72] The Testament of Cresseid & Seven Fables

ROBERT HENRYSON (*c.*1430–*c.*1506), MIDDLE SCOTS

First published in a bilingual edition by Faber & Faber in 2009. A letterpress edition of only 'The Testament of Cresseid' – titled *The Testament of Cresseid: A retelling of Robert Henryson's Poem* – was published in London by Enitharmon Editions in 2004 with images by

Hughie O'Donoghue (*TCSF*, 3–47; *TSH*, 422–38). SH published one of the fables, 'The Two Mice' (*TCSF*, 65–81; *TSH*, 442–8), twice and in the same year: in *Agni* 54 (2001, 191–7) and in *Last Before America. Essays in Honour of Michael Allen*, edited by Fran Brearton and Eamonn Hughes and published by the Blackstaff Press in 2001 (29–35).

This is SH's complete translation of *The Testament of Cresseid* (1532) and seven of the thirteen fables in *The Morall Fabillis of Esope the Phrygian, Compylit in Eloquent & Ornate Scottis* (1570). The text in this edition is drawn from the Faber & Faber edition (2009).

In the introduction to his translation SH says that he found with Henryson, a 'sensation of intimacy with a speaker at once sober and playful' that inspired him to translate his animal fables (*TCSF*, viii). On seeing an illustrated manuscript of 'The Cock and the Jasp' at the British Library, SH was 'so taken by the jaunty, canty note of its opening lines' that he felt 'an urge' to get it into his own words – 'the use of the Scots word "canty" (lively)', as Anne McKim notes, 'expressively illustrating his sense of kinship through language' (*TCSF*, xiii; Sonzogni 2021, 302).

As McKim also notes, SH 'developed a special affinity with his fellow Scottish poets' (Sonzogni 2021, 330–1) and *The Testament of Cresseid & Seven Fables* is the 'culmination of his infatuation with Scottish literature' (Fazzini 2016, 57). And it was through this translation, McKim observes, that SH 'explored his "hidden Scotland"' just as in *Sweeney Astray* SH had explored his 'hidden Ireland' and in *Beowulf* his 'hidden England' (Sonzogni 2021, 301; Homem 2001, 27; *SS*, 365). Henryson's language was 'animating' to SH because it brought him 'back to an underlying Scottish strain' in his own 'first speech'. As SH explains, 'the mid-Ulster vernacular retains traces of the language spoken by the Lowlanders and Londoners who came over during the Plantation in the early seventeenth century' (*SS*, 426). 'This awareness of connection through language', McKim points out, soon led to SH's 'delighted realisation' that he was 'entirely at home' with Henryson's 'sound of sense,' (*TCSF*, xiii), as SH puts it, quoting Robert Frost, and 'so much in tune with his note' (*TCSF*, xiii) – Henryson's 'freighted' note (*TCSF*, xi) – 'and his pace and his pitch' (Sonzogni 2021, 302; *TCSF*, xiii).

'There is a particularly "snug" fit,' Helen Cooney states, 'between Heaney and Robert Henryson, poet, translator and fellow-interpreter of "coded books"' (Cooney 2009, 37). SH, McKim observes, 'clearly appreciates that Henryson's is a version of the story, a response to Chaucer's version, and that translations as retellings can enable different versions and telling variations' (Sonzogni 2021, 304). As McCarthy notes, SH's 'reworking of *The Testament of Cresseid*' can be viewed as 'contextualized by engagement with Scotland' but also read 'as part of a twofold engagement with materials relating to the Trojan war' – by SH and other Irish writers and also by Henryson's 'medieval antecedents' (McCarthy 2008, 136).

When SH is approached with the idea of adapting Henryson's charming tales into animations, he suggests that the actor and comedian Billy Connolly narrate the films. Connolly agrees and the result is a series of five short films, *Five Fables* (2014) – 'The Two Mice'; 'The Fox, the Wolf and the Farmer'; 'Preaching of the Swallow'; 'The Fox, the Wolf and the Carter'; 'The Mouse and the Lion' – made by Belfast-based animators Flickerpix and first broadcast on the BBC on 13 March 2014. The animations are introduced by SH himself, who did not live to see this project completed.

[73] The Apple Orchard — [74] After the Fire — [75] Roman Campagna

RAINER MARIA RILKE (1875–1926), GERMAN

First published in the *London Review of Books* (5 May 2005, 10) under the title 'Three Poems', but referenced on the front page as 'Three Rilke Translations'.

'After the Fire' and 'The Apple Orchard' are collected in *District and Circle* (16 and 68). 'Roman Campagna' is uncollected.

These are SH's complete translations of '*Der Apfelgarten*', '*Die Brandstätte*', and '*Römische Campagna*' (1907/8). The texts in this edition are drawn from *District and Circle* (2006) for 'The Apple Orchard' and 'After the Fire' and from the *London Review of Books* (2005) for 'Roman Campagna'. The translations follow the order in which SH published them in the *London Review of Books*.

As Stephan Resch points out, after many years of 'half-avoiding and half-resisting the opulence and extensiveness' of poets such as Rainer Maria Rilke (*CP*, 13), SH 'had a renewed, albeit coincidental, encounter' (Sonzogni 2021, 119) with Rilke: 'one of those sudden reimmersions', as SH puts it, 'started off by opening Edward Snow's big volume of *New Poems* in translation' (*SS*, 387).

'For Rilke,' Resch argues, 'things became poetic triggers as his attention shifted from the object itself to the way he perceived it.'

Rilke referred to this way of perceiving as '*einfaches Schauen*' or 'simple vision'. 'Yet, beyond the new perception,' Resch observes, 'there is also an admiration for the tradesmanship of the sculptor that extends to his own poetry.' And 'In Heaney's *District and Circle*, there is a similar preoccupation with the surrounding tangible world.' According to Resch, the 'remarkable preoccupation with the physical world, its (in)stability and attempts at preventing it from vanishing' that permeates *District and Circle* is what connects the collection with the concept of Rilke's '*Dinggedicht*' or 'poem of things' (Sonzogni 2021, 120–1). As Joanna Cowper notes, '*Electric Light* saw the poet define himself in relation to the people and places that populated his memory,' whereas '*District and Circle* takes a closer look at the more challenging question of how the self continues, when the people and places that once helped·define it are gone'. SH, Cowper argues, 'questions the validity of a personal identity premised upon things that no longer exist' (Brewster 2009, 168).

Rilke enters SH's poetry in the early 1980s. SH tells O'Driscoll that when he was writing 'An Artist' (*SI*, 116) he was reading 'Rilke's letters about his infatuation with Cézanne and some of Rilke's words are included' (*SS*, 263; Rilke 1988, 179–89). Key words are 'anger' (*l.* 1), 'green apples' (*l.* 3), and 'mountain' (*l.* 15); and key images are the 'dog barking/at the image of himself barking' (*ll.* 4–5), 'working as the only thing that worked' (*l.* 7), and the artist's 'forehead like a hurled *boule*' (*l.* 13).

'After the Fire' is among the translations SH reads in his 2008 Robert Lowell Memorial Lecture, where it follows 'Anything Can Happen' [57]. As SH explains, the bewilderment of the boy in Rilke's poem the morning after a sudden fire has destroyed his home and 'the world is changed' seemed 'to match the mood of bewilderment after the balefire of September 11' (Heaney 2008b, 38:39–40:20).

[76] The First Step — [77] Dionysos in Procession — [78] The Satrapy — [79] Sculptor of Tyana — [80] The Displeasure of Selefkides — [81] 'The rest I'll speak of to the ones below in Hades'

CONSTANTINE P. CAVAFY (1863–1933), GREEK

First published with the title 'Poets, Sculptors, Sophists and Other Clients: Six Poems by Constantine Cavafy' in *Hermathena* 17 (Winter 2005, 7–12).

'The rest I'll speak of to the ones below in Hades' is collected with revisions in *District and Circle* (73).

These are SH's complete translations of 'Τὸ πρῶτο σκαλὶ', 'Ἡ Συνοδεία τοῦ Διονύσου', 'Ἡ Σατραπεία', 'Τυανεὺς Γλύπτης', 'Ἡ Δυσαρέσκεια τοῦ Σελευκίδου', and 'Τὰ δ' ἄλλα ἐν Ἅδου τοῖς κάτω μυθήσομαι', in the polytonic orthography followed by Cavafy (1905–15). The texts in this edition are drawn from *Hermathena* (2005) for 'The First Step', 'Dionysos in Procession', 'The Satrapy', 'Sculptor of Tyana' and 'The Displeasure of Selefkides'. The text of 'The rest I'll speak of to the ones below in Hades', collected in *District and Circle* (2006) and in this edition, has a variant: SH revises *l.* 8 from 'but everything we guard here' to 'but all we cover up here'.

Asked by Dennis O'Driscoll to elaborate on the appearance of Cavafy in *District and Circle*, SH says that it was 'coincidence', since he had 'just recently written a preface to a volume of translations of his poems by Stratis Haviaras, and was wakened up all over again to the nonpareil combination of "grief and reason", to use a Brodsky phrase, in his tone and his understanding'. SH explains that his 'first response to Cavafy was like everybody else's: immediate susceptibility to the clear steady gaze at the world and himself, at the stealth in passion and power politics' (*SS*, 387–8).

The words of the poem title 'The rest I'll speak of to the ones below in Hades' are in ancient Greek in Cavafy's original as they are the last words spoken by Ajax in Sophocles' eponymous drama (*Ajax*, v. 865). Having disgraced himself by being tricked by Athena, Ajax commits suicide by impaling himself on his sword. SH read *Ajax* while working on his translation of *Antigone* and translated a passage [69].

In 2007 C. P. Cavafy's *The Canon: The Original One Hundred and Fifty-Four Poems*, translated by Stratis Haviaras (1935–2020), was published by Harvard University Press with a Foreword by SH, where he describes the translations of his Harvard colleague and fellow poet as 'guaranteed and informed' (Cavafy 2007, vii). SH found the poetry of Cavafy 'wonderful and tempting', and considered co-translating all the poems with Haviaras – a collaboration which he believed could be 'as rewarding as that with Barańczak on Kochanowski' but decided not to pursue this (Heaney 2004a).

SH had included a Cavafy poem, 'As Much as You Can' ('Ὅσο μπορεῖς', 1905–15), in the anthology *The Rattle Bag*, co-edited with Ted Hughes and published by Faber & Faber in 1982 (42). The English translation is by Edmund Keeley and Philip Sherrard (1975).

Translation remains central to SH's writing right to the end of his life and beyond: poem-length and book-length translations from French, Irish, Italian, Latin and Old English are published, some after the poet's death on 30 August 2013.

In 2012, two literary events in Italy, one in Bologna in April and one in Mantua in September, give momentum to the completion of two book-length translations from the Italian of Pascoli and the Latin of Virgil that SH has started as poem-length translations in previous decades.

The Last Walk and *Aeneid Book VI* are published posthumously in 2013 and 2016 respectively.

[82] Deor

ANONYMOUS (NINTH CENTURY?), OLD ENGLISH

First published in *The Word Exchange: Anglo-Saxon Poems in Translation*, edited by Greg Delanty and Michael Matto and published by W. W. Norton in 2011 (47–9; SH also wrote the Foreword, xi–xiii).
    Uncollected.

This is SH's complete translation of 'Deor'. The text in this edition is drawn from *The Word Exchange: Anglo-Saxon Poems in Translation* (2011).

The original text is preserved in the *Exeter Book* (fol. 100^a–100^b), 'an anthology of Anglo-Saxon poetry that was donated to the Exeter cathedral library, where it still is, in 1071, by Leofric, the first bishop of Exeter', Harry Thomas explains in a note to his own translation of 'Deor'. The poem, Thomas notes, 'is probably the work of a *scop* of the 9th century' and 'contains lines of Christian consolation' which were almost certainly a later addition by the scribe (Thomas 2014).

As S. A. J. Bradley notes, 'The poem has been classed in the genre of begging-poems better known from later medieval examples; but its purpose is surely more generous, more didactic, and universal.' Bradley also notes that 'the strophic form of "Deor" and its use of refrain make it a rhetorical enterprise extremely rare in the surviving AS poetic corpus' (Bradley 1982, 362–3).

The Word Exchange, SH writes in his foreword, 'contains translations of the finest poetry that has survived from the Anglo-

Saxon period of English history, the six hundred years from the middle of the fifth to the middle of the eleventh century'. The anthology is 'a reminder that Anglo-Saxon poetry isn't all stoicism and melancholy, isn't all about battle and exile and a grey dawn breaking'. It can be 'unexpectedly rapturous' or 'happily didactic' or 'intimate and domestic', and 'rejoices in its own word-craft, its inventiveness, its appositive imagining and fundamental awareness of itself as a play of language'. This play of language, SH emphasises, 'is resumed by the poets who have translated the work included here, proof that the lifeline to and from this poetry has not been broken, that all language is an entry in further language' (Delanty 2012, xi–xii).

SH recorded his version of 'Deor' for *Poems Out Loud* (W. W. Norton) on 11 November 2010 (Heaney 2010).

[83] Charles IX to Ronsard

ATTRIBUTED TO CHARLES IX (1550–1574), MIDDLE FRENCH

First published with the French original in *Forty: Dublin Writers' Festival presents The Gallery Press 40th anniversary Poetry Celebration* (12), a keepsake published by the Gallery Press for a celebration in the Abbey Theatre on 6 June 2010, at which SH was guest speaker.
    Uncollected.

This is SH's translation of *ll.* 1–12 of '*L'art de faire des vers, dût-on s'en indigner*', one of three elegies attributed to King Charles IX of France. The text in this edition is drawn from *Forty: Dublin Writers' Festival* (2010).

As Paul Laumonier, Raymond Lebègue and Isidore Silver note in their edition of Pierre de Ronsard's complete works (Laumonier 2015, vii–viii), the third elegy appeared for the first time in Jean Royer de Prade's *Histoire de France depuis Pharamond jusqu'à Louis XIII, avec les éloges des roys en vers; réduitte en sommaire par I. R. de Prade* (de Prade 1652, 548) and thus is considered by some scholars as his.

The French original corresponding to SH's translation can be found easily, online and in print, embedded in a longer text – the result, possibly, of seventeenth- and nineteenth-century 'collage'. Given SH's preference for thrillers as off-duty reading, there could be an alternative source where the French text corresponds exactly to SH's translation: *La Reine Margot*, a historical novel of suspense

and drama published in 1845 by Alexander Dumas *père*. The plot
is centred on the 'peace-keeping' marriage, on 18 August 1572,
between Marguerite of Valois, a Catholic and the sister of Charles
IX, and Henri de Bourbon, King of Navarre, a Protestant. The
marriage led to a bloodbath known as the St Bartholomew's Day
Massacre when many Huguenots were killed in the predominantly
Catholic city of Paris.

The novel was immediately translated into English in two versions
– one of which, published by David Bogue in London in 1846, was
'so frequently reissued,' as David Coward notes, 'that it became the
standard text' (Coward 1997, xxii). Titled *Marguerite de Valois:
A Historical Romance*, it is an abridged translation and does not
include the passage translated by SH. One anonymous and full
translation, titled *Marguerite de Valois* and published in New York
by T. Y. Crowell in 1900, does contain the passage in question (29) –
and is also available online through Harvard Library and Project
Gutenberg (the latter, however, was released in September 2010, and
thus was too late to be SH's source).

If the French Wars of Religion would have resonated with SH's
personal experience of sectarian conflicts between Catholics and
Protestants in Northern Ireland, so would the contents of Chapter III,
title 'The Poet-King', where Charles IX says to Coligny:

> For the title of poet, you see, is what I am ambitious, above
> all things, to gain; and as I said a few days ago to my master
> in poetry:
>
> > The art of making verse, if one were criticised,
> > Should ever be above the art of reigning prized.
> > The crowns that you and I upon our brows are wearing,
> > I as the King receive, as poet you are sharing.
> > Your lofty soul, enkindled by celestial beams,
> > Flames of itself, while mine with borrowed glory gleams.
> > If 'mid the gods I ask which has the better showing,
> > Ronsard is their delight: I, but their image glowing.
> > Your lyre, which ravishes with sounds so sweet and bold,
> > Subdues men's minds, while I their bodies only hold!
> > It makes you master, lifts you into lofty regions,
> > Where even the haughty tyrant ne'er dared claim allegiance.
>
> > > (Dumas 1900, 29)

It is possible that these sentiments underpinning this text – the value
of poetry shared by Charles IX and Ronsard, their friendship and

mutual support – are the reason SH chose to translate these lines to celebrate the fortieth anniversary of Peter Fallon's Gallery Press, SH's lifelong Irish publisher.

The age difference between Ronsard and Charles when they met, and between SH and Fallon when they met, could have played a role in the choice of these lines. Fallon was twenty years of age when he met SH, becoming over the years one of SH's closest friends and first readers. In conversation with Dennis O'Driscoll, SH explains that his relationship with Fallon 'goes back a long way' and remembers Fallon arriving at his door in Belfast 'just before Christmas in 1971'. A 'long-haired youth with John Lennon glasses', Fallon was 'carrying a set of broadsheets that had been done on a hand press in Trinity College': a limited edition of a Heaney poem 'which he'd brought from Dublin for signing'. SH remarks that Fallon was already 'operating on two fronts, writing his own poems and publishing other people's, low-key and resolute, very much his own man'. Over the years SH and PF's friendship 'just grew because of confidences exchanged and trusts maintained, because of humour about things in general and an earnest particular interest in poetry'. As SH humorously glosses, the books he has done with Fallon 'may be short' but their connection 'is a long one'. In 1995 Fallon was 'a guest at the Nobel ceremonies on two counts – as personal friend and my Irish publisher' (*SS*, 285–6).

[84] Actaeon

OVID (43 BCE–CE 17/18), CLASSICAL LATIN
TITIAN (1488/90–1576), OIL PAINTING

First published in *Metamorphosis: Poems Inspired by Titian*, edited by Nicholas Penny and published by the (British) National Gallery in 2012 (41) to accompany the exhibition 'Metamorphosis: Titian 2012' (London, 11 July–23 Sept.) and reprinted in the *Guardian* (The Saturday Poem: 6 July 2012) and in *Granta* (17 July 2012) and in *Stone from Delphi* (115).

This is SH's ekphrasis of Titian's unfinished painting *The Death of Actaeon* (*Morte di Atteone*, 1559–76) based on *ll.* 206–50 from *Metamorphoses*, Book III. The text in this edition is drawn from *Stone from Delphi* (2012).

SH's language, 'like the Petrarchan form of the poem', Helen Vendler observes, 'pays tribute to the sixteenth-century context of Titian's paintings of the metamorphosis' (*SD*, 13).

As stated on the National Gallery's website, *Metamorphosis: Poems Inspired by Titian* was 'part of a unique collaboration between the National Gallery and the Royal Opera House' and involved 'fourteen leading poets' (Titian 2012). The poets were 'invited to respond to three great masterpieces by the Renaissance painter Titian, who read Ovid's *Metamorphoses* in a contemporary translation in Italian'. As Fiona Macintosh notes, Lodovico Dolce's 'highly influential' vernacular translation of Ovid's *Metamorphoses* (1553) 'appeared three years before Titian began his paintings – the Italian poet is generally regarded as his main source and his interlocutor' (Macintosh 2019, 436–7).

The paintings in question – *Diana and Callisto*, *Diana and Actaeon* and *The Death of Actaeon* – were inspired by Ovid's *Metamorphoses* and 'depict the fatal consequences of a mortal tragically caught up in the affairs of the gods' (Titian 2012). In his introduction Nicholas Penny, Director of the National Gallery 2008–15, documents how Titian integrated specific elements from Ovid's poetry in his paintings and discusses some of the best-known translations in English.

In a video filmed for the National Gallery, SH explains how he approached the task: 'I felt either you do this immediately or you won't do it at all: it will be too slow, you'll get anxious and it will build up. So I plunged in with the Actaeon I knew, basically [*The Death of Actaeon*].' SH 'worked on a free range, so to speak, on a blank canvas almost', adding that if he had 'stayed with the picture beforehand and dwelt with it,' it might have 'hampered' him because 'it is so absolute and so much itself' that he would not 'know what else you could do with it' (Heaney 2012c, 0:22–0:59). In conversation with Alan Yentob, SH reads his poem and remarks that Ovid is 'operating' in a 'mythosphere', adding that 'one of the artist's tasks was to give form to that by which he or she is formed' and thus 'the possibility of re-forming it for a new moment is there all the time' (Heaney 2012d, 17:18–18:42; Macintosh 2019, 436).

SH had previously written two ekphrastic poems: 'Summer 1969' and 'A Basket of Chestnuts'. 'In one, he engages in meditation upon Goya's paintings at the Prado', as Christelle Serée-Chaussinand records, 'In the other, he speculates upon his own portrait by Edward Maguire.' In the painting that inspired SH, Serée-Chaussinand notes, 'the myth goes full circle – that is, Actaeon metamorphoses into a stag as a result of Diana's reprisal and is hunted down by his own hounds and companions'. And 'along with the irony of the story of the hunter becoming hunted', Serée-Chaussinand points out, SH 'is fascinated by the violence of the scene, and by the process of metamorphosis' (Serée-Chaussinand 2014, 120, 125). In conversation with Martin Herbert, SH states that he 'always thought of the stag as the thing in that painting' and that 'it was the physical weight of the antlers' that he 'felt' (Heaney 2012e). Serée-Chaussinand maintains that SH 'is also drawn to the universality of the myth, as it tells something about desire'. His response, she argues, 'veers away from Titian's original work' in that Actaeon and not Diana is the centre of SH's attention: the poem, she notes, 'is written in the third-person singular from the young mortal's point of view' (Serée-Chaussinand 2014, 125).

According to Sarah Annes Brown, in SH's 'Actaeon' there is 'a further destabilisation of roles': his 'description of the transformed hunter', she observes, 'makes manifest his fractured identity' (Brown 2019, 145). SH's ekphrasis implies 'a further possible stage of metamorphosis': Actaeon 'has turned into a female beast'. And 'Given that the female in this myth is predator rather than prey', Brown argues, 'it seems oddly fitting that Actaeon's feeling that he was to blame, that he had been the aggressor, should be linked to acquiring female characteristics'. In 'a further reversal', Brown notes, 'Diana is also fleetingly cast as an animal, a prey whose scent allows her to be hunted down by hounds who only at the last minute switch their attentions to Actaeon in yet another clue at a buried connection between goddess and hunter' (Brown 2019, 145). Brown detects 'a possible echo here of the opening of *Twelfth Night*, when Orsino describes how the sight of Olivia transformed him into an Actaeon: "O, when mine eyes did see Olivia first,/Methought she purg'd the air of pestilence!/That instant was I turn'd into a hart;/And my desires, like fell and cruel hounds,/E'er since pursue me"' (Brown 2019, 145). Brown suggests that SH's Actaeon feels 'the urge to burden himself with a retrospective yet apparently unearned guilt'. SH's poem, she concludes, 'typifies a significant trend in the exhibition, a tendency (strongest in the male contributors) to identify with the doomed Actaeon' and '[i]n asserting a sympathetic kinship with the hunter, a capacity to map his suffering onto something in their own lives', SH follows in Ovid's footsteps (Brown 2019, 146).

[85] A Herbal

EUGÈNE GUILLEVIC (1907–1997), FRENCH

First published in *Franco-Irish Connections: Essays, Memoirs and Poems in Honour of Pierre Joannon*, edited by Jane Conroy and published by Four Courts in 2009 (123–8).
    Collected with revisions in *Human Chain* (35–43).

This is SH's abridged translation of '*Herbier de Bretagne*' ('Brittany Herbal', 1979). The text in this edition is drawn from *Human Chain* (2010).

As Phyllis Gaffney remarks, SH 'having initially translated some 230 of the source poem's 248 lines, he kept cutting. The Festschrift version runs to 157 lines, reduced to 147 in *Human Chain*' (Sonzogni 2021, 109).

SH is drawn to Guillevic's 'delightful "*Herbier*" because 'it evoked a childhood spent in a natural world that had some affinities with his own boyhood experience' (Sonzogni 2021, 107): 'It is one of those poems you wish you had thought of first,' SH remarks, as he too 'had grown up with heather and bracken and gorse ("whins" to us) and graveyards and grass and honeysuckle'. SH's 'desire to translate it' is countered by knowing how hard it would be 'to get the right fragrance and intimacy into the translated names of plants and weeds' (Heaney 2009c, 227).

As Murphy observes, Guillevic's '*Herbier de Bretagne*', becomes 'a herbal of Derry, as the graveyard flowers of Brittany become the whin and docken and broom of Northern Ireland, imparting a local flavour and fragrance to the self-elegiac memento mori ambiance of the sequence'. Indeed, a typescript housed at the National Library of Ireland shows that SH initially titled this translation 'A Bellaghy Herbal'. 'In paring Guillevic's already sparse and elemental evocation of the Brittany landscape by almost a hundred lines and carefully rearranging the closing sections of the sequence,' Murphy notes, SH is 'more interested in what Denise Levertov calls in her translations of Guillevic "reconstituting" the poem than in reproducing it as such' (Murphy 2016, 353; Guillevic 1969, xii). In a collection like *Human Chain* where SH, as Murphy puts it, 'envisions the entire span of his existence, from his imagined moment of conception to his imagined moment of mortal rupture', the translation of Guillevic's '*Herbier de Bretagne*' provides 'a meditative interval' as well as 'a distillation of the fragile sense of mortality that pervades the entire volume' (Murphy 2016, 353).

In conversation with Dennis O'Driscoll, SH explains that Guillevic's *Living in Poetry* – published in Paris in 1980 and in Dublin in 1999 – was one of the 'auspicious precedents' he considered when he agreed 'to an interview book' (*SS*, vii).

[86] The Kite

GIOVANNI PASCOLI (1855–1912), ITALIAN

'The Kite' is first published in *Auguri: To Mary Kelleher*, edited by Fergus Mulligan and published by the Royal Dublin Society in 2009 (4–6; SH also contributes a note titled 'A Poem for Mary Kelleher', 4) and reprinted with revisions in *Rivista pascoliana*, 24–25 (2012–13), *Pascoli e l'immaginario degli italiani*, edited by Andrea Battistini, Marco A. Bazzocchi and Gino Ruozzi (39–40); and in Gabriella Morisco, 'Two Poets and a Kite: Seamus Heaney and Giovanni Pascoli', *Linguæ & – Rivista di Lingue e Culture Moderne*, 12 (2013, 40, 42 and 44). An abridged (*ll.* 31–64) version of this translation is included with the title 'From "The Kite"' in *The FSG Book of Twentieth Century Italian Poetry: An Anthology*, edited by Geoffrey Brock and published by Farrar, Straus and Giroux in 2012 (15 and 17).

   SH reworked *ll.* 10–15 and *ll.* 25–33 of this translation into an original poem: titled 'A Kite for Aibhín' and dedicated to the poet's second granddaughter (born in 2008), it is collected as the last poem in his last book, *Human Chain* (85), and posthumously included in *New Selected Poems 1988–2013* (*NSP2014*, 217) and *100 Poems* (*100P*, 168).

This is SH's complete translation of '*L'aquilone*' (1904). The text in this edition is drawn from *Rivista pascoliana* (2012–13).

   SH explains the personal and literary genesis of this translation: 'I translated this poem for Mary Kelleher because of her love of Italy, Italian people and Italian culture. It's a thanks offering for a very happy evening Marie and I spent *chez* Kelleher a few years ago, round a table where Massimo Bacigalupo was our guest of honour and the company rose to the occasion with the wit and warmth a literary visitor expects in Dublin; and it's a memento of a couple of cheerful days we all spent subsequently in the Cinque Terre – flying our kite, in a manner of speaking, in Lerici beside the Golfo dei Poeti.' SH points out other Italian-Irish connections, 'not least the phrase "Urbino's windy hill", which is pinched from Yeats's poem "To a Wealthy Man who Promised a Second Subscription etc."' and which he quoted when he was 'the recipient of an honorary degree from the University of Urbino and the subject of a *laudatio* by Professor Gabriella Morisco'. During that visit Professor Morisco supplied SH with the text of Pascoli's '*L'aquilone*': 'she knew,' SH noted, 'that Yeats's phrase lurked in the Italian text' and 'knew moreover' that SH had written his 'own kite poem' ('A Kite for Michael and Christopher': *SI*, 44). SH concluded that 'Sooner or later' he was 'bound to go "fishing in the sky" (as the Chinese put it) one more time' (Heaney 2009a, 4).

As Gabriella Morisco remarks, when SH went to Urbino in 2001 to receive the honorary degree, he stayed for three days, and she showed him around. When they arrived at Capuchin Hill, she 'explained to him that this was the place that inspired our poet Giovanni Pascoli to write "*L'aquilone*", a poem that recalls the time he spent in Urbino as a boy in Raffaello boarding school, when he and his schoolmates flew kites'. Morisco explains that this is 'an old tradition, and even today, every year in September, children, young people and adults from the different areas of the town challenge one another in a fierce competition'. She points out that SH heard about Pascoli for the first time on that occasion and later asked her for a literal translation of the poem. Years later SH reminded Morisco that after their walk on Capuchin Hill 'she had found a postcard for him of a painting that showed a boy flying his kite outside the city gates'. SH kept that postcard 'long afterwards' because, as he told Morisco, he 'had not finished with the image of that boy and his plaything' (Morisco 2013, 35–6). The version SH sent Morisco indicates that the poet has stepped in and the translation is beginning to morph into an original poem.

SH's 'stripped down' version of 'The Kite', retitled 'A Kite for Aibhín', is 'devoted purely to the wistful images of innocent and happy childhood', Tim Smith notes, and 'removes any explicit mention of the death that shapes "*L'aquilone*"'. And even though SH's voice 'takes over' (Morisco 2013, 38), 'A Kite for Aibhín' is 'still a translation', Smith argues, 'recontextualised to "Anahorish Hill" instead of "Urbino's windy hill", which explicitly gives the poem a local Irish setting' (Sonzogni 2021, 186).

As Murphy notes, 'the Pascoli poem that Heaney translated from the Italian and published as "The Kite"' and 'the one he transforms into "A Kite for Aibhín"' are 'translations of a very different order' (Murphy 2016, 362). While 'The speaker of the Pascoli poem, prompted by a vision of kites above his beloved city of Urbino, remembers the exhilarating kite flying of his childhood and, further, recalls the early death of one of his childhood friends,' Murphy explains, in 'A Kite for Aibhín' SH 'purposefully transforms and truncates the original', transposing 'Pascoli's Urbino to the Anahorish Hill of his own childhood in Co. Derry' and translating the kite flying of Pascoli to a memorable kite-flying scene of his own childhood' (Murphy 2016, 362–3).

SH ends his last reading at 92NY Unterberg Poetry Center in New York on 26 September 2011 with 'A Kite from Aibhín', which he describes as 'a translation that has been appropriated' and 'Hibernicised to some extent' (Heaney 2011, 48:49–51:40).

[87] August X — [88] The Owl — [89] The Fallen Oak — [90] The Foxglove

GIOVANNI PASCOLI (1855–1912), ITALIAN

First published, with the title 'Pascoli tradotto' and including 'The Kite' [86], in *Rivista pascoliana*, 24–25 (2012–13), *Pascoli e l'immaginario degli italiani*, edited by Andrea Battistini, Marco A. Bazzocchi and Gino Ruozzi (37–42). SH also contributes an essay, 'On Home Ground' (19–26), based on the address he delivered on 3 April 2012 at the Archiginnasio in Bologna as part of 'Pascoli e l'immaginario degli italiani. Convegno internazionale di studi', an international conference organised by the University of Bologna to commemorate the centenary of Pascoli's death. A letterpress limited edition (seventy-five numbered copies) of 'The Owl' was produced by the Graphic Studio Dublin as part of the 2013 Sponsors Portfolio (Brandes 2014, 88).

These are SH's complete translations of 'X agosto', 'L'assiuolo', 'La quercia caduta', and 'Digitale purpurea' (1891–1904). The texts in this edition are drawn from *Rivista pascoliana* (2012–13).

Antony Oldcorn provided SH with literal versions and brief commentaries on 'The Owl' and 'The Foxglove'; and Gabriella Morisco a prose version of 'The Fallen Oak' (Battistini 2013, 21).

As the title of SH's contribution to the 'historic occasion' of Pascoli's centenary suggests, there are 'important similarities' between Pascoli's home ground and SH's (Battistini 2013, 19). As SH explains, the landscape of Pascoli's poetry reminds him 'very much of the home ground of my own childhood – open countryside with breezes blowing, flowers blooming, berries on briars, robins in hedges and a general feeling of fresh and airy life' (Battistini 2013, 20).

Pascoli's world was thus familiar, 'poetically and terrestrially' as Tim Smith puts it. Pascoli's 'treatment of the domestic, the *"piccole cose"* in life,' Smith observes, 'set him apart from his contemporaries,' and 'Even before Heaney's discovery and exploration of Pascoli's poetry, there were obvious parallels between the subject matter and poetic language of each poet's work' (Sonzogni 2021, 183).

[91] The Dapple-Grey Mare

GIOVANNI PASCOLI (1855–1912), ITALIAN

First published in *Peter Fallon: Poet, Publisher, Editor and Translator*, edited by Richard Rankin Russell and published by Irish Academic Press in 2013 (241–43).
Uncollected.

This is SH's complete translation of *La cavalla storna* (1903), with 'L'aquilone' ('The Kite' [86]) one of Pascoli's best-known poems, taught to this day in Italian schools and universities. The text in this edition is drawn from *Peter Fallon: Poet, Publisher, Editor and Translator* (2013).

Both Oldcorn and Morisco provided SH with a version of this poem (Battistini 2013, 21). SH found this poem 'easiest to translate'. As SH notes, 'To have a mare respond with recognition to a name uttered by a human voice asks us to suspend belief further than we are reasonably prepared to.' Still, he adds, 'the whole point of the poem is to subvert the reasonable, to magic the murder, as it were'. SH describes the verse of this poem as having an 'incantatory quality', a 'mood of omen and expectation', a 'haunting ballad-like appeal' and 'a sense of fatality and inevitability'. The 'archetypal quality' of this poem 'makes it at home in any context', SH argues, linking it to another poem 'which the Irish reader will think of immediately'. The poem in question is 'a lament, composed spontaneously at a moment when the great traditional practice of women keening a death was still prevalent in Gaelic culture'. A practice, SH explains, that is 'as old as Homer' but 'happened in 1784 in the south of Ireland, in Co. Cork, when a young Irish captain called Art Ó Laoghaire (O'Leary) was killed on the road by a group of English soldiers, and his horse famously came home with blood on the bridle'. SH also notes that, 'Equally famously and unforgettably', O'Leary's widow 'tells us in her great outcry that she rode to find him and mourned over his corpse where it lay by the roadside'. The widow's cry, SH maintains, is 'primal', and 'closer to the utterance of mourners around Hector's funeral pyre or

Beowulf's than to the pathos of "The Dapple-Grey Mare"'. However, SH concludes that Pascoli's poem 'has its own perfect pitch, and its music and moods are in the same twilit register as other poems being written in Ireland in the late 19th century, in a movement originated by William Butler Yeats and known as the Celtic Twilight – our own foreshadowing of the Italian *crepuscularists*' (Heaney 2013b, 23–4).

As Smith points out, 'The Dapple-Grey Mare' also recalls 'Follower' (*DN*, 12): 'Both are replete with rural settings from their youth and their fathers, even if their respective tones differ markedly' (Sonzogni 2021, 189). SH's concern with the aftermath of violence is reflected in the choice of this and another widely read Pascoli poem SH translated, '*X agosto*' ('August X' [87]) – both about the murder of Pascoli's father. In Pascoli's poem the poet's mother converses with the horse that witnessed the murder of her husband, shot on his way home in a horse-drawn buggy. She seeks and receives confirmation from the animal about the identity of the unpunished killer.

[92] The Last Walk

GIOVANNI PASCOLI (1855–1912), ITALIAN

First published posthumously in Ireland by the Gallery Press in 2013 with illustrations by Martin Gale. 'In a Huddle' (XII) and 'Washerwomen' (IV) are published in the *New Yorker* (11 Nov. 2013, 34; *LW*, [26] and [13]; *TSH*, 488–9 and 486).

This is SH's complete translation of (1891), a sequence of sixteen sonnets in Pascoli's *Myricae*. The text in this edition is drawn from the Gallery Press edition (2013).

On 11 August 2013 SH sent me an email with two Word documents attached: an advanced draft of his translation of '*L'ultima passeggiata*' and a letter in which he mentioned using versions online and in print as reference and asked me to read and comment on his version. I emailed as well as posted him the typescript with my initial impressions on Friday, 30 August. That evening a text message from the Dublin-based, Italian journalist Concetto La Malfa broke the news that SH had passed away. Some weeks later I shared my comments with the family as well as with Peter Fallon, with whom SH had made a provisional agreement for publication. The family decided to go ahead with the publication as SH and his Irish publisher had planned, and two suggestions I had offered were implemented.

In the Editor's Note, Fallon explains the genesis of 'a special limited edition' of SH's translation of Pascoli's *'L'ultima passeggiata'* that would include illustrations by Martin Gale and would be published in November 2013. On 22 August, in Dublin's Canal Bank Café, Fallon showed SH '"rough" proofs' and 'copies of Martin's specially completed drawings and paintings'. A few days later, in St Vincent's Hospital, Fallon and SH discussed and revised the translations. Fallon recalls questioning SH's use of 'bagpipes', for example, and 'thorny' to describe mulberry bushes. When SH died, the publisher and the family decided, in the words of the Editor's Note, 'to proceed towards publication as planned' (*LW*, [36]).

'Many of the scenes presented in *"L'Ultima Passeggiata"*, evoking rural life in late 19th century Italy,' SH notes in his Bologna address, 'were still there to be witnessed in mid-20th century Ireland.' SH provides a detailed description: 'Men ploughing the fields – with oxen in his case, with horses in mine; a lark in the morning rising from its nest; a housewife in the farmyard feeding her free-range hens; a railway running through fields where the steam train thunders and whistles, past cows grazing on the embankments, past telegraph poles and under telegraph wires; a man asleep on top of his cartload, a dog barking at him from a farmyard gate.' SH also notes that 'these scenes' are 'rendered in lovely miniature, as if they were a book of hours' and that 'the best thing about Pascoli's book of hours is not its attractive subject matter but its artfulness'. As SH puts it, Pascoli's 'miniature treatment of these scenes could easily have ended up as little stimulants for nostalgia but instead they are tautly constructed artifacts' (Battistini 2013, 21).

SH's 'tendency to conflate the source text and his own poetics', Smith points out, is poignantly present in his final work of poetry. SH, argues Smith, was drawn to *'L'ultima passeggiata'* because of 'its earthy, rural, domestic imagery' and because the sequence 'comprises some of Heaney's own common topoi'. 'The Last Walk', Smith notes, 'immediately recalls some of Heaney's earlier poetry. 'In his response to Pascoli's "condensed" poetics,' Smith remarks, SH 'revels in dressing up – in thickening – the poetic language of the source with his own lexicon, making the sequence seem Heaney's own unique creation'. *'L'ultima passeggiata'*, Smith concludes, provided SH 'with fertile ground in which to dig: one could plough further and identify myriad images that recur in Heaney's previous poetry' (Sonzogni 2021, 188–9).

As Rachel Falconer observes, SH's 'conviction of the serious purpose of poetry far transcends the current, in-house divisions of ecocriticism' and 'also restores a sense of poetry as playful, pleasurable, and health-enhancing to the individual reader or poet'. SH was drawn to Pascoli's *'L'ultima passeggiata'* also 'because this sequence of slight, finely turned poems, while celebrating the rhythms of rural life, seems farthest removed from any explicitly political or environmentalist agenda' (Falconer 2019, 3).

[93] Du Bellay in Rome

JOACHIM DU BELLAY (1522–1560), MIDDLE FRENCH

First published in *New England Review*, 34. 2 (2012–13, 7). Uncollected.

This is SH's complete translation of *'Nouveau venu, qui cherches Rome en Rome'*, the third sonnet in the sequence *Les Antiquités de Rome* (1558). The text in this edition is drawn from *New England Review* (2012–13).

In the note that accompanies this translation, 'one of the last poems he wrote before he died this past August', Paul Muldoon describes it as 'timely in several senses'. Muldoon points out how 'Du Bellay's witty engagement with paradoxes about permanence and immanence, fixity and flux, raises questions not only about those great themes but, coincidentally, about the nature of literary fame.' And even though the French sonneteer is 'hardly a household name', observes Muldoon, 'his impact on Spenser and Shakespeare, to name but two renowned poets, is absolutely crucial'. Muldoon considers SH's translation 'all the more poignant' because 'shortly after completing it, he would himself become a victim of what Shakespeare terms "devouring time"' (Muldoon 2013, 7). Phyllis Gaffney describes Du Bellay's sonnet as a 'meditation on the changes wrought by time. Inviting the traveller to contrast the grandeur of Ancient Rome with its current state of decay, it draws a paradoxical moral lesson: in conquering the world, Rome also conquered herself. Thus, the one enduring monument to the city's ancient splendour is its ruins, and only the river Tiber escapes time's relentless march.' Gaffney also notes that 'behind this sonnet, as behind some other poems of his, lurks a Latin original': *'Qui Romam in media quæris, novus advena, Roma'*, which she describes as 'a neo-Latin epigram' by Janus Vitalis from Palermo (1485–c. 1560), 'a contemporary Sicilian humanist' (Sonzogni 2021, 99). 'More than other translators', including Edmund Spenser, SH 'exploits' the language of the original 'to enhance the inherent wordplay of the poem's didactic message and to conjure up the multifaceted meanings of the city's name – without stressing the unavoidable new resonances that "Rome" has acquired in the religious history of Ireland' (Sonzogni 2021, 102).

Gaffney highlights SH's rendition of Du Bellay's 'Latinate *dompter* and *se dompter* (Latin *domitare*)' with 'sway', which is 'a word of Germanic origin that appealed to him when translating' (Sonzogni 2021, 103). In conversation with Robert Hass, SH explains that he 'liked another phrase which was still used in the country, about people who were famous or in control. It was said that "they held sway"' (Heaney 2000b, 10). As Gaffney notes, SH used this phrase 'in a draft opening to his *Beowulf* translation [50] and to close a fine translation from Charles IX, eulogising Ronsard' [83] (Sonzogni 2021, 103).

[94] 'Wind fierce to-night' — [95] 'Pent under high tree canopy'

ANONYMOUS (NINTH CENTURY), OLD IRISH

First published in *The Irish Hand*, edited by Timothy O'Neill and published by Cork University Press in 2014 (30). 'Wind fierce to-night' is reprinted in *The Finest Music*, edited by Maurice Riordan and published by Faber & Faber in 2014 (11), where it appears with the first line of the Irish original as title, and in *The Map and the Clock*, edited by Carol Ann Duffy and Gillian Clarke and published by Faber & Faber in 2016 (17), where it appears with the first line of the English translation as title.

These are SH's complete translations of '*Is aicherin-gáeth in-nocht*' and '*Dom-farcai fidbaide fál*'. The texts in this edition are both drawn from *The Irish Hand* (2014).

The earliest extant versions of both poems, whose translations SH co-authored with Timothy O'Neill in 2007, are written in the margins of a copy of Priscian's *Latin Grammar* housed in the Stiftsbibliothek in St Gallen, Switzerland (112 and 203). In 2007 Timothy O'Neill wrote out on vellum three copies of 'The Scribes' (*SI*, 111) and SH wrote these translations into the margins of this scripted piece. One of the skins was presented to the Stiftsbibliothek on 2 November 2007. 'Pent under high tree canopy' is included among the monastic poems in Gerard Murphy's *Early Irish Lyrics* with the title 'The Scribe in the Woods' (Murphy 1956, 4–5).

The mood of these two glosses – thousands of them were 'added to Priscian's text in tiny minuscule' – is opposite: a tense wait shadows the first, whereas playfulness colours the second. 'Shortly after being written, the manuscript was in continental Europe where a poem eulogising Archbishop Gunther of Cologne was added,' O'Neill explains. 'This and other notes', he continues, 'point to a connection with the circle of Sedulius Scottus, a renowned teacher who attracted many fellow Irish scholars to Liège, where he enjoyed the patronage of the local bishop.' However, 'increased harassment by Viking raiders' around the middle of the ninth century 'caused some scholars to seek new careers abroad'. The first Priscian poem translated by SH 'reflects this anxiety' (O'Neill 2014, 30).

As O'Neill points out, 'In the mid-ninth century, on a summer's day somewhere in Ireland, probably in Leinster, a scribe took a break from the tedious business of copying a Latin grammar book for the monastic school and wrote these verses in the margin of p. 203.' O'Neill notes that 'On the previous page he seemed worried about what the master would think of his work, seeking the intercession "of Patrick and Brigit on Mael Brigte, that he may not be angry with me for the writing that has been written this time"'. O'Neill argues that 'It may not have been his fault entirely that the writing was not up to standard, as the materials were possibly defective.' Indeed, 'they certainly caused problems on page 217, as he complained: "New vellum, bad ink, O, I say nothing more."' As O'Neill points out, 'Liquid of a different sort may explain *latheirt* ("hangover"), written in ogham on top of p. 204' (O'Neill 2014, 30). The second Priscian poem translated by SH reflects this idiosyncrasy.

'Pent under high tree canopy' is one of the translations from Irish that SH reads in his 2008 Robert Lowell Memorial Lecture, adding that this poem is 'sometimes called "The Scribe in the Woods"' (Heaney 2008b, 01:06:00–01:06:50).

[96] 'Towards Ireland a grey eye'

ANONYMOUS (TWELFTH CENTURY), MIDDLE IRISH

First published in *Human Chain* (73) and reprinted in *The Finest Music*, edited by Maurice Riordan and published by Faber & Faber in 2014 (62), where it appears with the first line of the Irish original as title.

This is SH's complete translation of '*Fil súil nglais*', which is included under the title 'A Blue Eye Will Look Back' among the poems connected with the life of Colmcille in Gerard Murphy's *Early Irish Lyrics* (Murphy 1956, 64–5). The text in this edition is drawn from *The Finest Music* (2014).

As Murphy notes in the subtitle to his translation, these words are ascribed to 'Colum Cille' 'about to leave Ireland, AD 563' (Murphy 1956, 65) and sail into exile for having allegedly transcribed a text without permission. The change in colour from blue to grey reflects the feelings of repentance and atonement that envelop Colmcille's farewell to his homeland. The poems in *Human Chain* exhale 'The living breath of things', as Colm Tóibín notes in his review for the *Guardian*. This translation, too, demonstrates how SH's late poems are 'true to memory and loss' and offer, 'at times miraculously', what Tóibín describes as 'a vision of what is beyond them or above them' (Tóibín 2010, 6). This is the last translation in the triptych titled 'Colum Cille Cecinit' (*HC*, 72–3). The other two poems, in the order SH put them, are '*Is scíth mo chrob ón scríbainn*' ([45] 'Colmcille the Scribe'), and '*Is aire charaim Doire*' ([60] 'Colmcille's Derry').

This cluster of eleventh- or twelfth-century Irish poems attributed to Colmcille, Kevin Murphy argues, 'seems at first simply one Irish writer's distant salute to another'. However, the three poems, depicting 'the Irish saint's stoical embrace of his work as a scribe and scholar' as well as 'his love for the town of Derry' and 'his lament as he sailed into exile from Ireland', Murphy notes, 'have both subtle and specific linkage to Heaney's life and work' (Murphy 2016, 353).

A comparative analysis of SH's translation of 'Colum Cille Cecinit' and earlier translations by Kuno Meyer and Flann O'Brien led Michael Parker to argue that SH 'links Colmcille's forbearing stance toward writing to the diction and values of his own work' and that 'What we seem to be witnessing here is both identification and expropriation as Heaney self-consciously translates himself book after book in his quest for self-renewal' (Parker 2012, 340). Murphy also points out that, 'within the intertextuality of *Human Chain* itself', SH 'conflates Colmcille's writing and that of his father as a cattle drover' in the third part of 'Lick the Pencil' (*HC*, 81). 'Most poignantly', Murphy notes, in the second part of 'Album' (*HC*, 5) SH 'elliptically cites the line of Colmcille's exile lament ("a grey eye will look back")' when, aged twelve, he was left at his boarding school in Derry and 'separated both from his parents and from the thatched-roof-cottage world of his childhood at Mossbawn'. This 'sense of exile', Murphy emphasises, is 'associated with the act of writing' and in 'The Conway Stewart' (*HC*, 9) is 'sealed by the parents marking the occasion with the gift of an elegant fountain pen' (Murphy 2016, 354).

[97] 'Birdsong from a willow tree'

ANONYMOUS (NINTH CENTURY), OLD IRISH

First published in *The Finest Music*, edited by Maurice Riordan and published by Faber & Faber in 2014 (17) and reprinted in *The Map and the Clock*, edited by Carol Ann Duffy and Gillian Clarke and published by Faber & Faber in 2016 (12).
    Uncollected.

This is SH's complete translation of '*Int én gaires asin tsail*', a poem that is included under the title 'The Blackbird Calling from the Willow' among the monastic poems in Gerard Murphy's *Early Irish Lyrics* (Murphy 1956, 6–7) and under the title 'The Blackbird's Song' in Greene and O'Connor's *A Golden Treasury of Irish Poetry* (Greene 1967, 206–7). The text in this edition is drawn from *The Map and the Clock* (2016).
    SH includes this translation among the blackbird poems he reads in his 2008 Robert Lowell Memorial Lecture (Heaney 2008b, 1:05:46–1:05:59). This is the last of the translations SH worked on with Timothy O'Neill:

> No. 7:
>
> Birdsong from the willow tree.
> Whet-beak, note-blurt, clear, airy.
> Yellow quill-bill, ink-cowled crafty:
> Blackbird, practicing his scale.

[98] Brothers

LAOISEACH MAC AN BHAIRD (*fl.* LATE SIXTEENTH CENTURY), EARLY MODERN IRISH

First published in *The Penguin Book of Irish Poetry*, edited by Patrick Crotty, published by Penguin in 2010 (197–9) and reprinted in *The Map and the Clock*, edited by Carol Ann Duffy and Gillian Clarke and published by Faber & Faber in 2016 (138–40).
    Uncollected.

This is SH's complete translation of '*A fhir ghlacas a ghalldacht*', one of very few poems by Laoiseach Mac an Bhaird to have survived. The text in this edition is drawn from *The Map and the Clock* (2016).

As Osborn Bergin explains, this poem 'is apparently meant as a reproach to someone who had adopted the dress and manners of a Tudor courtier' and is 'contrasted with another, perhaps his brother, who had chosen the harder but more adventurous life of a rebel'. Bergin also notes that 'the classical poets had no scruple about using the foreign word to denote foreign thing, so that in this short piece we find several English loan-words' (Bergin 1912, 473).

Sarah E. McKibben argues that this late sixteenth-century, eleven-stanza bardic satire 'constitutes an insistently *political* form of poetic speech – namely, a potent contestation of English colonialism – rather than a trivial complaint or a mere curiosity' (McKibben 2001, 262). The 'highly gendered language that still resonates today' and the 'strict syllabic metre' are used by Mac an Bhaird 'to attack an Irishman for having adopted an English hairstyle, clothing and manners in place of those native to him'. The poem, she notes, 'ridicules this change not merely as unattractive and uncomfortable, but as an index of individual and societal endangerment: anglicization represents a form of subordination that compromises the addressee's masculinity and thus his very identity' (McKibben 2001, 262–3). Within the context of sixteenth-century tensions with the north of Ireland, McKibben remarks, 'this abandonment of community norms also symbolises subordination': the poet as well as his English and Anglo-Irish commentators, she argues, 'share the understanding that the adoption of the other's culture is a sign of submission' (McKibben 2001, 266). In particular, 'dishonour, disloyalty, and cowardly submission' are made satirically manifest in the protagonist's decision to cut his hair 'in an English style as desired by English authorities'. This is a 'cultural violation' which renders him 'unfit either for praise or [. . .] any social standing whatsoever' since 'flowing hair', McKibben notes, 'was a key sign of manly, regal beauty in traditional Irish society and its literature' (McKibben 2010, 67–8).

It is not surprising that the cultural tensions underscoring this poem resonated with SH, who would have sympathised with the angst expressed by his Northern Irish predecessor in both personal and political terms. SH's decision to dig with a pen rather than with a spade placed SH in two seemingly separate worlds and made his poetry, in a sense, a lifelong commitment to keep them together. The political vein of Mac an Bhaird's poem that the scholars emphasise could be linked to another sense of in-betweenness, if not ambivalence, experienced by SH.

In conversation with Dennis O'Driscoll SH recalls a situation, which he also addressed in 'From the Frontier of Writing' (*HL*, 6), of similar 'submission'. 'On the evening when the body of Francis Hughes – a neighbour's son and the second hunger striker to die – was being waked in his home in County Derry', O'Driscoll reminds him, 'You were not only in Oxford when he died, but staying – of all places – in a British cabinet minister's rooms.' This coincidence, SH replies, was 'bewildering'. At the time, SH explains, neither 'the IRA's self-image as liberators' nor 'the too-brutal simplicity' of Margaret Thatcher 'work much magic' with him. SH's 'own mantra in those days' was 'the remark by Miłosz' that he quotes in 'Away from it All' (*SI*, 16): 'I was stretched between contemplation/of a motionless point/and the command to participate/actively in history' (*SS*, 259–60).

[99] The Drowned Blackbird

SÉAMAS DALL MAC CUARTA (*c.*1650–1733), IRISH

First published in *The Penguin Book of Irish Poetry*, edited by Patrick Crotty and published by Penguin in 2010 (255) and reprinted in *The Map and the Clock*, edited by Carol Ann Duffy and Gillian Clarke and published by Faber & Faber in 2016 (164).

Uncollected.

This is SH's complete translation of '*An lon dubh báite*', a poem 'meant to console a child whose pet blackbird has been drowned in a tub of whitewash' (O'Connor 2011, 141). The text in this edition is drawn from *The Map and the Clock* (2016).

This translation completes a cycle of poems inspired by a bird that was familiar to SH for personal as well as poetic reasons. In conversation with Dennis O'Driscoll, SH says that 'The Blackbird of Glanmore' – which is the last poem in *District and Circle* (75–6) and makes a moving pair when read alongside this other blackbird story – 'contains a memory' of SH's young brother Christopher. SH told O'Driscoll that the first time he returned home from St Columb's College, he saw his brother, who was 'just about two or three', frolicking and rolling 'around the yard for pleasure', blackbird-like. That sight stayed with SH forever 'and came up more than fifty years later in the poem' (*SS*, 408).

Paul Muldoon has done two translations of '*An lon dubh báite*': one in 1970, published in the *Irish Press* (17 January 1970, 340) and one in 1998, published in the *Journal of Irish Studies* 16 (2001, 7). The second translation, for inclusion in Pádraigín Ní Uallacháin's *A Hidden Ulster* (2003), was done because Muldoon 'couldn't locate a copy of the version published in the *Irish Press*' (O'Connor 2011, 141). O'Connor quotes from 'a related unpublished early essay' titled 'The Drowned Blackbird' where Muldoon 'associates MacCuarta with English metaphysical verse and with the cryptic lyric concision of early medieval Irish verse' (O'Connor 2011, 143) – qualities SH admired too. It is plausible that SH read at least one of the two translations published by Muldoon, the second more likely than the first (Muldoon 2018). Muldoon also titled his 2017 Inaugural Annual College Lecture for University College Dublin's College of Arts and Humanities 'The Drowned Blackbird: An Introduction to 18th Century Ulster Poetry'.

[100] The Fisherman

MARIO LUZI (1914–2005), ITALIAN

First published in Mario Luzi's *Il filo della vita/The Thread of Life/ Snáithe na beatha*, edited by Alessandro Gentili and published by Fondazione Mario Luzi Editore in 2014 (48–51); reprinted in *L'Ermetismo e Firenze: Atti del convegno internazionale di studi, Firenze, 27–31 ottobre 2014*, Volume II: *Luzi, Bigongiari, Parronchi, Bodini, Sereni*, edited by Anna Dolfi and published by Firenze University Press, 2016 (268–9), and in Mario Luzi's *Persone nel viaggio/People on a Journey*, edited by Alessandro Gentili and published by Valigie Rosse in 2021 (38–41).
   Uncollected.

This is SH's complete translation of Mario Luzi's '*Il pescatore*' (1957). The text in this edition is drawn from *Persone nel viaggio/ People on a Journey* (2021).
   SH was invited to translate a Luzi poem for inclusion in a publication marking the centenary of the Italian poet's birth in 2014. As Alessandro Gentili notes, Mario Luzi 'loved Ireland, and visited on a number of occasions' between the 1970s and the 1990s. In 1987 Luzi was awarded an honorary degree by SH's alma mater, Queen's University Belfast, and in 1991 received the European Prize for Literature in Dublin, European City of Culture. The year before, 'while at the Italian Cultural Institute', Luzi 'inscribed his poem

"E il lupo" on a vellum folio for *The Great Book of Ireland* (1991), the only Italian poet featuring in that extraordinary volume, a poetry anthology and art gallery combined' (Luzi 2021, 15) in which SH also inscribed a poem, 'Punishment' (*North*, 30–1).

Il filo della vita, featuring thirteen Irish poets, and its expanded companion, *Persone nel viaggio*, featuring twenty Irish poets, are a celebration 'of Luzi's poetry in a chorus of Irish poetical voices, each distinct, but all assembled to interpret and renew one single voice' and 'an expression of gratitude for the affection of an Italian poet for their country' (Luzi 2021, 15).

Thomas McCarthy's foreword to *Persone nel viaggio* echoes Gentili's twofold salute. McCarthy first pays tribute to 'a Luzi relationship that began with the legendary Ghan Shyam Singh of Queen's University Belfast, tended lovingly over the years by the brilliant UCC scholar Catherine O'Brien, and maintained to this day by the indefatigable Gentili' (Luzi 2021, 8). He then remembers the Irish poets who have since died – 'heroes of their day like Heaney and O'Grady, Montague and Mahon' – and who 'are preserved forever in this living language of Luzi'. This anthology of Irish poets honouring Luzi, McCarthy concludes, 'serves as an Irish bijou garden of remembrance, the wild flowers of their words blowing in the breeze from his Italian hillsides'.

The thematic and expressive affinities between the Italian poet and his Irish poet-translator to be detected in '*Il pescatore*' are evident. The opening lines – 'People arrive by water, unspeaking ones/keeping close to the hulls of the anchored ships' – could belong to SH's translation of *Beowulf* or *Aeneid Book VI*. And the closing lines – 'I crane my neck/to follow with anxious eyes the fisherman/who comes over to the breakwater and hauls/from the sea what the sea allows,/a few gifts from its never-ending turmoil' – evoke canonical SH lines from poems such as 'A Lough Neagh Sequence' (*DD*, 28–35), 'Limbo' (*WO*, 58), 'The Strand at Lough Beg' (*FW*, 9–10), 'Casualty' (*FW*, 14–17) or 'Eelworks' (*HC*, 28–32)

As Antonella Francini and Thomas McCarthy observe, through SH's translation Luzi's '*Il pescatore*' acquires the 'atmosphere' and 'resonance' of another Irish Nobel Laureate, W. B. Yeats (Dolfi 2016, 265, 267). And it is the shadow of W. B. Yeats's own fisherman that strengthens the affinities between Luzi and Heaney, each willing to probe into and trust the eyes of 'This wise and simple man' whom Yeats described: 'The freckled man who goes/To a grey place on a hill/In grey Connemara clothes/At dawn to cast his flies' (W. B. Yeats, 'The Fisherman').

[101] Aeneid Book VI

VIRGIL (70–19 BCE), CLASSICAL LATIN

First published posthumously in the UK by Faber & Faber in 2016; published in the USA by Farrar, Straus and Giroux in a bilingual edition in 2016.

SH published six excerpts. The first excerpt is 'The Golden Bough' (*ll.* 98–211 of the standard Latin edition, R. A. B. Mynors's *P. Vergili Maronis Opera* (Oxford Classical Texts, 1969), hereafter OCT; *ABVIa*, 8–13; *TSH*, 494–7), in *Translation: The Journal of Literary Translation*, XII (Fall 1989, 197–201). This version is reprinted in *The Golden Bough*, published by Imprenta de los Tropicos and In de Bonnefant in 1992 (9), and with revisions in the *Guardian* (27 Feb. 2016). A shorter and revised version (OCT, *ll.* 98–148; *ABVIa*, 8–10; *TSH*, 494–6), reprinted in *Poetry Review* (Spring 1991, 72–4) and in *Stone from Delphi* (54–5), is collected in *Seeing Things* (1–3). The second excerpt is 'Palinurus' (OCT, *ll.* 349–83; *ABVIa*, 20–2; *TSH*, 502–3), in *Parnassus: Poetry in Review* 30. 1/2 (2008, 78–80). The third excerpt is 'The Riverbank Field' (OCT, *ll.* 704–15 and *ll.* 748–51; *ABVIa*, 38 and 40; *TSH*, 514–15), in *The Riverbank Field*, published by the Gallery Press in 2007 (n.p.), and collected with revisions in *Human Chain* (46–7). The fourth excerpt is 'Three "Freed Speeches" from *Aeneid* VI' ('1. Aeneas': OCT, *ll.* 42–76; *ABVIa*, 5–7; '2. The Sybil': OCT, *ll.* 77–97; *ABVIa*, 7–8; '3. Anchises': OCT, *ll.* 847–54; *ABVIa*, 45–6; *TSH*, 492–3; 493–4 and 519) in *Modern Poetry in Translation*, 3. 12 (2009, 58–62). The fifth excerpt is 'The Fields of Light (OCT, *ll.* 638–78; *ABVIa*, 35–7; *TSH*, 512–13), in *Archipelago*, II (Spring 2008, 9–10), reprinted with revisions as 'The Elysian Fields' in *Stone from Delphi* (110–11). The sixth excerpt is 'Charon and the Underworld' (OCT, *ll.* 295–362; *ABVIa*, 18–21; *TSH*, 500–2), in *Stone from Delphi* (112–14).

This is SH's complete translation of *Ænĕis* VI. The text in this edition is drawn from *Aeneid Book VI* (2016).

The posthumously published text was compiled by SH's publisher and family from author-corrected proofs of a limited, letterpress edition that SH had in preparation with In de Bonnefant Press in the Netherlands, and from amendments subsequent to those proofs made by SH in a typescript he marked 'final'. That typescript had been SH's primary working document since its creation on 3 May 2008 (possibly based on an earlier document of March 2008) and was last saved by him on 31 July 2013, a month before his death. It contains two full drafts of the poem, working variants for each draft, an incomplete introductory note and a draft of an apparently discrete poem (Faber & Faber Archive and the Estate of

Seamus Heaney). The typescript, which SH had intended to deliver to his London publisher was, as Catherine Heaney and Matthew Hollis explain in a Note on the Text, 'still in his keeping on his death' (*ABVIa*, 51).

The In de Bonnefant proofs from 2010–11, which feature marked corrections by SH, provided the basis of the text for *ll.* 1–787 (OCT), *ll.* 1–1064 (*ABVIa*, 3–42). But SH continued to rework the concluding sections of the poem (OCT, *ll.* 788–901; *ABVIa*, 42–8, TSH, 517–20, *ll.* 1065–1222) 'in typescript after that proof had been corrected', and it is for this reason that 'the last typescript becomes the preferred text from this point onward'. The posthumously published text of 1,222 lines (SH's rendition expanded the 901 lines of the original Latin) is thus SH's 'complete rendering of Book VI': 'It follows the author's latest instructions, and contains no editorial interventions beyond the correction of literals.' SH would probably have revised the translation and the translator's note had he seen production through to completion: his marking of the typescript as 'final', therefore, is a more precise description of the text than 'finished', 'as well as one in keeping with the Aeneid's own halted composition' (*ABVIa*, 52–3).

SH's poetic intentions ultimately override other motivations. All excerpts underwent revision as SH worked on completing the translation of Book VI. The text of 'The Golden Bough', which opens *Seeing Things* (1991, 1–3) and was done in response to the death of SH's father (1986), is revisited in the context of a complete translation of Book VI (and after translating Book X and XI from Ovid's *Metamorphoses*, included in 'The Midnight Verdict', published in 1993). 'The Riverbank Field' and above all 'Palinurus' – 'a three-act drama' in 'loose terza rima' and 'rhythmically midway between "Route 110" and *Aeneid Book VI*', which Falconer regards as 'a little-known work of major significance' because it acts as 'a sounding line' into SH's late poetry and poetics (Falconer 2022, 11, 24 and 178) – illustrate SH's genius in commingling translated and original texts.

As Stephen Harrison puts it, SH's 'micro-strategies of translation' reveal his 'considerable gifts in rendering the formal and elevated classics of Latin poetry readable for a modern audience in a form which is both dignified and natural' (Harrison 2019, 13). 'Similarities in diction' in SH's 'earliest and latest translations,' as Ruth Macklin points out, demonstrate that SH valued 'the daring and precision of the lyric gift over literal translations' and the 'lifelong poetic dialogue between his Latin translations and his own original compositions also suggests his increasing confidence as a poet' (Sonzogni 2021, 192).

In his 'Translator's Note', prepared in two drafts in 2010, SH describes his translation of *Aeneid* Book VI as 'neither a "version" nor a crib' but 'more like classics homework' – 'the result', he explains, of 'a lifelong desire' to honour the memory of Father Michael McGlinchey, his Latin teacher at St Columb's College (*ABVIa*, vii). While the set text for the A-level exam in 1957 was *Aeneid* IX, SH recalls, McGlinchey wished it were Book VI. For this reason, over the years SH 'gravitated towards that part of the poem', taking 'special note of it' after the death of his father, 'since the story it tells is that of Aeneas' journey to meet the shade of his father Anchises in the land of the dead'. The 'impulse to go ahead with a rendering of the complete book', however, 'arrived in 2007' after SH wrote 'Route 110': an autobiographical sequence in twelve poems 'to greet the birth of a first granddaughter' that plots 'incidents' from the poet's own life 'against certain well-known episodes in Book VI' (*ABVIa*, vii–viii).

It is interesting to note that Virgil's *Aeneid* is mentioned only five times in *Stepping Stones,* published in 2008 – described by Rachel Falconer as an *annus mirabilis* in terms of his dialogue with Virgil. As she notes, SH 'drafted his translation of Virgil's *Aeneid* VI in its entirety for the first time, produced a broadcast essay on Virgil for BBC Radio 3, gave an interview about Virgil and *The Riverbank Field* on RTÉ, and published a free translation of Virgil's Palinurus episode, along with other extracts from the forthcoming translation' (Falconer 2022, 10–11). And in one of their conversations, O'Driscoll reminds SH that Tom Paulin – in his citation for SH's 2005 Irish PEN Award – suggested that Virgil's *Aeneid* is 'a seminal and founding text' for SH and that SH's oeuvre has been a Virgilian epic journey. O'Driscoll then asks SH if he is 'conscious of having undertaken such a journey'. SH replies 'not conscious' but adds that 'one Virgilian journey' had indeed been 'a constant presence' – Aeneas' 'venture into the underworld' (*SS*, 389).

Indeed, SH explained 'The motifs' of Book VI – 'the golden bough, Charon's barge, the quest to meet the shade of the father' and other episodes that are 'commingled with scenes from the poet's own life and times', acquiring 'totemic significance' (Falconer 2022, 3) – had been 'in his head for years' (*SS*, 389), and he liked 'that book of the *Aeneid* so much' that he was 'inclined to translate it as a separate unit, as Sir John Harington did in the seventeenth century' (*SS*, 440). And he did.

'The very trajectory of Virgil's life, from farmer's son to famous poet,' Falconer observes, offered SH 'a companionable biography with which he could closely identify'. As she notes, SH 'had begun reading Virgil from a very young age'. As a schoolboy at St Columb's College in the 1950s, SH studies parts of the *Aeneid* in Latin as well as the whole work in J. W. Mackail's prose translation in English, and he is still a teenager when he buys an edition of Book VI. This early exposure, Falconer argues, is 'one reason for the particular intimacy, warmth and affection that mark his engagement with Virgil in his later poetry and prose' where Virgil 'reappears to him as a "familiar compound ghost", summoned directly from his own childhood and adolescent memories, as well as mediated through his later reading of Dante and T. S. Eliot'. It is no surprise therefore that Virgil's poetry – translated or adapted – features 'prominently' in SH's work. As Falconer puts it, Virgil is SH's 'inner interlocutor' (Falconer 2022, 1 and 2).

SH's 'dialogue with Virgil', Falconer points out, 'runs much deeper than is generally acknowledged' (Falconer 2022, 1) and his translation of *Aeneid* Book VI should be confined neither to him abandoning his religious faith in the mid-1980s and replacing it with the classics, nor to him choosing pre-Christian myths to counter the Christian narratives of his Catholic background (Impens 2017, 59; *SD*, 10). Rather, Helen Vendler argues, SH hopes for 'a viable ethical synthesis of the best in Christian and classical systems' and 'pursued, throughout his writing life, a just estimation of his double inheritances, Christian and pre-Christian' (*SD*, 25). And if 'Celtic and Scandinavian myths were indispensable to his earlier work,' she concludes, 'in more recent years . . . it is the classical past that has suffused his poetry, contributing to it a sustaining mythology, a stern justice, and renewed fortitude against the devastations of Fate' (*SD*, 25).

As Rachel Falconer emphasises, SH was drawn to Virgil and to *Aeneid* Book VI especially because he found 'examples of the good of poetry' both 'in its capacity for remembering and forwarding the past' and 'in its capacity to break from the past, let fly and strike its own, fresh note' (Falconer 2022, 5–6) – and, with SH's own words, in poetry 'as a point of entry into the buried life of the feelings or as a point of exit for it' (*Preoccupations*, 52).

Evoking Derrida's suggestion in *Spectres of Marx* that 'all existence is haunted by spectres of the past', Ian Hickey argues that SH's work is 'deeply indebted to, and haunted by, literary and cultural inheritances of the past' and the place of Virgil's *Aeneid* within SH's work 'is indebted to the sense of inheritance and transmission of spectres of which Derrida speaks' (Hickey 2020, 101 and 104). As Derrida puts it, 'It is a proper characteristic of the spectre, if there is any, that no one can be sure if by returning it testifies to a living past or to a living future.' The *revenant*, Derrida explains, 'may already mark the promised return of the spectre of living being'. (Derrida 2006, 123). According to Hickey, 'This return of spectres of the past is nowhere more visible in their disadjustment of the contemporary within the translation than when we probe the extent to which it is haunted by Heaney's previous poetic dealings with Virgil' (Hickey 2020, 114).

This visibility manifests itself in SH's 'capacity to unite familial affection with larger literary ambition': a 'key characteristic' of his 'Virgilian reception' in general and of his translation of *Aeneid* Book VI in particular as it can be read in the context of SH's own life and experiences (Harrison 2019, 7; Hickey 2020, 114). As Falconer notes, however, it is Virgil's 'ability to bestride two worlds, to speak in two languages and two poetic traditions at once' that made visible to SH a way of standing – linguistically, culturally and politically – 'over the ground of a conflicted community' from an individual as well as collective viewpoint (Falconer 2022, 8).

SH 'mused on the shape of Virgil's life and the enduring impact of his writing' (Falconer 2022, 5) in two broadcasts: a treatise on Virgil for BBC Radio 3's *The Essay* (15 July 2008, the second of a four-part series titled 'Greek and Latin Voices') and an interview about Virgil and *The Riverbank Field* with the Irish poet Gerald Dawe for RTÉ 1's *The Poetry Programme* (4 Oct. 2008).

If Book VI of the *Aeneid* has earned SH a place in Philip Hardie's *The Last Trojan Hero: A Cultural History of Virgil's Aeneid* (2014) and in Susanna Braund and Zara Martirosova Torlone's *Virgil and His Translators* (2018), 'Twenty Ways of Reading Seamus Heaney's *Aeneid Book VI*' (2022) – an international workshop of poets, editors, classicists and scholars of Heaney's poetry – has demonstrated that we have just begun to grasp the depth and scope of this translation. It also alerted us that SH's personal and poetic motives outsmart scholarly exegesis and comparison.

Writing about Book VI of the *Aeneid* – which he refers to as SH's 'miraculous return from the literary afterlife', a 'brilliant capstone to the imposing edifice of his writing', and the poet's 'passport to the literary future' – Bernard O'Donoghue argues why it 'may come to be recognised as his finest translation of all, as well as the one most personal to him'. If SH 'rises unfailingly to the demands of these high moments in his wonderful and unflagging translation', he notes, 'What is perhaps less predictable, given his expressed reservations, is that he is also totally successful in bringing to vigorous life the less appealing part of the poem' (O'Donoghue 2016, 11).

As Nicholas Lezard observes, SH 'started proper work on this after his father died', and 'It is the last work he finished before his own death in 2013.' *Aeneid Book VI*, he adds, is 'in a way, his farewell to the land of the living' (Lezard 2017, 17) as he himself crossed over through the door that 'stands open day and night' – 'Death's dark door' (*ABVIa*, 9; *TSH*, 495, *l.* 175). Reading *Aeneid Book VI*, Brooke Clark observes, one feels that it is 'a literary touchstone' SH 'has carried with him and thought about for a long time'. This translation, concludes Clark, 'represents a synthesis of that material with his own idea of poetry, and his approach to writing it' (Clark 2016).

In SH's final typescript for *Aeneid Book VI*, held in the archives of Faber & Faber and his Estate, there is an abandoned fragment, without any punctuation to conclude it, that seems to express something of the synthesis between the crossing of life, poetry and translation. It reads,

> Amazed, bourne, continuous, regions of air

Biographical Notes

CHARLES BAUDELAIRE (1821–67) was a French poet, translator, essayist and literary and art critic. He was one of the most influential writers of nineteenth-century Europe.

JOACHIM DU BELLAY (1522–60) was a French poet and leader of the literary group known as La Pléiade. He was a pioneer of new literary forms in French.

ANA BLANDIANA (Otilia Valeria Coman, *b.*1942) is a Romanian poet, editor and essayist. Her numerous volumes of writing have been translated into many languages.

J. C. BLOEM (Jakobus Cornelis Bloem, 1887–1966) was a prominent Dutch jurist, poet and essayist. He was nominated for the Nobel Prize in Literature.

ST BRIGID (438/452–524/526) is one of Ireland's three patron saints together with Patrick and Columba. She is celebrated throughout Celtic countries for performing domestic miracles.

JOSEPH BRODSKY (Iosif Aleksandrovich Brodsky, 1940–96) was a Russian–American poet, translator and essayist. He was awarded the Nobel Prize in Literature in 1987.

CÆDMON (*fl. c.*657–84) was the earliest poet known to be writing in English. He was believed to have received the art of sacred song in a dream.

CONSTANTINE P. CAVAFY (1863–1933) was a Greek poet, journalist and civil servant. He did not publish his poetry in book form in his lifetime.

CHARLES IX (Charles Maximilien, 1550–74) became king of France when he was ten years old. He enjoyed a special friendship with the court poet Pierre de Ronsard (1524–82).

GABRIELLE DE COIGNARD (*c.*1550–86/94) was a French devotional poet who turned to writing verse as spiritual and physical consolation. Her poetry was published posthumously.

DANTE (Dante Alighieri, 1265–1321) was an Italian poet, philosopher and politician. His use of the vernacular in literature contributed to the standardisation of the Italian language.

EUGÈNE GUILLEVIC (1907–97) was a widely published French poet and for many years served with the Ministry of Finance and Economic Affairs.

ROBERT HENRYSON (c.1430–c.1506) was a Scottish poet and early fabulist. It is believed he was a schoolmaster at a Benedictine abbey school.

HORACE (Quintus Horatius Flaccus, 65–8 BCE) was a leading lyric poet during the time of Augustus in Rome. He took part in the Battle of Philippi (42 BCE), a milestone in Roman history.

JOHN OF THE CROSS (Juan de Yepes y Álvarez, 1542–91) was a Carmelite priest, mystic and poet. He was strongly influenced by St Teresa of Avila and was canonised in 1726.

ARTHUR JOHNSTON (c.1579–1641) was a Scottish poet and physician who published in Latin. His elegiac verse in Latin imitates Ovid's.

OZEF KALDA (Josef Kalda, 1871–1921) was a prolific writer from the Moravian Wallachia region of what is now the Czech Republic. Some of his work appeared anonymously.

JAN KOCHANOWSKI (1530–84) was the foremost poet of Renaissance Poland. He often wrote in Latin but is best remembered for developing the literary use of the Polish vernacular.

MARIO LUZI (1914–2005) was one of the most prominent Italian poets and essayists of the twentieth century, and a Lifetime Senator. He was nominated for the Nobel Prize in Literature.

LAOISEACH MAC AN BHAIRD (fl. late sixteenth century) was an Irish poet from a Connacht family famous for poetry and learning. Only two of his works survive.

SÉAMAS DALL MAC CUARTA (James McCuairt/James Courtney, c.1650–1733) was an Irish poet associated with an Irish-language school of poets in the Leinster–Ulster border region.

CATHAL BUÍ MAC GIOLLA GHUNNA (1680–1756) was one of the best-known Irish poets of south Ulster and north Leinster. He trained for the priesthood but abandoned his studies before ordination.

SORLEY MACLEAN (Somhairle MacGill-Eain, 1911–96) was a Scottish Gaelic poet, credited with achieving wider recognition and appreciation of Gaelic poetry in the twentieth century.

BRIAN MERRIMAN (Brian Mac Giolla Meidhre, c.1750–1805) was an Irish-language poet, a farmer and master of a school of mathematics.

NUALA NÍ DHOMHNAILL (b.1952) is an Irish poet who writes exclusively in Irish. She served as the second Ireland Professor of Poetry (2001–3).

SEÁN Ó COILEÁIN (John Collins, c.1754–1817) was an Irish poet and schoolmaster. His ancestors were driven from their original estates to settle near Timoleague.

TADHG ÓG Ó HUIGINN (1370–1448) was a leading Irish poet of his time, born into a Connacht family of bards. His surviving poems testify to his prominent contemporary reputation.

ANTOINE Ó RAIFTEIRÍ (Anthony Raftery, 1779/84–1835) is remembered as the last wandering bard and musician. None of his poems were written down in his lifetime.

AODHAGÁN Ó RATHAILLE (Egan O'Rahilly, c.1675–1729), was an Irish poet and bard. He created the *aisling*, a type of dream poem in which Ireland appears to the poet personified as a woman.

CATHAL Ó SEARCAIGH (b.1956) is an Irish-language poet who was born into and grew up in a Gaeltacht area. He is a much-translated writer of poetry, plays and travelogues.

EOGHAN RUA Ó SUILLEABHÁIN (Owen Roe O'Sullivan, 1748–84) was one of the last great Gaelic poets. His *aisling* poems, unpublished during his lifetime, were often set to song.

OVID (Publius Ovidius Naso, 43 BCE–CE 17/18) was a Roman poet who lived during the reign of Augustus. His *Metamorphoses* is one of the most influential sources of classical mythology.

GIOVANNI PASCOLI (1855–1912) was an Italian classical scholar, translator and poet. Some consider him to be the finest Latin poet since the Augustans.

ALEXANDER PUSHKIN (Aleksandr Sergeevich Pushkin, 1799–1837) was a poet, novelist, dramatist and short-story writer, and is regarded as the father of Russian literature.

RAINER MARIA RILKE (1875–1926) was an Austrian poet and novelist whose works positioned him as the bridge between traditional and modernist writers.

SOPHOCLES (c.496–406 BCE) is regarded as one of the three great Greek tragedians along with Aeschylus and Euripides. His Antigone is one of the most powerful female characters in world theatre.

MARIN SORESCU (1936–96) was a prolific Romanian poet, playwright and novelist. Some of his poetry could not be published until the end of Nicolae Ceauşescu's Communist dictatorship.

TITIAN (Tiziano Vecellio, 1488/90–1576) is recognised as one of the most important Italian painters and the main exponent of the Venetian Renaissance.

VIRGIL (Publius Vergilius Maro, 70–19 BCE) is known as the Augustan poet par excellence. In Dante's *Divine Comedy* he acts as the author's guide through Hell and Purgatory.

Bibliography

Almqvist 1990	Bo Almqvist, 'Of Mermaids and Marriages: Seamus Heaney's "Maighdean Mara" and Nuala Ní Dhomhnaill's "an Mhaighdean Mhara" in the Light of Folk Tradition', *Béaloideas*, 58 (1990): 1–74
Baker 2015	Deborah Lesko Baker, 'Gabrielle de Coignard's "Sonnets spirituels": Writing Passion within and against the Petrarchan Tradition', *Renaissance and Reformation/Renaissance et Réforme*, 38.3 (Summer/Été 2015): 41–59
Bakhtin 1981	Mikhail Bakhtin, *The Dialogic Imagination: Four Essays* (ed. Michael Holquist, tr. Caryl Emerson and Michael Holquist), Austin: University of Texas Press, 1981
Barańczak 1995	Stanislaw Barańczak and Seamus Heaney, 'Translators' Note', *Graph*, second series, 1 (1995): 41
Battersby 2002	Eileen Battersby, 'Stalked by an agenda', *Irish Times* (5 Oct. 2002): 10
Battistini 2013	Andrea Battistini, Marco A. Bazzocchi and Gino Ruozzi (eds), 'Pascoli e l'immaginario degli italiani', *Rivista pascoliana*, 24–25 (2012–13), Bologna: Pàtron Editore, 2013
Bergin 1912	Laoisioch Mac an Bhaird and Osborn Bergin, 'Courtier and Rebel', *Irish Review*, 2. 21 (Nov. 1912): 471–3
Bourke 1993	Angela Bourke, 'Fairies and Anorexia: Nuala Ní Dhomhnaill's "Amazing Grass"', *Proceedings of the Harvard Celtic Colloquium*, 13 (1993): 25–38
Bradley 1982	S. A. J. Bradley (ed. & tr.), *Anglo-Saxon Poetry*, London: Dent, 1982
Brandes 2008a	Rand Brandes and Michael J. Durkan, *Seamus Heaney: A Bibliography*, 1959–2003, London: Faber & Faber, 2008
Brandes 2008b	Rand Brandes, 'Seamus Heaney's Working Titles: From "Advancements of Learning" to "Midnight Anvil"', *The Cambridge Companion to Seamus Heaney* (ed. Bernard O'Donoghue), Cambridge: Cambridge University Press, 2009: 19–36

Brandes 2014	Rand Brandes (ed.), *Seamus Heaney: A Life Well Written. Selections from the Collections of Carolyn & Ward Smith, Alan M. Klein, and Rand Brandes*, New York: Grolier Club, and Hickory, NC: Lenoir-Rhyne University, 2014
Brereton 1958	Geoffrey Brereton (ed.), *The Penguin Book of French Verse*, Vol. 2: *Sixteenth to Eighteenth Centuries*, Harmondsworth: Penguin, 1958
Brewster 2009	Scott Brewster and Michael Parker (eds), *Irish Literature Since 1990: Diverse Voices*, Manchester: Manchester University Press, 2009
Briggs 1999	A.D.P. Briggs, 'New Translations by A.D.P. Briggs of Poems by Alexander Pushkin', *New Zealand Slavonic Journal* (1999): 63–90
Brodsky 1992	Joseph Brodsky, Рождественские стихи (Christmas Poems), Moscow: *Nezavisimaya Gazeta*, 1992
Brodsky 2001	Joseph Brodsky, *Nativity Poems*, New York: Farrar, Straus and Giroux, 2001
Broom 1998	Sarah Broom, 'Returning to Myth: From *North* to "Mycenae Lookout"', *Canadian Journal of Irish Studies*, 24. 1 (July 1998): 51–74
Brown 2019	Sarah Annes Brown, 'Metamorphosis: Poems Inspired by Titian: Reversals and Reflection', *Classical Receptions Journal*, 11. 2 (2019): 137–56
Burke 2022	Tony Burke, '*The Infancy Gospel of Thomas*: Irish' (online), (n.d.)
Carney 1958	James Carney, 'Two Old Irish Poems', *Ériu*, 18 (1958): 1–43
Cavafy 2007	C.P. Cavafy, *The Canon: The Original One Hundred and Fifty-Four Poems* (ed. Dana Bonstorm, tr. Stratis Haviaras, with a Foreword by Seamus Heaney), Cambridge, MA: Harvard University Press, 2007
Clark 2016	Brooke Clark, 'Does the New Translation of Virgil Sound Too Much Like Heaney?', *Partisan* (online) (28 June 2016)
Clune 1996	Anne Clune, 'Mythologizing Sweeney', *Irish University Review*, 26. 1 (Spring–Summer 1996): 48–60
Codrescu 2007	Andrei Codrescu, 'Introduction to Focus: Contemporary Romanian Poetry in Translation

and in Interstitial English', *American Book Review*, 28. 5 (2007): 3

Connolly 2016   Sally Connolly, *Grief and Metre: Elegies for Poets after Auden*, Charlottesville, VA: University of Virginia Press, 2016

Conroy 2009   Jane Conroy (ed.), *Franco-Irish Connections: Essays, Memoirs and Poems in Honour of Pierre Joannon*, Dublin: Four Courts Press, 2009

Cooney 2009   Helen Cooney, 'Sense-Clearing: *The Testament of Cresseid & Seven Fables by Robert Henryson*, Seamus Heaney', *Poetry Ireland Review*, 98 (July 2009): 36–7

Corcoran 1998   Neil Corcoran, *The Poetry of Seamus Heaney: A Critical Study*, London: Faber & Faber, 1998

Cosgrove 2018   Brian Cosgrove, 'Seamus Heaney's Last Words: Provenance and Context for "Noli Timere"', *The Furrow*, 69. 7/8 (July/Aug. 2018): 398–406

Coward 1997   David Coward, 'Introduction', Alexandre Dumas, *La reine Margot* (ed. David Coward), Oxford: Oxford University Press, 1997: vii–xxiv

Craig 1991   Patricia Craig, 'Irish Branching Out', *Times Literary Supplement* (8 Feb. 1991): 20

Crawford 2019   Robert Crawford, email to Marco Sonzogni (4 July 2019)

Crotty 2001   Patrick Crotty, 'All I Believe That Happened There Was Revision', *The Art of Seamus Heaney* (ed. Tony Curtis), Bridgend: Seren Books, 2001: 191–204

Crotty 2010   Patrick Crotty (ed., with a Preface by Seamus Heaney), *The Penguin Book of Irish Poetry*, London: Penguin Classics, 2010

Crowder 2017   Ashby Bland Crowder, 'Christmas Greetings from Seamus Heaney', *New Hibernia Review/ Iris Éireannach Nua*, 21. 3 (Fómhar/Autumn 2017): 34–58

Cruise O'Brien 1968   Conor Cruise O'Brien, 'Views', *The Listener* (24 Oct. 1969): 526

Cruise O'Brien 1974   Conor Cruise O'Brien, *States of Ireland*, London: Panther Books, 1974

DeForrest 1994   Matthew M. DeForrest, 'Seamus Heaney's *The Cure at Troy*: Individuality and the Psychological', *Éire-Ireland*, 29. 3 (Fómhar/Fall 1994): 126–36

Delanty 2012   Greg Delanty and Michael Matto (eds, with
                      a Foreword by Seamus Heaney), *The Word
                      Exchange: Anglo-Saxon Poems in Translation*,
                      New York: W. W. Norton & Co., 2012
Demel 1997   Jiří Demel, 'Kdo je autorem Zápisníku
                      zmizelého?' ['Who is the Author of the Diary of
                      One Who Disappeared?'], *Opus Musicum*, 29
                      (1997): 93–6
Dennison 2015   John Dennison, *Seamus Heaney and the
                      Adequacy of Poetry*, Oxford: Oxford University
                      Press, 2015
Dervan 2001   Michael Dervan, 'Poetic license: Nobel Prize-
                      winning Irish poet Seamus Heaney's new
                      translation of *Diary of One Who Vanished*
                      comes to New York', *Opera News*, 65 (2001): 39
Derrida 2006   Jacques Derrida, *Spectres of Marx* (*Spectres
                      de Marx*, 1993) (tr. Peggy Kamuf), London:
                      Routledge, 2006
Dolfi 2016   Anna Dolfi (ed.), *L'Ermetismo e Firenze: Atti
                      del convegno internazionale di studi, Firenze,
                      27–31 ottobre 2014*, Volume II: *Luzi, Bigongiari,
                      Parronchi, Bodini, Sereni*, Firenze: Firenze
                      University Press, 2016
Donnelly 2009   Brian Donnelly, '*The Digging Skeleton* after
                      Baudelaire', *Irish University Review*, 39. 2
                      (Autumn/Winter 2009): 246–54
Downum 2009   Denell Downum, 'Sweeney Astray: The
                      Other in Oneself', *Éire-Ireland*, 44: 3–4
                      (Earrach/Samhradh–Fall/Winter 2009): 75–93
Duffy 2016   Carol Ann Duffy and Gillian Clarke (eds),
                      *The Map and the Clock: A Laureate's Choice of
                      the Poetry of Britain and Ireland*, London: Faber
                      & Faber, 2016
Dumas 1900   Alexandre Dumas, *Marguerite de Valois*,
                      New York: T. Y. Crowell & Co., 1900
Eagleton 1999   Terry Eagleton, 'Hasped and Hooped and
                      Hirpling', *London Review of Books*, 11
                      (Nov. 1999): 75–93
Evans 1972   George Ewart Evans and David Thomson,
                      The Leaping Hare, London: Faber & Faber, 1972
                      (reprinted 2002)
Fairleigh 1996   John Fairleigh (ed.), *When the Tunnels Meet:
                      Contemporary Romanian Poetry*, Newcastle
                      upon Tyne: Bloodaxe Books, 1996

Falconer 2019	Rachel Falconer, 'Heaney, Pascoli and the Ends of Poetry', *The Ends of Poetry: California Italian Studies*, 8 (2019): 1–20
Falconer 2022	Rachel Falconer, *Seamus Heaney, Virgil and the Good of Poetry*, Edinburgh: Edinburgh University Press, 2022
Fazzini 2016	Marco Fazzini, '"At the Back of My Ear": A Note on Seamus Heaney and Scottish Poetry', *Journal of European Studies*, 46. 1 (2016): 51–9
Fumagalli 1997a	Maria Cristina Fumagalli, '"What Dante Means to Me": Seamus Heaney's Translation of the First Three Cantos of Dante's Inferno', *Agenda*, 34. 3–4 (1997): 204–34
Fumagalli 1997b	Maria Cristina Fumagalli, 'The Eternal Fountain of Poetic Imagination: Seamus Heaney's Translation of Juan de la Cruz's "Cantar del alma que se huelga de conocer a Dios por fee"', *Agenda*, 35. 2 (1997): 162–73
Greene 1954	David Greene, 'St Brigid's Alefeast', *Celtica*, II (1954): 150–3
Greene 1967	David Greene and Frank O'Connor (ed. & tr.), *A Golden Treasury of Irish Poetry: AD 600 to 1200*, London: Macmillan, 1967
Gregory 1907	Lady Augusta Gregory, *A Book of Saints and Wonders Put Down Here by Lady Gregory According to the Old Writings and the Memory of the People of Ireland*, London: John Murray, 1907
Guillevic 1969	Eugène Guillevic, *Selected Poems* (tr. Denise Levertov), New York: New Directions, 1969
Guzzo 2021	Leonardo Guzzo and Marco Sonzogni, 'La luce del Paradiso. Leggendo Dante a Newgrange', *L'Osservatore Romano* (17 April 2021): 6
Gwiazda 2016	Piotr Gwiazda, 'Magdalena Kay: In Gratitude for All the Gifts: Seamus Heaney and Eastern Europe', *Journal of European Studies*, 46. 1 (2016): 60–3
Hardwick 2016	Lorna Hardwick, 'Interview with Seamus Heaney' (recorded Sept. 2007), *Practitioners' Voices in Classical Reception Studies*, 7, Department of Classical Studies at the Open University, 2016
Harrison 2019	Stephen Harrison, Fiona Macintosh and Helen Eastman (eds), *Seamus Heaney and the Classics:*

	Bann Valley Muses, Oxford: Oxford University Press, 2019
Hart 1987	Henry Hart, 'Seamus Heaney's Poetry of Meditation: *Door into the Dark*', *Twentieth Century Literature*, 33. 1 (Spring 1987): 1–17
Hart 1992	Henry Hart, *Seamus Heaney: Poet of Contrary Progressions*, Syracuse, NY: Syracuse University Press, 1992
Havely 1998	Nick Havely (ed.), *Dante's Modern Afterlife: Reception and Response from Blake to Heaney*, London: Palgrave Macmillan, 1998
Heaney 1968	Seamus Heaney, 'Old Derry's Walls', *The Listener* (24 Oct. 1968): 521–3
Heaney 1972	Seamus Heaney, 'Stag of the Cabbages' (review of *The Leaping Hare* by George Ewart Evans and David Thomson), *The Listener* (21 Dec. 1972): 869
Heaney 1980	Seamus Heaney and Gloria Hunniford, *A Sense of Ireland* (film), UTV, 1980
Heaney 1985	Seamus Heaney, 'Envies and Identifications: Dante and the Modern Poet', *Irish University Review*, 15. 1 (1985): 5–19
Heaney 1986	Seamus Heaney, 'Introduction', *Sorley MacLean: Critical Essays* (ed. Raymond J. Ross and Joy Hendry), Edinburgh: Scottish Academic Press, 1986: 1–7
Heaney 1987	Seamus Heaney, 'Brodsky's Nobel: What the Applause Was About', *New York Times* book review (8 Nov. 1987): 1, 63, 65
Heaney 1988a	'Anglo-Irish Occasions', *London Review of Books* (5 May 1988): 9
Heaney 1988b	Seamus Heaney and George O'Brien, *The Writing Life: An Afternoon with Seamus Heaney* (video), Howard Community College, MD, 1988
Heaney 1989a	Seamus Heaney, 'Earning a Rhyme', *The Art of Translation: Voices from the Field* (ed. Rosanne Warren), Boston, MA: Northeastern University Press (1989): 13–20; reprinted from *Poetry Ireland* (Spring 1989): 95–100; reprinted in an abridged edition in *Finders Keepers: Selected Prose 1971–2001* (London: Faber & Faber, 2002): 59–66
Heaney 1989b	Seamus Heaney and Sue Lawley, *Desert Island Discs*, BBC Radio 4 (19 Nov. 1989)

Heaney 1995	Seamus Heaney and Robert Druce, *An Evening with Irish Poet (video)*, The John Adams Institute, Amsterdam (26 Jan. 1995)
Heaney 1996	Seamus Heaney and Charlie Rose, *Charlie Rose: The Power of Questions*, PBS (video) (19 April 1996)
Heaney 1998a	Seamus Heaney, fax to John Kinsella (4 Aug. 1998)
Heaney 1998b	'Whiting Foundation Keynote Address' (online), New York ([Spring] 1998)
Heaney 1999a	Seamus Heaney, fax to John Kinsella (12 Jan. 1999)
Heaney 1999b	Seamus Heaney, 'Report on Section 7: "Several Translations of the Same Text"', *Translation of Poetry and Poetic Prose: Proceedings of Nobel Symposium 110* (ed. Sture Allén), Singapore: World Scientific, 1999: 330–3
Heaney 1999c	Seamus Heaney, 'Fretwork: On Translating *Beowulf*', *In Other Words: The Journal for Literary Translators* (Autumn/Winter 1999/2000): 23–33; reprinted as 'The Drag of the Golden Chains: On Translating *Beowulf*', *Times Literary Supplement* (12 Nov. 1999): 14–16
Heaney 1999d	Seamus Heaney, 'A Gate Left Open: On Translating the Songs of Janáček's *Journal d'un disparu*', *Translation Ireland*, 13. 4 (Dec. 1999): 1–2
Heaney 1999e	Seamus Heaney and Jon Snow, 'I Can't Keep Writing Elegies', *Channel 4 News* (1999)
Heaney 2000a	Seamus Heaney, fax to John Kinsella (5 Jan. 2000)
Heaney 2000b	Seamus Heaney and Robert Hass, *Sounding Lines: The Art of Translating Poetry*, Berkeley: Doreen B. Townsend Center for the Humanities, 2000
Heaney 2000c	Seamus Heaney and Bei Ling, 'Can a Poem Stop a Tank: Bei Ling and Seamus in the Conversation Beijing Tried to Stop', *Los Angeles Times* book review (13 Dec. 2000): 6–9
Heaney 2002	Seamus Heaney, 'The Trance and the Translation', *Guardian* (30 Nov. 2002): 4, 6
Heaney 2004a	Seamus Heaney, letter to Dennis O'Driscoll, 21 Feb. 2004

Heaney 2004b	'Oraçao académica de Seamus Heaney', *Biblos: Revista da Faculdade de Letras*, University of Coimbra, Portugal, 2004: 635–7
Heaney 2004c	Seamus Heaney, fax to Maria Makuch, 18 Aug. 2004
Heaney 2004d	Seamus Heaney, 'The Jayne Lecture: Title Deeds: Translating a Classic', *Proceedings of the American Philosophical Society*, 148. 4 (Dec. 2004): 411–26
Heaney 2005	Seamus Heaney, '"Me" as in "Metre": On Translating Antigone', *Rebel Women: Staging Ancient Greek Drama Today* (ed. John Dillon and S. E. Wilmer), London: Bloomsbury, 2005: 169–76
Heaney 2006	Seamus Heaney, 'Translator's Note', *Poetry* (April 2006): 5
Heaney 2007	Seamus Heaney, 'Towers, Trees, Terrors: A Reverie in Urbino', *In forma di parole: Seamus Heaney poeta dotto*, 23. 2 (2007): 145–56
Heaney 2008a	Seamus Heaney, letter to Stephanie Schwerter (2 April 2008)
Heaney 2008b	Seamus Heaney, 'Robert Lowell Memorial Lecture' (video), Boston University, Boston, MA (2 Oct. 2008)
Heaney 2008c	Seamus Heaney and Paul Muldoon, *History and Homeland* (video), The New Yorker Festival (4 Oct. 2008)
Heaney 2008d	Seamus Heaney and Gerald Dawe, 'The Riverbank Field', *The Poetry Programme*, RTÉ (4 Oct. 2008)
Heaney 2009a	Seamus Heaney, 'A Poem for Mary Kelleher', *Auguri: To Mary Kelleher* (ed. Fergus Mulligan), Dublin: Royal Dublin Society, 2009: 4–6
Heaney 2009b	Seamus Heaney and Charlie McCarthy, *Out of the Marvellous*, film documentary, RTÉ/Icebox Films, 2009
Heaney 2009c	Seamus Heaney, letter to Michael Brophy (10 May 2007), in Guillevic: *La poésie à la lumière du quotidien* (ed. Michael Brophy), Berne, Switzerland: Peter Lang, 2009: 227
Heaney 2010	Seamus Heaney, 'Seamus Heaney Reads Deor', *Poems Out Loud* (15 Nov. 2010) (podcast)
Heaney 2011	Seamus Heaney, 'Seamus Heaney Reads From His Work' (video), Poetry Season,

	92NY Unterberg Poetry Center, New York (26 Sept. 2011)
Heaney 2012a	Seamus Heaney, *Stone from Delphi: Poems with Classical References* (ed. Helen Vendler), San Francisco: Arion Press, 2012
Heaney 2012b	Seamus Heaney, 'Mossbawn via Mantua: Ireland in/and Europe: Cross-Currents and Exchanges', *Irish Studies in Europe* (ed. Werner Huber, Sandra Meyer and Julia Novak), Trier: Wissenschaftlicher Verlag Trier, 2012: 19–27
Heaney 2012c	Seamus Heaney, 'Poems inspired by Titian' (video), National Gallery, London, 2012
Heaney 2012d	Seamus Heaney and Alan Yentob, *Imagine: Dancing with Titian*, BBC One (24 July 2012)
Heaney 2012e	Seamus Heaney and Martin Herbert, 'Metamorphosis: Titian 2012 – poetry in paint', *Daily Telegraph* (9 July 2012)
Heaney 2013a	Seamus Heaney, 'An evening with the poet', a film by Séamas McSwiney, Centre Culturel Irlandais in conjunction with the Périphérie du Marché de la Poésie, Paris (13 June 2013)
Heaney 2013b	Seamus Heaney, 'On Home Ground', in 'Pascoli e l'immaginario degli italiani', *Rivista pascoliana*, 24–25 (2012–13), Bologna: Pàtron Editore, 2013: 19–26
Heydel 2022	Magda Heydel, email to Marco Sonzogni (15 June 2022)
Hickey 2020	Ian Hickey, 'Derrida, Heaney and the Translation of Virgil's *Aeneid*, Book VI', *Études irlandaises*, 45. 2 (2020): 101–17
Holsinger 2007	Bruce Holsinger, 'The Parable of Caedmon's "Hymn": Liturgical Invention and Literary Tradition', *Journal of English and Germanic Philology*, 106. 2 (April 2007): 149–75
Homem 2001	Rui Carvalho Homem, 'On Elegies, Eclogues, Translations, Transfusions: an Interview with Seamus Heaney', *European English Messenger*, 10. 2 (2001): 25–30
Howard 2013	Ben Howard, Letters to the Editor, *Times Literary Supplement*, 5764 (20 Sept. 2013): 6
Impens 2017	Florence Impens, '"Help me please my hedge-school master": Virgilian Presences in the Work of Seamus Heaney', *Irish University Review*, 47. 2 (2017): 251–65

Jackson 1971	Kenneth Hurlstone Jackson (ed.), *A Celtic Miscellany. Translations from the Celtic Literatures*, Harmondsworth: Penguin, 1951, 1971
Jones 1997	Richard C. Jones III, '"Talking amongst Ourselves": Language, Politics, and Sophocles on the Field Day Stage', *International Journal of the Classical Tradition*, 4. 2 (Fall 1997): 232–46
Joyce 1916	James Joyce, *A Portrait of the Artist as a Young Man*, New York: B. W. Huebsch, 1916
Kay 2012	Magdalena Kay, *In Gratitude for All the Gifts: Seamus Heaney and Eastern Europe*, Toronto: University of Toronto Press, 2012
Kean 2021	Rachel Falconer, 'Terra Tremens: Katabasis in Seamus Heaney's *District and Circle* (2006)', Margaret Kean (ed.) *The Literatures of Hell*, Cambridge: D. S. Brewer, 2021: 133–58
Keller 2001	Johanna Keller, 'Making Another's Poetry His Own: Interview with Seamus Heaney', *New York Times* (27 May 2001): 19
Kennelly 1984	Brendan Kennelly, 'Soaring from the Treetops', *New York Times* book review (27 May 1984), 14
Kinahan 1982	Frank Kinahan, 'Artists on Art: An Interview with Seamus Heaney', *Critical Inquiry* 8.3 (Spring 1982): 405–14
Kinsella 1999	John Kinsella, 'Introduction' ('Localities: Intercultural Poetics'), *Kunapipi*, 20. 3 (1998) [1999]: vii–viii
Kraz 2012	Maren Gise Kraz, '"O poet guiding me": Dante and Contemporary Irish Poetry', Doctoral dissertation, Faculty of Modern Languages, Heidelberg University, 2011–12
Laumonier 2015	Paul Laumonier, Raymond Lebègue and Isidore Silver (eds), *Pierre de Ronsard, Œuvres complètes*, 7 vols, Paris: STFM, 2015
Lavan 2020	Rosie Lavan, *Seamus Heaney and Society*, Oxford: Oxford University Press, 2020
Lezard 2017	Nicholas Lezard, '*Aeneid VI* by Seamus Heaney Review – Through "Death's Dark Door" with Virgil', *Guardian* (7 March 2017): 17
Lonergan 2020	Corinna Salvadori Lonergan, '"E se non piangi, di che pianger suoli" *Inferno* XXXIII in lettura con Benigni, Heaney, O'Donoghue, Beckett', Franco Musarra, Manola Gianfranceschi,

	Pacifico Ramazzotti, Laura Nocchi (eds), *Lettere dell' Inferno di Roberto Benigni*, Firenze: Franco Cesati Editore, 2020
Lowell 1961	Robert Lowell, *The Voyage and Other Versions of Poems by Baudelaire*, New York: Farrar, Straus and Giroux, 1961; London: Faber & Faber, 1968
Lunday 2008	Elizabeth Lunday, 'Violence and Silence in Seamus Heaney's "Mycenae Lookout"', *New Hibernia Review/Iris Éireannach Nua*, 12.1 (Errach/Spring 2008): 11–27
Luzi 2021	Mario Luzi, *Persone in viaggio/People on a Journey: Twenty poems translated by twenty poets* (ed. Alessandro Gentili), Pisa: Valigie Rosse, 2021 (expanded from *Il filo della vita/The Thread of Life/Snáithe na beatha* (ed. Alessandro Gentili), Rome: Fondazione Mario Luzi Editore, 2014
McCarthy 2008	Conor McCarthy, *Seamus Heaney and Medieval Poetry*, Cambridge: D. S. Brewer, 2008
McClements 2017	Freya McClements, 'Seamus Heaney: The Christmas Card Maker', *Irish Times* (18 Dec. 2017)
McGowan 2002	Joseph McGowan, 'Heaney, Cædmon, "Beowulf"', *New Hibernia Review/Iris Éireannach Nua*, 6. 2 (Summer 2002): 25–42
Macintosh 2019	Fiona Macintosh, 'Ovid and Titian 2012', *International Journal of the Classical Tradition*, 26. 4 (2019): 433–44
McKibben 2001	Sarah E. McKibben, 'Laoiseach Mac an Bhaird and the Politics of Close Reading', *Proceedings of the Harvard Celtic Colloquium*, 20/21 (2000/2001): 262–84
McKibben 2010	Sarah E. McKibben, 'Bardic Poetry, Masculinity, and the Politics of Male Homosociality', *A Companion to Irish Literature*, Vol. 2 (ed. Julia M. Wright), Oxford: Wiley-Blackwell, 2010
Mac Réamoinn 1982	Seán Mac Réamoinn (ed.), *The Pleasures of Gaelic Poetry*, London: Allen Lane, 1982
Meyers 2020	Jeffrey Meyers, 'Seamus Heaney and Joseph Brodsky: A Poetic Friendship', *The Article* (online) (6 Sept. 2020)

Miłosz 1983	Czesław Miłosz, *The History of Polish Literature*, Berkeley: University of California Press, 1983
Miłosz 1996	Czesław Miłosz, 'Bringing a Great Poet Back to Life', *New York Review of Books* (15 Feb. 1996): 26, 28
Morisco 2013	Gabriella Morisco, 'Two Poets and a Kite: Seamus Heaney and Giovanni Pascoli', *Linguæ & Rivista di Lingue e Culture Moderne*, 12.1 (2013): 35–45
Muldoon 2013	Paul Muldoon, 'A note on Seamus Heaney's "Du Bellay in Rome"', *New England Review*, 34:2 (Jan. 2013): 7
Muldoon 2018	Paul Muldoon, email to Marco Sonzogni, 6 March 2018
Murphy 1956	Gerard Murphy (ed.), *Early Irish Lyrics: Eighth to Twelfth Century*, Oxford: Clarendon Press, 1956
Murphy 2001	Gerry Murphy, 'Pushkin's Arion', *Poetry Ireland Review*, 68 (Spring 2001): 17
Murphy 2016	Kevin Murphy, 'Heaney Translating Heaney: Coupling and Uncoupling the Human Chain', *Texas Studies in Literature and Language*, 58. 3 (2016): 352–68
Mynors 1969	R. A. B. Mynors (ed.), *P. Vergili Maronis Opera*, Oxford Classical Texts, London: Clarendon Press, 1969
Němcová 1998	Alena Němcová, 'Appendix', *Tajemství P.S. aneb Odhalení autora textu Janá kova Zápisník zmizelého* [*Mystery P.S. or Revealing the Author of Janáček's Diary of One who Disappeared*] (ed. Jan Mikeska), Vizovice, CZ: Nakladatelstvi 'LÍPA'-A.J. Rychlik, 1998
Ní Dhomhnaill 2014	Nuala Ní Dhomhnaill, 'In Memoriam Séamus Heaney'/'In Memoriam Seamus Heaney', *Irish Pages*, 8 (2014): 162–6
Nobel 1995	The Nobel Prize in Literature 1995 (online)
O'Brien 2004	Eugene O'Brien, '"More than a Language . . . No More of a Language": Merriman, Heaney, and the Metamorphoses of Translation Author(s)', *Irish University Review*, 34. 2 (Autumn–Winter 2004): 277–90

O'Connor 2011	Laura O'Connor, 'The Bilingual Routes of Paul Muldoon/Pól Ó Maoldúin', *Irish Studies Review*, 19. 2 (2011): 135–55
O'Curry 1878	Eugene O'Curry, *Lectures on the Manuscript Materials of Ancient Irish History*, Dublin: William A. Hinch, 1878
O'Donoghue 1999	Bernard O'Donoghue, 'The Master's Voice-Right', *Irish Times* (9 Oct. 1999): 67
O'Donoghue 2016	Bernard O'Donoghue, '*Aeneid* Book VI: Seamus Heaney's Miraculous Return from Literary Afterlife', *Irish Times* (27 Feb. 2016): 11
O'Neill 2013	Timothy O'Neill, notes to 'Seven Old Irish Poems. Translated by Seamus Heaney and Tim O'Neill' (November 2013)
O'Neill 2014	Timothy O'Neill, *The Irish Hand: Scribes and their Manuscripts from the Earliest Times*, Cork: Cork University Press, 2014
O'Rawe 2001	Des O'Rawe, 'The Poet as Translator', *Irish Review*, 27 (Summer 2001): 180–3
Ó Ríordáin 1996	John J. Ó Ríordáin, *The Music of What Happens: Celtic Spirituality – A View from the Inside*, Dublin: Columba Press, 1996
Ó Searcaigh 1993	Cathal Ó Searcaigh, *An Bealach 'na Bhaile: Rogha Dánta/Homecoming: Selected Poems*, Indreabhán: Cló Iar-Chonnacht, 1993
Parker 1993	Michael Parker, *Seamus Heaney. The Making of the Poet*, Dublin: Gill and Macmillan, 1993
Parker 2012	Michael Parker, '"His nibs": Self-Reflexivity and the Significance of Translation in Seamus Heaney's *Human Chain*', *Irish University Review: A Journal of Irish Studies*, 42. 2 (2012): 327–50
Parker 2013	Michael Parker, 'Past Master: Czesław Miłosz and his Impact on the Poetry of Seamus Heaney', *Textual Practice*, 27. 5 (2013): 825–50
Parker 2017	Michael Parker, 'Back in the Republic of Conscience: Seamus Heaney's *The Cure at Troy*, its Politics, Ethics and Aesthetics', *Textual Practice*, 31. 4 (2017): 747–81
Penny 2012	Nicholas Penny (ed.), *Metamorphosis: Poems inspired by Titian*, London: The National Gallery Company, 2012
Piette 1991	Adam Piette, 'New Air and Relish', *Cambridge Quarterly*, 20. 2 (1991): 95–117

Potts 2001	Robert Potts, 'The View from Olympia', *Guardian* (7 April 2001): 8
de Prade 1652	I. R. de Prade, *L'Histoire de France depuis Pharamond jusqu'à Louis XIII, avec les éloges des roys en vers; réduitte en sommaire par I. R. de Prade*, Paris: Antoine de Sommaville, 1652
Pretto 2020	Rossella Pretto, 'Seamus Heaney: attraversare il Lete', *Studi Cattolici*, 717 (Nov. 2020): 756–61
Quinn 2009	Justin Quinn, 'Heaney and Eastern Europe', *The Cambridge Companion to Seamus Heaney* (ed. Bernard O'Donoghue), Cambridge: Cambridge University Press, 2009
Regan 2015	Stephen Regan, 'Seamus Heaney and the Making of *Sweeney Astray*', *Hungarian Journal of English and American Studies*, 21. 2 (Fall 2015): 317–39
Rilke 1988	Rainer Maria Rilke, 'The Cezanne Inscape' (tr. Jane Bannard Greene), *Writers on Artists* (ed. Daniel Halpern), San Francisco: North Point Press, 1988: 179–89
Riordan 2014	Maurice Riordan (ed.), *The Finest Music: Early Irish Lyrics*, London: Faber & Faber, 2014
Ross 1932	A. S. C. Ross, 'The Middle English Poem on the Names of a Hare', *Proceedings of the Leeds Philosophical and Literary Society, Literary and Historical Section*, 3 (1932–5): 347–7
Ross 1986	Brendan Devlin, 'In Spite of Sea and Centuries: An Irish Gael Looks at the Poetry of Somhairle Mac Gill-Eain', Raymond J. Ross and Joy Hendry (eds) with an introduction by Seamus Heaney, *Sorley MacLean: Critical Essays*, Edinburgh: Scottish University Press, 1986: 81–9
Ross 2004	David Ross, 'Time Steps Back to Hallaig Wood with Poet's Tribute to MacLean. Heaney Follows in Path of Writer Who Gave Voice to Victims of Clearances', *The Herald* (27 May 2004): 3
Schwerter 2013	Stephanie Schwerter, *Northern Irish Poetry and the Russian Turn: Intertextuality in the Work of Seamus Heaney, Tom Paulin and Medbh McGuckian*, Basingstoke: Palgrave Macmillan, 2013
Serée-Chaussinand 2014	Christelle Serée-Chaussinand. 'Actaeon Revisited: Seamus Heaney and Sinéad Morrissey Respond to Titian', *New Hibernia Review/Iris*

	Éireannach Nua, 18. 4 (Geimhreadh/Winter 2014): 119–30
Smith 2016	Margaret Smith, 'Kinship and Kingship: Identity and Authority in the Book of Lismore', *Eolas: Journal of the American Society of Irish Medieval Studies*, 9 (2016): 77–85
Sonzogni 2021	Marco Sonzogni and Marcella Zanetti (eds), *Raids & Settlements: Seamus Heaney as Translator*, Wellington, NZ: Cuba Press, 2021
Sorescu 1987	Marin Sorescu, *The Biggest Egg in the World* (ed. Edna Longley, tr. David Constantine, D. J. Enright, Michael Hamburger, Seamus Heaney, Ted Hughes, Michael Longley, Paul Muldoon, Ioana Russell-Gebbett and William Scammell), Newcastle upon Tyne: Bloodaxe Books, 1987
Sorescu 1991	Marin Sorescu, *Hands Behind My Back: Selected Poems* (tr. Gabriela Dragnea, Stuart Friebert and Adriana Varga, with an introduction by Seamus Heaney), Oberlin, OH: Oberlin College Press, 1991
Sorescu 2000	Marin Sorescu, *Dánta deireadh saoil. Poemele Sfârsítului* (tr. Aodh Ó Canainn and Anamaria Maior, with a foreword by Seamus Heaney), Dublin: Coiscéim, 2000
Thomas 2014	'Deor' (tr. Harry Thomas), *Berfrois* (online) (10 Dec. 2014); in Harry Thomas, *Some Complicities*, Boston, MA: Un-Gyve Press, 2013
Titian 2012	*Metamorphosis: Titian 2012* (video films), The National Gallery, Sainsbury Wing, London (11 July–23 Sept. 2012)
Tochigi 2000	Nobuaki Tochigi, 'Cathal Ó Searcaigh and Aspects of Translation', *Éire-Ireland*, 35. 1–2 (Earrach/Samhradh–Spring/Summer 2000): 139–49
Tóibín 2010	Colm Tóibín, 'The Living Breath of Things', *Guardian* (21 Aug. 2010): 6
Tommasini 2001	Anthony Tommasini, 'The Irish poet's foray into Janáček', *New York Times* (2 June 2001): B9
van de Kamp, 1994	Peter van de Kamp (ed., with an introduction by Theo D'Haen), *Turning Tides: Modern Dutch & Flemish Verse in English Versions by Irish Poets*, Fort Wayne, IN: Story Line Press, 1994
Vendler 2001	Helen Vendler, 'Heaney, the Survivor', *Irish Times* (24 March 2001): 52

Vendler 2015   Helen Vendler, 'Speech at the Funeral Service
                        for Stanisław Barańczak' (3 Jan. 2015), privately
                        printed
Wilmer 2002   Stephen E. Wilmer, 'Finding a Post-Colonial
                        Voice for Antigone: Seamus Heaney's *Burial at
                        Thebes*', *Classics in Post-Colonial Worlds* (ed.
                        Lorna Hardwick and Carol Gillespie), Oxford:
                        Oxford University Press, 2002: 228–42
Witczak 2003   Krzysztof Tomasz Witczak, 'El río del olvido',
                        Veleia, 20 (2003): 355–9
Wright 1841   Thomas Wright and James Orchard Halliwell,
                        *Reliquiae Antiquae: Scraps from Ancient
                        Manuscripts Illustrating Chiefly Early English
                        Literature and the English Language*, London:
                        John Russell Smith, 1841

Acknowledgements

Going through the 'single things' to include in this volume, the image of the astronaut in the closing lines of 'Alphabets' (*HL*, 3) who 'from his small window . . ./Sees all that he has sprung from' kept coming to mind. And with it, feelings of wonder and worry; of doubt and devotion; of scrutiny and solace. A human chain of 'aid workers' (*HC*, 18) – editors, publishers, translators, readers, scholars, students, and librarians from around the world – helped me turn 'lug' into 'lift': Giuliana Adamo, Fahim Afarinasadi, Ulrico Agnati, Clifford Ando, Rosellina Archinto, Massimo Bacigalupo, Catherine Bailey, John Barnes, Mary Beard, Claudia Bernardi, Piotr Blumczynski, Piero Boitani, Sam Boless, Brian Boyd, Rand Brandes, Terence Brown, Diana Burton, Duncan Campbell, Diwen Cao, Anna Chahoud, Hamish Clayton, Aedín Ní Bhróithe Clements, Renata Colorni, Barrie Cooke, Odette Copat, Alessandra Corbetta, Elena Cotta Ramusino, Robert Crawford, Michael Cronin, Patrick Crotty, Eleanor Crow, Flaminia Cruciani, Nina Cuccurullo, John F. Deane, Irene De Angelis, Hansgerd Delbrück, Domenico De Martino, John Dennison, Terence Dolan, Brian Donnelly, Alexandra Dumitrescu, Robert Easting, Rachel Falconer, Peter Fallon, Samira Fatih, Marco Fazzini, Jane Feaver, Paolo Febbraro, Marco Fernandelli, Markku Filppula, Gabriel Fitzmaurice, Chris Fletcher, Alessandro Fo, Faran Foley, Karen Foote, Alberto Fraccacreta, Phyllis Gaffney, Jonathan Galassi, Emanuel E. Garcia, Alessandro Gentili, Zbigniew Gniatkowski, Jana Grohnert, Anna Gubinskaya, Leonardo Guzzo, Lorna Hardwick, Isolde Harpur, Stephen Harrison, Lisa Harrop, James Harte, Robert Hass, Nick Havely, Catherine Heaney, Christopher Heaney, Marie Devlin Heaney, Michael Heaney, Magdalena Heydel, Sally Hill, Matthew Hollis, Rui Carvalho Homem, Jerzy Illg, Maria Magdalena Kaczor, Diarmuid Kennedy, Brendan Kennelly, Declan Kiberd, James Kierstead, Concetto La Malfa, Jo Margherita Lander, Mauricio Lopez Langenbach, Rosie Lavan, Michele Leggott, Ida Li, Giacomo Lichtner, Katie Liptak, Roger Little, Corinna Salvadori Lonergan, Lisa Lowe, Margot MacGillivray, Fiona Macintosh, Ruth Macklin, Federico Magrin, Maria Makuch, Mariangela Maio, Bill Manhire, Federica Massia, Cathal McCabe, Lucy McCabe, Michael McCann, Courtney McDonald, Rory McKenzie, Anne McKim, Helen Melody, Giorgia Meriggi, Roberto Monzani, Gabriella Morisco, Leslie A.

Morris, Anthony Mortimer, Paul Muldoon, Eiléan Ní Chuilleanáin, Micheál Ó Cearúil, Cormac Ó Cuilleanáin, Bernard O'Donoghue, Dennis O'Driscoll, Anthony Oldcorn, Timothy O'Neill, Maria O'Shea, Vincent O'Sullivan, Chris Park, Michael Parker, Tim Parks, Simon Perris, Robert Pinsky, Marilena Poggi, Giuseppe Polimeni, Antiniska Pozzi, Stuart Prior, Babette Puetz, Tony Quinn, Elena Cotta Ramusino, Christopher Reid, Stephan Resch, Harry Ricketts, Maurice Riordan, Elisabetta Risari, Jane Robertson, Anthony Roche, Eugene Roche, Andrea Rodighiero, Peter Ryan, Maria Chiara Savi, Christopher Sawyer-Lauçanno, Leigh Schlecht, Julia Maria Seemann, Frank Sewell, Sydney Shep, Bill Shipsey, Kathy Shoemaker, Paul Simon, Lavinia Singer, Peter Sirr, Anna Siyanova, Timothy Smith, Donald Sommerville, Gabriele Sonzogni, Maria Irene Ramalho de Sousa Santo, Lydia Stewart, Britta Stöckmann, Stephen Stuart-Smith, Olga Suvorova, Jeff Tatum, Heidi Thomson, Teresa Travaglia, Paddy Twigg, Susie Tyrrell, Helen Vendler, Peter Whiteford, Ross Woods, Stuart Young, Marcella Zanetti. My gratitude to Yuanyuan Liang 'is not a thing for which one can render formal thanks in formal words' and so 'I store it in the treasure-house of my heart' (Oscar Wilde, *De Profundis*). The best guidance an editor can receive is listening to Heaney explain his work – at readings and lectures; in interviews and conversations; in videos and recordings that continue to become available online. And the best advice is in one of his poems, one of the two he considered most representative of his work, 'A Drink of Water' (*FW*, 16): '*Remember the Giver*'.

MS

Index of Titles and First Lines

Just as an olive seedling, when it tries 270